The GENERAL SCIENCE COMPENDIUM

For IAS Prelims Paper 1 & State PSC EXAM

Corporate Office : 45, 2nd Floor, Maharishi Dayanand Marg, Corner Market, Malviya Nagar, New Delhi-110017

Tel. : 011-49842349 / 49842350

Chief Editor : Satya Prakash
Complied & Edited by: J. Kumar

Typeset by Disha DTP Team

Printed at Repro Knowledgecast Limited, Thane

For further information about the books from DISHA,

Log on to **www.dishapublication.com** or email to **info@dishapublication.com**

CONTENTS

BIOLOGY   C-1-78

Chapter 1

MEASUREMENTS & MOTION

MEASUREMENTS

The process of comparing an unknown physical quantity with respect to a known quantity is known as measurement. Measurement of any physical quantity consists of two parts – (i) a numerical value and (ii) the known quantity. The known quantity is called the unit of that physical quantity. Measurement is an integral part of physics.

PHYSICAL QUANTITIES

Quantities which can be measured are called physical quantities. Velocity, acceleration, force, area, volume, pressure, etc. are some examples of physical quantities.

Kinds of Physical Quantities

There are two kinds of physical quantities

Fundamental physical quantities: Fundamental physical quantities are those which do not depend on other quantities and also independent of each other. They are seven in number *viz*; *length, mass, time, thermodynamic temperature, electric current, luminous intensity and amount of substance.*

Derived physical quantities: Derived physical quantities are those which are derived from fundamental physical quantities. For example, *velocity* is derived from the fundamental quantities length and time, hence it is a derived physical quantity.

UNITS

To measure a physical quantity it is compared with a standard quantity. This standard quantity is called the unit of that quantity.

Types of Units

There are two types of units :

Fundamental units: Fundamental units are those units which cannot be derived from any other unit, and they cannot be resolved into any basic or fundamental unit. Also, the units of fundamental physical quantities are called fundamental units.

The following table shows the seven fundamental units of S.I. System.

S. No.	Fundamental Physical quantity	Fundamental Unit	Symbol
1.	Length	metre	m
2.	Mass	kilogram	kg
3.	Time	second	s
4.	Electric current	ampere	A
5.	Temperature	kelvin	K
6.	Luminous intensity	candela	cd
7.	Amount of substance	mole	mol

The Metre is the length of the path travelled by light in vaccum during a time interval of 1/299, 792, 458 of a second.

The Kilogram is equal to the mass of the International prototype of the kilogram [a platinum iridium alloy cylinder] kept at international Bureau of Weights and Measures, at Sevres, near Paris, France.

The Second is the duration of 9,192,631,770 periods of the radiation corresponding to the transition between the two hyperfine levels of the ground state of the cesium –133 atom.

The Ampere is that constant current which, if maintained in two straight parallel conductors of infinite length, of negligible circular cross-section, and placed 1 metre apart in vacuum, would produce between these conductors a force equal to 2×10^{-7} newton per metre of length.

The Kelvin, is the fraction $\frac{1}{273.16}$ of the thermodynamic temperature of the triple point of water.

The Mole is the amount of substance of a system, which contains as many elementary entities as there are atoms in 0.012 kilogram of carbon - 12.

The Candela is the luminous intensity, in a given direction, of a source that emits monochromatic radiation of frequency 540×10^{12} hertz and that has a radiant intensity in that direction of 1/683 watt per steradian.

Derived units: Any unit which can be obtained by the combination of one or more fundamental units are called derived unit.

Examples: *Area, speed, density, volume, momentum, acceleration, force* etc.

Derived units of some physical quantities are as follows:

S. No.	Derived Physical quantity	Derived Unit
1.	Area	m^2
2.	Volume	m^3
3.	Density	kg/m^3
4.	Speed	m/s
5.	Acceleration	m/s^2
6.	Momentum	$kg\,m/s$
7.	Force	$kg\,m/s^2$ or newton
8.	Work	$kg\,m^2/s^2$ or joule
9.	Power	$kg\,m^2/s^3$ or watt
10.	Charge	ampere-sec or coulomb
11.	Potential	joule/coulomb or volt
12.	Resistance	volt/ampere or ohm

Systems of Units

Depending upon the units of fundamental physical quantities, there are four main systems of units, namely

- **CGS** (Centimeter, Gramme or Gram, Second)
- **FPS** (Foot, Pound, Second)
- **MKS** (Meter, Kilogram, Second)
- **SI** (Systeme Internationale d' Unites)

The first three of these systems recognize only three fundamental quantities i.e. length (L), mass (M) and time (T) while the last one recognizes seven fundamental quantities. i.e. length (L), mass (M), time (T), electric current (I or A), thermodynamic temperature (K or θ), amount of substance (mol) and luminous intensity (I_v).

An international organization, the **Conference Generale des Poids et Mesures, or CGPM** is internationally recognized as the authority on the definition of units. In english, this body is known as *"General Conference on Weights and Measure"*. **The Systeme International de Unites, or SI system** of units, was set up in 1960 by the CGPM.

Characteristics of a Standard Unit

A standard unit must have following features to be accepted world wide. It should

- have a convenient size.
- be very well defined.
- be independent of time and place.

Supplementary Units of SI System

The following table shows the two supplementary units of SI. System.

S.No.	Physical quantity	Supplementary Unit	Symbol
1.	Plane angle	radian	rad
2.	Solid angle	steradian	sr

1. **radian (rad):** The radian is the plane angle between two radii of a circle that cut off on the circumference an arc equal in length to the radius.
2. **steradian (sr):** The steradian is the solid angle that, having its vertex at the center of a sphere, cuts off an area of the surface of the sphere equal to that of a square with sides of length equal to the radius of the sphere.

DIMENSIONS

The Dimensions of the physical quantity are the powers to which the fundamental units are raised in order to obtain the units of that quantity.

All physical quantities have a fundamental dimension that is independent of the units of measurement. The basic physical dimensions are: mass, length, time, temperature, electrical current, and luminous intensity.

S.No.	Physical Quantity	Symbol	Primary Dimension	SI Unit
1	Mass	m	M	kg (kilogram)
2	Length	L	L	m (metre)
3	Time	t	T	s (second)
4	Temperature	T	K	K (Kelvin)
5	Electric current	I	Q	A (ampere)
6	Luminous intensity	C	C	cd (candela)

All other dimensions can be derived as combinations of these primary dimensions. These are called derived dimensions.

S.No.	Physical Quantity	Symbol	Derived Dimension	Unit
1.	Force	F	MLT^{-2}	N (Newton = kg. m/s^2)
2.	Acceleration	a	LT^{-2}	m/s^2
3.	Pressure	p	$ML^{-1}T^{-2}$	N/m^2, i.e. Pa (Pascal)
4.	Energy	E	$ML^2T{-2}$	J (Joule = N. m)
5.	Power	P	ML^2T^{-3}	W (watt = J/s)
6.	Area	A	L^2	m^2
7.	Volume	V	L^3	m^3
8.	Velocity	v	LT^{-1}	m/sec
9.	Work	W	ML^2T^{-2}	Kg m^2/sec^2
10.	Impulse	J	MLT^{-1}	Kg m/sec
11.	specific weight	g	$ML^{-2}T^{-2}$	Kg m^{-2}/sec^2
12.	Electric current	I	QT^{-1}	Ampere(C/sec)
13.	EMF/Voltage/ Potential	E	$ML^2T^{-2}Q^{-1}$	Volt (Kg m^2/sec^{2}C)
14.	Resistance / Impedance	R	$ML^2T^{-1}Q^{-2}$	Ohm (Kg m^2 /sec C^2)
15.	Capacitance	C	$M^{-1}L^{-2}T^2Q^2$	Farad (sec^{2}C^2/Kgm^2)
16.	Current density	J	$QT^{-1}L^{-2}$	Ampere per square meter (C/sec m^2)

17.	Magnetic intensity	H	$QL^{-1}T^{-1}$	Ampere per meter (C/m sec)
18.	Dielectric constant	k	$M^0L^0T^0$	None
19.	Permittivity	e	$T^2Q^2M^{-1}L^{-3}$	farad per meter (sec^2C^2/Kgm^3)
20.	Magnetic flux	B	$MT^{-1}Q^{-1}$	webcr per square meter (Kg/sec C)

Thus we can express the unit of force as products of different powers of the fundamental units of mass, length and time.

i.e., Force = $[MLT^{-2}]$

Thus the dimensions of a physical quantity are the powers to which the fundamental quantities mass, length and time must be raised to represent it.

> A spring balance on the moon will give different reading from that on Earth but a beam balance will give the same reading as spring balance requires gravity to measure. Mass remains same throughout but weight changes with gravity. Mass will only change if there is any change in the volume of matter in the body.

MOTION

Movement of any object from one position to another position with respect to the observer is called as **Motion**.

Position: Motion of any object is defined by its position with respect to the observer. Position is the location of the object. If object changes its position with the passage of time, it is said to be in motion.

Reference point: It is the point from which the location of object is measured. It is often called as origin.

Any object can be located only with the help of reference point and its direction.

Distance

It is a measure of the interval between two locations measured along the *actual path* connecting them.

Displacement

It is a measure of the interval between two locations measured along the *shortest path* connecting them.

VECTOR

Vector is a quantity which have both mangitude and direction.

e.g. Displacement, Force, Velocity etc.

SCALAR

Scalar is a qunatity with magnitude only and without direction.

e.g. Distance, Speed etc.

Uniform Motion

→ When a body travels equal distance in equal interval of time, then the motion is said to be uniform motion.

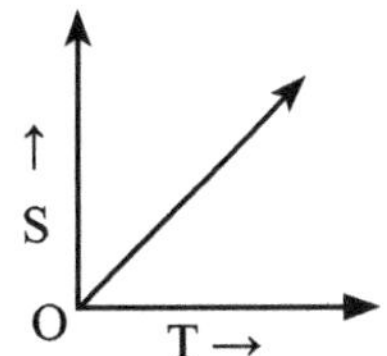

Non-uniform Motion

→ In this type of motion, the body will travel unequal distances in equal intervals of time.

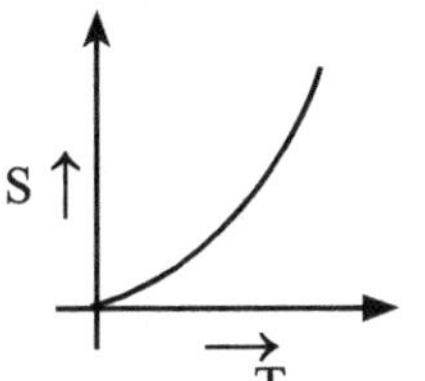 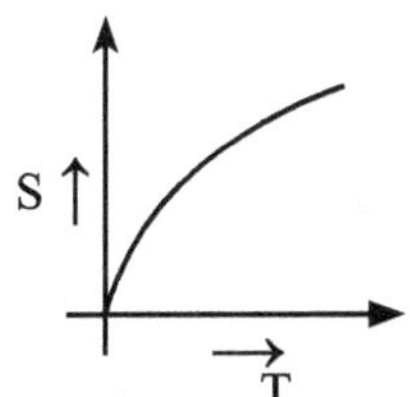

Continuous increase in slope of curve indicates accelerated non-uniform motion.

Continuous decrease in slope of curve indicates decelerate non-uniform motion.

Speed

It is the Distance travelled by an object in unit time. It is a scalar quantity since there is no consideration of direction.

Velocity

It is the distance travelled by an object in a specific direction in unit time. It is a Vector quantity since there is consideration of direction.

Acceleration

It is the rate of change of velocity of an object with time. Since velocity is a vector quantity therefore acceleration is also vector.

Retardation

It is negative acceleration or deceleration. Retardation is the rate of decrease in velocity.

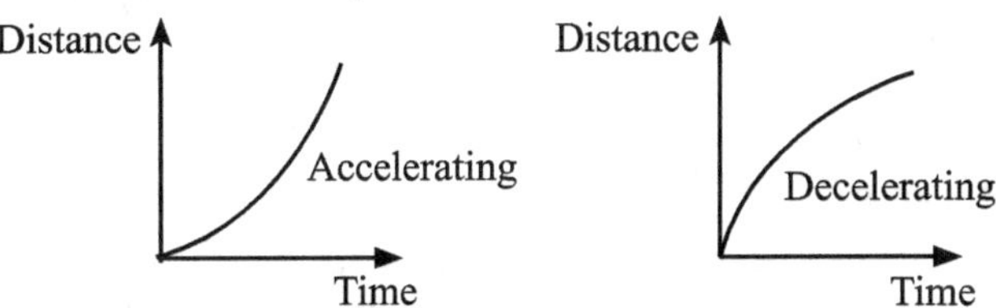

REST AND MOTION

Rest : An object is said to be at rest if it does not change its position with respect to its surroundings with the passage of time.

Types of Motion on the basis of Dimensions

One-Dimensional Motion: It is the motion in which the position of the object changes only in one direction. In this case the object moves along a line. For example – motion of a train along a straight line, freely falling object under gravity, etc.

Two-Dimensional Motion: It is the motion in which the position of the object changes in two directions. In this case the object moves on a plane. For example– projectile motion.

Three-Dimensional Motion: It is the motion in which the position of the object changes in three directions. In this case the object moves in a space. For example– a bird flying in the sky.

THE RATE OF MOTION
Average Speed

It is defined as *the total distance travelled divided by the time interval to travel that distance.*

Average speed $V_{av} = \dfrac{d}{t}$, d is distance travelled, and t is time interval (change in time).

The average speed of Cheetah is 70 m/s for 30 seconds

Instantaneous Speed

It is the speed at a particular time instant (t is infinitesimal small or close to zero).

Uniform and Non-uniform Speed

A body is said to be moving with uniform speed if it covers equal distances in equal time intervals and with non-uniform or variable speed if covers unequal distances in the same time intervals.

SPEED WITH DIRECTION (VELOCITY)
Average Velocity

It is defined as *the ratio of change in position or displacement to the time taken.*

$$\bar{v} = v_{av} = \frac{x_2 - x_1}{t_2 - t_1} = \frac{\Delta x}{\Delta t}$$

Here x_1 and x_2 are the positions of the particle at time t_1 and t_2 respectively. Also, $\Delta x = x_2 - x_1$ = change in position and $\Delta t = t_2 - t_1$ = change in time. Its unit is ms^{-1}, cms^{-1} or $km\ h^{-1}$.

Instantaneous Velocity

Velocity of a body at a particular instant or moment of time is called instantaneous velocity.

RATE OF CHANGE OF VELOCITY [ACCELERATION]

Positive acceleration : If the velocity of an object increases in the same direction, the object has a positive acceleration.
Negative acceleration (Retardation): If the velocity of a body decreases in the same direction, the body has a negative acceleration or it is said to be retarding e.g, a train slows down.

GRAPHICAL REPRESENTATION OF MOTION IN A STRAIGHT LINE
Displacement-Time Graphs

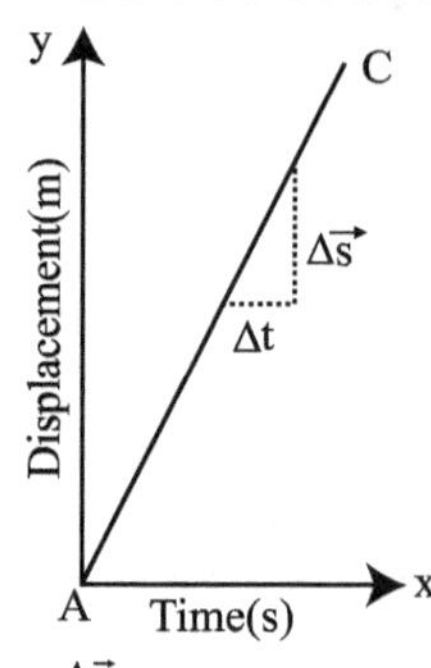

A graph showing the displacement of the cyclist from A to C: This graph shows us how, in t seconds time, the cyclist has moved from A to C.
We know the gradient (slope) of a graph is defined as the change in y divided by the change in x, i.e., $\dfrac{\Delta y}{\Delta x}$.

In this graph the gradient of the graph is just $\dfrac{\Delta \vec{s}}{\Delta t}$ and this is just the expression for velocity.

The slope of a displacement-time graph gives the velocity. The slope is the same all the way from A to C, so the cyclist's velocity is constant over the entire displacement he travels. Observe the following displacement-time graphs.

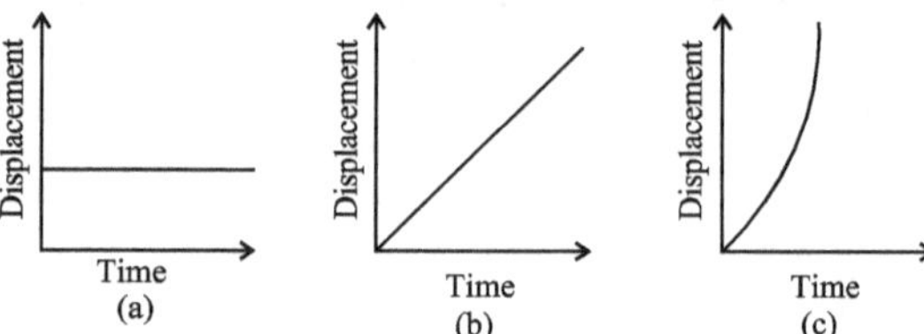

Graph (a) shows the object is stationary over a period of time. The gradient is zero, so the object has zero velocity.
Graph (b) shows the object is moving at a constant velocity. You can see that the displacement is increasing as time goes on. The gradient, however, stays constant so the velocity is constant. Here the gradient is positive, so the object is moving in the direction we have defined as positive.
Graph (c) shows the object is moving at a constant acceleration. You can see that both the displacement and the velocity (gradient of the graph) increases with time. The gradient is increasing with time, thus the velocity is increasing with time and the object is accelerating.

> The x-t graph of an object having uniform motion is a straight line inclined to the time-axis. The slope of straight line x-t graph gives velocity of the uniform motion of the object.

Velocity-Time Graphs

This is the velocity-time graph of a cyclist travelling from A to B at a constant acceleration, i.e. with steadily increasing velocity.

The gradient of this graph is just $\dfrac{\Delta \vec{s}}{\Delta t}$ and this is just the expression for acceleration. Because the slope is the same at all points on this graph, the acceleration of the cyclist is constant.

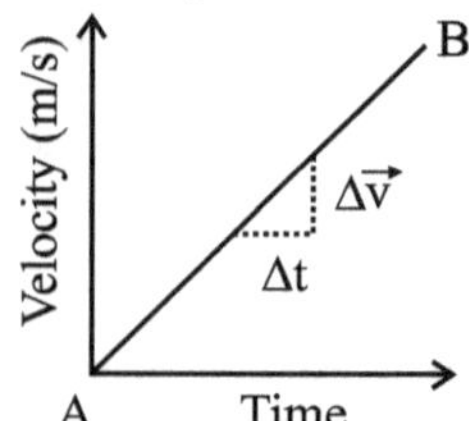

The *slope of a velocity-time graph gives the acceleration.* Observe the following velocity-time graphs.

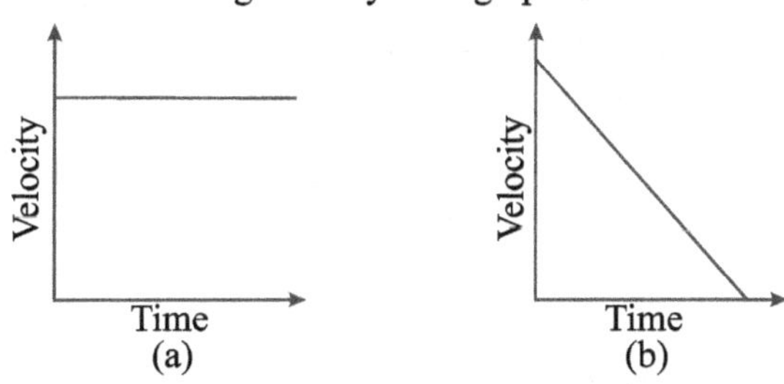

| (a) | (b) |

Graph (a) shows the object is moving at a constant velocity over a period of time. The gradient is zero, so the object is not accelerating.

Graph (b) shows an object which is decelerating. You can see that the velocity is decreasing with time. The gradient, however, stays constant so the acceleration is constant. Here the gradient is negative, so the object is accelerating in the opposite direction to its motion, hence it is decelerating.

Acceleration-Time Graphs

Observe the following acceleration-time graphs.

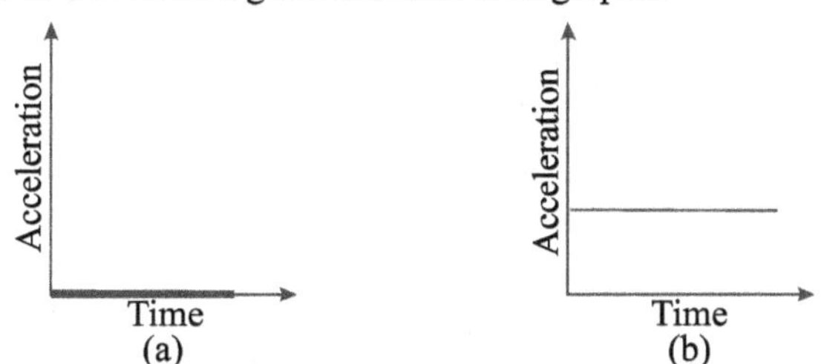

| (a) | (b) |

Graph (a) shows an object which is either stationary or travelling at a constant velocity. Either way, the acceleration is zero over time.

Graph (b) shows an object moving at a constant acceleration. In this case the acceleration is positive - remember that it can also be negative.

EQUATIONS OF MOTION

Kinematic equations can be used to describe the motion with constant acceleration.

First equation (Equation for velocity-time relation):

Final velocity
= initial velocity + acceleration × time interval

or $v = u + at$

Second equation (Equation for position-time relation):

Displacement = initial velocity × time interval + $\dfrac{1}{2}$ × acceleration × time interval^2

or $s = ut + \dfrac{1}{2}at^2$

Third equation (Equation for position-velocity relation) : $v^2 = u^2 + 2as$

Final velocity^2 = initial velocity^2 + 2 × acceleration × displacement

or $v^2 = u^2 + 2as$

RELATIVE MOTION

The motion of an object B w.r.t. object A which is moving or stationary is called as relative motion.

Relative velocity of an object B w.r.t. object A when both are in motion is the rate of change of position of object B w.r.t. object A.

Relative velocity of object B w.r.t. object A, $\overrightarrow{V_{BA}} = \overrightarrow{V_B} - \overrightarrow{V_A}$

MOTION UNDER GRAVITY

It is a common experience that when a body is dropped form a certain height it experiences acceleration due to gravity and its motion is in a straight path. Similarly, when a body is thrown vertically up, it goes to a certain height and then starts falling again, experiencing acceleration due to gravity throughout the motion.

The *value of acceleration due to gravity (g) is taken as 9.8 m/s^2, 980 cm/s^2 or 32 ft/s^2.*

Let us consider the three cases discussed below.

Case-I: Body thrown downward :

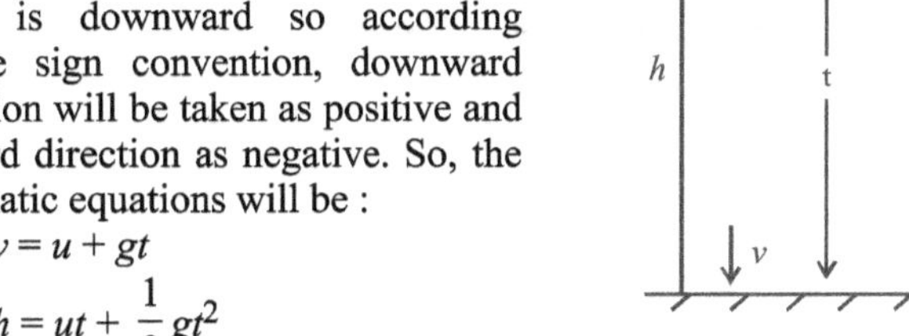

In this case, initial motion of the body is downward so according to the sign convention, downward direction will be taken as positive and upward direction as negative. So, the kinematic equations will be :

(i) $\quad v = u + gt$

(ii) $\quad h = ut + \dfrac{1}{2}gt^2$

(iii) $\quad v^2 = u^2 + 2gh$

(iv) $\quad h^{nth} = h + \dfrac{1}{2}g(2n - 1)$

In a special case when the body is dropped/let falls i.e., initial velocity $(u) = 0$, then equation becomes

$$v = gt \; ; \; h = \dfrac{1}{2}gt^2 \; ; \; v^2 = 2gh \; ; \; h^{nth} = \dfrac{1}{2}g(2n - 1)$$

Case-II: Body thrown upward:

If a body is thrown vertically up with an initial velocity (u). Hence $a = -g$. Kinematic equations will be:

(i) $\quad v = u - gt \qquad$ (ii) $\quad h = ut - \dfrac{1}{2}gt^2$

(iii) $\quad v^2 - u^2 = -2gh \quad$ (iv) $\quad h_n = u - g\left(n - \dfrac{1}{2}\right)$

Maximum height reached by the body

From equation $v^2 = u^2 + 2gh$

$$H = \dfrac{u^2}{2g} \qquad [\because v = 0]$$

Therefore, the maximum height reached by the body is directly proportional to the square of the initial velocity.

Time of ascent (t_a): The time taken by a body thrown up to reach maximum height 'h' is called its time of ascent.

$$t_a = \dfrac{u}{g}$$

Hence time of ascent t_a is directly proportional to the initial velocity u.

Time of descent (t_d): The time taken by a freely falling body to reach the ground is called the time of descent.

$$t_d = \sqrt{\frac{2h}{g}}$$

and $h = \dfrac{v^2}{2g}$, $t_d = \dfrac{v}{g}$

$a = +g$

$u \quad v = u$

But, we know that $u = v$ i.e., projected velocity of a body is equal to the velocity of the body on reaching the ground.

$$\therefore \qquad t_d = \frac{u}{g} = \text{time of ascent } (t_a)$$

Time of ascent = time of descent

Case-III: Body projected vertically up from the top of a tower :

If a body is projected vertically up from the top of a tower of height 'h' with velocity 'u'. Then

Displacement after time t is $s = ut - \dfrac{1}{2}gt^2$

Velocity after time t is $v = u - gt$.

Velocity on reaching the ground is $\sqrt{u^2 + 2gh}$

Maximum height above the ground is $\{h + (u^2/2g)\}$

PROJECTILE MOTION

Projectile is the name given to a body thrown with some initial velocity in any arbitrary direction and then allowed to move under the influence of a constant acceleration. The motion of a projectile is called projectile motion.

Example : A football kicked by the player, a stone thrown from the top of building, a bomb released from a plane.

The path followed by a projectile is called its **trajectory**, mostly, the trajectory of a projectile is parabolic.

Maximum height (H): When a projectile moves, it covers a maximum distance in vertical direction. This maximum distance is called the maximum height attained by the projectile.

$$\text{Maximum height} \quad H = \frac{u^2 \sin^2 \alpha}{2g}$$

Horizontal range (R): The horizontal distance between the point of projection and the point of landing of a projectile.

$$\text{Maximum range} \quad R = \frac{u^2 \sin 2\alpha}{g}$$

Time of flight (T): The time taken by the projectile to reach the point of landing from the point of projection.

$$\text{Time of flight} \quad T = \frac{2u \sin \alpha}{g}$$

MULTIPLE CHOICE QUESTIONS

1. An inertial observer sees two events E_1 and E_2 happening at the same location but 6 µs apart in time. Another observer moving with a constant velocity v (with respect to the first one) sees the same events to be 9 µs apart. The spatial distance between the events, as measured by the second observer, is approximately
   (a) 300 m   (b) 1000 m
   (c) 2000 m   (d) 2700 m

2. Two particles A and B move with relativistic velocities of equal magnitude v, but in opposite directions, along the x-axis of an inertial frame of reference. The magnitude of the velocity of A, as seen from the rest frame of B, is

   (a) $2v \Big/ \left(1 - \dfrac{v^2}{c^2}\right)$ (b) $2v \Big/ \left(1 + \dfrac{v^2}{c^2}\right)$

   (c) $2v \sqrt{\dfrac{c-v}{c+v}}$ (d) $2v \Big/ \sqrt{1 - \dfrac{v^2}{c^2}}$

3. Match List I (Units) with List II (Physical quantity) and select the correct answer using the codes given below the lists. **[CDS]**

List I	List II
(Units)	**(Physical quantity)**
(A) Watt	1. Electric charge
(B) Tesla	2. Power
(C) Coulomb	3. Luminous intensity
(D) Candela	4 Magnetic field

   Codes

	A	B	C	D
(a)	1	4	1	3
(b)	1	2	3	4
(c)	1	2	4	3
(d)	2	4	3	1

4. Match List I (Physical quantity) with List II (Units) and select the correct answer using the codes given below the lists.

List I	List II
(Physical quantity)	**(Units)**
A. Power	1. kg ms^{-1}
B. Energy	2. kg m^{2}s^{-1}
C. Momentum	3. Nm^{-2}
D. Pressure	4. kW
	5. kWh

   Codes

	A	B	C	D
(a)	4	5	1	3
(b)	4	5	1	2
(c)	5	4	1	2
(d)	5	4	2	3

5. What is the correct sequence in which the lengths of the following units increase?

   1. Angstrom   2. Micron   3. Nanometer

   Select the correct answer using the code given below:

   [NDA]

   (a) 1, 2, 3   (b) 3, 1, 2
   (c) 1, 3, 2   (d) 2, 3, 1

6. Which one of the following is not a dimension less quantity?

   (a) Strain   (b) Relative density
   (c) Frequency   (d) Angle

7. Match List 'I' (Physical quantity) with list II (Dimension) and select the correct answer by using the codes given below the lists.

List I (Physical quantity)	List II (Dimension)
A. Density	1. $[MLT^{-2}]$
B. Force	2. $[ML^{-3}]$
C. Energy	3. $[MLT^{-1}]$
D. Momentum	4. $[ML^2T^{-2}]$

   Codes

	A	B	C.	D
(a)	3	2	4	1
(b)	1	2	3	4
(c)	2	1	4	3
(d)	3	2	1	4

8. 'Farad' is the unit of   **[SSC CGL]**

   (a) resistance   (b) conductance
   (c) capacitance   (d) inductance

9. S.I. unit of surface tension is

   (a) degree/cm   (b) N/m
   (c) N/m^2 (d) N m

10. Match List I (Physical quantity) with list II (Units) and select the correct answer by using the codes given below the lists.

List I (Physical quantity)	List II (Units)
A. Solid angle	1. pascal
B. Impulse	2. steradian
C. Viscosity	3. Newton-second
D. Pressure	4. Pascal-second

    Codes

	A	B	C.	D
(a)	2	4	3	1
(b)	2	3	4	1
(c)	1	4	3	2
(d)	1	3	4	2

11. Which one of the following pairs does not have the same dimension?   **[NDA]**

    (a) Potential energy and kinetic energy
    (b) Density and specific gravity
    (c) Focal length and height
    (d) Gravitational force and frictional force

12. **Assertion :** Density is a derived physical quantity.

    Reason : Density cannot be derived from the fundamental physical quantities.

    (a) If both **Assertion** and **Reason** are **correct** and Reason is the **correct explanation** of Assertion.
    (b) If both **Assertion** and **Reason** are correct, but Reason is **not the correct explanation** of Assertion.
    (c) If **Assertion** is **correct** but **Reason** is **incorrect**.
    (d) If **Assertion** is **incorrect** but **Reason** is **correct**.

13. The numerical ratio of displacement to the distance covered is always.

    (a) less than one
    (b) equal to one
    (c) equal to or less than one
    (d) equal to or greater than one

14. An iron ball and a wooden ball of same radius are released from a height 'h' in vacuum. Which of the two balls would take more time to reach the ground?

    (a) Iron ball
    (b) Both would take same time
    (c) Wooden ball
    (d) None of these

15. If an object undergoes a uniform circular motion, then its
    [NDA]

    (a) acceleration remains uniform
    (b) velocity changes
    (c) speed changes
    (d) velocity remains uniform

16. Which one of the following remains constant while throwing a ball upward ?   **[NDA]**

    (a) Displacement   (b) Kinetic energy
    (c) Acceleration   (d) Velocity

17. A passenger in a moving train tosses a five rupee coin. If the coin falls behind him, then the train must be moving with a uniform

    (a) acceleration   (b) deceleration
    (c) speed   (d) velocity

18. Which of the following distance-time graph (x-t) represents one-dimensional uniform motion?   **[IAS Prelim]**

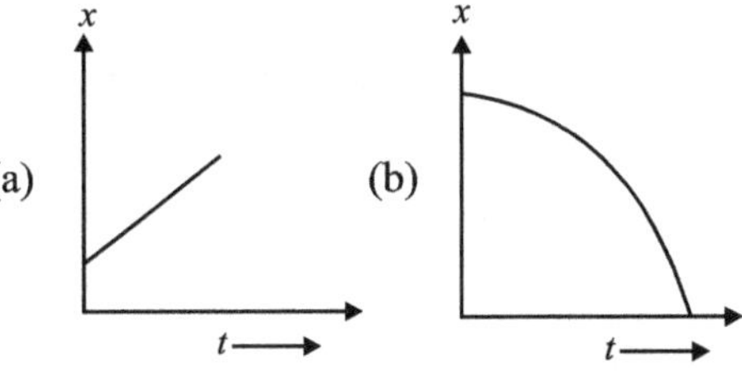

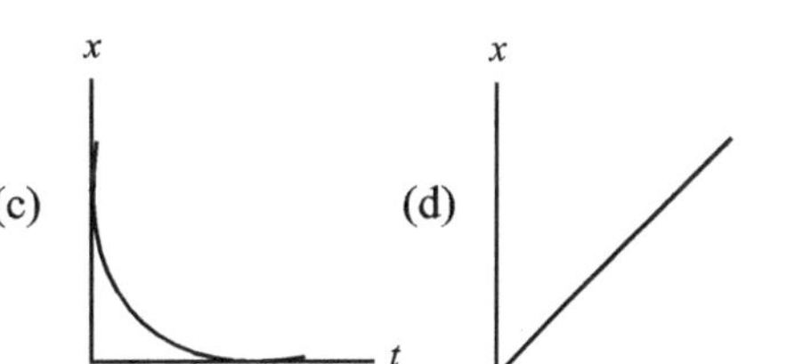

19. A stone is thrown vertically upwards with an initial velocity u from the top of a tower of height $\dfrac{12u^2}{g}$. With what velocity does the stone reach the ground ? **[NDA]**

(a) u   (b) 4u

(c) 5u   (d) $2\sqrt{6}\,u$

20. Which one of the following characteristics of the particle does the shaded area of the velocity-time graph shown represent? **[NDA]**

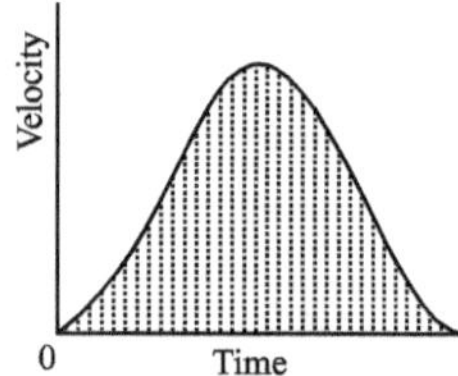

(a) Momentum   (b) Acceleration

(c) Distance covered   (d) speed

21. A parachutist jumps from a height of 5000 metre. The relationship between his falling speed, v and the distance fallen through d is best represented as : **[IAS Prelim]**

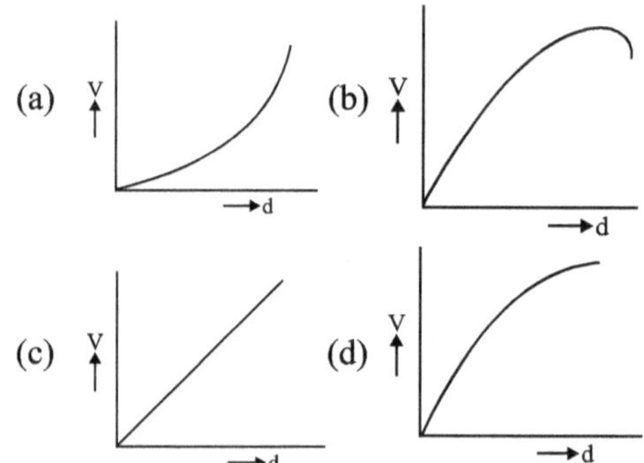

22. A spherical body moves with a uniform angular velocity (ω) around a circular path of radius r. Which one of the following statements is correct? **[IAS Prelim]**

(a) The body has no acceleration

(b) The body has a radial acceleration $\omega^2 r$ directed toward centre of path

(c) The body has a radial acceleration $2/5\,\omega^2 r$ directed away from the centre of the path

(d) The body has an acceleration ω^2 tangential to its path

23. If d denotes the distance covered by a car in time t and $\vec{S}$ denotes the displacement by the car during the same time, then : **[NDA]**

(a) $d \le |\vec{S}|$ (b) $d = |\vec{S}|$ only

(c) $d \ge |\vec{S}|$ (d) $d < |\vec{S}|$

24. The displacement of a particle at time t is given by $\bar{x} = a\hat{i} + bt\hat{j} + \dfrac{c}{2}t^2\hat{k}$ where a, b and c are positive constants. Then the particle is **[NDA]**

(a) accelerated along $\dfrac{18}{5}$ direction

(b) decelerated along $\dfrac{18}{5}$ direction

(c) decelerated along $\hat{j}$ direction

(d) accelerated along $\hat{j}$ direction

25. A body is projected vertically upwards with a velocity of 96 ft/s. What is the total time for which the body will remain in the air?

(a) 3 s   (b) 6 s

(c) 9 s   (d) 12 s

26. A motor vechicle is moving on a circle with a uniform speed. The net acceleration of the vehicle is **[NDA]**

(a) zero

(b) towards the centre of circle

(c) away from the centre along the radius of the circle

(d) perpendicular to the radius and along the velocity

27. A swinging pendulum has its maximum acceleration at **[NDA]**

(a) the bottom of the swing

(b) the two extremities of the swing

(c) every point on the swing

(d) no particular portion of the pendulum

28. An object is in uniform circular motion on a plane. Suppose that you measure its displacement from the centre along one direction, say, along the x-axis. Which one among the following graphs could represent this displacement (x)? **[NDA]**

(a)
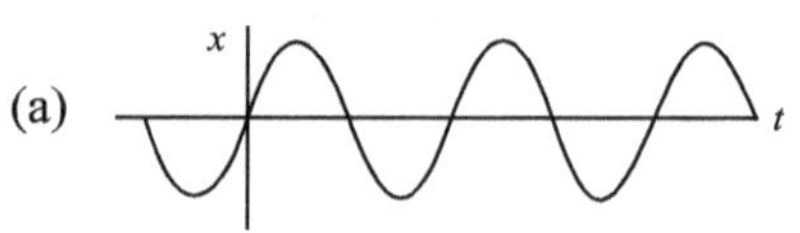

(b)
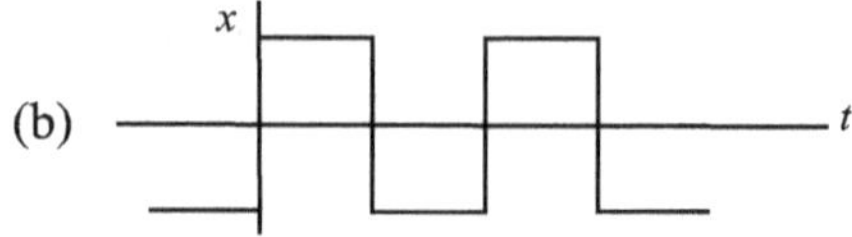

(c)
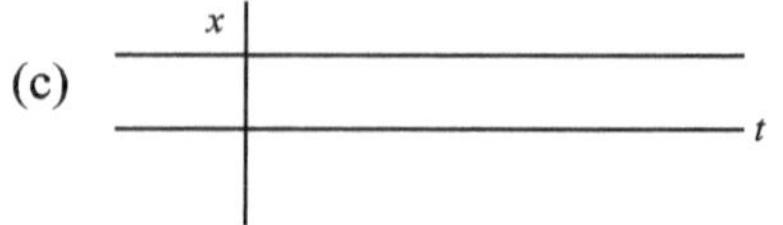

(d)
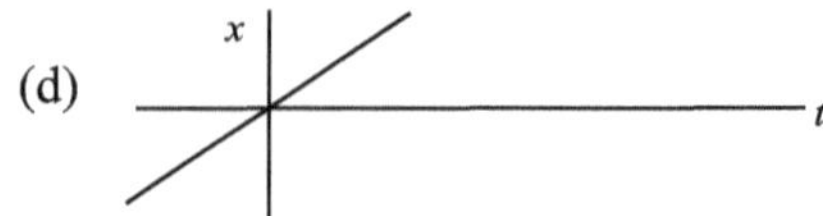

29. A particle starts from rest, accelerates uniformly for 3 seconds and then decelerates uniformly for 3 seconds and comes to rest.

    Which one of the following displacement (x)-time (t) graphs represents the motion of the particle? **[NDA]**

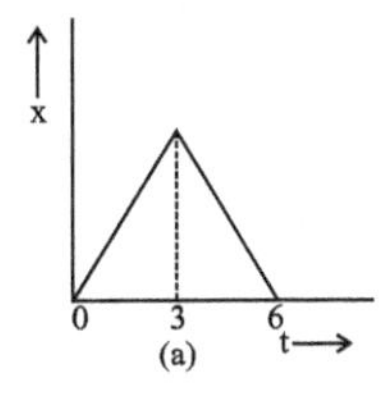
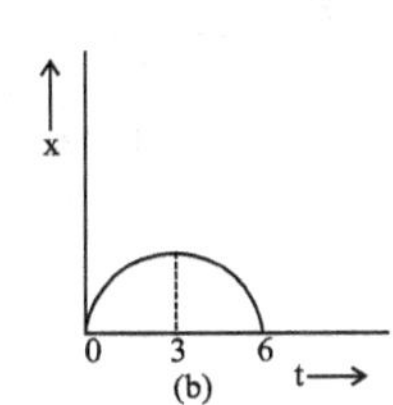
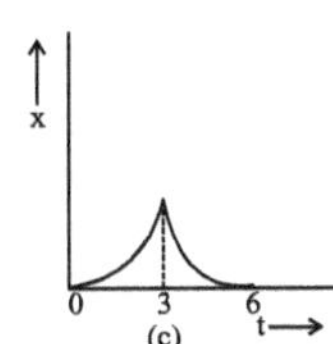
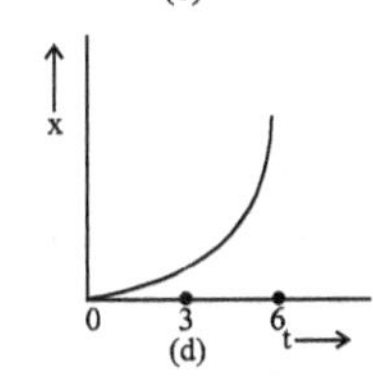

30. In the system shown, the masses are released from rest. What shall be the acceleration of the moving masses? **[NDA]**

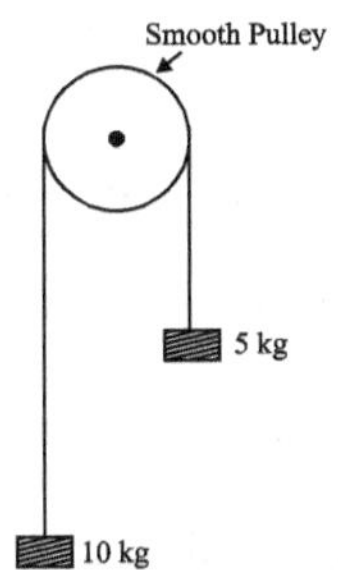

    (a) g
    (b) 2g/3
    (c) g/3
    (d) g/2

31. Which one of the following elements is used as a timekeeper in atomic clocks? **[CDS 2018-I]**
    (a) Potassium
    (b) Caesium
    (c) Calcium
    (d) Magnesium

32. Which one of the following is the value of one nanometer? **[CDS 2018-I]**
    (a) 10^{-7} cm
    (b) 10^{-6} cm
    (c) 10^{-4} cm
    (d) 10^{-3} cm

33. Which one of the following physical quantity has the same unit as that of pressure? **[NDA 2017-I]**
    (a) Angular momentum
    (b) Stress
    (c) Strain
    (d) Work

34. The symbol of SI unit of inductance is H. It stands for **[NDA 2017-II]**
    (a) Holm
    (b) Halogen
    (c) Henry
    (d) Hertz

35. Light year is a measure of **[NDA 2017-II]**
    (a) time
    (b) distance
    (c) total amount of light falling on the Earth in a year
    (d) average intensity of light falling on the Earth in a year

36. Consider the following velocity and time graph: **[NDA 2018-II]**

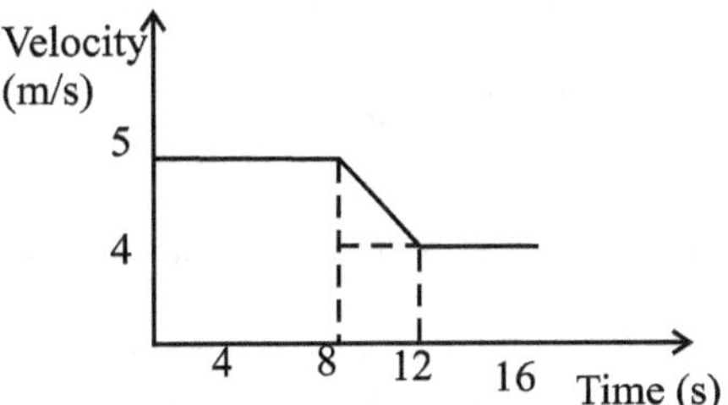

    Which one of the following is the value of average acceleration from 8 s to 12 s?
    (a) 8 m/s²
    (b) 12 m/s²
    (c) 2 m/s²
    (d) −1 m/s²

37. A ball is released from rest and rolls down an inclined plane, as shown in the following figure, requiring 4s to cover a distance of 100 cm along the plane: **[NDA 2018-II]**

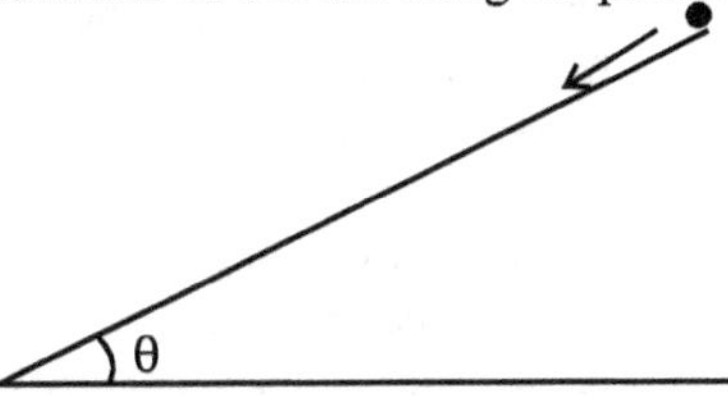

    Which one of the following is the correct value of angle θ that the plane makes with the horizontal? (g = 1000 cm/s²)
    (a) $\theta = \sin^{-1}(1/9.8)$
    (b) $\theta = \sin^{-1}(1/20)$
    (c) $\theta = \sin^{-1}(1/80)$
    (d) $\theta = \sin^{-1}(1/100)$

ANSWER KEY																			
1.	(c)	2.	(b)	3.	(a)	4.	(a)	5.	(c)	6.	(c)	7.	(c)	8.	(c)	9.	(b)	10.	(b)
11.	(b)	12.	(c)	13.	(c)	14.	(b)	15.	(b)	16.	(c)	17.	(a)	18.	(d)	19.	(c)	20.	(c)
21.	(d)	22.	(b)	23.	(c)	24.	(a)	25.	(b)	26.	(b)	27.	(b)	28.	(a)	29.	(c)	30.	(c)
31.	(b)	32.	(a)	33.	(b)	34.	(c)	35.	(b)	36.	(d)	37.	(c)						

LAWS OF MOTION AND FORCE

Everybody in this universe stays in a state of rest i.e., no change in position of a body wrt time or of uniform motion i.e., change in position of a body wrt time. This chapter is concerned about the cause of rest or motion (i.e., force) and its effect (i.e., acceleration or deceleration) and their relationship.

NEWTON'S LAWS OF MOTION

Newton's First Law of Motion

According to this law, *an object continues in a state of rest or in a state of motion at a constant speed along a straight line, unless compelled to change that state by a net force.* In other words, if a body is in a state of rest, it will remain in the state of rest and if it is in the state of motion, it will remain moving in the same direction with the same velocity unless an external unbalanced force is applied on it. This law is also called **law of inertia**. It gives qualitative definition of force.

Inertia and Mass

A greater net force is required to change the velocity of some objects than of others. The net force that is just enough to cause a bicycle to pick up speed will cause an imperceptible change in the motion of a freight train. In comparison to the bicycle, the train has a much greater tendency to remain at rest. Accordingly, we say that the train has more inertia than the bicycle. Quantitatively, the inertia of an object is measured by its mass. *Inertia is the natural tendency of an object to remain at rest or in motion at a constant speed along a straight line.* The mass of an object is a quantitative measure of inertia. The *greater the mass, the greater is the inertia of body.*

Types of Inertia

Inertia of rest : *The tendency of the body to continue in state of rest even when some external unbalanced force is applied on it is called inertia of rest.*

Inertia of motion : The tendency of the body to continue in its state of motion even when some unbalanced force is applied on it is called the inertia of motion.

Newton's Second Law of Motion

It states that *the rate of change of momentum of a body is directly proportional to the applied unbalanced force.*

i.e., Rate of change of momentum $\propto$ force applied

or, $\quad F \propto \dfrac{\Delta p}{\Delta t}$

If a body is moving with initial velocity u and after applying a force F on it. Its velocity becomes v in time t, then

$$F \propto \frac{m\,(v-u)}{t}$$

Here $\quad \dfrac{v-u}{t} = a$ (acceleration)

So $F \propto ma$ or $F = k\,ma$, where k is proportionality constant.

Momentum

The momentum of a moving body is defined as the *product of its mass and velocity*. If we represent the mass and velocity of a body by m and $\vec{v}$ respectively, then momentum is given by
$$\vec{p} = m\,\vec{v}$$
The direction of momentum of a body is same as that of its velocity.

The SI unit of momentum is kilogram meter per second (kgm/s).

Impulse or Change in Momentum

From Newton's second law, $\vec{F} = \dfrac{\Delta \vec{p}}{\Delta t}$, one can derive the **impulse-momentum theorem**. This theorem states that impulse is equal to the change in momentum, or,

$\vec{F}\Delta t = \Delta \vec{p} = \vec{p} - \vec{p}_0$

where $\vec{F}\Delta t$ is called impulse, $\vec{F}$ is the average force and Δt is the time interval the force is in action.

NEWTON'S THIRD LAW OF MOTION

It states that *to every action there is always an equal and opposite reaction.*

This law of motion states that 'if a body A exerts a force $+F$ on a body B, then body B exerts a force $-F$ on A, that is a force of the same magnitude and along the same line of interaction but in the opposite direction'.

CONSERVATION OF MOMENTUM

The principle of conservation of momentum states that *"if there is a direction in which there is zero unbalanced force acting on a system then the total momentum of that system in that direction is constant even if the bodies act on each other'.*

Also, the total momentum of the system remains constant, if no external force acts on a system of constant mass.

$$m_1 \vec{v_1} + m_2 \vec{v_2} + m_3 \vec{v_3} + ... = \text{constant}$$

Ex. The pull of the Earth, do act on the bodies, but the result can still be used if there is a direction in which the external forces are balanced.

FORCE

Force is that physical quantity which tries to change or changes the state of rest or of uniform motion of a body.

Units of force: The S.I. unit of force is newton.
In C.G.S. system, the unit of force is dyne.
1 newton = 10^5 dyne
In MKS system, the unit of force is the kilogramme force (kgf).
1 kgf = 9.8 newton (or 9.8 N)

Basic Forces in Nature

There are four basic forces in nature and they are

(i) **Gravitational Force:** Every body in the universe attracts each other, this force is known as gravitational force. This is the weakest force among all other forces which is existing.

(ii) **Weak Nuclear Force:** These forces are 10^{25} times stronger than gravitational force.

(iii) **Electromagnetic Force:** The electromagnetic forces are the forces between the charged particles. When charges are at rest, then the force is called as electrostatic force. This force is much stronger than gravitational force and it dominates atomic and molecular phenomena.

(iv) **Strong nuclear forces :** This is the strongest force found in nature. These forces acts between the proton and the neutron in order to bind them in the nucleus.
This force is 10^{38} times stronger than gravitational forces, 10^2 times stronger than electrostatic forces and 10^{13} times stronger than weak nuclear forces.

FRICTION

Friction is the resistance to the relative motion between two objects in contact (in case of solid objects) or the body and its surroundings (in case object is moving in a fluid). Actually, when two objects are kept in contact, a reaction force R acts between the two objects as shown in the figure.

This reaction force R has two components $-F$, along the surface and N, perpendicular to the surface. The force F which acts along the surface is called the force of friction.

The results of experimental investigation into the behaviour of frictional forces confirm that:

- frictional force opposes the movement of an object across the surface of another with which it is in rough contact.

- the direction of the frictional force is opposite to the potential direction of motion.

- The magnitude of the frictional force is only just sufficient to prevent movement and increases as the tendency to move increases, up to a limiting value. When the limiting value is reached, the frictional force cannot increase any further and motion is about to begin (limiting equilibrium). When the frictional force F reaches its limit, its value then is related to the normal reaction N in the following way $F = \mu N$
The constant μ is called the coefficient of friction and each pair of surfaces has its own value for this constant.

$$\left[\begin{array}{l} \text{Coefficient of friction} \\ \quad (\mu) = \frac{F}{N} \end{array} \right]$$

Angle of Friction

It is the angle between the normal reaction (N) and the resultant of limiting friction (F) and normal reaction.

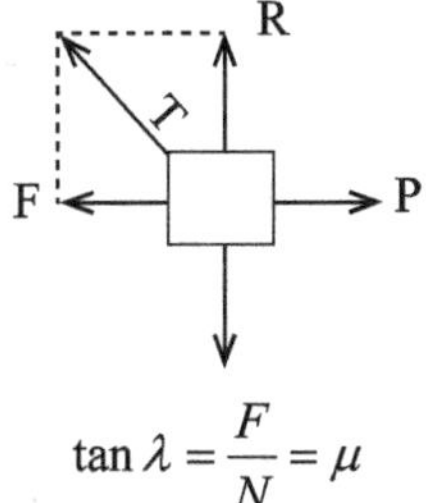

$$\tan \lambda = \frac{F}{N} = \mu$$

Angle of Repose

It is the minimum angle of inclination of a plane at which body starts moving down the plane under its own weight

$$\tan \theta = \mu_s = \tan \lambda$$
$$\text{i.e. } \theta = \lambda$$

Maximum frictional force betweentwo bodies (f_{max})

$$f_{max} \propto \text{nature of surfaces}$$
$$\propto \text{normal contact force}$$

f_{max} independent of contact area.

Types of Friction

Static frictional force: When there is no relative motion between the contact surfaces, frictional force is called static frictional force. It is a self-adjusting force, it adjusts its value according to requirement.

The maximum value of static friction is called **limiting friction**.

Kinetic frictional force: Once relative motion starts between the surfaces in contact, the frictional force is called as kinetic frictional force. The magnitude of kinetic frictional force is also proportional to normal force

i.e., $$f_k = \mu_k N$$

- **Sliding friction:** When one body slides over the surface of another body, the resistance to its motion is called as sliding friction. It is always more than rolling friction.

- **Rolling friction:** When one body rolls over the surface of another body, the resistance to its motion is termed as rolling friction. Friction in this case is very small.

  The coefficient of rolling friction (μ_R) is the least and coeficient of static friction is maximum, i.e., $\mu_R < \mu_K < \mu_S$.

Friction: A necessary Evil

Friction is **necessary** for doing various activities in our daily life.

- We could not hold articles such as glass tumbler and other things without friction. It becomes very difficult to hold a greasy glass.
- We could not write with pen or pencil if there is no friction.
- Friction helps objects to move, stop or to change the direction of motion. We cannot walk without friction.

Friction is an evil

- It causes wear and tear. For example, soles of shoes, ball bearings, steps of a stair, parts of machines etc.
- Friction produces heat. When a machine is operated, heat generated causes damage to the machinery.

Fast moving objects such as cars, bullet trains, aeroplanes are all streamlined-designed with curved and sloping surfaces to cut through the air and reduce drag. Boats can also be streamlined to reduce water resistance.

Motion in a Lift

The weight of a body is simply the force exerted by earth on the body. If body is on an accelerated platform, the body experiences fictitious force, so the weight of the body appears changed and this new weight is called apparent weight. Let a man of weight $W = Mg$ be standing in a lift.

Case (a): If the lift is moving with constant velocity v upwards or downwards.

Apparent weight, $W' =$ actual weight W

Case (b): If the lift is accelerated i.e., a = constant and in upward direction.

Apparent weight,
$$W' = W + F_0 = Mg + Ma = M(g + a)$$

Case (c): If the lift is accelerated downward with acceleration $a < g$:

Apparent weight,
$$W' = W + F_0 = Mg - Ma = M(g - a)$$

Case (d): If the lift is accelerated downward with acceleration $a > g$:

Apparent weight, $W' = M(g - a)$ is negative.

CENTRIPETAL FORCE

If m be the mass of object then it experiences a force which directs towards the centre of the circular path and has a magnitude given by

$$F_c = ma_c = \frac{mv^2}{r} \quad \text{or} \quad F = mr\,\omega^2 \quad [\because \ v = r\omega]$$

This force is known as centripetal force.

CENTRIFUGAL FORCE

The virtual force which balances the centripetal force in uniform circular motion is called as centrifugal force. It is not the real force as it is due to the acceleration of rotating frame. When a body is rotating in a circular path and the centripetal force vanishes, the body would leave the circular path.

APPLICATIONS

- **Cream Separator :** It is device which works on the principle of centrifugal force. It contains a vessel which has milk, when it rotated the lighter particles i.e. the cream is collected in a cylindrical layer around the axis and the milk is drained through an outlet attached to the vessel.
- **Washing Machine Drier :** When wet clothes are packed tightly in a cylindrical vessel with perforated walls and rotated with very high speed, water particles move out through the walls of the vessel.

CIRCULAR MOTION

Motion of a particle along a circle or circular path is called a circular motion. If the body covers equal distances along the circumference of the circle, in equal intervals of time, the motion is said to be a **uniform circular motion**. A uniform circular motion is a motion in which speed remains constant but direction changes so velocity.

Examples of uniform circular motion are

- motion of moon around the earth.
- motion of satellite round its planet.

BANKING OF ROAD

The tilting of the vehicle is achieved by raising the outer edge of the circular track, slightly above the inner edge. This is known as banking of curved track. $\left[\text{Angle of banking } (\theta) = \dfrac{V^2}{Rg}\right]$

CONDITION OF OVERTURNING

If speed is greater than limiting speed, then condition of overturning is occurred.

Maximum speed of Car in a circular motion
(i) On a level path $\quad V_{max} = \sqrt{\mu_s Rg}$
(ii) On a banked path $\quad V_{max} = \left[Rg\dfrac{\mu_s + \tan\theta}{1 - \mu_s \tan\theta}\right]^{1/2}$
Where, μ_s = coefficient of static friction $\quad\quad\quad R$ = Radius of circular path $\quad\quad\quad g$ = Acceleration due to gravity

WORK, ENERGY AND POWER

The meaning of work in physics is different from its meaning in common language. Actually, in physics work has a meaning only when a displacement is caused in a body by the applied force on it. If there is no displacement in a body by an applied force in the direction of force, no work is said to be done.

WORK

Work is defined as the product of the force and displacement in the direction of applied force or product of displacement and force in the direction of displacement.

W = Force × displacement in the direction of force

$= F.S = FS \cos \theta$

where θ is the angle between F and S.

The SI unit of work is newton-metre is also called joule (J)

1 joule $= 10^7$ erg

Work done by a force applied at an angle

W = *component of force in the direction of displacement × magnitude of displacement = F cos θ s*

Work done by a force can be positive, negative or zero as the value of $\cos \theta$ is positive, negative or zero.

($\because$ F and s, being magnitudes, are always positive)

- Work is a scalar quantity but there can be positive and negative work.

ENERGY

Energy is defined as the capacity to do work.

The SI unit of energy is the joule (J) same as that of work. The commonly used unit for electrical-energy consumption is the **kilowatt-hour (kWh).**

Thus, 1kWh = 1kW × 1 hour

$= (1000 \text{ W}) \times (3600 \text{ s})$

$= (1000 \text{ J/s}) \times (3600 \text{ s})$

$= (3600000 \text{ joules}) = 3.6 \times 10^6 \text{J}.$

For electrical-energy consumption in houses, factories, shops, etc., kilowatt-hour is simply called 'unit' (Board of trade unit B.O.T.U.).

Kinetic Energy (K.E.)

Energy possessed by a body by virtue of its state of motion is called kinetic energy. Kinetic energy is always positive and is a scalar.

$$\text{K.E.} = \frac{1}{2}mv^2 = \frac{p^2}{2m}$$

Potential Energy (P.E.)

Potential energy is energy due to position. If a body is in a position such that if it were released it would begin to move, it has potential energy.

$$\text{P.E.} = mgh$$

For **example**, energy of water in a water tank on the roof, energy of small spring in ball-pen, etc.

Gravitational potential energy

When an object is allowed to fall from higher level to a lower level it gains speed due to gravitational pull, i.e. it gains kinetic energy.

The magnitude of its gravitational potential energy is equivalent to the amount of work done by the weight of the body in causing the descent.

If a mass m is at a height h above a lower level, the P.E. possessed by the mass is mgh.

Since h is the height of an object above a specified level, an object below the specified level has negative potential energy.

Work-Energy Theorem

According to the work-energy theorem, total work done on a system by forces equals to the change in kinetic energy.

LAW OF CONSERVATION OF ENERGY

According to this law, energy can only be converted from one form to another, it can neither be created nor destroyed. The total energy before and after the transformation always remains the same.

Transformation of Energy

The conversion of one form of energy to the other form is termed as transformation of energy. The phenomenon in which energy is transformed from useful from to useless form is known as dissipation of energy.

Mass-Energy equivalence Relation

According to this relation mass (m) and energy (E) are inter-convertible

$$E = mc^2$$

Where, $c = 3 \times 10^8$ ms^{-1} is the velocity of light in vaccum or air.

POWER

The time rate of doing work is defined as power (P). If equal works are done in different times, power will be different. More quickly work is done, power will be more.

$$\text{Power (P)} = \frac{\text{Work (W)}}{\text{time (t)}}$$

The S.I. unit of power is the *joule per second* and is called the *watt (W)*. 1 H.P (Horse power) = 746 W

Physical formula unit Dimension quantity

Physical Quantity	Formula	Unit	Dimension
Work (W)	$W = f.d$	J	ML^2T^{-2}
Kinetic energy (K)	$K = \frac{1}{2}mv^2$	J	ML^2T^{-2}
Mechanical energy (E)	$E = K + V$	J	ML^2T^{-2}
Potential energy (V_x)	$\frac{-dv(x)}{dx} = F(x)$	J	ML^2T^{-2}
Power (P)	$P = F.v$	W	ML^2T^{-3}

COLLISIONS

Collision is an event in which two or more than two bodies interact with one another for a short time and exchange momentum and kinetic energy. Collisions are of two types :

- Elastic collision
- Inelastic collision

Elastic Collision

A collision in which there is no loss of kinetic energy is called elastic or perfectly elastic collision. The basic characteristics of perfectly elastic collision are

- linear momentum is conserved
- kinetic energy is conserved
- total energy is conserved
- coefficient of restitution is unity ($e = 1$)

Inelastic Collision

In an inelastic collision kinetic energy is lost during collision. The basic characteristic of an inelastic collision are :

- linear momentum is conserved
- kinetic energy is not conserved
- total energy is conserved
- coefficient of restitution is $0 < e < 1$

In case of perfectly inelastic collision the two bodies get stuck together and move with common velocity, that is why for perfectly inelastic collision.

CENTRE OF MASS AND ROTATIONAL MOTION

The motion through space in which the position of the centre of mass of the object changes is considered as translational motion.

CENTRE OF MASS (COM)

For a system of particles, **centre of mass,** is that point at which its total mass is supposed to be concentrated.

Rigid Body

A body which does not deform on the application of whatsoever large force is called a rigid body. Ideally such type of body will not exist but practically, large, extended object can be treated as rigid body. For example, door is a rigid body.

Centre of Mass of Some Symmetrical Regular Shaped Objects

When bodies are symmetrical in shape and have uniform densities then their centre of mass would lie on their geometrical centres.

The position of centre of mass depends on following two factors:

- The geometrical shape of the body
- The distribution of mass in the body

Velocity of the centre of mass of a system of particles is given by,

$V = P/M$,

Where P = Linear momentum of the system.

The centre of mass moves as if all the mass of the system is concentrated at this point and all the external forces act at it. If the total external force on the system is zero, then the total linear momentum of the system is constant.

ROTATIONAL MOTION

A rigid body performs a pure rotational motion, if each particle of the body moves in a circle, and the centre of all the circles lie on a straight line, called the axis of rotation.

Examples : Motion of a ceiling fan, motion of a potter's wheel, etc.

Angular Displacement ($\Delta\theta$)

The change in position of a particle moving in a circular path with respect to the center is known as it's angular displacement. . Its **SI unit** is radian.

Angular Velocity (ω)

The rate of change of angular displacement of a body.

Average angular velocity $\omega = \dfrac{\theta_2 - \theta_1}{t_2 - t_1} = \dfrac{\Delta\theta}{\Delta t}$

Also, angular velocity, $\omega = 2\pi n$ where, n = number of revolutions per second.

Its SI unit is radian/s

Relation between angular velocity (ω), linear velocity (v) and radius of circular path (r)

$$v = r\,\omega \qquad \text{or} \qquad \omega = \frac{v}{r}$$

MOMENT OF INERTIA

The property of a body by virtue of which it opposes any change in its state of rest or of rotational motion is defined as its moment of inertia. The moment of inertia of a particle in rotational motion is equal to the product of its mass (m) and square of its distance (r) from the axis.

Moment of inertia, $I = mr^2$

It is neither a scalar nor a vector but it is considered as a **tensor.**

Its **SI unit** is kg m^2

Body	Axis	Moment of Inertia (I)
Thin circular Ring	Perpendicular to ring (at the centre)	$M R^2$
	Diameter	$M R^2/2$
Circular disc	Perpendicular to disc (at the centre)	$M R^2/2$
	Diameter	$M R^2/4$
Hollow cylinder	Axis of cylinder	$M R^2$
Solid cylinder		$M R^2/2$
Solid sphere	Diameter	$2M R^2/5$
Thin rod	Perpendicular	$M L^2/12$

TORQUE

Torque is the turning or twisting action on a body about the axis of rotation due to a force $\vec{F}$.

$$\vec{\tau} = (\vec{r} \times \vec{F}).\hat{n} \,,$$

Rigid body in Equilibrium

A rigid body is in equilibrium, if it has zero translational acceleration and zero angular acceleration.

Principle of Moments for a Lever

Load × load arm = effort × effort arm

Mechanical advantage (M.A.) of lever

$$= \frac{\text{load}}{\text{effort}} = \frac{\text{effort arm}}{\text{load arm}}$$

Couple

When two equal and parallel forces having different line of action acts on a body then it makes a couple. It has always the unidirectional rotational effect.

Couple = force × force arm

ANGULAR MOMENTUM

In translational motion the measure of quantity of motion possessed by a body is linear momentum and the physical quantity analogous to it in rotational motion is angular momentum, it is represented by L and it is a vector quantity. Angular momentum $L = I\omega$. Its S.I. unit is joule-second.

Relation Between Torque (τ) and Angular Momentum (L)

$$\frac{dL}{dt} = \tau \qquad (\text{As } \tau = I\,\alpha)$$

Conservation of Angular momentum

Suppose on a system of particles of a rigid body no external force is acting then its angular momentum remains conserved, this is known as conservation of angular momentum.

Physical Quantity	Formula	Unit	Dimension
Moment of Inertia (I)	$I = \Sigma\, m_i r_i^2$	$Kg\ m^2$	$[ML^{-2}]$
Angular Velocity (ω)	$v = \omega \times r$	rad sec^{-1}	$[T^{-1}]$
Angular momentum (L)	$L = r \times P$	J s	$[ML^2 T^{-1}]$
Torque (τ)	$\tau = r \times F$	N m	$[ML^2 T^{-2}]$

MULTIPLE CHOICE QUESTIONS

1. A ball weighing 100 gm, released from a height of 5 m, bounces perfectly elastically off a plate. The collision time between the ball and the plate is 0.5 s. The average force on the plate is approximately.
   - (a) 3 N
   - (b) 2 N
   - (c) 5 N
   - (d) 4 N

2. A disc of mass m is free to rotate in a plane parallel to the xy plane with an angular velocity $\omega\hat{z}$ about a massless rigid rod suspended from the roof of a stationary car (as shown in the figure below). The rod is free to orient itself along any direction.

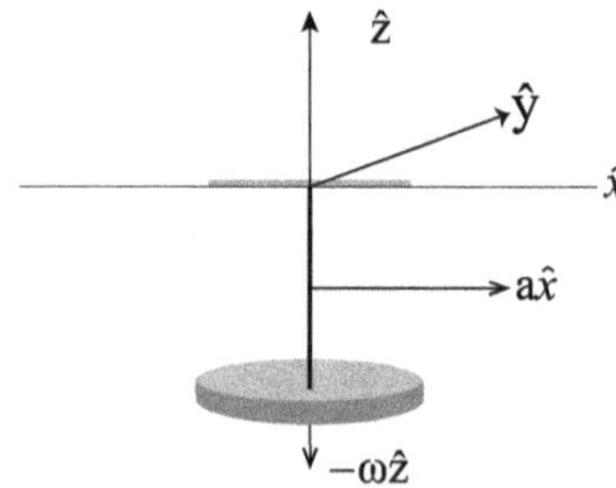

   The car accelerates in the positive x–direction with an acceleration $a > 0$. Which of the following statements is true for the coordinates of the centre of mass of the disc in the reference frame of the car?
   - (a) only the x and the z coordinates change
   - (b) only the y and the z coordinates change
   - (c) only the x and the y coordinates change
   - (d) all the three coordinates change

3. Newton's laws of motion do not hold good for objects
   - (a) at rest
   - (b) moving slowly
   - (c) moving with high velocity
   - (d) moving with velocity comparable to velocity of light

4. A jet engine works on the principle of conservation of **[NDA]**
   - (a) linear momentum
   - (b) angular momentum
   - (c) energy
   - (d) mass

5. Which one among the following is correct for resultant of balanced forces? **[NDA]**
   - (a) It is zero
   - (b) It is non-zero
   - (c) It varies continuously
   - (d) None of the above

6. When a moving bus suddenly applies brakes, the passengers sitting in it fall in the forward direction. This can be explained by **[NDA]**
   - (a) the theory of relativity
   - (b) Newton's first law
   - (c) Newton's second law
   - (d) Newton's third law

7. A book is kept on the surface of a table. If the gravitational pull of the earth on the book is the force of action, then the force of reaction is exerted by **[NDA]**
   - (a) the book on the table
   - (b) the book on the earth
   - (c) the table on the book
   - (d) the table on the earth

8. The pressure exerted on the ground by a man is greatest **[CDS]**
   - (a) when the lies down in the ground
   - (b) when the stands on the toes of one foot
   - (c) when the stands with both foot flat on the ground
   - (d) all of the above yield the same pressure

9. If a ship moves from freshwater into seawater, it will **[CDS]**
   - (a) sink completely
   - (b) sink a little bit
   - (c) rise a little higher
   - (d) remain unaffected

10. A man is at rest in the middle of a horizontal plane of perfectly smooth surface of ice. He can move himself to the shore by making use of Newton's **[NDA]**
    - (a) first law of motion
    - (b) second law of motion
    - (c) third law of motion
    - (d) first, second and third laws of motion

11. If an object having mass of 1 kg is subjected to a force of 1 N it moves with **[CDS]**
    - (a) a speed of 1 m/s
    - (b) a speed of 1 km/s
    - (c) an acceleration of 10 m/s^2
    - (d) an acceleration of 1 m/s^2

12. An athlete diving off a high springboard can perform a variety of exercises in the air before entering the water below. Which one of the following parameters will remain constant during the fall? **[CDS]**
    - (a) The athlete's linear momentum
    - (b) The athlete's moment of inertia
    - (c) The athlete's kinetic energy
    - (d) The athlete's angular momentum

13. **Statement A :** While drawing a line on a paper, friction force acts on paper in the same direction along which line is drawn on the paper.

    Statement B : Friction always opposes motion.
    - (a) Statement A is correct.
    - (b) Statement B is correct.
    - (c) Both statements are correct.
    - (d) Both statements are incorrect.

14. **Assertion (A) :** A man standing on a completely frictionless surface can propel himself by whistling.

    Reason (R) : If no external force acts on a system, its momentum cannot change. **[IAS Prelim]**
    - (a) Both A and R are true and R is the correct explanation of A
    - (b) Both A and R are true but R is not a correct explanation of A
    - (c) A is true but R is false
    - (d) A is false but R is true

15. A spherical body moves with a uniform angular velocity (w) around a circular path of radius r. Which one of the following statements is correct? **[IAS Prelim]**
    (a) The body has no acceleration
    (b) The body has a radial acceleration $\omega^2 r$ directed toward centre of path
    (c) The body has a radial acceleration $2/5\omega^2 r$ directed away from the centre of the path
    (d) The body has an acceleration ω^2 tangential to its path

16. On the basis of following features identify the correct option.
    A. It is measured in units of kg m/s.
    B. Its direction is same as that of velocity of body.
    (a) Momentum   (b) Inertia
    (c) Both A and B   (d) Neither A and B

17. In cricket match, while catching a fast moving ball, a fielder in the ground gradually pulls his hands backwards with the moving ball to reduce the velocity to zero. The act represents **[CDS]**
    (a) Newton's first law of motion
    (b) Newton's second law of motion
    (c) Newton's third law of motion
    (d) Law of conservation of energy

18. **Statement A:** Pulling a lawn roller is easier than pushing it.
    Statement B : Pushing increases the apparent weight and hence the force of friction. **[CDS]**
    (a) Statement A is correct.
    (b) Statement B is correct.
    (c) Both statements are correct.
    (d) Both statements are incorrect.

19. It is difficult to cut things with a blunt knife because **[CDS]**
    (a) the pressure exerted by knife for a given force increases with increase in bluntness
    (b) a sharp edge decreases the pressure exerted by knife for a given force
    (c) a blunt knife decreases the pressure for a given force
    (d) a blunt knife decreases the area of intersection

20. **Statement A :** When a gun is fired it recoils, i.e., it pushes back, with much less velocity than the velocity of the bullet.
    Statement B : Velocity of the recoiling gun is less because the gun is much heavier than the bullet. **[CDS]**
    (a) Statement A is correct.
    (b) Statement B is correct.
    (c) Both statements are correct.
    (d) Both statements are incorrect.

21. Two teams are pulling a rope with equal and opposite forces each of 5 kN in a tug of war so that a condition of equilibrium exists. What will be the tensile force in the rope? **[NDA]**
    (a) Zero   (b) 2.5 kN
    (c) 5 kN   (d) 10 kN

22.

Column-I		Column-II
A.	Rocket propulsion	P. Force
B.	Agent which causes acceleration	Q. Momentum
C.	Product of mass and velocity	R. S.I. unit of force
D.	Newton	S. Law of conservation of momentum

    (a) A → S; B → P; C → R; D → Q
    (b) A → P; B → S; C → R; D → Q
    (c) A → S; B → P; C → Q; D → R
    (d) A → P; B → S; C → Q; D → R

23. **Statement A :** While walking on ice, one should take small steps to avoid slipping.
    Statement B : This is because smaller steps ensure smaller friction.
    (a) Statement A is correct.
    (b) Statement B is correct.
    (c) Both statements are correct.
    (d) Both statements are incorrect.

24. Thomas and Mary are playing carom board. They arrange the seeds in the vertical order. Thomas strikes on the seeds with the striker, with a great speed. He finds that, the stakes do not fall down. On the other hand, when he strikes the seeds with less speed, all the seeds of the stakes fell down. Which property of force this shows?
    (a) Newton's third law (b) Motion
    (c) Inertia   (d) Reaction of force

25. A man getting down a running bus, falls forward because-
    (a) due to inertia of rest, road is left behind and man reaches forward
    (b) due to inertia of motion upper part of body continues to be in motion in forward direction while feet come to rest as soon as they touch the road
    (c) he leans forward as a matter of habit
    (d) of the combined effect of all the three factors stated in (a), (b) and (c)

26. The work done becomes zero if
    (a) force perpendicular to the displacement
    (b) displacement is zero
    (c) force acting on the body is zero
    (d) All of the above

27. When an incandescent electric bulb glows **[CDS]**
    (a) the electric energy is completely converted into light
    (b) the electric energy is partly converted into light energy and partly into heat energy
    (c) the light energy is converted into electric energy
    (d) the electric energy is converted into magnetic energy

28. The sum of the change in kinetic and potential energy is always **[SSC CGL]**
    (a) Zero   (b) Positive
    (c) Negative   (d) None of the above

29. The potential energy is always the same for an object with the same
    (a) Velocity   (b) Speed
    (c) Acceleration   (d) Position

30. If velocity of a body is twice of previous velocity, then kinetic energy will become **[NDA]**
    (a) 2 times   (b) 1/2 times
    (c) 4 times   (d) 1 times

31. In case of negative work the angle between the force and displacement is
    (a) 0°   (b) 45°
    (c) 90°   (d) 180°

32. How much time will it take to perform 440 J of work at a rate of 11 W?
    (a) 50 s   (b) 40 s
    (c) 30 s   (d) 20 s

33. When a stone tied to a string is whirled in a circle, the work done on it by the string is
    (a) positive
    (b) negative
    (c) zero
    (d) undefined

34. Match the Column I and Column II.

Column-I		**Column-II**	
A.	Electric motor	P.	Electrical energy to sound energy
B.	Electric bell	Q.	Electrical energy to mechanical energy
C.	Electric bulb electrical	R.	Light energy to energy
D.	Photoelectric mechanical	S.	Heat energy to cell energy
E.	Steam engine light energy	T.	Electric energy to

    (a) A-P; B-Q; C-T; D-R; E-S
    (b) A-Q; B-P; C-T; D-T; E-S
    (c) A-Q; B-P; C-T; D-S; E-R
    (d) A-Q; B-P; C-T; D-R; E-S

35. Which one of the following physical quantities is represented by the shaded area in the given graph?

    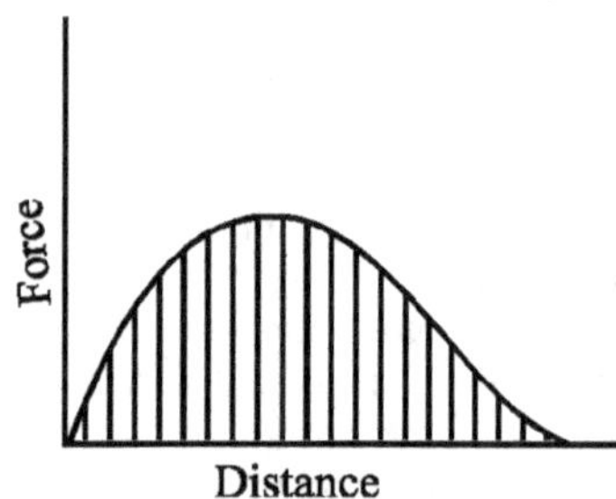

    (a) Torque
    (b) Impulse
    (c) Power
    (d) Work done

36. Two masses m and 9 m are moving with equal kinetic energies. The ratio of the magnitudes of their momenta is
    (a) 1 : 1
    (b) 1 : 3
    (c) 3 : 1
    (d) 1 : 9

37. A particle oscillates in one dimension about the equilibrium position subject to a force $F_x(x)$ that has an associated potential energy $U(x)$. If k is the force constant, which one of the following relations is true? **[NDA]**
    (a) $F_x(x) = -kx^2$
    (b) $F_x(x) = -kx$
    (c) $U(x) = \frac{1}{2}kx$
    (d) $U(x) = \frac{1}{2}k^2x$

38. If a light body and a heavy body have equal momentum, then **[NDA]**
    (a) the lighter body has greater energy than the heavier body
    (b) the lighter body has lesser kinetic energy than the heavier body
    (c) the kinetic energy of the lighter body is equal to the kinetic energy of the heavier body
    (d) the kinetic energy of both the bodies are independent of momentum.

39. A rubber ball dropped from 24 m height loses its kinetic energy by 25%. What is the height to which it rebounds.
    (a) 6 m
    (b) 12 m
    (c) 18 m
    (d) 24 m

40. The potential energy of a freely falling object decreases progressively.
    (a) The law of conservation of energy is violated
    (b) Potential energy gets converted into kinetic energy progressively
    (c) Sum of Potential Energy and Kinetic Energy at any point during the free fall remains constant
    (d) Both (b) and (c)

41. In which of the following examples, work done is negative?
    (a) Work done by the force of gravity on a moving aeroplane
    (b) Work done by the force of gravity on a ball thrown upwards
    (c) Work done by the force of gravity on a freely falling object
    (d) Work done by the force of gravity on a satellite revolving around the earth

42. **Assertion :** A man gets completely exhausted in trying to push a stationary wall.

    Reason : Work done by the man on the wall is zero.
    (a) If both **Assertion** and **Reason** are **correct** and **Reason** is the **correct explanation** of **Assertion**.
    (b) If both **Assertion** and **Reason** are **correct**, but **Reason** is not the **correct** explanation of **Assertion**.
    (c) If **Assertion** is **correct** but **Reason** is **incorrect**.
    (d) If **Assertion** is **incorrect** but **Reason** is **correct**.

43. A boy has four options to move a body through 3m as indicated. In which case is maximum work done?
    (a) Push over an inclined plane
    (b) Lift vertically upwards
    (c) Push over smooth rollers
    (d) Push on a plane horizontal surface

44. An electrical appliance of 500 W is used for 5 hours per day. Energy consumed in 30 days will be
    (a) 2.5 kW h
    (b) 25 kW h
    (c) 75 kW h
    (d) None of these

45. Two persons do the same amount of work, one in 10 s and the other in 20 s. Find the ratio of the power used by the first person to that by the second person.
    (a) 6 : 4
    (b) 2 : 1
    (c) 5 : 2
    (d) 4 : 3

46. Rahul takes 1 minute to raise a box to a height of 1 metre and Rohan takes 1/2 minute to do so. Comment on the energy by the two.
    (a) Energy spent by the Rahul is more.
    (b) Energy spent by both Rahul and Rohan is same.
    (c) Energy spent by the Rohan is more
    (d) Cannot be said

47. Gravitational potential energy of an object will
    (a) increase by increasing the path along which the object is moved
    (b) decrease by increasing the path along which the object is moved
    (c) not effected by changing the path, provided the overall height is same
    (d) None of these

48. Two identical particles move towards each other with velocity 2v and v respectively. The velocity of centre of mass is
(a) v
(b) v/3
(c) v/2
(d) zero

49. A solid sphere is rotating in free space. If the radius of the sphere is increased keeping mass same which one of the following will not be affected ?
(a) Angular velocity
(b) Angular momentum
(c) Moment of inertia
(d) Rotational kinetic energy

50. A simple machine helps a person in doing: **[IAS Prelim]**
(a) less work
(b) the same amount of work with lesser force
(c) the same amount of work slowly
(d) the same amount of work much faster

51. For a particle revolving in a circular path, the acceleration of the particle is **[NDA]**
(a) along the tangent
(b) along the radius
(c) zero
(d) along the circumference of the circle

52. A fan is moving around its axis, What will be its motion regarded as ?
(a) Pure rolling
(b) Rolling with shipping
(c) Skidding
(d) Pure rotation

53. During summersault, a swimmer bends his body to
(a) increase moment of Inertia
(b) decrease moment of Inertia
(c) decrease the angular momentum
(d) reduce the angular velocity

54. For a given mass and size, moment of inertia of a solid disc is
(a) more than that of a ring
(b) less than that of a ring
(c) equal to that of a ring
(d) depend on the material of ring and disc

55. A gymnast takes turns with her arms & legs stretched. When she pulls her arms and legs **[CDS]**
(a) the angular velocity decreases
(b) the moment of inertia decreases
(c) the angular velocity stays constant
(d) the angular momentum increases

56. For which one of the following does the centre of mass lie outside the body? **[CDS 2017-I]**
(a) A fountain pen
(b) A cricket ball
(c) A ring
(d) A book

57. A person is standing on a frictionless horizontal ground. How can he move by a certain distance on this ground? **[CDS 2017-II]**
(a) By sneezing
(b) By jumping
(c) By running
(d) By rolling

58. A person thrown an object on a horizontal frictionless plane surface. It is noticed that there are two forces acting on this object– (i) gravitational pull and (ii) normal reaction of the surface. According to the third law of motion, the net resultant force is zero. Which one of the following can be said for the motion of the object? **[CDS 2017-II]**
(a) The object will move with acceleration.
(b) The object will move with deceleration.
(c) The object will move with constant speed, but varying direction.
(d) The object will move with constant velocity.

59. Consider the following statements : **[CDS 2018-I]**
1. There is no net moment on a body which is in equilibrium.
2. The momentum of a body is always conserved.
3. The kinetic energy of an object is always conserved.
Which of the statements given above is/are correct?
(a) 1, 2 and 3
(b) 2 and 3 only
(c) 1 and 2 only
(d) 1 only

60. The speed of a car travelling on a straight road is listed below at successive intervals of 1: **[NDA 2017-I]**

Time (s)	0	1	2	3	4
Speed (m/s)	0	2	4	6	8

Which of the following is/are correct?
The car travels
1. with a uniform acceleration of 2 m/s^2.
2. 16 m in 4 s.
3. with an average speed of 4 m/s.
Select the correct answer using the code given below:
(a) 1, 2 and 3
(b) 2 and 3 only
(c) 1 and 2 only
(d) 1 only

61. The following figure shows displacement versus time curve for a particle executing simple harmonic motion : **[NDA 2017-I]**

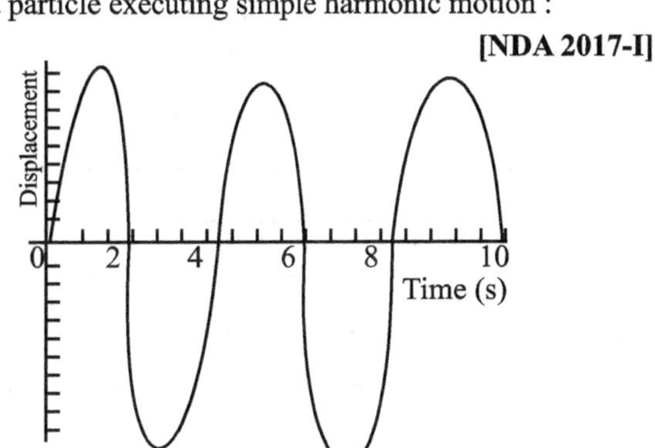

Which one of the following statements is correct?
- (a) Phase of the oscillating particle is same at $t = 1$ s and $t = 3$ s
- (b) Phase of the oscillating particle is same at $t = 2$ s and $t = 8$ s
- (c) Phase of the oscillating particle is same at $t = 3$ s and $t = 7$ s
- (d) Phase of the oscillating particle is same at $t = 4$ s and $t = 10$ s

62. Which one of the following is the correct relation between frequency f and angular frequency ω? **[NDA 2017-I]**
- (a) $f = \pi\omega$
- (b) $\omega = 2\pi f$
- (c) $f = 2\omega/\pi$
- (d) $f = 2\pi\omega$

63. The force acting on a particle of mass m moving along the x-axis is given by $F(x) = Ax^2 - Bx$. **[NDA 2017-II]** Which one of the following is the potential energy of the particle
- (a) $2Ax - B$
- (b) $-\dfrac{x^2}{6}(2Ax\,\dfrac{3}{\lambda}B)$
- (c) $Ax^3 - Bx^2$
- (d) Zero

64. If an object moves with constant velocity then which one of the following statements is NOT correct? **[NDA 2018-I]**
- (a) Its motion is along a straight line
- (b) Its speed changes with time
- (c) Its acceleration is zero
- (d) its displacement increases linearly with time

65. An object is moving with uniform acceleration a. Its initial velocity is u and after time t its velocity is v. The equation of its motion is v = u + at. The velocity (along y-axis) time (along x-axis) graph shall be a straight line **[NDA 2018-I]**
- (a) passing through origin
- (b) with x-intercept u
- (c) with y-intercept u
- (d) with slope u

66. Which one of the following has maximum inertia? **[NDA 2018-I]**
- (a) An atom
- (b) A molecule
- (c) A one-rupee coin
- (d) A cricket ball

67. Which one of the following statements about the mass of a body is correct? **[NDA 2018-I]**
- (a) It changes from one place to another
- (b) It is same everywhere
- (c) It depends on its shape
- (d) It does not depend on its temperature

ANSWER KEY

1.	(d)	2.	(d)	3.	(d)	4.	(a)	5.	(a)	6.	(b)	7.	(c)	8.	(b)	9.	(c)	10	(c)
11.	(d)	12.	(d)	13.	(c)	14.	(b)	15.	(b)	16.	(a)	17.	(b)	18.	(a)	19.	(c)	20.	(a)
21.	(c)	22.	(c)	23.	(a)	24.	(c)	25.	(c)	26.	(d)	27.	(b)	28.	(a)	29.	(d)	30.	(c)
31.	(d)	32.	(b)	33.	(c)	34.	(d)	35.	(d)	36.	(b)	37.	(b)	38.	(c)	39.	(c)	40.	(d)
41.	(b)	42.	(a)	43.	(b)	44.	(c)	45.	(b)	46.	(b)	47.	(c)	48.	(c)	49.	(b)	50.	(b)
51.	(b)	52.	(d)	53.	(b)	54.	(b)	55.	(b)	56.	(c)	57.	(a)	58.	(d)	59.	(c)	60.	(a)
61.	(c)	62.	(b)	63.	(b)	64.	(b)	65.	(c)	66.	(d)	67.	(b)								

FORCE OF GRAVITY, SOLIDS & FLUIDS

FORCE OF GRAVITY

Earth attracts every body towards itself with a force known as 'gravity'. Due to the force of gravity the ball thrown upwards doesn't go upwards but it falls downwards after covering some vertical distance.

Actually, every object attracts every other object towards itself with a force. This force is called the gravitational force. Gravitational force is one among the four fundamental forces. It is always attractive in nature.

NEWTON'S UNIVERSAL LAW OF GRAVITATION

Newton came to the conclusion that any two objects in the Universe exert gravitational attraction on each other.

Any two particles of matter anywhere in the universe attract each other with a force which is directly proportional to the product of their masses and inversely proportional to the square of the distance between them,

i.e. $\quad F \propto \dfrac{m_1 m_2}{r^2}$ or $\qquad F = \dfrac{G m_1 m_2}{r^2}$

Here, the constant of proportionality G is known as the **universal gravitational constant**. It is termed a "universal constant" because it is thought to be the same at all places and all times.

$G = 6.673 \times 10^{-11} \ \mathrm{N}m^2/\mathrm{kg}^2$.

The value of universal gravitational constant, G is very small-hence gravitational force is very small, unless one (or both) of the masses is huge.

Important Characteristics of Gravitational Force

- Gravitational forces are always attractive and always acts along the line joining the two masses.
- Gravitational force is a mutual force hence it is action-reaction force, i.e., $\vec{F}_{12} = -\vec{F}_{21}$.
- Value of G is small, therefore, gravitational force is weaker than electrostatic and nuclear forces.
- Gravitational force is a central force because $F \propto \dfrac{1}{r^2}$.
- The gravitational force between two masses is independent of the presence of other objects and medium between the two masses.

Importance of the Universal Law of Gravitation

The universal law of gravitation successfully explained several phenomena which were believed to be unconnected.

- the force that binds us to the earth
- the motion of the moon around the earth
- the motion of planets around the Sun and
- the tides due to the moon and the Sun.

MASS AND WEIGHT

The quantity of matter in a body is known as the mass of the body. Mass is quantitative measure of inertia. Mass is an intrinsic property of matter and does not change as an object is moved from one location to another.

Weight, in contrast, is the gravitational force that the earth exerts on the object and can vary, depending on how far the object is above the earth's surface or whether it is located near another body such as the moon.

The **relation between weight W and mass m**

$$W = \frac{GM_E m}{r^2} \ ; \qquad W = mg$$

As $\qquad g_{\text{moon}} = \dfrac{1}{6} \ g_{\text{earth}}$ therefore,

$$w_{\text{moon}} = \frac{1}{6} \ w_{\text{earth}}$$

Inertial and Gravitaional Mass

The mass of a body is the quantity of matter possessed by a body.

Inertial Mass: Inertial mass of a body is related to its inertia of linear motion, and is defined by Newton's second law of motion.

$$F = m_i a \text{ or } m_i = \frac{F}{a}$$

The mass m_i of the body in this sense is the inertial mass of the body.

Infact, inertial mass of a body is the measure of the ability of the body to oppose the production of acceleration in its motion by an external force.

Properties of inertial mass

- It is proportional to the quantity of matter contained in the body.
- It is independent of size, shape and state of the body.
- It does not depend upon the temperature of the body.

Gravitational Mass

Gravitational mass of a body is related to gravtitational pull on the body and is defined by Newton's law of gravitation.

If a body of mass m_G is placed on the surface of earth of radius R and mass M, then gravitational pull on the body is given by

$$F = \frac{GMm_G}{R^2} \Rightarrow m_G = \frac{F}{\left(GM / R^2\right)}$$

The mass m_G of the body in this sense is the gravitational mass of the body.

ACCELERATION DUE TO GRAVITY OF THE EARTH

When a body is dropped from a certain height above the ground, it begins to fall towards the earth under gravity. The acceleration produced in the body due to gravity is called the acceleration due to gravity. It is denoted by g. Its value close to the Earth's surface is 9.8 m/s^2.

$$g = \frac{F}{m} \text{ or } g = \frac{GM}{R^2}$$

This is the **relation between acceleration due to gravity (g) and universal gravitational constant (G).**

Aceeleration due to gravity,

$$g = \frac{GM}{R^2} \text{ or } g = \frac{4}{3}\pi G R \rho$$

Difference between acceleration due to gravity (g) and universal gravitational constant (G)

Acceleration due to gravity (g)	Universal gravitational constant (G)
It is the acceleration produced in a freely falling object under the action of the earth's gravitational force.	It is the gravitational force of attraction between two objects of unit masses separated by a unit distance
The value of g is different at different places on the earth as well as other planets.	The value of G remains same everywhere in the universe.
g = 9.8 m/s^2	G = 6.673 × 10^{-11} Nm^2/kg^2

VARIATION IN ACCELERATION DUE TO GRAVITY

The value of 'g' acceleration due to gravity, varies from place to place on the surface of earth. It also varies as we go above or below the surface of the Earth.

Variation in g with height or altitude:

$$g' = g\left(1 - \frac{2h}{R_e}\right)$$

i.e. The decrease in the value of g on going up a height 'h' above the surface of earth by a factor $\left(1 - \frac{2h}{R_e}\right)$

Variation in g with depth:

$$g' = g\left(1 - \frac{d}{R_e}\right)$$

Thus the value of g decreases by a factor $\left(1 - \frac{d}{R_e}\right)$ as we go down below the surface of the earth.

ESCAPE VELOCITY

Escape velocity is the minimum velocity that should be given to the body to enable it to escape away from the gravitational field of earth.

If the mass of the planet is M and its radius is R, then the escape velocity from its surface will be

$$V_e = \sqrt{(2GM / R)} \text{ or } \qquad V_e = \sqrt{(2gR)}$$

Escape velocity from the surface of earth is 11.2 Km/sec.

The escape velocity of a body from a planet depends upon the size (mass and radius) of the planet and hence the value of acceleration due to gravity on its surface. It does not depend upon mass of the body. To throw an ant or an elephant out of the gravitational field, the required velocity of projection is same.

KEPLER'S LAWS OF PLANETARY MOTION

Kepler worked out three laws, which govern the motion of planets and are known as *Kepler's laws of planetary motion.*

Law of orbits (first law): All planets revolve in elliptical orbits around the sun and the sun is situated at one of the two foci of the elliptical path.

SATELLITES

Just as the planets revolve around the sun, in the same way few celestial bodies revolve around these planets. These bodies are called 'Satellites'.

For example moon is the natural satellite of Earth. Artificial satellites are launched from the Earth. Such satellites are used for telecommunication, weather forecast etc. The path of these satellites are elliptical with the centre of Earth at a focus.

Characteristics of Motion of Satellites

Orbital velocity (v_0) : Let a satellite of mass m revolves around the Earth in circular orbit of radius r with speed v_0. The gravitational pull between satellite and earth provides the necessary centripetal force.

Orbital velocity $(v_0) = \sqrt{(Gm/R)} = \sqrt{(gR)}$

Relation between escape velocity (v_e) and orbital velocity (v_0):
$$v_e = \sqrt{2}v_0$$

- Value of orbital velocity does not depend on the mass of satellite but it depends on the mass and radius of the planet around which the rotation is taking place.
- The orbital velocity for a satellite near the surface of earth is 7.92 km/sec.
- **Energy of satellite :** A satellite revolving around a planet has both kinetic and potential energy.

  Kinetic energy : The kinetic energy of the satellite is due to motion of the satellite.
  $$K = \frac{GMm}{2r}$$
  Potential energy : Potential energy of the satellite,
  $$U = -\frac{GMm}{r}$$
  The negative sign is because of zero potential energy at infinity.
- **Binding energy :** The energy required to remove the satellite from its orbit to infinity is called binding energy of the system.

  Binding energy of satellite, $E = \dfrac{GMm}{2r}$
- When the satellite is orbiting in its orbit, then no energy is required to keep it in its orbit.
- When the energy of the satellite is negative then it moves in either a circular or an elliptical orbit.

TYPES OF SATELLITES

Geo-stationary Satellite

A satellite which appears to be stationary for a person on the surface of the Earth is called geostationary satellite.

It is also known as Communication Satellite or Synchronous Satellite.

Features of Geo-stationary Satellite

- The orbit of the satellite must be circular and in the equatorial plane of the Earth.
- The angular velocity of the satellite must be in the same direction as the angular velocity of rotation of the earth i.e., from west to east.
- The period of revolution of the satellite must be equal to the period of rotation of earth about its axis.
  i.e., 24 hours = 24 × 60 × 60 = 86400 sec.
- Height from the surface of the earth is nearly 35600 km.
- The orbital velocity of this satellite is nearly 3.08 km/sec.
- The relative velocity of geostationary satellite with respect to earth is zero. This type of satellite is used for communication purposes. The orbit of a geostationary satellite is called '*Parking Orbit*'.

Applications of Geo-stationary Satellite

- In weather forecasting, broadcasting and in predictions of the flood and droughts.
- In telecommunication and radio transmissions.

Polar Satellite

Polar Satellites go around the poles of the earth in north-south direction and the earth rotates around its axis in east-west direction. The altitude of polar satellite is around 500 to 800 km and its time period is around 100 minutes.

FREE FALL

The motion of a body under the influence of gravity alone is called a free fall. When a body falls freely towards the earth, its velocity continuously increases. The acceleration developed in its motion is called acceleration due to gravity (g).

$$g = \frac{GM}{R^2}$$

This gives the acceleration due to gravity on the surface of the earth. $g = 9.8$ m/s^2

WEIGHTLESSNESS

The phenomenon of "weightlessness" occurs when there is no force of support on your body.

FORCE ON SOLIDS AND FLUIDS

Viscosity is the internal resistance or friction, offered to an object moving through a fluid.

ELASTICITY

The property of the body by virtue of which it tends to regain its original shape and size after removing the deforming force is called **elasticity**. If the body regains its original shape and size completely, after the removal of deforming forces, then the body is said to be **perfectly elastic**.

The property of the body by virtue of which it tends to retain its deformed state after removing the deforming force is called **plasticity**. If the body does not have any tendency to recover its original shape and size, it is called **perfectly plastic**.

- Bridges are designed using the concept of elasticity so that it can withstand heavy load of traffic and force of strongly blowing wind.
- The thickness of the metallic rope used in the crane in order to lift a given load is decided from the knowledge of elastic limit of the material.

STRESS AND STRAIN

Stress

The internal restoring force acting per unit area of a body is called stress.

i.e., Stress = Restoring force/ Area

Strain

When a deforming force is applied on a body, there is a change in the configuration of the body. The body is said to be strained or deformed. The ratio of change in configuration to the original configuration is called strain.

$$\text{i.e., Strain} = \frac{\text{Change in configuration}}{\text{Original configuration}}$$

Strain being the ratio of two like quantities has **no unit** and **dimension**.

HOOKE'S LAW

Elastic limit is the upper limit of deforming force up to which, if deforming force is removed, the body regains its original form completely and beyond which if deforming force is increased, the body loses its property of elasticity and gets permanently deformed.

Within the elastic limit, stress is proportional to strain.

i.e., Stress $\propto$ strain or, stress = E × strain

This constant E is known as **modulus of elasticity** or **coefficient of elasticity**. It depends upon the nature of the materials.

Types of Modulus of Elasticity

Corresponding to three types of strain, there are three types of modulus of elasticity:

Young's Modulus of Elasticity (Y)

$$Y = \frac{\text{normal stress}}{\text{longitudinal strain}}$$

Bulk or Volume Modulus of Elesticity (K)

$$K = \frac{Normal\ stress}{Volumetric\ strain}$$

If p is the increase in pressure applied on the spherical body then, $F/A = P$

The reciprocal of bulk modulus of elasticity of a material is called its **Compressibility.**

$$Compressibility = \frac{1}{K}$$

Brittle, Ductile and Malleable solids

There are some materials which break as soon as the stress is increased beyond the elastic limit. They are called **brittle**, e.g. glass, ceramics etc.

Materials which have large plastic range of extension are called **ductile**. Using this property, materials can be drawn into thin wires, e.g. copper, aluminium etc.

Materials which can be hammered into thin sheets are called **malleable** e.g. gold, silver, lead, etc.

Elastomers : Rubber has a large elastic region. It can be stretched several times its original length. On the removal of stress it returns to its original state. But the stress-strain graph is not a straight line. This means, it does not obey Hooke's law e.g. rubber, elastic tissue of aorta etc.

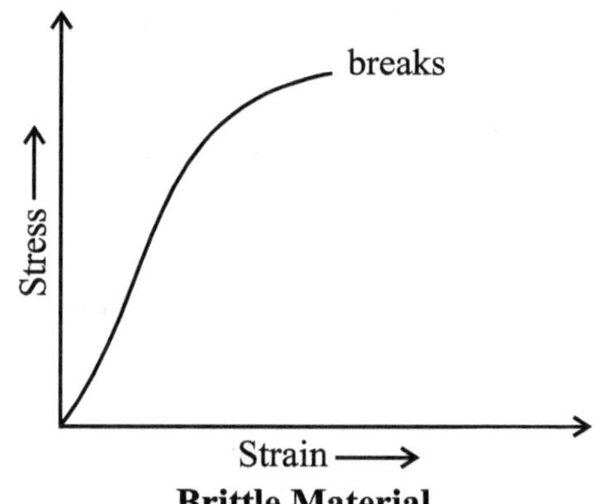

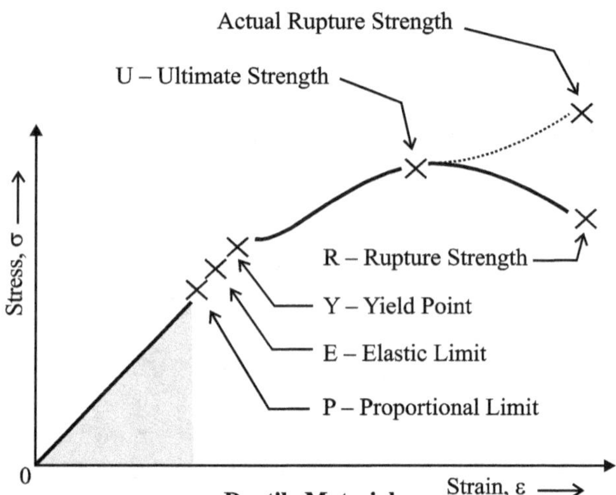

FLUIDS

Fluids include liquids and gases and begin to flow when a shearing stress is applied. Fluids have no definite shape. It assume the shape of containing vessel.

Density (ρ)

Mass per unit volume is defined as *density*.

$$\text{Density, } \rho = \frac{mass\ (m)}{volume\ (V)}$$

SI unit : kg/m^3

Specific Weight or Weight Density (W)

$$\text{Specific weight, } W = \frac{\text{Weight}}{\text{Volume}}$$

$$= \frac{mg}{V} = \left[\frac{m}{V}\right]g = \rho g$$

S I Unit: N/m^3

Specific weight of pure water at 4°C is 9.81 kN/m^3

Relative Density

$$\text{Relative density (R.D.)} = \frac{\text{Density of given liquid}}{\text{Density of pure water at 4°C}}$$

The density of water is maximum at 4°C and is equal to $1.0 \times 10^3\ \text{kgm}^{-3}$.

Specific Gravity

It is defined as the ratio of the specific weight of the given fluid to the specific weight of pure water at 4°C.

Specific gravity =

$$\frac{\text{Specific weight of given liquid}}{\text{Specific weight of pure water at 4°C (9.81 kN/m}^3)}$$

$$= \frac{\rho_\ell \times g}{\rho_w \times g} = \frac{\rho_\ell}{\rho_w} = \text{R.D. of the liquid}$$

Specific gravity of fluids

Fluid	Temperature (Deg°C)	Specific Gravity
Acetic Acid	25	1.052
Acetone	25	0.787
Alcohol, ethyl (ethanol)	25	0.787
Alcohol, methyl (methanol)	25	0.789
Alcohol, propyl	25	0.802
Ammonia (aqua)	25	0.826
Aniline	25	1.022
Benzene	25	0.876
Butane	25	0.601
Kerosene	60°F	0.82
Chloroform	25	1.469
Mercury	25	13.633
Oxygen	−183	1.14
Sea Water	25	1.028
Pure Water	212°F	1.000
Glycerol	25	1.129

PRESSURE IN A FLUID

The pressure exerted by a fluid is defined as the force per unit area at a point within the fluid.

$$P_{av} = \frac{\Delta F}{\Delta A}$$

When the force is constant over the surface , the above equation reduces to $P = F/A$

The **SI unit** of pressure is Nm^{-2} and is also called pascal (Pa). The other common pressure units are *atmosphere and bar*.

$1\,\text{atm} = 1.01325 \times 10^5$ Pa, 1 bar = 1.00000×10^5 Pa,

$1\,\text{atm} = 1.01325$ bar

Expression for liquid pressure and total pressure

The liquid pressure at a depth h is given by

$P = \rho g h$ where ρ is the density of the liquid.

and the total pressure at the same depth h

$P_{\text{total}} = P_{\text{atm}} + \rho g h$, where P_{atm} is atmospheric pressure.

ATMOSPHERIC PRESSURE, ABSOLUTE PRESSURE AND GAUGE PRESSURE

Atmospheric Pressure

Force exerted by air column on unit cross-section area of sea level is called *atmospheric pressure* (P_0)

$$P_0 = \frac{F}{A} = 101.3\,kN/m^2$$

Barometer is used to measure atmospheric pressure which was **discovered by Torricelli**.

Atmospheric pressure varies from place to place and at a particular place from time to time.

Absolute Pressure

Sum of atmospheric and gauge pressure is called absolute pressure.

$$P_{\text{abs}} = P_{\text{atm}} + P_{\text{gauge}}$$
$$\Rightarrow \quad P_{\text{abs}} = P_0 + h\rho g$$

Pascal's Law

According to Pascal's law– A pressure applied to a confined fluid at rest is transmitted equally undiminished to every part of the fluid and the walls of the container. This principle is used in a hydraulic presses, brakes, jack or lift, etc.

> - Passengers when travelling in an aeroplane remove ink from their fountain pen as the atmospheric pressure decreases when the aeroplane is up in the sky.
> - Bleeding from nose is caused when a person is there at higher altitudes, as the atmospheric pressure is less compared with blood pressure. Thus the blood vessels exposed inside the nose are more likely to burst and can cause bleeding.

ARCHIMEDES' PRINCIPLE

A body immersed in a fluid partly or wholly experiences an upward buoyant force equivalent to the weight of the fluid displaced by it. The buoyant force acts through the centre of gravity of the displaced fluid. The phenomenon of force exerted by fluid on the body is called buoyancy and the force is called buoyant force.

A body experiences buoyant force whether it floats or sinks, under its own weight or due to other forces applied on it.

Body **float**, if weight of it is less than buoyant force and **sink**, if weight of the body is greater than buoyant force.

SURFACE TENSION

Surface tension can be defined in the form of an imaginary line on the liquid surface or by relating it to the work done. The force acting per unit length of an imaginary line drawn on the free liquid surface at right angles to the line and in the plane of liquid surface, is known as surface tension.

Surface tension, $T = \dfrac{F}{L}$

Its **SI unit :** N/m or J/m^2.

Examples of surface tension

- Raindrops are spherical in shape.
- The hair of a shaving brush cling together when taken out of water.
- Oil spread on cold water but remains as a drop on hot water etc.

Factors Affecting Surface Tension

- Cohesive force
- Temperature
- Impurities
- Electrification

Surface Energy

According to molecular theory of surface tension the molecules in the surface have some additional energy due to their position. This additional energy per unit area of the surface is called surface energy.

i.e.,   Surface energy $= \dfrac{\text{Work done}}{\text{Increase in surface area}}$

Angle of Contact

The angle enclosed between the tangent plane at the liquid surface and the tangent plane at the solid surface at the point of contact inside the liquid is termed as the **angle of contact**.

The angle of contact depends on the nature of the solid and liquid in contact.

Shape of liquid surface : When a liquid is brought in contact with a solid surface, the surface of the liquid becomes curved (concave or convex) near the place of contact.

The free surface of a liquid which is near the walls of a vessel and which is curved because of surface tension is known as **meniscus**. Meniscus concave for glass water and meniscus convex for glass-mercury.

Angle of contact depends upon the surfaces in contact.

Water proofing agent : Angle of contact increases due to water proofing agent. It gets converted from acute to obtuse angle.

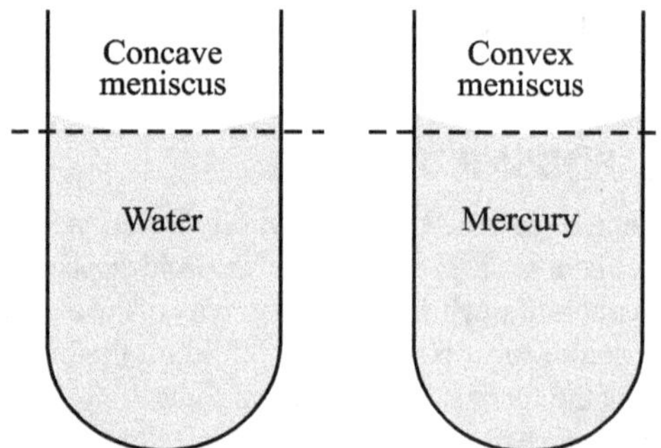

Capillary Rise

A glass tube with fine bore and open at both ends is known as **capillary tube**. *The property by virtue of which a liquid rise or fall in a capillary tube is known as **capillary rise or fall or capillarity**.* Rise or fall of liquid in tubes of narrow bore (capillary tube) is called *capillary action*.

FLOW OF LIQUID

Streamline Flow

When a liquid (fluid) flows, such that each particle of the liquid passing a point moves along the same path and has the same velocity as its predecessor then the flow is called stream line flow. It is also called laminar flow.

Turbulent Flow

When the velocity at a point in the liquid changes with time the flow is called unsteady flow.

BERNOULLI'S THEOREM

When incompressible, non-viscous, irrotational liquid i.e., ideal liquid flow from one position to other in streamline path then in its path at every point, the sum of pressure energy, kinetic energy and potential energy per unit volume remains constant.

VISCOSITY

It is the internal resistance or friction offered to an object moving through a fluid.

Effect of Temperature and Pressure on Viscosity

Effect of temperature: On increasing temperature viscosity of a liquid decreases.

Effect of pressure: On increasing pressure viscosity of a liquid increases except water whose viscosity decreases with pressure rise.

Viscosities of Common Materials (at 21°C)

Material	Viscosity (Centipoise)
Water	1 cps
Milk	3 cps
Castrol Oil	1,000 cps
Honey	10,000 cps
Chocolate	25,000 cps
Ketchup	50,000 cps
Peanut Butter	250,000 cps

Stoke's Law

When a solid moves through a viscous medium, its motion is opposed by a viscous force depending on the velocity and shape and size of the body.

Importance of Stoke's law

* It is used in the determination of electronic charge with the help of Milikan's experiment.
* It accounts the formation of clouds.
* It accounts why the speed of rain drops is less than that of a body falling freely with a constant velocity from the height of clouds.
* It helps a man coming down with the help of a parachute.

Terminal Velocity

It is the maximum constant velocity acquired by the body while falling freely in a viscous medium.

Physical Quantity	Formula	Unit	Dimension
Pressure (p)	$P = F/A$	Pascal	$[ML^{-1}T^{-2}]$
Density (ρ)	$\rho = m/v$	Kgm^{-3}	$[ML^{-3}]$
Coefficient of viscosity (η)	$\eta = Fl/vA$	Pl	$[ML^{-1}T^{1}]$
Reynold's Number (R_e)	$R_e = \rho vd/\eta$	None	None
Surface Tension	$S = F/d$	Nm^{-1}	$[MT^{-2}]$

MULTIPLE CHOICE QUESTIONS

1. Which one among the following is the correct value of the gravitational force of the Earth acting on a body of mass 1 kg?
   (a) 8. 9 N　　　　　(b) 9. 8 N
   (c) 89 N　　　　　(d) 98 N

2. A geostationary satellite
   (a) can move about any axis
   (b) must move about the polar axis
   (c) must move on an axis in the equatorial plane
   (d) Both (b) and (c)

3. The weight of a body is 9.8 N at the place where $g = 9.8$ ms^{-2}. Its mass is　　　**[NDA]**
   (a) zero　　　　　(b) 9.8 kg
   (c) 10 kg　　　　　(d) 1 kg

4. If the moon is to escape from the gravitational field of the earth forever, it will require a velocity　　**[SSC CGL]**
   (a) 11.2 km/s　　　　　(b) less than
   (c) slightly more than 111.2 km/s
   (d) 22.4 km/s

5. In respect of the difference of the gravitational force from electric and magnetic forces, which one of the following statements is true ?
   (a) Gravitational force is stronger than the other two.
   (b) Gravitational force is attractive only, whereas the electric and the magnetic forces are attractive as well as repulsive.
   (c) Gravitational force has a very short range.
   (d) Gravitational force is a long range force, while the other two are short range forces.

Directions (Qs. 6 and 7): Each of these questions contain two statements, Assertion and Reason. Each of these questions also has four alternative choices, only one of which is the correct answer. You have to select one of the codes (a), (b), (c) and (d) given below.

(a) Assertion is correct, reason is correct; reason is a correct explanation for assertion.
(b) Assertion is correct, reason is correct; reason is not a correct explanation for assertion
(c) Assertion is correct, reason is incorrect
(d) Assertion is incorrect, reason is correct.

6. **Assertion :** The tidal waves in sea are primarily due to the gravitational effect of earth.

   Reason : The intensity of gravitational field of earth is maximum at the surface of earth.

7. Consider the following statements:　　　**[NDA]**
   1. The gravitational force exerted by the sun on the moon is greater than the gravitational force exerted by the earth on the moon.

2. A heavy body falls at a faster rate than a light body in vaccum.

   Which of the following statements given above is/are correct ?
   (a) 1 only　　　　　(b) 2 only
   (c) Both 1 and 2　　　(d) Neither 1 nor 2

8. A body weighs 5 kg on equator. At the poles it is likely to weight　　　　　　　　　　　　**[NDA]**
   (a) 5 kg
   (b) less than 5 kg but not zero
   (c) 0 kg
   (d) more than 5 kg

9. A spring balance is graduated on sea level. A body of mass 1 kg is weighed at consecutively increasing heights from the earth's surface, then what would be the weight indicated by the balance?
   (a) Weight will go on increasing continuously
   (b) Weight will go on decreasing continuously
   (c) Weight will remain same
   (d) Weight will first increase and then decreases

10. The mass of a body on earth is 100 kg (acceleration due to gravity, $g_e = 10$ m/s^2. If acceleration due to gravity on the moon is $g_e / 6$, then the mass of the body on the moon is :
    [IAS Prelim]
    (a) 100/6 kg　　　　　(b) 60 kg
    (c) 100 kg　　　　　(d) 600 kg

11. Match the columns I and II.

Column I	Column II
(A) Weight	(1) Minimum
(B) $g_{equator}$	(2) Zero
(C) g_{poles}	(3) Vector
(D) g_{centre}	(4) Maximum

    (a) (A) → (2) ; (B) → (1) ; (C) → (3) ; (D) → (4)
    (b) (A) → (2) ; (B) → (2) ; (C) → (4) ; (D) → (3)
    (c) (A) → (3) ; (B) → (1) ; (C) → (4) ; (D) → (2)
    (d) (A) → (4) ; (B) → (3) ; (C) → (1) ; (D) → (2)

12. **Assertion (A) :** The weight of a body decreases with the increase of altitude on earth.

    Reason (R) : The earth is not a perfect sphere. **[IAS Prelim]**
    (a) Both A and R are true and R is the correct explanation of A
    (b) Both A and R are true but R is not a correct explanation of A
    (c) A is true but R is false
    (d) A is false but R is true

13. If the radius of the earth were to shrink by one percent, its mass remaining the same, the value of g on the earth's surface would: **[IAS Prelim]**
    - (a) increase by 0.5%
    - (b) increase by 2%
    - (c) decrease by 0.5%
    - (d) decrease by 2%

14. Consider the following statements:

    A body weighs less at the equator than at the poles because: **[NDA]**
    1. earth rotates about its axis.
    2. the ice cap at the poles increases gravitational pull.
    3. equatorial diameter is greater than the polar diameter.
    4. of some unknown facts.

    Which of the statements given above is/are incorrect?
    - (a) 1 and 2
    - (b) 3 only
    - (c) 1 and 3
    - (d) 4 only

15. **Assertion (A) :** Space rocket are usually launched in the equatorial line from west to east

    Reason (R) : The acceleration due to gravity is minimum at the equator.
    - (a) Both A and R are ture and R is the correct explanation of A
    - (b) Both A and R are true but R is not the correct explanation of A
    - (c) A is true but R is false
    - (d) A is false but R is true

16. A body is at rest on the surface of earth. Which of the following statements is correct? **[SSC CGL]**
    - (a) Only weight of the body acts on it.
    - (b) Only upward force acts on the body.
    - (c) Frictional force acts on the body.
    - (d) Net upward force is equal to the net downward force.

17. Consider a satellite going round the earth in a circular orbit. Which of the following statements is wrong?
    - (a) It is a freely falling body.
    - (b) It is moving with constant speed
    - (c) It is acted upon by a force directed away from the centre of the earth which counter-balances the gravitational pull.
    - (d) It is an accelerated motion

18. **Assertion :** The value of 'g' is greater at the equator than at the poles.

    Reason : Radius is more at the equator than at the poles.
    - (a) If both **Assertion** and **Reason** are **correct** and **Reason** is the **correct explanation** of **Assertion**.
    - (b) If both **Assertion** and **Reason** are **correct**, but **Reason** is not the **correct** explanation of **Assertion**.
    - (c) If **Assertion** is **correct** but **Reason** is **incorrect**.
    - (d) If **Assertion** is **incorrect** but **Reason** is **correct**.

19. Kerosene oil rises up in a wick of lantern because of
    - (a) capillarity
    - (b) buoyant force
    - (c) diffusion of oil through the wick
    - (d) None of the above

20. The tendency of a liquid drop to contract and occupy minimum area is due to : **[IAS Prelim]**
    - (a) surface tension
    - (b) viscosity
    - (c) density
    - (d) vapour pressure

21. Which type/types of pen uses/use capillary action in addition to gravity for flow of ink? **[CDS]**
    - (a) Fountain pen
    - (b) Ballpoint pen
    - (c) Gel pen
    - (d) Both ballpoint and gel pens

22. Purity of a metal can be determined with the help of
    - (a) Pascal's law
    - (b) Boyle's law
    - (c) Archimedes principle
    - (d) Conservation of mass principle

23. Flow velocities in an incompressible fluid can be measured with which one of the following? **[NDA]**
    - (a) Barometer
    - (b) Venturi tube
    - (c) Strain gauge
    - (d) Manometer

24. If a gas is heated at constant pressure its isothermal compressibility
    - (a) increases with temperature
    - (b) remains constant
    - (c) decreases with temperature
    - (d) decreases inversely with temperature

25. A liquid is flowing in a streamlined manner through a cylindrical pipe. Along a section containing the axis of the pipe, the flow profile will be : **[IAS Prelim]**

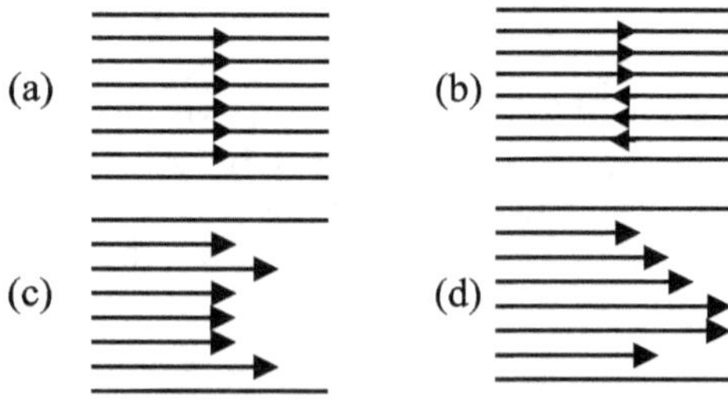

26. For which one of the following is capillarity not the reason? **[IAS Prelim]**
    - (a) Blotting of ink
    - (b) Rising of underground water
    - (c) Spread a water drop on a cotton cloth
    - (d) Rising of water from the roots of a plant to its foliage

27. In scuba-diving, while ascending towards the water surface, there is a danger of bursting the lungs. It is because of **[CDS]**
    - (a) Archimedes' principle
    - (b) Boyle's law
    - (c) Gay-Lussac's law of combining volumes
    - (d) Graham's law of diffusion

28. The specific gravity of a substance is measured by a hydrometer at the sea level. If the measurement is done at the top of a mountain, what would be the specific gravity ? **[NDA]**
    (a) Zero
    (b) More than that measured at the sea level
    (c) Less than that measured at the sea level
    (d) Same as that measured at the sea level

29. A block of ice is floating in a beaker containing liquid of specific gravity greater than one. When ice melts completely what happens to the level of liquid in the beaker? **[NDA]**
    (a) It will remain the same as before
    (b) It will go down
    (c) It will rise up
    (d) It may or may not change depending upon size of beaker

30. **Assertion (A) :** With the increase of temperature, the viscosity of glycerine increases. **[NDA]**
    Reason (R) : Rise of temperature increases kinetic energy of molecules.
    (a) Both A and R are true and R is the correct explanation of A
    (b) Both A and R are true but R is not a correct explanation of A
    (c) A is true but R is false
    (d) A is false but R is true

31. Three identical vessels A, B and C are filled with water, mercury and kerosene respectively up to an equal height. The three vessels are provided with identical taps at the bottom of the vessels. If the three taps are opened simultaneously, then which vessel is emptied first?
    (a) Vessel B **[IAS Prelim]**
    (b) All the vessels A, B and C will be emptied simultaneously
    (c) Vessel A
    (d) Vessel C

32. Consider the following statements : **[IAS Prelim]**
    If there were no phenomenon of capillarity
    1. it would be difficult to use a kerosene lamp
    2. one would not be able to use a straw to consume a soft drink
    3. the blotting paper would fail to function
    4. the big trees that we see around would not have grown on the Earth
    Which of the statements given above are correct?
    (a) 1, 2 and 3 only   (b) 1, 3 and 4 only
    (c) 2 and 4 only   (d) 1, 2, 3 and 4

33. Raw mangoes shrivel when pickled in brine. The phenomenon is associated with **[CDS]**
    (a) osmosis
    (b) reverse osmosis
    (c) increase of surface tension of fluid
    (d) decrease of surface tension of fluid

34. **Assertion (A) :** An iron ball floats on mercury but gets immersed in water.
    Reason (R) : The specific gravity of iron is more than that of mercury **[IAS Prelim]**
    (a) Both A and R are true and R is the correct explanation of A
    (b) Both A and R are true but R is not a correct explanation of A
    (c) A is true but R is false
    (d) A is false but R is true

35. A liquid is kept in a regular cylindrical vessel upto a certain height. If this vessel is replaced by another cylindrical vessel having half the area of cross-section of the bottom, the pressure on the bottom will **[CDS]**
    (a) remain unaffected
    (b) be reduced to half the earlier pressure
    (c) be increased to twice the earlier pressure
    (d) be reduced to one-fourth the earlier pressure

36. Dirty cloths containing grease and oil stains are cleaned by adding detergents to water. Stains are removed because detergent **[CDS]**
    (a) reduces drastically the surface tension between water and oil
    (b) increases the surface tension between water and oil
    (c) increases the viscosity of water and oil
    (d) decreases the viscosity in detergent mixed water

37. A liquid rises to a certain length in a capillary tube. The tube is inclined to an angle of 45°. The length of the liquid column will **[NDA]**
    (a) increase
    (b) decrease
    (c) remain unchanged
    (d) first decrease and then increase

38. Two identical blocks of ice, A and B, float in water as shown in the figure given below. Which one among the following statements in this regard is correct? **[NDA]**

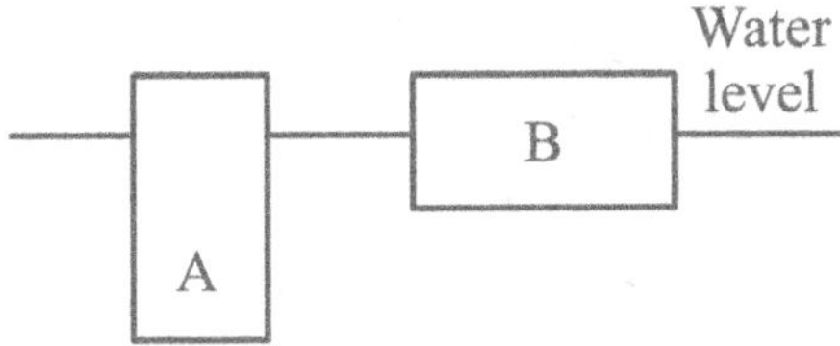

    (a) Block A displaces a greater volume of water since the pressure acts on a smaller bottom area
    (b) Block A displaces a greater volume of water since its submerged end is lower in the water.
    (c) Block B displaces a greater volume of water since its submerged end has a greater area in water
    (d) The two blocks displace equal volumes of water since they have the same specific gravity and same mass

39. When a ship floats on water   [NDA]
    (a) it displaces no water
    (b) the mass of water displaced is equal to the mass of the ship
    (c) the mass of water displaced is lesser than the mass of the ship
    (d) the mass of water displaced is greater than the mass of the ship

40. Why do two ice blocks join to form one block when pressed together?   [NDA]
    (a) Melting point of ice is lowered with increase in pressure
    (b) Melting point of ice increases with increase in pressure
    (c) Melting point of ice remains unchanged with increase in pressure
    (d) Melting point of ice is 0°C

41. Consider two hollow glass spheres, one containing water and the other containing mercury. Each liquid fills about one-tenth of the volume of the sphere. In zero gravity environment   [NDA]
    (a) water and mercury float freely inside the sphere
    (b) water forms a layer on the glass, while mercury floats
    (c) mercury forms a layer on the glass, while water floats
    (d) water and mercury both form a layer on the glass

42. **Assertion (A) :** A beaker filled with water at 4°C overflows if the temperature is decreased or increased.
    Reason (R) : Density of water is maximum at 4°C.
    (a) Both A and R are true and R is the correct explanation of A
    (b) Both A and R are true but R is not a correct explanation of A
    (c) A is true but R is false
    (d) A is false but R is true

43. The pressure of a fluid varies with depth h as $P = P0 + rgh$, where r is the fluid density. This expression is associated with   [CDS 2018-I]
    (a) Pascal's law   (b) Newton's law
    (c) Bernoulli's principle   (d) Archimedes' principle

44. Which one of the following statements is true for the relation $F = \dfrac{Gm_1 m_2}{r^2}$? (All symbols have their usual meanings)   [NDA 2017-I]
    (a) The quantity G depends on the local value of g, acceleration due to gravity
    (b) The quantity G is greatest at the surface of the Earth
    (c) The quantity G is used only when earth is one of the two masses
    (d) The quantity G is a universal constant

45. In a vacuum, a five-rupee coin, a feather of a sparrow bird and a mango are dropped simultaneously from the same height. The time taken by them to reach the bottom it t_1, t_2 and t_3 respectively. In this situation, we will observe that   [NDA 2017-II]
    (a) $t_1 > t_2 > t_3$ (b) $t_1 > t_3 > t_2$
    (c) $t_3 > t_1 > t_2$ (d) $t_1 = t_2 = t_3$

46. If some object is weighed when submerged in water, what will happen to its weight compared to its weight in air?   [NDA 2017-II]
    (a) Increase
    (b) Decrease
    (c) Remain exactly the same
    (d) Increase or decrease cannot be predicted

47. Which one of the following statements about gravitational force is NOT correct?   [NDA 2018-I]
    (a) It is experienced by all bodies in the universe
    (b) It is a dominant force between celestial bodies
    (c) It is a negligible force for atoms
    (d) It is same for all pairs of bodies in our universe

48. Whether an object will float or sink in a liquid, depends on   [NDA 2018-I]
    (a) mass of the object only
    (b) mass of the object and density of liquid only
    (c) difference in the densities of the object and liquid
    (d) mass and shape of the object only

49. Which of the following statements about a fluid at rest in a cup is/are correct?   [NDA 2018-I]
    1. Pressure is same at all the points in the fluid.
    2. Pressureis exerted on the walls.
    3. Pressure exists everywhere in the fluid.
    Select the correct answer using the code given below:
    (a) 1 and 2 only   (b) 2 and 3 only
    (c) 1 only   (d) 1, 2 and 3

50. A planet has a mass M_1 and radius R_1. The value of acceleration due to gravity on its surface is g_1. There is another planet 2, whose mass and radius both are two times that of the first planet. Which one of the following is the acceleration due to gravity on the surface of planet 2?   [NDA 2018-II]
    (a) g_1 (b) $2g_1$
    (c) $g_1/2$ (d) $g_1/4$

51. The coefficient of areal expansion of a material is $1.6 \times 10^{-5}\ K^{-1}$. Which one of the following gives the value of coefficient of volume expansion of this material?   [NDA 2018-II]
    (a) $0.8 \times 10^{-5}\ K^{-1}$ (b) $2.4 \times 10^{-5}\ K^{-1}$
    (c) $3.2 \times 10^{-5}\ K^{-1}$ (d) $4.8 \times 10^{-5}\ K^{-1}$

ANSWER KEY

1.	(b)	2.	(c)	3.	(d)	4.	(a)	5.	(b)	6.	(d)	7.	(a)	8.	(d)	9.	(b)	10.	(c)
11.	(c)	12.	(b)	13.	(b)	14.	(b)	15.	(b)	16.	(d)	17.	(c)	18.	(d)	19.	(a)	20.	(a)
21.	(a)	22.	(c)	23.	(b)	24.	(b)	25.	(a)	26.	(b)	27.	(b)	28.	(c)	29.	(c)	30.	(d)
31.	(d)	32.	(b)	33.	(a)	34.	(c)	35.	(a)	36.	(a)	37.	(c)	38.	(d)	39.	(d)	40.	(a)
41.	(b)	42.	(a)	43.	(a)	44.	(d)	45.	(d)	46.	(b)	47.	(d)	48.	(c)	49.	(b)	50.	(c)
51.	(b)																		

SOUND, OSCILLATIONS, HEAT & THERMODYNAMICS

Sound is a form of energy that we hear. A vibrating object i.e., anything that moves back and forth, to-and-fro from side to side, in and out and up and down produces sound, as the object (vibrating) has a certain amount of energy. Sound requires material medium-a solid, a liquid or a gas to travel.

If there is no medium to vibrate then no sound is possible, sound cannot travel in a vacuum. Air is a poor conductor of sound compared with solids and liquids.

WAVE

Due to the vibratory motion of the particles of the medium a periodic disturbance is produced in a material medium. This is called a **wave**. In the absence of medium solid, liquid or gas sound wave is not being propagated but light (electromagnetic) waves travel through the vacuum.

Types of Waves

On the basis of the requirement of medium, waves are of two types

Mechanical Waves

A mechanical wave is a periodic disturbance which requires a material medium for its propagation. The properties of these waves depend on the medium so they are known as *elastic waves*, such as sound-waves, water waves, waves in stretched string etc. On the basis of motion of particles the mechanical waves are classified into two parts.

Transverse wave: When the particles of the medium vibrate in a direction perpendicular to the direction of propagation of the wave, the wave is known as the *transverse wave*. For example, waves produced in a stretched string, waves on the surface liquid.

These waves travel in the form of crests and troughs. These waves can travel in solids and liquids only.

Longitudinal wave: When the particles of the medium vibrate along the direction of propagation of the wave then the wave is known as the longitudinal wave. For example sound wave in air, waves in a solid rod produced by scrabbing etc.

These waves travel in the form of compressions and rarefactions. These waves can travel in solids, liquids and gases.

Electromagnetic Waves

The waves which do not require medium for their propagation are called electromagnetic waves. This means that these waves can travel through vacuum also. For example, light waves, X-rays, γ-rays, infrared waves, radio waves, microwaves, etc. These waves are transverse in nature.

Difference between sound waves and electromagnetic waves

- Sound waves are longitudinal whereas electromagnetic waves are transverse.
- Sound waves travel at a speed of 340 m/s whereas electromagnetic waves travel at a speed of 3×10^8 m/s

- Sound waves do not pass through a vacuum but electromagnetic waves (light) do.

Basic Terms Related to Sound Waves

Time Period (T): Time taken in one complete vibration (full cycle) is called it's time period.

Frequency (ν): Frequency is defined as the number of vibrations (or oscillations) completed by a particle in one second.

Frequency, $\nu = \dfrac{1}{T}$

Its SI unit is hertz

Wavelength (λ): The distance travelled by the wave during the time in which any one particle of the medium completes one vibration about its mean position.

Amplitude: The maximum displacement of the wave particle from its mean position.

Wave Velocity: The distance i.e., wavelength (λ) covered by a wave in one time period

Therefore, Wave velocity $= \dfrac{\text{wavelength}}{\text{time taken}}$

or $\qquad v = \lambda/T \ = \nu\lambda$

or $\qquad$ Wave velocity = Frequency × Wavelength

Speed of sound is maximum in solids and minimum in gas.

Factors Affecting the Speed of Sound

Temperature: Speed of sound is directly proportional to the square root of absolute temperature i.e., $v \propto \sqrt{T}$.

Pressure: The speed of sound is independent of pressure.

Density: Speed of sound is inversely proportional to the square root of density of the gas.

$$v = \sqrt{\frac{\gamma P}{\rho}} \Rightarrow v \propto \frac{1}{\sqrt{\rho}} \text{ or, } \frac{v_1}{v_2} = \sqrt{\frac{\rho_2}{\rho_1}}$$

Humidity: Humid air is lighter than dry air that is why speed of sound increase as humidity increases.

CHARACTERISTICS OF SOUND

Pitch

Pitch is the sensation (brain interpretation) of the frequency of an emitted sound and is the characteristic which distinguishes a shrill (or sharp) sound from a grave (or flat) sound. Faster the vibration of the source, higher is the frequency and higher is the pitch. Similarly low pitch sound corresponds to low frequency. A high pitch sound is called a shrill sound (humming of a bee, sound of guitar).

A low pitch sound is called a hoarse sound (roar of a lion, car horn, etc.)

The pitch of female voice is higher than the pitch of male voice.

Loudness

Loudness or softness of a sound wave is the sensation that depends upon its amplitude. The loudness of sound is a measure of the sound energy reaching the ear per second. When we strike a table top with more force, it vibrates and produces loud sound waves which have more amplitude.

The loudness depends on intensity as well as upon the sensitiveness of ear.

Loudness of sound is co-related with the sound level measured in **decibel (dB)**,

Sound above 80dB is unpleasant for human ear.

Quality (Timbre)

Quality or timbre of a sound wave is that characteristic which helps us in distinguishing one sound from another having same pitch and loudness. We recognise a person (without seeing) by listening to his sound as it has a definite quality. *(A pure sound of single frequency is called a tone).* An impure sound produced by mixture of many frequencies is called a **note**. It is pleasant to listen. Notes of the same pitch played upon different musical instruments are distinguished from each other by their quality. The quality of a note depends on the wave form. The waves produced by different instruments differ in their forms.

REFLECTION OF SOUND

It is a common experience that when we shout into a well or inside an empty hall, or inside a dome, we hear our own sound after a short time. It happens because our sound is reflected from the walls. When sound waves strike a surface, they return back into the same medium. This phenomenon is called reflection of sound.

Laws of Reflection of sound

* Angle of incidence $\angle i$ is equal the angle of reflection $\angle r$.
* The incident wave, the reflected wave and the normal all lie in the same plane.

ECHO

The Phenomenon of hearing back our own sound is called an *echo*. It is due to successive reflection from the surfaces of obstacles.

Conditions for the formation of Echoes

* The minimum distance between the source of sound and the reflecting body should be 17.2 metres.
* The wavelength of sound should be less than the height of the reflecting body.
* The intensity of sound should be sufficient so that it can be heard after reflection.

DOPPLER EFFECT

The Doppler Effect is a mean by which wave properties particularly frequencies are altered by the relative movement of source or listener.

Situation where the motion is oriented in a line between the listener L and the source S, with the direction from the listener to the source as the positive direction. The velocities v_L and v_s are the velocities of the listener and source relative to the wave medium, then the apparent frequency is given by,

$$f_L = [(v + v_L)/(v + v_S)]f_S$$

$$(f_L) = \text{frequency heard by the listener}$$

$$(f_S) = \text{frequency of the source}$$

$$v = \text{Speed of Sound}$$

-When the source and observer is moving with speed in the same direction then apparent frequency is given by,

$$f_L = [(v - v_L)/(v - v_S)] f_S$$

-When the listener is at rest, then $v_L = 0$, and if the source is at rest, then $v_S = 0$.

If neither the source nor the listener are moving, then $f_L = f_S$

-When the speed of observer or source becomes more than the speed of sound, then Doppler's formula does not apply.

REVERBERATION

Persistence of sound after its production is stopped, is called reverberation. When a sound is produced in a big hall, its waves reflect from the walls and travel back and forth. Due to this, energy does not reduce and the sound persist.

RANGE OF HEARING

Normal human ears can hear the sound of frequency 20 Hz to 20,000 Hz. Sound of frequency less than 20 Hz is called **infrasonic**. Sound of frequency greater than 20,000 Hz is called **ultrasonic**. Children under the age of five and dogs, owls can hear upto 25 kHz. Whales and elephants produce sound in the infrasonic range. Rhinoceroes make communication between themselves by using a frequency as low as 5 Hz.

Ultrasound

Frequencies higher than 20,000 Hz are called ultrasound. Ultrasound can be produced by Galton's whistle. Some animals, such as dolphins can produce ultrasound. Bats can produce and hear ultrasound. On being high frequency waves, ultrasound possesses high intensity, and therefore can penetrate any solid or liquid medium.

SONAR

SONAR stands for **s**ound **n**avigation **a**nd **r**anging. SONAR is a device which is used to find depth of sea or to detect the position of submarine hidden inside water. Sonar consists of a transmitter and a detector.

INTERFERENCE OF WAVES

When two waves of equal frequency and nearly equal amplitude travelling in same direction having same state of polarisation in medium superimpose, then intensity is different at different points. At some points intensity is large, whereas at other points it is nearly zero.

For Constructive Interference (Maximum Intensity)

Phase difference, $\phi = 2n\pi$ or path difference $= n\lambda$
where n = 0, 1, 2, 3, ...

For Destructive Interference (Minimum Intensity)

Phase difference, $\phi = (2n+1)\pi$, or path difference $= \left(2n-1\right)\dfrac{\lambda}{2}$
; where n = 0, 1, 2, 3, ...

STATIONARY LONGITUDINAL WAVES AND AIR COLUMNS

When two longitudinal waves of same frequency and amplitude travel in a medium in opposite directions then by superposition, standing waves are produced. These waves are produced in air columns in cylindrical tube of uniform diameter. These sound producing tubes are called **organ pipes.**

Vibration of Air Column in Closed Organ Pipe

The tube which is closed at one end and open at the other end is called closed organ pipe.
If ℓ is length of pipe and λ be the wavelength and v be the velocity of sound in organ pipe then,

Case (a), $L = \dfrac{\lambda}{4} \Rightarrow \lambda = 4L \Rightarrow n_1 = \dfrac{v}{\lambda} = \dfrac{v}{4\,L}$
Fundamental frequency or first harmonic.

Case (b), $L = \dfrac{3\lambda}{4} \Rightarrow \lambda = \dfrac{4L}{3} \Rightarrow n_2 = \dfrac{v}{\lambda} = \dfrac{3v}{4L}$
First overtone or third harmonic

Case (c), $L = \dfrac{5\lambda}{4} \Rightarrow \lambda = \dfrac{4L}{5} \Rightarrow n_3 = \dfrac{v}{\lambda} = \dfrac{5v}{4L}$
Second overtone or fifth harmonic.

Vibration of Air Column in Open Organ Pipe

The tube which is open at both ends is called an open organ pipe.

Case (a), $L = \dfrac{\lambda}{2} \Rightarrow \lambda = 2L \Rightarrow n_1 = \dfrac{v}{\lambda} = \dfrac{v}{2L}$
Fundamental frequency or first harmonic.

Case (b), $L = \dfrac{2\lambda}{2} \Rightarrow \lambda = \dfrac{2L}{2} \Rightarrow n_2 = \dfrac{v}{\lambda} = \dfrac{2v}{2L}$
First overtone or second harmonic.

Case (c), $L = \dfrac{3\lambda}{2} \Rightarrow \lambda = \dfrac{2L}{3} \Rightarrow n_3 = \dfrac{v}{\lambda} = \dfrac{3v}{2L}$
When open organ pipe vibrate in m^{th} overtone then

$$L = (m+1)\dfrac{\lambda}{4} \quad \text{so,} \quad \lambda = \dfrac{4L}{m+1} \Rightarrow n = (m+1)\dfrac{v}{2L}$$

Second overtone or third harmonic.
Hence frequency of overtones i.e. of both odd and even harmonics and is given by the relation
$$n_1 : n_2 : n_3 \,\ldots\ldots\ldots= 1 : 2 : 3 \ldots\ldots$$

BEATS

When two sound waves of nearly same frequency are produced simultaneously, then the intensity of resultant sound wave increases and decreases with time. This change in the intensity of sound is called as the phenomenon of '*beats*'.
The time interval between two successive beats is called *beat period* and the number of beats per second is called the *beat frequency.*

If f_1 and f_2 are the frequencies ($f_1 > f_2$) of the two waves, then the beat frequency
$$b = f_1 - f_2$$

Important Features

- At frequency difference greater than about 6 or 7 Hz, we no longer hear individual beats.

SIMPLE HARMONIC MOTION (S.H.M.)

Oscillatory motion in which the acceleration of the particle is directly proportional to the displacement and directs towards a fixed point in a direction opposite to displacement is called simple harmonic motion abbreviated as S.H.M.
If a particle performs oscillatory motion such that its acceleration (a) and displacement (x) are related as below
$$a \propto -x,$$
then the motion of particle is simple harmonic.
The force (F) acting on the particle is obviously proportional to x and directs in opposite to it. i.e.,
$$F \propto -x$$
or $\quad F = -kx$, where k is a constant force law
This force F is known as the restoring force as it always restore the position of the particle.

Equation of S.H.M.

The equation of S.H.M. represents the displacement (x) of the particle at any time (t).
It is generally given by
$$x = A\sin(\omega t + \phi) \quad \text{or} \quad x = A\cos(\omega t + \phi)$$
Here, $\quad$ A = amplitude and ω = angular frequency
ϕ = phase constant or initial phase
Amplitude (A): It is the maximum distance on the either side of the mean position of oscillating particle. It is represented by A, its S.I. unit is metre (m).
Phase: Phase of a vibrating particle at any instant is the state of the vibrat ing particle regarding its displacement and direction of vibration at that particular instant.
The *cosine* in equation $x = A\cos(\omega t + \phi_0)$ gives the phase of oscillation at time t.
Velocity
The displacement of a particle executing S.H.M. is given by
$$x = A\sin(\omega t + \phi)$$
Time period: It is the time taken by the oscillating particle to complete one oscillation. It is represented by T.
Kinetic energy: A particle executing SHM possesses kinetic energy by virtue of its motion.

$$K.E = \dfrac{1}{2}mv^2 = \dfrac{1}{2}m\omega^2(A^2 - x^2) \quad (v = \omega\sqrt{A^2 - x^2})$$

Potential energy : A particle executing SHM possesses potential energy due to its displacement from its mean position.

$$P.E = \dfrac{1}{2}kx^2 \Rightarrow P.E = \dfrac{1}{2}m\omega^2 x^2 \quad (k = m\omega^2)$$

At mean position, $x = 0 \Rightarrow$ P.E. $= 0$
At extreme position, $x = A$
$$\Rightarrow \quad (P.E)_{\max} = \dfrac{1}{2}m\omega^2 A^2 = \dfrac{1}{2}k\omega^2$$

Simple Pendulum

An ideal simple pendulum consists of a heavy point mass (bob) suspended by a weightless, inextensible and perfectly flexible string from a rigid support about which it is free to oscillate.

Time period of a simple pendulum,

$T = 2\pi \sqrt{\dfrac{l}{g}}$ where, l = length of pendulum

and g = acceleration due to gravity.
Time period of second pendulum is 2 seconds.

Resonance

The phenomenon of increase in amplitude when the driving force is close to the natural frequency of the oscillator.

HEAT AND THERMODYNAMICS

Heat is a form of energy which is responsible for the change in thermal condition of a body. It is also described as energy flow due to difference in temperature. The branch of science which deals with the conversion of heat into mechanical work and vice-versa is *Thermodynamics*.

HEAT

Heat or thermal energy is the sum of all types of kinetic energies (translational, vibrational, rotational) of all the molecules of the body.

The SI unit of heat energy is joule (J), practical unit of heat energy is Calorie. "One calorie is the amount of heat required to raise temperature of one gram of water from 14.5°C to 15.5°C."

1 Calorie = 4.186 joule

TEMPERATURE

Temperature is defined as the degree of hotness or coldness of a body. To measure temperature above 800°C, we use **Pyrometer**.

Absolute Temperature

The lowest temperature of –273.16 °C at which a gas is supposed to have zero volume and zero pressure and at which entire molecular motion stops is called absolute zero temperature. A new scale of temperature starting with –273.16°C by Lord Kelvin as zero. This is called Kelvin scale or absolute scale of temperature.

T(K) = t°C + 273.16

Temperature Scale

In order to measure the temperature, two-points are fixed, the lower fixed point is ice point and upper fixed point is boiling point of water.

Celsius Scale (°C): This scale was designed by Andre Celsius in 1710. In this scale the melting point of ice is taken as 0°C and the boiling point of water is taken as 100°C and the space between the two points is divided into 100 equal parts.

Fahrenheit Scale (°F): This scale was designed by Gabriel Fahrenheit in 1717. In this scale the melting point of ice is taken as 32°F and the boiling point of water is taken as 212°F and the space between the points is divided equally into 180 parts.

Kelvin Scale (K): This was designed by Kelvin. In this scale the melting point of ice is taken as 273K and boiling point of water is taken as 373K and the space between the points is divided equally into 100 parts.

Relation between various temperature scales

$$\left(\dfrac{C}{5} = \dfrac{F-32}{9} = \dfrac{K-273}{5} \right)$$

- At –40° temperature, the celsius and fahrenheit scales read the same.
- At 574.25° temperature, the fahrenheit and kelvin scales read the same.

TRIPLE POINT OF WATER

The state at which three phases of water-ice, liquid water and water vapour are equally stable and co-exist in equilibrium.
It is unique because it occurs at a specific temperature of 273.16 K and a specific pressure of 0.46 cm of Hg column.

HUMIDITY

Absolute Humidity : It is the amount of water vapour present in a unit volume of air.
Relative humidity: It is defined as the ratio of the amount of water vapour present in a given volume of air at a given temperature to the amount of water vapour required to saturate the same volume of air at the same temperature.

The relative humidity during rainy season increases and the rate of vaporisation decreases. This is why clothes dry earlier in winter than in rainy season.

IDEAL-GAS EQUATION

The equation PV = nRT, where n = no. of moles in the sample of gas, R = Universal gas constant (= 8.31 J mol^{-1} K^{-1}) is known as *Ideal-gas equation*.

It is the combination of following three laws.

Boyle's Law: When temperature is held constant, the pressure is inversely proportional to volume.

i.e., $P \propto \dfrac{1}{V}$ (at constant temperature)

Charle's Law: When the pressure is held constant, the volume of the gas is directly proportional to the absolute temperature.
i.e., $V \propto T$ (at constant pressure)

Avogadro's Law: When the pressure and temperature are kept constant, the volume is directly proportional to the number of moles of the ideal gas in the container.

i.e., $V \propto n$ (at constant pressure and temperature)

THERMAL EXPANSION

When a body (almost all) is heated it expands. The expansion can take place in the length, area or volume of the body. Depending upon the expansion in length, area or volume we have three types of expansion.

Linear Expansion

Let l_1 be the length of a wire at temperature 'θ_1' when temperature is increased to θ_2, length increases to l_2 then

$$\alpha = \dfrac{\Delta l}{l_1 \Delta \theta} \quad \text{or} \quad l_2 = l_1(1 + \alpha \, \Delta \theta)$$

($\Delta l = l_1 - l_2$ change in length & change in temperature $\Delta\theta = \theta_1 - \theta_2$)

Where α is **coefficient of linear expansion**. Its unit is /°C or /K. It depends upon the nature of material. The value of 'α' also depends on temperature but very slightly.

Superficial or Areal Expansion:

Increase in surface area of a solid when temperature is increased. If A_1 and A_2 be the surface area at temperature θ_1 and θ_2 respectively then

$$\beta = \frac{\Delta A}{A_1 D\theta} \quad \text{or,} \quad A_2 = A_1(1 + \beta\Delta\theta)$$

'β' is **coefficient of superficial expansion** of a solid. Its unit is /°C and /K, it depends upon nature of material.

Cubical or Volume Expansion:

Increase in volume of a substance on heating. If V_1 and V_2 are volumes of a substance at temperature θ_1 and θ_2 respectively, then

$$\gamma = \frac{\Delta V}{V_1 \Delta\theta} \quad \text{or,} \quad V_2 = V_1(1 + \gamma\Delta\theta)$$

Where 'γ' is **coefficient of cubical expansion** of solid. Its unit is /°C or /K and it depends upon the nature of material.

The relation between (α, β and γ is $\alpha = \dfrac{\beta}{2} = \dfrac{\gamma}{3}$

$\Rightarrow \alpha : \beta : \gamma = 1 : 2 : 3$)

> - A small gap is left between the iron nails of railway tracks.
> - Space is left between the girders used for supporting bridges.
> - Clock pendulums are made of invar. Invar has extremely small temperature coefficient of expansion, so the length of invar pendulum does not change with the change of season. i.e., temperature.

EXPANSION OF LIQUIDS

When we heat a liquid which is kept inside a container then liquid as well as the container both expand. In this case the observed expansion of liquid will be apparent expansion. But if the container were not expand then the expansion will be real expansion.

Coefficient of real expansion γ_r

$$= \frac{\text{real increase in volume}}{\text{original volume} \times \Delta\theta}$$

Coefficient of apparent expansion γ_a

$$= \frac{\text{apparent increase in volume}}{\text{original volume} \times \Delta\theta}$$

If γ_g is coefficient of volume expansion of material of container then

$$\gamma_r = \gamma_g + \gamma_a$$

Anomalous Expansion of Water

Almost all liquids expand on heating but water when heated from 0°C to 4°C its volume decreases and hence density increases until its temperature reaches 4°C as its density is maximum at 4°C and on further heating its density decreases. This behaviour of water is called anomalous behaviour of water.

This allows aquatic animals to remain alive and move freely near the bottom.

CALORIMETRY

We know that there is spontaneous transfer of heat from a hot body to colder body. If heat exchange with the surrounding is negligible then the total heat lost by a hot body is always equal to the heat gained by the cold body, this is the **principle of calorimetry or, law of mixture.**

Specific Heat Capacity

When we supply heat to a body, its temperature rises. If m is mass, $\Delta\theta$ is temperature rise and Q is the heat supplied, then

$$Q \propto M \Rightarrow Q \propto \Delta\theta \text{ or } Q = Ms\Delta\theta \Rightarrow s = \frac{Q}{M\Delta\theta}$$

Where 's' is constant called *specific heat* which depends upon the nature of material and its surrounding.

Specific heat capacity of a material is equal to the heat required to raise temperature of unit mass from 14.5°C to 15.5°C.

Molar Heat Capacity and Heat Capacity

Molar heat capacity of a substance is the amount of heat required to raise the temperature of one mole of a substance by unit degree.

$$s_m = \frac{Q}{n\Delta\theta} \qquad n = \text{number of moles}$$

Heat capacity of a substance is the amount of heat required to raise temperature of a body by unit degree. It is represented by C, its unit is J/°C or cal °C. Heat capacity depends upon nature of material and its mass.

$$\text{Heat capacity,} \quad C = \frac{Q}{\Delta\theta} = ms$$

Water Equivalent and Latent Heat

Water Equivalent of a body is defined as the mass of water which has the same heat capacity as that of the body. It is represented by W.

Latent Heat or Hidden Heat: When state of a substance changes, change of state takes place at constant temperature (m.pt. or B. pt.) heat is released or absorbed and is given by

$Q = mL$ where L is latent heat. The S.I. unit of latent heat is J/kg.

Latent heat of fusion or melting (L_f): It is the amount of heat required to change unit mass of solid into liquid state at its melting point. It is represented by L_f. For ice its value is 80 cal g^{-1}.

$$Q = mL_f$$

Latent heat of vaporisation or boiling (L_v): It is the amount of heat required to change unit mass of liquid into its vapors at its boiling point. It is represented by L_v

For water $L_v = 540$ cal g^{-1}.

$$Q = mL_v$$

Sublimation: It is the conversion of a solid directly into vapours.

$$\text{Solid} \xrightarrow{\text{Heat}} \text{Vapour}$$

Boiling Point

Boiling point of a liquid is the temperature at which the saturated vapour pressure of that liquid becomes equal to external atmospheric pressure. Boiling point increases with increase in external pressure.

Regelation

The phenomenon in which ice melts when pressure is increased and again freezes when pressure is removed is called *regelation*.

BOILING POINT & ABSOLUTE PRESSURE			
Boiling point of Water [°C]	Absolute pressure [mm Hg]	Boiling point of Water [°C]	Absolute pressure [mm Hg]
100	760	114	1241
101	776	121	1551
102	827	151	3620
104	879	181	7757
112	1138	310	74091

HEAT TRANSFER

Heat energy can be transferred from a body at higher temperature to a body at lower temperature by three different ways viz. conduction, convection and radiation.

Conduction

Conduction is the process in which heat is transmitted from one point to the other through the substance without the actual motion of the particles. When one end of a metal is heated, the molecules at the hot end start vibrating with higher amplitudes (kinetic energy) and transmit this K.E. to the next molecule and so on. However, the molecules still remain in their mean positions of equilibrium. This process of conduction is prominent in the case of solids.

Convection

Convection is the process in which heat is transmitted from one place to the other by the actual movement of the vibrating particles. It is prominent in the case of liquids and gases.

Land and **sea breezes** and **trade winds** are formed due to convection. Convection plays an important part in ventilation, gas filled electric lamps and heating of buildings by hot water circulation.

It is the process of transfer of heat in a fluid by the movement of the fluid itself.

Radiation

Radiation is the process in which heat is transmitted from one place to the other directly without the necessity of any intervening medium. We get heat radiations directly from the sun without affecting the intervening medium. Heat radiations can pass through vacuum. Heat radiations are a part of the electromagnetic spectrum.

Radiation has the following properties

- Radiant energy travels in straight line and when some object is placed in the path, it's shadow is formed at the detector.
- It is reflected and refracted or can be made to interfere. The reflection or refraction are exactly as in case of light.
- It can travel through vacuum.
- Intensity of radiation follows the law of inverse square.
- Thermal radiation can be polarised in the same way as light by transmission through a nicol prims.

THERMAL CONDUCTIVITY

It is the measure of ability of the solid to conduct heat through it. Examples: silver, copper, etc. are good conductors of heat and glass, wood are bad conductors of heat.

The coefficient of thermal conductivity (K) is defined as the amount of heat flowing in unit time across the opposite faces of a cube of side having unit length maintained at unit temperature difference.

$$\text{Coefficient of thermal conductivity } K = \frac{(\Delta Q / \Delta t)}{(A \Delta T / \Delta x)}$$

Black Body

A black body absorbs the entire thermal radiation incident on it. Practically there is no body which absorbs 100% radiations incident on it. Ferry designed a black body which a spherical enclosure painted black from inside with a small hole in the wall.

Any radiation through this hole goes inside and get absorbed after multiple reflections. There is cone directly opposite to the hole due to which incident radiation is not reflected back through the hole.

Wien's Displacement Law

According to Wien's displacement law, wavelength corresponding to highest intensity (λ_m) is inversely proportional to the absolute temperature of the body.

Kirchhoff's Law

Good absorbers of radiation are also good radiators of radiation and this statement is quantitatively explained by Kirchoff's law. According to this law, at any given temperature the ratio of emissive power to the absorptive power is constant for all bodies and this constant is equal to the emissive power of perfect Black Body at the same temperature.

$$E/a_{body} = E_{Black\ Body}$$

- **Emissive Power** - It denotes the energy radiated per unit area per unit solid angle normal to the area.

  $E = \Delta u / [(\Delta A) (\Delta w) (\Delta t)]$

  where, Δu is the energy radiated by area ΔA of surface in solid angle Δw in time Δt.

- **Absorptive Power** - It is defined as the fraction of the incident radiation that is absorbed by the body

  a(absorptive power) = energy absorbed / energy incident

THERMODYNAMIC PROCESSES

Thermodynamic process is said to take place if some change occurs in the state of a thermodynamic system, i.e. the thermodynamic variables of the system – pressure, volume, temperature and entropy change with time.

In practice, the following types of thermodynamic processes can take place :

Isothermal process: A thermodynamic process that takes place at constant temperature.

Isobaric process: A thermodynamic process that takes place at constant pressure.

Isochoric process: A thermodynamic process that takes place at constant volume.

Adiabatic process: A thermodynamic process in which no heat enters or leaves the system.

Cyclic process: A thermodynamic process in which the system returns to its original state.

LAWS OF THERMODYNAMICS
Zeroth Law of Thermodynamics

If objects A and B are separately in thermal equilibrium with a third object C then objects A and B are in thermal equilibrium with each other.

First Law of Thermodynamics

If some quantity of heat is supplied to a system capable of doing external work, then the quantity of heat absorbed by the system is equal to the sum of the increase in the internal energy of the system and the external work done by the system.

i.e., $\qquad \Delta Q = \Delta U + \Delta W$

The first law of thermodynamics is essentially a restatement of the law of conservation of energy i.e., energy can neither be created nor be destroyed but may be converted from one form to another.

Second Law of Thermodynamics

Kelvin-Planck statement : It is impossible for an engine working between a cyclic process to extract heat from a reservoir and convert completely into work. In other words, 100% conversion of heat into work is impossible.

HEAT ENGINES

Heat engine is a device which converts heat energy into work. A heat engine, in general, consists of three parts :
- A source or high temperature reservoir at temperature T_1.
- A working substance.
- A sink or low temperature reservoir at temperature T_2.

The efficiency of internal combustion engine is approximately 40% to 60%.

Carnot Theorem

No irreversible engine (I) can have efficiency greater than Carnot reversible engine (R) working between same hot and cold reservoirs.

Refrigerators and Heat Pumps

Air conditioners, refrigerators and heat pumps, utilize heat transfer of energy from low to high temperatures, and work reverse of that heat engines do. Heat transfers energy Q_c from a cold reservoir and delivers energy Q_h into a hot one. This requires work input, W, which produces a transfer of energy by heat. Therefore, the total heat transfer to the hot reservoir is given by,

$$Q_c = Q_h + W$$

A simple heat pump has four basic components: an evaporator, a compressor, a condenser, and an expansion value. In the heating mode, heat transfers Q_c to the working fluid in the evaporator from the colder, outdoor air, turning it into a gas. The electrically driven compressor increases the temperature and pressure of the gas and forces it into the condenser coils inside the heated space. Because the temperature of the gas is higher than the temperature in the room, heat transfers energy from the gas to the room as the gas condenses into a liquid. The working fluid is then cooled as it flows back through an expansion valve to the outdoor evaporator coild.

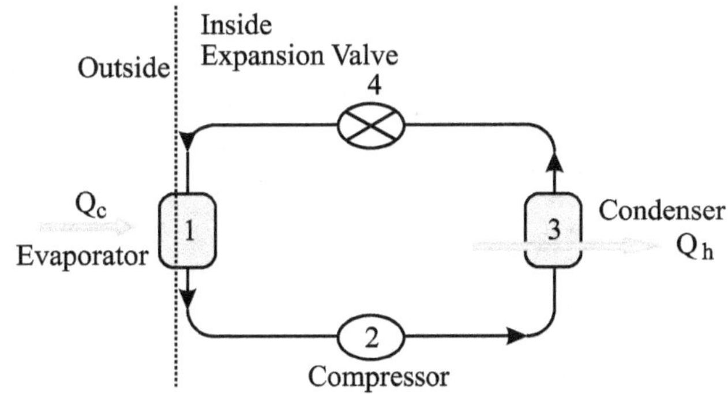

MULTIPLE CHOICE QUESTIONS

1. The sound travels fastest in
 (a) solids   (b) liquids
 (c) gases   (d) none of these

2. Two identical piano wires have same fundamental frequency when kept under the same tension. What will happen if tension of one of the wire is slightly increased and both the wires are made to vibrate simultaneously? **[CDS]**
 (a) Noise   (b) Beats
 (c) Resonance   (d) Non-linear effects

3. Why is sound heard with more intensity through CO_2 than through the air ? **[NDA]**
 (a) Density of CO_2 is more than that of air
 (b) Density of CO_2 is less than that of air
 (c) Air is bad conductor of heat
 (d) CO_2 is a compound, but air is a mixture of gases.

4. How does time period *(T)* of a seconds pendulum vary with length *(l)*? **[NDA]**
 (a) $T \alpha \sqrt{l}$ (b) $T \alpha l^2$
 (c) $T \alpha l$ (d) T does not depend on l

5. Which one of the following properties distinguishes ultrasound from normal audible sound? **[NDA]**
 (a) Intensity   (b) Speed of propagation
 (c) Frequency   (d) Quality

6. Consider the following statements :
 If the same note is played on a flute and a sitar, one can still distinguish between them because they differ in
 [NDA]
 1. frequency   2. intensity
 3. quality
 Which of the statements given above is/are correct?
 (a) 1 and only   (b) 2 and 3 only
 (c) 3 only   (d) 2 only

7. Consider the following statements :
 Sound waves can undergo
 [NDA]
 1. reflection   2. refraction
 3. interference
 (a) 1 and 2 only   (b) 2 and 3 only
 (c) 1 and 3 only   (d) 1, 2 and 3

8. Consider the following parts of spectra **[NDA]**
 1. Visible   2. Infrared
 3. Ultraviolet   4. Microwave
 Which one of the following is the correct sequence in which their wavelengths increase ?
 (a) $4-3-1-2$ (b) $4-1-2-3$
 (c) $3-2-1-4$ (d) $3-1-2-4$

9. In a sitar wire which one of the following types of vibration is produced? **[NDA]**
 (a) Progressive longitudinal
 (b) Stationary longitudinal
 (c) Progressive transverse
 (d) Stationary transverse

10. Which one of the following is not electromagnetic in nature? **[NDA]**
 (a) Cathode-rays   (b) X-rays
 (c) Gamma-rays   (d) Infrared-rays

11. 'Pitch' is a characteristic of sound that depends upon its **[NDA]**
 (a) intensity   (b) fequency
 (c) quality   (d) None of these

12. Timbre is called the quality of sound. One can recognise the voice of a familiar human being or instrument without actually seeing them. This quality is associated with
 (a) material of the body
 (b) overtones present in the sound
 (c) shape of the body
 (d) all of the above

13. Suppose a tunnel is dug along a diameter of the earth. A particle is dropped from a point, a distance h directly above the tunnel, the motion of the particle is
 (a) simple harmonic   (b) parabolic
 (c) oscillatory   (d) non-periodic

14. Which one of the following types of waves are used in a night vision apparatus? **[IAS Prelim]**
 (a) Radio waves   (b) Microwaves
 (c) Infra-red waves   (d) None of the above

15. C   D   K   L
 B   J   I
 A   E   M
 F   G   H

Figure given above shows the part of a long string in which transverse waves are produced. Which pair of points is in phase? **[NDA]**
 (a) A and E   (b) B and J
 (c) D and J   (d) C and G

16. Consider the following statements with reference to observations made by an astronaut on the surface of moon:
 1. The astronaut finds that a simple pendulum continues to oscillate for a much longer time, than that on the earth.
 2. No atmosphere exists there.
 Which of the statements given above is/are correct ?
 [NDA]
 (a) Only 1   (b) Only 2
 (c) Both 1 and 2   (d) Neither 1 nor 2

17. If the length of second's pendulum is increased by 2%, how many seconds will it lose per day? **[NDA]**
 (a) 3600 s   (b) 3456 s
 (c) 1728 s   (d) 846 s

18. A man standing between two parallel hills fires a gun and hears two echoes, one 2.5 s and the other 3.5 s after the firing. If the velocity of sound is 330 ms^{-1}, how long will it take him to hear the third echo? **[NDA]**
    (a) 4s (b) 5s
    (c) 6s (d) 8s

19. The simple harmonic motion of a particle is given by y = 3 sin ωt + 4 cos ωt. Which one of the follwing is the amplitude of this motion? **[NDA]**
    (a) 1 (b) 5
    (c) 7 (d) 12

20. 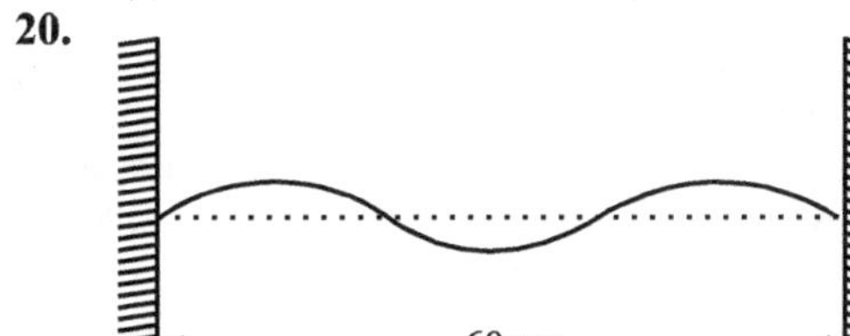

    The standing wave pattern along a string of length 60 cm is shown in the above diagram. If the speed of the transverse waves on this string is 300 m/s, in which one of the following modes is the string vibrating ? **[NDA]**
    (a) Fundamental (b) First overtone
    (c) Second overtone (d) Third overtone

21. A sonometer wire having a length of 50 cm is vibrating in the fundamental mode with a frequency of 100Hz. Which of the following is the type of propagating wave and its speed? **[NDA]**
    (a) Longitudinal, 50 m/s (b) Transverse, 50 m/s
    (c) Longitudinal, 100 m/s (d) Transverse, 100 m/s

22. The Visible light has a wavelength range from about 380 nm (violet) to 780 nm (red). If an excited object emits light with wavelength of 15 nm, to which one of the following ranges does it belongs? **[NDA]**
    (a) X-ray (b) Gamma ray
    (c) Infrared (d) Ultraviolet

23. Sound moves with higher velocity if **[NDA]**
    (a) pressure of the medium is decreased
    (b) temperature of the medium is increased
    (c) humidity of the medium is increased
    (d) Both (b) and (c) above

24. Bats can ascertain distance, directions, nature and size of the obstacles at night. This is possible by reflection of the emitted **[NDA]**
    (a) ultrasonic waves from the bat
    (b) ultrasonic waves from the distant objects
    (c) supersonic waves from the bat
    (d) supersonic waves from the distant objects

25. The regions of compressions and rarefractions of sound wave are·establisbed because
    (a) the sound wave undergoes diffraction behind obstacles
    (b) the reflected sound wave at fixed end interferes with the incident wave
    (c) the longitudinal movement of air molecules produce pressure fluctuations ·
    (d) the speed of the sound wave changes as it travels through a medium

26. A thermodynamic function
    $$G(T, P, N) = U - TS + PV$$
    is given in terms of the internal energy U, temperature T, entropy S, pressure P, volume V and the number of particles N. Which of the following relations is true? (In the following μ is the chemical potential.)
    (a) $S = -\dfrac{\partial G}{\partial T}\Big|_{N.P}$ (b) $S = \dfrac{\partial G}{\partial T}\Big|_{N.P}$
    (c) $V = -\dfrac{\partial G}{\partial P}\Big|_{N.T}$ (d) $\mu = -\dfrac{\partial G}{\partial N}\Big|_{P.T}$

27. The sound from an open pipe is more pleasant than the sound from a closed pipe. This is because :
    (a) sound is heard from both the sides of an open pipe
    (b) there are more overtone combinations in an open pipe than in a closed one
    (c) it is very easy to operate an open pipe
    (d) the length of the open pipe is shorter

28. Which one of the following is the mode of heat transfer in which warm material is transported so as to displace a cooler material ? **[NDA]**
    (a) Conduction only
    (b) Convection only
    (c) Radiation
    (d) Both conduction and convection

29. Low temperatures (cryogenics) find application in : **[IAS Prelim]**
    (a) space travel, surgery and magnetic levitation
    (b) surgery, magnetic levitation and telemetry
    (c) space travel, surgery and telemetry
    (d) space travel, magnetic levitation and telemetry

30. Which zone of a candle flame is the hottest ?
    (a) Dark innermost zone **[NDA]**
    (b) Outermost zone
    (c) Middle luminous zone
    (d) Central zone

31. **Assertion (A):** Steam is more harmful for human body than the boiling water in case of burn.
    Reason (R) : Boiling water contains more heat than steam. **[CDS]**
    (a) Both A and R are true and R is the correct explanation of A
    (b) Both A and R are true, but R is not the correct explanation of A
    (c) A is true, but R is false
    (d) A is false, but R is true

32. **Assertion (A):** In a pressure cooker food is cooked above boiling point.
    Reason (R): Boiling point of water increases as the pressure increases. **[CDS]**
    (a) Both A and R are true and R is the correct explanation of A
    (b) Both A and R are true, but R is not the correct explanation of A
    (c) A is true, but R is false
    (d) A is false, but R is true

33. Strips of two metals A and B are firmly jointed together as shown in the figure. **[IAS Prelim]**

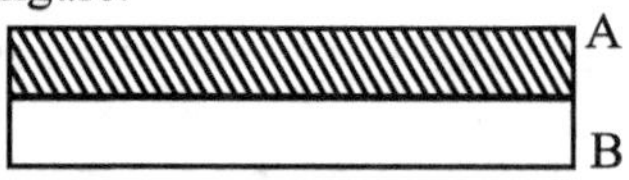

On heating, A expands more than B does. If this jointed strip is heated, then it will appear as

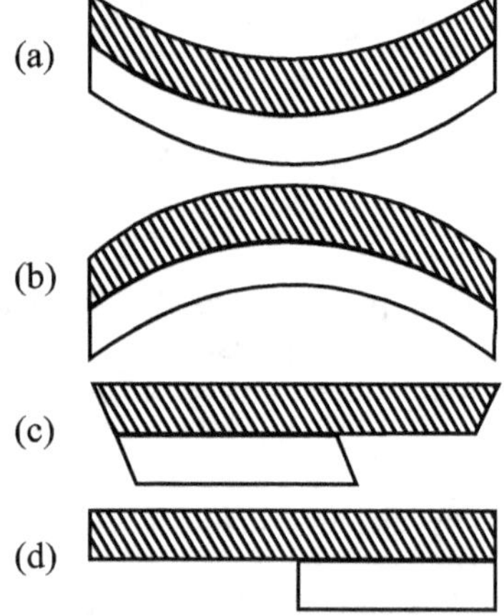

(a)

(b)

(c)

(d)

34. Which one among the following statements about thermal conductivity is correct ? **[NDA]**
   (a) Steel > Wood > Water (b) Steel > Water > Wood
   (c) Water > Steel > Wood (d) Water > Wood > Steel

35. Cloudy nights are warmer compared to clear cloudless nights, because clouds: **[IAS Prelim]**
   (a) prevent clod waves from the sky from descending on earth
   (b) reflect back the heat given off by earth
   (c) produce heat and radiate it towards earth
   (d) absorb heat from the atmosphere and send it towards earth

36. A solid is melted (above the melting point) and allowed to cool down at normal condition.Its variation of temperature as a function of times is as shown in the figure given below. What is the reason for the plateau(flat position) in the central region of the cooling curve as shown in the figure? **[NDA]**
   (a) Latent heat of fusion of the solid
   (b) Specific heat of the solid
   (c) Thermal conductivity of the solid
   (d) Thermal capacity of the solid.

37. If the door of a running refrigerator in a closed room is kept open, what will be the net effect on the room? **[CDS]**
   (a) It will cool the room
   (b) It will heat the room
   (c) It will make no difference on the average
   (d) It will make the temperature go up and down

38. The surface of a lake is frozen in severe winter, but the water at its bottom is still liquid. What is the reason ? **[IAS Prelim]**
   (a) Ice is a bad conductor of heat.
   (b) Since the surface of the lake is at the same temperature as the air, no heat is lost.
   (c) The density of water is maximum at 4°C.
   (d) None of the statements (a), (b) and (c) given is correct.

39. Which of the following properties are most desirable for a cooking pot ? **[NDA]**
   (a) High specific heat capacity and low conductivity
   (b) Low specific heat capacity and high conductivity
   (c) High specific heat capacity and high conductivity
   (d) Low specific heat capacity and low conductivity

40.

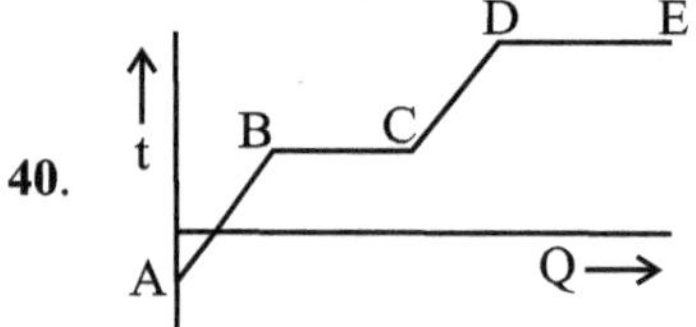

The graph given above indicates change in temperature (Δt) when heat (Q) was given to a substance. Which among the following parts of the graph correctly depict the latent heat of the substance? **[NDA]**
   (a) AB and BC   (b) BC and DE
   (c) CD and DE   (d) DE and AB

41. Consider the following statements: . **[CDS]**
   1. Steam at 100°C and boiling water at 100°C contain same amount of heat.
   2. Latent heat of fusion of ice is equal to the latent heat of vaporization of water.
   3. In an air-conditioner, heat is extracted from the room air at the evaporator coils and is rejected out at the condenser coils.
   Which of these statements is/are correct?
   (a) 1 and 2   (b) 2 and 3
   (c) Only 2   (d) Only 3

42. Mr X was advised by an architect to make outer walls of his house with hollow bricks. The correct reason is that such walls **[CDS]**
   (a) make the building stronger
   (b) help keeping inside cooler in summer and warmer in winter
   (c) prevent seepage of moisture from outside
   (d) protect the building from lightning

43. Why are inner lining of hot water geysers made up of copper? **[CDS]**
   (a) Copper has low heat capacity
   (b) Copper has high electrical conductivity
   (c) Copper does not react with steam
   (d) Copper is good conductor of both heat and electricity

44. A Centigrade thermometer and Fahrenheit thermometer are dipped in boiling water. The temperature of water is lowered till the Fahrenheit thermometer registers half of its upper fixed point. What is the corresponding fall temperature registered by the Centrigrade thermometer? **[NDA]**
   (a) Half of its range of temperature between the upper and the lower fixed points
   (b) Approximately 41°C
   (c) Approximately 59°C
   (d) 18°C

45. When water is heated from 0°C to 20°C, how does its volume change?
   (a) It shall increase
   (b) It shall decrease
   (c) It shall first increase and then decrease
   (d) It shall first decrease and then increase

46. Thermal conductivity of aluminium, copper and stainless steel increases in the order
(a) Copper < Aluminium < Stainless Steel
(b) Stainless Steel < Aluminium < Copper
(c) Aluyminium < Copper < Stainless Steel
(d) Copper < Stainless Steel < Aluminium

47. Which of the following statements is/ are false about mode of heat transfer?
I. In radiation, heat is transfered from one medium to another without affecting the intervening medium
II. Radiation and convection are possible in vaccum while conduction requires material medium.
III. Conduction is possible in solids while convection occurs in liquids and gases.
(a) I only   (b) II only
(c) II and III   (d) I, II and III

48. When pressure on piece of ice is increases its melting point
(a) decreases
(b) increases
(c) remains unchanged
(d) first increases and then decreases

49. Consider the following three statements
1. Heating 1 kg of water from 10°C to 50°C
2. Melting 600 g of ice at 0°C
3. Converting 300 g of ice at 0°C to water at 50°C
Which one of the following shows the correct arrangement of the quantity of heat required in the above process in increasing order of magnitude?
Choose the correct answer from the codes give below
(a) 1, 2, 3   (b) 2, 1, 3
(c) 3, 2, 1   (d) 3, 1, 2

50. **Assertion (A) :** The boiling point of water decreases as the altitude increases.
Reason (R) : The atmospheric pressure increases with altitude.   **[IAS Prelim]**
(a) Both A and R are true and R is the correct explanation of A
(b) Both A and R are true but R is not a correct explanation of A
(c) A is true but R is false
(d) A is false but R is true

51. **Assertion (A) :** A piece of copper and a piece of glass are heated to the same temperature. When touched, thereafter, the copper piece appears hotter than the glass piece.
Reason (R) : The density of copper is more than that of glass.   **[IAS Prelim]**
(a) Both A and R are true and R is the correct explanation of A
(b) Both A and R are true but R is not a correct explanation of A
(c) A is true but R is false
(d) A is false but R is true

52. Ultrasonic waves are produced by making use of
[CDS 2017-II]
(a) ferromagnetic material (b) ferrimagnetic material
(c) piezoelectric material (d) pyroelectric material

53. Which of the following represents a relation for 'heat lost = heat gained'?   **[CDS 2018-I]**

(a) Principle of thermal equilibrium
(b) Principle of colors
(c) Principle of calorimetry
(d) Principle of vaporization

54. Sound waves cannot travel through a   **[CDS 2018-I]**
(a) copper wire placed in air
(b) silver slab placed in air
(c) glass prism placed in water
(d) wooden hollow pipe placed in vacuum

55. Which one of the following is the correct relation between the Kelvin temperature (T) and the Celsius temperature (tc)?   **[CDS 2018-I]**
(a) These are two independent temperature scales
(b) T = tc
(c) T = tc − 273.15
(d) T = tc + 273.15

56. The speed of a body that has Mach number more than 1 is
[NDA 2017-I]
(a) supersonic   (b) subsonic
(c) 300 m/s   (d) about 10 m/s

57. Which one of the following statements is NOT correct?
[NDA 2017-I]
(a) In the conduction mode of transference of heat, the molecules of solid pass heat from one molecule to another without moving from their positions
(b) The amount of heat required to raise the temperature of a substance is called its specific heat capacity
(c) The process of heat transfer in liquids and gases is through convection mode
(d) The process of heat transfer from a body at higher temperature to a body at lower temperature without heating the space between them is known as radiation

58. The amount of heat required to change a liquid to gaseous state without any change in temperature is known as
[NDA 2017-I]
(a) specific heat capacity
(b) mechanical equivalent of heat
(c) latent heat of vaporization
(d) quenching

59. The time period of a simple pendulum made using a thin copper wire of length L is T. Suppose the temperature of the room in which this simple pendulum is placed increases by 30°C, what will be the effect on the time period of the pendulum?   **[NDA 2017-I]**
(a) T will increase slightly
(b) T will remain the same
(c) T will decrease slightly
(d) T will become more than 2 times

60. A Kelvin thermometer and a Fahrenheit thermometer both give the same reading for a certain sample. What would be the corresponding reading in a Celsius thermometer?
[NDA 2017-I]
(a) 574   (b) 301
(c) 273   (d) 232

61. Why is it difficult to measure the coefficient of expansion of a liquid than solid?   **[NDA 2017-I]**
(a) Liquids tend to evaporate at all temperatures
(b) Liquids conduct more heat
(c) Liquids expand too much when heated
(d) Their containers also expand when heated

62. Bats detect obstacles in their path by receiving the reflected **[NDA 2017-II]**

- (a) Infrasonic waves
- (b) Ultrasonic waves
- (c) Radio waves
- (d) Microwaves

63. The statement that 'heat cannot flow by itself from a body at a lower temperature to a body at a higher temperature', is known as **[NDA 2017-II]**

- (a) Zeroth law of thermodynamics
- (b) First law of thermodynamics
- (c) Second law of thermodynamics
- (d) Third law of thermodynamics

64. Which one of the following statements is not correct? **[NDA 2017-II]**

- (a) Ultrasonic waves cannot get reflected, refracted or absorbed.
- (b) Ultrasonic waves are used to detect the presence of defects like cracks, porosity, etc. in the internal structure of common structure materials.
- (c) Ultrasonic waves can be used for making holes in very hard materials like diamond.
- (d) Ultrasonic waves cannot travel through vacuum.

65. Which one of the following statements is correct? **[NDA 2018-I]**

- (a) Any energy transfer that does not involve temperature difference in some way is not heat
- (b) Any energy transfer always requires a temperature difference
- (c) On heating the length and volume of the object remain exactly the same
- (d) Whenever there is a temperature difference, heat is the only way of energy transfer

66. If T is the time period of an oscillating pendulum, which one of the following statements is NOT correct? **[NDA 2018-I]**

- (a) The motions repeats after time T only once
- (b) T is the least time after which motion repeats itself
- (c) The motion repeats itself after nT, where n is a positive integer
- (d) T remains the same only for small angular displacements

67. Which one of the following frequency ranges is sensitive to human ears? **[NDA 2018-I]**

- (a) $0 - 200$ Hz
- (b) $20 - 20,000$ Hz
- (c) $200 - 20,000$ Hz only
- (d) $2,000 - 20,000$ Hz only

68. Which of the following statements about latent heat for a given substance is/are correct? **[NDA 2018-I]**

1. It is fixed at a given temperature.
2. It depends upon the temperature and volume.
3. it is independent of temperature and volume.
4. It depends on the temperature but independent of volume.

Select the correct answer using the code given below:

- (a) 2
- (b) 1 and 3
- (c) 4 only
- (d) 1 and 4

69. Which of the following statements about specific heat of a body is/are correct? **[NDA 2018-I]**

1. It depends upon mass and shape of the body
2. It is independent of mass and shape of the body
3. It depends only upon the temperature of the body

Select the correct answer using the code given below:

- (a) 1 only
- (b) 2 and 3
- (c) 1 and 3
- (d) 2 only

70. Which one of the following is an example of the force of gravity of the earth acting on a vibrating pendulum bob? **[NDA 2018-I]**

- (a) Applied force
- (b) Frictional force
- (c) Restoring force
- (d) Virtual force

71. Thermal capacity of a body depends on the **[NDA 2018-I]**

- (a) mass of the body only
- (b) mass and shape of the body only
- (c) density of the body
- (d) mass, shape and temperature of the body

Directions : The following items consist of two statements, Statement I and Statement II. Examine these two statements carefully and select the correct answer using the code given below.

    code: **[NDA 2018-II]**

- (a) Both the statements are individually true and Statement II is the correct explanation of Statement I
- (b) Both the statements are individually true but Statement II is not the correct explanation of Statement I
- (c) Statement is the true but Statement II is false
- (d) Statement I is false but Statement II is true

72. Statement I :

The pitch of the sound wave depends upon its frequency.

Statement II :

The loudness of the sound wave depends upon its amplitude.

73. Statement I :

Sound wave cannot propagate in vacuum.

Statement II :

Sound waves are elastic waves and require a medium to propagate.

74. The frequency of ultrasound waves is

- (a) less than 20 Hz
- (b) between 20 Hz and 2 kHz
- (c) between 2 kHz and 20 kHz
- (d) greater than 20 kHz

75. The absolute, zero temperature is 0 Kelvin. In °C unit, which one of the following is the absolute zero temperature?

- (a) 0 °C
- (b) –100°C
- (c) –273.15°C
- (d) –173.15°C

76. The time period of oscillation of a simple pendulum having length L and mass off the bob m is given as T. If the length of the pendulum is increased to 4L and the mass of the bob is increased to 2m, then which one of the following is the new period of oscillation?

  (a) T   (b) 2T

  (c) 4T   (d) T/2

77. The connecting cable of electrical appliances like electric iron, water heater or room heater contains three insuated copper wires of three different colours-red, green and black. Which one of the following is the correct colour code?

  (a) Red-live wire, Green-neutral wire, Black-ground wire

  (b) Red-neutral wire, Green-ground wire, Black-live wire

  (c) Red-live wire, Green-ground wire, Black-neutral wire

  (d) Red-ground wire, Green-live wire, Black-neutral wire

78. The graphs between current (l) and voltage (v) for three linear resistors 1, 2 and 3 are given below:

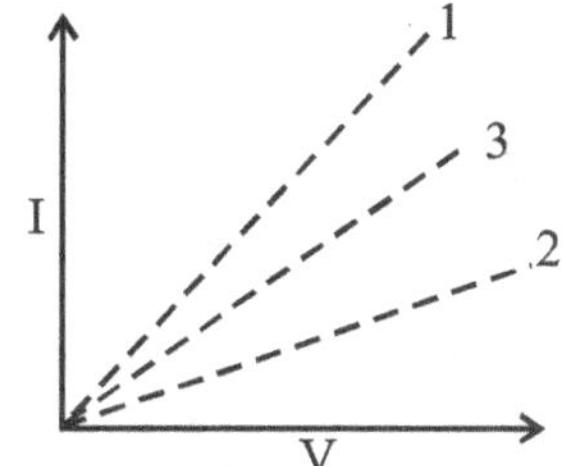

If R_1, R_2 and R_3 are the resistances of these resistors, then which one of the following is correct?

  (a) $R_1 > R_2 > R_3$

  (b) $R_1 < R_3 < R_2$

  (c) $R_3 < R_1 < R_2$

  (d) $R_3 > R_2 > R_1$

79. Consider the following statements about a microscope and a telescope

1. Both the eyepiece and the objective of a microscope are convex lenses.

2. The focal length of the objective of a telescope is larger than the focal length of its eyepiece.

3. The magnification of a telescope increases with the increases in focal length of its objective.

4. The magnification of a microscope increases with the increases in focal length of its objective.

Which of the statements given above are correct?

  (a) 1 and 3 only

  (b) 1 and 4

  (c) 2, 3 and 4

  (d) 1, 2 and 3

		ANSWER KEY																	
1.	(a)	2.	(c)	3.	(a)	4.	(a)	5.	(c)	6.	(c)	7.	(d)	8.	(d)	9.	(d)	10.	(a)
11.	(b)	12.	(d)	13.	(c)	14.	(c)	15.	(d)	16.	(c)	17.	(d)	18.	(c)	19.	(b)	20.	(c)
21.	(d)	22.	(a)	23.	(d)	24.	(a)	25.	(c)	26.	(a)	27.	(b)	28.	(b)	29.	(a)	30.	(b)
31.	(c)	32.	(a)	33.	(b)	34.	(b)	35.	(b)	36.	(a)	37.	(b)	38.	(a)	39.	(b)	40.	(b)
41.	(d)	42.	(b)	43.	(d)	44.	(b)	45.	(d)	46.	(b)	47.	(b)	48.	(b)	49.	(d)	50.	(c)
51.	(b)	52	(c)	53	(c)	54	(d)	55	(d)	56.	(a)	57.	(b)	58.	(c)	59.	(a)	60.	(b)
61.	(d)	62.	(b)	63.	(c)	64.	(a)	65.	(a)	66.	(a)	67.	(b)	68.	(d)	69.	(b)	70.	(c)
71.	(a)	72.	(b)	73.	(a)	74.	(d)	75.	(c)	76.	(b)	77.	(c)	78.	(b)	79.	(d)		

ELECTRICITY, MAGNETISM & LIGHT

ELECTRICITY, MAGNETISM

Electricity is the branch of physics in which we study electric charges, at rest (electrostatics or static electricity) and in motion (current electricity).

An electric current flowing in a conductor produces a magnetic field or magnetism around it.

ELECTRIC CHARGES

Charge is something associated with matter due to which it produces and experiences electric and magnetic effects.

Every atom contains two types of charged particles:

(i) *Positive charge* (Proton) and (ii) *Negative charge* (electron) The magnitude of elementary positive or negative charge is same and is equal to 1.6×10^{-19} C.

Charge is a scalar quantity and its **SI unit** is ampere second or **coulomb** (C).

Basic Properties of Electric Charge
(i) *Similar charges repel and opposite charges attract.*
(ii) Charge is conserved i.e., the charge can neither be created nor be destroyed but it may simple be transferred from one body to other. Charge is transferable.

CONDUCTORS AND INSULATORS

The materials which allow electric charge (or electricity) to flow freely through them are called **conductors**.

The materials which do not allow electric charge to flow through them are called **nonconductors** *or* **insulators**.

Examples of good conductors are metals, impure water etc.

Examples of insulators are quartz, glass, air, rubber, etc.

Silver is the best conductors of electricity.

CLOUD FORMATION, THUNDERING AND LIGHTNING

Clouds are very small droplets of water in the form of vapour. Clouds roam about in the sky with the wind. Generally, a patch of cloud develops an electric charge on it by friction. As a result of friction the upper layers of cloud (which are away from earth) get positively charged and the lower layers of cloud (which are facing earth) get negatively charged.

Dry air and pure water are bad conductors of electricity, hence clouds continue to carry the charge on them till the intensity of charge between the two gets too high.

When two patches of cloud bearing different charges come face to face they get attracted to one another and the electrons from negatively charged cloud jump to the positively charged cloud. The jumping of electrons between the clouds results in a big spark. The heat from the spark results in sudden expansion of air setting the air in violent waves which are heard by us as **thunder**. The spark is seen as a flash of **lightning** first and then followed by a thunder, a little later.

To protect tall buildings from damage by lightning, a lightning conductor is fixed on them.

COULOMB'S LAW

The force exerted by one *point charge* (when separation between charged bodies is much larger than their linear sizes) on another, acts along the line joining the two charges and it varies inversely as the square of the distance separating the charges and is proportional to the product of the charges. The force is repulsive if the charges have the same sign and attractive if the charges have opposite signs.

i.e., $\quad F = \dfrac{k|q_1 q_2|}{r^2}$

Where k is an experimentally determined constant called the Coulomb constant, which has the value
$$k = 9 \times 10^9 \, \mathrm{Nm^2/C^2}$$

It is common practice to express k in terms of another constant ε_0, by writing $k = 1/(4\pi\varepsilon_0)$; ε_0 is called the **permittivity of free space** or **absolute electrical permittivity** and has a value of $\varepsilon_0 = 1/(4\pi k)$ $= 8.85 \times 10^{-12} \, C^2/(Nm^2)$.

ELECTRIC POTENTIAL AND CURRENT
Electric Potential
Potential at a point can be physically interpreted as the work done by the field in displacing a unit + ve charge from some reference point to the given point.

i.e., $\quad V = \dfrac{w}{q_0}$

$\qquad V = - \int\limits_{\infty}^{} \vec{E} \; d\vec{s} \;$ i.e. $E = - \dfrac{dv}{dr}$

It is a scalar quantity.

Its **SI unit** is volt or joule coulomb^{-1}.

Electrostatic potential produced by a point charge,

$V = \dfrac{Kq}{r}$

Electric current

The time rate of flow of charge or electrons through any cross-section is called electric current.

Current through the conductor is, $I = \dfrac{q}{t} = \dfrac{ne}{t}$

where n is an integer.
Charge of one electron is 1.6×10^{-19} C.
Number of electrons flowing through a conductor in t second is

$$n = \dfrac{I \times t}{e}$$

Electric current is measured in **ampere (A).** It is a scalar fundamental physical quantity.

OHM'S LAW

According to Ohm's law *"The current passing through a conductor is directly proportional to the potential difference between its ends, provided the physical conditions such as temperature of conductor remain unchanged."*

    i.e., $V \propto I$ or $V = RI$

where R is a constant which is called **resistance** of the material. *Resistance of a material depends on its length, area of cross-section, and nature of material etc.*

i.e., $R = \rho \dfrac{l}{A}$ where, ρ = resistivity of material.

The **SI unit** of resistance is ohm (Ω).
The conductors, which obey the Ohm's law are called the ohmic conductors or linear resistances. All metallic conductors (such as silver, aluminium, copper, iron, etc.) are the **ohmic conductors or linear resistances**.
The conductors, which do not obey the Ohm's law are called the **non-ohmic conductors** or **non-linear resistances**. Examples are, diode valve, triode valve, transistors, electrolyte, etc.

[RESISTIVITY & CONDUCTIVITY OF DIFFERENT MATERIALS]

Material	Resistivity at 20° C	Conductivity at 20° C
Silver	1.59×10^{-8}	6.30×10^{7}
Copper	1.68×10^{-8}	5.96×10^{7}
Gold	2.44×10^{-8}	4.10×10^{7}
Aluminum	2.82×10^{-8}	3.50×10^{7}
Tungsten	5.60×10^{-8}	1.79×10^{7}
Zinc	5.90×10^{-8}	1.69×10^{7}
Nickel	6.99×10^{-8}	1.43×10^{7}
Iron	9.71×10^{-8}	1.00×10^{7}
Platinum	1.06×10^{-7}	9.43×10^{6}
Tin	1.09×10^{-7}	9.17×10^{6}
Carbon (graphite)	$2.50 \times 10^{-6} – 5.00 \times 10^{-6}$	$2 \times 10^{5} - 3 \times 10^{5}$
Lead	2.20×10^{-7}	4.55×10^{6}
Titanium	4.20×10^{-7}	2.38×10^{6}
Carbon (Graphene)	1.00×10^{-8}	1.00×10^{8}
Mercury	9.80×10^{-7}	1.02×10^{6}

Electroplating

Electroplating is the process of depositing a thin film (coating a layer) of finer (non-corrosive and costly) metal over the objects made from corrosive and cheaper metal with the passing of electric current through an electrolyte.
The objective of electroplating is to
(i)   protect the surface of the corrosive and cheaper metal.
      For example chromium and nickel plating of bicycle handlebar made from iron. Tin plating of iron containers for storing food articles (oil and picles).
(ii) decoration by giving a shine to the objects. For example silver or gold coating on cutlery.
(iii) Making of artificial jewellery and zari for embroidery from copper or other cheaper metals electroplated with silver or gold.

COMBINATION OF RESISTORS – SERIES AND PARALLEL

Series Combination of Resistors

$R_s = R_1 + R_2 + R_3 + \,........\, + R_n$
The equivalent resistance is greater than largest of individual resistance.

Parallel Combination of Resistors

$$\dfrac{1}{R_p} = \dfrac{1}{R_1} + \dfrac{1}{R_2} + \dfrac{1}{R_3} + ... + \dfrac{1}{R_n}$$

The equivalent resistance is smaller than smallest of individual resistance.

> - Special resistors are comonly used as single-use fuse. The conductive material in the fuse gets completely destroyed when threshold current is reached. These are used to protect various electrical appliances.
> - Resistors are also used as sensors for various applications like gas sensors, lie detectors etc.

MEASURING INSTRUMENT

Galvanometers
These are instruments used for detection and measurement of small currents.

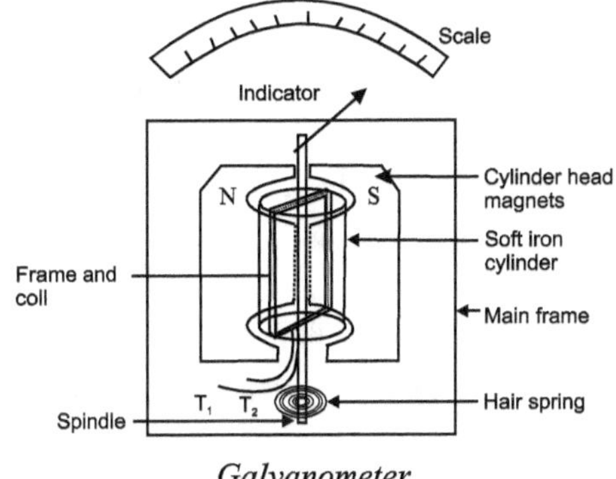

Galvanometer

Ammeter
An ammeter is a low resistance galvanometer used to measure strength of current in an electrical circuit.

(i) An ammeter is always connected in series in a circuit because, when an ammeter is connected in series it does not appreciably change the resistance of circuit and hence the main current flowing through the circuit.

(ii) An ideal ammeter has zero resistance.

Conversion of galvanometer into ammeter :

A galvanometer can be converted to an ammeter by connecting a low resistance or shunt in parallel to coil of galvanometer.

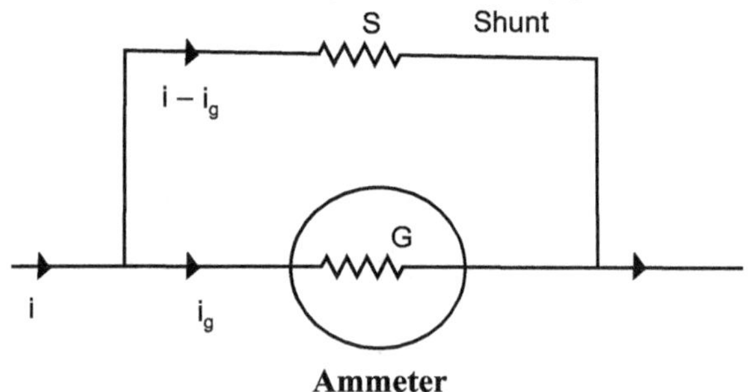

Voltmeter

A voltmeter is a high resistance galvanometer used to measure potential difference.

(i) A voltmeter is connected in parallel to a circuit element because, when connected in parallel it draws least current from the main current. So it measures nearly accurate potential difference.

(ii) An ideal voltmeter has infinite resistance.

Conversion of galvanometer into voltmeter :

A galvanometer is converted to a voltmeter by connecting a high resistance in series with the coil of galvanometer.

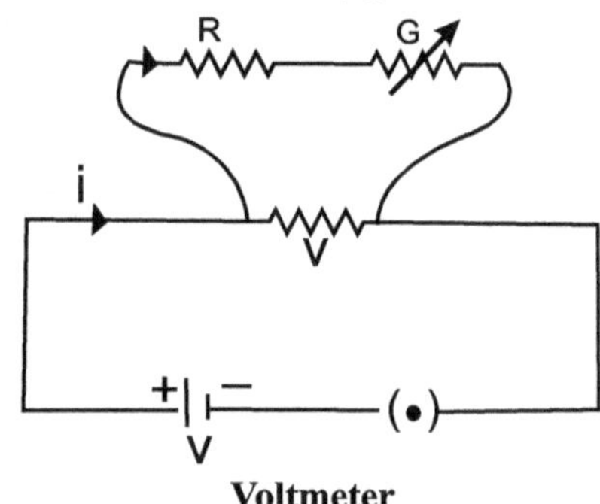

HEATING EFFECT OF ELECTRIC CURRENT

Joule's Law of Heating: When a current I is made to flow through a conductor of resistance R for time t, heat Q is produced such that,

i.e., $Q = I^2 Rt = P \times t = VIt = \dfrac{V^2}{R}t$

SI unit of electric heat or energy is *joule*.

Electric Power : $P = VI = \dfrac{V^2}{R} = I^2 R$ **SI unit :** Watt

HOUSEHOLD CIRCUITS

Switches

A switch is a key in a circuit which is used to make or break the circuit. It is always connected in the live wire of the circuit so that when it is off, you can safely touch the exposed live wire.

Safety Fuse

A fuse is a device containing short length of thin wire which melts and breaks the circuit if the current exceeds a safe value. The fuse wire is made up of a material which has *high resistance and low melting point* so that as soon as excessive current passes through, it gets melted. Generally, an **alloy of tin and lead** is used to make a fuse wire.

Earthing

Earthing is a safety process which is used to prevent the shocks due to leakage, short circuiting, etc. The cable coming from an appliance has three wires. One is live, the other neutral and the third one is earth. The earth wire is connected to the outer part of body metallic framework of the appliance.

Short Circuit and Overloading

Short circuit is a condition in which live wire comes in direct contact with a neutral wire and excessive current flows in the circuit.

When a large current (as compared to normal current) flows in a circuit which causes overheating, the circuit is said to be overloading of the electrical circuit.

Excessive continued overloading of an electrical circuit may lead to electric fires.

PERMANENT MAGNETS AND ELECTROMAGNETS

The **permanent artificial magnets** are made of some metals and alloys like Carbon-steel, Alnico, Platinum-cobalt, Alcomax, Ticonal etc. The permanent magnets are made of ferromagnetic substances with large coercivity and retentivity and can have desired shape like bar-magnet, U shaped or horse-shoe magnet and magnetic needle etc. These magnets retain its attracting power for a long time.

The **temporary artificial magnets** like electromagnets are prepared by passing current through coil wound on soft iron core. These cannot retain its strength for a long time. Electromagnets are stronger than permanent magnet.

The **strength of an electromagnet** depends on

(i) the number of turns in the coil (n)

(ii) the strength of current (I)

(iii) the nature of the core material.

Properties of Magnet

(i) A freely suspended magnet always points in the north-south direction (directive property)

(ii) Like magnetic poles repel each other and unlike magnetic poles attract each other.

(iii) Magnetic poles always exist in pairs. It is not possible to have either S-pole alone or N-pole alone.

Uses of Magnets

Magnets have their lot of applications in daily life.

(i) In the refrigerators to keep the door close.

(ii) In the Electric bells, speakers which can convert the electrical energy into sound energy.

(iii) In telephones and in tape recorders.

(iv) Electromagnets are used for removing pieces of iron and steel from the non-magnetic heap of metal scrap.

(v) Doctors use the magnets to cure arthritis, gout, and to stimulate the nerves in human body.

MAGNETIC EFFECT OF CURRENT

Magnetic effect of electric current means-an electric current flowing in a conductor produces a magnetic field in the space around it. In 1820, Hans Christian Oersted Showed that electricity and magnetism are related phenomena.

Oersted discovered a magnetic field around a conductor carrying electric current.

(a) A magnet at rest produces a magnetic field around it while an electric charge at rest produces an electric field around it.

(b) A current carrying conductor has a magnetic field and not an electric field around it. On the other hand, a charge moving with a uniform velocity has an electric as well as a magnetic field around it.

Burglar Alarms, Microphones, loud speakers, car horns and electric bells, A.C. generator, D.C. motor, transformer, etc. are based on magnetic effect of electric current.

A.C. Generator or Dynamo

An a.c. generator or dynamo is a device which converts mechanical energy into electrical energy, an electric generator is based on the principle of electromagnetic induction, according to which *if a closed coil is rotated about an axis perpendicular to a uniform magnetic field, an induced e.m.f. is set up across the coil whose direction is governed by Fleming's right hand rule.*

DC Motor

A D.C. motor converts direct current energy from a battery into mechanical energy of rotation.

It is based on the fact that when a coil carrying current is held in a magnetic field, it experiences a torque, which rotates the coil.

Uses of D.C Motor :

1. The D.C. motors are used in D.C. fans (exhaust, ceiling or table) for cooling and ventilation.
2. They are used for pumping water.
3. Big D.C. motors are used for running tram-cars and even trains.

Transformer

It is a device used for transforming a low alternating voltage of high current into a high alternating voltage of low current and vice versa, without increasing power or changing frequency.

Principle : It works on the phenomenon of mutual induction.

If a low voltage is to be transformed into a high voltage, then the number of turns in secondary is more than those in primary. The transformer is called a **step-up transformer.**

If a high voltage is to be transformed into a low voltage, then the number of turns in secondary is less than those in primary. The transformer is called a **step-down transformer.**

Transformation ratio of the transformer,

$$K = \frac{Number\ of\ turns\ in\ secondary\ (N_s)}{Number\ of\ turns\ in\ primary\ (N_p)}$$

THE EARTH'S MAGNETISM

The branch of Physics which deals with the study of earth's magnetic field is called **terrestrial magnetism.**

Some Definitions

Geographic axis : It is straight line passing through the geographic poles of the earth. It is the axis of rotation of the earth. It is known as polar axis.

Geographic meridian : It is a vertical plane passing through geographic north and south pole of the earth.

Geographic equator : A great circle on the surface of the earth in a plane perpendicular to geographical axis is called geographic equator. All places on geographic equator are at equal distances from geographical poles.

Magnetic axis : It is a straight line passing through the magnetic poles of the earth. It is inclined to geographic axis at nearly 17°.

Magnetic meridian : It is a vertical plane passing through the magnetic north and south pole of the earth.

Magnetic equator : A great circle on the surface of the earth in a plane perpendicular to magnetic axis is called magnetic equator. All places on magnetic equator are at equal distance from magnetic poles.

Elements of Earth's Magnetic Field

Angle of declination (ϕ) : *The angle between the magnetic meridian and geographical meridian at a place is called angle of declination.*

(a) **Isogonic lines :** Lines drawn on a map through places that have same declination are called isogonic lines.

(b) **Agonic lines :** The lines drawn on a map through places that have zero declination is known as an agonic lines.

Angle of dip or inclination (θ) : *The angle through which the N pole dips down with reference to horizontal is called the angle of dip.* At magnetic north and south pole, angle of dip is 90°. At magnetic equator, the angle of dip is 0°.

Horizontal component of earth's magnetic field : The total intensity of the earth's magnetic field makes an angle θ with horizontal. It has

(a) component in horizontal plane called **horizontal component B_H.**

(b) component in vertical plane called **vertical component B_V.**

DIA, PARA AND FERROMAGNETIC SUBSTANCES

Diamagnetic Substances

The substances which when placed in a magnetic field are feebly magnetised in a direction opposite to that of the magnetising field are called diamagnetic substances. e.g., Cu, Zn, Bi, Ag, Au, Pb, He, Ar, $NaCl$, H_2O, marble, glass etc.

Paramagnetic Substances

The substances which when placed in a magnetic field are feebly magnetised in the direction of magnetising field are called paramagnetic substances. e.g., -

Al, Na, Sb, Pt, $CuCl_2$, Mn, Cr, liquid oxygen etc.

Ferromagnetic Substances

The substances which when placed in a magnetic field are strongly magnetised in the direction of the magnetising field are called ferromagnetic substances. Iron, cobalt, nickel etc. are some examples of ferromagnetic substance.

LIGHT

The branch of physics which deals with nature, source, properties and the effects of light is called **optics.** It is mainly through light and the sense of vision that we know and interpret the world around us.

LIGHT AND ITS CHARACTERISTICS

Light is a form of energy that produces the sensation of vision on our eyes. It is an electromagnetic radiation, such as that emitted by the Sun, which acts like a wave in a wavelength range from 400 nm to 750 nm that the human eye can perceive. It is a combination of electric and magnetic oscillations in mutually perpendicular directions, but the light wave itself propagates in a direction perpendicular to both the oscillations.

Characteristics of Light

(i)   Light travels along a straight line in a medium or vacuum. The path of light changes only when the medium changes. This is also called the rectilinear propagation of light. The path is *called a ray of light*, and bundle of such rays constitutes *a beam of light.*

(ii) Light travels with a speed nearly equal to 3×10^8 m/s in vacuum. According to current theories, no material particle can travel at a speed greater than the speed of light.

(iii) The speed of light depends on the medium through which they pass.

(iv) Light shows different behaviour such as reflection, refraction, interference, diffraction, polarisation etc.

REFLECTION OF LIGHT

The turning back of light in the same medium is called reflection of light.

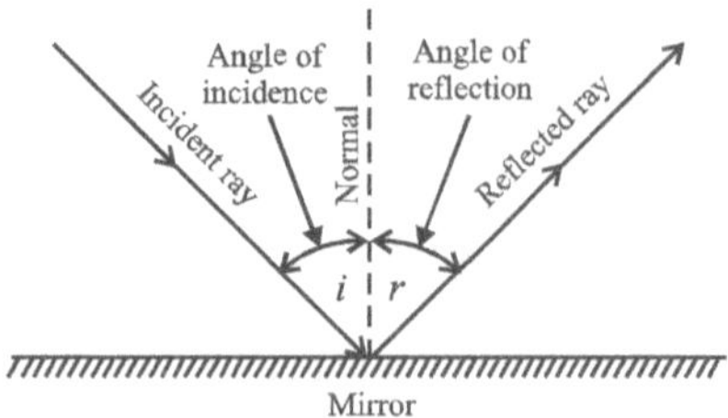

Laws of Reflection

*   The angle of incidence (i) is always equal to the angle of reflection (r). i.e., $\angle i = \angle r$

*   The incident ray, the normal, and the reflected ray all lie in the same plane.

Characteristics of Image Formed by Plane Mirror

(i)   A plane mirror always forms virtual and erect image of the object.

(ii) Distance of object from mirror = distance of image from mirror.

(iii) The image is laterally inverted (better word perversion), i.e., the left of the object becomes the right of the image and vice versa.

(iv) The size of the image is the same as that of the object

SPHERICAL MIRROR, ITS TYPES AND USES

A highly polished curved surface whose reflecting surface is a cut part of a hollow sphere of a glass or any polished metal is called spherical mirror. Spherical mirrors are of two types:

Concave or Convergent Mirrors

Imagine a sphere of hollow glass. If we cut out a spherical cap and polished it with silver on the outside, we have a concave mirror

Convex or Divergent Mirrors

If we polished the inner surface of a concave mirror with silver and look at the outward bulge, we have a convex mirror.

Image Formed by Convex Mirror

The image is always virtual, erect, smaller than the object and is located between the pole and the focus no matter where in front of the mirror the object is placed.

Terms Related to Spherical Mirror

Centre of curvature (C) : It is the centre of sphere of which the mirror is a part.

Radius of curvature (R) : It is the radius of the sphere of which the mirror is a part.

Pole (P) : It is the geometrical centre of the spherical reflecting surface. All distances are measured from the pole.

Principal axis : It is the straight line joining the centre of curvature to the pole.

Focus (F) : When a narrow beam of rays of light, parallel to the principal axis and close to it (known as paraxial rays), is incident on the surface of a mirror, the reflected beam is found to converge (concave mirror) or appear to diverge (convex mirror) from a point on principal axis. This point is called focus.

Focal length (f) : It is the distance between the pole and the principal focus. For spherical mirrors, $f = R/2$.

Uses of Concave Mirror

Makeup and shaving mirrors are concave mirrors. Concave mirrors are also used in a new method for displaying the speed of a car, as a dentist mirror, in floodlight, in solar cooker etc.

Uses of Convex Mirror

Convex mirrors, give a wider field of view than do other types of mirrors. Therefore, they are often used for security purposes and rear view mirror in vehicles.

MIRROR FORMULA AND MAGNIFICATION

Mirror Formula

A relationship among the object distance (u), the image distance (v) and the focal length (f) of a mirror

i.e., $$\frac{1}{f} = \frac{1}{u} + \frac{1}{v}$$

Magnification

If the mirror is plane, the size of the image is always equal to the size of the object i.e., **magnification is unity**. But the case is different for a curved mirror. The size of the image is different from the size of the object in such a 'mirror'. Image may be greater or smaller in size than the object depending upon the nature of the mirror or the location of the object.

Let I and O be the size of the image and the object respectively then

Magnification, $m = \dfrac{I}{O} = -\dfrac{v}{u}$

This is also called linear magnification.

Image formation

By Concave Mirror

Position of the object	Position of image	Size of image	Nature of the image
At infinity	At the focus	Highly diminished to a point	Real, inverted
Between centre of curvature and infinity	Between focus and centre of curvature	Diminished	Real, inverted
At centre of curvature	At centre of curvature	Same size as object	Real, inverted
Between centre of curvature and focus	Between centre of curvature and infinity	Magnified	Real, inverted
At focus	At infinity	Highly magnified	Real, inverted
Between focus and pole	Behind the mirror	Magnified	Virtual and upright

By Convex Mirror

Position of the object	Position of image	Nature of the image	Size of the image
At infinity	At focus	Virtual and upright	Diminished to a point size.
Between pole and infinity	Behind the mirror between focus and pole	Virtual and upright	Diminished

REFRACTION OF LIGHT

The bending of the light ray from its path in passing from one medium to the other medium is called refraction of light.

If the refracted ray bends towards the normal relative to the incident ray (Passing obliquely), then the second medium is said to be denser than the first medium. But if the refracted ray bends away from the normal, then the second medium is said to be rarer than the first medium.

If a ray of light passing normally i.e., at right angles from one medium to another optical medium then it does not bend or deviate from its path.

Cause of refraction of light: Refraction of light takes place due to change in the speed of light as it enters from one medium to another medium.

Laws of Refraction

There is two laws of refraction

* The incident ray, the refracted ray, and the normal to the refracting surface at the point of incidence are in the same plane.
* The ratio of *sine* of angle of incidence to the *sine* of angle of refraction is constant for a pair of media

i.e. $\dfrac{\sin i}{\sin r}$ = constant ($^1\mu_2$)

where $^1\mu_2$ is the refractive index of medium 2 w.r.t. medium 1. This law is also known as **snell's law.**

REFRACTIVE INDEX

Light travels through a vacuum at a speed $c = 3.00 \times 10^8$ m/s. It can also travel through many materials, such as air, water and glass. Atoms in the material absorb, remit and scatter the light, however. Therefore, light travels through the material at a speed that is less than c, the actual speed depending on the nature of the material.

To describe the extent to which the speed of light in a material medium differs from that in a vacuum, we use a parameter called the index of refraction (or refractive index).

The ratio of speed of light in free space c to that in a given medium v is called **absolute refractive index**

i.e., μ or $n = \dfrac{c}{v}$

Relative refractive index : When light passes from one medium to the other, the refractive index of medium 2 relative to 1 is written as $^1\mu_2$ and is defined as $_1\mu_2 = \dfrac{\mu_2}{\mu_1} = \dfrac{(c/v_2)}{(c/v_1)} = \dfrac{v_1}{v_2}$

Real and Apparent Depths

When an object is seen from other medium, we don't see its actual or real depth or height. The depth we see is called apparent depth.

* When object in denser medium and observer in rarer medium, then

$$\mu = \frac{\text{real depth}}{\text{apparent depth}}$$

And in this case,
real depth > apparent depth

* When object in rarer medium and observer in denser medium, then

$$\mu = \frac{\text{apparent depth}}{\text{real depth}}$$

And in this case,
apparent depth > real depth

TOTAL INTERNAL REFLECTION

When a light ray, travelling from a denser medium to a rarer medium is incident at the interface at an angle of incidence greater than critical angle (c) i.e., the angle of incidence in a denser medium for which the angle of refraction in rarer medium becomes 90°, then light rays reflected back into the denser medium. This phenomenon is called total internal reflection (TIR).

Sparkling of diamond, optical fibres etc. are the applications of total internal reflection.

Critical angle: The angle of incidence in a denser medium for which the angle of refraction in rarer medium becomes 90° is called critical angle.

Refractive index of denser medium $\mu = \dfrac{1}{\sin c}$

[Examples of Total Internal Reflection]

- Optical fibre – based on total internal reflection, is used in telecommunication, and to send laser light rays inside the human body.
- Brilliance of diamond is based on total internal reflection. Critical angle for diamond and air interface = 24° is very small. Thus by cutting diamond suitably, multiple total internal reflection are made to occur.
- Mirage is an optical illusion of water which appears in the desert in hot summer. This is due to total internal reflection.

LENS

A lens is a piece of transparent material with two refracting surfaces such that at least one is curved and refractive index of used material is different from that of the surroundings.

Convex lens: A thin spherical lens with refractive index greater than that of surrounding behaves as a convergent or convex lens i.e. converges parallel rays. Its central (i.e. paraxial) portion is thicker than marginal one.

Concave lens: If the central portion of a lens (with $\mu_L > \mu_M$) is thinner than marginal, it diverges parallel rays and behaves as a divergent or a concave lens.

Uses of Convex Lens and Concave Lens

Uses of convex lens : As a magnifying glass, search lights, spotlights in the theatres, in microscope, telescope, photographic camera etc.

Uses of concave lens : In spectacles for the correction of myopia, Gallilean telescope etc.

TERMS RELATED TO THIN SPHERICAL LENS

Optical centre (O) - It is the geometrical centre of the lens or a point for a given lens through which any ray passes undeviated.

Principal axis (C_1C_2) - It is a line passing through optical centre and perpendicular to the lens. The centre of curvature of curved surface always lie on the principal axis.

Principal focus (F) - A lens has two surfaces and hence two focal points, first focal point is an object point on the principal axis for which image is at infinity while second focal point is an image point on the principal axis for which object is at infinity.

Focal length (f) - The distance between optical centre of a lens and the principal focus.

Aperture - In reference to lens, aperture means to effective diameter of its light transmitting area so that brightness i.e. intensity of image formed by a lens which depends on the light passing through the lens will depend on the square of aperture. i.e. $I \propto (\text{aperture})^2$

For Divergent or Concave lens

(i) If object is at infinity image will be formed at focus on the same side of the lens as the object, virtual, erect and point sized.

(ii) If object is in front of lens, anywhere between the optical centre and infinity image will be formed between focus and the optical centre, on the same side of the lens, highly diminished, virtual and erect.

Image Formation

By Convex Lens

Position of object	Position of image	Nature of image	Size of image
At infinity	At principal focus on the other side of the lens	Real and inverted	Extremely diminished
Beyond 2f1	Between f2 and 2f2 on the other side of the lens	Real and inverted	Diminished
At 2f1	At 2f2 on the other side of the lens	Real and inverted	Equal to the object
Between f1 and 2f1	Beyond 2f2 on the on the other side of the lens	Real and inverted	Enlarged
At the focus	At infinity on the other side of the lens	Real and inverted	Extremely magnified
Between the focus and optical centre	On the same side of the lens as the object	Virtual and erect	Magnified

By Concave Lens

Position of object	Position of image	Nature of image	Size of image
At infinity	At the focus, on the same side of the lens as object.	Virtual and erect	Extremely diminished
Anywhere between optical centre and infinity	Between focus and optical centre, on the same side of lens as the object.	Virtual and erect	Diminished
At a distance equal to focal length	At mid point between the focus and optical centre on the side of the object	Virtual and erect	Diminished

LENS FORMULA

If an object is placed at a distance u from the optical centre 'O' of a lens and its image is formed at a distance v (from the optical centre) and focal length of this lens is f then

$$\frac{1}{f} = \frac{1}{v} - \frac{1}{u}$$

MAGNIFICATION

If a thin object of linear size O situated vertically on the axis of a lens at a distance u from the optical centre and its image of size I is formed at a distance v (from the optical centre) then

Magnification, $m = \dfrac{I}{O} = \dfrac{v}{u}$

POWER OF A LENS

If focal length of a lens is measured in metre (m) then its reciprocal gives the power (P) of the lens.

i.e., Power of a lens, $P = \dfrac{1}{f\,(\text{in m})}$

The S.I. unit of power is diopter (D).
Power of a combination of lenses:

$$P = P_1 + P_2 + ...P_n$$

INTERFERENCE OF LIGHT

When two light waves of exactly same frequency travels in a medium, in the same direction simultaneously then due to their superposition, the intensity of light is maximum at some points while the intensity is minimum at some other points. This phenomenon is called interference of light. *The colours in soap bubbles and oil slicks are due to this property of light.*

DIFFRACTION OF LIGHT

The wavelength of light is of the order of angstroms. So, when light waves encounter obstacles of very small sizes, the light waves bend around the edges of the obstacle and travel. This is known as diffraction of light.

POLARISATION OF LIGHT

An ordinary source of light such as bulb consists of a large number of waves emitted by atoms or molecules in all directions symmetrically. Such light is called unpolarized light

THE HUMAN EYE

The eye allows us to see and interpret the shapes, colors, and dimensions of objects by processing the light they reflect or emit. The eye is able to see in bright light or in dim light, but it cannot see objects when light is absent.

Eye lens : It is a convex lens made of transparent and flexible jelly like material. Its curvature can be adjusted with the help of ciliary muscles.

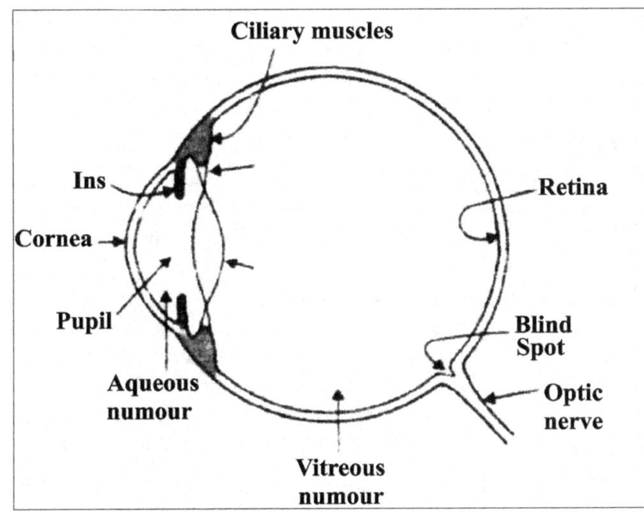

Power of Accommodation

The ability of the eye lens to change its shape to focus near and distant objects clearly is called *power of accommodation.*

The minimum distance, at which objects can be seen most distinctly without strain, is called the least distance of distinct vision. It is also called the near point(N.P.) of the eye. For a young adult with normal vision, the near point is about 25 cm.

DEFECTS OF VISION AND THEIR CORRECTION

Myopia or Short-Sightedness

A person with myopic eye can see nearby objects clearly but cannot see far off objects distinctly.

Remedy: This defect can be corrected by using a concave lens of suitable focal length. A concave lens diverges the rays coming from the object so that they get focused at the retina.

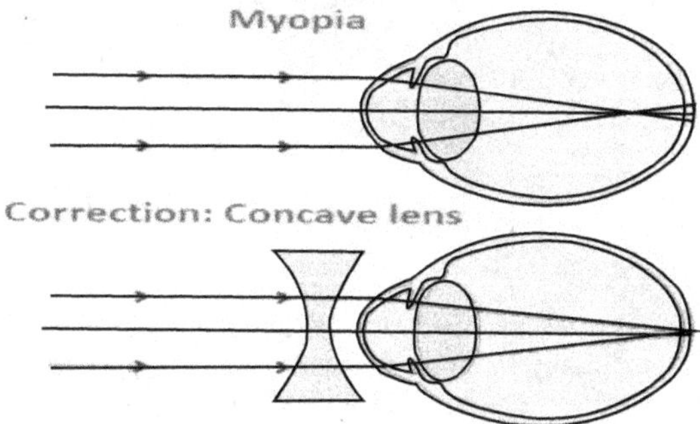

Hypermetropia or Far-sightedness

A person with hypermetropic eye can see far off objects clearly but cannot see nearby objects clearly.

Remedy: Eyeglass with convex lens is used to rectify this problem.

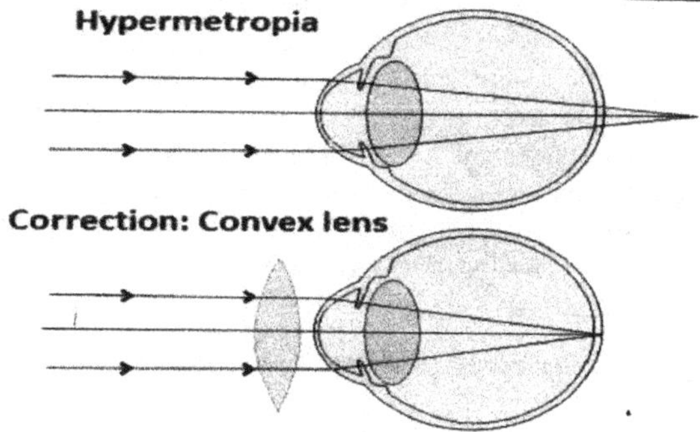

Presbyopia

Presbyopia is due to a lessening of flexibility of the crystalline lens, as well as to a weakening of the ciliary muscles which control lens focusing, both attributable to the ageing process.

Remedy: Person suffering from presbyopia require bifocal lenses. A common type of bi-focal lenses consists of both concave and convex lenses. The upper portion consists of a concave lens. It facilitates distant vision. The lower part is a convex lens. It facilitates near vision.

Astigmatism

Astigmatism is the most common problem responsible for blurry vision.

Remedy: cylindrical lens is use to correct astigmatism.

Cataract

A cataract is a clouding of the lens in the eye.

DISPERSION OF WHITE LIGHT BY A GLASS PRISM

The *phenomenon of decomposition of the white light into seven component colours when passing through a prism or through a transparent object delimited by non parallel surfaces is called dispersion of light.* A beam of light containing all the visible spectrum of the light is white, because the sum of all the colors generates the white color. Normally the light we use is white. It's the light containing all the colors mixed together. The light is decomposed in all the component colours, i.e., Violet, Indigo, Blue, Green, Yellow, Orange and Red, called as VIBGYOR.

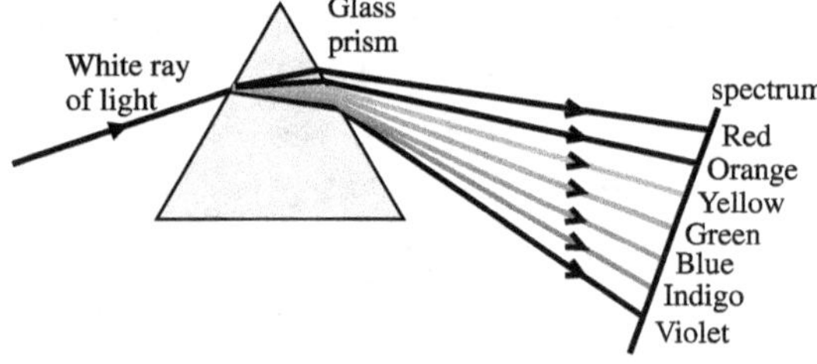

RAINBOW

A rainbow is a natural spectrum of sunlight in the form of bows appearing in the sky when the sun shines on raindrops after the rain. Rainbows are generated through refraction and total internal reflection of light in small rain drops. The sun is always behind you when you face a rainbow, and that the center of the circular arc of the rainbow is in the direction opposite to that of the sun. After rain, there are still some tiny water droplets remained in the air. If there is sunshine, a white sunbeam will be reflected and refracted by these tiny droplets. Different colors of light have different refractivity. They will be reflected in slightly different directions inside a water droplet. Since, water is more dense than air, light is refracted as it enters the drop-red is bent less, blue more. Some of the light will reflect off the back of the drop if the angle is larger than the critical angle (48° for water)

The light is then refracted again as it leaves the drop (act like a small prism), the colours of white light have been dispersed.

- Violet light will leave the drop at an angle of 40° from the beam of sunlight
- Red light will leave the drop at an angle of 42° from the beam of sunlight.

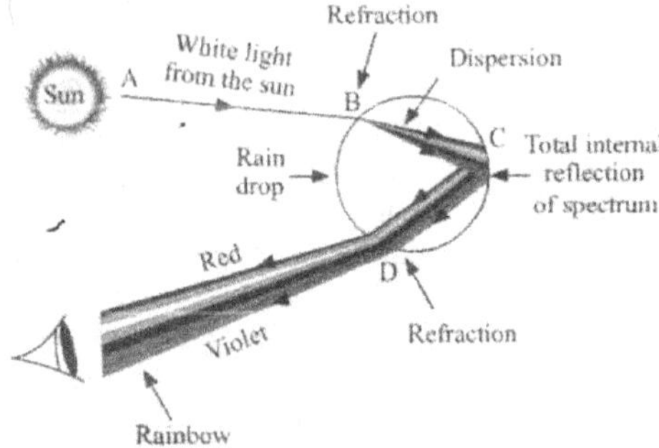

ATMOSPHERIC REFRACTION

The density of air in the atmosphere is not the same everywhere. It is greatest at the earth's surface and goes on decreasing as we move higher. The refractive index of air depends on its density-higher the density of air, greater its refractive index. The changes in refractive index of earth's atmosphere or air give rise

to many phenomena like twinkling of stars, advance sunrise and delayed sunset etc.

Twinkling of Stars

The scientific name for the twinkling of stars is stellar scintillation (or astronomical scintillation). Stars twinkle when we see them from the Earth's surface because we are viewing them through thick layers of turbulent (moving) air in the Earth's atmosphere. Stars (except the Sun) appear as tiny dots in the sky; as their light travels through the many layers of the Earth's atmosphere, the light of the star is bent (refracted) many times in random directions (light is bent when it hits a change in density-like a pocket of cold air or hot air). This random refraction results in the twinkling of stars.

Advance Sunrise and Delayed Sunset (Approximately 2 minutes)

The actual sunrise takes place when the sun is just above the horizon. When the sun is just below the horizon, the light rays coming from it, on entering the earth's atmosphere suffer atmospheric refracton from a rarer medium to a denser medium. So, they bend towards the normal at each refraction. Due to the continuous refraction of light rays at each layer of the atmosphere, it follows a curved path as shown in Figure and reaches the eyes of the observer at O.

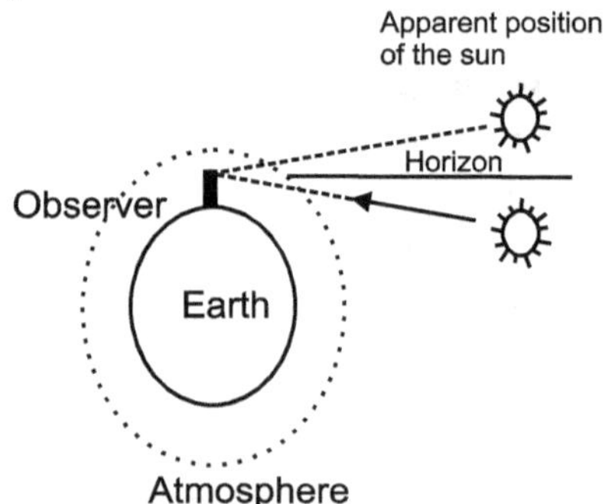

SCATTERING OF LIGHT

The interplay of light with objects around us gives rise to several spectacular phenomena in nature like the blue colour of the sky, colour of water in deep sea, the reddening of the sun at sunrise and the sunset etc. When sunlight enters the earth atmosphere, air and water vapour molecules absorb part of the light and reradiate it to all directions. This is called *scattering of light.*

Tyndall Effect

When a beam of sunlight enters a dusty (or smoke filled) room through a window then path becomes visible due to scattering of light by dust or smoke particles this phenomenon is called tyndall effect.

The reddening of the Sun at Sunrise and Sunset

At noon, the light of sun travels relatively shorter distance through earth's atmosphere thus appears white as only a little of blue and violet colours are scattered. Near the horizon , most of the blue and green light and shorter wavelengths are scattered and hence the sun appears reddish at sunrise and sunset.

OPTICAL INSTRUMENTS

Simple Microscope (Magnifying Glass or Reading Lens)

It consists of a convergent lens with object between its focus and optical centre and eye close to it. The image formed by it is erect, virtual, enlarged and on same side of lens between object and infinity.

Magnifying Power of a simple microscope

The magnifying power (MP) of a simple microscope

When image is formed at the near point

Then, $M = 1 + \dfrac{D}{f}$

In the case of when eye is placed behind the lens at a distance a, then

$$M = 1 + \dfrac{(D-a)}{f}$$

When the image is formed at, the infinity.

$$M = \dfrac{D}{f}$$

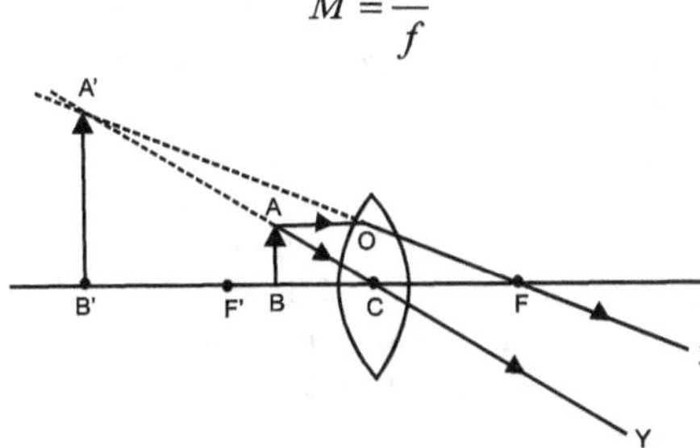

[Image formation by simple Microscope]

Compound Microscope

It consists of two convergent lenses $f_{eye\ lens} > f_{objective}$ and $(diameter)_{eyelens} > (diameter)_{objective}$ arranged co-axially. The separation between objective and eye-piece can be varied.

Magnification produced by a compound microscope :

$M = m_{objective} \times m_{eye\ piece}$

Magnifying power of a compound microscope

$$M = -\dfrac{L}{f_o}\left(1 + \dfrac{D}{f_e}\right)$$

where, L = length of telescope

f_o = focal length of objective and

f_e = focal length of eyes lens　　　　　(1)

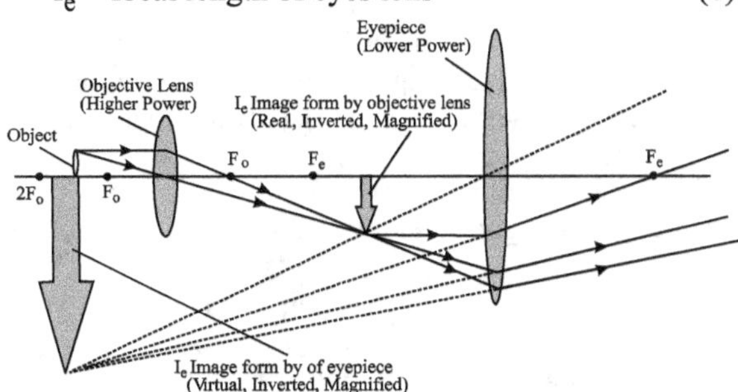

[Image formation by compound microscope]

Telescope

It is used to provide angular magnification of distant objects. i.e., to see far off objects.

Astronomical Telescope (Refracting Type)

It consists of objective, i.e., a converging lens, of larger focal length f_0 and larger aperture, and an eyepiece, also a converging lens, of smaller focal length f_e and smaller aperture, placed coaxially.

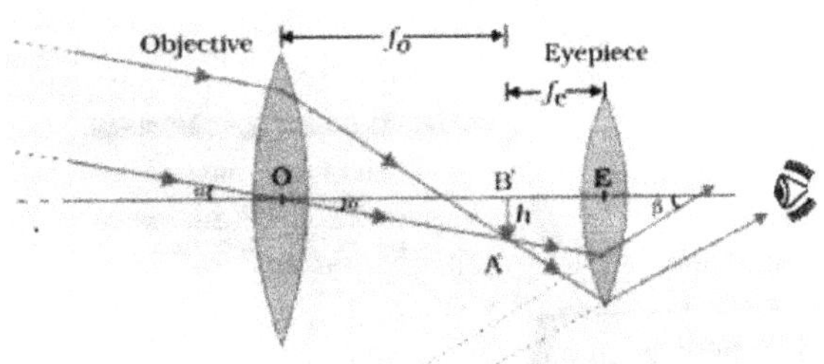

[Image formation by Astronomical telescope refracting type]

Magnifying Power (M)

Magnifying power (M), also called angular magnification of a telescope is defined as the ratio of the visual angle subtended by the final image at the eye and the visual angle subtended by the object when the object lies in the actual position.

Astronomical telescope is used to see heavenly bodies and terrestrial telescope to see far off objects on earth.

Magnifying power of a telescope

m = angle β subtended at the eye by the image/ angle α subtended at the eye by the object.

m = f_o/f_e

f_o = focal length of the objective, and

f_e = focal lengths of the eyepiece

Telescope (Reflection type) or Cassegrian telescope

Reflecting telescope differs from refracting or astronomical telescope as one objective lens is replaced by a concave parabolic mirror of larger aperture, free from chromatic and spherical aberrations.

Reflecting type telescope works on the principle of reflection and not refraction. In absence of refraction, dispersion of white light will not occur and there will be no chromatic aberration.

Magnifying power is given by,

$$m = \dfrac{f_o}{f_e} = \dfrac{R}{\dfrac{2}{f_e}}$$

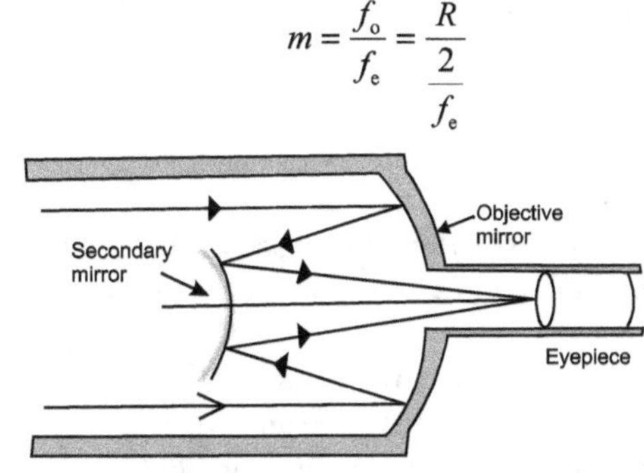

(Reflecting type telescope)

PRIMARY AND SECONDARY COLOURS OF LIGHT

Primary colours

The group of colours which can be used to form all other colours by mixing.

Examples: red, green, blue., White = Blue + Green + Red

Secondary colours

These are created by combining two or more primary colours.

Examples : Red + Blue = Magenta,

Red + Green = Yellow,　　Blue + Green = Cyan

MULTIPLE CHOICE QUESTIONS

1. A rectangular piece of dielectric material is inserted partially into the (air) gap between the plates of a parallel plate capacitor. The dielectric piece will
   (a) remain stationary where it is placed
   (b) be pushed out from the gap between the plates
   (c) be drawn inside the gap between the plates and its velocity does not change sign
   (d) execute an oscillatory motion in the region between the plates

2. The figure below describes the arrangement of slits and screens in a Young's double slit experiment. The width of the slit in S_1 is a and the slits in S_2 are of negligible width. If the wavelength of the light is λ, the value of d for which the screen would be dark is

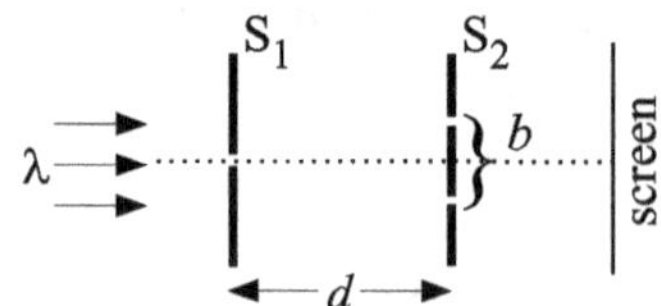

   (a) $b\sqrt{\left(\dfrac{a}{\lambda}\right)^2 - 1}$ (b) $b/2\sqrt{\left(\dfrac{a}{\lambda}\right)^2 - 1}$

   (c) $\dfrac{a}{2}(b/\lambda)^2$ (d) $(ab)/\lambda$

3. Path of a ray of light between two mirrors is shown in the diagram. If the length of each mirror is 'ℓ', what is the total path length of the ray between the mirrors?

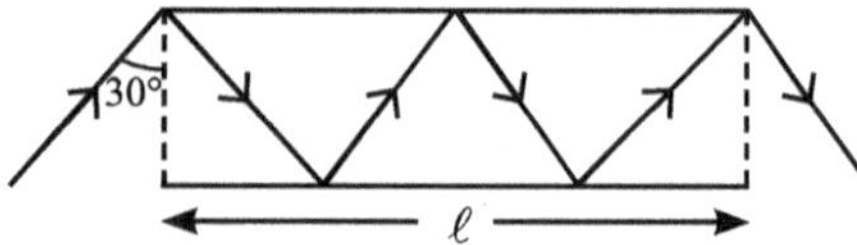

   (a) $(3/4)\ \ell$ (b) $(4/3)\ \ell$
   (c) $(3/2)\ \ell$ (d) $2\ \ell$

4. An electric lamp of 100 watt is used for 10 hours per day. The 'units' of energy consumed in one day by the lamp is **[NDA]**
   (a) 1 unit   (b) 0.1 unit
   (c) 10 units   (d) 100 units

5. The main power supply in India is at 220 V, whereas that in the US is at 110 V. Which one among the following statements in this regard is correct? **[NDA]**
   (a) 110 V is safer but more expensive to maintain
   (b) 110 V is safer and cheaper to maintain
   (c) 110 V leads to lower power loss
   (d) 110 V works better at higher latitudes

6. Two pieces of conductor of same material and of equal length are connected in series with a cell. One of the two pieces has cross-sectional area double that of the other. Which one of the following statements is correct in this regard ? **[NDA]**

   (a) The thicker one will allow stronger current to pass through it.
   (b) The thinner one would allow stronger current to pass through it.
   (c) Same amount of electric current would pass through both the pieces producing more heat in the thicker one.
   (d) Same amount of electric current would pass through both the pieces producing more heat in the thinner one.

7. Magnetism of a bar magnet can be destroyed if it is **[NDA]**
   I. kept in the magnetic meridian.
   II. placed in a direction opposite to that of the Earth's horizontal intensity.
   III. heated to a temperature known as Curie temperature.
   Select the correct answer using the code given below
   (a) I and III only   (b) II only
   (c) II and III only   (d) I, II and III

8. A wire of resistance 16 W is bent in the form of a circle. What is the effective resistance between diametrically opposite points? **[NDA]**
   (a) 1 W   (b) 2 W
   (c) 4 W   (d) 8 W

9. Fluorescent tubes are fitted with a choke. The choke coil : **[IAS Prelim]**
   (a) steps up the line voltage
   (b) steps-down the line voltage
   (c) reduces current in the circuit
   (d) chokes low frequency current

10. Electrically charged particles from space travelling at speeds of several hundred km/sec can severely harm living beings if they reach the surface of the Earth. What prevents them from reaching the surface of the Earth? **[IAS Prelim]**
    (a) The Earth's magnetic field diverts them towards its poles
    (b) Ozone layer around the Earth reflects them back to outer space
    (c) Moisture in the upper layers of atmosphere prevents them from reaching the surface of the Earth
    (d) None of the statements (a), (b) and (c) given above is correct

11. Match List I with List II and select the correct answer using the code given below the Lists : **[NDA]**

List I (Magnet)	List II (Property)
A. Artificial magnet	1. Long lived
B. Permanent magnet	2. Last for infinitely long period
C. Temporary magnet	3. Short lived
D. Earth as a magnet	4. Induced magnet

	A	B	C	D
(a)	3	1	4	2
(b)	3	4	1	2
(c)	2	1	4	3
(d)	2	4	1	3

12. Two pieces of metallic wire having equal lengths and equal volume placed in air have different resistances. The two wires must **[NDA]**
    (a) have different cross-sections
    (b) have different temperatures
    (c) be of different materials
    (d) be of same density

13. Graphene is frequently in news recently. What is its importance? **[IAS Prelim]**
    1. It is a two-dimensional material and has good electrical conductivity.
    2. It is one of the thinnest but strongest materials tested so far.
    3. It is entirely made of silicon and has high optical transparency.
    4. It can be used as 'conducting electrodes' required for touch screens, LCDs and organic LEDs.
    Which of the statements given above are correct?
    (a) 1 and 2 only (b) 3 and 4 only
    (c) 1, 2 and 4 only (d) 1, 2, 3 and 4

14. If the electrical resistance of a typical substance suddenly drops to zero then the substance is called **[NDA]**
    (a) superconductor (b) semiconductor
    (c) conductor (d) insulator

15. Which one of the following is correct?
    Lightning is formed, when **[NDA]**
    (a) similar charges of electricity rush towards each other and then get repelled
    (b) clouds strike against impurities in air and hte friction burns up these impurities
    (c) strong opposite charges in different clouds break down the resistance offered by intervening air
    (d) water vapour produces electricity in the clouds

16. Consider the following statements:
    An ordinary light bulb has a rather short life because the: **[IAS Prelim]**
    1. filament wire is not uniform.
    2. bulb cannot be evacuated completely.
    3. wires supporting the filament melt at high temperatures.
    Which of the above statements are correct?
    (a) 1 and 3 (b) 2 and 3
    (c) 1 and 2 (d) 1, 2 and 3

17. Consider the following statements regarding a motor car battery: **[IAS Prelim]**
    1. The voltage is usually 12 V.
    2. Electrolyte used is hydrochloric acid.
    3. Electrodes are lead and copper.
    4. Capacity is expressed in ampere-hour.
    Which of the above statements are correct?
    (a) 1 and 2 (b) 2 and 3
    (c) 3 and 4 (d) 1 and 4

18. In which one of the following cases Ohm's law is not valid? **[NDA]**
    (a) Wire bound resistor
    (b) Potentiometer
    (c) Junction diode
    (d) Electric bulb

19. A current I flows through a potential difference V in an electrical circuit containing a resistance R. The product of V and I, i.e., VI may be understood as **[NDA]**
    (a) resistance R
    (b) heat generated by the circuit
    (c) thermal power radiated by the circuit
    (d) rate of change of resistance

20. When light waves travel from air to glass, which variables are affected? **[NDA]**
    (a) Wavelength, frequency and velocity
    (b) Velocity and frequency only
    (c) Wavelength and frequency only
    (d) Wavelength and velocity only

21. Consider the following statement:
    The principle of total internal reflection is applicable to explain the **[NDA]**
    1. Formation of mirage in desert.
    2. Formation of image in microscope.
    3. Colour of evening sky.
    4. Operation of optical fibres.
    Which of the statement given above are correct?
    (a) 1 and 4 (b) 3 and 4
    (c) 2 and 3 (d) 1 and 2

22. When an optician prescribes a – 5D lens, what does it mean? **[NDA]**
    (a) Concave lens of 20 cm focal length
    (b) Convex lens of 5 cm focal length
    (c) Concave lens of 5 cm focal length
    (d) Convex lens of 5 cm focal length

23. A spherical air bubble is embedded in a piece of glass. For a ray of light passing through the bubble, it behaves like a **[NDA]**
    (a) converging lens
    (b) diverging lens
    (c) plano-converging lens
    (d) plano-diverging len

24. What is the phenomenon of the moon to appear bigger in size as it approaches the horizon, called ? **[NDA]**
    (a) Atmospheric refraction of light
    (b) Diffraction of light
    (c) Scattering of light
    (d) Total internal reflection of light by water vapours

25. Which one among the following is used to make periscope? **[NDA]**
    (a) Concave lens (b) Concave mirror
    (c) Plane mirror (d) None of the above

26. What is the essential difference between a terrestrial telescope and an astronomical telescope? **[NDA]**
    (a) One of the lenses in a terrestrial telescope is concave
    (b) The final image formed in a terrestrial telescope is virtual
    (c) A terrestrial telescope forms an erect image while an astronomical telescope forms an inverted image
    (d) A terrestrial telescope forms an inverted image while an a stronomical telescope forms an erect image

27. A ray of ligh is incident normally on one of the faces of right angled isosceles prism as shhown above. It undergoes total internal reflection from hypotenuse. Which one of the following is the minimum refractive index of the material of the prism? **[NDA]**

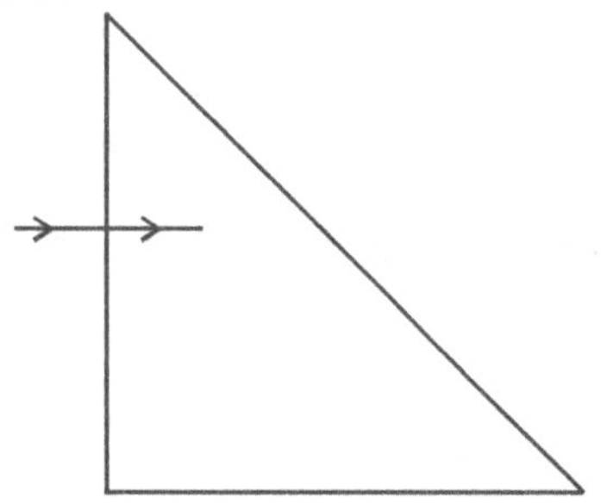

   (a) 1.0   (b) 1.33
   (c) 1.414   (d) 1.6

28. A far-sighted person has a near point at 100 cm. What must be the power of the correcting lens? **[NDA]**
   (a) -0.8 D   (b) -3.0 D
   (c) $+0.8$ D   (d) $+3.0$ D

29. An object is kept 5 cm in front of a concave mirror of focal length 15 cm. What will be the nature of the image? **[NDA]**
   (a) Virtual, not magnified
   (b) Virtual, magnified
   (c) Real, not magnified
   (d) Real, magnified

30.

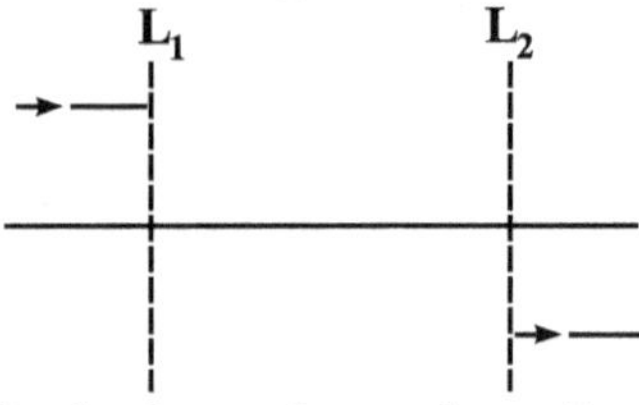

In the figure shown above, L_1 and L_2 are two lenses and are kept along the same axis. A parallel beam of light falling on L_1 leaves L_2 as a parallel beam: **[NDA]**
Consider the following statements.
1. Both L_1 and L_2 can be convex lenses.
2. The distance between the two lenses can be equal to sum of their focal lengths.
Which of the statements given above is/are correct ?
   (a) Only 1   (b) Only 2
   (c) Both 1 and 2   (d) Neither 1 nor 2

31. Refractive index of an optical medium changes with
1. the nature of the medium.
2. the change in the angle of incidence of the ray.
3. colour of the incident ray. **[NDA]**
Select the correct answer using the code given below:
   (a) 1 and 3 only   (b) 2 and 3 only
   (c) 1 and 2 only   (d) 1, 2 and 3

32. Yellow colour light is used as fog light because yellow colour **[NDA]**
   (a) light is most scattered by fog
   (b) has the longest wavelength among all colours
   (c) has the longest wavelength among all colours except red and orange but the red colour is already used for brake light and stop light whereas orange colour is avoided due to its similarity with red
   (d) has the shortest wavelength among all colours not already reserved for other purpose

33. A refracting telescope consists of **[NDA]**
   (a) one concave mirror and one convex lens
   (b) two convex lenses of equal focal length
   (c) two concave mirrors of different focal lengths
   (d) two convex lenses of unequal focal lengths

34. An object is placed at the focus of a concave mirror. The image will be **[NDA]**
   (a) real, inverted, same size at the focus
   (b) real, upright, same size at the focus
   (c) virtual, inverted, highly enlarged at infinity
   (d) real, inverted, highly enlarged at infinity

35. Consider the following statements **[CDS]**
1. Clear sky appears blue due to poor scattering of blue wavelength of visible light.
2. Red part of light shows more scattering than blue light in the atmosphere.
3. In the absence of atmosphere, there would be no scattering of light and sky will look black.
Which of the statements given above is/are correct?
   (a) Only 1   (b) 1 and 2
   (c) Only 3   (d) All of these

36. **Assertion (A) :** A myopic person is advised to use concave lens.
Reason (R) : The eye lens of a myopic person focuses the parallel rays coming from distant objects in front of the retina. **[NDA]**
   (a) Both A and R are individually true and R is the correct explanation of A
   (b) Both A and R are individually true but R is NOT the correct explanation of A
   (c) A is true but R is false
   (d) A is false but R is true

37. If the focal length of the biconvex lens is 25 cm, then the power of the lens will be **[NDA]**
   (a) $+4$ dioptre   (b) -4 dioptre
   (c) $+0.04$ dioptre   (d) -0.04 dioptre

38. Two thin convex lenses of focal lengths 4 cm and 8 cm are separated by a distance of 4 cm in air. The combination will have the focal length **[NDA]**
   (a) 4 cm   (b) 8 cm
   (c) 12 cm   (d) 32 cm

39. **Assertion (A) :** Convex mirror is used as a driver mirror.
Reason (R) : Images formed by convex mirror are diminished in size. **[NDA]**
   (a) Both A and R are individually true and R is the correct explanation of A
   (b) Both A and R are individually true but R is NOT the correct explanation of A
   (c) A is true but R is false
   (d) A is false but R is true

40. Match the column - I and Column - II.

Column-I		**Column-II**
A.	Myopia	P.	Convex lens
B.	Hypermetropia	Q.	Concave lens
C.	Presbyopia	R.	Cylindrical lens
D.	Astigmatism	S.	Bifocal Lens

    (a) A-P; B-Q; C-S; D-R
    (b) A-P; B-Q; C-R; D-S
    (c) A-Q; B-P; C-S; D-R
    (d) A-Q; B-P; C-R; D-S

41. **Assertion (A) :** A person stands at a distance of 1m in front of a concave mirror. If the radius of curvature of the mirror is 4m, the image of the person lies at a distance 2m behind the mirror.
    Reason (R) : The general mirror equation confirms the location of the image from the mirror and it could be a real image. **[NDA]**
    (a) Both A and R are individually true and R is the correct explanation of A
    (b) Both A and R are individually true but R is NOT the correct explanation of A
    (c) A is true but R is false
    (d) A is false but R is true

42. After using for some time, big transformers get heated up. This is due to the fact that **[CDS 2017-II]**
    1. current produces heat in the transformers
    2. hysteresis loss occurs in the transformers
    3. liquid used for cooling gets heated
    Select the correct answer using the code given below.
    (a) 1 only   (b) 2 and 3 only
    (c) 1 and 2 only (d) 1, 2 and 3

43. Suppose voltage V is applied across a resistance R, The power dissipated in the resistance is P. Now the same voltage V is applied across a parallel combination of three equal resistors each of resistance R. Then the power dissipated in the second case will be **[CDS 2017-I]**
    (a) P   (b) 3P
    (c) P/3   (d) 2P/3

44. A parallel-plate capacitor, with air in between the plates, has capacitance C. Now the space between the two plates of the capacitor is filled with a dielectric of dielectric constant 7. Then the value of the capacitance will become **[CDS 2017-I]**
    (a) C   (b)
    (c) 7C   (d) 14C

45. Consider the electromagnetic radiations having wavelengths 200 nm, 500nm and 1000 nm. Which wavelength(s) of the following can make visual sensation to a human eye? **[CDS 2017-I]**
    (a) 200 nm and 500 nm
    (b) 500 nm and 1000 nm
    (c) 500 nm only
    (d) 200 nm and 1000 nm

46. The optical phenomenon that is primarily responsible for the observation of rainbow on a rainy day is **[CDS 2017-I]**
    (a) diffraction   (b) interference
    (c) dispersion   (d) reflection

47. A ray of light is incident on a plane mirror at an angle of 40° with respect to surface normal. When it gets reflected from the mirror, it undergoes a deviation of **[CDS 2017-II]**
    (a) 40°   (b) 100°
    (c) 90°   (d) 80°

48. The wires are made having same length l and area of cross-section A. Wire 1 is made of copper and wire 2 is made of aluminium. It is given that the electrical conductivity of copper is more than that of aluminium. In this context, which one of the following statements is correct? **[CDS 2017-II]**
    (a) The resistance of wire 1 will be higher than that of wire 2.
    (b) The resistance of wire 2 will be higher than that of wire 1.
    (c) The resistance of both the wires will be the same.
    (d) If same current is flown through both the wires, the power dissipated in both the wires will be the same.

49. Why is argon gas used along with tungsten wire in an electric bulb? **[CDS 2018-I]**
    (a) To increase the life of the bulb
    (b) To reduce the consumption of electricity
    (c) To make the emitted light colored
    (d) To reduce the cost of the bulb

50. Working of safety fuses depends upon **[CDS 2018-I]**
    1. magnetic effect of the current
    2. chemical effect of the current
    3. magnitude of the current
    4. heating effect of the current
    Select the correct answer using the code given below.
    (a) 1, 2, 3 and 4   (b) 1, 2 and 3 only
    (c) 3 and 4 only   (d) 4 only

51. Two metallic wires made from copper have same length but the radius of wire 1 is half of that of wire 2. The resistance of wire 1 is R. If both the wires are joined together in series, the total resistance becomes **[CDS 2018-I]**
    (a) 2R   (b) $\dfrac{R}{2}$
    (c) $\dfrac{5}{4}R$ (d) $\dfrac{3}{4}R$

52. When the Sun is near the horizon during the morning or evening, it appears reddish. The phenomenon that is responsible for this observation is **[CDS 2018-I]**
    (a) reflection of light   (b) refraction of light
    (c) dispersion of light   (d) scattering of light

53. A wire of copper having length l and area of cross-section A is taken and a current I is flown through it. The power dissipated in the wire is P. If we take an aluminium wire having same dimensions and pass the same current through it, the power dissipated will be **[CDS 2018-I]**
    (a) P   (b) < P
    (c) > P   (d) 2P

54. Which one of the following devices changes low voltage alternating current to high voltage alternating current and vice versa? **[NDA (I) 2017]**

    (a) Generator   (b) Motor
    (c) Transformer   (d) Vibrator

55. An optical illusion which occurs mainly in deserts during hot summer is based on the principle of   **[NDA (I) 2017]**
    (a) Reflection   (b) Interference
    (c) Dispersion   (d) Total internal reflection

56. Match List I with List II and select the correct answer using the code given below the Lists :   **[NDA (I) 2017]**

Lists I (Disease)		Lists II (Remedy)
A.	Hypermetropia	1. Concave lens
B.	Presbyopia	2. Bifocal lens
C.	Myopia	3. Surgery
D.	Cataract	4. Convex lens

Code:

	A	B	C	D
(a)	4	2	1	3
(b)	4	1	2	3
(c)	3	1	2	4
(d)	3	2	1	4

57. A circular coil of single turn has a resistance of 20 Ω. Which one of the following is the correct value for the resistance between the ends of any diameter of the coil?   **[NDA (I) 2017]**
    (a) 5 Ω (b) 10 Ω
    (c) 20 Ω (d) 40 Ω

58. In a solenoid, the current flowing through the wire is I and number of turns per unit length is n. This gives a magnetic field B inside the solenoid. If number of turn per unit length is increased to 2n, what will be the value of magnetic field in the solenoid?   **[NDA (I) 2017]**
    (a) B   (b) 2 B
    (c) B / 2   (d) B / 4

59. Which one of the following statements is correct about the magnification of an optical microscope? **[NDA (I) 2017]**
    (a) Magnification increases with the increase in focal length of eyepiece
    (b) Magnification increases with the increase in focal length of objective
    (c) Magnification does not depend upon the focal length of eyepiece
    (d) Magnification decreases with the increase in focal length of eyepiece

60. The radii of curvature of the faces of a double convex lens are 10 cm and 20 cm. The refractive index of the glass is 1.5. What is the power of this lens (in units of dioptre)?   **[NDA (I) 2017]**
    (a) +7.5 D   (b) –7.5 D
    (c) +2.5 D   (d) +5.0 D

61. Which one of the following physical quantities does NOT affect the resistance of a cylindrical resistor?   **[NDA (I) 2017]**
    (a) The current through it
    (b) Its length
    (c) The resistivity of the material used in the resistor
    (d) The area of cross-section of the cylinder

62. Suppose a rod is given a negative charge by rubbing it with wool. Which one of the following statements is correct in this case?   **[NDA (I) 2017]**
    (a) The positive charges are transferred from rod to wool
    (b) The positive charges are transferred from wool to rod
    (c) The negative charges are transferred from rod to wool
    (d) The negative charges are transferred from wool to rod

63. The mirrors used as rear-view mirrors in vehicles are   **[NDA (II) 2017]**
    (a) concave   (b) convex
    (c) cylindrical   (d) plane

64. Concave mirror is used in headlights of vehicles, because it   **[NDA (II) 2017]**
    (a) focuses light from the bulb onto nearby vehicles
    (b) sends parallel rays
    (c) fits well into the shape of the headlight
    (d) is cheaper than other mirrors

65. Step-up transformers are used for   **[NDA (II) 2017]**
    (a) increasing electrical power
    (b) decreasing electrical power
    (c) decreasing voltage
    (d) increasing voltage

66. A rainbow is produced due to which one of the following phenomena?   **[NDA (II) 2017]**
    (a) Dispersion of light
    (b) Interference of light
    (c) Diffraction of light
    (d) Scattering of light by atmospheric dust

67. Which one of the following statements is not correct?   **[NDA (II) 2017]**
    (a) Human eye is a refracting system containing a diverging lens.
    (b) The retina of the human eye contains millions of light sensitive cells, called rods and cones, which convert the light into electrical messages.
    (c) Every image that is focused on the retina is upside down.
    (d) We need both eyes to judge the relative positions of objects accurately.

68. What is the net force experienced by a bar magnet placed in a uniform magnetic field?   **[NDA (I) 2018]**
    (a) Zero
    (b) Depends upon length of the magnet
    (c) Never zero
    (d) Depends upon temperature

69. Which one of the following devices is non-ohmic?   **[NDA (I) 2018]**
    (a) Conducting copper coil
    (b) Electric heating coil
    (c) Semi conductor diode
    (d) Rheostat

70. Which one of the following is the natural phenomenon based on which a simple periscope works?   **[NDA (I) 2018]**
    (a) Reflection of light
    (b) Refraction of light

(c)   Dispersion of light
(d)   Total internal reflection of light

71. Which one of the following statements about the refractive index of a material medium with respect to air is correct?   **[NDA (I) 2018]**
(a)   It can be either positive or negative
(b)   It can have zero value
(c)   It is unity for all materials
(d)   It is always greater than one

72. Which one of the following statements about magnetic field lines is NOT correct?   **[NDA (I) 2018]**
(a)   They can emanate from a point
(b)   They do not cross each other
(c)   Field lines between two poles cannot be precisely straight lines at the ends
(d)   There are no field lines within a bar magnet

73. Two convex lenses with power 2 dioptre are kept in contact with each other. The focal length of the combined lens system is   **[NDA (I) 2018]**
(a)   0.10 m   (b)   2 m
(c)   4 m   (d)   0.25 m

74. Which of the following statements about electromagnetic waves, sound waves and water waves is/are correct?
1.   They exhibit reflection   **[NDA (I) 2018]**
2.   They carry energy
3.   They exert pressure
4.   They can travel in vacuum
Select the correct answer using the code given below:
(a)   1, 2 and 3   (b)   2 and 4
(c)   1 and 3 only   (d)   1 only

75. The magnetic field strength of a current- carrying wire at a particular distance from the axis of the wire   **[NDA (II) 2018]**
(a)   depends upon the current in the wire
(b)   depends upon the radius of the wire
(c)   depends upon the temperature of the surroundings
(d)   None of the above

76. Consider the following circuit: **[NDA (II) 2018]**

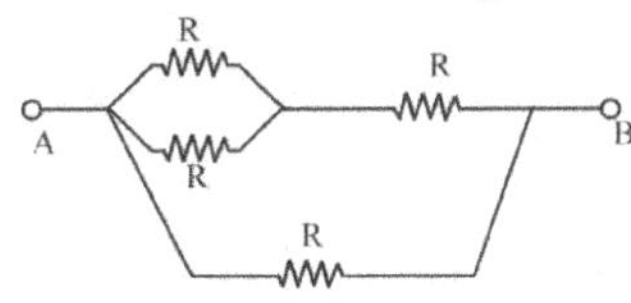

Which one of the following is the value of the resistance between points A and B in the circuit given above?
(a) $\dfrac{2}{5}R$ (b) $\dfrac{3}{5}R$
(c) $\dfrac{3}{2}R$ (d)   4R

77. If the focal length of a convex lens is 50 cm, which one of the following is its power?   **[NDA (II) 2018]**
(a)   +2 dioptre   (b)   +0.02 dioptre
(c)   −0.5 dioptre   (d)   +0.5 dioptre

78. The refractive indices of two media, are dentoed by n_1 and n_2, and the velocities of light in these two media are respectively v_1 and v_2. If n_2/n_1 is 1.5, which one of the following statements is correct?   **[NDA (II) 2018]**
(a) v_1 is 1.5 times v_2.   (b) v_2 is 1.5 times v_1.
(c) v_1 is equal to v_2.   (d) v_1 is 3 times v_2.

79. Which one of the following statements is correct for a plane mirror?   **[NDA (II) 2018]**
(a)   Its focal length is zero.
(b)   The size of the image of an object placed in front of the mirror is sightly less than that of the object.
(c)   The image is virtual, erect and laterally inverted.
(d)   Its focal length is 200 cm.

80. An object is placed in front of a convex mirror. Which one of the following statements is correct?   **[NDA (II) 2018]**
(a)   It will never form an inverted image.
(b)   The image moves towards the focus when the object moves towards the mirror.
(c)   Depending on the position of the object with respect to the mirror, the image can be inverted and real.
(d)   The size of the image becomes larger than that of the object when the object is placed at a distance equal to half the focal length.

81. A circular coil of radius R having N number of turns carries a steady current I. The magnetic induction at the centre of the coil is 0.1 tesla. If the number of turns is doubled and the radius is halved, which one of the following will be the correct value for the magnetic induction at the centre of the coil?   **[NDA (II) 2018]**
(a)   0.05 tesla   (b)   0.2 tesla
(c)   0.4 tesla   (D)   0.8 tesla

ANSWER KEY																				
1.	(c)	2.	(d)	3.	(d)	4.	(a)	5.	(a)	6.	(d)	7.	(c)	8.	(c)	9.	(c)	10.	(a)
11.	(a)	12.	(c)	13.	(c)	14.	(a)	15.	(c)	16.	(d)	17.	(d)	18.	(c)	19.	(c)	20.	(d)
21.	(a)	22.	(a)	23.	(b)	24.	(a)	25.	(c)	26.	(c)	27.	(c)	28.	(d)	29.	(b)	30.	(c)
31.	(d)	32.	(c)	33.	(d)	34.	(d)	35.	(c)	36.	(a)	37.	(a)	38.	(a)	39.	(b)	40.	(c)
41.	(c)	42.	(d)	43.	(b)	44.	(c)	45	(c)	46.	(c)	47.	(d)	48.	(b)	49.	(a)	50.	(c)
51.	(c)	52.	(d)	53.	(c)	54.	(c)	55.	(d)	56.	(a)	57.	(a)	58.	(b)	59.	(d)	60.	(a)
61.	(a)	62.	(d)	63.	(b)	64.	(b)	65.	(d)	66.	(a)	67.	(a)	68.	(a)	69.	(c)	70.	(a)
71.	(d)	72.	(d)	73.	(d)	74.	(a)	75.	(a)	76.	(b)	77.	(a)	78.	(a)	79.	(c)	80.	(a)
81.	(c)																		

MODERN PHYSICS

The basic building blocks of all the electronic circuits are the devices in which a controlled flow of electrons can be obtained. This chapter deals with the components of electronics such as semiconductors, diodes, transistors, integrated chips. Also describes the discovery of electron, proton, neutron and explains the latest technologies of the communication system such as Internet, Mobile Telephony etc.

STRUCTURE OF THE ATOMIC NUCLEUS

An atom (size 10^{-10} m) consists of a positively charged nucleus (size 10^{-15} m) which is surrounded by electrons moving around it in different shells. Nucleus of an atom consists of protons and neutrons together called **nucleons** i.e., mass number (A) Radius of nucleus is related to mass number as $R = R_0 A^{1/3}$ where constant $R_0 = 1.25 \times 10^{-15}$ m.

Electron

Electron (e^-) was discovered by sir J.J. Thomson in 1897 when he was studying the properties of cathode rays.

(i)   Electrons are negatively charged particles with e/m ratio 1.76×10^8 c/g

(ii) The charge of an electron was measured by R. Millikan in oil drop experiment as -1.6×10^{-19}C

(iii) Mass of an electron is 9.1×10^{-28} gram.

(iv) Electron is approximately 2000 times lighter than hydrogen

Proton

In 1909, Rutherford discovered proton (p^+) in his gold foil α–particle scattering experiment

(i)   Protons are positively charged particles.

(ii) The charge of a proton is $+1.6 \times 10^{-19}$ C (same as magnitude of an electron).

(iii) Mass of a proton is 1.672×10^{-24} gram.

(iv) The atomic number of an element represents the number of protons in the nucleus.

Neutron

In 1932, James Chadwick discovered neutron (n).

(i)   Neutron is an uncharged particle.

(ii) Mass of neutron is 1.674×10^{-24} gm

(iii) The mass number is the sum of number of protons and neutrons.

FUNDAMENTAL PARTICLES (ELEMENTARY PARTICLES)

Fundamental particles act as the smallest building blocks of the universe and thus have no internal structure. Fundamental particles are broadly classified into two types

Fermions

These are the elementary particles that make up all matter. Fermions have an odd half-integer (like 1/2, 3/2,) spin. Quarks, leptons, protons and neutrons, are all fermions. Fermions have only one state as these obey the Pauli Exclusion Principle and therefore cannot co-exist in the same state at same location at the same time.

Fermions have wave functions which are anti-symmetric under the interchange of identical particles. These particles obey Fermi-Dirac statistics, showing destructive interference of identical single particle wave functions.

Fermions are divided into two groups: Leptons and Quarks.

Leptons have six different varieties known as flavors; these are Electron, Electron Neutrino, Muon, Muon Neutrino, Tau and Tau Neutrino. Fermions also contain Baryons and quarks additionally. Quarks unlike leptons only exist in composite particles with other quarks, are also divided into flavors.

Leptons spin = 1/2		
Flavor	**Mass GeV/c^2**	**Electric charge**
ν_e electron neutrino	$<1 \times 10^{-8}$	0
e electron	0.000511	−1
ν_μ muon neutrino	<0.0002	0
μ muon	0.106	−1
ν_τ tau neutrino	<0.02	0
τ tau	1.7771	−1

Quarks spin = 1/2		
Flavor	**Approx. Mass GeV/c^2**	**Electric charge**
u up	0.003	2/3
d down	0.006	−1/3
c charm	1.3	2/3
s strange	0.1	−1/3
t top	175	2/3
b bottom	4.3	−1/3

Baryon

A hadron made from three quarks. The proton (up-up-down) and the neutron (up-down-down) are both baryons. They may also contain additional quark-antiquark pairs.

Bosons

These elementary particles are force carrier. Bosons have an integer spin (0, 1, 2...). Bosons have wave functions which are symmetric under the interchange of identical particles. These particles obey Bose-Einstein statistics, showing constructive interference of identical single particle wave functions.

Bosons

Unified Electroweak spin = 1		
Name	**Mass GeV/c^2**	**Electric charge**
γ photon	0	0
W$^-$	80.4	-1
W$^+$	80.4	$+1$
Z^0	91.187	0

Force carriers spin = 0, 1, 2, ...		
Strong (color) spin = 1		
Name	**Mass GeV/c^2**	**Electric charge**
g gluon	0	0

Mesons q$\bar{\text{q}}$					
Mesons are bosonic hadrons.					
There are about 140 types of mesons					
Symbol	**Name**	**Quark content**	**Electric charge**	**Mass GeV/c^2**	**Spin**
π^+	pion	$u\bar{d}$	$+1$	0.140	0
K^-	kaon	$s\bar{u}$	-1	0.494	0
ρ^+	rho	$u\bar{d}$	$+1$	0.770	1
B^0	B-zero	$d\bar{b}$	0	5.279	0
η_c	eta-c	$c\bar{c}$	0	2.980	0

PHOTOELECTRIC EFFECT

The phenomenon of emission of electrons from the surface of metal when light of suitable frequency falls on it is called photoelectric effect.

The ejected electrons are called **photoelectrons** and the current produced due to emitted electrons is called **photocurrent**.

Einstein's photoelectric equation

$$\frac{1}{2}\, mv^2_{max} = h\,(v - v_0) = hc\left(\frac{1}{\lambda} - \frac{1}{\lambda_0}\right) = eV_S$$

The Einstein's photoelectric equation is in accordance with conservation of energy.

MASS ENERGY RELATION AND NUCLEAR BINDING ENERGY

Einstein established the equivalence of mass and energy through a relation known as **Einsteins mass-energy equivalence relation.**

$$E = mc^2$$

where   C $= 3 \times 10^8$ m/s (speed of light in vacuum)

This relation supports both the *law of conservation of mass* and *law of conservation of energy.*

Nuclear Binding Energy

The energy required to break a nucleus into its constituent nucleons and place them at infinite distance is called nuclear binding energy or binding energy. This is the energy with which the nucleons are held together.

The difference between the rest mass of nucleus and sum of rest masses of nucleons constituting the nucleus is known as **mass defect.**

Binding Energy per Nucleon

The binding energy per nucleon of a nucleus is the average energy required to extract a nucleon from the nucleus.

Binding energy per nucleon

$$\bar{B} = \frac{Total\ binding\ energy}{Total\ number\ of\ nucleons} = \frac{BE}{A} = \frac{\Delta mc^2}{A}$$

RADIOACTIVITY

The phenomenon of spontaneous emission of radiations α, β or γ-rays from a substance is called radioactivity. .

Radioactivity is a spontaneous process which is independent of all external conditions. It is not affected by temperature, pressure, electric or magnetic field.

The number of decays per unit time or decay rate is called activity.

Activity $A = N\lambda$

where N$_0$ λ = A$_0$ is initial activity

Half life *is the time in which activity of radioactive substance is reduced to half.*

$$T_{1/2} = \frac{0.693}{\lambda}$$

Radioactive Series

- The heavy natural nuclides can decay to stable end products by four paths. The four paths have mass number given as 4n, 4n + 1, 4n + 2 and 4n + 3 where n is integer.
- Last element of series is stable and has a decay constant zero.

Properties of α, β & γ-rays

(A) **Properties of α-rays**

(a) It is a positively charged particle $\left(^4_2\text{He}^{2+}\right)$ and contains a charge of 3.2×10^{-19} coulomb(exactly double the charge of electron).

(b) The mass of α-particles is 6.645×10^{-27}kg (It is equal to mass of a helium nucleus). Actually α-particle is nucleus of helium, hence it is called doubly ionised helium.

(c) They (α-particles) get deflected in both electric and magnetic fields.

(d) The velocity of α-particle is very less than the velocity of light i.e., $v_\alpha \approx \dfrac{c}{10}$, where c is velocity of light.

(e) The penetrating power of α particle is lowest (in comparison to β and γ particles). It is 1/100 times of β-particles & 1/10,000 times of γ-rays.

(B)　Properties of β rays or β-particles

(a)　The beta particles (i.e., β^-) are electrons contain -1.6×10^{-19} C of charge. Actually β^- is electron and β^+ is positron.

(b)　They get deflected in both electric and magnetic field.

(c)　The velocity of β-particle varies between 0.01c to .99c, where c is velocity of light.

(d)　The mass of β particle is relativistic, because its velocity is comparable to velocity of light

(e)　They have both ionisation and penetration power. Ionisation power less than α-particle and penetration power more than α-particle and less than γ -ray.

(C)　Properties of γ-rays (or gamma radiation)

(a)　They are electromagnetic waves as x-rays.

(b)　They are not deflected in electric and magnetic field, it means that they are chargeless.

(c)　The velocity of γ-particle is equal to velocity of light.

(d)　The ionisation power of gamma rays is less than β and α rays but penetration power more than β and α-rays.

(e)　When γ-rays photon strikes nucleus then it gives rise to a phenomenon of pair production i.e.,

$$h\nu \longrightarrow \beta^- + \beta^+$$
$$(\gamma-\text{rays or photon}) \quad \quad (\text{Pair production})$$

Uses of Radioactive Isotopes

In medicine

(i)　Co^{60} for treatment of cancer

(ii)　Na^{24} for circulation of blood

(iii)　I^{131} for thyroid problem or goitre

(iv)　Sr^{90} for treatment of skin and eye

(v)　Fe^{59} for location of brain tumor

In industries

(i)　for detecting leakage in water and oil pipe lines

(ii)　for investigation of wear and tear, study of plastics and alloys, also in thickness measurement.

In agriculture

(i)　$_6C^{14}$ to study plant photosynthesis

(ii)　$_{15}P^{32}$ to find nature of phosphate which is best for given soil and crop

(iii)　$_{27}Co^{60}$ for protecting potato crop from earthworm

(iv)　For pest control

In scientific research

(i)　K^{40} to find age of meteorites

(ii)　S^{35} in factories

In carbon dating

(i)　It is used to find age of earth and fossils

(ii)　The age of earth is found by Uranium disintegration and fossil age by disintegration of C^{14}

X-RAYS

•　The X-rays were discovered by Prof. Roentgen, a German scientist in 1885. He was awarded Nobel Prize for this discovery in 1901. X-rays are electromagnetic waves.

•　The modern apparatus for the production of X-rays was developed by Dr. Coolidge in 1913.

•　X-rays are produced when fast moving electrons are suddenly stopped on a metal of high atomic number.

Properties of X-rays

(i)　They are not deflected by electric or magnetic field.

(ii)　They travel with the speed of light.

(iii)　There is no charge on X-rays.

(iv)　X-rays show both particle and wave nature.

(v)　They are invisible.

Applications of X-rays

Following are some important and useful applications of X-rays.

Scientific applications: Various diffraction patterns are used to determine internal structure of crystals.

Industrial applications: Since X-rays can penetrate through various materials, they are used in industry to detect defects in metallic structures in big machines, railway tracks and bridges.

In radio therapy: X-rays can cause damage to the tissues of body (cells are ionized and molecules are broken). So X-rays damages the malignant growths like cancer and tumors which are dangerous to life, when is used in proper and controlled intensities.

In medicine and surgery: The cracks or fracture in bones can be easily located. Similarly intestine and digestive system abnormalities are also detected by X-rays.

NUCLEAR REACTIONS

Nuclear Fission

Nuclear fission is the disintegration (Splitting) of a heavy nucleus upon bombardment by a projectile, such that the heavy nucleus splits up into two or more lighter nuclei of comparable masses with an enormous release of energy. 200 MeV per fission of U^{235} nuclei.

$$_{92}^{235}U + _0^1 n \rightarrow _{53}^{141}Ba + _{36}^{92}Kr + 3\left(_0^1 n\right) + 200 \text{ MeV}$$

It is the principle of **atom bomb** (destructive use).

Nuclear reactor has been devised for this purpose.

The main parts of nuclear reactor are

(a)　**Nuclear fuel :** U^{233}, U^{235}, Pu^{239} etc.

(b)　**Moderator :** Graphite, heavy water (D_2O). To slow down the neutrons (or slow down the nuclear reaction).

(c)　**Control rods :** (Cadmium, boron). To absorb excess neutrons. It controls the chain reaction.

(d)　**Coolant :** (water etc). To remove the heat produced in the core to heat exchanger for production of electricity.

Nuclear Fusion :

It is the fusion of two or more light nuclei to form a heavy nucleus with a release of huge amount of energy.

The nuclear fusion reaction, which is the source of the energy of sun/ star are proton-proton cycle.

SEMICONDUCTORS

The materials whose conductivity lies between conductors ($10^2 - 10^8$ sm^{-1}) and insulators ($10^{-11} - 10^{-19}$ sm^{-1}) are called semiconductors ($10^5 - 10^{-6}$ sm^{-1})

There are two types of semiconductor.

Intrinsic Semiconductor: These semiconductors are pure in which the thermal vibrations of the lattice have liberated charge carriers (i.e., electrons and holes). In intrinsic semiconductor, the number of electrons are equal to the number of holes. i.e., $n_i = n_e = n_h$ e.g. Si, Ge,

Extrinsic Semiconductor: They are impure semiconductors in which traces of impurity introduces mobile charge carriers [which may be + ve (holes) or –ve (electrons)] in addition to those liberated by thermal vibration.

Again there are two types of extrinsic semiconductors

(i) N-type semiconductor

(ii) P-type semiconductor.

N-type Semiconductor

When a pure semiconductor (Si or Ge) is doped by pentavalent impurity (P, As, Sb, Bi) then four electrons out of the five valence electrons of impurity take part in covalent bonding, with four silicon atoms surrounding it and the fifth electron is set free. These impurity atoms which donate free e^- for conduction are called as **donor impurity** (N_D). Here free e^- increases very much so it is called as n- type semiconductor and impurity ions known as **"immobile donor positive ions"**. Free e^- called as majority charge carriers and holes called as minority charge carriers.

P-type Semiconductor

When a pure semiconductor (Si or Ge) is doped by trivalent impurity (B, Al, In, Ga) then outer most three electrons of the valence band of impurity take part, in covalent bonding with four silicon atoms surrounding it and one electron from semiconductor makes hole in semiconductor. These impurity atoms which accept bonded e^- from valence band are called as **acceptor impurity** (N_A). Here holes increases very much so it is called as p- type semiconductor and impurity ions known as **"immobile acceptor negative ions"**. Free e^- are called as minority charge carries and holes are called as majority charge carriers.

P-N JUNCTION DIODE

When a P-type semiconductor is suitably joined to an N-type semiconductor, then resulting arrangement is called P-N junction or P-N junction diode.

Forward and Reverse Biasing

Forward biasing : *If we apply a voltage V such that P-side of the P-N junction diode is positive and N-side is negative then it is called forward biasing.*

Reverse biasing : *If we apply a voltage V such that P-side is negative and N-side is positive then it is called reverse biasing.*

P-N Junction Diode as a Rectifier

Rectifier is a device which converts ac to unidirectional pulsating output. In other words it converts ac to dc. It is of following types.

(i) Half wave rectifier

(ii) Full wave rectifier

P-N Junction diode as an Inverter

It is a device which converts direct current (d.c) to alternating current (a.c.)

TRANSISTOR

Transistor in general is known as bipolar junction transistor. It is a current operated device. It consists of three main regions

Emitter (E): It provides majority charge carriers by which current flows in the transistor. Therefore the emitter semiconductor is heavily doped.

Base (B): The based region is lightly doped and thin.

Collector (C): The size of collector region is larger than the two other regions.

Transistors are of Two Types

N-P-N Transistor : *If a thin layer of P-type semiconductor is sandwitched between two thick layers of N-type semiconductor is known as NPN transistor.*

P-N-P Transistor : *If a thin layer of N-type of semiconductor is sandwitched between two thick layer of P-type semiconductor is known as PNP transistor.*

Transistor as an Amplifier

A device which increases the amplitude of the input signal is called amplifier.

Transistor as a switch

Transistors can be used in an electronic circuit as a simple switches. A transistor conducts current across the collector emitter path only when a voltage is applied to the base. When no base voltage is present, the switch is off when base voltage is present, the switch is on.

Transistor as an Oscillator

Oscillator *is a device which delivers a.c. output wave form of desired frequency from d.c. power even without input signal excitation.*

Transistors are used in variety of applications such as

- High current transistors are used in car power inverters.
- Audio equipment uses transistors.
- Transistors are used in hearing aids.

OPTOELECTRONIC DEVICES

Zener diode : *A properly doped crystal diode which has sharp breakdown voltage is known as Zener diode. It is always connected in reverse bias condition. It is used as a voltage regulator. In forward biased case, it works as a simple diode.*

Photodiode : *A junction diode made from light or photosensitive semiconductor is called a photodiode.*

Light emitting diode (LED) : When a junction diode is "forward biased" energy is released at junction in the form of light due to recombination of electrons and holes. In case of Si or Ge diode, the energy released is in infra-red region.

In the junction diode made of GaAs, InP etc. energy is released in visible region such a junction diode is called **"light emitting diode" (LED)**.

LEDs are used in various real life projects such as

- Solar powered LED street light.
- LED based automatic emergency light.
- Displaying dialed telephone numbers on seven segment display, etc.

INTEGRATED CIRCUITS

An integrated circuit (IC), sometimes called a **chip** or **microchip,** is a semiconductor wafer on which thousands or millions of tiny resistors, capacitors and transistors are fabricated. An IC can function as an amplifier, oscillator, timer, counter, computer memory or microprocessor.

Uses of ICs

(i) In cars (automotive controls) televisions, computers, microwaves, laptops, MP3, play stations, cellular phones, aeroplanes, space crafts etc.

(ii) In switching telephone circuits, data processing, military equipments.

(iii) In digital watchs, scientific calculator and computers (flip-flops, logic gates, temperature sensors etc.)

COMMUNICATION

Communication means transmission of information. Every communication system has three essential elements-*Transmitter, medium/channel and receiver.*

Transmitter, converts the message signal produced by the source of information into a form suitable for transmission through the channel and receiver receives transmitted signal.

Modes of Communication

There are two basic modes of communication:

(i) **Point-to-point communication mode :** In this mode, communication takes place over a link between a single transmitter and receiver as in telephone.

(ii) **Broadcast mode of communication :** In this mode, there are a large number of receivers corresponding to a single transmitter. Radio and television are most common examples of broadcast mode of communication.

Modulation and Demodulation

Modulation : The original low frequency message/information signal cannot be transmitted to long distances. So, at the transmitter end, information contained in the low frequency message signal is superimposed on a high frequency wave, which acts as a carrier of the information. This process is known as modulation.

Demodulation: The process of retrieval of original information from the carrier wave at the receiver end is termed as demodulation. This process is the reverse of modulation.

WAVE PROPAGATION

Ground Wave or Surface Wave Propagation

*The radio waves which travel through atmosphere following the surface of earth are known as **ground waves or surface waves** and their propagation is called **ground wave propagation** or **surface wave propagation**.*

The ground wave propagation is suitable for low and medium frequency i.e., upto 20 MHz only.

Sky Wave Propagation

The sky waves are the radiowaves of frequency between 2MHz to 30 MHz.

The highest frequency of radio waves which when sent straight i.e., normally towards the layer of ionosphere gets reflected from ionosphere and returns to the earth is called **critical frequency.**

Space Wave Propagation

The space waves are the radiowaves of very high frequency i.e., between 30 MHz to 300 MHz or more.

INTERNET AND MOBILE TELEPHONY

Internet

The Internet is a worldwide, publicly accessible series of interconnected computer networks that transmit data by packet switching using the standard Internet Protocol (IP).

File transfer : In computing, file transfer is a generic term for referring to the act of transmitting files over a computer network. While the term "file transfer" is often linked to the File Transfer Protocol (FTP), there are numerous ways to transfer files over a network. Servers which provide a file transfer service are often called file servers.

There are 2 Types of file transfers:

"Pull-based" file transfers where the receiver initiates a file transmission request.

"Push-based" file transfers where the sender initiates a file transmission request.

Some protocols for file transfer may provide both of these, and they are often referred to as "uploading" or "downloading", from the client's perspective.

The World Wide Web (commonly shortened to the www) is a system of interlinked hypertext documents accessed via the Internet. The World Wide Web was created in 1989 by Sir Tim Berners-Lee, working at CERN in Geneva, Switzerland and released in 1992.

Mobile Telephony

The central concept of this system is to divide the service area into a suitable number of cells centred on an office called MTSO (Mobile Telephone Switching Office). Each cell contains a low-power transmitter called a base station and customers. When a mobile receiver crosses the coverage area of one base station, it is necessary for the mobile user to be transferred to another base station. This procedure is called handover or handoff. This process is carried out very rapidly, to the extent that the consumer does not even notice it. Mobile telephones operate typically in the UHF range of frequencies about 800-950 MHz.

SOURCES OF ENERGY

Everything we do is connected to energy in one form or another, Energy, defined as "the ability to do work."

Various forms of energy includes: Biomass energy - energy from plants, Electricity, Geothermal energy, Fossil Fuels - Coal, Oil and Natural gas, Hydro power Ocean energy, Nuclear energy, Wind energy etc.

Energy sources are divided into two groups — renewable and non-renewable Renewable and non-renewable energy sources can be used to produce secondary energy sources including electricity.

GOOD SOURCES OF ENERGY

A source of energy is that which can provide adequate usable energy at a steady rate over a long period of time. A good source of energy possesses the following characteristics: (i) large amount of work per unit volume or mass (ii) be easily accessible, (iii) be easy to store and transport, and (iv) be economical. So evaluation criteria for good source of energy are:

Capital costs, Operating costs, Efficiency, Is it renewable?, Energy storage requirements, Pollution, Environmental modification, Levelized cost to the consumer, Feasibility on large scale, Unit capacity, Proper ignition temperature, High calorific value etc.

- Calorific value of a fuel is the amount of heat produced by unit mass or unit volume of that fuel.
- Ignition temperature of fuel is the temperature at which the fuel starts burning or producing energy.

Calorific Values of Common fuels

Fuels	Gross calorific value in MJ/kg
Wood (15% water)	16
Ethanol	30
Methanol	23
Anthracite (4% water)	36
Coal tar fuels	36–41
General purpose coal (5–10% water)	32–42
High-volatile coking coals (4% water)	35
Low temperature coke (15% water)	26
Diesel fuel	46
Gas oil	46
Heavy fuel oil	43
Kerosene	47
Medium fuel oil	43
Petrol	44.8–46.9

CLASSIFICATION OF SOURCES OF ENERGY
(on the basis of recycling period)

Renewable Sources of Energy

Renewable sources of energy are those which can be generated by us or which are constantly being generated by natural processes or whose supply is unlimited. Examples : The sun, wind, flowing water, etc.

Non-Renewable Sources of Energy

Non-renewable sources of energy are those which were produced in the past by natural processes, whose supply is limited and which we cannot generate again in short interval of time, these will be exhausted in future. Examples : Coal, petroleum, natural gas, etc.

CONVENTIONAL SOURCES OF ENERGY

The sources of energy which are extensively used by man due to their easy availability.

For example: Fossil fuels, wind energy, energy from biomass etc.

Fossil Fuels

Fossil fuels are hydrocarbon based natural resources that were formed over 300 hundred millions of years ago by the fossilization of prehistoric plants and animals. There are three major forms of fossil fuels: coal, oil and natural gas.

Drawbacks of Fossils Fuels

- Fossil fuels are non-renewable resources and are limited.
- Global warming is directly associated with the increase in greenhouse gases produced from the burning of fossil fuels.
- On burning fossil fuels releases acidic oxides which leads to acid rain and thus affecting soil and water resources.
- Environmental pollution : Burning of fossil fuels causes air pollution.

Thermal Power Plant

A thermal power station comprises all of the equipment and systems required to produce electricity by using a steam generating boiler fired with fossil fuels or biofuels to drive an electrical generator. Such power stations are most usually constructed on a very large scale and designed for continuous operation.

Majority of total electricity production in India is from Coal Based Thermal Power Station. A coal based thermal power plant converts the chemical energy of the coal into electrical energy. This is achieved by raising the steam in the boilers, expanding it through the turbine and coupling the turbines to the generators which converts mechanical energy into electrical energy.

Working of Power plant

Coal based thermal power plant works on the principal of modified Rankine Cycle. In a coal based power plant coal is transported from coal mines to the power plant by railway in wagons or in a merry-go-round system. Coal is unloaded from the wagons to a moving underground conveyor belt. This coal from the mines is of no uniform size. So it is taken to the Crusher house and crushed to a size of 20mm. From the crusher house the coal is either stored in dead storage(generally 40 days coal supply) which serves as coal supply in case of coal supply bottleneck or to the live storage(8 hours coal supply) in the raw coal bunker in the boiler house. Raw coal from the raw coal bunker is supplied to the Coal Mills by a Raw Coal Feeder. The Coal Mills or pulverizer pulverizes the coal to 200 mesh size. The powdered coal from the coal mills is carried to the boiler in coal pipes by high pressure hot air. The pulverized coal air mixture is burnt in the boiler in the combustion zone. Generally in modern boilers tangential firing system is used i.e. the coal nozzles/ guns form tangent to a circle. The temperature in fire ball is of the order of 1300°C. The boiler is a water tube boiler hanging from the top. Water is converted to steam in the boiler and steam is separated from water in the boiler

Drum. The saturated steam from the boiler drum is taken to the Low Temperature Superheater, Platen Superheater and Final Superheater respectively for superheating. The superheated steam from the final superheater is taken to the High Pressure Steam Turbine (HPT). In the HPT the steam pressure is utilized to rotate the turbine and the resultant is rotational energy. From the HPT the out coming steam is taken to the Reheater in the boiler to increase its temperature as the steam becomes wet at the HPT outlet. After reheating this steam is taken to the Intermediate Pressure Turbine (IPT) and then to the Low Pressure Turbine (LPT). The outlet of the LPT is sent to the condenser for condensing back to water by a cooling water system. This condensed water is collected in the Hotwell and is again sent to the boiler in a closed cycle. The rotational energy imparted to the turbine by high pressure steam is converted to electrical energy in the Generator. Generator also known as alternator is the electrical end of a turbo-generator set. It is generally known as the piece of equipment that converts the mechanical energy of turbine into electricity. The generation of electricity is based on the principle of electromagnetic induction.

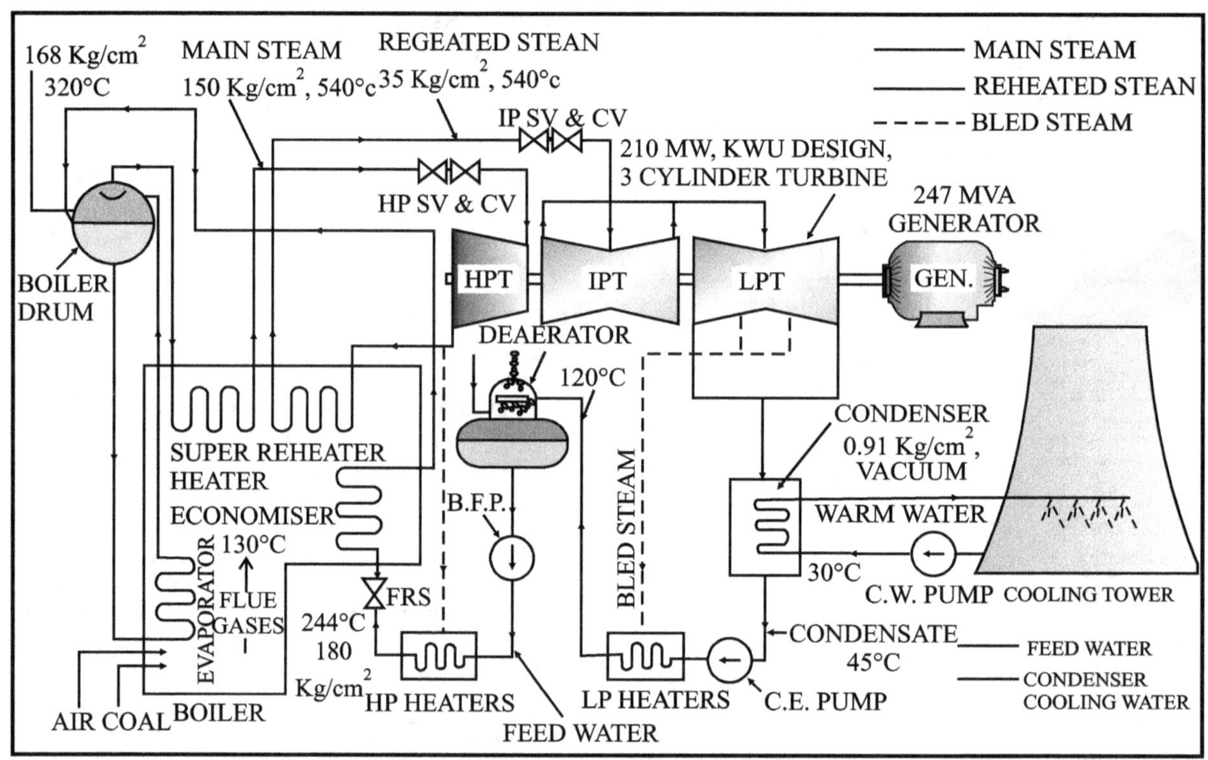

Components of Coal based Thermal Power Plant

Advantages of coal based thermal Power Plant

- Production cost of coal based fuel is cheaper in comparison with that of diesel based
- Steam engines and turbines can work under 25 % of overload continuously
- A portion of the steam generated can be used as a process steam in different industries
- These power plants can respond to rapidly changing loads without difficulty

Hydro Power Plant

Hydro power means making electricity from water power. It is the largest source of renewable power worldwide. A quarter of our energy requirement in India is met by hydro-power plants.

Hydroelectric power uses the kinetic energy of moving water to make electricity. Dams can be built to stop the flow of river. Water behind a dam often forms a reservoir.

The water from the high level is carried through pipes in order to rotate the turbine. As the turbine rotates, the armature of the generator also rotates and thus produces electricity.

About 20% of the power generated in India comes from hydroelectric power stations.

Advantages of Hydroelectricity

- This technique does not cause any environmental pollution.
- It is one of the cheapest sources of energy.
- Dams constructed on rivers helps in irrigation and also in controlling floods.

Components of Hydro Power Plant

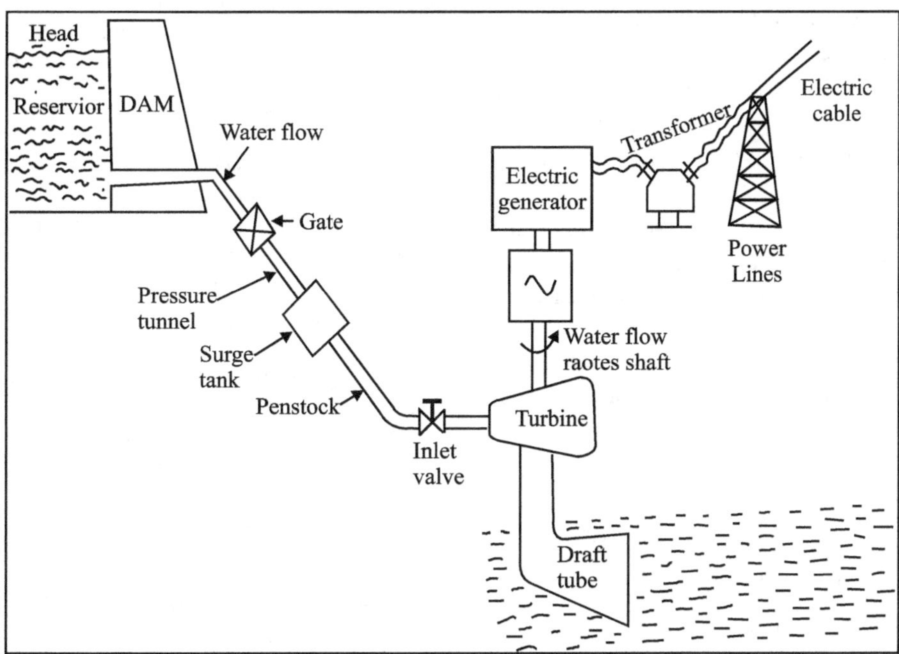

BIO-MASS

Biomass is a renewable energy source because the energy it contains comes from the sun. Through the process of photosynthesis, chlorophyll in plants captures the sun's energy and converting carbon dioxide from the air and water from the ground into carbohydrates, complex compounds composed of carbon, hydrogen, and oxygen. When these carbohydrates are burned, they turn back into carbon dioxide and water and release the sun's energy they contain. In this way, biomass functions as a sort of natural battery for storing solar energy. As long as biomass is produced sustainably with only as much used as is grown then this battery will last indefinitely.

Bio-mass as a Fuel :
* Wood as a fuel. i.e., firewood.
* Animal dung as a fuel.

BIO-GAS

Bio-gas is made from organic waste matter after it is decomposed. The decomposition breaks down the organic matter, releasing various gases. The main gases released are methane, carbon dioxide, hydrogen and hydrogen sulphide. Bacteria carry out the decomposition or fermentation.

Uses
* In industries and also as a domestic fuel for cooking, lighting, etc.
* In pumping sets used for irrigation.

Advantages of Bio-gas
* It causes less pollution, as burns without smoke.
* High Calorific i.e., heat producing value.
* It is a clean fuel as it leaves no residue.
* This method is environment friendly as it is an efficient method of waste disposal and supplies energy and manure.

WIND ENERGY

Along with sun, it was the air, which showed man its power. Even before the solar energy, it was the wind energy that man used for his work. Initially, it was used in two main ways; to drive wind mills on land and to drive sailboat at sea. The first use of windmills were to grind food grains and to run pumps to irrigate. Farmers have been using wind energy for many years to pump water from wells using windmills. Now with the advancement of science and technology, we have windmills generating electricity. Naturally, now this energy can be used for many more works.

Advantages of Wind Energy
* It is a renewable source of energy.
* It does not cause pollution.
* It does not require any recurring expenses.

Disadvantages or Limitations of Wind Energy
* It requires high maintainance and large area for installation.
* These farms can be established in the areas where wind blows for most part of the year.

NON-CONVENTIONAL SOURCES OF ENERGY

Solar Energy

The energy obtained from the sun is called solar energy. The inner temperature of the sun is very high (10^7K). Energy of the sun reaching every year on earth is about 1.6×10^8 KWh (Kilo watt hour). Value of energy used by all the living beings on the earth is 7×10^{13} KWh per year.

Solar Cell

Solar cell is such a device which converts solar energy into electric energy. Solar cells are also known as photo or photoelection cell (PV cell) because it works on the principle of photo-voltaic effect. Solar cells can be found on many small appliances, like calculators, and even on spacecraft. They are made of silicon, a Semi-conductor. Silicon (Si) is abundant in nature but availability of the special grade silicon for making solar cells is limited. A single cell of 4 cm^2 silicon develops a voltage of 0.5-1V and can produce about 0.7 W of electricity when exposed to sun.

The group of solar cells connected in specific pattern to produce desired potential difference and magnitude of solar cell panel.

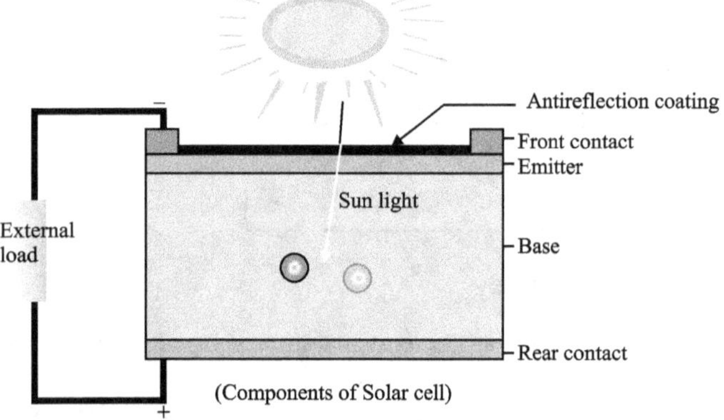

(Components of Solar cell)

Applications of Photoelectric Cells

* In television cameras for telecasting scenes and photo telegraphy.
* In production of sound in motion pictures.
* To switch on and off the street lights automatically.
* To control temperature in furnaces and chemical reactions.
* In fire and burglar's alarm, to open and close the doors automatically and in counting devices.

Solar Cooker

A solar cooker is a device that uses the energy in sunlight to generate sufficient temperatures to be able to cook food. Swiss naturalist Horace de Saussure was known to have been experimenting with solar cookers as early as 1767. Three basic solar cooker designs exist:

• Parabolic Reflector • Box Cookers • Panel Cookers

> The earth receives about 1.4 kW of direct solar radiations per square meter per second is called solar constant.

ENERGY FROM THE SEA

Tidal Energy

Tide arise due to the gravitational pull of mainly the moon on the water and spinning earth. The tide moves a huge amount of water twice each day, and harnessing it could provide a great deal of energy. Tide is the alternate rise and fall in the water level of oceans and seas.

Advantages

(i) It is an inexhaustible and renewable source of energy.

(ii) It does not cause any environmental pollution.

(iii) It does not produce any harmful waste.

Wave Energy

Kinetic energy exists in the moving waves of the ocean. Waves are a powerful source of energy. That energy can be used to power a turbine. There are several methods of getting energy from waves, but one of the most effective works like a swimming pool wave machine in reverse.

Ocean Thermal Energy

The energy from the sun heats the surface water of the ocean. In tropical regions, the surface water can be 40° celsius or more degrees warmer than the deep sea water. This temperature difference can be used to produce electricity.

The energy available due to the difference in the temperature between the water at the surface and water at depths is called ocean thermal energy (OTE).

Geothermal Energy

Energy present in the depth of the earth is called *geothermal energy*. Temperature in the earth at a distance of 10 kilometres is about 120°C and it increases to 300°C at the depth of 320 kilometres. It is evident that temperature increases with depth. Melted liquid, **magma** is present in the depth of earth. It is surrounded by various layers of soil, sand and water. Whenever there is some passage, it comes in contact with water present between these layers and converts this water into the steam of sufficient pressure. This vapour pressure can be used for production of energy.

> In Iceland, virtually every building in the country is heated with hot spring water. In fact, Iceland gets more than 50 per cent of its energy from geothermal sources. In Reykjavik, (population 115,000), hot water is piped in from 25 kilometers away, and residents use it for heating and for hot tap water.

NUCLEAR ENERGY

Nuclear power is an alternative energy source that can be obtained from either the splitting of the bigger nucleus of atoms (nuclear fission) or the combining of the lighter nuclei of atoms (nuclear fusion).

Atom bomb is based on the principle of nuclear fission and **Hydrogen bomb** is based on the principle of nuclear fusion.

Nuclear Fission

Nuclear reactions liberate a large amount of energy compared to chemical reactions. One fission event results in the release of about 200 MeV of energy, or about 3.2×10^{-11} watt-seconds. Thus, 3.1×10^{10} fissions per second produce 1 W of thermal power. The fission of 1 g of uranium or plutonium per day liberates about 1 MW. This is the energy equivalent of 3 tons of coal or about 600 gallons of fuel oil per day, which when burned produces approximately 1/4 tonne of CO_2.

Nuclear reactors manufacture their own fuel, since they produce ^{239}Pu from ^{238}U. With the total worldwide installed nuclear capacity of 3.4×10^5 MWe (megawatt electrical), one can estimate that more than 100 tonnes of ^{239}Pu are produced each year in reactors whose primary energy source is the fission of ^{235}U. This ^{239}Pu can be reprocessed from used fuel rods and used to power other reactors.

The isotope ^{235}U, with an abundance of only 0.7% in natural uranium, is commonly used to produce electricity in nuclear fission reactors. This isotope has the distinctive and useful property of undergoing nuclear fission through interaction with thermal-energy neutrons (neutrons with average speeds of only a few km/s). The other main isotope of uranium, ^{238}U, does not undergo nuclear fission with thermal neutrons, but it does capture neutrons to form the isotope ^{239}Np that then decays to ^{239}Pu. This isotope of plutonium undergoes nuclear fission with thermal neutrons with a higher probability than that of ^{235}U. The energy released in the fission of 2^{235}U and ^{239}Pu, mainly in the form of kinetic energy of the fission fragments, provides the heat to run the turbines that generate electricity at a nuclear fission power plant.

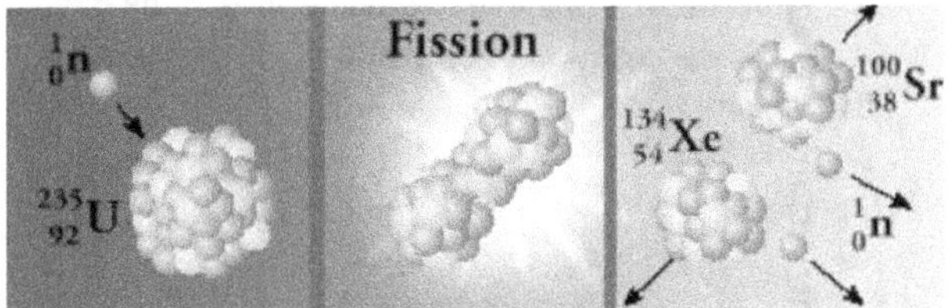

Nuclear Fission Reaction

Nuclear Fusion

Nuclear fusion is the source of energy in the sun and stars where high temperatures and densities allow the positively charged nuclei to get close enough to each other for the (attractive) nuclear force to overcome the (repulsive) electrical force and allow fusion to occur.

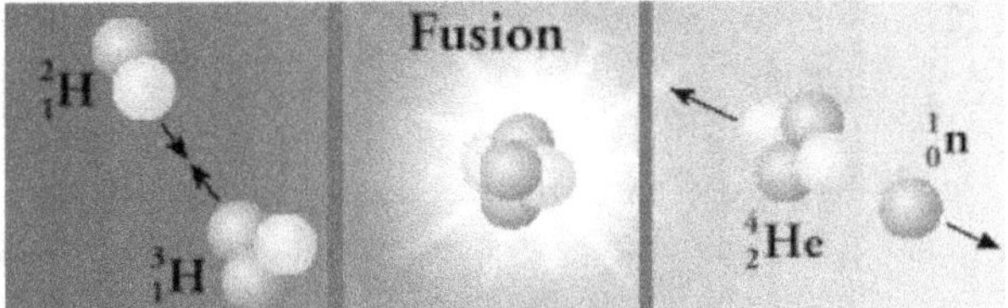

Nuclear Fission Reaction

The most promising fusion reaction,

$$^{3}\text{H} + {}^{2}\text{H} \rightarrow {}^{4}\text{He} + n + 17.6 \text{ MeV}$$

involves the radioactive nuclide tritium (^{3}H), available from the nuclear production reaction

$$^{6}\text{Li} + n \rightarrow {}^{3}\text{H} + {}^{4}\text{He}$$

To produce energy using this reaction, both the magnetic confinement reactor with a high-temperature plasma (a gas that has been completely ionized) and the inertial confinement reactor (which utilizes laser implosion technologies) have been investigated. Extremely high plasma temperatures are required in the magnetic confinement reactor and difficult laser

implosion techniques are required for the inertial confinement reactor. Although significant progress has been made in these investigations, no working reactor that produces more energy than it consumes has been built. Unfortunately, the funding for continuing this work has declined, and the work is proceeding at a slower pace. Although these types of reactors would not have the fission product waste disposal problem of fission reactors, fusion reactors generate large number of fast neutrons, leading to large quantities of radioactive byproducts.

In colliding-beam fusion (CBF) approach of nuclear fusion aneutronic power (power without neutrons) and non-radioactive nuclear energy is used. One aneutronic method features the,

$$^{2}\text{H} + {}^{3}\text{He} \rightarrow {}^{1}\text{H} + {}^{4}\text{He}.$$

However, this requires ^{3}He, which only has limited availability on the Earth. The Moon is a potential source of ^{3}He produced by cosmic-ray protons hitting the Moon directly and not being absorbed by an atmosphere as on Earth. Another potential approach for colliding beam fusion is the ^{11}B + ^{1}H reaction leading to the three ^{4}He nuclei. The energy release is in the form of charged particles whose kinetic energy can be converted to electricity with a very high efficiency. Current research predicts that this energy source has an extremely high degree of cleanness and efficiency. In all current energy sources, approximately two-thirds of the energy is lost in the form of waste heat or thermal pollution.

In the CBF approach, there is virtually no waste. This design favors small size for the greatest efficiency (100 MWe or less), and would lead to either power plants with several reactors or decentralization of energy production.

Nuclear fusion reactors, if they can be made to work, promise virtually unlimited power for the indefinite future. This is because the fuel, isotopes of hydrogen, is essentially unlimited on Earth.

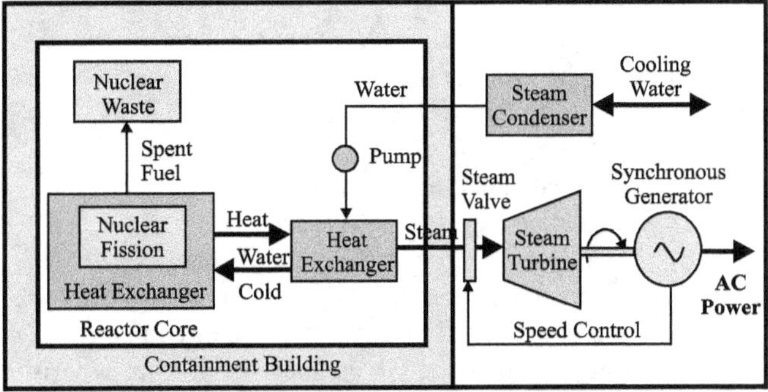

Layout of a Nuclear Reactor

Advantages of Nuclear Energy

- Production cost of nuclear reactor is lower in comparison to produce equal amount of energy through coal or oil based

- Cleaner energy production method as the nuclear power plant itself does not emit any Greenhouse gases.

- Nuclear Energy produced by a power plant can run interrupted for years hence can supply power without any delay and hence a reliable source of energy.

MULTIPLE CHOICE QUESTIONS

1. Consider a quantum system of non-interacting bosons in contact with a particle bath. The probability of finding no particle in a given single particle quantum state is 10^{-6}. The average number of particles in that state is of the order of
  (a) 10^3 (b) 10^6
  (c) 10^9 (d) 10^{12}

2. The maximum intensity of solar radiation is at the wavelength of $\lambda_{sun} \sim 5000$ Å and corresponds to its surface temperature $T_{sun} \sim 10^4$ K. If the wavelength of the maximum intensity of an X–ray star is 5 Å, its surface temperature is of the order of
  (a) 10^{16} K   (b) 10^{14} K
  (c) 10^{10} K   (d) 10^{7} K

3. Electromagnetic radiations are emitted by which of the following? **[NDA]**
  (a) Only by radio and television transmitting antennas
  (b) Only by bodies at temperature higher than their surroundings
  (c) Only by red-hot bodies
  (d) By all bodies

4. If an α-particle is projected normally through a uniform magnetic field, then the path of the α-particle inside the field will be **[NDA]**
  (a) circular   (b) parabolic
  (c) elliptical   (d) a straight line

5. Which one of the following is correct?
The wavelength of the X-rays **[NDA]**
  (a) is longer than the wavelength of sound waves
  (b) is longer than the wavelength of the yellow sodium light
  (c) is longer than the wavelength of radio waves
  (d) is of the order of 0.1 nanometer

6. Light Emitting Diode (LED) converts **[CDS]**
  (a) light energy into electrical energy
  (b) electrical energy into light energy
  (c) thermal energy into light energy
  (d) mechanical energy into electrical energy

7. A deuteron d captures a charged pion π^- in the $l = 1$ state, and subsequently decays into a pair of neutrons (n) via strong interaction. Given that the intrinsic parities of π^-, d and n are -1, $+ 1$ and $+ 1$ respectively, the spin-wavefunction of the final state neutrons is a
  (a) linear combination of a singlet and a triplet
  (b) singlet
  (c) triplet
  (d) doublet

8. Sun emits energy in the form of electromagnetic radiation. The following help in the generation of solar energy. Arrange them in the right sequence beginning from the starting of the cycle : **[NDA]**
  1. Hydrogen is converted to helium at very high temperatures and pressures.
  2. The energy finds its way to sun's surface.
  3. A vast quantity of energy is generated by nuclear fusion.
Select the correct answer using the code given below.
  (a) 1-2-3   (b) 2-3-1
  (c) 3-2-1   (d) 1-3-2

9. The neutron, proton, electron and alpha particle are moving with equal kinetic energies. How can the particles be arranged in the increaseing order of their velocities? **[NDA]**
  (a) alpha particle-neutron-proton- electron
  (b) proton-electron-neutron-alpha paraticle
  (c) electron-proton-neutron-alpha paraticle
  (d) neutron-proton-electron-alpha paraticle

10. Match the Column I and Column II.

Column – I	Column – II
(A) Isotopes	(1) Mass number same but different atomic number
(B) Isobars	(2) Atomic number same but different mass number.
(C) Isotones	(3) Number of nentrons plus number of protons
(D) Nucleons	(4) Number of nentrons same but different atomic number

  (a) (A) → (3); (B) → (1); (C) → (2); (D) → (4)
  (b) (A) → (2); (B) → (1); (C) → (4); (D) → (3)
  (c) (A) → (1); (B) → (2); (C) → (3); (D) → (4)
  (d) (A) → (1); (B) → (3); (C) → (2); (D) → (4)

11. Select the correct statement(s) from the following.
  I. In conductors, the valence and conduction bands may overlap.
  II. Substances with energy gap of the order of 10 eV are insulators.
  III. The resistivity of a semiconductor increases with increase in temperature.
  IV. The conductivity of a semiconductor increases with increase in temperature.
  (a) I and II only   (b) I and III only
  (c) I, II and IV   (d) I, II, III and IV

12. Which of the following cannot be fabricated on an IC?
  (a) Transistors   **[CDS]**
  (b) Inductors and transformers
  (c) Diodes
  (d) Resistors

13. At absolute zero, Si acts as
  (a) non-metal   (b) metal
  (c) insulator   (d) None of these

14. Telephony is an example of _________ mode of communication

   (a) point-to-point   (b) broadcast
   (c) both (a) and (b)   (d) None of these

15. **Column – I**   **Column – II**
   (A) Hydrogen bomb   (1) Fission
   (B) Atom bomb   (2) Fusion
   (C) Binding energy   (3) Critical mass
   (D) Nuclear reactor   (4) Mass defect
   (a) (A) → (3); (B) → (2); (C) → (1); (D) → (4)
   (b) (A) → (2); (B) → (1); (C) → (4); (D) → (3)
   (c) (A) → (3); (B) → (1); (C) → (2); (D) → (4)
   (d) (A) → (4); (B) → (2); (C) → (3); (D) → (1)

16. Which of the following statements is/are correct ?
   I.   Pure Si doped with trivalent impurities gives a p-type semiconductor
   II. Majority carriers in a n-type semiconductor are holes
   III. Minority carriers in a p-type semiconductor are electrons
   IV. The resistance of intrinsic semiconductor decreases with increase of temperature
   (a) I only   (b) I, III and IV
   (c) I and IV   (d) II only

17 The active component in an IC are
   (a) Resistors
   (b) Capacitors
   (c) Transistors and diodes
   (d) None of these

18. The waves used in telecommunication are   **[SSC]**
   (a) IR   (b) UV
   (c) Microwave   (d) Cosmic rays

19. Television signals are
   (a) frequency modulated
   (b) amplitude modulated
   (c) both frequency and amplitude modulated
   (d) phase modulated

20. Repeaters used in telephone links are: **[NDA]**
   (a) Rectifiers   (b) Oscillators
   (c) Amplifiers   (d) Transformers

21. The transistor are usually made of   **[CDS]**
   (a) metal oxides with high temperature coefficient of resistivity
   (b) metals with high temperature coefficient of resistivity
   (c) metals with low temperature coefficient of resistivity
   (d) semiconducting materials having low temperature coefficient of resistivity

22. A moderator is used in nuclear reactors in order to
   (a) slow down the speed of the nuetrons
   (b) acceleerate the neutrons
   (c) increase the number of neutrons
   (d) decrease the number of neutrons

23. The main constituent of biogas is
   (a) methane   (b) carbon dioxide
   (c) hydrogen   (d) hydrogen sulphide

24. Which one of the following is the correct sequence of the wavelengths of radiations ?   **[NDA]**
   (a) UV > Green> IR > Hard X-rays
   (b) IR > Green> UV > Hard X-rays

   (c) UV > Hard X-rays> IR > Green
   (d) IR > Hard X-rays> Green> UV

25. The most familiar form of radiant energy in sunlight that causes tanning and sunburning of human skin, is called
   (a) ultraviolet radiation   **[CDS]**
   (b) visible radiation
   (c) infrared radiation
   (d) microwave radiation

26. Which one among the following radiations carries maximum energy?   **[NDA]**
   (a) Ultraviolet rays   (b) Gamma-rays
   (c) X-rays   (d) Infra-red rays

27. In a hydro power plant
   (a) potential energy possessed by stored water is converted into electricity
   (b) kinetic energy possessed by stored water is converted into potential energy
   (c) electricity is extracted from water
   (d) water is converted into steam to produce electricity

28. Which part of the solar cooker is responsible for green house effect?
   (a) Coating with black colour inside the box
   (b) Mirror
   (c) Glass sheet
   (d) Outer cover of the solar cooker

29. A perfect black body has the unique characteristic feature as   **[CDS]**
   (a) a good absorber only
   (b) a good radiator only
   (c) a good absorber and a good radiator
   (d) neither a radiator nor an absorber

30. Which of the following does NOT allow harmful ultraviolet radiations from the sun to reach the earth?
   (a) O_2 (b) NO_2
   (c) CO_2 (d) O_3

31. Solar cells generate little amount of electricity, but are becoming popular because
   (a) its raw material Silicon is available in large quantities in India
   (b) it can be set up in remote and inaccessible hamlets without laying transmission lines
   (c) electricity generated from solar cells can be stored and used when required
   (d) All of these

32. Geothermal energy is
   (a) energy of magma inside the earth crust
   (b) energy stored as heat in the earth
   (c) amount of energy obtained from coal and petroleum inside earth crust.
   (d) amount of minerals obtained from earth crust

33. Tidal energy is a
   (a) form of energy obtained from kinetic energy of moving ocean water
   (b) form of energy which is obtained from the river in the form of tidal waves

(c) form of energy which is obtained from the lake in the form of tidal waves

(d) form of energy which is obtained from the ocean in the form of tidal waves.

34. Which among the following statements are the requirements of good source of energy?

A. It should do a large amount of work per unit volume or mass.

B. It should be easily accessible.

C. It should be easy to store and transport.

D. It should be economical.

(a) A, B   (b) A, B, C

(c) B, C, D   (d) All of these generator

35. Which of the following statement is/are the applications of photovoltaic cells?

A. They are used to detect opacity of solids, defects in materials.

B. They are used to switch on and off the street lights automatically

C. They are used to compare illuminating power of two sources.

D. To control temperature in furnaces and chemical reactions

(a) B and C   (b) B, C, D

(c) A, B, C   (d) All of these

36. Which one of the following is not a semiconductor? **[CDS 2017-I]**

(a) Silicon   (b) Germanium

(c) Quartz   (d) Gallium arsenide

37. A photon of X-ray has energy of 1 keV. A photon of visible radiation has energy of 3 eV. In this context, which one of the following statements is not correct? **[CDS 2017-I]**

(a) The wavelength of X-ray photon is less than the wavelength of visible radiation photon.

(b) Both the photons have different energies.

(c) The speeds of both the photons in vacuum are different.

(d) The frequency of X-ray photon is higher than the frequency of visible radiation photon.

38. Which one of the following statements is not correct? **[CDS 2017-I]**

(a) The cathode rays originate from cathode and proceed towards the anode in a cathode-ray discharge tube.

(b) The television picture tubes are nothing but cathode-ray tubes.

(c) The cathode rays themselves are not visible.

(d) The characteristics of cathode rays depend upon the nature of the gas present in the cathode-ray tube.

39. When a piece of pure silicon is doped with aluminium, then

(a) the conductivity of the doped silicon piece will remain the same   **[CDS 2017-I]**

(b) the doped silicon piece will become n-type

(c) the doped silicon piece will become p~type

(d) the resistivity of the doped silicon piece will increase

40. The majority charge carriers in a p-type semiconductor are   **[NDA (II) 2017]**

(a) free electrons   (b) conduction electrons

(c) ions   (d) holes

41. Which one of the following metals is used in the filaments of photo-electric cells that convert light energy into electric energy? **[NDA (I) 2018]**

(a) Tungsten   (b) Copper

(c) Rubidium   (d) Aluminium

42. The full form of LED is   **[NDA (II) 2018]**

(a) Light Emitting Diode

(b) Light Emitting Device

(c) Light Enhancing Device

(d) Light Enhancing Diode

43. If a free electron moves through a potential difference of 1 kV, then the energy gained by the electron is given by **[NDA (II) 2018]**

(a) 1.6×10^{-19}J   (b) 1.6×10^{-16}J

(c) 1.0×10^{-19}J   (d) 1×10^{-16}J

44. Consider the following statements about visible light, UV light and X-rays: **[NDA (II) 2018]**

1. The wavelength of visible light is more than that of X-rays.

2. The energy of X-ray photons is higher than that of UV light photons.

3. The energy of UV light photons is less than that of visible light photons.

Which of the statements given above is/are correct?

(a) 1, 2 and 3   (b) 1 and 2 only

(c) 2 and 3 only   (d) 1 only

45. The wavelength of X-rays is of the order of **[NDA (II) 2018]**

(a) 1A°   (b) $1\,\mu$ m

(c) 1 mm   (d) 1 cm

ANSWER KEY

1	(b)	2	(d)	3	(d)	4	(a)	5	(d)	6	(b)	7	(b)	8	(d)	9	(a)	10	(b)
11	(c)	12	(b)	13	(c)	14	(a)	15	(b)	16	(b)	17	(c)	18	(c)	19	(c)	20	(c)
21	(a)	22	(c)	23	(a)	24	(b)	25	(a)	26	(b)	27	(a)	28	(c)	29	(c)	30	(d)
31	(d)	32	(b)	33	(d)	34	(d)	35	(d)	36	(c)	37	(c)	38	(d)	39	(c)	40.	(d)
41.	(c)	42.	(a)	43.	(b)	44.	(b)	45.	(a)										

APPENDIX

NOBEL PRIZE IN PHYSICS [1901-2018]

Year	Nobel Prize Winner	Nationality	Contribution
1901	Wilhelm Roentgen	German	Discovery of X-rays
1903	A. H. Henry Pierre Curie Marie Sklodowska Curie	French French French	Discovery of spontaneous radioactivity. Study of radioactivity. Discovery of radium and polonium.
1905	Lenard Phillip	German	Worked on cathode rays
1906	J. J. Thomson	British	Discovery of electron
1907	A. A. Michelson	American	Optical instrument
1908	Gabriel Lipman	French	Interference coloured photography
1909	Guglielmo Marconi Braud Ferdmand	Italian German	Development of wireless telegraphy Development of wireless telegraphy
1910	J. D. van der Waals	Dutch	Equation of gases and liquids
1913	Kamerling Onnes. Heeke	Dutch	Low temperature and liquid helium
1914	Max Von Lave	German	X-ray diffraction in crystals
1915	W. H. Bragg	British	Crystal structure by X-rays
1916	W. L. Bragg	British	Crystal structure by X-rays
1918	Max Planck	German	Quantum theory
1921	Albert Einstein	German	Explanation of quantum theory of light and photoelectric effect.
1922	Niels Bohr	Danish	Theory of atomic structure.
1923	Robert A. Milikan	American	Experiment on charge on electron and photoelectric effect.
1927	Arthur Holly Compton Charles T. R. Wilson	American British	Discovery of compton effect which proved quantum theory. Developed the method to observe the motion of charged particles (Wilson cloud chamber)
1928	Owen William Richardson	British	Worked on thermal evolution
1929	Louis V. de Broglie	French	Discovered the wave nature of electron
1930	Chandrashekhar Venkata Raman	Indian	Discovered Raman effect
1935	James Chadwick	British	Discovered neutron
1936	Hess F. Victor Carl D. Anderson	Austrian American	Discovered cosmic rays Discovered positron
1938	Enrico Fermi	Italian	Slow neutron reactions and artificial radioactivity
1939	Ernest O. Lawrence	American	Development of cyclotron
1945	W. Pauli	American	Exclusion Principle
1947	E. Appleton	British	Study of ionosphere
1948	P.M.S. Blacken	British	Discovered and studied cosmic rays
1949	H. Yukawa	Japanese	Prediction of meson

Year	Name	Nationality	Contribution
1956	John Bardeen William Shockley Walter Braittain	American American American	Invention of transistor
1983	S. Chandrashekhar William Fowler	American of Indian origin American	Evolution of stars and their structure
1984	Carlo Rubbia Simon Van der	Switzerland Switzerland	Evolution of stars Discovery of field particles
1985	Prof. Klausvon Klitzing	German	Discovery of Quantised Hall effect
1986	Ernst Ruska Gerd Binning Hensic Rohrer	German Switzerland Switzerland	Invention of first electron microscope Invention of scanning tunneling microscope
1987	Dr. K. Allex Muller Dr. George Bednoz	Switzerland German	Discovery of super conducting in ceramic substances - do -
1988	Leo Ladderman Malvin Schwartz Jack Steinberger	American American America	Discovery of muon neutrino - do - - do -
1989	Dr. Norman F. Ramsey Dr. Hans. G. Dehmelt Dr. Wolfgang Paul	American American German	Invention of oscillatory field methods Invention of Ion trap technique - do -
1990	Jerome I. Friedman Henry W. Kendall Richard E. Taylor	American American Canadian	For deep inelastic scattering of electrons on protons and bound neutrons.
1991	Thiere Giilace D. Jennace	French	Important research in the conversion of crystalline substance into non-crystalline.
1992	Joje Schepak	French	Development of detectors in high energy physics.
1993	Russel A. Hulse Joseph H. Taylor	American American	Discovery of binary pulsar in 1974 - do -
1994	Bertram N. Brockhouse Chficirre G. Shull	Canadian American	Development of methods of the study of condensed substances - do -
1995	Maxtin L. Pearl Frederick Reines	American American	Pioneering experimental contribution in Lepton Physics. - do -
1996	David M. Lee Douglas D. Osberoff Robert C. Richardson	American American American	Discovery of supertluidity in Helium-3 - do - - do -
1997	Prof. Steven Chu. Dr. William D. Phillips Prof. Claude Cohen Tannoudji	American American French	Discovery of cooling a molecule to extremely low temperatures by laser action.
1998	Prof. Robert B. Laughlin Prof. Hurst L. Stoemer Prof. Daniel C. Tsui	American American American	Discovery of new quantum fluid - do - - do -
1999	Dr. Gerardus T. Hooft Dr. Martinus Veltman	Dutch Dutch	Explanation of quantum structure of electroweak interactions

2000	Zhores I. Alferov Herbert Krocmer Jack Kilby	Russian American American	Invention and developments related to integrated circuits, microchip pocket calculator
2001	Eric Cornell Corl Weisman Wolfgang Kelierlee	American American German	Discovery of principles related to behaviour of substances.
2002	Raymond Davis Jr. Masatoshi Koshiha Riccardo Giacconi	American Japanese American	Contribution to the information regarding the facts of Astrophysics and 'Nuclear Furnace' of sun.
2003	Alexi A. Abrikosov Vitaly L. Ginzburg Anthony J. Legge	American (Russian origin) Russian British	Important (research in the field of superconductivity and superfluidity in Quantum Physics.
2004	David J. Grass H. David Pulitzer Frank Wilezek	American American American	For developing a theory that explains quarks nature's triniest building blocks to better understand and explain how people can smell a lilac flower on spring morning and still recall it years after.
2005	John 1. Hall Theodor W. Hacnsch	American German	Contribution to the development of laser based precision spectroscopy.
2005	Ray J. Glauber	American	Contribution to the quantum theory of optical coherence.
2006	John C. Mather George F. Smoot	American American	For discovery of the cosmic microwave background radiation as well as its small variation indifferent directions.
2007	Albert Fert Peter Grunberg	German German	Research in the field of nano-technology. Their discovery led to miniaturising the hard disk for gadgets like i-Pod and cell phone.
2008	Makoto Kobayashi Toshihide Maskawa Yoichiro Nambu	Japan Japan American (Tokyohorn)	Discoveries in sub-atomic particles. Separate work that helped explain why the universe is made mostly of matter and not of anti-matter, via processes known as broken symmetries.
2009	Charles Kao Billiard Boyle George Smith	USA & Britain USA USA	Information technology revolution. Fibre optic cable enabling transmission of data at speed of light.
2010	Andre Geim Konstantin Novoselov	U.K. U.K.	Digital sensor i.e., the digital camera's electronic eye. invention of imaging semiconductor circuit. The charge coupled device (CCD) sensor which is the 'electronic eye' of the digital camera. For important work two dimensional substance Graphene.
2011	Saul Perlmutter Adam Riess Brian Schmidt	U.S.A. U.S.A. U.S.A. -Australia	For discovering that the expansion of universe is accelerating, a finding that implies that the cosmos will end in frozen nothing-ness.
2012	Serge Haroche J. Wineland	France U.S.A.	"For ground breaking experimental methods that enable measuring and manipulation of individual quantum systems."
2013	Francois Englert Peter Higgs	Belgium Braitain	For theoretical discovery of elementary matter to form starts and planets.

2014	Isamu Akasaki Hiroshi Amano Shuji Nakamura	Japan Japan Japan United States	"For the invention of efficient blue light-emitting diodes which has enabled bright and energy-saving white light sources"
2015	Takaaki Kajita Arthur B. McDonald	Japan Canada	"For the discovery of neutrino oscillations, which shows that neutrinos have mass"
2016	1. David J. Thouless 2. F. Duncan M. haldane 3. J. Michael Kosterlitz	USA USA USA	For theroretical discoveries of topological phase transitions and topological phases of matter.
2017	1. Rainer Weiss 2. Barry C Barish 3. Kip S. Thorne	USA USA USA	For contributions to LIGO detector and observation of gravitational waves.
2018	1. Arthur Ashkin 2. Gerard Mourou 3. Donna Strickland	USA France Canada	For groundbreaking inventions in the field of laser Physics

Chapter 1

MATTER & ITS COMPOSITION

MATTER AND ITS COMPOSITION

The universe is made up of matter and energy.

Matter: Matter describes the physical things around us: the earth, the air we breathe, etc.

Energy: It is the ability to cause change or do work. Some forms of energy include light, heat, chemical, nuclear, electrical and mechanical energy.

The matter can be classified in two different ways;

- According to its physical state
- According to its chemical composition

The Physical States of Matter

Matter is found in three physical states, i.e. Solid, Liquid and Gas. These states are also known as *phases of matter. The difference in the physical states of matter is due to the arrangement of the particles of which the matter is made of.*

Almost all chemical substances can exist in more than one physical state (phase) depending on external pressure and temperature.

States of Matter

Solid	Liquid	Gas	Plasma	Bose-Einstein Condensate (BEC)
• Definite shape • Definite volume • Highest density • Cannot flow • Maximum force of attraction amongst the particles • Particles are tightly packed • Cannot be compressed • Particles cannot move, rather they vibrate only at their fixed position • Kinetic energy of the particles is minimum	• Indefinite shape; takes the shape of the container • Definite volume • Density is lower than solid • Flow • Less force of attraction amongst the particles. • Particles are loosely packed as compared to solids • Cannot be compressed • Particles can slide over one another	• Indefinite shape • Indefinite volume • Lower density • Flow • Negligible force of attraction amongst the particles • Particles are loosely packed • Can be compressed • Particles can move freely	• No definite shape • No definite volume • Electrically conductive • Produce magnetic fields • Produce electric fields • Mixture of disassociated electrons and ions	• Occurs at low temperature/supercritical temperature • Large fraction of bosons/atoms occupy the lowest quantum state • Consisting of large numbers of bosons whose total number is conserved in collisions • Display Coherence i.e. whole condensate behaves like one big entity

Eric A. Cornell, Wolfgang Ketterle, and Carl E. Wieman received the Nobel Prize in Physics (2001) for the achievement of Bose-Einstein condensation in dilute gases of alkali atoms (^{87}Rb, ^{23}Na) and for early fundamental studies of the properties of the condensates

Solid

Solids can be divided into two distinct classes.

<table>
<tr><td colspan="2" align="center">Solid</td></tr>
<tr><td>Crystalline Solids
• Have characteristic geometrical shape.
• Possesses highly ordered three-dimensional arrangements of particles.
• Bounded by Planes or faces
• Planes of a crystal intersect at particular angles.
• Have sharp melting and boiling points.
Examples:
Copper Sulphate ($CuSO_4$), $NiSO_4$, Diamond, Graphite, NaCl, Sugar, etc.</td><td>Amorphous Solids
• Solids that don't have a definite geometrical shape.
• Particles are randomly arranged in three dimensions.
• Don't have sharp melting points.
• Formed due to sudden cooling of liquid.
• Melt over a wide range of temperature.
Examples:
Coal, Coke, Glass, Plastic, rubber, etc.</td></tr>
</table>

Liquid

Like solids, the volume of a liquid is slightly altered by variations in temperature and pressure.

Liquids have three typical physical properties:

- **Vapour pressure:** A Liquid when kept in a closed container vaporizes into the free space above it. The process of vaporization will continue till the equilibrium is reached between liquid and vapor. *The pressure at which the liquid and vapour can co-exist is called the vapour pressure of the liquid at a given temperature.*

- **Surface tension:** The surface of a liquid is always in a state of tension because a molecule at the surface is attracted towards the bulk by a force much greater than that drawing it toward the vapor where the attracting molecules are more widely spread. The spherical shape of *liquid* **bubble** and **capillary** movement can be explained with the help of surface tension.

- **Viscosity:** It determines the flow of the liquid. *It is the internal friction between layers of the liquid.*

Gases

Gas is the third state of the matter. Gases have three characteristic properties:

- they are easy to compress
- they expand to fill their containers, and
- they occupy far more space than the liquids or solids from which they form.

Plasma

It is the 4th state of matter. Like gases, plasmas have no definite shape and volume. These are made up of electrically charged particles and strongly influenced by electric and magnetic fields. Plasmas are made up of atoms in which some or all of the electrons have been stripped away and positively charged nuclei move freely.

Plasma makes up the sun and stars, and it is the most common state of matter in the universe as a whole.

Bose-Einstein Condensate (BEC)

Bose-Einstein Condensate (BEC) conceptualized by Indian Physicist S. N. Bose and Albert Einstein. It is widely regarded as 5th state of matter.

At Ultra-low temperatures non-interacting particles undergo a phase transition which is termed as Bose-Einstein condensation. Atoms in the Bose-Einstein Condensate are all at the same energy and oscillate together. During this phase transition phenomenon a significant fraction of the particles occupy a single quantum state.

> The field of science is ever-evolving and various probable states of matter like Excitonium, Fermionic condensate, Rydberg Polarons, Quantum spin liquid etc. are in the process of consideration.

EFFECT OF TEMPERATURE AND PRESSURE ON STATES OF MATTER

Physical change of matter from one phase to another phase occurs on adding energy to matter. For example:

- adding thermal energy, i.e. heat to liquid **water** causes it to become **steam** or **vapour,** i.e. a gas.
- taking away energy also causes physical change, such as when liquid **water** becomes ice, i.e., a **solid,** when heat is removed.

Physical change also can be caused by motion and pressure.

Physical processes undergone by matter leading to changes in the phases of the system are:

Melting and freezing

The melting point (or, also sometimes called liquefaction point) of a solid is the temperature at which it changes state from solid to liquid at atmospheric pressure.

- At the *melting point* the solid and liquid phases exist in equilibrium. If we continue to apply heat to the sample, the temperature will not rise above the melting point until the entire sample has been liquefied.
- The heat energy, **called latent heat of fusion,** is being used to convert the solid into the liquid form.

> A solid mixture, such as a metal alloy, can often be separated into its constituent parts by heating the mixture and extracting the liquids as they reach their different melting points.

The freezing point is the temperature at which a liquid changes to a solid. As the liquid is cooled, particle motion slows.

Most liquids contract as they freeze. One of the important characteristics of water is that it expands when it freezes, so ice floats.

Adding dissolved substances, or solutes, to a liquid will depress the freezing point.

Super Cooled liquid

Liquids can be cooled to temperatures well below their melting point before they begin to solidify. Such liquids are said to be **"super cooled"** and often require the presence of a dust particle or **"seed crystal"** to start the process of crystallization.

The freezing point of pure water is 0°C, but that melting point can be decreased by adding freezing or salt. The use of ordinary salt (sodium chloride, i.e. NaCl) on icy roads in the winter helps to melt the ice from the roads by lowering the melting point of the ice.

Sublimation

Sublimation is a chemical process where a solid turns into a gas without going through the liquid phase.

Examples of substance which sublime

*   The best known of these substances is CO_2 or *"dry ice"* which sublime to gas.
*   Other common substances which sublime are *ammonium nitrate, camphor, anthracene, iodine* and *naphthalene.*

Vapourisation

Vapourisation is the conversion of a liquid to a gas.

Evaporation	Boiling
• Evaporation takes place at all temperatures,	• Boiling occurs at a particular temperature.
• Evaporation takes place from the surface	• Boiling is a bulk phenomenon.

The temperature at which a liquid boils is called boiling point.
*   Boiling point is dependent upon the pressure the substance is subjected to.
*   A liquid under higher pressure will require more heat before vapour bubbles can form within it.

Food takes longer time to get cooked at high altitude. At high altitudes, the atmospheric pressure is lower than that at sea level, so the boiling point at high altitudes is quite low, which means water boils very fast at low temperatures. The food inside it does not get enough heat to get cooked and thus food is difficult to be cooked at high altitudes. Using a pressure cooker at such conditions helps **increase the boiling time** as the pressure inside the pressure cooker increases due to the vapour produced inside it.

Condensation and Deposition

Condensation is the change of the physical state of matter from gas phase into liquid phase.

Condensation is the opposite of evaporation.

When the gas transforms directly into a solid, without going through the liquid phase, it is called deposition or de-sublimation.

Example: Conversion of water vapour in the atmosphere into frost or ice at subfreezing temperatures. Frost tends to outline solid blades of grass and twigs because the air touching these solids cools faster than air that is not touching a solid surface.

ELEMENT, MIXTURE AND COMPOUNDS

According to chemical composition, matter can be classified as

*   *Pure substances* (or simply known as substance) are those matter that has distinct properties and a composition that does not vary from sample to sample. Water and ordinary table salt are examples of pure substances
*   *Mixtures* are combinations of two or more substances in which each substance retains its own chemical identity. The substances making up a mixture are called components of the mixture.

ELEMENTS

Elements are the simplest form of chemical substances that cannot be broken down by ordinary chemical means. Examples are hydrogen (H), sulphur (S) or gold (Au), etc.

The building blocks of the Universe are the elements. The term *element* was first used by *Robert Boyle.*

Most of the elements are *solids*, while *eleven* of them are *gases* and only *two* are *liquids*. Of the two liquids, *mercury* is a *metal* and *bromine* is non-metal. However, two other metals can also exist in the liquid state at around 30°C. These two are *gallium* and *caesium.*

COMPOUNDS

A compound is a substance composed of two or more elements which are chemically combined. Examples of compounds are water, sugar and salt, etc.

Compounds

Specific elements present	**Bonding in the compound**	**Reactivity-types of chemical reactions**
For example: • **Oxides** contain one or more oxygen atoms, **hydrides** contain one or more hydrogen atoms, and **halides** contain one or more halogen. • **Organic and inorganic compounds** contains carbon and few other elements like hydrogen, oxygen, nitrogen, sulphur, halogens. Earlier, these were obtained from animals and plants. • **Inorganic compounds** contain any two or more elements out of 118 elements. These are usually obtained from minerals and rocks.	For example: • **Ionic compounds** contain ions and are held together by the attractive forces among the oppositely charged ions. Common salt (sodium chloride) is one of the best-known ionic compounds. • **Molecular compounds** contain discrete molecules, which are held together by sharing electrons (*covalent bonding*). **Examples:** Water (H_2O) methane (CH_4) etc.	For example: • **Acids** are compounds that produce H^+ ions (protons) when dissolved in water to produce aqueous solutions. The most common acids are aqueous solutions of HCl (hydrochloric acid), H_2SO_4 (sulphuric acid), HNO_3 (nitric acid), and H_3PO_4 (phosphoric acid). • **Bases** are proton acceptors. e.g. NaOH (Sodium hydroxide), etc.

MIXTURES

Mixtures

Homogeneous mixtures	**Heterogeneous mixtures**
• same composition throughout • do not separate into phases when left alone. • any homogeneous mixtures are solutions that consist of a solute and a solvent. **Example**: An alloy is a solution of two or more elements, at least one of which is a metal, where the resulting material has metallic properties.	• no definite composition • separate into phases when left alone. • can be separated by ordinary physical means. **Example:** Blood, Oil and water, etc.

Methods of Separation of the Components of Mixtures

To separate different components of a mixture, varieties of physical techniques are available. ***Based on difference in the physical properties of the components present in the mixture.***

Separation by Using Separating Funnels

A separating funnel is used for the separation of components of a mixture between two immiscible liquid phases. One phase is the aqueous phase and the other phase is an organic solvent. This separation is based on the differences in the densities of the liquids.

Separation by Evaporation

The separation of liquid (solvent) and solid (solute) from a solution is done by removing the liquid (solvent) by heating or by solar evaporation. By evaporation we can recover the solute component only in solid or powder form.

Separation by Filtration

Filtration is a better method for separating solids from liquids in heterogeneous mixtures. In filtration the solid material is collected as a residue on filter paper and the liquid phase is obtained as filtrate.

Applications: Salt (water soluble) and sand(water insoluble) using water as solvent

Sulphur (soluble in CS_2) and glass powder (insoluble in CS_2) using CS_2 as solvent.

Centrifugation

Sometimes the solid particles in a liquid are very small and can pass through a filter paper. For such particles, the filtration technique cannot be used for separation. Such mixtures are separated by centrifugation. So, *centrifugation is the process of separation of insoluble materials from a liquid where normal filtration does not work well.*

During centrifugation the denser particles are forced to the bottom and the lighter particles stay at the top when spun rapidly.

Applications: Used in
- Diagnostic laboratories for blood and urine tests.
- Dairies and home to separate butter from cream.
- Washing machines to squeeze water from wet clothes.

Simple Distillation

Simple distillation is a method used for the separation of components of a mixture containing two miscible liquids that boil without decomposition and have sufficient difference in their boiling points.

Applications:
- Separation of acetone and water.
- Distillation of alcohol.

Fractional Distillation

Fractional distillation is used for the separation of a mixture of two or more miscible liquids for which the difference in boiling points is less than 25K.

Applications: Separation of
- Different fractions from crude oil.
- A mixture of methanol and ethanol.
- Different gases from liquid air.

Name of the fraction (% in crude oil)	No. of C-atoms	Boiling range	Use
Fuel Gas, LPG, refinery gas (1-2%)	1 to 4 (mainly propane & butane which can be liquified`	25°C	Bottled gas
Petrol	5 to 7	25 to 75°C	Fuel for cars
Naptha (20-40%)	6 to 10	75 to 190°C	Making chemical
Paraffin, kerosene (10-15%)	10 to 16	190 to 250°C	Airecraft fuel
Diesel (15-20%)	14 to 20	250 to 350°C	Fuel for cars, lorries, buses
Fuel oil, lubricating oils, waxes and bitumen (40-50%)	over 20 to several hundred	high boiling liquids or low melting solids thal boil over 350°C	Fuel oil is used as fuel for ships, power stations. Bitumen is used for roads and roops.

Chromatography

Chromatography involves passing a mixture of different dissolved substances in a "mobile phase" through another material called a *stationary phase*, which separates the analyte to be measured from other molecules in the mixture and allows it to be isolated.

The mobile phase may be a gas or liquid. The mobile phase is then passed through stationary phase. The stationary phase may be a solid packed in a glass plate or a piece of chromatography paper.

The various chromatographic techniques are:
- Column Chromatography,
- Thin Layer Chromatography (TLC)
- Paper Chromatography
- Gas chromatography.

Paper chromatography is one of the important chromatographic methods.

Applications: To separate
- Colours in a dye.
- Pigments from natural colors.
- Drugs from blood.

SOLUTION

A **solution** (a homogeneous mixture) is formed when one or more substances (the **solute**) are completely dissolved in another substance (the **solvent**). Depending on the nature of the solvent and solute we can have following kinds of solutions.

Different kinds of solution			
Solute	**Solvent**	**State of Resulting Solution**	**Example**
Gas	Gas	Gas	Air
Gas	Liquid	Liquid	Soda water (CO_2 in water)
Gas	Solid	Solid	H_2 gas in palladium
Liquid	Liquid	Liquid	Ethanol in water
Solid	Liquid	Liquid	NaCl in water
Solid	Solid	Solid	Brass (Cu/Zn), solder (Sn/Pb)

When a substance dissolves in a solvent it is said that the particular solute is **soluble** in that particular solvent. If it does not dissolve then it is **insoluble**.

Water as a solvent

Water is a commonly used solvent as it dissolves a large number of substances. Because of this property water is called a **universal solvent**.

Strengths of Solution

Quantitative study of a solution requires its *concentration,* that is, the amount of solute present in a given amount of solution.

$$\textbf{Molarity (M)} = \frac{\text{Number of moles of solute}}{\text{Volume of Solution in litre}} = \frac{n}{v}$$

$$\textbf{Molality (m)} = \frac{\text{Number of moles of solute}}{\text{Weight of solvent in kg}} = \frac{n}{w}$$

$$\textbf{Normality (N)} = \frac{\text{gram equivalent weight}}{\text{liter of solution}}$$

Normality (N) = Molarity (M) × number of equivalents

Strength = Molarity × Molecular weight

$$\textbf{Mass percentage} = \frac{\text{Mass of solute}}{\text{Mass of solution}} \times 100$$

Parts per million (ppm)

$$= \frac{\text{Number of parts of the compound}}{\text{Total number of parts of all components of the solution}} \times 10^6$$

Mole Fraction = Moles of the component/Total moles of the original solution

Dilution formula

$M_1 \cdot V_1 = M_2 \cdot V_2$

M_1 = the molarity of the original solution

V_1 = the volume of the original solution

M_2 = the molarity of the diluted solution

V_2 = the volume of the diluted solution

Colligative Properties of Solutions

Several important properties of solutions depend on the number of solute particles in solution and not on the nature of the solute particles. These properties are called **colligative properties** because they are bound together by a common origin; The colligative properties are:

- Vapour-pressure lowering
- Boiling-point elevation
- Freezing-point depression
- Osmotic pressure

Osmotic Pressure

Osmotic pressure may be defined as the external pressure applied to the solution in order to stop the osmosis of solvent into solution separated by a semi permeable membrane.

> *Reverse osmosis* is one of the processes that makes desalination (or removing salt from seawater) possible. It is the process of osmosis in reverse. Where osmosis occurs naturally without energy required, to reverse the process of osmosis, energy is required to be applied to the more saline solution.

SUSPENSION AND COLLOID

Depending on the size of the particles suspended, or dispersed in the surrounding medium, heterogeneous mixtures can be divided into the followings:

- **Suspension:** Materials of smaller particle size, insoluble in a solvent but visible to naked eyes, form suspension. The size of particles in suspension is over 1000 nanometers (nm).
- **Colloid:** A colloid contains smaller particles ranging in size from 1 to 1000 nanometers (nm).In case of true solutions the size of the particles are less than 1 nm.

The following table summarizes the major properties and points of distinction between each type of solution with respect to different properties.

Properties of colloids, true solutions and suspension

Properties	True Solution	Colloidal Solutions	Suspension
Size of the particles	< 1nm	1 – 1000nm	>1000nm
Nature	Homogeneous	Heterogeneous	Heterogeneous
Filterability (Diffusion through parchment paper)	Particles of true Solution diffuse rapidly through filter paper as well as parchment paper.	Colloidal particles pass through filter paper but not through parchment paper.	Suspension particles do not pass through filter paper and parchment paper.

Visibility	Particles of True Solution are not visible to naked eye.	Colloidal particles are not seen to naked eye but can be studied through ultra microscope.	Suspension particles are big enough to be seen by naked eye.
Tyndall effect	True Solution does not show Tyndall effect.	Colloids show Tyndall effect.	Suspension may or may not show Tyndall effect.
Appearance	Transparent	Translucent	Opaque

Classification of Colloids

Colloids are also called colloidal dispersions because the substances remain dispersed and do not settle to the bottom of the container.
- The substance being dispersed is referred to as being in the *dispersed phase*,
- The substance in which it is dispersed is in the continuous phase is called *dispersion phase*.

Different Kinds of Colloids

Dispersed Phase	Dispersion Medium	Type of Colloid	Example
Solid	Solid	Solid sol	Ruby glass, Gem stone
Liquid	Solid	Solid emulsion/gel	Pearl, cheese
Gas	Solid	Solid foam	Lava, pumice
Solid	Liquid	Sol	Paints, cell fluids
Liquid	Liquid	Emulsion	Milk, oil in water
Gas	Liquid	Foam	Soap suds, whipped cream
Solid	Gas	Aerosol	Smoke
Liquid	Gas	Aerosol	Fog, mist

Gases cannot form a colloidal solution between themselves, because they form homogenous mixtures.

Determination of a Colloid

Following two methods can be used to determine whether a mixture is colloid or not.
- **Tyndall Effect**: When light is shined through a *true solution*, the light passes cleanly through the solution, however when light is passed through a *colloidal solution*, the substance in the dispersed phases scatters the light in all directions, making it readily seen. An example of this is shining a flashlight into fog. The beam of light can be easily seen because the fog is a colloid. *Blue colour* of the *sky* and *sea water, twinkling of stars*, etc. are also examples of tyndall effect.
- **Dialysis:** The substance is allowed to pass through a semi permeable membrane. The larger dispersed particles in a colloid would be unable to pass through the membrane; while the surrounding liquid molecules can .This process is known as dialysis.

Applications of suspensions and colloids
- **Suspensions** have many applications in medical sciences. For example Barium sulfate in suspension is frequently used medically as a radio contrast agent for x-ray imaging and other diagnostic procedures. **Colloids** are also very important in the medical field because they can be used to manipulate blood conditions. To be specific, colloids are often used to regulate colloidal osmotic pressure, a pressure applied by proteins in the blood to pull water in the vascular system.

PHYSICAL AND CHEMICAL CHANGES

To understand the difference between a pure substance and a mixture, let us understand the difference between a physical and a chemical change.

Physical Change

During physical changes a substance changes its physical appearance, but not its composition. All changes of state (for example, from liquid to gas or from liquid to solid) are physical changes.

Characteristics of Physical Changes
- It is a temporary change.
- No new substances are formed.
- No change in mass takes place.
- Can be reversed by reversing the conditions.
- Change in physical state, size and appearance.

Some Examples Involving Physical Changes

Physical changes	Observation	Change on physical property
• Switching of an electric bulb.	The bulb glows and gives out heat and light energy.	The physical appearance of the bulb changes.
• Rubbing a permanent magnet on a steel rod.	The steel rod gets magnetised. If it is brought near iron nails, they get attracted.	The steel rod acquires the property of attracting pieces of iron.
• Action of heat on iodine	The brownish grey crystals of iodine change to form violet vapours. On cooling the vapours condenses to for form crystals.	Change in state and colour.
• Dissolving of common salt in water.	The white crystalline salt disappears in water. However, the water tastes exactly like common salt. Moreover, common salt can be recovered by evaporation.	Change of state.

Chemical Change

A chemical change is one in which the identity of the original substance is changed and a new substance or new substances are formed.
e.g. souring of milk, burning of paper, buring of candle, etc.
In the burning of candle, the wax of a candle burns into ash and smoke.

Characteristics of a Chemical Change

- A chemical change is permanent change and cannot be reversed to give back the original substance.
- One or more new substances (called products) are formed.
- Change in mass of a substance takes place.
- The composition of the product is different from that of the starting substance.
- A chemical change is always accompanied by the change in energy.

Some Examples Involving Chemical Changes:

Chemical change	Observation	Chemical equation
• Burning of magnesium in air	When a magnesium ribbon is heated in a flame of Bunsen burner, it catches fire and burns with dazzling white flame to form white ash.	Magnesium + Oxygen $\longrightarrow$ Magnesium oxide
• Rusting of iron	When iron (silver grey) is left exposed to moist air for a few days, reddish brown powdery mass (rust) is found on its surface.	(from air) $\longrightarrow$ Iron + Oxygen + Water vapours $\longrightarrow$ Rust
• Burning of LPG	When LPG (liquefied petroleum gas) is burnt, it burns with a pale blue flame and liberates colourless gas carbon dioxide along with steam.	Butane (LPG) + Oxygen $\longrightarrow$ Carbon dioxide + Water

MULTIPLE CHOICE QUESTIONS

1. Who among the following is called 'The father of modern chemistry?
   - (a) Michael Faraday
   - (b) Lavoisier
   - (c) Proust
   - (d) Linus Pauling

2. Match the following
   - A. Azidothymidine
   - B. cis-Platin and taxol
   - C. Streptomycin
   - D. Paracetamol
   - 1. Antibiotic
   - 2. Drugs for AIDS patient
   - 3. Drugs for treating cancer patients
   - 4. Antipyretic
   - (a) A - 2, B - 3, C - 1, D - 4
   - (b) A - 1, B - 2, C - 4, D - 3
   - (c) A - 4, B - 2, C - 3, D - 1
   - (d) A - 1, B - 2, C - 3, D - 4

3. The chemical formula for 'laughing gas' is
   - (a) N_2O (Nitrous oxide)
   - (b) NO (Nitric oxide)
   - (c) NO_2 (Nitrogen dioxide)
   - (d) N_2O_5 (Nitrogen pentoxide)

4. The compound used as 'artificial sweetener' is
   - (a) Saccharine
   - (b) Tartaric acid
   - (c) citric acid
   - (d) octane

5. The chemical name of 'Marsh gas' is
   - (a) Ethene
   - (b) Methane
   - (c) Propane
   - (d) Hexane

6. The chemical formula of Borax is
   - (a) $Na_2B_4O_7$
   - (b) $CaOCl_2$
   - (c) $BaSO_4$
   - (d) $Ca(SO_4)_2$

7. The chemical formula of plaster of paris is **[BPSC]**
   - (a) $CaSO_4 \cdot 5H_2O$
   - (b) $2CaSO_4 \cdot H_2O$
   - (c) $(CaSO_4) \cdot 2H_2O$
   - (d) $COSO4 \cdot MGO$

8. The chemical name of lime stone is **[UPPCS]**
   - (a) Calcium chloride
   - (b) Calcium oxide
   - (c) Calcium carbonate
   - (d) Calcium

9. Blue vitriol is **[UPPCS]**
   - (a) Copper sulphate
   - (b) Calcium sulphate
   - (c) Iron sulphate
   - (d) Sodium sulphate

10. The main component of Gobar gas is? **[CDS]**
    - (a) Chlorine
    - (b) Hydrogen
    - (c) Ethylene
    - (d) Methene

11. The main component of Biogas is
    - (a) Methane
    - (b) Ethane
    - (c) Propane
    - (d) Butane

12. Which chemical was an important symbol in our freedom struggle ? **[CDS]**
    - (a) Glucose
    - (b) Fertilizer
    - (c) Medicine
    - (d) Sodium chloride

13. Match the following columns ? **[NDA]**

Column I (Fuel Gas)	Column II (Major constituent)
A. CNG	1. Carbon monoxide, hydrogen
B. Coal gas	2. Butane, propene
C. LPG	3. Methane, ethane
D. Water gas	4. Hydrogen, methane, carbon monoxide

   - (a) A - 2, B - 1, C - 3, D - 4
   - (b) A - 2, B - 4, C - 3, D - 1
   - (c) A - 3, B - 4, C - 2, D - 1
   - (d) A - 3, B - 1, C - 2, D - 4

14. Which one of the following is used in the preparation of antiseptic solution? **[CDS]**
    - (a) Potassium nitrate
    - (b) Iodine
    - (c) Iodine chloride
    - (d) Potassium chloride

15. Aqua-regia used by alchemists to separate silver and gold is a mixture of **[CDS]**
    - (a) hydrochloric acid (concentrated) and nitric acid (concentrated)
    - (b) hydrochloric acid (concentrated) and sulphuric acid (concentrated)
    - (c) nitric acid (concentrated) and sulphuric acid (concentrated)
    - (d) hydrochloric acid (dilute) and sulphuric acid (dilute)

16. Nail polish remover contains **[CDS]**
    - (a) acetone
    - (b) benzene
    - (c) formaldehyde
    - (d) acetic acid

17. Which one among the following is a sin smelling agent added to LPG cylinder to help the detection of gas leakage? **[CDS]**
    - (a) Ethanol
    - (b) Thioethanol
    - (c) Methane
    - (d) Chloroform

18. Which of the following is a good lubricant ? **[CDS]**
    - (a) Diamond powder
    - (b) Graphite powder
    - (c) Molten carbon
    - (d) Alloy of carbon and iron

19. The main constituent of vinegar is **[NDA]**
    - (a) Acetic acid
    - (b) Ascorbic acid
    - (c) Citric acid
    - (d) Tartaric acid

20. To weld metals together, high temperature is required. Such a high temperature is obtained by burning **[NDA]**
    - (a) Acetylene in oxygen
    - (b) LPG in oxygen
    - (c) Methane in oxygen
    - (d) Acetylene in nitrogen

21. What happens when a fixed amount of oxygen gas is taken in a cylinder and compressed at constant temperature?
    - A. Number of collisions of oxygen molecules at per unit area of the wall of the cylinder increase.
    - B. Oxygen (O_2) gets converted into ozone (O_3).
    - C. Kinetic energy of the molecules of oxygen gas increases.
    - (a) A and C
    - (b) B and C
    - (c) C only
    - (d) A only

22. Boyle's law states that the
    (a) pressure of a gas is directly proportional to the temperature at constant volume
    (b) pressure of a gas is inversely proportional the volume at constant temperature
    (c) volume is directly proportional to the temperature at constant pressure
    (d) None of the above

23. When we put some crystals of potassium permanganate in a beaker containing water, we observe that after sometime whole water has turned pink. This is due to
    (a) boiling
    (b) melting of potassium permanganate crystals
    (c) sublimation of crystals
    (d) diffusion

24. Which of the following processes is known as fusion?
    (a) change of liquid to solid
    (b) change of solid to liquid
    (c) change of liquid to vapour
    (d) change of gaseous state to solid state

25. When a gas is compressed keeping temperature constant, it results in
    (a) increase in speed of gaseous molecules
    (b) increase in collision among gaseous molecules
    (c) decrease in speed of gaseous molecules
    (d) decrease in collision among gaseous molecules.

26. A pungent smell often present near the urinals is due to
    (a) sulphurdioxide   (b) chlorine
    (c) ammonia   (d) urea

27. Kerosene is a mixture of
    (a) aromatic hydrocarbons
    (b) aliphatic hydrocarbons
    (c) saturated hydrocarbons
    (d) alicyclic hydrocarbons

28. The oxide of which of the following elements is used as a coolant?
    (a) Silicon   (b) Nitrogen
    (c) Carbon   (d) Phosphorus

29. Which one of the following is not a mixture?   [NDA]
    (a) Air   (b) Mercury
    (c) Milk   (d) Cement

30. Which one among the following statements regarding the properties of mixtures and compounds is not correct?   [NDA]
    (a) A mixture shows the properties of its constituents but the properties of a compound are entirely different from its constituents
    (b) A mixture may be homogeneous or heterogeneous but a compound is a homogeneous substance
    (c) The constituents of a mixture can be separated by physical methods but those of a compound cannot be separated by physical methods
    (d) Energy is either absorbed or evolved during the preparation of a mixture but not in the preparation of a compound

31. Which one among the following is *not* a mixture?
    (a) Graphite   (b) Glass
    (c) Brass   (d) Steel

32. The latest discovered state of matter is   [NDA]
    (a) solid
    (b) Bose-Einstein condensation
    (c) plasma   (d) liquid

33. What type of mixture is smoke?   [CDS]
    (a) Solid mixed with a gas
    (b) Gas mixed with a gas
    (c) Liquid mixed with a gas
    (d) Gas mixed with a liquid and a solid

34. Iron sheet kept in moist air covered with rust. Rust is   [CDS]
    (a) an element
    (b) a compound
    (c) a mixture of iron and dust
    (d) a mixture of iron, oxygen and water

35. What is the term used to denote the critical temperature at which the air becomes saturated with vapour and below which the condensation is likely to begin ?   [NDA]
    (a) Condensation point
    (b) Evaporation point
    (c) Dew point
    (d) Point of critical temperature

36. Tails of comets are visible due to
    (a) Tyndall Effect   (b) Reflection
    (c) Brownian movement
    (d) None of these

37. The process used to separate oil and water is
    (a) distillation   (b) sublimation
    (c) separating funnel   (d) chromatography

38. Amalgam is a solution of
    (a) solid in solid   (b) solid in liquid
    (c) liquid in solid   (d) liquid in liquid

39. Which one of the following is correct? Butter is   [CDS]
    (a) a supercooled oil (b) an emulsion
    (c) a molecular solid (d) None of these

40. Which one of the following petroleum refinery products has the lowest boiling point?   [CDS]
    (a) Kerosene   (b) Diesel
    (c) Gasoline   (d) Lubricating oil

41. Which one of the following is not a mixture?   [CDS]
    (a) Tootpaste   (b) Toilet soap
    (c) Baking soda   (d) Vinegar

42. Iodised salt is a   [CDS]
    (a) mixture of potassium iodide and common salt
    (b) mixture of molecular iodide and common salt
    (c) compound formed by combination of potassium iodide and common salt
    (d) compound formed by molecular iodine and common salt

43. At NTP, the least volume will be occupied by 15 g of which one of the following ?   [NDA]
    (a) NH_3 (b) O_2
    (c) N_2 (d) Ne

44. What is the weight of one atom of Hydrogen in grams?   [NDA]
    (a) 6.023×10^{-23} (b) 1.66×10^{-24}
    (c) 6.62×10^{-24} (d) None of these

45. Which one of the following elements shows variable equivalent mass?   [NDA]
    (a) Zinc   (b) Silver
    (c) Calcium   (d) Iron

46. The atomic weights are expressed in terms of atomic mass unit. Which one of the following is used as a standard?
   (a) $^1H_1$ (b) $^{12}C_6$ **[NDA]**
   (c) $^{16}O_8$ (d) $^{35}C_{17}$

47. Which one of the following mixtures is homogeneous?
   (a) Starch and sugar **[NDA]**
   (b) Methanol and water
   (c) Graphite and charcoal
   (d) Calcium carbonate and calcium bicarbonate

48. In which one of the following situations a chemical reaction does not occur? **[NDA]**
   (a) Common salt is exposed to air
   (b) Coal is burnt in air
   (c) Sodium is placed in water
   (d) Iron is kept in moist air

49. Which of the following is the best example of the law of conservation of mass? **[NDA]**
   (a) When 12 gm of carbon is heated in vacuum, there is no change in mass
   (b) Weight of platinum wire is the same before and after heating
   (c) A sample of air increases in volume when heated at constant pressure but mass remains unchanged
   (d) 12 gm of carbon combines with 32 gm of oxygen to give 44 gm of carbondioxide.

50. An intense purple colour (Plasmon band) is exhibited by a colloid consisting of spherical
   (a) silver particles of 10 mm diameter
   (b) silicon particles of 5 mm diameter
   (c) gold particles of 5 nm diameter
   (d) iron particles of 3 mm diameter

51. Consider aqueous solutions of two compounds A and B of identical concentrations. The surface tension of the solution of A is smaller than that of pure water while for B it is greater than that of pure water under identical conditions. From this one infers that
   (a) surface concentration of A is smaller that its bulk concentration
   (b) surface concentration of B is larger than its bulk concentration
   (c) surface concentration of A is larger than that of B
   (d) surface concentration of A is smaller than that of B

52. Which one of the following is an example of chemical change? **[CDS 2016-I]**
   (a) Burning of paper
   (b) Magnetization of soft iron
   (c) Dissolution of cane sugar in water
   (d) Preparation of ice cubes from water

53. Which one of the following is a physical change?
   (a) Burning of coal **[CDS 2017-I]**
   (b) Burning of wood
   (c) Heating of a platinum crucible
   (d) Heating of potassium chlorate

54. What is the maximum number of states of matter?
   (a) Three (b) Four **[CDS 2017-I]**
   (c) Five (d) Variable

55. The molecular mass of sulphuric acid is 98. If 49 g of the acid is dissolved in water to make one litre of solution, what will be the strength of the acid? **[CDS 2017-I]**
   (a) Two normal (b) One normal
   (c) 0.5 normal (d) Four normal

56. An emulsion consists of **[CDS 2017-II]**
   (a) one liquid and one solid
   (b) one liquid and one gas
   (c) two liquids (d) two solids

57. Which one of the following is not a characteristic of a compound? **[CDS 2018-I]**
   (a) Composition is variable.
   (b) All particles of compound are of only one type.
   (c) Particles of compound have two or more elements.
   (d) Its constituents cannot be separated by simple physical methods.

58. Glass is a **[NDA 2017-I]**
   (a) liquid (b) colloid
   (c) non-crystalline amorphous solid
   (d) crystalline solid

59. A homogeneous mixture contains two liquids. How are they separated? **[NDA 2017-I]**
   (a) By filtration (b) By evaporation
   (c) By distillation (d) By condensation

60. 20 g of common salt is dissolved in 180 g of water. What is the mass percentage of the salt in the solution?
   (a) 5% (b) 9% **[NDA 2017-I]**
   (c) 10% (d) 15%

61. The compound $C_6H_{12}O_4$ contains **[NDA 2017-II]**
   (a) 22 atoms per mole
   (b) twice the mass precent of H as compared to the mass percent of C
   (c) six times the mass percent of C as compared to the mass percent of H
   (d) thrice the mass percent of H as compared to the mass percent of O

62. Which one of the following is a heterogenous mixture?
   (a) Hydrochloric acid (b) Vinegar
   (c) Milk (d) Soda water

ANSWER KEY															
1	(b)	**2**	(a)	**3**	(a)	**4**	(a)	**5**	(b)	**6**	(a)	**7**	(c)	**8**	(c)
9	(a)	**10**	(d)	**11**	(a)	**12**	(b)	**13**	(c)	**14**	(b)	**15**	(a)	**16**	(a)
17	(b)	**18**	(b)	**19**	(a)	**20**	(a)	**21**	(d)	**22**	(b)	**23**	(d)	**24**	(b)
25	(d)	**26**	(c)	**27**	(b)	**28**	(c)	**29**	(b)	**30**	(d)	**31**	(a)	**32**	(c)
33	(d)	**34**	(b)	**35**	(c)	**36**	(a)	**37**	(c)	**38**	(c)	**39**	(d)	**40**	(c)
41	(c)	**42**	(c)	**43**	(c)	**44**	(b)	**45**	(d)	**46**	(b)	**47**	(b)	**48**	(a)
49	(a)	**50**	(c)	**51**	(c)	**52**	(a)	**53**	(c)	**54**	(c)	**55**	(b)	**56**	(c)
57	(b)	**58**	(c)	**59**	(c)	**60**	(c)	**61**	(c)	**62**	(c)				

ATOMS, MOLECULES & NUCLEAR CHEMISTRY

ATOMS AND MOLECULES

The combination of different elements to form compounds is governed by some basic rules. These rules, collectively called 'laws of chemical combination'.

LAW OF CHEMICAL COMBINATIONS

Law of Conservation Mass

Lavoisier, who is widely regarded as the father of modern chemistry, gave the the law of conservation of mass. *This law states that in any chemical reaction, the mass of the substances that react equals the mass of the products that are formed.*

Law of Definite Proportions

This law was given by Joseph Proust, a French chemist, in 1799. Proust's **law of definite proportions** states that *different samples of the same compound always contain its constituent elements in the same proportion by mass.*

Law of Multiple Proportions

In 1803 Dalton gave this law. *As per this law if two elements combine to form more compounds, the masses of one element that combine with a fixed mass of the other element, are in the ratio of small whole numbers.*

The Law of Gaseous Volume

When gases react, the volumes consumed and produced, measured at the same temperature and pressure, are in ratios of small whole numbers. This is also known as Gay-Lussac's Law.

Dalton's Atomic Theory

The hypotheses about the nature of matter on which Dalton's atomic theory is based can be summarized as:

- Matter consists of indivisible atoms.
- All the atoms of a given chemical element are identical in mass and in all other properties.
- Different chemical elements have different kinds of atoms and in particular such atoms have different masses.
- Atoms are indestructible and retain their identity in chemical reactions.

Laws of Chemical Combination and Dalton's Theory

- Dalton's fourth postulate explains the law of conservation of mass.
- The fifth postulate is an attempt to explain the law of definite proportions.

ATOMS

Atoms are building blocks of all matter. On the basis of Dalton's atomic theory, we can define an *atom as the basic unit of an element that can enter into chemical combination.*

The size of an atom is extremely small and not visible to eye. The comparative idea regarding the size of atom can be had from the following:

Relative sizes	
Radius (in meter)	**Example**
10^{-10}	Atoms of hydrogen
10^{-4}	Grain of sand
10^{-1}	Water melon
0.2×10^{-1}	Cricket ball

Atomic Symbols

It was Jon Jacob Berzelius who devised the modern convenient system of using letters of the alphabet to represent elements. The systems of naming the elements are enumerated below:

- The symbols of the most common elements, mainly nonmetals, use the first letter of their English name. Examples: H (hydrogen), B (Boron), C (Carbon), N (nitrogen), O (Oxygen), F(Flourine), P (Phosphorous), S (Sulphur), I (iodine), etc.
- If the name of the element has the same initial letter as another element, then the symbol uses the first and second letters of their English name. Examples: He(Helium), Li(Lithium), Be(Beryllium), Ne(Neon), Al (Aluminium)

Atomic Number, Mass Number and Isotopes

The subatomic particles present in atom are-*neutron, proton* and *electron.* All atoms can be identified by the number of protons and neutrons they contain.

Atomic number

The number of protons in the nucleus of an atom decides which element it is. This very important number is called the atomic number (Z). In a neutral atom the number of protons is equal to the number of electrons, so the atomic number also indicates the number of electrons present in the atom. The chemical identity of an atom can be determined solely by its atomic number.

Mass number

The mass number (A) is the total number of neutrons and protons present in the nucleus of an atom of an element.

Mass number = number of protons + number of neutrons
= atomic number + number of neutrons

The number of neutrons in an atom is equal to the difference between the mass number and the atomic number, or $(A - Z)$.

ISOTOPES

Atoms that have the same atomic number but different mass numbers are called **isotopes.**

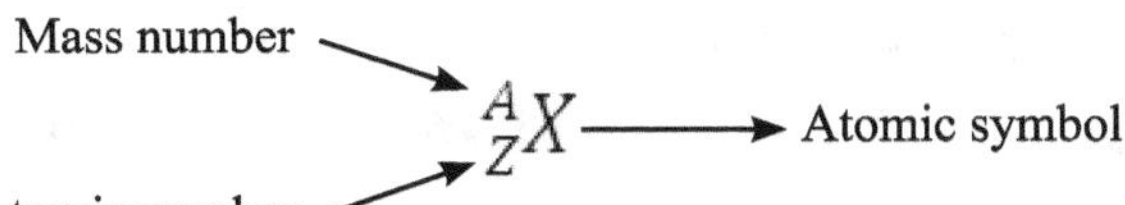

The first isotope of uranium is used in nuclear reactors and atomic bombs, whereas the second isotope lacks the properties necessary for these applications.

> The chemical properties of an element are determined primarily by the protons and electrons in its atoms; neutrons do not take part in chemical changes under normal conditions. Therefore, isotopes of the same element have similar chemistry, forming the same types of compounds and displaying similar relativities.

Isobars

Thus, elements atoms of different elements having same mass number (A) but different atomic number(z) are termed as isobars.

Examples : $^{14}_{7}N$ and $^{14}_{6}C$ $^{24}_{11}Na$ and $^{24}_{12}Mg$

Isotones

The atoms of an element which have *atomic numbers and mass number both different but the number of neutrons in atomic nuclei are same called isotones.*

Atomic Mass

A property closely related to an atom's mass number is its **atomic mass.** The mass of an atom depends on the number of electrons, protons, and neutrons it contains.

*   A value is assigned to the mass of one atom of a given element so that it can be used as
    standard. By international agreement, *atomic mass* (sometimes called *atomic weight*) is *the mass of the atom in atomic mass units (amu).*
*   One *atomic mass unit (*also called one Dalton) is defined as *a mass exactly equal to one-twelfth the mass of one carbon-12 atom.*

Carbon-12 is the carbon isotope that has six protons and six neutrons. Setting the atomic mass of carbon-12 at 12 amu provides the standard for measuring the atomic mass of the other elements.

MOLECULE

Amedeo Avogadro, an Italian chemist, first coined the term molecule in 1801 in order to explain the Gay-Lussac's law.
Molecule may be defined as a combination of two or more than two atoms of the same or different elements in a definite arrangement. These atoms are held together by chemical forces or *chemical bonds.*

Difference between Atoms and Molecules

*   An atom is the smallest particle of a substance which cannot exist freely whereas molecules can be considered as the smallest particle of an element or of a compound which can exist alone or freely under ordinary conditions.
*   A molecule of a substance shows all chemical properties of that substance.

Representing a Molecule Chemically

The chemical composition of a molecule can be expressed with the help of symbols of elements and formulae.

*   Oxygen molecule is made of two atoms of oxygen and therefore it is a *diatomic molecule* (represented by O_2), hydrogen, nitrogen, fluorine, chlorine, bromine and iodine are other examples of diatomic molecules and are represented as H_2, N_2, F_2, Cl_2, Br_2 and I_2 respectively.
*   Some other elements exist as more complex molecules. Phosphorus molecule consists of four atoms (denoted by P_4) whereas sulphur exists as eight atom molecule (S_8).
*   Normally, molecules consisting of more than three or four atoms are considered under the category of *polyatomic molecules*.

Molecular Formula

Formulae are combinations of symbols that represent a compound. A formula indicates:

*   The elements involved in the molecule.
*   The number of atoms of each element contained in the molecule. In writing formulae, we use subscripts, coefficients, and parentheses in addition to the symbols of the elements.
*   **Subscripts** indicate the number of atoms of an element, as in H_2 where two is the subscript meaning two hydrogen atoms. If there is no subscript with a symbol, it is assumed there is only one atom of that element.
*   **Coefficients** are numbers in front of the formula; indicate the number of molecules of compound, as in 4HCl where four is the coefficient indicating four molecules of HCl.
*   **Parentheses** are used to separate a radical from the rest of the formula when it would be confusing not to do so.

Steps in Formula Writing

In writing formulae for compounds, there are four steps that should be followed:

*   Determine the symbols for the elements in a compound.
*   Determine the valence of each of the atoms or radicals.
*   Write the positive element's symbol first, followed by that of the negative element.
*   Make the compound electrically neutral by using subscripts.

For example, the formula for calcium chloride may be written as follows:

*   Symbols of Calcium = Ca and Chloride = Cl.
*   Ca valence is +2, Cl valence is –1.
* $Ca^{+2} 2Cl^{-1}$. If we add the charges, we find that this compound is not neutral $(+2 - 1 = +1)$. Therefore, we must proceed to step (4).
*   To have two negative charges to balance the two positive charges, we must have two
    Cl^{-1} ions $(-1 \times 2 = -2)$. Thus, the formula would be $CaCl_2$.

Empirical Formula

The empirical formula of a compound is the simplest formula which expresses its percentage composition. It is the ratio of the different elements present in a chemical compound. Empirical formula does not show the exact number of elements present. For example, molecular formula of Benzene is C_6H_6.

Structural Formula

Structural formula of a molecule represents the structure of the molecule. Structural formula shows how the atoms are bonded to each other.

Molecular Mass

Molecular formula of a compound is normally used for determining the molecular mass of that compound.

- The *molecular mass is the sum of atomic masses of all the atoms present in that molecule.*
  For example:
  The molecular mass of CO_2 is obtained as:
  C= 1×12.0 u = 12.0 u
  For two O = 2×16.0 u = 32.0 u
  Mass of CO_2 = 44.0 u
  Hence, we write molecular mass of CO_2 = 44.0 u.

Equivalent Mass

The formula to calculate the equivalent mass of an element is given by :

$$\text{Equivalent mass} = \frac{\text{Atomic Mass}}{\text{Valency}}$$

IONS

An ion is an atom or a group of atoms that has a net positive or negative charge.

- The number of positively charged protons in the nucleus of an atom remains the same during ordinary chemical changes (called chemical reactions), but negatively charged electrons may be lost or gained.
- The loss of one or more electrons from a neutral atom results in a *cation, an ion with a net positive charge.* For example, a sodium atom (Na) can readily lose an electron to become a sodium cation.
- On the other hand, an *anion* is *an ion whose net charge is negative* due to an increase in the number of electrons. A bromine atom (Br), for instance, can gain an electron to become the bromide ion Br^-.

AVOGADRO'S LAW (AVOGADRO'S THEORY; AVOGADRO'S HYPOTHESIS)

This law states that equal volumes of gases at the same temperature and pressure contain the same number of molecules regardless of their chemical nature and physical properties. Avogadro's number is 6.022×10^{23}. It is the number of molecules of any gas present in a volume of 22.4 L and is the same for the lightest gas (hydrogen) as for a heavy gas such as carbon dioxide or bromine.

Avogadro's law provides a method to determine molecular weights of gaseous element.

Avogadro's Number and Molar mass of an element

In the SI system the *mole (mol) is the amount of a substance that contains as many elementary entities (atoms, molecules, or other particles) as there are atoms in exactly 12 g (or 0.012 kg) of the carbon-12 isotope.* The actual number of atoms in 12 g of carbon-12 is determined experimentally. This number is called **Avogadro's number (N_A),** in honor of Amedeo Avogadro. The currently accepted value is, N_A = 6.0221415×10^{23} Generally, Avogadro's number is rounded to 6.022×10^{23}. *This mass of carbon-12 is its molar mass (M), defined as the mass (in grams or kilograms) of 1 mole of units (such as atoms or molecules) of a substance.*

ATOMIC STRUCTURE AND NUCLEAR CHEMISTRY

Matter is made up of atoms, and therefore an understanding of the structure of atom is very important.

- In 1879, Sir William Crooks discovered cathode rays. Cathode rays are produced in vacuum tubes equipped with two electrodes.
- Using a cathode ray tube in 1897, J.J. Thomson determined that all matter, whatever its source, contains particles of the same kind that are much less massive than the atoms of which they form a part.
- Thomson originally called these as **corpuscles** which later came to be known as **electrons**.

FUNDAMENTAL PARTICLES OF ATOM

Electrons, Protons and neutrons are called fundamental particles. Characteristics of the fundamental particles are given below:

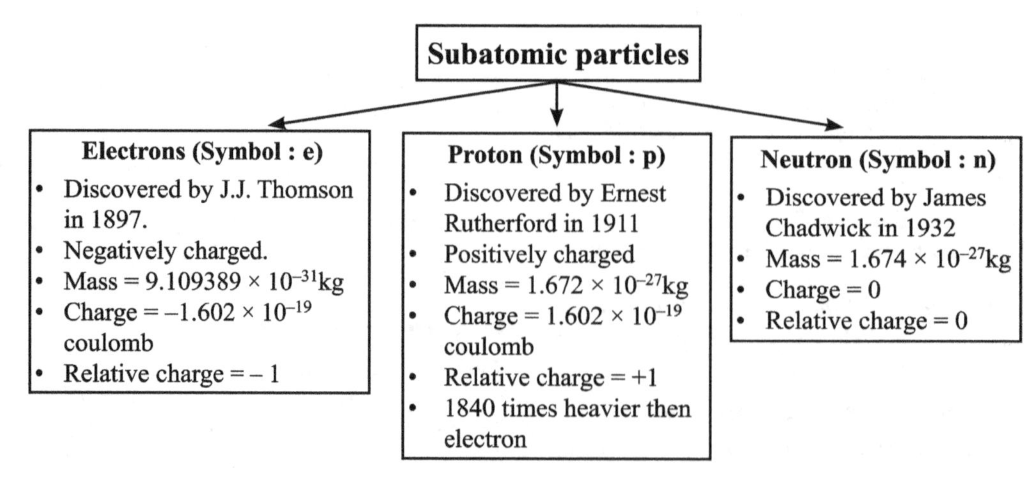

The discovery of the sub-atomic particles led to the enunciation of different models of the atoms which tried to explain the internal structure of the atom.

MODELS OF ATOM

Thomson Model

- J.J.Thomson proposed that atoms can be considered as a large positively charged body with a number of small negatively charged electrons scattered throughout it. This model was called as *Plum pudding* model of the atom.
- The electrons represent the plums in the pudding made of positive charge.
- Thomson model was discarded because it could not explain certain experimental observations like alpha particle scattering experiment by thin metal foils conducted by Ernest Rutherford.

Rutherford's Model

In 1909, Rutherford discovered proton in his famous *gold foil experiment*. In this experiment, Rutherford bombarded a beam of alpha particles on an ultrathin gold foil and then detected the scattered alpha particles in zinc sulfide (ZnS) screen.

Results
- Most of the particles pass through the foil without any deflection.
- Some of the alpha particles deflect at small angle.
- Very few even bounce back (1 in 20,000).

Conclusion
Based on his observations, Rutherford proposed the following structural feature of an atom:
- Most of the atom's mass and its entire positive charge are confined in a small core, called *nucleus*. The positively charged particle is called *proton*.
- Most of the volume of an atom is empty space.

- The number of negatively charged electrons dispersed outside the nucleus is same as number of positively charge in the nucleus. It explains the overall electrical neutrality of an atom.

Bohr's Model

The assumptions of Bohr's Theory are as follows:
- Electrons revolve round the nucleus in definite orbits called stationary states.
- Each stationary state is associated with a definite energy, which is called an energy level.
- As long as electrons revolve in the *stationary states*, they don't lose or gain energy.
- Electrons may jump from one orbit to another, in which case energy is absorbed or emitted in fixed quantities only (known as 'quanta').

Modern Atomic Model

The present accepted model of atom, called **quantum mechanical or wave-mechanical concept of atom**, is basically mathematical in nature. This was proposed by Erwin Schrödinger- an Austrian physicist in 1926.

HEISENBERG'S UNCERTAINTY PRINCIPLE

An important consequence of the wave-particle duality of matter and radiation was discovered by Werner Heisenberg in 1927 and is called the **Uncertainty Principle**. According to this principle, it is not possible to simultaneously measure both the position and momentum (or velocity) of an electron accurately.

The characteristics of each of the quantum numbers are given below:

Quantum numbers

Principal quantum number (denoted by n)	Azimuthal quantum number (denoted by l)	Magnetic quantum number (denoted by m_l)	The Spin quantum number (denoted by m_s)
• Specifies the energy level (or principal shell) of the electron within the atom and size of the orbital. • Can take only positive non-zero integral values i.e 1,2,3,4 etc. • The shells or energy levels are designated as K, L, M, N etc. depending on the values of n i.e. 1,2,3,4 etc. respectively. • The number of electrons that can be accommodated in one shell is $2n^2$.	• Specifies the **shape** of an orbital with a particular principal quantum number. • Divides the shells into smaller groups of orbitals called **subshells (sublevels)**. • l may be zero or a positive integer-less than or equal to (n–1) (n is the principal quantum number), i.e. = 0,1,2,3... (n–1). • Different values correspond to different types of subshells and each subshell contains orbitals of a given shape as shown below: ◄ $l = 0$ (*s* orbital): Spherical ◄ $l = 1$ (*p*-orbital): Dumb-bell ◄ $l = 2$ (*d*-orbital): cloverleaf	• Describes the direction or orientation of the orbital in space. • Takes-up any integral value from $-\ell$ to $+\ell$. (For example, for $\ell = 1$; m_l can have the values as $-1,0$ and 1.That means the p-orbital can have three orientation i.e. there are three p orbitals- p_x, p_y and p_z.)	describes the spin of the electron, i.e. whether it is clockwise or anticlockwise. This quantum number was introduced later, it's not an outcome of the solution of Schrodinger Equation.

ARRANGEMENT OF ELECTRONS IN AN ATOM

- Each electron in an atom is described by four different **quantum numbers**. The first three (n, l, m_l) specify the particular orbital of interest, and the fourth (m_s) specifies how many electrons can occupy that orbital.

Table of Allowed Quantum Numbers

n	l	m_l	Number of orbitals	Orbital Name	Number of electrons
1	0	0	1	$1s$	2
2	0	0	1	$2s$	2
	1	-1, 0, +1	3	$2p$	6
3	0	0	1	$3s$	2
	1	-1, 0, +1	3	$3p$	6
	2	-2, -1, 0, +1, +2	5	$3d$	10
4	0	0	1	$4s$	2
	1	-1, 0, +1	3	$4p$	6
	2	-2, -1, 0, +1, +2	5	$4d$	10
	3	-3, -2, -1, 0, +1, +2, +3	7	$4f$	14

- The *Pauli Exclusion Principle* (Wolfgang Pauli, Nobel Prize in 1945) states that *no two electrons in the same atom can have identical values for all four of their quantum numbers.*
- The distribution of electrons among the orbitals of an atom is called the *electronic configuration*. The electrons are filled in according to a scheme known as the *Aufbau principle* ("building-up"), which corresponds to increasing energy of the subshells as below:

1s → 2s→2p→3s→3p→4s→3d→ 4p → 5s → 6s → 4f → 5d → 6p → 7s → 5s

Because an electron spins, it creates a magnetic field, which can be oriented in one of two directions. For two electrons in the same orbital, the spins must be opposite to each other; the spins are said to be **paired**. These substances are not attracted to magnets and are said to be **diamagnetic**. Atoms with more electrons that spin in one direction than another contain **unpaired** electrons. These substances are weakly attracted to magnets and are said to be **paramagnetic**.

NUCLEAR CHEMISTRY

Radioactivity may be defined as disintegration or decay of unstable atoms accompanied by emission of radiation

Radioactivity can be of two types-Natural and artificial or induced radioactivity.

Nature of Radiations

The invisible radioactive radiations are of three types:

- **Alpha (α) particle:** a helium nucleus ($_2^4\alpha$ or $_2^4$He) without electrons. These are positively charged and largest particle emitted by radioactive nuclei. Also has the highest charge.
- **Beta (β) particle:** a beta particle ($_{-1}^0\beta$ or $_{-1}^0$e) is an electron emitted from an atomic nucleus.
- **Positron:** the antiparticle of an electron/beta particle, $_1^0\beta$ or $_1^0$e. The same size as an electron but with a positive charge.
- **Gamma (γ) rays:** high-energy rays (like X-rays).

$$In\frac{N_t}{N_0} = -kt$$

N_t = mass of radioactive material at time interval (t)
N_0 = mass of the original amount of radioactive material
k = decay constant
t = time interval ($t_{1/2}$ for the half-life)

- Radioactivity is due to instability of atomic nuclei. Instability is due to deviation from the ratio of neutron to proton to 1:1 for light nuclei and 3:2 for heavy nuclei.
- The *decay constant (λ)* is the fraction of the number of atoms that *decay per* second.

$$dN/dt = -\lambda N$$

dN/dt is the number of *decays* per second (or activity) and N is the number of atoms present.

- *Half-Life ($T_{1/2}$)* - Time taken for the decay of 50% of initial number of nuclei present in a radioactive sample

$T_{1/2}$ = ln 2/λ= τ ln 2

- *Mean Life (τ)*-Time at which number of nuclei has been reduced to e^{-1} of its initial value

Comparison of the Properties of Alpha, Beta, and Gamma Rays

Property	α ray	β ray	γ ray
Nature	Helium nuclei, $_2^4$He	Fast electrons	Electro-magnetic radiation
Velocity	One-tenth of the velocity of light	Velocity of light	Velocity of light
Penetrating power	Low	moderate	high
Stopped by	Paper of 0.01 mm thick	1 cm of aluminium	Several cm thick lead/concrete layer

Nuclear Reactions

A nuclear reaction is that which proceeds with a change in the composition of the nucleus resulting in the formation of an atom of a new element.

Therefore, the process in which the artificial transmutation of a stable nuclide leads to the formation of radioactive isotope is called *artificial radioactivity or induced radioactivity.*

DIFFERENCE BETWEEN NUCLEAR REACTIONS AND CHEMICAL REACTIONS

	Chemical Reaction	Nuclear Reaction
Changes	Rearrangement of elements	Change in nucleus
Nature	Loss/gain/ and sharing of electrons.	Nuclear decomposition
Site of reaction	Outside nucleus.	Inside nucleus
Change in Mass	Mass of reactants = Mass of products	Mass of reactants $\neq$ Mass of products
Change in Energy	Low energy change	High energy change.

Nuclear Fusion

Nuclear fusion refers to a nuclear reaction in which two light nuclei fuse together to form heavy nucleus with release of large amount of energy.

Nuclear Fission

Nuclear fission is a nuclear reaction in which a heavy atomic nucleus (such as that of uranium) disintegrates into two nearly equal fragments with release of large amount of energy.

Application of Nuclear Reactions

It has been possible to control fission of U-235 so that energy is released slowly at a usable rate. *Controlled fission is carried out in a specially designed plant called a nuclear power reactor or simply nuclear reactor.* The chief components of a nuclear reactor are:

- **U-235 fuel rods** constitute the 'fuel core'. The fission of U-235 produces heat energy and neutrons that start the chain reaction.
- **Moderator** slows down or moderates the neutrons. The most commonly used moderator is ordinary water. Graphite rods are sometimes used. Neutrons slow down by losing energy due to collisions with atoms/molecules of the moderator.
- **Control rods** control the rate of fission of U-235. These are made of boron-10 or cadmium that absorbs some of the slowed neutrons. Thus the chain reaction is prevented from going too fast.
- **Coolant** cools the fuel core by removing heat produced by fission. Water used in the reactor serves both as moderator and coolant. Heavy water (D_2O) is even more efficient than light water.
- **Concrete shield** which protects the operating personnel and environment from destruction in case of leakage of radiation.

Nuclear power is a major source of energy for electrical generation worldwide.

Hydrogen Bomb

This destructive device makes use of the nuclear fusion of the isotopes of hydrogen. It consists of a small plutonium fission bomb with a container of isotopes of hydrogen.

$$^1H_2 + {}^1H_3 \longrightarrow {}^2He_4 + {}^0n_1 + \text{Energy}$$

Uses of Radioactive Substances and Radiation

Radioactive substance and radiation have been used for the benefit of people also.

Medicine

Radionuclides are used to directly treat illnesses. For example radioactive iodine is used, which is taken up almost exclusively by the thyroid, to treat cancer or hyperthyroidism. Radioactive tracers and dyes are also used to accurately map a specific area or system, such as in a cardiac stress test, which may use a radioactive isotope like Technetium-99 to identify areas of the heart and surrounding arteries with diminished blood flow. Cobalt-60 is also used to treat cancer patients. In Positron emission tomography (PET), a computer imaging diagnostic technique, radioactivity of some substances is utilized.

Smoke Detectors

Some smoke detectors also use radioactive elements as part of their detection mechanism, usually americium-241. The ionizing radiation of the alpha particles is used to cause and then measure changes in the ionization of the air immediately around the detector. A change due to smoke in the air will cause the alarm to sound.

Radiography

Essentially high-powered versions of the types of X-ray machines used in medicine, industrial radiography cameras use X-rays or even gamma sources (such as Iridium-192, Cobalt-60, or Cesium-137) to examine hard to reach or hard to see places. This is frequently used to examine welds for defects or irregularities, or examining other materials to locate structural anomalies or internal components.

Food Safety

Food irradiation is the process of using radioactive sources to sterilize foodstuffs. The radiation works by killing bacteria and viruses, or eliminating their ability to reproduce by severely damaging their DNA or RNA.

Archaeology

One important contribution that nuclear science has made in this area is the ability to determine the age of ancient artifacts. There are several techniques for doing this, but the most common process for dating objects of up to about 50,000 years is called *radiocarbon dating.*

Tracer

Unstable nuclei have also been used as *radioactive tracers* in scientific research. *A tracer is a radioactive element whose pathway through a chemical reaction can be followed.* For example, scientists have used carbon-14 to study many aspects of photosynthesis. Likewise, phosphorus-32 atoms can be used to trace phosphorus-containing chemicals as they move from the soil into plants.

MULTIPLE CHOICE QUESTIONS

1. Which of the following are the constituents of matter?

   A.   Atoms   B.   Molecules

   C.   Solid

(a) A and B only   (b) A and C only

(c) B and C only   (d) A, B and C

2. What mass of hydrogen and oxygen will be produced on complete electrolysis of 18g of water?

(a) 2g hydrogen and 32g oxygen

(b) 2g hydrogen and 16g oxygen

(c) 4g hydrogen and 32g oxygen

(d) 4g hydrogen and 14g oxygen

3. Which of the following statements is /are correct?

According to Dalton's theory

   A.   An atom is the smallest particle of matter

   B.   An atom is the smallest particle of an element

   C.   An atom is the smallest indivisible particle of an element that can take part in a chemical change

   D.   An atom is the radioactive emission

(a) A, B and C   (b) B, C and D

(c) A, C and D   (d) A and D

4. Which one among the following statements about an atom is not correct? **[CDS]**

(a) Atoms always combine to form molecules

(b) Atoms are the basic units from which molecules and ions are formed

(c) Atoms are always neutral in nature

(d) Atoms aggregate in large numbers to form the matter that we can see, feel and touch

5. Which one among the following is correct regarding ^{20}Ne, $^{23}Na^+$, $^{19}F^-$ and $^{24}Mg^{2+}$? **[CDS]**

(a) They are isomers of each other

(b) They are isotopes of each other

(c) They are isoelectronic with each other

(d) All of the above

6. Which of the following pairs is/are correctly matched?

   1.   **Isotopes:** Atoms with same atomic number but different atomic mass

   2.   **Isobars:** Atoms with same number of neutrons but different atomic number

   3.   **Isotones:** Atoms with same mass number but different atomic number

Select the correct answer using the code given below:

[NDA]

   Code:

(a) 1, 2 and 3   (b) 1 only

(c) 1 and 2 only   (d) 2 only

7. The nucleus of a singly ionized carbon atom contains **[NDA]**

(a) 6 protons and 6 neutrons

(b) 5 protons and 6 neutrons

(c) 6 protons, 6 neutrons and 6 electrons

(d) 12 protons, 6 neutrons and 6 electrons

8. The following questions consist of two statements, one labelled as the Assertion (A) and the other as 'Reason (R), You are to examine these two statements carefully and select the answers to these items using the codes given below:

Assertion (A): Atomic weights of most of the elements are not whole numbers.

Reason (R): Atoms of most of the elements contain mixture of isotopes having different atomic weights. **[NDA]**

(a) Both A and R are individually true and R is the correct explanation of A

(b) Both A and R are individually true but R is NOT the correct explanation of A

(c) A is true but R is false

(d) A is false but R is true

9. An oxide of nitrogen has molecular weight 30. What is the number of electrons in one molecule of the compound? **[NDA]**

(a) 14   (b) 15

(c) 22   (d) 23

10. What is the weight of one atom of Hydrogen in grams? **[NDA]**

(a) 6.023×10^{-23} (b) 1.66×10^{-24}

(b) 6.62×10^{-24} (d) None of these

11. The atomic weights are expressed in terms of atomic mass unit. Which one of the following is used as a standard? **[NDA]**

(a) $^{1}H_{1}$ (b) $^{12}C_{6}$

(c) $^{16}O_{8}$ (d) $^{35}Cl_{17}$

12. What is the number of water molecules present in a tiny drop of water (volume 0.0018 ml) at room temperature? **[NDA]**

(a) 4.84×10^{17} (b) 4.184×10^{18}

(c) 6.023×10^{19} (d) 6.023×10^{23}

13. The number of neutrons in $^{27}Al_{7}$ is **[NDA]**

(a) 40   (b) 27

(c) 14   (d) 13

14. The nucleus of a singly ionized carbon atom contains **[NDA]**
(a) 6 protons and 6 neutrons
(b) 5 protons and 6 neutrons
(c) 6 protons, 6 neutrons and 6 electrons
(d) 12 protons, 6 neutrons and 6 electrons

15. An atom of carbon has 6 protons. Its mass number is 12. How many neutrons are present in an atom of carbon? **[NDA]**
(a) 12　　　　　　　(b) 6
(c) 10　　　　　　　(d) 14

16. What is the number of mole(s) of $H_2(g)$ required to saturate one mole benzene? **[NDA]**
(a) 1　　　　　　　(b) 2
(c) 3　　　　　　　(d) 4

17. How many moles of hydrogen atom are present in one mole of Aluminium hydroxide ? **[NDA]**
(a) one mole　　　　(b) Two moles
(c) Three moles　　　(d) Four moles

18. Protons and neutrons are bound in a nucleus by the **[NDA]**
(a) short range 'weak interaction'
(b) short range 'strong interaction'
(c) long range 'electromagnetic interaction'
(d) long range 'gravitational interaction'

19. Which one among the following most correctly determines the atomic number of an element? **[NDA]**
(a) Number of protons
(b) Number of protons and electrons
(c) Number of ions
(d) Number of nucleons

20. The number of protons in a negatively charged atom (anion) is **[NDA]**
(a) more than the atomic number of the element
(b) less than the atomic number of the element
(c) more than the number of elecrons in the atom
(d) less than the number of electrons in the atom

21. Which one among the following is correct regarding ^{20}Ne, $^{23}Na^+$, $^{19}F^-$ and $^{24}Mg^{2+}$? **[NDA]**
(a) They are isomers of each other
(b) They are isotopes of each other
(c) They are isoelectronic with each other
(d) All of the above

22. Which of the following pairs is/are correctly matched? **[NDA]**
1. **Isotopes:** Atoms with same atomic number but different atomic mass
2. **Isobars:** Atoms with same number of neutrons but different atomic number
3. **Isotones:** Atoms with same mass number but different atomic number
Select the correct answer using the code given below:
Code:
(a) 1, 2 and 3　　　　(b) 1 only
(c) 1 and 2 only　　　(d) 2 only

23. Which one among the following transitions of electron of hydrogen atom emits radiation of the shortest wavelength? **[NDA]**
(a) n = 2 to n = 1　　(b) n = 3 to n = 2
(c) n = 4 to n = 3　　(d) n = 5 to n = 4

24. Which formula gives the maximum number of electrons in a shell?
(a) n^2　　　　　　(b) $2n^2$
(c) $3n^2$　　　　　　(d) $4n^2$

25. In which one of the following is the valence electronic configuration, ns^2np^3 found ? **[NDA]**
(a) Carbon　　　　　(b) Oxygen
(c) Nitrogen　　　　　(d) Argon

26. An α-particle consists of which of the following? **[CDS]**
(a) 2 protons and 2 neutrons
(b) 1 proton and 1 electron
(c) 2 protons and 4 neutrons
(d) 1 proton and 1 neutron

27. Which one of the following is heavy water used in nuclear reactor? **[CDS]**
(a) Water having molecular weight 18 u
(b) Water having molecular weight 20 u
(c) Water at 4°C but having molecular weight 19 u
(d) Water below the ice in a frozen sea

28. Which one of the following is not needed in a nuclear fission reactor? **[CDS]**
(a) Moderator　　　　(b) Coolant
(c) Accelerator　　　　(d) Control device

29. Heavy water implies **[CDS]**
(a) water which is used in heavy industries such as thermal power plants
(b) water which contains SO_4^{2-} and Cl^- of calcium and magnesium
(c) deuterated water
(d) water which has maximum density

30. Age of fossil may be found out by determining the ratio of two isotopes of carbon. The isotopes are **[CDS]**
(a) C-12 and C-13　　(b) C-13 and C-14
(c) C-12 and C-14　　(d) C-12 and carbon black

31. Which one of the following reactions is the main cause of the energy radiation from the Sun? **[CDS]**
(a) Fusion reaction　　(b) Fission reaction
(c) Chemical reaction　(d) Diffusion reaction

32. In fission of ^{235}U atom the energy released is 200 MeV. In one day fission of 1 kg ^{235}U will give power (in MW) approximately.
(a) 550　　　　　　(b) 650
(c) 950　　　　　　(d) 1250

33. In the phase diagram of water, the solid-liquid boundary has a negative slope. The reason for this unusual behaviour can be traced to decrease in
(a) density of the system on melting
(b) volume of the system on melting
(c) entropy of the system on melting
(d) enthalpy of the system on melting

34. In the gamma decay of a nucleus   [CDS 2016-II]
   (a) the mass number of the nucleus changes whereas its atomic number does not change
   (b) the mass number of the nucleus does not change whereas its atomic number changes
   (c) both the mass number and the atomic number of the nucleus change
   (d) neither the mass number nor the atomic number of the nucleus changes

35. Consider the following statements :   [CDS 2017-II]
   1. The chain reaction process is used in nuclear bombs to release a vast amount of energy, but in nuclear reactors, there is no chain reaction.
   2. In a nuclear reactor, the reaction is controlled while in nuclear bombs, the reaction is uncontrolled.
   3. In a nuclear reactor, all operating reactors are 'critical', while there is no question of 'criticality' in case of a nuclear bomb.
   4. Nuclear reactors do not use moderators, while nuclear bombs use them.
   Which of the above statements about operational principles of a nuclear reactor and a nuclear bomb is/are correct?
   (a) 1 and 3   (b) 2 and 3
   (c) 4 only   (d) 1 and 4

36. Which of the following radioactive substances enters/enter the human body through food chain and causes/cause many physiological disorders?
                                [CDS 2017-II]
   (a) Strontium-90   (b) Iodine-131
   (c) Cesium-137   (d) All of the above

37. Which one of the following elements will be an isobar of calcium if the atomic number of calcium is 20 and its mass number is 40?   [CDS 2018-I]
   (a) Element with 20 protons and 18 neutrons
   (b) Element with 18 protons and 19 neutrons
   (c) Element with 20 protons and 19 neutrons
   (d) Element with 18 protons and 22 neutrons

38. Consider the following chemical reaction: [CDS 2018-I]
   In the balanced chemical equation of the above, which of the following will be the values of the coefficients a, b, c and d respectively?
   (a) 3, 2, 3, 1   (b) 1, 3, 2, 3
   (c) 2, 3, 3, 1   (d) 3, 3, 2, 1

39. Rutherford's alpha-particle scattering experiment was responsible for the discovery of   [NDA 2017-I]
   (a) Electron   (b) Proton
   (c) Nucleus   (d) Helium

40. The species that has the same number of electrons as $^{35}_{17}Cl$ is   [NDA 2017-II]
   (a) $^{35}_{16}S$ (b) $^{34}_{16}S^+$
   (c) $^{40}_{18}Ar^+$ (d) $^{35}_{16}S^{2-}$

41. The proposition 'equal volumes of different gases contain equal numbers of molecules at the same temperature and pressure' is known as   [NDA 2017-II]
   (a) Avogadro's hypothesis
   (b) Gay-Lussac's hypothesis
   (c) Planck's hypothesis
   (d) Kirchhoff's theory

42. A sample of oxygen contains two isotopes of oxygen with masses 16 u and 18 u respectively. The proportion of these isotopes in the sample is 3 : 1. What will be the average atomic mass of oxygen in this sample?   [NDA 2018-II]
   (a) 17.5 u   (b) 17 u
   (c) 16 u   (d) 16.5 u

43. What is the formula mass of anhydrous sodium carbonate? (Given that the atomic masses of sodium, carbon and oxygen are 23 u, 12 u and 16 u respectively)   [NDA 2018-II]
   (a) 286 u   (b) 106 u
   (c) 83 u   (d) 53 u

44. Which one of the following statements about the law of conservation of mass is correct?   [NDA 2018-II]
   (a) A given compound always contains exactly same proportion of elements.
   (b) When gases combine in a reaction, they do so in a simple ratio by volume, provided all gases are at room temperature.
   (c) Matter can neither be created nor destroyed.
   (d) Equal volumes of all gases at same temperature and pressure contain equal number of molecules.

ANSWER KEY																			
1.	(a)	**2.**	(b)	**3.**	(a)	**4.**	(d)	**5.**	(c)	**6.**	(b)	**7.**	(a)	**8.**	(a)	**9.**	(c)	**10.**	(b)
11.	(b)	**12.**	(c)	**13.**	(c)	**14.**	(a)	**15.**	(b)	**16.**	(c)	**17.**	(c)	**18.**	(b)	**19.**	(a)	**20.**	(d)
21.	(c)	**22.**	(b)	**23.**	(a)	**24.**	(b)	**25.**	(c)	**26.**	(a)	**27.**	(b)	**28.**	(c)	**29.**	(c)	**30.**	(c)
31.	(a)	**32.**	(c)	**33.**	(b)	**34.**	(d)	**35.**	(b)	**36.**	(d)	**37.**	(d)	**38.**	(b)	**39.**	(c)	**40.**	(c)
41.	(a)	**42.**	(d)	**43.**	(c)	**44.**	(c)												

ELEMENTS CLASSIFICATION & CHEMICAL BONDING

Chapter 3

CLASSIFICATION OF ELEMENTS

Four major attempts made for classification of the elements are follows:
- Dobereiner's Triads
- Newlands' Law of Octaves
- Mendeleev's Periodic Law & Periodic Tables
- Modern Periodic Table

Dobereiner's Triads

In 1829, J.W. Dobereiner, a German chemist made groups of three elements each and called them triads.
- All three elements of a triad were similar in their physical and chemical properties. He proposed a law known as *Dobereiner's law of triads*.
- According to this law, when elements are arranged in order of increasing atomic mass, the atomic mass of the middle element was nearly equal to the arithmetic mean of the other two and its properties were intermediate between those of the other two.

Newlands' Law of Octaves

John Alexander Reina Newlands in 1863–64 noted that every eighth element showed similar physical and chemical properties, when the elements are placed in the increasing order of their atomic masses. **This was called the Newlands law of octaves.**

The law states that when elements are placed in the increasing order of atomic masses, the properties of the eighth elements are repeated.

Mendeleev's Periodic Law and Periodic Table

On arranging the elements in the increasing order of atomic masses, it was observed that the elements with similar properties repeat periodically.

In 1869, Mendeleev stated his observation in the form of the following statement which is known as the **Mendeleev's Periodic Law**

The chemical and physical properties of elements are periodic function of their atomic masses.

Mendeleev arranged the elements in the form of a table which is known as the **Mendeleev's Periodic Table** as below:
- Elements were arranged in increasing order of their atomic masses in horizontal rows till element whose properties were similar to those of the first element was came across.

Salient Features of Mendeleev's Periodic Table

The following are the main features of this periodic table:
- The elements are arranged in rows and columns in the periodic table.
- The horizontal rows are called **periods**. There are six periods in the periodic table. These are numbered from 1 to 6 (Arabic numerals). Each one of the 4th, 5th and 6th periods have two series of elements.
- All the elements present in a particular group are chemically similar in nature. They also show a regular gradation in their physical and chemical properties from top to bottom.

Modern Periodic Law and Periodic Table

The Modern Periodic Law states that the chemical and physical properties of elements are periodic functions of their atomic numbers, i.e. if elements are arranged in the order of their increasing atomic number, the elements with similar properties are repeated after certain regular intervals.

The periodic table based on the modern periodic law is called the Modern Periodic Table. Presently, the accepted modern periodic table is the *Long Form of Periodic Table:*

Long Form of Periodic Table

s-Block Elements; d-Block Elements; p-Block Elements; f-Block Elements

Period	1 / IA	2 / IIA	3 / IIIB	4 / IVB	5 / VB	6 / VIB	7 / VIIB	8 / VIII	9 / VIII	10 / VIII	11 / IB	12 / IIB	13 / IIIA	14 / IVA	15 / VA	16 / VIA	17 / VIIA	18 / VIIIA
1	1 H																	2 He
2	3 Li	4 Be											5 B	6 C	7 N	8 O	9 F	10 Ne
3	11 Na	12 Mg											13 Al	14 Si	15 P	16 S	17 Cl	18 Ar
4	19 K	20 Ca	21 Sc	22 Ti	23 V	24 Cr	25 Mn	26 Fe	27 Co	28 Ni	29 Cu	30 Zn	31 Ga	32 Ge	33 As	34 Se	35 Br	36 Kr
5	37 Rb	38 Sr	39 Y	40 Zr	41 Nb	42 Mo	43 Tc	44 Ru	45 Rh	46 Pd	47 Ag	48 Cd	49 In	50 Sn	51 Sb	52 Te	53 I	54 Xe
6	55 Cs	56 Ba	57 La	72 Hf	73 Ta	74 W	75 Re	76 Os	77 Ir	78 Pt	79 Au	80 Hg	81 Tl	82 Pb	83 Bi	84 Po	85 At	86 Rn
7	87 Fr	88 Ra	89 Ac	104 Rf	105 Db	106 Sg	107 Bh	108 Hs	109 Mt	110 Ds	111 Rg	112 Uub	113	114 Uuq	115	116 Uuh	117	118 ?

Lanthanides (f-Block Elements)

58 Ce	59 Pr	60 Nd	61 Pm	62 Sm	63 Eu	64 Gd	65 Tb	66 Dy	67 Ho	68 Er	69 Tm	70 Yb	71 Lu

Actinides (f-Block Elements)

90 Th	91 Pa	92 U	93 Np	94 Pu	95 Am	96 Cm	97 Bk	98 Cf	99 Es	100 Fm	101 Md	102 No	103 Lr

Element data (atomic number, symbol, name, atomic mass, electron configuration):

No.	Symbol	Name	Atomic Mass	Configuration
1	H	Hydrogen	1.008	$1s^1$
2	He	Helium	4.003	$1s^2$
3	Li	Lithium	6.941	$2s^1$
4	Be	Beryllium	9.0121	$2s^2$
5	B	Boron	10.811	$2s^2 2p^1$
6	C	Carbon	12.011	$2s^2 2p^2$
7	N	Nitrogen	14.007	$2s^2 2p^3$
8	O	Oxygen	15.999	$2s^2 2p^4$
9	F	Fluorine	18.998	$2s^2 2p^5$
10	Ne	Neon	20.180	$2s^2 2p^6$
11	Na	Sodium	22.990	$3s^1$
12	Mg	Magnesium	24.305	$3s^2$
13	Al	Aluminium	26.982	$3s^2 3p^1$
14	Si	Silicon	28.086	$3s^2 3p^2$
15	P	Phosphorus	30.974	$3s^2 3p^3$
16	S	Sulphur	32.066	$3s^2 3p^4$
17	Cl	Chlorine	35.453	$3s^2 3p^5$
18	Ar	Argon	39.948	$3s^2 3p^6$
19	K	Potassium	39.098	$4s^1$
20	Ca	Calcium	40.078	$4s^2$
21	Sc	Scandium	44.956	$3d^1 4s^2$
22	Ti	Titanium	47.867	$3d^2 4s^2$
23	V	Vanadium	50.942	$3d^3 4s^2$
24	Cr	Chromium	51.996	$3d^5 4s^1$
25	Mn	Manganese	54.938	$3d^5 4s^2$
26	Fe	Iron	55.845	$3d^6 4s^2$
27	Co	Cobalt	58.933	$3d^7 4s^2$
28	Ni	Nickel	58.693	$3d^8 4s^2$
29	Cu	Copper	63.546	$3d^{10} 4s^1$
30	Zn	Zinc	65.39	$3d^{10} 4s^2$
31	Ga	Gallium	69.723	$3d^{10} 4s^2 4p^1$
32	Ge	Germanium	72.61	
33	As	Arsenic	74.922	
34	Se	Selenium	78.96	
35	Br	Bromine	79.904	
36	Kr	Krypton	83.30	
37	Rb	Rubidium	85.468	$5s^1$
38	Sr	Strontium	87.62	$5s^2$
39	Y	Yttrium	88.906	$4d^1 5s^2$
40	Zr	Zirconium	91.224	$4d^2 5s^2$
41	Nb	Niobium	92.906	$4d^4 5s^1$
42	Mo	Molybdenum	95.94	$4d^5 5s^1$
43	Tc	Technetium	(98)	$4d^5 5s^2$
44	Ru	Ruthenium	101.07	$4d^7 5s^1$
45	Rh	Rhodium	102.906	$4d^8 5s^1$
46	Pd	Palladium	106.42	$4d^{10}$
47	Ag	Silver	107.868	$4d^{10} 5s^1$
48	Cd	Cadmium	112.411	$4d^{10} 5s^2$
49	In	Indium	114.818	
50	Sn	Tin	118.710	
51	Sb	Antimony	121.760	
52	Te	Tellurium	127.60	
53	I	Iodine	126.904	
54	Xe	Xenon	131.29	
55	Cs	Cesium	132.905	$6s^1$
56	Ba	Barium	137.327	$6s^2$
57	La	Lanthanum	138.906	$5d^1 6s^2$
72	Hf	Hafnium	178.49	$4f^{14} 5d^2 6s^2$
73	Ta	Tantalum	180.948	$4f^{14} 5d^3 6s^2$
74	W	Tungsten	183.84	$4f^{14} 5d^4 6s^2$
75	Re	Rhenium	186.207	$4f^{14} 5d^5 6s^2$
76	Os	Osmium	190.23	$4f^{14} 5d^6 6s^2$
77	Ir	Iridium	192.217	$4f^{14} 5d^7 6s^2$
78	Pt	Platinum	195.078	$4f^{14} 5d^9 6s^1$
79	Au	Gold	196.967	$4f^{14} 5d^{10} 6s^1$
80	Hg	Mercury	200.59	$4f^{14} 5d^{10} 6s^2$
81	Tl	Thallium	204.383	
82	Pb	Lead	207.2	
83	Bi	Bismuth	208.980	
84	Po	Polonium	(209)	
85	At	Astatine	(210)	
86	Rn	Radon	(222)	
87	Fr	Francium	(223)	$7s^1$
88	Ra	Radium	(226)	$7s^2$
89	Ac	Actinium	(227)	$6d^1 7s^2$
104	Rf	Rutherfordium	(261)	$5f^{14} 6d^2 7s^2$
105	Db	Dubnium	(262)	$5f^{14} 6d^3 7s^2$
106	Sg	Seaborgium	(263)	$5f^{14} 6d^4 7s^2$
107	Bh	Bohrium	(262)	$5f^{14} 6d^5 7s^2$
108	Hs	Hassium	(265)	$5f^{14} 6d^6 7s^2$
109	Mt	Meitnerium	(266)	$5f^{14} 6d^7 7s^2$
110	Ds	Darmstadtium	(269)	$5f^{14} 6d^8 7s^2$
111	Rg	Rontgenium	(272)	$5f^{14} 6d^9 7s^2$
112	Uub	Ununbium	(277)	$5f^{14} 6d^{10} 7s^2$
114	Uuq	Ununquadium		$5f^{14} 6d^{10} 7s^2 7p^2$
116	Uuh	Ununhexium		$5f^{14} 6d^{10} 7s^2 7p^4$
118	?			
58	Ce	Cerium	140.116	$4f^1 5d^1 6s^2$
59	Pr	Praseodymium	140.908	$4f^3 6s^2$
60	Nd	Neodymium	114.908	$4f^4 6s^2$
61	Pm	Promethium	(145)	$4f^5 6s^2$
62	Sm	Samarium	150.36	$4f^6 6s^2$
63	Eu	Europium	151.964	$4f^7 6s^2$
64	Gd	Gadolinium	157.25	$4f^7 5d^1 6s^2$
65	Tb	Terbium	158.925	$4f^9 6s^2$
66	Dy	Dysprosium	162.50	$4f^{10} 6s^2$
67	Ho	Holmium	164.930	$4f^{11} 6s^2$
68	Er	Erbium	167.26	$4f^{12} 6s^2$
69	Tm	Thulium	168.934	$4f^{13} 6s^2$
70	Yb	Ytterbium	173.04	$4f^{14} 6s^2$
71	Lu	Lutetium	174.967	$4f^{14} 5d^1 6s^2$
90	Th	Thorium	232.038	$6d^2 7s^2$
91	Pa	Protactinium	231.036	$5f^2 6d^1 7s^2$
92	U	Uranium	238.029	$5f^3 6d^1 7s^2$
93	Np	Neptunium	(237)	$5f^4 6d^1 7s^2$
94	Pu	Plutonium	(244)	$5f^6 7s^2$
95	Am	Americium	(243)	$5f^7 7s^2$
96	Cm	Curium	(247)	$5f^7 6d^1 7s^2$
97	Bk	Berkelium	(247)	$5f^9 7s^2$
98	Cf	Californium	(251)	$5f^{10} 7s^2$
99	Es	Einsteinium	(252)	$5f^{11} 7s^2$
100	Fm	Fermium	(257)	$5f^{12} 7s^2$
101	Md	Mendelevium	(258)	$5f^{13} 7s^2$
102	No	Nobelium	(259)	$5f^{14} 7s^2$
103	Lr	Lawrencium	(262)	$5f^{14} 6d^1 7s^2$

Modern Periodic table is divided into seven horizontal rows of elements. Each row of elements is called "PERIOD". It has 18 vertical columns called groups. These groups are numbered 1 to 18 from the left, using Arabic numerals.

The electron arrangements of atoms are linked to position in the periodic table.

- Elements in the same group have the same number of electrons in their outer shell.
- For the main group elements, the number of group is the number of electrons in the outer shell.
- The number of period shows the shells of electrons the atoms have.

CLASSIFICATION OF THE ELEMENTS

The elements in the periodic table may be broadly classified as follows:

Main Group Elements

The elements present in groups 1 and 2 on left side and groups 13 to 17 on the right side of the periodic table are called **representative or main group** elements. Their outermost shells have less than eight electrons and hence are incomplete.

Noble Gases

Group 18 on the extreme right side of the periodic table contains noble gases. Their outermost shells contain 8 electrons except He which contains only 2 electrons.

Their main properties are:

- Possesses 8 electrons in their outermost shell (except He which has 2 electrons).

Transition Elements

The middle block of periodic table (groups 3 to 12) contains transition elements. Their two outermost shells are incomplete. Since these elements represent a transition (change) from the most electropositive element to the most electronegative element, they are named as transition elements.

Their important properties are as follows:

- All these elements are metals having high melting and boiling points.
- These elements are good conductors of heat and electricity.

Inner Transition Elements

These elements, also called *rare-earth elements*, are shown separately below the main periodic table. These are two series of 14 elements each. The first series called **lanthanides** consists of elements having atomic number 58 to 71 (Ce to Lu). The second series of 14 rare-earth elements ia called actinoids.

In all rare-earths (lanthanoids and actinoids), three outermost shells are incomplete. They are therefore called **inner transition elements**.

> It may be noted that the element *lanthanum* (atomic no. 57) is not a lanthanoid and the element *actinium* (atomic no. 89) is not an actinoid.

Metals

Metals are present in the left hand portion of the periodic table. The strong metallic elements; alkali metals (Li, Na, K, Rb, Cs, Fr) and alkaline earth metals (Be, Mg, Ca, Sr, Ba, Ra) occupy groups 1 and 2 respectively.

Non-metals

Non-metals occupy the right hand portion of the periodic table. Strong non-metallic elements i.e. halogens (F, Cl, Br, I, At) and chalcogens (O, S, Se, Te, Po) occupy group 17 and 16 respectively.

Metalloids

Metalloids are located along the staircase separating the metals from the nonmetals on the periodic table. Boron, silicon, germanium, arsenic, antimony, and tellurium all have metal and nonmetal properties.

Trends in a Periodic Table (Periodic Properties)

Definite trends of certain properties of the elements are observed in the periodic table. These properties are called periodic properties. The following table depicts and describes the important periodic property and their variations:

Periodic property	Definition	Variation	
		Along a period	**Down a group**
Atomic Radius	Half of the distance between the centers of two atoms of that element that are just touching each other	Decreases	Increases
Ionization Energy	Energy required to completely remove an electron from a gaseous atom or ion.	Increases	Decreases
Electron Affinity	Energy change that occurs when an electron is added to a gaseous atom	Increases (*except* for Noble Gas whose Electron Affinity is near Zero)	
Electronegativity	Measure of the attraction of an atom for the electrons in a chemical bond.	Increase	Decreases
Metallic Character	Used to define the chemical properties that metallic elements present.	Decreases	Increases

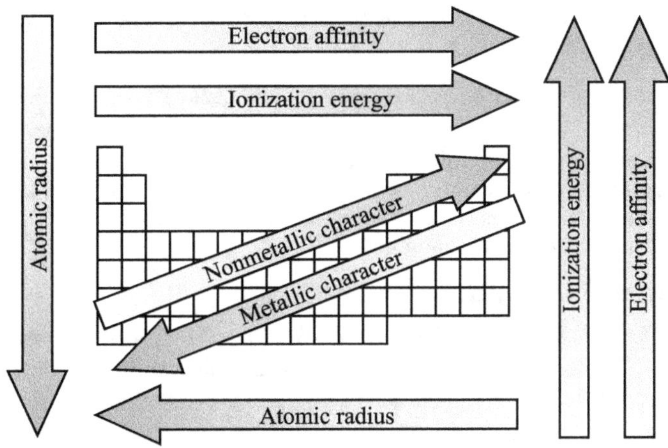

CHEMICAL BONDING AND REACTIONS

Chemical Bond may be defined as a force that acts between two or more atoms to hold them together as a stable molecule.
- Bonds can be formed between atoms of the same element, or between atoms of different elements.

LEWIS DOT STRUCTURE

A Lewis dot symbol consists of the symbol of an element and one dot for each valence electron in an atom of the element. The Lewis dot structure of few elements are given below:

·Li   ·Be   ·B   ·C.   :N·   :O·   :F·   :Ne:

OCTET RULE

Noble gases namely helium, neon, argon, krypton, xenon and radon do not react with other elements to form compounds i.e. they are non-reactive.

Electronic configuration of Noble gases

Name	Symbol	Atomic No.	Electronic Configuration	No. of electrons in the outermost cell
Helium	He	2	2	2
Neon	Ne	10	2,8	8
Argon	Ar	18	2,8,8	8
Krypton	Kr	36	2,8,8,8	8
Xenon	Xe	54	2,8,18,18,8,8	8
Radon	Rn	86	2,8,18,32,18,8	8

It has been concluded that
- Atoms having 8 electrons in their outermost shell are very stable and they don't form compounds.
- Other atoms such as hydrogen, sodium, chlorine, etc. which do not have 8 electrons in their outermost shell undergo chemical reactions. They can stabilize by combining with each other and attain the above configurations of noble gases, i.e. 8 electrons (or 2 electrons in case of helium) in their outermost shells.
- Thus, atoms tend to attain a configuration in which they have 8 electrons in their outermost shells. This is the basic cause of chemical bonding.

This attainment of eight electrons for stable structure is called the octet rule. The octet rule explains the chemical bonding in many compounds.

TYPES OF BONDING

Ionic Bonding

The chemical bond formed by transfer of electron from a metal to a non-metal is known as ionic or electrovalent bond.

Example of Ionic bond formation

$$Na^· \; :\ddot{C}l: \longrightarrow Na^+ \; :\ddot{C}l:^-$$

During formation of Sodium Chloride (NaCl), the sodium atom donates its single valence electron to the chlorine atom. This led to creation of sodium cation (Na^+) and chlorine (Cl^-).

$$:\ddot{C}l· \; Mg \; :\ddot{C}l: \longrightarrow :\ddot{C}l:^- \; Mg^{2+} \; :\ddot{C}l:^-$$

During formation of Magnesium Chloride ($MgCl_2$), magnesium atom donates both of its valence electrons to chlorine atoms. Each chlorine atom can only accept 1 electron before it can achieve its noble gas configuration for these 2 atoms of chlorine are required to accept the 2 electrons donated by the magnesium.

Properties of Ionic Compounds

Ionic compounds contain ions (cations and anions) which are held together by the strong electrostatic forces of attraction. They show the following general characteristic properties:

High melting and boiling points: Ionic bonds are very strong. A lot of energy is needed to break them. So ionic compounds have high melting and boiling points.

Conductive when liquid: Ionic compounds can only conduct electricity if their ions are free to move. Ionic compounds do not conduct electricity when they are solid. But these compounds conduct electricity when dissolved in water or melted.

> Ionic compounds have high melting and boiling points. The melting point of sodium chloride is 1074 K (801°C) and its boiling point is 1686K (1413°C). The melting and boiling points of ionic compounds are high because of the strong electrostatic forces of attraction present between the ions.

Covalent Bond

A covalent bond is a chemical link between two atoms or ions where the electron pairs are shared between them. A covalent bond may also be termed as molecular bond.

Example of covalent bond formation

$$:\ddot{C}l· \; ·\ddot{P}· \; ·\ddot{C}l: \longrightarrow :\ddot{C}l:\ddot{P}:\ddot{C}l: \\ :\ddot{C}l· \qquad\qquad :\ddot{C}l:$$

During formation of Phosphorus trichloride (PCl_3), single phosphorous atom shares its 3 unpaired electrons with 3 chlorine atoms. These led to possession of 8 valence electrons for all the four molecules (1 Phosphorus and 3 Chlorine atoms) and complete the octet.

$$2:\ddot{O}· \longrightarrow \;^x_x\ddot{O}^x_x\ddot{O}\,^·_·$$

During formation of oxygen molecule (O_2), oxygen atom needs 2 additional electrons to complete its valence energy shell. For this 2 pairs of electrons must be shared between the 2 oxygen atoms to complete the octet.

Properties of covalent molecular compounds

- **Low melting points and boiling points:** A relatively small amount of energy is required to overcome the weak attractions between covalent molecules, so these compounds melt and boil at much lower temperatures than metallic and ionic compounds do.
- **Low enthalpies of fusion and vapourisation:** These properties are usually smaller than they are for ionic compounds.
- **Soft or brittle solid forms:** The weak intermolecular forces make the solid form of covalent molecular compounds easy to distort or break.
- **Poor electrical and thermal conductivity:** Covalent molecular compounds do not conduct electricity well.

Because of the weak forces of attraction present between discrete molecules, called *intermolecular forces,* the covalent compounds exist as a gas or a liquid or a solid. For example O_2, N_2, CO_2 are gases; water and CCl_4 are liquids and iodine is a solid.

The melting points and boiling points of covalent compounds are lower than those of ionic compounds. For example, melting point of naphthalene which is a covalent compound is 353 K (80°C). Similarly, the boiling point of carbon tetrachloride which is another covalent liquid compound is 350 K (77°C).

Types of covalent bonds

- **Nonpolar covalent bond:** A bond between two nonmetal atoms that have the same electronegativity and therefore have equal sharing of the bonding electron pair.
- **Polar covalent bond:** A bond between two nonmetal atoms that have different electronegativities and therefore have unequal sharing of the bonding electron pair.

Polar Molecule: A molecule in which the bond dipoles present do not cancel each other out and thus results in a *molecular dipole.*

Co-ordinate Covalent Bond

Boron reacts with the halogens to form a class of compounds having the general formula BX_3, where X is a halogen atom. **These are examples of compounds having incomplete octets.**

This type of bond is called a coordinate covalent bond (also referred to as dative bond), defined as a covalent bond in which one of the atoms donates both electrons.

Exceptions to Octet Rule

The octet rule applies mainly to the second-period elements. However there are certain exceptions to the octet rules. That is there are certain compounds in which the octet rule is not satisfied. Exceptions to the octet rule fall into three categories:

An odd number of electrons

There are some molecules containing an *odd* number of electrons. For example, nitric oxide (NO) and nitrogen dioxide (NO_2). As we need an even number of electrons for complete pairing (to reach eight), the octet rule clearly cannot be satisfied for all the atoms in any of these molecules. Odd-electron molecules are sometimes called *radicals*.

More than eight electrons around the central atom

Atoms of the second-period elements cannot have more than eight valence electrons around the central atom, but atoms of elements in and beyond the third period of the periodic table form some compounds in which more than eight electrons surround the central atom. That is the central atom has expanded octet. One example of such a compound is SF_6.

Metallic Bonding

The structures formed by metals are held together by metallic bond.
- Metals form giant structures in which electrons in the outer shells of the metal atoms are free to move.
- The metallic bond is the force of attraction between these free electrons and positive metal ions.

Metals are good conductors of electricity and heat, because the free electrons carry a charge or heat energy through the metal. The free electrons allow metal atoms to slide over each other, so metals are malleable and ductile

Intermolecular Forces Between Molecules

A **hydrogen bond** is the attractive force between the hydrogen attached to an electronegative atom of one molecule and an electronegative atom of a different molecule.

Van der Waals forces are forces of attraction which exist between all atoms and molecules. These forces result from weak electrostatic attraction between temporary dipoles and induced dipoles caused by movement of electrons in atoms and molecules.

CHEMICAL REACTIONS AND CHEMICAL EQUATIONS

Chemical changes result from chemical reactions taking place between different substances. It is a process in which a substance (or substances) is changed into one or more new substances.

In chemical reaction, the substance which undergoes a chemical change is called the ***reactant*** and the substance which is formed as a result of a chemical change is called the ***product***.

Balancing Chemical Equations

According to Law *of conservation of mass,* the mass and the number of atoms present in the reactant(s) should be equal to the mass and number of atoms present in product(s).

The Equation can be balanced by placing the appropriate coefficient (2 in this case) in front of H_2 and H_2O:

$$2H_2 + O_2 \longrightarrow 2H_2O$$

This *balanced chemical equation* shows that *"two hydrogen molecules can combine or react with one oxygen molecule to form two water molecules"*.

STP in chemistry is the abbreviation for standard temperature and pressure. STP is most commonly used when performing calculation on gases, such as gas density. The standard temperature is 273K (0° celsius or 32° Fahrenheit) and the standard pressure is 1 atmospheric (atm.) pressure.

Types of Chemical Reactions

The types of Chemical Reaction are discussed below with examples.

• Combination reactions

In combination reactions, as the name indicates, *two or more substances (elements or compounds) simply combine to form a new substance.* For example, when a substance burns it combines with oxygen present in the air.

$$\text{e.g.,} \quad \underset{\text{(coal)}}{C} \quad + \quad O_2 \quad \longrightarrow \quad CO_2$$

• Decomposition reactions

A decomposition reaction is the one in which a compound decomposes into two or more than two substances (elements or compounds). For example, lime stone when heated gives lime and carbon dioxide.

$$\text{e.g.,} \quad CaCO_3 \xrightarrow{\text{Heat}} CaO + CO_2$$

• Displacement reaction

The displacement reaction is one in which one element displaces another element from its compounds.

$$\text{e.g.,} \quad Pb + CuCl_2 \longrightarrow PbCl_2 + Cu$$

• Double displacement reaction

The reactions in which mutual exchange of radicals takes place are known as double decomposition reactions. As a result of double decomposition reactions two new substances are formed.

$$\text{e.g.,} \quad AgNO_3 + NaCl \longrightarrow AgCl + NaNO_3$$

Oxidation and reduction reaction

When a substance gains oxygen during a reaction, it is said to be oxidized and when a substance loses oxygen during a reaction, it is said to be reduced.

Thus in this reaction, during the reaction process, one reactant gets oxidized while the other gets reduced. Such reactions are called ***oxidation reduction reaction or Redox Reactions.***
There is no oxidation without reduction and there is no reduction without oxidation, i.e. oxidation and reduction take place simultaneously.

As per modern concept, oxidation and reduction is explained in terms of loss and gain of electrons not in terms of gain and loss of oxygen and hydrogen.

- *Oxidation is loss of electrons.*
- *Reduction is gain of electrons.*

OXIDATION NUMBER

Oxidation Number shows the total number of electrons which have been removed from an element (a positive oxidation state) or added to an element (a negative oxidation state) to get to its present state.

By knowing how the oxidation number of an element changes during a reaction, we can tell whether it is being oxidised or reduced.

- *Increase in oxidation number is oxidation*
- *Decrease in oxidation number is reduction.*

Rules to Calculate Oxidation Numbers

- The oxidation number for an atom of any free (uncombined) element is ZERO.
  Examples: Na, Mg have zero oxidation number.

- The oxidation number of an element in self-combination is always ZERO.
  Examples: H_2, Cl_2, P_4 have zero oxidation number.
- In most hydrogen containing compounds, oxidation number of hydrogen is $+1$. (Exception is when H combines with alkali metals or alkaline earth to form hydrides of metals such as: NaH, LiH, CaH_2. Then, the oxidation number of H is -1).
- In compounds involving the alkali metals, the elements are assigned oxidation number of $+1$.
- In combinations of non-metals **not** involving hydrogen and oxygen, the nonmetal that is more electronegative is considered negative.

REDOX REACTIONS IN DAY-TO-DAY LIFE

Redox reactions are very important in our lives. Two very common phenomena- corrosion and rancidity are results of redox reactions. These are discussed below:

Corrosion:

For most of us, Corrosion is the degradation of metals and is often called rust. Chemically we can define it as an irreversible interfacial reaction of a material (metal, ceramic, polymer) with its environment which results in consumption of the material.

Most metals corrode on contact with water (and moisture in the air), acids, bases, salts, oils, aggressive metal polishes, and other solid and liquid chemicals. Metals will also corrode when exposed to gaseous materials like acid vapors, formaldehyde gas, ammonia gas, and sulphur containing gases. *Corrosion specifically refers to any process involving the deterioration or degradation of metal components.* The best known case is that of the rusting of steel. Corrosion processes are usually electrochemical in nature.

Factors Influencing Corrosion

Following factors influence the corrosion. These are the

- Reactivity of metals
- Presence of moisture and atmospheric gases like CO_2, SO_2 etc.
- Presence of impurities.
- Strains in the metal
- Presence of electrolyte.

Methods to Prevent Corrosions

- To minimize corrosion, protective coatings are applied to prevent the direct contact of moisture and oxygen with the metal. This process is called *galvanising*. It involves coating of Zn metal on iron surface.

- Electrochemical principles can also be applied to inhibit corrosion. This is known as *cathodic protection.*

- Another way to protect iron and other metals from oxidation is to coat them with a corrosion-resistant metal, such as chromium, platinum or gold. This process of coating one metal with another by electrolysis is called *electroplating.*

Rancidity

What we perceive is an unpleasant change in the flavor and odour of a food, called rancidity. Unsaturated fats are more susceptible to oxidation than are saturated fats. Factors which accelerate fat oxidation include trace metals (iron, zinc, etc.), salt, light, water, bacteria, and molds. Fat oxidation can be retarded by use of antioxidants (Antioxidants are compounds that inhibit chemical reactions with oxygen such as BHT, BHA, vitamin E, and vitamin C), by use of spices such as sage and rosemary, and by use of light and/or air tight wrapping.

ENERGY CHANGES IN CHEMICAL REACTIONS

When chemical reactions take place they are often accompanied by **heat changes**.

* *Exothermic reactions*
* *Endothermic reactions*

Exothermic Reactions

Reactions in which product formation is accompanied by release of heat are called exothermic chemical reactions.

Examples

Calcium oxide reacts vigorously with water to produce slaked lime (calcium hydroxide) releasing a large amount of heat.

$$CaO + H_2O \longrightarrow Ca(OH)_2 + Heat$$

Fuels such as methane burns in presence of Oxygen produce Carbon dioxide and water with release of heat.

$$CH_4 + 2O_2 \longrightarrow CO_2 + 2H_2O + Heat$$

Endothermic Reactions

Reactions in which product formation is accompanied by absorption of heat are called endothermic chemical reactions.

Examples

Ammonium Chloride when mixed with little water produces a cooling effect

$$NH_4Cl + H_2O \longrightarrow NH_4OH + HCl - heat$$

Ammonium chloride when mixed in barium hydroxide solution produces ammonia gas and a cooling effect due to heat absorption.

$$2NH_4Cl + Ba(OH)_2 \longrightarrow BaCl_2 + 2H_2O + 2NH_3 - heat$$

MULTIPLE CHOICE QUESTIONS

1. The early attempt to classify elements as metals and non-metals was made by
   (a) Mendeleev   (b) Lother Meyer
   (c) Lavoisier   (d) Henry Moseley
2. The long form of periodic table consists of
   (a) seven periods and eight groups
   (b) seven periods and eighteen groups
   (c) eight periods and eighteen groups
   (d) eighteen periods and eight groups
3. Which one of the following is most electropositive element?
   (a) Sodium   (b) Calcium
   (c) Aluminium   (d) Silicon
4. Which of the following is not isoelectronic with O^{2-}?
   (a) N^{3-} (b) Na^+
   (c) F^- (d) Ti^+
5. On the basis of following features identify correct option
   A. Gaps were left for undiscovered elements
   B. No correct position of hydrogen
   C. The isotopes of same element will be given different position
   (a) Mendeleev's periodic table
   (b) Modern periodic table
   (c) Newland's arrangement of elements
   (d) Both (a) and (b)
6. According to Newland's law of octaves, which element is the repetition of the first element in the periodic table?
   (a) Oxygen   (b) Nitrogen
   (c) Chlorine   (d) Sulphur
7. Which one of the following is a diagonally related pair?
   (a) H, Be   (b) Na, Mg
   (c) B, Si   (d) K, Ca
8. Which element is more electronegative among halogens?
   (a) Br   (b) Cl
   (c) F   (d) I
9. Which of the following is correct set of Dobereiner Triads?
   (a) Na, Si, Cl   (b) Be, Mg, Ca
   (c) F, Cl, I   (d) Li, Na, Be
10. On moving horizontally across a period, the number of electrons in the outermost shell increases from ...... to ....
    (a) 2, 8   (b) 2, 18
    (c) 1, 8   (d) 1, 18
11. Which of the following elements A, B, C, D and E with atomic number 3, 11, 15, 18 and 19 respectively belong to the same group?
    (a) A, B, C   (b) B, C, D
    (c) A, D, E   (d) A, B, E
12. Which of the following statement is not true about noble gases?
    (a) They are non-metallic in nature
    (b) They exist in atomic form
    (c) They are radioactive in nature
    (d) Xenon is the most reactive among them
13. Which among the following atoms has high atomic radi?
    (a) Na   (b) Rb
    (c) K   (d) Cs
14. Which of the following is an actinide?
    (a) Plutonium   (b) Polonium
    (c) Promethium   (d) Palladium
15. Which one of these group of elements is also called the halogen family?
    (a) Group 16   (b) Group 18
    (c) Group 10   (d) Group 17

16. The elements with atomic numbers 2, 10, 18, 36, 54 and 86 are all –
(a) halogens   (b) noble gases
(c) noble metals   (d) light metals

17. Which one of the following properties changes with valency?   **[CDS]**
(a) Atomic weight   (b) Equivalent weight
(c) Molecular weight   (d) Density

18. The elements of a group in the periodic tabic   **[CDS]**
(a) have similar chemical properties
(b) have consecutive atomic numbers
(c) are isobars
(d) are isotopes

19. Which element forms the highest number of compounds in the periodic table?   **[CDS]**
(a) Carbon   (b) Oxygen
(c) Silicon   (d) Sulphur

20. Which one of the following is not a periodic property i.e., does not show any trend on moving from one side to the other in the periodic table?   **[CDS]**
(a) Atomic size   (b) Valency
(c) Radioactivity   (d) Electronegativity

21. Which one of the following elements is a metalloid?   **[NDA]**
(a) P   (b) Al
(c) As   (d) Po

22. What is the correct increasing order of electronegativity for the most common oxidation states among the following elements?   **[NDA]**
(a) $F < O < N < C$ (b) $C < N < C < F$
(c) $C < N < F < O$ (d) $C < N < O < F$

23. Consider the following statements with reference to the periodic table of chemical elements: **[IAS Prelim]**
1. Ionisation potential gradually decreases along a period
2. In a group of elements, electron affinity decreases as the atomic weight increases
3. In a given period, electronegativity decreases as the atomic number increases
Which of these statement (s) is/are correct?
(a) 1 only   (b) 2 only
(c) 1 and 3   (d) 2 and 3

24. The octet rule is *not* valid for which one of the following molecules?   **[NDA]**
(a) CO_2 (b) H_2S
(c) NH_3 (d) BF_3

25. The rusting of iron nail   **[CDS]**
(a) decreases its weight
(b) increases its weight
(c) does not affect weight but iron is oxidised
(d) does not affect weight but iron is reduced

26. Which one of the following when dissolved in H_2O gives hissing sound?   **[CDS]**
(a) Limestone   (b) Slaked lime
(c) Sodalime   (d) Quicklime

27. Consider the following statements:
1. Maximum covalency of carbon is 4, whereas maximum covalency of silicon is 6.
2. The maximum covalency of an element is limited to 6.
Which of the statements given above is/are correct?   **[NDA]**
(a) 1 only   (b) 2 only
(c) Both 1 and 2   (d) Neither 1 nor 2

28. An ionic compound when dissolved in water has produced $m A^{n-}$, $n B^{m-}$ ions. What is the formula of the compound?   **[NDA]**
(a) $A_m B_n$ (b) $A_n B_m$
(c) $A_m B_m$ (d) $A_n B_n$

29. What are the types of bonds present in $CuSO_4.5H_2O$?   **[NDA]**
(a) Electrovalent and covalent
(b) Electrovalent and coordinate covalent
(c) Electrovalent, covalent, coordinate covalent and hydrogen bonds
(d) Covalent and coordinate covalent

30. Consider the following equation for the formation of ammonia from nitrogen and hydrogen: **[NDA]**
$$N_2 + 3H_2 = 2NH_3$$
How many hydrogen molecules are required to react with 100 molecules of nitrogen?
(a) 100   (b) 200
(c) 300   (d) 400

31. As compared to covalent compounds, electrovalent compounds, generally have   **[NDA]**
(a) low melting point and low boiling point
(b) low melting point and high boiling point
(c) high melting point and low boiling point
(d) high melting point and high boiling point

32. Calcium carbonate is naturally available as limestone and can also be synthesized from quick lime. It is seen that the compositions of the elements in both the natural and synthetic calcium carbonate are same. The validity of which one among the following laws is confirmed by this observation?   **[NDA]**
(a) Law of conservation of mass
(b) Law of definite proportion
(c) Law of multiple proportion
(d) Avogadro's law

33. *This question consist of two statements, Statement I and Statement II. You are to examine these two statements carefully and select the answer to these items using the codes given below.*
Statement I: Conversion of blue copper sulphate to black cupric oxide on heating is a physical change.
Statement II: A change in which chemical composition does not change is called physical change.   **[NDA]**

(a) Both the statements individually true and Statement II is the correct explanation of Statement I.

(b) Both the statements are individually true but Statement II is not correct explanation of Statement I.

(c) Statement I is true but Statement II is false.

(d) Statement I is false but Statement II is true.

34. In $KMnO_4$ molecule, the oxidation states of the elements Potassium (K), Manganese (Mn) and Oxygen (O) are respectively **[NDA]**

(a) $+1, +5, -2$ (b) $+1, +7, -2$

(c) $0, 0, 0$ (d) $+1, +7, 0$

35. In the reaction $4Fe + 3O_2 \longrightarrow 4Fe^{3+} + 6O^{2-}$ **[NDA]** Which of the following statements is incorrect?

(a) It is a redox reaction

(b) Metallic iron acts as a reducing agent

(c) O_2 acts as an oxidising agent

(d) Metallic iron is reduced to Fe^{3+}

36. Most of the explosions in mines occur due to the mixing of **[IAS Prelim]**

(a) hydrogen with oxygen

(b) oxygen with acetylene

(c) methane with air

(d) carbon dioxide with ethane

37. Match List-I (Oxidation number) with List II (The element) and select the correct answer using the codes given below the lists: **[IAS Prelim]**

List-I	List-II
(Oxidation number)	(The elements)
A. 2	1. Oxidation number of Mn in MnO_2
B. 3	2. Oxidation number of S in $H_2S_2O_7$
C. 4	3. Oxidation number of Ca in CaO
D. 6	4. Oxidation number of Al in $NaAlH_4$

Codes:

(a) A-3; B-4; C-1; D-2   (b) A-4; B-3; C-1; D-2

(c) A-3; B-4; C-2; D-1   (d) A-4; B-3; C-2; D-1

38. If a limestone piece is dipped in water, a bubble evolves. The bubbling is due to **[CDS]**

(a) hydrogen   (b) oxygen

(c) water vapour   (d) carbon dioxide

39. Which one of the following reducing agents can also act as an oxidising agent? **[CDS]**

(a) H_2 (b) H_2S

(c) SO_2 (d) HI

40. A woman desires to clean the surface of her gold ornaments by a chemical approach. For this she requires to use **[CDS]**

(a) aqua-regia

(b) concentrated H_2SO_4

(c) concentrated NaOH

(d) sodium thiosulphate solution

41. Among the elements Zn, Ga, Ge and As, the one with the lowest first Ionization energy is

(a) As   (b) Zn

(c) Ga   (d) Ge

42. Which element forms the highest number of compounds in the periodic table? **[CDS 2013 - II]**

(a) Carbon   (b) Oxygen

(c) Silicon   (d) Sulphur

43. Which one of the following statements is correct? **[CDS 2016-II]**

(a) The oxidation number for hydrogen is always zero.

(b) The oxidation number for hydrogen is always +1.

(c) The oxidation number for hydrogen is always -1.

(d) Hydrogen can have more than one oxidation number.

44. Bright light is found to emit from photographer's flashgun. This brightness is due to the presence of which one of the following noble gases? **[CDS 2018-I]**

(a) Argon   (b) Xenon

(c) Neon   (d) Helium

45. Which one of the following elements is least reactive with water? **[NDA 2017-I]**

(a) Lithium   (b) Sodium

(c) Potassium   (d) Cesium

46. The valency of an element depends upon the

(a) total number of protons in an atom

(b) mass number of an atom

(c) total number of neutrons is an atom

(d) total number of electrons in the outer most shell of an atom

47. Match List I with List II and select the correct answer using the code given below the Lists : **[NDA 2017-I]**

List I	List II
(Noble gas)	(Use)
A. Argon	1. In lights for advertising display
B. Neon	2. Airport landing lights and in light houses
C. Krypton	3. Light in photographer's flash gun
D. Xenon	4. In tungsten filament to last longer

Code :

	A	B	C	D
(a)	3	1	2	4
(b)	3	2	1	4
(c)	4	2	1	3
(d)	4	1	2	3

48. Radon is **[NDA 2017-I]**

(a) an inert gas   (b) an artificial fibre

(c) an explosive   (d) a metal

49. The ionization energy of hydrogen atom in the ground state is **[NDA 2017-II]**

(a) 13.6 MeV   (b) 13.6 eV

(c) 13.6 Joule   (d) Zero

50. Which one of the following gases is placed second in respect of abundance in the Earth's atmosphere? **[NDA 2017-II]**
(a) Oxygen   (b) Hydrogen
(c) Nitrogen   (d) Carbon dioxide

51. Which one of the following is a chemical change? **[NDA 2017-II]**
(a) Cutting of hair
(b) Graying of hair naturally
(c) Swelling of resin in water
(d) Cutting of fruit

52. How much CO_2 is produced on heating of 1 kg of carbon? **[NDA 2017-II]**
(a) $\dfrac{11}{3}$ kg   (b) $\dfrac{3}{11}$ kg
(c) $\dfrac{4}{3}$ kg   (d) $\dfrac{3}{4}$ kg

53. Consider the following reaction:

$$CH_4 + 2O_2 \longrightarrow CO_2 + 2H_2O$$

Which of the following about the reaction given above is/are correct? **[NDA 2017-II]**
1. Carbon is oxidized.
2. Hydrogen is oxidized.
3. Hydrogen is reduced.
4. Carbon is reduced.
Select the correct answer using the code given below:
(a) 1 only   (b) 1 and 2 only
(c) 2 and 3 only   (d) 2 and 4 only

54. Which one of the following alkali metals has lowest melting point? **[NDA 2018-I]**
(a) Sodium   (b) Potassium
(c) Rubidium   (d) Caesium

55. Which one of the following metals is alloyed with sodium to transfer heat in a nuclear reactor? **[NDA 2018-I]**
(a) Potassium   (b) Calcium
(c) Magnesium   (d) Strontium

56. Which one of the following metals is used in the filaments of photo-electric cells that convert light energy into electric energy? **[NDA 2018-I]**
(a) Tungsten   (b) Copper
(c) Rubidium   (d) Aluminium

57. The atomic number of an element is 8. How many electrons will it gain to form a compound with sodium? **[NDA 2018-II]**
(a) One   (b) Two
(c) Three   (d) Four

58. A stainless steel chamber contains Ar gas at a temperature T and pressure P. The total number of Ar atoms in the chamber is n. Now Ar gas in the chamber is replaced by CO_2 gas and the total number of CO_2 molecules in the chamber is n/2 at the same temperature T. The pressure in the chamber now is P'. Which one of the following relations holds true? (Both the gases behave as ideal gases) **[NDA 2018-II]**
(a) P' = P   (b) P' = 2P
(c) P' = P/2   (d) P' = P/4

59. Which one of the following reactions will give NO (nitric oxide) gas as one of the products? **[NDA 2018-II]**
(a) $3\,Cu + 8HNO_3$ (dilute) $\rightarrow$
(b) $Cu + 4HNO_3$ (conc.) $\rightarrow$
(c) $4Zn + 10HNO_3$ (dilute) $\rightarrow$
(d) $Zn + 4HNO_3$ (conc.) $\rightarrow$

60. Which one of the following is an oxidation-reduction reaction? **[NDA 2018-II]**
(a) $NaOH + HCl \rightarrow NaCl + H_2O$
(b) $CaO + H_2O \rightarrow Ca(OH)_2$
(c) $2Mg + O_2 \rightarrow 2MgO$
(d) $Na_2SO_4 + BaCl_2 \rightarrow BaSO_4 + 2NaCl$

ANSWER KEY																	
1	(c)	2	(b)	3	(a)	4	(d)	5	(a)	6	(a)	7	(c)	8	(c)	9	(b)
10	(c)	11	(d)	12	(c)	13	(d)	14	(a)	15	(d)	16	(b)	17	(b)	18	(a)
19	(a)	20	(c)	21	(c)	22	(d)	23	(b)	24	(d)	25	(b)	26	(d)	27	(a)
28	(a)	29	(c)	30	(c)	31	(d)	32	(b)	33	(d)	34	(b)	35	(d)	36	(b)
37	(a)	38	(d)	39	(c)	40	(a)	41	(c)	42	(a)	43	(d)	44	(b)	45	(a)
46	(d)	47	(d)	48	(a)	49	(b)	50	(a)	51	(b)	52	(a)	53	(b)	54	(d)
55	(a)	56	(c)	57	(b)	58	(c)	59	(a)	60	(c)								

Chapter 4

ACIDS, BASES, SALTS & METALS

ACIDS, BASES AND SALTS

CONCEPTS OF ACIDS AND BASES

Arrhenius Concept

According to Arrhenius, *an acid is a compound that releases H^+ ions in water; and a base is a compound that releases OH^- ions in water.*

Bronsted–Lowry Concept

In 1923 J.N. Bronsted and J.M. Lowry independently proposed a broader concept of acids and bases. According to this concept,
- An acid is any molecule or ion that can donate a proton (H^+)
- A base is any molecule or ion that can accept a proton
- An acid is a proton donor while a base is a proton acceptor.
- Water that accepts a proton is a Bronsted base.

Conjugate Acid-Base pairs

An important concept that emanates from Bronsted-Lowry concept is **conjugate acid-base pairs.** In an acid-base reaction the acid (HA) gives up its proton (H^+) and produces a new base (A^-).
- The new base that is related to the original acid is called a **conjugate** (*meaning related*) **base.**
- Similarly the original base (B^-) after accepting a proton (H^+) gives a new acid (HB) which is called a **conjugate acid.**

Classes of Bronsted Acids and Bases

Bronsted acids can be classified as per its capacity to furnish protons as follows:
- **Monoprotic acids** are capable of donating one proton only,
- **Polyprotic acids** are capable of donating two or more protons, *e.g.* H_2SO_4, H_3PO_4, carbonic acid (H_2CO_3), hydrosulphuric acid, etc.
- **Monoprotic bases** can accept one proton.
- **Polyprotic bases** can accept two or more protons, *e.g.* anions of diprotic and triprotic acids.

Strength of Bronsted Acids and Bases

The strength of a Bronsted acid depends upon its tendency to donate a proton. The strength of a Bronsted base depends on its ability to accept a proton.

For example, HCl is nearly 100% ionised in water. Its reaction with water can be depicted by the equation:

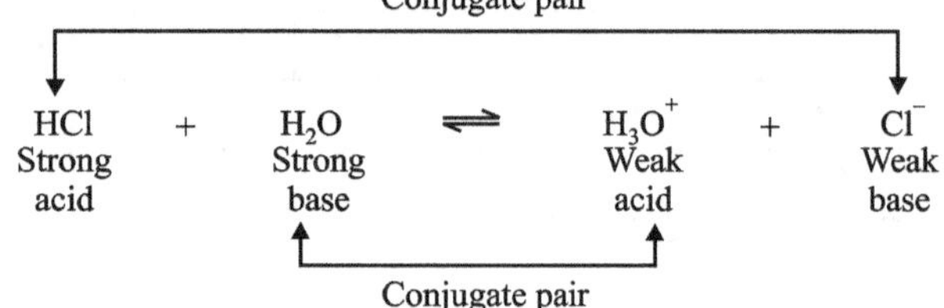

The above reaction has proceeded almost completely to the right; that indicates that HCl has a strong tendency to lose a proton. Also, the base H_2O has a strong ability to accept a proton. The overall situation is that the acid and base on the left are each stronger than the conjugate acid and conjugate base on the right. That is why the equilibrium is displaced to the right. Thus it may be stated that:
- *a strong acid has a weak conjugate base*
- *a strong base has a weak conjugate acid*

Strong Acids: HCl, HBr, HI, HNO_3, H_2SO_4, $HClO_3$, $HClO_4$

Strong Bases: Alkali metal hydroxides, $Ba(OH)_2$, $Sr(OH)_2$, $Ca(OH)_2$, $Mg(OH)_2$

Lewis Concept of Acids and Bases

In the early 1930s, G.N. Lewis gave an even a more general model of acids and bases. According to Lewis theory:
- *an acid is an electron-pair acceptor*
- *a base is an electron-pair donor*

Lewis visualized an acid and base as sharing the electron pair provided by the base. As a result a covalent bond (or coordinate bond) between the **Lewis acid** and the **Lewis base** is formed. The resulting combination is called a **Complex.**

pH SCALE-THE MEASURE OF ACIDITY

The concentrations of H^+ and OH^- ions in aqueous solutions are frequently very small and hence not convenient to work with.

- It was Danish chemist Soren Sorensen who in 1909 proposed a more useful quantity called pH. The **pH** of a solution is defined as **the negative logarithm of the hydrogen ion concentration (in mol/L):**

  $$pH = -\log[H_3O^+] \qquad \text{or} \qquad pH = -\log[H^+]$$

- The above equation gives a convenient numbers to work with. The negative logarithm gives a positive number for pH, which otherwise would be negative due to the small value of $[H^+]$. The pH of a solution is a dimensionless quantity.

- pH is simply a way to express hydrogen ion concentration, acidic and basic solutions at 25°C can be distinguished by their pH values, as follows:

- A pOH scale analogous to the pH scale can be devised using the negative logarithm of the hydroxide ion concentration of a solution. Thus, we define pOH as:

  $$pOH = -\log[OH^-]$$

- In general, from the definitions it follows that

  $$pH + pOH = 14.00$$

- The pH scale ranges from 0 to 14 on this scale. pH 7 is considered neutral, below 7 acidic and above 7 basic. Farther from 7, more acidic or basic the solution is.

pH in Humans and Animals

Most of the biochemical reactions taking place in our body are in a narrow pH range of 7.0 to 7.8. Even a small change in pH hampers the processes. Any condition in which blood pH drops below 7.35 is known as *acidosis*, if pH rises above 7.45-then it is called *alkalosis*.

Acid Rain

When the pH of rain water goes below 5.6, it is called **acid rain**. Acid rain is a major environmental disaster.

pH in Plants

Soils need to be of optimum pH for plants to have an adequate growth .It should be neither highly alkaline nor highly acidic.

In digestive system

pH plays an important part in the digestion of food. Our stomach produces hydrochloric acid (formic acid) which helps in digestion of food. When we eat spicy food, stomach produces too much of acid which causes 'acidity' i.e. irritation and sometimes pain too. In order to get cured from this we use 'antacids' which are bases like '*milk of magnesia*' (suspension of magnesium hydroxide in water).

Self-defence of Animals and Plants

Bee sting causes severe pain and burning sensation. It is due to the presence of *methanoic acid* (formic acid) in it. Use of a mild base like baking soda can provides relief from pain. Some plants like '*nettle plant*' have fine stinging hair which inject *methanoic acid* into the body of any animal or human being that comes in its contact.

BUFFER SOLUTIONS

Generally pH of an aqueous solution decreases on addition of a small amount of HCl because of the increase in the concentration of H^+ ions. On the other hand, if a small amount of NaOH is added, the pH of the solution increases. However, there are some solutions which resist the change in pH on addition of small amount of strong acid or alkali. Such solutions are called *buffer solutions*. For example, solution of ammonium acetate, blood, a equimolar mixture of $NH_4OH + NH_4Cl$, $CH_3COOH + CH_3COONa$, etc.

Types of Buffer Solution

- **Acidic buffer:** Acidic buffer solution contains equimolar quantities of a weak acid and its salt with strong base. For example, acetic acid (CH_3COOH) and sodium acetate (CH_3COONa). A solution containing equimolar quantities of acetic acid and sodium acetate maintains its pH value around 4.74.
- **Basic buffer:** Basic buffer solution contains equimolar quantities of a weak base and its salt with a strong acid. For example, ammonium hydroxide (NH_4OH) and ammonium chloride (NH_4Cl).

SALTS

A salt is an ionic compound which dissociates to yield a positive ion other than hydrogen ion [H^+] and a negative ion other than hydroxide ion [OH^-]

Example:
$NaCl \rightarrow Na^+ + Cl^-$ (fused/ Aq. soln)

Classification of Salts

- **Normal Salt:** In case the acid and base neutralise completely the salt formed is a normal salt. e.g. $NaCl$, $CuSO_4$
- **Acidic Salt:** If a polybasic acid is neutralised partly by a base, the salt formed is acidic. e.g. H_2SO_4, H_3PO_4
- **Basic Salts:** This type of salts are formed by incomplete neutralization of a base with an acid or by partial replacement of hydroxy radicals of a diacids or triacidic base with an acid radical.
  e.g. $Cu(OH)NO_3$ - Basic copper nitrate.
- **Double Salt** - Such a salt is formed by mixing saturated solution of two simple salts followed by crystallisation of the saturated solution.
  e.g. $FeSO_4 \cdot (NH_4)_2SO_4 6H_2O$ (Mohr's salt) is a mixture of $FeSO_4$ (Simple salt) and $(NH_4)_2SO_4$ (Simple salt)
- **Mixed Salts** - There is no general method for the formation of this type of salt.
  e.g. Sodium potassium sulphate $NaKSO_4$ (two basic radicals, Na^+, K^+)
- **Complex salt** - Such a salt is formed by mixing saturated solution of simple salts followed by crystallisation of the solution similar to double salts. e.g. $K_3F_e(CN)_6$

SOME COMMON USEFUL SALTS

A large number of salts are useful for our homes and industry for various purposes. Some are discussed below:

Baking Soda

Chemically baking soda is sodium hydrogen carbonate; $NaHCO_3$.
- It is an important part of food.
- Baking soda is manufactured by Solvay's process.
- It is mainly used for manufacturing washing soda but baking soda is obtained as an intermediate.
- On heating, sodium hydrogen carbonate is converted into sodium carbonate and carbon dioxide is given off:
  $$2NaHCO_3 \xrightarrow{\text{heat}} Na_2CO_3 + H_2O + CO_2\uparrow$$

Uses

- It is used as a component of baking powder.
- It is used as a *tenderizer* and *leavening* agent in *baking* (In combination with a liquid and acid it releases CO_2)
- It is used as deodorizer because of its neutralizing action.
- It is used in laundry work for enhancing the detergents effectiveness because it stabilizes the pH level (acts as a buffer)
- *It is used in fire extinguishers.* Baking soda undergoes a chemical reaction that gives off CO_2 that makes it useful in extinguishing small grease or electrical fires.
  $$2NaHCO_3 \xrightarrow{\text{heat}} Na_2CO_3 + H_2O + CO_2 \uparrow$$
- It is used as abrasive cleaner.

Washing Soda

- Washing soda is used for washing of clothes. Chemically, washing soda is sodium carbonate decahydrate, $Na_2CO_3 \cdot 10H_2O$.
- Washing soda is manufactured by Solvay's process.

Uses

- It is used in the manufacture of caustic soda, glass, soap powders, borax and in paper industry.
- For removing permanent hardness of water.
- As a cleansing agent for domestic purpose.

Plaster of Paris

Also called POP, chemically, it is $2CaSO_4.H_2O$ or $CaSO_4.1/2H_2O$ (calcium sulphate hemi hydrate)

- Gypsum, $(CaSO_4.2H_2O)$ is used as the raw material to manufacture POP.
- The only difference between gypsum $(CaSO_4.2H_2O)$ and plaster of Paris $(CaSO_4.1/2H_2O)$ is the less amount of water of crystallization.

Uses

- In medicine, used for making plaster casts to hold fractured bones in place while they set. It is also used for making casts in dentistry.
- For making fire proof materials.

Bleaching Powder

Bleaching is a process of removing colour from a cloth to make it whiter. Bleaching powder has been used for this purpose since long. Chemically, it is calcium oxychloride $CaOCl_2$.

Uses

- Used in textile industry for bleaching of clothes.
- In paper industry for bleaching of wood pulp.
- It makes wool unshrinkable.
- Used as disinfectant and germicide for sterilization of drinking water and swimming pool water.
- For the manufacture of chloroform $(CHCl_3)$
- Used as an oxidizing agent in chemical industry.

Sodium Hydroxide

Also known as Caustic Soda, chemically it is NaOH. Industrial methods of its production are:

- Causticisation process (Gossage process)
- Castner Kellner cell
- Chlor-Alkali process

Uses

- It is used in many industries, mostly as a strong chemical base in the manufacture of pulp and paper, textiles, soaps, dyes, cellulose, detergents etc.
- It is used in petroleum refining.

> Magnesium hydroxide $(MgOH_2)$ is an important component of antacids and laxatives. Milk of magnesia is a suspension of magnesium hydroxide in water. It is used as an antacid and laxative.

> It acts as antacid by lowering the amount of acid in the stomach and is used for the treatment of heartburn, indigestion etc.
> It also acts as laxative by drawing water into the intestines which causes movement of the intestines.

Sodium Carbonate

Also called soda ash, its chemical formula is Na_2CO_3

It exists in various forms, namely anhydrous sodium carbonate Na_2CO_3 (Soda-ash). Monohydrate $Na_2CO_3.H_2O$ (crystal carbonate), heptahydrate. $Na_2CO_3.7H_2O$ and decahydrate $Na_2CO_3.10H_2O$ (washing soda or sal soda)

Sodium carbonate is generally prepared now a days by *ammonia soda* or *Solvay process*. The ingredients of this process are readily available and inexpensive. These are *Salt brine* (NaCl) (from sea), ammonia (NH_3) and *lime stone* $CaCO_3$ (from mines). The process consists of many sections, $CaCl_2$ is an important by product obtained.

Uses

- It is used for softening of hard water. For this purpose hydrated sodium carbonate, $Na_2CO_3.10H_2O$ known as *washing soda* is used.
- A mixture of sodium carbonate (Na_2CO_3) and potassium carbonate (K_2CO_3) is used as fusion mixture.
- It is used in paper, paint and textile industries
- It is used for the manufacture of glass, borax, soap and caustic soda (NaOH)

PROPERTIES, EXTRACTION AND USES OF METALS

Out of 118 chemical elements known till date, 103 has been well characterized in terms of their properties. The systematic classification of these 103 elements shows their numbers as:

- Metals=79
- Non-metals=17
- And metalloids=7

COMPARISON OF METALS AND NON-METALS

Metals and non-metals differ both in physical and chemical properties.

The characteristic physical properties of metals and non-metals are listed in following table:

Serial No.	Metals	Non-metals
1.	Metals have lustre. They reflect light from polished or freshly cut surface	Non-metals do not have lustre (exceptions – Diamond and Iodine)
2.	Metals generally have high density.	Non-metals generally have low density.
3.	They are good conductors of heat and electricity.	They are usually bad conductors of heat (exception – carbon in the form of gas carbon and graphite)

4.	Metals are malleable and ductile. They can be beaten into thin sheets and drawn into wires.	Non-metals are not malleable and ductile. They can be crushed into powder.
5.	They have a three dimensional crystal structure with metallic bonds	They have different types of structures with covalent and van-der-Waals' bonds
6.	Metals are generally hard.	Non-metals are generally soft (Exception: Diamond)
7.	Metals generally have 1 to 3 electrons in their outermost shell	Non-metals generally have 4 to 8 in their outermost shell of the atom.
8.	They show valency 1 to 4.	They show valency 1 to 7.
9.	They are electropositive in nature.	They are electronegative in nature.
10.	They generally form basic oxides.	They generally form acidic oxides.
11.	They act as reducing agents.	They act as oxidizing agents.
12.	Active metals react with cold and hot water.	Non-metals usually do not react with cold or hot water.
13.	Active metals react with non- oxidizing acids to form their oxides or oxyacids.	Solid non-metals react with oxidizing acids to form hydrogen gas.
14.	They react with non-metals under different conditions to form salts.	They react with metals as well as non metals under different conditions to form salts.

CHEMICAL PROPERTIES OF METAL

The chemical reactions undergone by metals are furnished below:

Reaction with Oxygen

Most of the metals react with oxygen and form oxides. The reaction may take place without heating as in sodium, calcium or potassium, while some *metals* react with oxygen on heating to form oxides.

- Oxides of metals are *basic* in nature as they react with water and form bases, e.g. Na_2O, CaO, MgO, K_2O, etc.
- Oxides of aluminium (Al_2O_3), zinc (ZnO), tin (SnO) and iron (Fe_2O_3) are *amphoteric* in nature as they react with acids as well as with bases.

Reaction of Metals with Acids

Metals react with common acids like dilute HCl and dilute H_2SO_4 with evolution of H_2.

Reaction of Metals with Water

Many metals react with water to form hydroxides. Hydroxides are basic in nature. Sodium and potassium react with cold water.
- Magnesium reacts with hot water
  $$Mg(s) + H_2O(l) \rightarrow Mg(OH)_2(aq) + H_2(g)$$
- Metals like Al or Fe react on heating with water or with steam. In these conditions metals form metal oxides.

Reaction of Metals with Common Bases

Some metals like aluminium and zinc react with common bases.
$$Sn(s) + 2NaOH\ (aq) + H_2O\ (l) \rightarrow Na_2SnO_3$$
$$\text{sodium stannate}$$
$$Zn(s) + 2NaOH\ (aq) \rightarrow \quad Na_2ZnO_2$$
$$\text{Sodium zincate}$$

REACTIVITY SERIES

A metal that can lose electrons more easily in comparison to other metal is more electropositive and would be more active in nature then other metal. Such a metal when dipped in a solution of salt of a less active metal would displace it.

The arrangement of metals in the decreasing order of their activity is known as activity or reactivity series. It is also known as electrochemical series.

K	Potassium	Most Reactive at the top
Na	Sodium	
Ca	Calcium	
Mg	Magnesium	
Al	Aluminium	
Zn	Zinc	Reactivity decreases down the series
Fe	Iron	
Pb	Lead	
H	Hydrogen	
Cu	Copper	
Hg	Mercury	
Ag	Silver	Least Reactive at the bottom
Au	Gold	

EXTRACTION OF METALS-METALLURGY

The process of extraction of metal from its ore is called **metallurgy.**
- **Minerals** are naturally occurring compounds of metals.
- **Ores** are those minerals from which metals can be economically extracted.

Examples
- Aluminium is the most common metal in the Earth's crust, occurring in all sorts of minerals. However, it isn't economically worthwhile to extract it from most of these minerals. Instead, the usual ore of aluminum is bauxite - which contains from 50 - 70% of aluminium oxide.

Examples of Ores

Some important ores and the metals present in these ores are listed in the following table:

Type of ore	Metals
Native Metals (Found in Free State)	Gold (Au), silver (Ag)
Oxide ores	Iron (Haematite, Fe_2O_3); Aluminium (Bauxite, $Al_2O_3 . 2H_2O$); Tin(Cassiterite, SnO_2); Copper Cuprite, Cu_2O); Zinc (Zincite, ZnO); Titanium (Ilmenite, $FeTiO_3$, Rutile, TiO_2)
Sulphide ores	Zinc (Zinc blende, ZnS); Lead (Galena, PbS); Copper (Copper glance, Cu_2S); Silver (Silver glance or Argentite, Ag_2S); Iron (Ironpyrites, FeS_2)
Carbonate ores	Iron (Siferite, $FeCO_3$); Zinc (Calamine, $ZnCO_3$), Lead (Cerrusite, $PbCO_3$)
Sulphate ores	Lead(Anglesite, $PbSO_4$)
Halide ores	Silver (Horn silver, $AgCl$); Sodium (Common salt or Rock salt, $NaCl$); Aluminium(Cryolite, Na_3AlF_6)
Silicate ores	Zinc (Hemimorphite, $Zn_4Si_2O_7(OH)_2.H_2O$

The method used to extract metals from the ore in which they are found depends on their reactivity.

Steps Involved in the Extraction of Metals from Ores

Metallurgical Steps

Few steps involved in extracting the metal as shown above are discussed below:

Concentrating the Ore

This means getting rid of as much of the unwanted rocky material (called **gangue** or **matrix**) as possible before the ore is converted into the metal.

Some methods are:

Froth floatation: The ore is first crushed and then treated with something which will bind to the particles of the metal compound that are required and make those particles hydrophobic. "Hydrophobic" stands for "water fearing".

Magnetic separation: Magnetic ores like pyrolusite (MnO_2) and chromite ($FeO.Cr_2O_3$) are enriched by this method by making use of the difference in the magnetic properties of the ore and gangue particles.

Conversion of concentrated ore to oxide

It is easier to obtain a metal from its oxide form as compared to its sulphide, carbonate or any other form. Therefore, prior to reduction usually the metal is converted to its oxide form. Following methods are used to convert the concentrated ore to its oxide form.

Calcination: It is a process in which the ore is heated strongly in absence of air. The ore is heated at a temperature well below its melting point.

This method is generally used for carbonate and hydrated ores.

Roasting: It is a process wherein the ore is heated either alone or with some other material in excess of air below the fusion point of the ore.

- Usually, this method is used for sulphide ores.
- Ores of metals like zinc, lead, copper and nickel, when roasted in air, are converted to their oxides.
- The purpose of roasting is to convert the ore in a form suitable to reduce. The gaseous product of sulphide roasting, sulphur dioxide is often used to produce sulphuric acid.

Reducing the metal compound to the metal

- **Carbon reduction**
  Carbon (as coke or charcoal) is cheap. It not only acts as a reducing agent, but it also acts as the fuel to provide heat for the process.
- **Reduction using a more reactive metal**
  Titanium is produced by reducing titanium chloride using a more reactive metal such as sodium or magnesium. This is the only way of producing high purity metal.
- **Reduction by electrolysis**
  This is a common extraction process for the more reactive metals - for example, for aluminum and metals above it in the electrochemical series.

An advantage is that it can produce very pure metals.

Refining of metals

Refining of metals is done to obtain metals in very pure form by removing impurities present in it. *Electrolytic refining* is widely used method for this purpose.

Important Elements and Ores

S.No.	Element	Ore	Formula
1.	Aluminium (Al)	Corundum, Red Ruby	Al_2O_3
		Bauxite	$Al_2O_3.2H_2O$
		Diaspore	$Al_2O_3.H_2O$
		Cryolite	Na_3AlF_6
2.	Antimony (Sb)	Sübenite	Sb_2S_3
3.	Arsenic (As)	Arsenic pyrite or Mispikel	FeAsS
		Cobaltite	CoAsS
		Nickel Glance	NiAsS
		Orpoment	As_2S_3
4.	Barium (Ba)	Heavy spar or Barytes	$BaSO_4$
		Withrite	$BaCO_3$
5.	Bismuth (Bi)	Bismuthite	Bi_2S_3
6.	Cadmium (Cd)	Greenocite	CdS
7.	Calcium (Ca)	Chalk, limestone, ice-land spar or calcite	$CaCO_3$
		Dolomite	$CaCO_3.MgCO_3$
		Gypsum	$CaSO_4.2H_2O$
		Anhydrite sulphate	$CaSO_4$
		Fluorspar	CaF_2
		Floropetite	$3Ca_3(PO_4)_2.CaF_2$
		Phosphorite	$Ca_3(PO_4)_2$
8.	Chromium (Cr)	Chromite	$FeO.Cr_2O_3$
		Chrokoite	$PbCrO_4$
9.	Cobalt (Co)	Smelite	$CoAsS_2$
10.	Copper (Cu)	Cuprite or ruby copper	Cu_2O
		Malachite	$CuCO_3.Cu(OH)_2$
		Azurite	$2CuCO_3.Cu(OH)_2$
		Chalcopyrite or Copper-pyrites	$CuFeS_2$
		Chalcocite or Copper glance	Cu_2S
11.	Gold (Au)	Calaverite	$AuTe_2$
		Petsite	$(Ag, Au)_2Te$
		Silvenites	$(Ag, Au)Te_2$
12.	Iron (Fe)	Haemetite	Fe_2O_3
		Magnetite	Fe_3O_4
		Limonite	$2Fe_2O_3.3H_2O$
		Siderite	$FeCO_3$
		Iron pyrites	FeS_2
13.	Potassium (K)	Carnalite	$KCl.MgCl_2.6H_2O$
		Silvine	KCl
		Carnite	$K_2SO_4\ MgSO_4\ MgCl_2.6H_2O$
		Felspar	$KAlSi_3O_3$
		Saltpetre	KNO_3
14.	Lead (Pb)	Galena	PbS
		Cerrusite	$PbCO_3$
		Anglesite	$PbSO_4$

15.	Magnesium (Mg)	Magnesite Dolomite Kiesserite Epsom salt Carnalite Talc Asbestos	$MgCO_3$ $MgCO_3.CaCO_3$ $MgSO_4 H_2O$ $MgSO_4.7H_2O$ $KCl.MgCl_2.6H_2O$ $3MgO.4SiO_2.H_2O$ $CaMg_3(SiO_3)_4.$
16.	Manganese (Mn)	Pyrolusite Bronite Magnite Hausmanite	MnO_2 Mn_2O_3 $Mn_2O_3.H_2O$ Mn_3O_4
17.	Mercury (Hg)	Cinnabar	HgS
18.	Nickel (Ni)	Milarite	Nis
19.	Silver (Ag)	Ruby Silver Horn silver Argentite	$3Ag_2S.Sb_2S_3$ $AgCl$ Ag_2S
20.	Sodium (Na)	Chile Saltpeter Borax Trona	$NaNO_3$ $Na_2B_4O_7.10H_2O$ $Na_2CO_3.2NaHCO_3.10H_2O$
21.	Strontium (Sr)	Strontianite Silestine	$SrCO_3$ $SrSO_4$
22.	Tin (Sn)	Casseterite	SnO_2
23.	Zinc (Zn)	Zinc blende Zincite Calamine	ZnS ZnO $ZnCO_3$

ALLOYS

Alloys are metallic materials prepared by mixing two or more molten metals.
These are used for many purposes, such as construction, and are central to the transportation and electrical industries. Composition of some common alloys and their uses are given in the following table.

	Alloy	**Composition**	**Uses**
1.	Brass	Cu = 80%, Zn = 20%	For making utensils and cartridges.
2.	Bronze	Cu = 90%, Sn = 10%	For making statues, medals, ships, coins and machines
3.	Solder	Sn = 50%, Pb = 50%	For joining metals, solding wire and electronic components etc.
4.	Duraluminum	Al = 95.5%, Cu = 3%, Mn = 1.0%, Mg = 0.5%	Used in bodies of aircrafts, kitchen parts etc. ware and automobile
5.	German Silver	Cu = 60%, Zn = 20%, Ni = 20%	For making utensils and ornaments
6.	Gun metal	Cu = 90%, Sn = 10%	For Gears and castings etc.
7.	Bell metal	Cu = 80%, Sn = 20%	For bells, gangs etc.
8.	Magnalium	Al = 90%, Mg = 10%	For balance beams, light instruments.
9.	Type metal	Pb = 82%, Sb = 15%, Sn = 3%	For casting type
10.	Stainless steel	Fe, Ni, Cr, C	For utensils, cutlery etc.

- In **homogeneous alloys**, atoms of the different elements are distributed uniformly. Examples include brass, bronze, and the coinage alloys.
- **Heterogeneous alloys**, such as tin-lead solder and the mercury amalgam sometimes used to fill teeth, consist of a mixture of crystalline phases with different compositions.

An **amalgam** is an alloy of mercury with one or more metals. Most of the metals form amalgams with mercury except iron and platinum. Amalgams of sodium and aluminium are good reducing agents. Amalgam of silver, tin, cadmium and copper have been utilized as *dental fillings*.

SOME IMPORTANT METALS AND THEIR USES

Iron(Fe)

Iron is the most abundant metal which occurs in the earth's crust. The most commonly used iron ores are **haematite**, Fe_2O_3, and **magnetite**, Fe_3O_4.

Cast Iron

The molten iron from the bottom of the furnace can be used as *cast iron*. However, it is very impure, containing about 4% of carbon. This carbon makes it very hard, but also very brittle. If you hit it hard, it tends to shatter rather than bend or dent.

Use: Cast iron is used for things like manhole covers, cast iron pipes, valves and pump bodies in the water industry, guttering and drainpipes, cylinder blocks in car engines, AGA-type cookers, and very expensive and very heavy cookware.

Wrought iron

If all the carbon is removed from the iron to give high purity iron, it is known as wrought iron. Wrought iron is quite soft and easily worked and has little structural strength.

Use: It was once used to make decorative gates and railings, but these days mild steel is normally used instead.

Mild steel

Mild steel is iron containing up to about 0.25% of carbon. The presence of the carbon makes the steel stronger and harder than pure iron. The higher the percentage of carbon, the harder the steel becomes.

Use: Mild steel is used for lots of things - nails, wire, car bodies, ship building, girders and bridges amongst others.

High carbon steel

High carbon steel contains up to about 1.5% of carbon. The presence of the extra carbon makes it very hard, but it also makes it more brittle.

Use: Used for cutting tools and masonry nails (nails designed to be driven into concrete blocks or brickwork without bending). It tends to fracture rather than bend if you mistreat it.

Special steels

These are iron alloyed with other metals. Examples are given in the following table:

Variety	Addition	Special Properties	Uses
Stainless steel	chromium and nickel	resists corrosion	cutlery, cooking utensils, kitchen sinks, industrial equipment for food and drink processing
Titanium steel	titanium	withstands high temperatures	gas turbines, spacecraft
Manganese steel	manganese	very hard	rock-breaking machinery, some railway track (e.g. points), military helmets

The hardness and elasticity of steel can be controlled by heat treatment. The steel is heated to a temperature below redness. It is then cooled slowly. The process is called **tempering of steel**. It is used to bring the steel to a suitable state of hardness and elasticity.

Hard steel can be softened by heating it to a high temperature and then allowing it to cool down slowly. This process is called **annealing**.

Steel produced in this way is known as quenched steel and the process of making such steel is known as **quenching or hardening of steel**.

Some important compounds of iron

Green Vitriol: Iron sulphate or ferrous sulphate is the chemical compound with the formula. $FeSO_4 . 7H_2O$ is called Green vitriol. It is used as:

- A reducing agent, mostly for the reduction of chromate in cement.
- As nutritional supplement to patients suffering from iron deficiency.
- As a colorant.

Mohr's Salt: Ammonium iron sulphate, or Mohr's Salt, is a double salt of iron sulphate and ammonium sulphate, with the formula $(NH_4)_2 Fe (SO_4)_2 \cdot 6H_2O$ and used in the laboratory.

Copper(Cu)

Copper is malleable and ductile and is a good conductor of both heat and electricity. The important ores of copper is chalcopyrite, $CuFeS_2$ (also known as *copper pyrites*)

Copper has multifarious uses like:

- **Making brass:** Brass is a copper-zinc alloy. Alloying produces a metal harder than either copper or zinc individually. Bronze is another copper alloy - this time with tin.
- **Coinage:** Used for masking coins in its alloy forms.

Some important compounds of Copper

- **Blue vitriol**

Copper sulphate is the compound with the formula $CuSO_4$. This salt exists as a series of compounds that differ in their degree of hydration. The anhydrous form is a pale green or gray-white powder, whereas the penta hydrate($CuSO_4 \cdot 5H_2O$), the most commonly encountered salt, is bright blue.

- **Black oxide of copper**

Copper oxide or cupric oxide (CuO) is the higher oxide of copper. As a mineral, it is known as **tenorite**.

Uses

- Cupric oxide is used as a pigment in ceramics to produce blue, red, and green (and sometimes gray, pink, or black) glazes.
- To produce cuprammonium hydroxide solutions, used to make rayon.
- Occasionally used as a dietary supplement in animals, against copper deficiency.
- Copper oxide has application as a p-type semiconductor, because it has a narrow band gap.

- **Red oxide of copper**

Copper oxide or cuprous oxide is the inorganic compound with the formula- Cu_2O. It is one of the principal oxides of copper.

Uses

Cuprous oxide is commonly used as a pigment, a fungicide, and an antifouling agent for marine paints.

Rectifier based on this material have been used industrially.

Aluminium

The usual aluminium ore is *bauxite*. Bauxite is essentially an impure aluminium oxide. The major impurities include iron oxides, silicon dioxide and titanium dioxide. Bauxite actually contains one of a variety of hydrated aluminium oxides some of which can be written as Al_2O_3, xH_2O.

Uses: Aluminum is used in aircraft making, container vehicle bodies, tube trains, in making saucepans, etc.

Anodizing of Aluminium: In anodising the aluminium is first etched with sodium hydroxide solution to remove the existing oxide layer, and then making the aluminium article the anode in electrolysis of dilute sulphuric acid. The oxygen given off at the anode reacts with the aluminium surface, and form a film of oxide up to about 0.02 mm thick.

Zinc (Zn)

It is extracted from ores like zinc blende (ZnS).

- Zinc is an essential trace element, necessary for plants, animals, and microorganisms.
- It is typically the second most abundant transition metal in organisms after iron and it is the only metal which appears in all enzyme classes.
- Zinc is used in galvanizing. *Galvanization* is a metal coating process in which a ferrous part is coated with a thin layer of zinc.

MULTIPLE CHOICE QUESTIONS

1. The Compound that gives a basic solution in HF is
   (a) AsF_5 (a) PF_5
   (c) BF_3 (d) BrF_3

2. Which one of the following salts when dissolved in water makes the solution basic? **[NDA]**
   (a) Sodium chloride
   (b) Copper sulphate
   (c) Ferric chloride
   (d) Sodium acetate

3. Which of the following salts are insoluble in water? **[NDA]**
   (a) Chlorides of Fe and Mn
   (b) Nitrates of Ag and Pb
   (c) Carbonates of Pb and Cu
   (d) Phosphates of Na and NH_4

4. Two elements gallium and oxygen combine to form a compound Ga_2O_3. Which among the following is the valency of gallium? **[NDA]**
   (a) 1   (b) 2
   (c) 3   (d) 4

5. Arrange the following bases in increasing order of their, basic strength **[NDA]**
   1. Sodium hydroxide
   2. Magnesium hydroxide
   3. Aluminium hydroxide
   4. Ammonium hydroxide
   Select the correct answer using the code given below
   Codes:

	A	B	C	D
(a)	4	2	1	3
(b)	4	1	2	3
(c)	4	3	2	1
(d)	1	2	3	4

6. Which one among the following is not a property of salt? **[NDA]**
   (a) Salts have ordered packing arrangements called lattices
   (b) Salts have low melting points but high boiling points
   (c) Salts are brittle
   (d) Salts conduct electricity when dissolved in water or even in the molten state

7. Which among the following statements with regard to pH scale is/are correct? **[NDA]**
   I. It is a logarithmic scale.
   II. The scale is limited to 0-14 because the ionic product of water is about 10^{-14}
   III. The lower the value of pH, the greater is the acidity of the solution.
   Select the correct answer using the code given below
   (a) I and II only
   (b) I, II and III
   (c) I and III only
   (d) II only

8. **Statement I:** Metal ions are Lewis acids.
   Statement II: Metal ions are electron pair acceptors. **[NDA]**
   (a) Both the statements individually true and Statement II is the correct explanation of Statement I.
   (b) Both the statements are individually true but Statement II is not correct explanation of Statement I.
   (c) Statement I is true but Statement II is false.
   (d) Statement I is false but Statement II is true.

9. Neutral water with pH about 7 becomes slightly acidic when aerated. This is because **[NDA]**
   (a) oxygen from air is dissolved in the water which makes the water acidic
   (b) dirt, which get contaminated with the water during aeration makes the water acidic
   (c) ultraviolet radiation dissociates water molecules and makes water acidic
   (d) carbon-dioxide from air is dissolved

10. The concentration of hydrochloric acid in a given solution is 10^{-8} M. What is the value of pH for this solution? **[NDA]**
    (a) 7   (b) > 7 but not 14
    (c) < 7   (d) 14

11. Human stomach produces acid 'X' which helps in digestion of food. Acid 'X' is **[NDA]**
    (a) acetic acid   (b) methanoic acid
    (c) hydrochloric acid   (d) citric acid

12. Bases turn red litmus blue and acids turn blue litmus red. A student tested a liquid with a red litmus paper and it stayed red with no change. This shows that the liquid **[NDA]**
    (a) must be pure water
    (b) must be an acid
    (c) is not a base
    (d) is neither a base nor an acid

13. Which of the following statements regarding oxidation and reduction are correct?
    1. In oxidation, loss of electron takes place whereas in reduction, gain of electron takes place.
    2. In oxidation, gain of electron takes place whereas in reduction, loss of electron takes place.
    3. Oxidizing agent decreases the oxidation number but reducing agent increases the oxidation number.
    4. Oxidizing agent increases the oxidation number but reducing agent reduces the oxidation number. **[NDA]**
    Select the correct answer using the code given below:
    Code:
    (a) 1 and 3   (b) 2 and 4
    (c) 2 and 3   (d) 1 and 4

14. The following equation is an example of a redox reaction, in which Cl_2 is the oxidizing agent and $FeBr_3$ is the reducing agent:
    $$2FeBr_3 (aq) + 3Cl_2 (g) = 2FeCl_3 (aq) + 3Br_2 (1)$$

Which one among the following statements is *incorrect* for this redox reaction? **[NDA]**
(a) Oxidizing agents are themselves reduced
(b) Reducing agents gain or appear to gain electrons
(c) Reducing agents are themselves oxidized
(d) Oxidizing agents oxidize other substances

15. Which one among the following is the correct order of strength of acids? **[NDA]**
(a) $H_2SO_4 > H_3PO_3 > CH_3COOH$
(b) $H_3PO_3 > H_2SO_4 > CH_3COOH$
(c) $CH_3COOH > H_3PO_3 > H_2SO_4$
(d) $CH_3COOH > H_2SO_4 > H_3PO_3$

16. Which one among the following is an electrochemical cell that cannot be charged? **NDA]**
(a) Electrolytic cell
(b) Storage cell
(c) Primary cell
(d) Fuel cell

17. The pH of fresh milk is 6. When it turns sour, the pH **[NDA]**
(a) becomes < 6
(b) remains the same i.e., 6
(c) becomes > 6
(d) becomes neutral, i.e., 7

18. Which one among the following is a double salt? **[NDA]**
(a) $K_4[Fe(CN)_6]$
(b) $K_2SO_4 \cdot Al_2(SO_4)_3 \cdot 24H_2O$
(c) $CuSO_4 \cdot 5H_2O$
(d) NaCl

19. **Statement I:** Addition of water to an aqueous solution of HC1 decreases the pH. **[CDS]**
Statement II: Addition of water suppresses the ionisation of HC1.
(a) Both the statements are individually true and Statement II is the correct explanation of Statement I
(b) Both the statements are individually true but Statement II is not the correct explanation of Statement I
(c) Statement I is true, but Statement II is false
(d) Statement I is false, but Statement II is true

20. The pH of fresh ground water slightly decreases upon exposure to air because **[CDS]**
(a) carbon dioxide from air is dissolved in the water
(b) oxygen from air is dissolved in the water
(c) the dissolved carbon dioxide of the ground water escapes into air
(d) the dissolved oxygen of the ground water escapes into air

21. Antacids are commonly used to get rid of acidity in the stomach. A commonly used antacid is **[CDS]**
(a) sodium hydrogen phthalate
(b) magnesium hydroxide
(c) calcium hydroxide
(d) manganese acetate

22. Aluminium is used in thermite welding because –
(a) aluminium is a light metal
(b) aluminium has more affinity for oxygen
(c) aluminium is a strong oxidising agent
(d) aluminium is a reactive metal

23. Which method is employed for obtaining a pure metal?
(a) Froth floatation
(b) Electrolytic refining
(c) Magnetic separation
(d) Gravity separation

24.

Column-I		Column-II
A.	Hardest Non-metal	P. Graphite
B.	Non-metal conducts electricity	Q. Sulphur
C.	Non-metal with lustre	R. Diamond (Carbon)
D.	Non-metal used as fungicide	S. Iodine

(a) A – R; B – P; C – S; D – Q
(b) A – Q; B – P; C – S; D – R
(c) A – P; B – R; C – S; D – Q
(d) A – R; B – P; C – Q; D – S

25.

Column-I (Alloy)		Column-II (Composition of Elements)
A.	Steel	P. Cu and Sn
B.	Brass	Q. Cu and Zn
C.	Bronze	R. Fe, C and Cr
D.	Magnalium	S. Al and Mg

(a) A – Q; B – R; C – P; D – S
(b) A – R; B – Q; C – P; D – S
(c) A – Q; B – R; C – S; D – P
(d) A – R; B – Q; C – S; D – P

26.

Column-I (Product)		Column-II (Name of alloy)
A.	Aircrafts	P. Stainless steel
B.	Utensils	Q. Bronze
C.	Medals	R Magnalium
D.	Balance beam	S Duralumin

(a) A – S; B – P; C – Q; D – R
(b) A – P; B – S; C – Q; D – R
(c) A – S; B – P; C – R; D – Q
(d) A – P; B – S; C – R; D – Q

27. What is anode mud?
(a) Fan of anode
(b) Metal of anode
(c) Impurities collected at anode in electrolysis during purification of metals
(d) All of these

28. Food cans are coated with tin and not with zinc because **[CDS]**
(a) zinc is costlier than tin.
(b) zinc has a higher melting point than tin.
(c) zinc is more reactive than tin.
(d) zinc is less reactive than tin.

29.

Column-I		Column-II
A.	Titanium	P. Coinage metal
B.	Palladium	Q. Fuel
C.	Uranium	R. Catalyst
D.	Platinum	S. Strategic metal

(a) A – S; B – R; C – Q; D – P
(b) A – P; B – R; C – Q; D – S
(c) A – R; B – S; C – Q; D – P
(d) A – S; B – Q; C – R; D – P

30. 'Yellow cake', an item of smuggling across border is
    (a) a crude form of heroin   **[IAS Prelim]**
    (b) a crude form of cocaine
    (c) uranium oxide
    (d) unrefined gold
31. Which one of the following materials is very hard and very ductile?   **[IAS Prelim]**
    (a) Carborundum   (b) Tungsten
    (c) Cast iron   (d) Nichrome
32. Match List I with List II and select the correct answer using the codes given below the lists   **[IAS Prelim]**

List-I	List-II
A. Blue vitriol	1. Sodium bicarbonate
B. Epsom salt	2. Sodium hydroxide
C. Baking soda	3. Magnesium sulphate
D. Caustic soda	4. Copper sulphate

    Codes:
    (a) A-3; B-4; C-2; D-1
    (b) A-4; B-3; C-2; D-1
    (c) A-3; B-4; C-1; D-2
    (d) A-4; B-3; C-1; D-2
33. Match List-I with List-II and select the correct answer using the codes given below the lists: **[IAS Prelim]**

List-I	List-II
A. Potassium bromide	1. Fertiliser
B. Potassium nitrate	2. Photography
C. Potassium sulphate	3. Bakery
D. Monopotassium tartarate	4. Gun powder

    Codes:
    (a) A-2; B-4; C-1; D-3
    (b) A-2; B-3; C-1; D-4
    (c) A-4; B-2; C-3; D-1
    (d) A-4; B-2; C-1; D-3
34. Match List-I with List-II and select the correct answer using the codes given below the lists: **[IAS Prelim]**

List I (Mineral)	List II (Industries in which largely used)	**[CDS]**
A. Limestone	1. Cement	
B. Copper	2. Electrical goods	
C. Bauxite	3. Manufacture of aeroplanes	
D. Manganese	4. Steel	

    Codes: **[CDS]**

	A	B	C	D
(a)	3	4	1	2
(b)	1	2	3	4
(c)	3	2	1	4
(d)	1	4	3	2

35. German silver is used to make decorative articles, coinage metal, ornaments, The name is given because: **[CDS 2016-I]**
    (a) it is an alloy of copper and contains silver as one of its components
    (b) Germans were the first to use silver
    (c) Its appearance is like silver
    (d) It is an alloy of silver
36. In paper manufacturing, degumming of the raw material is done using   **[CDS 2016-II]**
    (a) sulphuric acid
    (b) bleaching powder
    (c) caustic soda
    (d) nitric acid
37. Dolomite powder is applied in some agricultural lands. The purpose of applying it is to   **[CDS 2016-II]**
    (a) increase the pH of the soil
    (c) lower the pH of the soil
    (c) increase the phosphorus content of the soil
    (d) increase the nitrogen content of the soil
38. The pH value of a sample of multiple-distilled water is   **[CDS 2017-I]**
    (a) zero   (b) 14
    (c) very near to zero   (d) very near to seven
39. In the reaction between hydrogen sulphate ion and water, the water acts as   **[CDS 2017-II]**
    (a) an acid   (b) a base
    (c) a salt   (d) an inert medium
40. Which one of the following gases dissolves in water to give acidic solution?   **[CDS 2018-I]**
    (a) Carbon dioxide   (b) Oxygen
    (c) Nitrogen   (d) Hydrogen
41. Stung by hairs of nettle leaves causes burning pain. This is due to the injection of   **[NDA 2017-I]**
    (a) Acetic acid   (b) Methanoic acid
    (c) Sulphuric acid   (d) Hydrochloric acid
42. The chemical name of baking soda is   **[NDA 2017-I]**
    (a) Na_2CO_3 (b) $NaHCO_3$
    (c) $CaCO_3$ (d) $NaOH$
43. Which compound, when dissolved in water, conducts electricity and forms a basic solution?   **[NDA 2017-II]**
    (a) HCl (b) CH_3COOH
    (c) CH_3OH (d) $NaOH$
44. The principal use of hydrofluoric acid is   **[NDA 2017-II]**
    (a) in etching glass
    (b) as a bleaching agent
    (c) as an extremely strong oxidizing agent
    (d) in the preparation of strong organic fluorine compounds
45. Zinc is used to protect iron from corrosion because zinc is   **[NDA 2017-II]**
    (a) more electropositive than iron
    (b) cheaper than iron
    (c) a bluish white metal
    (d) a good conductor of heat and electricity
46. The desirable range of pH for drinking water is   **[NDA 2017-II]**
    (a) 6.5 to 8.5   (b) 5.0 to 6.5
    (c) 6.5 to 7.0   (d) 7.0 to 8.5

47. Which one of the following gives the highest amount of hydrogen ions (H^+)? **[NDA 2018-I]**
    (a) Sodium hydroxide solution
    (b) Milk of magnesia
    (c) Lemon juice
    (d) Gastric juice

48. Brine is an aqueous solution of **[NDA 2018-I]**
    (a) NaCl
    (b) NaOH
    (c) $NaHCO_3$
    (d) Na_2CO_3

49. Which one of the following is the chemical formula of Washing Soda? **[NDA 2018-I]**
    (a) $NaHCO_3$
    (b) $Na_2CO_3.10H_2O$
    (c) $Na_2CO_3.5H_2O$
    (d) NaOH

50. Which one of the following is a tribasic acid? **[NDA 2018-II]**
    (a) Hydrochloric acid
    (b) Nitric acid
    (c) Sulphuric acid
    (d) Phosphoric acid

51. The solution of which one of the following will have pH less than 7? **[NDA 2018-II]**
    (a) NaOH
    (b) KCl
    (c) $FeCl_3$
    (d) NaCl

ANSWER KEY															
1	(d)	2	(d)	3	(c)	4	(c)	5	(c)	6	(b)	7	(b)	8	(a)
9	(d)	10	(c)	11	(c)	12	(a)	13	(d)	14	(b)	15	(a)	16	(c)
17	(a)	18	(b)	19	(c)	20	(a)	21	(b)	22	(b)	23	(b)	24	(a)
25	(b)	26	(a)	27	(c)	28	(c)	29	(a)	30	(c)	31	(d)	32	(d)
33	(a)	34	(b)	35	(c)	36	(b)	37	(a)	38	(d)	39	(b)	40	(a)
41	(b)	42	(b)	43	(d)	44	(a)	45	(a)	46	(c)	47	(d)	48	(a)
49	(b)	50	(d)	51	(c)											

NON - METALS

NON - METALS

Non-metals occupy the upper right hand corner of the periodic table.

Seventeen elements are generally classified as nonmetals. Their names as per their states in the normal conditions are:

Gases : hydrogen, helium, nitrogen, oxygen, fluorine, neon, chlorine, argon, krypton, xenon and radon.

Liquid: bromine.

Solid: carbon, phosphorus, sulfur, selenium, and iodine.

PROPERTIES OF NON-METALS

Physical Properties

- Non-metals are neither malleable nor ductile.
- They are brittle (break easily).
- They do not conduct heat and electricity.
- They are not lustrous (not shiny). They are dull.
- They are generally soft (except diamond which is extremely hard non-metal).
- They may be solid, liquid or gases at the room temperature.
- They have comparatively low melting points and boiling points (except diamond which is a non-metal having a high melting point and boiling point).
- Non-metals have low densities, that is, non-metals are light substances.
- Non-metals are non-sonorous. They do not produce sound when hit with an object.

Chemical Properties of Non-Metals

Non-metals are more reactive with metals than with other non-metals. Generally non-metals react with each other at a high temperature.

Action of Air:

Non-metals do not react with air at room temperature except white phosphorus.

Action of water:

Generally, non-metals do not react with water. However, chlorine dissolves in water and form an acidic solution.

Displacement of one non-metal by another from salt solution:

Just like metals, non-metals also differ in their reactivities. Among halogen family (*i.e.* Cl, Br, I and F) the most reactive is chlorine (Cl). The order of reactivity is $Cl > Br > I$. Thus chlorine can displace Br and I from solutions of bromides (NaBr) and Iodides (NaI).

Reaction with metals:

Non metals with high electronegativity (F, Cl, Br etc.) generally reacts with alkali and alkaline earth metals to form ionic compounds.

Allotropes are different form of the same element. Different bonding arrengements between atoms result in different structures with different chemical and Phosphorus properties. For example: The allotropic forms of Phosphorus are white, red and black phosphorus.

SOME IMPORTANT NON-METALLIC ELEMENTS

Hydrogen

The discovery of hydrogen is credited to *Henry Cavendish* in 1766, although it had been isolated as early as 1671 by Robert Boyle.

Isotopes of Hydrogen

Three isotopes of hydrogen exist and all occur naturally.

- ^{1}H is sometimes called **Protium**, It is abundent in nature. It is the only hydrogen isotope lacking neutrons.
- The second isotope, ^{2}H, is called **deuterium**

D-element bonds are more difficult to break than H-element bonds and this fact allows the mechanisms of many chemical reactions to be examined. D_2O itself is important as a material that slows neutrons in nuclear reactors.

- The third isotope, ^{3}H, **Tritium** is radioactive.

Properties

- Hydrogen occupies a unique place in the periodic table, and while it usually appears above the alkali metals or the halogens (or both), its properties don't fall well within either group.
- The ionization energy of hydrogen is much higher than any of the alkali metals.
- Hydrogen is a colorless, odorless, tasteless gas at ambient temperature. It has very low boiling and melting points (only helium boils colder). It is poorly soluble in most solvents.

Uses

- Over two-thirds of this hydrogen produced is used to prepare ammonia (NH_3) by the Haber process. The large majority of this ammonia is then used in fertilizer production.
- Methanol, which is an industrially important compound, is prepared from the reaction of hydrogen with carbon monoxide:

Group 18: Noble Gases

- The elements in Group 18 are helium (He), neon (Ne), argon (Ar), krypton (Kr), xenon (Xe) and radon (Rn).
- All Group 18 elements are gases at room temperature.
- They are completely chemically inert with few exceptions.
- The first noble gas compound was prepared in 1962 by scientist Neil Bartlett. Bartlett noticed that the ionization energy of xenon is about the same as that of oxygen.

Group 17: Halogens

The halogens are fluorine (F), chlorine (Cl), bromine (Br), iodine (I) and astatine (Ats).

- Fluorine typically occurs in nature in minerals such as fluorite (fluorspar, CaF_2). The other halogens are generally isolated from salts dissolved in seawater. They are obtained by oxidation of the halide ion to the halogen in a molten salt, except fluorine which requires special conditions to prevent explosions.
- All halogens have high electronaffinities and ionization energies.

Uses of halogenated compounds

- Teflon– non-stick coating, is a polymer made of carbon and fluorine (CF_3 (CF_2)n(CF_2– CF_2–), n is very large).
- The compounds used in air-conditioners (now HCFCs) are compounds made up of carbon, fluorine, hydrogen, and chlorine (e.g. HCFC-22: CHF_2Cl). These substances are more environment friendly than the Freons. (HCFCs are Freons in which either a chlorine or fluorine atom has been replaced by a hydrogen atom to allow easier environmental degradation to occur.)
- Many plastics, organic solvents, pesticides, fungicides, and bactericides contain chlorine atoms. Chlorinated compounds are also used as disinfectants and bleaching agents.

Group16: Chalcogens

- The elements of the Group 16 of the periodic table are Oxygen (O), Sulphur(S), Selenium (Se), Telurium (Te) and Polonium (Po) which are also called **chalcogens.**

Oxygen

- Oxygen is the second most abundant element in the Earth's crust and in hydrosphere.
- Two *allotropes* of oxygen are; O_2: Oxygen and O_3: Ozone. Both occur naturally. Oxygen has a high electron affinity, electronegativity, and ionization energy. It tends to form compounds in the −2 oxidation state, although compounds with −1, −½, and +2 oxidation states also exist (in H_2O_2, KO_2, and OF_2 respectively).
- O_2 is an odorless, colorless, and tasteless gas at room temperature. It is quite reactive and form oxide ions or strong covalent single bonds to other elements. Oxygen is obtained by the fractional distillation of air.
- *Ozone* is a pale blue gas with an irritating odor. It is a significantly stronger oxidant than Dioxygen(O_2) because of its structure. Small amounts of ozone are generated by lightning striking the earth. We can even smell this ozone also. *Internal combustion engines* (cars, trucks, etc.) produce large quantities of *ozone* that frequently affect air quality in cities.

> The word oxygen comes from the Greek meaning 'acid former,' while ozone comes from the Greek meaning 'to smell.'

Sulphur

Sulphur (S) is a non-metallic solid with atomic number 16 and placed in VI-A group of the modern periodic table. It is the second member of the group VIA, first being Oxygen and others being Selenium, Tellurium and Polonium.

Being a member of group VIA, it has 6 electrons in valence shell. Sulphur shows variable valencies of 2, +4 and +6. It exists in different forms (in the same physical state). There are two important crystalline forms - rhombic or octahedral (α - sulphur), and monoclinic sulphur (β - sulphur).

Rhombic sulphur crystallizes at temperature below 96°C, while monoclinic sulphur crystallizes at temperature above 96°C (transitional temperature). Polymeric sulphur (S_8) is another allotrope of sulphur. It is an eight member ring molecule. At 160°C or higher temperatures, the sulphur molecule is energized and eventually ruptures. It is insoluble in organic media, natural and synthetic rubber, as well as in carbon disulphide.

Water (H_2O)

Water is the most abundant molecule on the earth. Approximately 70% of the Earth's surface is water. Water is also the only substance on Earth which naturally occurs in a solid, liquid and gas form. Water is also medium for many chemical reactions. That is why it is called "universal solvent".

Hardness of Water

Hardness of water is due to dissolved sulphate, chloride or carbonate salt of calcium and magnesium. There are two kinds of hardness of water.

- Temporary
- Permanent

Temporary hardness is due to dissolved bicarbonate salt of calcium and magnesium. Temporary hardness can be removed by boiling. Boiling causes formation of carbonate from the bicarbonate.

Permanent hardness is caused by chlorides and sulphate of calcium and magnesium. Permanent hard water can not be softened by boiling.

Though hard water is not considered harmful for drinking, it may cause other harms. Hard water can leave the clothes rough and worn out. More soap is required for washing clothes.

Properties of Water

- It is attracted to other polar molecules. This is also called adhesion. Adhesion leads to occurrence of capillary action.
- Water has high specific heat and high heat of vapourisation because of this water is used as coolant in moter vehicles
- It has high heat of evaporation. This property is responsible for its ability to resist evaporation in moderate temperature.
- Ice has lower density compared to water. This low density allow icebergs to float and is also the reason that only top part of the lakes are frozen.

- Water has high polarity. This makes water a powerful solvent as it attracts other less and polar molecules.

Group 15: Nitrogen

- Nitrogen is rare in the hydrosphere and lithosphere, though abundant in the atmosphere. Only $NaNO_3$ and KNO_3 are found in significant amounts as mineral deposits.
- Compounds of nitrogen occur in all oxidation states from –3 to +5. In this property, nitrogen differs from all other second-row elements except carbon which have very limited numbers of accessible oxidation states.
- Diamond consists of an infinite array of tetrahedral carbon atoms. It is the hardest naturally occurring substance and pure diamond is a colourless crystalline material. It is a very soft, black material that is quite slippery and is a good electrical conductor.

Group 14: Carbon

- Carbon has been known since pre-historic times. Carbon ranks only 17th amongst all elements (between sulfur and zirconium) in abundance in the Earth's crust.
- Carbon is one of the elements which shows allotropy.

Carbon-monoxide (CO)

- Carbon monoxide (CO) is a colorless, odorless, tasteless gas with a relatively low boiling point.
- It forms when carbon or hydrocarbons burn in a deficiency of oxygen.
- It is toxic in either high doses or prolonged (hours) exposure to low doses. Its toxicity arises because it binds to hemoglobin much like oxygen does, but more strongly

Uses

- Industrially, carbon monoxide is sometimes used as a fuel because it burns to carbon dioxide.
- It also is a valuable reducing agent. When reacted with hydrogen it generates methanol, an important organic solvent and basic reagent.

Carbon-dioxide(CO_2)

- Like carbon monoxide, carbon dioxide (CO_2) is colourless, odourless, and tasteless.
- It is much less toxic than CO, but will induce unconsciousness and death at very high concentrations even if it is not inhaled.

- Carbon dioxide is absorbed by plants in the presence of sunlight and chlorophyll (green colouring matter) to form glucose and higher carbohydrates. This process is known as *photosynthesis.*

Uses: The two major uses of carbon dioxide are as a refrigerant and for carbonating soft drinks.

Carbonic Acid and Carbonates

- When CO_2 dissolves in water, the weak acid, i.e. carbonic acid (H_2CO_3) forms.
- Carbonate minerals are plentiful in nature and include aragonite ($CaCO_3$), calcite ($CaCO_3$), dolomite ($CaMgCO_3$), gaylussite $Na_2Ca(CO_3)_2$, lanthanite (($La,Ce)_2(CO_3)_3$), magnesite ($MgCO_3$), and witherite ($BaCO_3$). Of the minerals, the calcium and magnesium containing varieties are most important.
- In particular, the stalactites and stalagmites in caves are composed of calcium carbonate are coral reefs.

Elemental silicon is a semiconductor and very pure material (99.9999%). It is used in the production of computer chips.

Glass

- Glass is simply quartz to which one or more other substances have been added. Because of this added substance, the temperature at which the quartz melts is lowered. This is important because quartz melts near 1000°C and getting flames that hot is very difficult.
- *Common glass* (also soft glass or soda-lime glass) is prepared by adding calcium carbonate and sodium carbonate to molten quartz. The heat drives carbon dioxide off, leaving calcium oxide and sodium oxide behind.
- *Lead crystal* results from adding lead oxide to quartz. The extra mass of the lead gives high quality crystal its heavier feel and the high refractive index that gives crystal its special look.
- *Pyrex* is obtained by adding boron oxide, B_2O_3, to quartz. This causes its coefficient of thermal expansion to decrease. Baking dish made of pyrex glass when moved from freezer to the oven do not crack. Also, stovetop cookware is possible with borosilicate glass, because it won't crack or melt under normal kitchen conditions.
- Coloured glass results from the addition of transition metal ions to the glass. The metal usually exists as an oxide in the structure. Examples are:

Colour	Element used	Colour	Element used
blue-violet	cobalt	green	chromium
canary	uranium	pale pink	tellurium
peacock blue	copper	violet	manganese
cranberry	gold	red	copper
photochromatic	AgCl/AgBr (changes color as surrounding lighting changes)		

- *Sulphur* is used in making compounds like sulpha drugs, sulphuric acid, in matches, in gun powder, for vulcanization of rubber, etc.
- *Boron*, in the form of compound borax, is used in making skin ointments.
- *Phosphorus* is used in making crackers.
- *Chlorine*, in the form of bleaching powder, is used for purification of water.
- *Carbon* is used as a fuel, as electrodes (graphite), as a reducing agent in metallurgy.
- *Oxygen, hydrogen and nitrogen* are used by all living things; they are the 'building blocks' of life.
- *Iodine* is used to prevent thyroid problems.
- *Bromine* is used in the preparation of dyes.
- Some compounds of *fluorine* (such as sodium fluoride, stannous fluoride) are added to toothpastes to prevent dental decays or formation of cavities.

MULTIPLE CHOICE QUESTIONS

1. Which of the following reacts with cold water vigorously?
   (a) carbon   (b) sodium
   (c) magnesium   (d) sulphur
2. Which of the following non-metals has shining lustrous surfaces?
   (a) Graphite and phosphorus
   (b) Graphite and iodine
   (c) Iodine and phosphorus
   (d) Phosphorus and chlorine
3. A non metal that catches fire at room temperature is-
   (a) Sodium   (b) Sulphur
   (c) Phosphorus   (d) Fluorine
4. Which of the following metals on reacting with sodium hydroxide solution produce hydrogen gas?
   A. Cu   B. Al
   C. Fe   D. Zn
   (a) B and C   (b) A and D
   (c) B and D   (d) B only
5. Which are the most abundant elements in the universe? **[NDA]**
   (a) Oxygen and Nitrogen (b) Hydrogen and Oxygen
   (c) Hydrogen and Helium (d) Carbon and Nitrogen
6. What is the colour of oxygen in solid state? **[NDA]**
   (a) Pale yellow   (b) Pale blue
   (c) Light green   (d) Greenish yellow
7. Why is nitrogen molecule chemically less active? **[NDA]**
   (a) It has small atomic radius
   (b) It has high electronegativity
   (c) It has high dissociation energy
   (d) It has stable electronic configuration
8. Yellow colour of usual nitric acid is due to the presence of which one of the following? **[NDA]**
   (a) N_2O (b) NO
   (c) N_2O_5 (d) NO_2
9. Which one of the following elements cannot displace hydrogen gas from a dilute acid? **[NDA]**
   (a) Zinc   (b) Copper
   (c) Magnesium   (d) Iron
10. Which of the following is not a nitrogenous fertilizer? **[NDA]**
    (a) $Ca(CN)_2$ (b) $CaCN_2$
    (c) NH_4NO_3 (d) Urea
11. Which one of the following is the correct order in which the gases H_2, Ne, O_2 and N_2 are evolved on fractional distillation of liquid air? **[NDA]**
    (a) H_2, Ne, O_2, N_2 (b) H_2, Ne, N_2, O_2
    (c) N_2, O_2, Ne, H_2 (d) O_2, N_2, H_2, Ne
12. Which of the following is an element which never exhibits positive oxidation state in any of its compounds? **[NDA]**
    (a) Oxygen   (b) Chlorine
    (c) Fluorine   (d) Carbon
13. Oxygen and ozone are **[NDA]**
    (a) allotropes   (b) isomers
    (c) isotopes   (d) isobars

14. A glass of water does not turn into ice as it reaches 0 °C. It is because **[NDA]**
    (a) water does not solidify at 0°C
    (b) a certain amount of heat must be supplied to the glass of water so as to solidify
    (c) a certain amount of heat must be taken out from the glass of water so as to solidify
    (d) water solidifies at 0 K only
15. Which one among the following does *not* have an allotrope? **[NDA]**
    (a) Oxygen   (b) Sulphur
    (c) Nitrogen   (d) Carbon
16. Deionised water is produced by
    (a) Calgon process   **[NDA]**
    (b) Ion-exchange resin process
    (c) Clark's process
    (d) Permutit process
17. Which one of the following is the secondary source of light in a fluorescent lamp? **[CDS]**
    (a) Neon gas   (b) Argon gas
    (c) Mercury vapour   (d) Fluorescent coating
18. Which one of the following is the softest? **[CDS]**
    (a) Sodium   (b) Aluminium
    (c) Iron   (d) Copper
19. Which among the following elements is abundant on the lunar surface and holds the potential to put an end to the energy crisis of the earth? **[CDS]**
    (a) Helium-I   (b) Helium-II
    (c) Helium-III   (d) Helium-IV
20. Which allotropy of carbon is in rigid three- dimensional structure? **[CDS]**
    (a) Graphite   (b) Fullerene
    (c) Diamond   (d) Carbon black
21. What are the elements which are liquids at room temperature and standard pressure? **[CDS]**
    1. Helium   2. Mercury
    3. Chlorine   4. Bromine
    Select the correct answer using the codes given below
    (a) 2 and 3   (b) 2, 3 and 4
    (c) 2 and 4   (d) 1 and 3
22. Both Potassium and sulfuric acid form intercalation compounds with graphite. The graphite layers are
    (a) reduced in both the cases
    (b) oxidized in both the cases
    (c) oxidized in the case of Potassium and reduced in the case of Sulphuric acid
    (d) reduced in the case of Potassium and oxidized in the case of sulphuric acid
23. Which one of the following is also called Stranger Gas? **[IAS Prelim]**
    (a) Argon   (b) Neon
    (c) Xenon   (d) Nitrous oxide

24. **Statement I:** Soaps do not form lather with water containing salts of calcium and magnesium. **[CDS]**
Statement II: Calcium and magnesium salts of long chain fatty acids are insoluble in water.
   (a) Both the statements are individually true and Statement II is the correct explanation of Statement I.
   (b) Both the statements are individually true but Statement II is not the correct explanation of Statement I.
   (c) Statement I is true, but Statement II is false.
   (d) Statement I is false, but Statement II is true.

25. The form of carbon known as graphite **[CDS 2014-II]**
   (a) is harder than diamond
   (b) contains a higher percentage of carbon than diamond
   (c) is a better electrical conductor than diamond
   (d) has equal carbon-to-carbon distances in all directions

26. Which of the following is a good lubricant ? **[CDS 2014-II]**
   (a) Diamond powder
   (b) Graphite powder
   (c) Molten carbon
   (d) Alloy of carbon and iron

27. Which one of the following is not true for diamond? **[CDS 2015-II]**
   (a) Each carbon atom is linked to four other carbon atoms
   (b) Three-dimensional network structure of carbon atoms is formed
   (c) It is used as an abrasive for sharpening hard tools
   (d) It can be used as a lubricant.

28. Which one of the following is not an allotrope of carbon? **[CDS 2016-II]**
   (a) Coal
   (b) Diamond
   (c) Graphite
   (d) Graphene

29. The paste of a white material in water is used to maintain a fractured bone fixed in place. The white material used is called **[CDS 2017-II]**
   (a) bleaching powder
   (b) plaster of Paris
   (c) powder of zinc oxide
   (d) lime powder

30. Tincture of iodine is an antiseptic for fresh wounds. It is a dilute solution of elemental iodine, which **does not** contain **[CDS 2017-II]**
   (a) water
   (b) acetone
   (c) alcohol
   (d) potassium iodide

31. Which of the following substances cause temporary hardness in water? **[CDS 2018-I]**
   1. $Mg(HCO_3)_2$
   2. $Ca(HCO_3)_2$
   3. $CaCl_2$
   4. $MgSO_4$
   Select the correct answer using the code given below:
   (a) 3 and 4
   (b) 2 and 3
   (c) 1 and 4
   (d) 1 and 2

32. Temporary hardness in water is due to which one of the following of Calcium and Magnesium? **[NDA 2017-I]**
   (a) Hydrogencarbonates
   (b) Carbonates
   (c) Chlorides
   (d) Sulphates

33. Which one of the following elements forms highest number of compounds? **[NDA 2017-I]**
   (a) Oxygen
   (b) Hydrogen
   (c) Chlorine
   (d) Carbon

34. Which one of the following elements is used in pencil-lead? **[NDA 2017-I]**
   (a) Zinc
   (b) Lead
   (c) Carbon (Graphite)
   (d) Tin

35. When pure water boils vigorously, the bubbles that rise to the surface are composed primarily of **[NDA 2017-II]**
   (a) air
   (b) hydogen
   (c) hydrogen and oxygen
   (d) water vapour

36. Why is potassium permanganate used for purifying drinking water? **[NDA 2017-II]**
   (a) It kills germs
   (b) It dissolves the impurities
   (c) It is a reducing agent
   (d) It is an oxidizing agent

37. Permanent hardness of water cannot be removed by which one of the following methods? **[NDA 2018-II]**
   (a) Treatment with washing soda
   (b) Calgon's method
   (c) Boiling
   (d) Ion exchange method

ANSWER KEY															
1	(b)	2	(b)	3	(c)	4	(b)	5	(a)	6	(a)	7	(c)	8	(d)
9	(b)	10	(a)	11	(b)	12	(c)	13	(a)	14	(c)	15	(c)	16	(b)
17	(d)	18	(a)	19	(c)	20	(c)	21	(c)	22	(d)	23	(c)	24	(a)
25	(c)	26	(b)	27	(d)	28	(d)	29	(b)	30	(b)	31	(d)	32	(a)
33	(d)	34	(c)	35	(c)	36	(d)	37	(c)						

Chapter 6

ORGANIC CHEMISTRY

ORGANIC CHEMISTRY

Organic chemistry is the study of carbon containing compounds and their properties. This includes the great majority of chemical compounds on the planet, but **some substances** such as **carbonates** and **oxides of carbon** are considered to be **inorganic** substances even though they contain carbon. There exists a large number of organic compounds.

Differences Between Organic and Inorganic Compounds

Following table compares the properties of the organic and inorganic compounds:

Organic Compounds	Inorganic Compounds
Use mostly covalent bonding	Mostly ionic bonding
Are gases, liquids or solids with low melting points	Are generally solids with high melting points
Mostly insoluble in water	Many are water soluble
Many are soluble in organic solvents such as petroleum, benzene and hexane	Most are not soluble in organic solvents
Solution in water generally do not conduct electricity	When dissolved in water conducts electrical current
Almost all burn	Most not combustible
Slow to react with other chemicals	Often undergo fast chemical reactions

CATENATION IN CARBON

Majority of organic compounds contain chains or rings of carbon atoms that contain other elements such as O, N, P, S, Cl, Br and I. The compounds of carbon are far more numerous than the known compounds of all the other elements put together. *This is because that carbon has the power to combine with other carbon atoms to form long chains; this property is not shown to such an extent by any other element. This property of carbon is known as catenation.*

FUNCTIONAL GROUPS

Classes of organic compounds can be distinguished according to functional groups they contain. *A functional group is a group of atoms that is largely responsible for the chemical behavior of the parent molecule.*

Classification of Organic Compounds

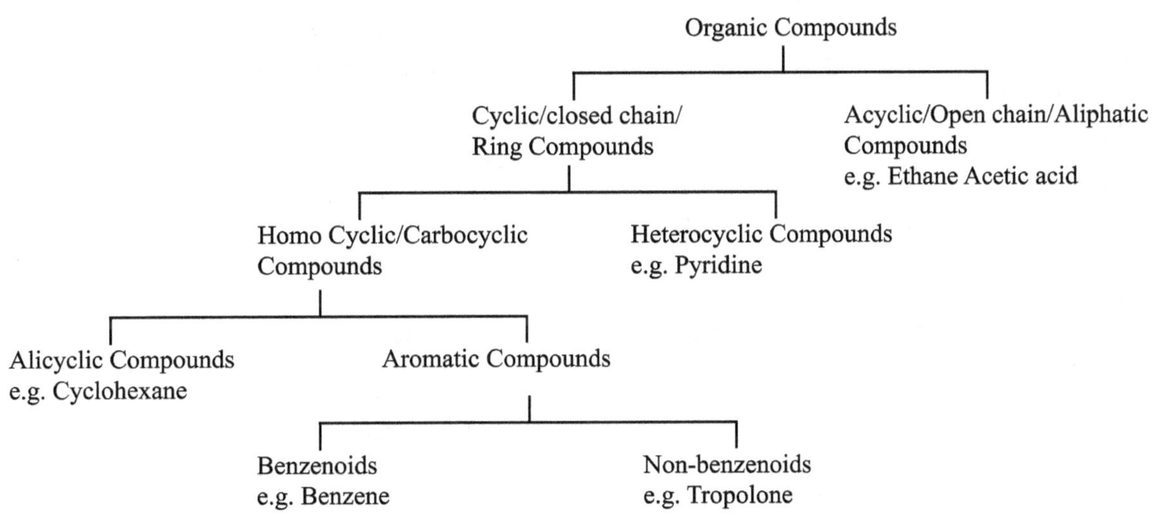

Important Functional Groups and the Corresponding Classes of Organic Compounds

S.No.	Functional Group		Class of compounds
	Formula	Name	
1.	$-X$ ($-F$, Cl, $-Br$, $-I$)	Halo (fluoro, chloro, bromo, iodo)	Alkyl halides or halogen compounds
2.	$-OH$	Hydroxy	Alcohol
3.	$-OR$	Alkoxy	Ethers
4.	$-SH$	Mercapto	Thioalcohols, mercaptans or thiols
5.	$-SR$	Thioether	Thioethers or sulphides
6.	$-CHO$	Aldehydic	Aldehydes
7.	$-CO-$	Ketonic	Ketones
8.	$-COOH$	Carboxyl	Carboxylic acids
9.	$-COOR$	Ester	Esters
10.	$-COX$ (X = Cl, Br or I)	Acyl halide	Acid halides or Acyl halides
11.	$-CONH_2$	Amide	Amides or acid amides
12.	$-CO.O.CO-$	Anhydride	Acid anhydrides
13.	$-NH_2$	Amino	Amines
14.	$-NH-$	Imino	Imines
15.	$-C \equiv N$	Cyano	Cyanides or Nitriles
16.	$-N \equiv C$	Isocyano	Isocyanides or Isonitriles
17.	$-NO_2$	Nitro	Nitro compounds
18.	$-N = O$	Nitroso	Nitroso compounds
19.	$-N = N-$	Azo	Azo compounds
20.	$-SO_2 - OH$	Sulphonic acid	Sulphonic acids

HYDROCARBONS

The simplest organic compounds are the hydrocarbons, which are composed solely of carbon and hydrogen.

Hydrocarbons can be classcified in two general groups *aliphatic* and *aromatic*. These compounds are the starting point for all organic compounds.

Aliphatic Hydrocarbons

Aliphatic hydrocarbons consist of straight or branched chains of carbon atoms with the other valence electrons involved in bonds with hydrogen. Examples are:

$$CH_3\text{-}CH_2\text{-}CH_2\text{-}CH_2\text{-}CH_3 \qquad CH_2 = CH_2$$
$$\text{Pentane} \qquad\qquad\qquad \text{Ethene}$$

Aliphatic hydrocarbons can be subdivided into two groups based on the types of carbon-carbon bonds the compounds contain.

Saturated aliphatic hydrocarbons

Saturated aliphatic hydrocarbons are hydrocarbons in which all of the carbon-carbon bonds are single bonds. These compounds are also referred to as *alkanes*, as mentioned for single bonds earlier. The simplest alkane is methane, CH_4.

- All other alkanes are formed by adding CH_2s to the formula. Hence the general formula for the alkanes is C_nH_{2n+2}.
- Alkanes are not very reactive chemically and are insoluble in water. They burn to form carbon dioxide and water (*combustion reaction*).
- *Alkanes also under go reactions induced by UV light.* Examples include the slow breakdown of plastics in the sun,

and halogenations reactions (reactions where halogen atoms such as Cl, Br, or I replace H in the molecule).

Unsaturated aliphatic hydrocarbons

Unsaturated hydrocarbons are those hydrocarbons, which contain at least one double or triple bond (that is, they are alkenes or alkynes) between two carbon atoms. Simplest of alkene (General formula of alkenes are: C_nH_{2n-2}) is ethene which consists of two double-bonded carbon atoms and four hydrogen atoms.

$$CH_2 = CH_2$$

- The general formula of alkyne is C_nH_{2n} and the simplest of alkyne is acetylene CH≡CH

Aromatic Hydrocarbons

- The second major group of the hydrocarbons is the aromatic hydrocarbons, which are hydrocarbons that contain a benzene ring as part of their structure.
- Benzene has the formula C_6H_6 and consists of six carbon atoms in a ring with three alternating double bonds.
- Aromatic compounds show completely different behavior to aliphatic compounds, and hence it is not difficult to deduce that they have a special chemical structure.

Representations of Benzene

There are two accepted ways of representing the structure of benzene. The first is the Kekule structure that is written as shown below. Two structures-called resonating structures- are required, as one structure cannot fully represent the molecule. The molecule is said to alternate very rapidly between the two structures.

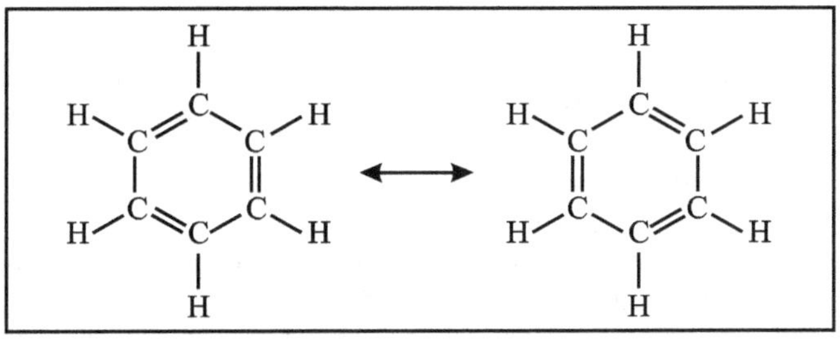

The resonance structures are hypothetical and individually do not represent any real molecule.

Properties of benzene

Benzene is totally insoluble in water, it is a volatile liquid at room temperature. The properties of other aromatics are reflective of benzene but vary according to the substituent added to the ring in place of one of the hydrogen atoms.

> The term "aromatic" has its origin in the fact that certain aromatic substances (for example: oil of bitter almonds, vanilla, and oil of wintergreen) contain the benzene ring. The possession of an odor is not characteristic, however, of all aromatic substances. Aromatic compounds containing benzene ring are known as benzenoids and those not containing benzene ring are known as non-benzenoids.

Aromatic hydrocarbons are the starting point for many medicinally important compounds.

ALCOHOL (ALKANOL)

- Alcohols are hydroxyl (-OH) derivatives of hydrocarbons formed by replacing a hydrogen with the hydroxyl radical and are of the general form R-OH where R represents the hydrocarbon.
- There are three categories of alcohols: primary, secondary, and tertiary.

> A reagent that brings an electron pair is called a nucleophile/nucleus seeking (Nu:) and the reaction is called nucleophilic. A reagent that takes away an electron pair/electron seeking (E+) and the reaction is called electrophilic.

- Ethanol (CH_3CH_2OH) has been prepared since antiquity by fermentation of sugars and starches, catalyzed by yeast. Sugars for fermentation come from a variety of sources, including grains, grape juice, various vegetables and agricultural wastes.
- Yeast secretes two enzymes called invertase and zymase. These enzymes act as catalyst for converting sugar to ethanol.

Properties of Alcohols

The low-molecular-weight alcohols are volatile liquids, and the high-molecular-weight alcohols (more than 13 carbons) are solids. The first three alcohols (C_1 to C_3) are completely miscible (mix in any proportion) with water.

Uses of Alcohols

- Alcohols are most commonly used as solvents in the pharmacy.
- They are also used as disinfectants and antiseptics.

ETHERS

Ethers are a class of organic compounds that contain an ether group—an oxygen atom connected to two alkyl or aryl groups—of general formula: R–O–R'. When the two alkyl groups are similar, then its *Symmetrical ether* otherwise we call it *Unsymmetrical ether*.

Properties of Ethers

Ether molecules cannot form hydrogen bonds with each other since they do not have a hydrogen atom attached directly to an oxygen atom. Therefore, they have about the same boiling points and melting points as alkanes of similar molecular weights.

Uses of Ethers

Ethers are used as general anesthetics in medicine. They also find use as solvents. Some important ethers include diethyl ether (which has been traditionally known as ether) that was used as a general anesthetic, and methyl phenyl ether (commonly called anisole) which is used extensively in the perfume industry.

AMINES

- Amines result from the replacement of one or more of the hydrogen atoms of ammonia with hydrocarbons and have the general formula $R\text{-}NH_2$.
- Amines are derivatives of ammonia that has three hydrogen.
- Amines are classified according to the number of hydrogen that are replaced by alkyl or phenyl groups in ammonia (NH_3)
- Whenever one of the hydrocarbon groups connected to the nitrogen atom contains a benzene ring, the compound is referred to as an aromatic amine.

Properties of Amines

The low-molecular-weight amines are all volatile liquids, and those having up to five carbons are soluble in water. The element nitrogen is in the same period of the periodic table as oxygen and has some similar properties--the most significant being the ability to form hydrogen bonds. The formation of hydrogen bonds between amines, and between amines and water, accounts for their higher boiling points (than alkanes) and their water solubility.

> Amines react with inorganic acids to form salts. (Amines react with organic acids to form amides, a class of organic compounds.) This reaction results in a hydrochloride salt of the amine and is a very important reaction in pharmacy. Many drugs contain an amine functional group, and if they contain many carbon atoms, they are not very soluble in water. The salts formed from amines, however, are very soluble in water. Therefore, if we wish to use a water solution of an amine drug that is insoluble, we can make it soluble by forming the salt of the amine.

Use of Amines

Amines are very important biological compounds and are responsible for most of the fishy odours that we detect in nature. They are also found in decomposing tissues (such as off meat). Amines are building blocks of many natural and synthetic materials – proteins, textiles, plastics, adhesives, and pharmaceuticals.

ALKANOIC ACID (CARBOXYLIC ACIDS)

Carboxylic acids are compounds which contain a -COOH group.

- Most of the simpler saturated carboxylic acids are found in nature.
  For example ethanoic acid (also referred to as acetic acid) is commonly found in vinegar and wine. Its structural formula is CH_3COOH. Butanoic acid (C_4H_9COOH) is found in cheeses, rancid butter, and under armpits of human; whilst hexanoic acid ($C_6H_{13}COOH$) is the odour associated with goats and goat cheeses. Ethanoic acid is an important industrial chemical.
- Alkanoic acids (Carboxylic acids) are produced in major quantities by the combustion of coal and wood. Long chain carboxylic acids have also been found in the atmosphere, the major source of the compounds being pollens and other plant products.

Properties of Carboxylic Acids

Carboxylic acids are very polar compounds due to the two oxygen atoms and can form two hydrogen bonds between themselves.

A carboxylic acid has a higher melting point than a different type of organic compound with a similar molecular weight. Consequently, they are all solids under normal conditions.

Uses of Carboxylic Acids: Many carboxylic acids have use in food industry.

- **Benzoic acid** – a common preservative used in beverages.
- **Citric acid** – used to provide a sour taste in fruit and vegetables.
- **Sorbic acid** – used as an acidic anti-microbial agent.
- **Lactic acid** – commonly found in cultured dairy products.
- **Malic acid** – commonly found in fruits.
- **Tartaric acid** – used extensively in cooking processes (it is also called cream of tartar)

ALDEHYDE (ALKANOLS)

Aldehydes and Ketones are characterised by the presence of carbonyl group $>C = O$ in their molecules. Aldehydes contain

group $\overset{H}{\underset{R}{>}}C = O$ and ketones the $\overset{R}{\underset{R}{>}}C = O$.

- Aldehydes have lower boiling points than corresponding alcohols or acids as they cannot form hydrogen bonds between themselves.
- The lower-molecular-weight aldehydes (up to five carbons) are soluble in water. Aldehydes are neutral in pH and undergo both oxidation and reduction reactions.
- They are easily oxidized to acids and reduced to alcohols.

Use

- Some aldehydes, such as vanillin and benzaldehyde, are frequently used in the pharmacy as flavouring agents. Others, such as formaldehyde, are often used as disinfectants.
- Both aldehyde (and ketones) occurs in natural and man-made products very frequently.
- All naturally occurring plant sugars (such as glucose) are aldehydes, ketones, or their products.

Aldehydes are also produced in the atmosphere from hydrocarbons as a result of a complicated process called *photo-oxidation*. These aldehydes contribute to smog; ethanal is the aldehyde most commonly identified in smog. Methanal is almost present in all air samples tested. Aldehydes produced by plants such as 2-hexenal has been found in forested atmospheres, in addition to methanal and ethanal.

KETONES (ALKANONE)

Ketones result from the oxidation of a secondary alcohol and have the general structural formula O where R and R' can be the same or different hydrocarbon groups.

$$R-C-R'$$

- Ketones are similar to aldehydes in their boiling points, which are lower than those of corresponding alcohols and carboxylic acids.
- Ketones are neutral compounds, being neither acids nor bases.

Ketones are also often responsible for the smell component of many natural body substances. e.g. the strange smelling breath of a diabetic is due to the presence of propanone.

ESTERS

Esters are formed from the reaction of a carboxylic acid with an alcohol and have the general structural formula RCOOR' where R and R' can be the same or different hydrocarbon groups.

- The simplest esters are liquids and have fragrant odours. An example is ethyl acetate, $CH_3-CH_2-OOC-CH_3$, which has the odour of pineapple.
- Esters have boiling points similar to alkanes of similar molecular weight as they cannot form hydrogen bonds between themselves.
- They can form hydrogen bonds with water. Therefore, esters that contain less than five carbon atoms are soluble in water.

Uses of Esters

- The sweet and pleasant odours and tastes of many foods are due to complex mixtures of organic compounds, of which esters are generally the most prevalent component. Some examples of esters that are used as flavouring agents and the corresponding flavours are:
  - methyl butanoate: apple
  - ethyl butanoate: strawberry
  - butyl butanoate: pineapple
  - pentyl ethanoate: banana
  - methyl 2-phenylethanoate: jasmine

MULTIPLE CHOICE QUESTIONS

1. The enzyme involved in the oxidation of ethanol to form vinegar is
   (a) zymase   (b) oxidase
   (c) dehydrgenase   (d) invertase

2. The main constituent of Vinegar is: **[NDA]**
   (a) Acetic acid   (b) Ascorbic acid
   (c) Citric acid   (d) Tartaric acid

3. Soaps are sodium salts of fatty acids. Which of the following fatty acid does not form soap?
   (a) Butyric acid   (b) Oleic acid
   (c) Palmitic acid   (d) Stearic acid

4. Identify the enzyme which converts glucose to ethyl alcohol.
   (a) Zymase   (b) Invertase
   (c) Maltase   (d) Diastase

5. Mineral acids are stronger acids than carboxylic acids because
   A. mineral acids are completely ionised
   B. carboxylic acids are completely ionised
   C. mineral acids are partially ionised
   D. carboxylic acids are partially ionised
   (a) A and D   (b) B and C
   (c) A and B   (d) C and D

6. 'Drinking alcohol' is very harmful and it ruins the health. 'Drinking alcohol' stands for:
   (a) drinking methyl alcohol
   (b) drinking ethyl alcohol
   (c) drinking propyl alcohol
   (d) drinking isopropyl alcohol

7. Which of the following has shortest carbon-carbon bond length?
   (a) C_2H_2 (b) C_2H_4
   (c) C_2H_6 (d) C_6H_6

8. Which of the following can be used distinguish between ethane and ethene?
   (a) A lighted splinter
   (b) Aqueous bromine
   (c) Litmus solution
   (d) Lime water

9.

Column-I		Column-II
A.	Carbon black	P.	Water filters.
B.	Diamond	Q.	Fuel
C.	Coke	R.	Jewellery
D.	Charcoal	S.	Filler in automobiles

   (a) A-Q; B-R; C-S; D-P
   (b) A-P; B-Q; C-Q; D-S
   (c) A-S; B-R; C-P; D-Q
   (d) A-S; B-R; C-Q; D-P

10.

Column-I		Column-II
A.	Polyethylene	P. wood glue
B.	Cellulose acetate	Q. Soft drinks
C.	Polyvinyl acetate	R. Descaling agents
D.	Dil. Acetic acid	S. Photographic film.

    (a) A-Q; B-S; C-P; D-R
    (b) A-S; B-Q; C-P; D-R
    (c) A-Q; B-S; C-R; D-P
    (d) A-S; B-Q; C-R; D-P

11. Gas welding used for welding broken pieces of iron, we normally use a mixture of:
    (a) ethane and oxygen
    (b) ethene and oxygen
    (c) ethyne and oxygen
    (d) ethene and air

12. On the basis of following features identify the correct option
    A. Drinks containing ethanol
    B. These drinks are major source of income to government
    (a) Alcoholic beverages
    (b) Soft drinks
    (c) Carbonated beverages
    (d) Rectified spirit

13. The flavour of apple is mainly due to which one of the following? **[CDS]**
    (a) Formalin   (b) Benzene
    (c) Ethanol   (d) Benzaldehyde

14. Which of the following has maximum density? **[CDS]**
    (a) Chloroform   (b) Water
    (c) Benzene   (d) Ice

15. Addition of ethylene dibromide to petrol **[CDS]**
    (a) increases the octane number of fuel
    (b) helps elimination of lead oxide
    (c) removes the sulphur compound in petrol
    (d) serves as a substitute of tetraethyl lead

16. The offending substance in the liquor tragedies leading to blindness etc., is **[IAS Prelim]**
    (a) ethyl alcohol   (b) amyl alcohol
    (c) benzyl alcohol   (d) methyl alcohol

17. The characteristic odour of garlic is due to **[IAS Prelim]**
    (a) a chloro compound   (b) a sulphur compound
    (c) a fluorine compound   (d) acetic acid

18. Which one of the following is an active component of oil of clove? **[IAS Prelim]**
    (a) Menthol   (b) Eugenol
    (c) Methanol   (d) Benzaldehyde

19. Consider the following statements about acetylene:
    1. It is used in welding industry
    2. It is a raw material for preparing plastics
    3. It is easily obtained by mixing silicon carbide and water
    of these statements **[IAS Prelim]**
    (a) 1 and 2 are correct   (b) 1 and 3 are correct
    (c) 2 and 3 are correct   (d) 1, 2 and 3 are correct

20. Which one of the following is the correct sequence in increasing order of molecular weights of the hydrocarbons?

[IAS Prelim]

(a) Methane, ethane, propane and butane
(b) Propane, butane, ethane and methane
(c) Butane, ethane, propane and methane
(d) Butane, propane, ethane and methane

21. Assertion (A): The main constituent of the liquefied petroleum gas is methane.

Reason (R): Methane can be used directly for burning in homes and factories where it can be supplied through pipelines. **[IAS Prelim]**

(a) Both A and R are true and R is the correct explanation of A
(b) Both A and R are true but R is not the correct explanation of A
(c) A is true but R is false
(d) A is false but R is true

22. A bee-sting leaves an acid which causes pain and irritation. The injected acid is **[NDA]**

(a) acetic acid　　　(b) sulphuric acid
(c) citric acid　　　(d) methanoic acid

23. The major product formed in the following reaction is

(a)

(b)

(c)

(d)

24. Molecules of which of the following has cage like structure? **[NDA-2017-I]**

1. Diamond　　　2. Graphite
3. Fullerenes

Select the correct answer using the code given below:

(a) 1, 2 and 3　　　(b) 2 and 3 only
(c) 2 only　　　(d) 3 only

25. How is carbon black obtained? **[NDA-2018-I]**

(a) By heating wood at high temperature in absence of air
(b) By heating coal at high temperature in absence of air
(c) By burning hydrocarbons in a limited supply of air
(d) By heating coal at high temperature in presence of air

26. Which one of the following properties is NOT true for graphite? **[NDA-2018-I]**

(a) Hybridisation of each carbon atom of sp^3
(b) Hybridisation of each carbon atom is sp^2
(c) Electrons are delocalized over the whole sheet of atoms
(d) Each layer is composed of hexagonal rings.

27. Which one of the following is the purest form of Carbon? **[NDA-2018-I]**

(a) Charcoal　　　(b) Coke
(c) Fullerene　　　(d) Carbon black

28. Which one of the following statements is not correct?

[NDA-2018-II]

(a) All carbons in diamond are linked by carbon-carbon single bond.
(b) Graphite is layered structure in which layers are held together by weak van der Waals forces.
(c) Graphite layers are formed by hexagonal rings of carbon atoms.
(d) Graphite layers are held together by carbon-carbon single bond.

ANSWER KEY															
1	(c)	**2**	(a)	**3**	(a)	**4**	(a)	**5**	(a)	**6**	(b)	**7**	(a)	**8**	(b)
9	(d)	**10**	(a)	**11**	(c)	**12**	(a)	**13**	(c)	**14**	(b)	**15**	(d)	**16**	(d)
17	(b)	**18**	(b)	**19**	(a)	**20**	(a)	**21**	(d)	**22**	(d)	**23**	(a)	**24**	(d)
25	(c)	**26**	(a)	**27**	(d)	**28**	(d)								

CHEMISTRY AND MANKIND

- Living systems are made of a number of complex organic compounds which are called bio-molecules. The various biomolecules are carbohydrates, amino acids, proteins, enzymes, lipids, hormones; etc. We may call these molecules of life also.

SOME IMPORTANT MOLECULES OF LIFE

Carbohydrate

The chemicals used by the body may be divided into two categories;
- **Macronutrients:** those substances that we need to eat regularly in fairly large quantities.
- **Micronutrients:** those substances that we need only in small quantities.

Carbohydrates are the main energy sources for the human body. Chemically, carbohydrates are organic molecules in which carbon, hydrogen, and oxygen bond together in the ratio : $C_X(H_2O)_Y$, where X and Y are whole numbers.

Animals obtain carbohydrates by eating foods like potatoes, rice, breads, and so on. These carbohydrates are manufactured by plants during the process of photosynthesis. Plants harvest energy from sunlight to run the reaction just described in reverse :

$$6CO_2 + 6H_2O + \text{energy (from sunlight)} \longrightarrow C_6H_{12}O_6 + 6O_2$$

There are two types of carbohydrates, the simple sugars and those that are made of long chains of sugars - the complex carbohydrates.

Simple Sugars

All carbohydrates are made up of units of sugar (also called saccharide units). Carbohydrates that contain only one sugar unit (monosaccharides) or two sugar units (disaccharides) are referred to as simple sugars. Simple sugars are sweet in taste and are broken down quickly in the body to release energy. Two of the most common monosaccharides are glucose and fructose. Glucose is the primary form of sugar stored in the human body for energy. Fructose is the main sugar found in most fruits. Both glucose and fructose have the same chemical formula ($C_6H_{12}O_6$); however, they have different structures. Disaccharides have two sugar units bonded together. For example, common table sugar is sucrose, a disaccharide that consists of a glucose unit bonded to a fructose unit.

Sweetening power of common sugars:

Fructose > Invert sugar > Sucrose > Glucose > Maltose > Lactose

Complex Carbohydrates

Complex carbohydrates are polymers of the simple sugars. In other words, the complex carbohydrates are long chains of simple sugar units bonded together. Therefore the complex carbohydrates can also be referred to as polysaccharides. Starch is an example of complex carbohydrate.

> Both starch and glycogen are polymers of glucose; however, starch is a long, straight chain of glucose units, wheras glycogen is a branched chain of glucose units. Another important polysaccharide is **cellulose**. Cellulose is yet a third polymer of the monosaccharide glucose. Cellulose differs from starch and glycogen in terms of extra stability. Cellulose, also known as plant fiber, cannot be digested by human beings, therefore cellulose passes through the digestive tract without being absorbed into the body. Cellulose fiber is essential in the diet because it helps exercise the digestive track and keep it clean and healthy.

OIL AND FATS

Fats consist of a wide group of compounds that are generally soluble in organic solvents and largely insoluble in water. Chemically, fats are generally triesters of glycerol and fatty acids. Fats may be either solid or liquid at room temperature, depending on their structure and composition.

> The saponification number or saponification value is the number of milligrams of KOH required to neutralize the fatty acids resulting from the complete hydrolysis of 1g of fat/wax/resin. It gives information concerning the character of the fatty acids of the fat.

Hydrogenation of Oils

Unsaturated vegetable fats and oils can be transformed through partial or complete hydrogenation into fats and oils of higher melting point. The hydrogenation process involves "sparging" the oil at high temperature and pressure with hydrogen in the presence of a catalyst, typically a powdered nickel compound. As each double-bond is broken, two hydrogen atoms each form single bonds with the two carbon atoms. The elimination of double-bonds by adding hydrogen atoms is called saturation; as the degree of saturation increases, the oil progresses towards being fully hydrogenated, An oil may be hydrogenated to increase resistance to rancidity (oxidation) or to change its physical characteristics. As the degree of saturation increases, the oil's viscosity and melting point increase.

$$\text{Oil} \atop \text{unsaturated} \quad + \text{H}_2 \xrightarrow[\substack{200°C \\ 5\,atm}]{Ni} \quad \substack{\text{Fat} \\ \text{(Saturated)}}$$

MAN-MADE MOLECULES

Polymers

A polymer may by defined as a high molecular weight compound formed by the combination of a large number of one or more types of small molecules of low molecular weight. The small unit (or units) of which the polymer is made is known as *monomer* (or monomers). Many polymeric substances occur in nature such as cellulose, starch, rubber, proteins, and resins.

The synthetic polymers are manufactured generally from the small units by the process known as polymerisation. *Polymerisation may be defined as a chemical combination of a number of similar or different molecules to form a single large molecule.*

Addition Polymerisation

This involves the self-addition of n-unsaturated molecules of one or two monomers without loss of any small molecule to form a single giant molecule, e.g., propylene polymerises to polypropylene.

Some of the polymers are obtained only from one type of monomer, whereas the others are obtained form two different types of monomers, the former polymers are known as *homopolymers* whereas the latter are known as *copolymers*. Polypropylene, polyethylene, polyisoprens, etc. are the examples of homopolymers; on the other hand, dacron, nylon, certain vinyl polymers, etc. constitute the examples of *copolymers*

Some Common Examples of Addition and Condensation Polymers and their uses:

Addition Polymers	Repeating Unit	Common Uses
Polyethylene (PE)	$\cdots\text{C}-\text{C}\cdots$ (with H, H above and H, H below)	Plastic bags, bottles
Polypropylene (PP)	$\cdots\text{C}-\text{C}\cdots$ (with H, H above and H, CH_3 below)	Indoor-outdoor carpets
Polystyrene (PS)	$\cdots\text{C}=\text{C}\cdots$ (with H, H above and H, C_6H_5 below)	Plastic utensils, insulation
Polyvinyl chloride (PVC)	$\cdots\text{C}=\text{C}\cdots$ (with H, H above and H, Cl below)	Shower curtains, tubing
Polyvinylidene chloride (Saran)	$\cdots\text{C}=\text{C}\cdots$ (with H, Cl above and H, Cl below)	Plastic wrap
Polytetrafluoroethylene (Teflon)	$\cdots\text{C}=\text{C}\cdots$ (with F, F above and F, F below)	Nonstick coating
Polyacrylonitrile (Orion)	$\cdots\text{C}=\text{C}\cdots$ (with H, H above and H, $\text{C}\equiv\text{N}$ below)	Yarn, paints

Polymer	Structure	Uses
Polymethyl methacrylate (Lucite, Plexiglas)	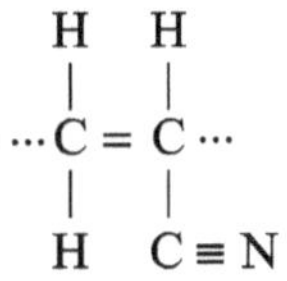 $\cdots C = C \cdots$ with H, H, H, $C \equiv N$	Windows, bowling balls
Polyvinyl acetate (PVA)	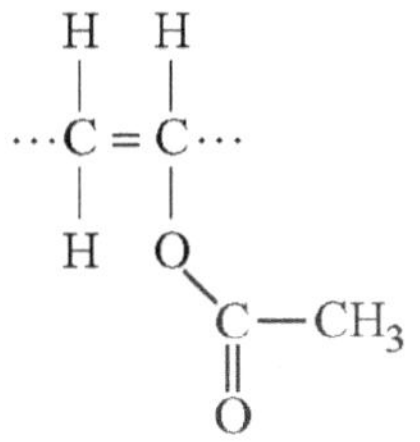 $\cdots C = C \cdots$ with H, H, H, $O-C(=O)-CH_3$	Adhesives, chewing gum
Nylon	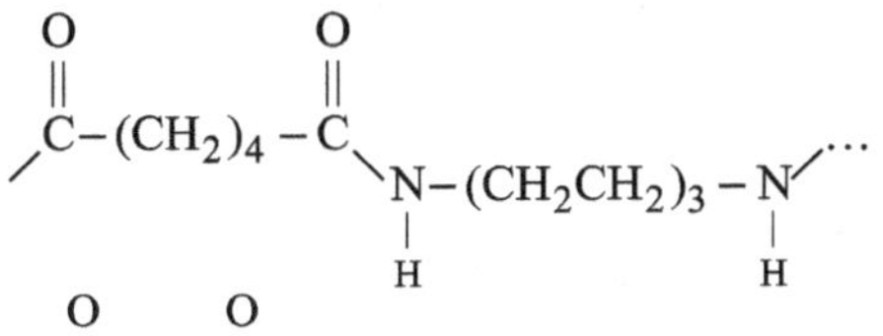 $-C(=O)-(CH_2)_4-C(=O)-N(H)-(CH_2CH_2)_3-N(H)-\cdots$	Carpeting, clothing
Polyethylene terephthalate	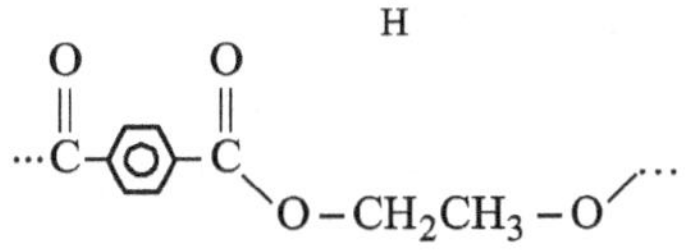 $\cdots C(=O)-\langle\text{ring}\rangle-C(=O)-O-CH_2CH_3-O-\cdots$	Clothing, plastic bottles
Melamine-formaldehyde resin (Melmac, Formica)	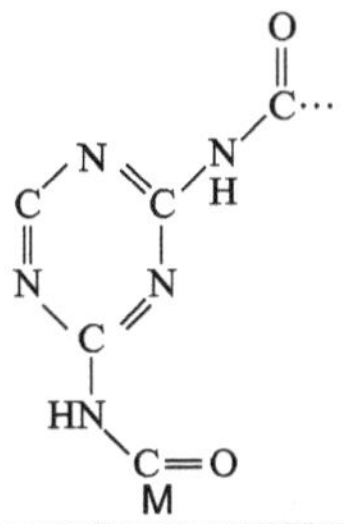 (triazine ring structure, M)	Dishes, countertops

Polymers may be divided into two categories

- *Natural polymers* - They are obtained from natural sources e.g. **polysaccharides** (starch, cellulose), **Proteins** (polymers of amino acids), gums, resins (cross linked polymers formed by compounds containing double or triple bonds slowly oxidised by atmospheric oxygen). **natural rubber** (polymer of isoprene), **Nucleic acids** (polymers of nucleotides) silk and wool (polymers of amino acids).

- *Synthetic polymers* - Polymers prepared by synthesis (man made), are known as synthetic polymers eg. polystyrene, nylon, PVC, etc.

  Rayon was originally called artificial silk but now a days it is a name given to artificial fibres derived form cellulose. Rayon can absorb over 90% of its own mass of water and it was not stick to wound.

  Natural silk contains nitrogen while artificial silk may not have nitrogen.

Rubber a well- known organic polymer and the **only true hydrocarbon polymer found in nature**. It is formed by the radical addition of the monomer **isoprene**. Polymerization can result in either poly-*cis*-isoprene or poly-*trans* isoprene—or a mixture of both, depending on reaction conditions. Natural rubber is poly-*cis*-isoprene, which is extracted from the tree *Hevea brasiliensis*

In 1839, the American chemist Charles Goodyear discovered that natural rubber could be cross-linked with sulfur (using zinc oxide as the catalyst) to maintain its elasticity even under external pressure. His process, known as *vulcanization,* paved the way for many practical and commercial uses of rubber, such as in automobile tires and dentures.

Most synthetic rubbers (called *elastomers*) are made from petroleum products such as ethylene, propene, and butadiene. For example, chloroprene molecules polymerize readily to form polychloroprene, commonly known as **neoprene**, which has properties that are comparable or even superior to those of natural rubber.

Dye

A dye can generally be described as a colored substance that has an affinity to the substrate to which it is being applied. The dye is generally applied in an aqueous solution, and may require a mordant to improve the fastness of the dye on the fiber.

The dyes were obtained from animal, vegetable or mineral origin, with no or very little processing.

Classification of dye

Dyes may be classified as discussed below:

Acid dyes: These are water-soluble anionic dyes that are applied to fibres such as silk, wool, nylon and modified acrylic fibres using neutral to acid dyebaths.

Basic dyes: These are water-soluble cationic dyes that are mainly applied to acrylic fibers, but find some use for wool and silk. Usually acetic acid is added to the dyebath to help the uptake of the dye onto the fiber. Basic dyes are also used in the coloration of paper.

Direct or substantive dyes: These kind of dyes are obtained when dyeing is normally carried out in a neutral or slightly alkaline dyebath, at or near boiling point, with the addition of either sodium chloride (NaCl) or sodium sulfate (Na_2SO_4). Direct dyes are used on cotton, paper, leather, wool, silk and nylon. They are also used as pH indicators and as biological stains.

Mordant dyes: These require a mordant, which improves the fastness of the dye against water, light and perspiration.

> The most important mordant dyes are the synthetic mordant dyes, or chrome dyes, used for wool; these comprise some 30% of dyes used for wool, and are especially useful for black and navy shades. The mordants, potassium dichromate, is applied as an after treatment.

Vat dyes: These are essentially insoluble in water and incapable of dyeing fibres directly.

Reactive dyes: These utilize a chromophore attached to a substituent that is capable of directly reacting with the fibre substrate. Reactive dyes are by far the best choice for dyeing cotton and other cellulose fibers at home or in the art studio.

Disperse dyes: These were originally developed for the dyeing of cellulose acetate, and are water insoluble. The dyes are finely ground in the presence of a dispersing agent and sold as a paste, or spray-dried and sold as a powder. Their main use is to dye polyster but they can also be used to dye nylon. cellulose triacetate, and acrylic fibres.

Pigments

Pigments are various organic and inorganic insoluble substances, which are widely used as surface coatings. They are also employed in the ink, plastic, rubber, ceramic, paper and linoleum industries to impart colour. The pigment industry is usually regarded as associated with paints, but in fact it is a separate industry.

Pigments are broadly classified into two types:
- White Pigments e.g. white lead, zinc oxide, etc.
- Coloured Pigments e.g. ultramarine blue.

Paints

Paints are stable mechanical mixtures of one or more pigments. The main function of the pigments is to impart the desired colour and to protect the paint film from penetrating radiation, such as U.V. rays.
- The pigments and the extenders are suspended in drying oils called **vehicle.** The vehicle or drying oil is a film forming material, to which other ingredients are added in varying amounts. The paint is applied on a metal or wood surface to give it a protective coating.
- **Driers** promote the process of film formation and hardening.
- **Thinners** maintain the uniformity of the film by reducing viscosity of the blend.

The important varieties of paints are emulsion paints, latex paints, metallic paints, epoxide resin paints, oil paints, water paints or distempers, etc.
- **Varnishes** differ from paints in that they have no pigments and in varnishes a part or whole of the oil is substituted by resin.

Drugs and Medicines

Chemical substances administered to a human body or to an animal, either for treatment of diseases or reduce suffering from pain are called medicines or drugs. The various types of medicinal compounds according to the purpose for which they are used are:

Antiseptics

The chemicals which prevent or check the sepsis of wounds. Examples are: *dettol* (chloroxylenol + terpeneol), *Bithional* (added to soaps). *Salol, Acriflavin, Savlon, Gention violet, Mercuro Chrome, Salicylic acid, picric acid, resorcinol, phenol, iodoform, boric acid, iodine, methylene blue, potassium permanganate.*

Disinfectants

The chemical substances which completely destroy the micro organisms or stop their growth but are harmful to human tissues are called disinfectants. Examples are: *1.0% phenol,* SO_2 etc. They are used to disinfect floors, clothes, utensils etc.

Antipyretics

They lower the body temperature i.e. fever reducing. Examples are: *aspirin, paracetamol, phenacetin, analgin.*

Analgesics

They are pain releiving. Examples are: *Aspirin* and *analgin,* both are antipyretic and analgesics. *Novalgin* is most widely used analgesic.

Certain narcotics like *Codeine, morphene, pethidine hydro-chloride, methadone* and *heroin* etc. are also used as analgesics.

Tranquilizers

Also called psycho-therapeutic drugs, reduce anxiety, induce sleep, and cure mental diseases. Examples are: *Barbituric acid* and its derivatives, *seconal, luminal, Methyldopa and Hydralazine, Equanil.*

Sedatives and Hypnotics

They are central nervous system depressants reduce restlessness, emotional tension and induce sleep. Examples are: *Phenobarbital, Glute thimide, Valium* etc.

Antianxiety Agents

Examples are: *Meprobamate* and *Diazepam.*

Tranquilizers, Sedatives & Hypnotics and *Antianxiety* **agents** are central nervous system stimulants.

Anaesthetics

The chemical substances which produce insensibility to the vital functions of all types of cell especially of nervous system temporarily are called anaesthetics. Examples are, *General anaesthetics - Chloroform, Fluothane, Local anaesthetics - Cocaine, α-Eucaine, β-Eucaine.*

Narcotics

The chemical substances which act as depressant and analgesic. Examples: *Heroin, Opium* and *Pethedine.*

Antibiotics

The chemical substances produced by micro-organisms that inhibit the growth of bacteria other microorganisms or even destroy them are called antibiotics. Examples: Penicillin is the first antibiotic discovered by Alexander Fleming. It is effective against pneumonia, bronchitis and sore throat etc.

Antimalarials

These are the drugs which cure malaria. Examples are: *Plasmoquin (Plasmochin), Atebrin* (Mepacrine), *Chloroquine.*

Antacids

Antacids are the drugs which neutralize excess acid in the gastric Juices and give relief from acid indigestion. They remove the excess acid and raise the pH to appropriate level in stomach. There are mainly weak bases.
Examples– $Mg(OH)_2$, $KHCO_3$

Contraceptives

Contraceptives drugs are used to control the fertilization process for population control. These are also known as antifertlity/birth control pills and contain a mixture of synthetic derivatives of hormones -estrogen and progesterone. Norethindrone is an example of synthetic progesterone derivative most widely used as antifertility drug and act by preventing ovulation. The estrogen derivative which is used in combination with progesterone derivative is ethynylestradiol (novestrol).
Examples- Mestranol & norethindrone; levonorgestrel & ethinyl estradiol

Fertilizer

A chemical fertilizer is defined as any inorganic material of wholly or partially synthetic origin that is added to the soil to sustain plant growth.

Classification of Fertilizers

Based on the availability of nutrients in them chemical fertilizers are divided into four groups:
- **Nitrogenous fertilizers:** NH_3 is the feed stock of all nitrogenous fertilizers such as anhydrous ammonium nitrate (NH_4NO_3) and urea ($CO(NH_2)_2$).NH_3 is obtained by **Born - Haber process**.
- **Phosphatic fertilizers:** e.g. superphosphate of lime, $Ca(H_2PO_4)_2$.
- **Potassic fertilizers:** Potash is a mixture of potassium minerals used to make potassium fertilizers.
- **Complex fertilizers:** Compound fertilizers, which contain N, P, and K, can often be produced by mixing straight fertilizers.

Pesticides

Pesticides are a class of synthetic chemicals used to control the pests of crops. Pests can be an insect, disease or weed or sometimes non - insect pest like rats.

Some important pesticides commonly used in agriculture are:
- **Organo-chlorine chemicals:** They are highly dangerous pesticides having the ability to persist in plant bodies and soil for long period to cause innumerable ecological and health hazards later. Examples: DDT, BHC, endosulfan, heptachlor and chlordane.
- **Organo-phosphorous chemicals:** They are also dangerous pesticides with ability to kill many useful bacteria besides killing the pests. They act as a source of pollution of agricultural land and ground water. Examples: Phorate, methyl parathion.
- **Carbonates:** They are used as insecticides, acaricides or nematicides to kill insects, mites and nematodes respectively. They can kill many aerobic and anaerobic bacteria in soil. They migrate into the underground water- when excess dosage is used.Examples: Carbofuran, aldicarb and carboryl.
- **Ethylene Di Bromide (EDB):**These are volatile liquids used to produce gaseous poisons to kill stored grain pests. They can leave traces of dangerous chemicals on grains and cause food pollution.

Cement

Portland cement is the basic ingredient of concrete. Concrete is formed when portland cement creates a paste with water (called hydration) that binds with sand and rock to harden. Bricklayer Joseph Aspdin of Leeds, England first made portland cement early in the 19th century by burning powdered limestone and clay.

Manufacture of Portland Cement

Portland cement is manufactured by crushing, milling and proportioning the following materials:
- Lime or calcium oxide, CaO(70%): from limestone, chalk, shells, shale or calcareous rock
- Silica, SiO_2(20%): from sand, old bottles, clay or argillaceous rock
- Alumina, Al_2O_3(5%): from bauxite, recycled aluminum, clay
- Iron, Fe_2O_3(3%): from clay, iron ore, scrap iron and fly ash
- Gypsum, $CaSO_4$. $2H_2O$(2%): found along with limestone

The most common way to manufacture portland cement is through a **dry method**:
70% of the cement produced in the world is Portland cement.

Safety Matches

The credit for developing friction matches that are presently still in use has been attributed to English chemist, John Walker, in 1826.
- Charles Sauria, a French chemist, invented the first phosphorus-based match, by replacing the antimony sulfide in Walker's matches with white phosphorus in 1830. But white phosphorus is toxic and was eventually banned. Subsequently red phosphorus was used in the place of white phosphorus which are allotropic forms of one another.
- The red phosphorus is located on the striking surface on the side of the box, mixed with an abrasive substance such as powdered glass.
- A small amount of the red phosphorus on the striking surface is converted into white phosphorus when match is stuck. The white phosphorous then ignites.

Ink

Ink is a colloidal system of fine pigment particles dispersed in a solvent. The pigment may or may not be coloured, and the solvent may be aqueous or organic. We can have two types of inks: Writing inks and Printing inks
- In **Writing inks** which are used in fountain pens, a fluid water-based dye system is applied. In ballpoint pens, pastelike oil-based dye systems are used. The thickness of the ink allows to flow consistently through capillary action. The ink does not spread unevenly, and dries easily compared to water-based systems.

- **Printing inks** may be of two varieties: ink for conventional printing and ink for digital nonimpact printing, which includes ink-jet and laser (electrophotographic) technologies. In **printing inks** colour is imparted by pigments rather than the dyes used in writing inks. Pigments are insoluble, whereas dyes are soluble. Ink pigments are both inorganic and organic.

Gun-powder

Gunpowder is a mixture of three different components:
- Potassium nitrate, KNO_3 (also called salt petre) (75% by weight)
- Charcoal (15% by weight), and sulphur (10% by weight).
  - Nitroglycerine
  - Picric acid
  - T.N.T(Tri-nitro toluene)
  - PETN (Pentaerythritol nitrate)
  - RDX (Research Department Explosive)

Nitroglycerine was first made in 1847. It is hazardous to make, use and transport. In 1886,Alfred Nobel found that nitroglycerine soaks into diatomaceous earth to give a pasty mixture that can be molded into sticks that don't detonate so easily. These were called dynamite and Nobel started the company Dynamite Nobel to manufacture dynamite. He made lots of money through dynamite business and later funded the Nobel prizes.

Soaps and Detergents

Soaps are water-soluble sodium or potassium salts of fatty acids.
- Soaps are made from fats and oils, or their fatty acids, by treating them chemically with a strong alkali. The fats and oils used in soap making come from animal or plant sources.
- Fatty acids are the components of fats and oils that are used in making soap. They are weak acids composed of two parts:
- A carboxylic acid group (-COOH), plus a hydrocarbon chain attached to the carboxylic acid group. Generally, it is made up of a long straight chain of carbon (C) atoms each carrying two hydrogen (H) atoms.

The common alkalis used in soap making are sodium hydroxide (NaOH), also called caustic soda; and potassium hydroxide (KOH), also called caustic potash.

Saponification of fats and oils is the most widely used soap making process. Saponification involves heating fats and oils and reacting them with a liquid alkali to produce soap and water (neat soap) plus glycerine.

Cleaning action of soaps and detergents

Water alone will not remove grease or oil from clothes because oil and grease present in soil repel the water molecules. Both soaps and detergents share a critical chemical property - they are surface-active agents, or surfactants. In other words, they reduce the surface tension of water. Because of reduction of surface tension, water soaks more easily in clothes and removes stains faster.

The carboxylate end of the soap molecule is attracted to water. It is called the hydrophilic (water-loving) end. The hydrocarbon chain is attracted to oil and grease and repelled by water. It is known as the hydrophobic (water-hating) end.

The water-hating end is repelled by water but attracted to the oil in the soil. At the same time, the water-loving end is attracted to the water molecules. These opposing forces loosen the soil and suspend it in the water. Warm or hot water helps dissolve grease and oil in soil. Washing machine agitation or hand rubbing helps pull the soil free.

Fuels

A fuel is a substance that releases energy. Some fuels (for example uranium) release energy from nuclear reactions.
- This energy is captured in chemical bonds through processes such as photosynthesis and respiration. Energy is released during oxidation.
- The most common form of oxidation is the direct reaction of a fuel with oxygen through combustion. Wood, gasoline, **coal** , and any number of other fuels have energy-rich chemical bonds created using the energy from the **Sun**, which is released when the fuel is burned (i.e., the release of chemical energy).
- Fossil fuels are principally hydrocarbons with minor impurities. They are so named because they originate from the decayed and fossilized remains of plants and animals that lived millions of years ago.

Types of Fossil Fuels

Fossil fuels can be separated into three categories:
- **Petroleum:** The first is **petroleum** or **crude** oil. This is a mixture of light, simple hydrocarbons dominated by the fractions with 6 to 12 carbons but also containing some light hydrocarbons (e.g., methane and ethane).
- **Coal:** The second most prominent and naturally most abundant fossil fuel is **coal**. Coal also was produced from decayed vegetative material buried years ago through a process that is slightly different, being less oxidizing. Coal is found as a solid not a liquid.
  Disadvantages: Coal is a very polluting fuel that produces a large amount of unburnt hydrocarbon, particulate, and significant quantities of sulphur dioxide byproducts.
- **Natural gas:** The third major fossil fuel is **natural gas**. This is a general term for the light hydrocarbon fractions found associated with most oil deposits. Natural gas is mostly methane with small quantities of ethane and other gases mixed in. It is hydrogen rich, since methane has a carbon to hydrogen ratio of 1:4. It is also an excellent fuel, burning with a high heat output and little in the way of unwanted pollution. Natural gas is also easy to transport through pressurized pipelines.

Factors to consider when choosing a fuel

Energy Value: Energy Value is the heat of combustion of a fuel given per gram of fuel. The higher the energy value, the more energy is released, the better the fuel.

Ignition Temperature: Ignition Temperature is the minimum temperature to which the fuel-oxidizer mixture (or a portion of it) must be heated in order for the combustion reaction to occur.

Propellants

Propellant is the chemical mixture burned to produce thrust in rockets and consists of a fuel and an oxidizer. A *fuel* burns when combined with oxygen producing gas for propulsion. An *oxidizer* is used that releases oxygen for combination with a fuel.

Ammonium nitrate, Ammonium dinitramide, Ammonium perchlorate, potassium nitrate are used as oxidizers
Propellants are classified into liquid, solid, or hybrid.

Liquid Propellants

In a liquid propellant rocket, the fuel and oxidizer are stored in separate tanks, and are fed through a system of pipes, valves, and turbo pumps to a combustion chamber where they are combined and burned to produce thrust.

Liquid oxygen (LOX), highly refined kerosene (RP-1), liquid hydrogen, Dinitrogen tetroxide (N_2O_4), hydrazine (N_2H_4) are some of the common liquid propellants.

Cryogenic propellants are liquefied gases stored at very low temperatures, most frequently liquid hydrogen (LH2) as the fuel and liquid oxygen (LOX) as the oxidizer. Hydrogen and oxygen remains liquid at temperatures of -253°C and -183°C respectively.

Solid Propellants

Solid propellant consists of a casing filled with a mixture of solid compounds (fuel and oxidizer) which burn at a rapid rate, expelling hot gases from a nozzle to produce thrust. When ignited, a solid propellant burns from the center out towards the sides of the casing. The shape of the center channel determines the rate and pattern of the burn, thus providing a means to control thrust. Unlike liquid propellant engines, solid propellant motors cannot be shut down. Once ignited, they will burn until all the propellant is exhausted.

Ammonium Perchlorate (AP) and Hydroxyl-terminated polybutadiene (HTPB) are common solid propellants

Hybrid Propellants

Hybrid propellant engines represent an intermediate group between solid and liquid propellant engines. One of the substances is solid, usually the fuel, while the other, usually the oxidizer, is liquid. The liquid is injected into the solid, whose fuel reservoir also serves as the combustion chamber.

Advantage of hybrid propellants based engines is that they have high performance, similar to that of solid propellants, but the combustion can be stopped, or moderated.

CHEMISTRY AND THE ENVIRONMENT

The environment consists of various segments such as **atmosphere, hydrosphere, lithosphere and biosphere.**

Atmosphere: The atmosphere is the protective layer of gases which is surrounding the earth. Its main functions are:

- Absorbs IR radiations emitted by the sun and reemitted from the earth and thus controls the temperature of the earth.
- Filters tissue damaging UV radiation of the sun.
- It acts as a source for CO_2 for plant photosynthesis and O_2 for respiration
- It acts as a source for nitrogen for nitrogen fixing bacteria and ammonia producing plants.
- The atmosphere transports water from ocean to land.

Hydrosphere: Hydrosphere is the part of earth on which all types of water resources exist,viz., *oceans, seas, rivers, lakes, glaciers, ice caps, ground water,* etc.

Lithosphere: Lithosphere is the part of the earth where all types of minerals, metals, organic matters, rocks, soils, etc. exist. Soil is a part of lithosphere.

Biosphere: The biosphere refers to the sphere of living organisms and their interactions with the environment (viz. atmosphere, hydrosphere and lithosphere). The biosphere is very large and complex and is divided into smaller units called *ecosystems.*

DAMAGE TO ENVIRONMENT

Environment may get damaged due to several reasons. The damage may be in the small area or may affect a much larger area and its ill-effects may by felt all over the globe. The environmental damages may be broadly classified as:

Regional Environmental Damage

Those environmental damages which affect the living and non-living things locally over a small area are termed as *regional environmental damages*.

Acid rain

Acid rain, or acid deposition, is a broad term that includes any form on precipitation with acidic components, such as sulphuric or nitric acid that fall to the ground from the atmosphere in wet or dry forms. This may include rain, snow, fog, hail or even dust that is acidic. Acid rain results when sulphur dioxide (SO_2) and nitrogen oxides (NO_X) are emitted into the atmosphere and transported by wind and air currents. The SO_2 and NO_X react with water, oxygen and other chemicals to form sulphuric and nitric acids. These then mix with water and other material before falling to the ground. The major sources of SO_2 and NO_X in the atmosphere are:

- Burning of fossil fuels to generate electricity. Two thirds of SO_2 and one fourth of NO_X in the atmosphere come from electric power generators.
- Vehicles and heavy equipments.
- Manufacturing, oil refineries and other industries.

The environmental effects of acid rain include:

- Washes away of nutrients from soil and
- Degradation of basic material such as limestone and marble. Acid rain affects building and structures, particularly. Those made of metal or stone.

> The Taj Mahal which is made of marble ($CaCO_3$) has been seriously affected by acid rain. To protect Taj Mahal, Govt. of India has notified 'Taj Trapezium'–an area surrounding it. In this area all industries have been asked to switch to LPG or natural gas in the place of coal or oil.

Global Environmental Damage

The environmental damages which affect the living and non living things globally or wider part of the earth are called global environmental damages.

Ozone layer depletion

Chloroflourocarbons (CFCs) are chemicals used in refrigerants, and various kinds of sprays or sols (eg. perfumes, air freshener, etc.). CFCs cause ozone holes in the ozone layer. Ozone hole refer to depletion of ozone layer due to the reaction of CFCs and ozone molecule. The ozone layer resides in the stratosphere and surrounds the entire Earth. UV radiation (280 to 315 nanometer wavelength) which comes from the Sun is partially absorbed in this layer. As a result, the amount of UV-radiation reaching the Earth's surface is greatly reduced. Due to depletion of ozone layer, human exposure to UV-radiation increases the risk of skin cancer, cataracts, and a suppressed immune system. UV-radiation exposure can also damage terrestrial plant life, single cell organisms, and aquatic ecosystems.

Green House effect

More ultraviolet radiations reach the earth through the ozone holes and the reflected radiations from the earth are absorbed by CO_2, water vapour, etc. The trapped radiations release more and more heat resulting in the phenomenon of Global Warming. This effect is also known as Green House Effect. Green house effect may lead to the rising of water level in the seas, changes in rainfall, increased frequency of extreme natural events, melting of the ice-caps or glaciers etc.

POLLUTION

Pollution refers to deterioration or unclean objectionable conditions in the quality of natural resources such as air, water and soil because of the action or presence of unwanted substances beyond a certain limit. Pollutants are the substances or effect introduced into the environment in significant amounts in solid, semi solid, liquid, gas or sub molecular particle form which has a detrimental effect on the environment. Pollutants can be natural or man-made (anthropogenic).

Some examples of **natural pollutants** are:

- Fires in forests may be caused when lightning strikes the trees. Burning of tree produces a lot of CO_2 which is released to the atmosphere.
- Soil erosion increases suspended particulate matter and dust in air. These may even enter water bodies as they are washed down by rain or natural water falls.
- Volcanic eruptions also add pollutants like SO_2 and solid particles to the environment.
- Volatile organic compounds from leaves, trees and dead animals naturally enter the atmosphere.
- Natural radioactivity and the other natural pollutants have been entering the environment since ages.

Anthropogenic pollutants are of two types:

Primary pollutants: Primary pollutants are added directly in a harmful form to the atmosphere.

e.g. CO_2 and CO from burning of fossil fuel; SO_2 and oxides of nitrogen from vehicular combustion, thermal power stations, etc.

Secondary Pollutants: Secondary pollutants are the products of reaction between the primary pollutants and normal environmental constituents.

Nitric oxide, a primary pollutant reacts with oxygen to give nitrogen-di-oxide which is a secondary pollutant.

$$2NO + O_2 \longrightarrow 2NO_2$$

The sources of anthropogenic pollutants can be of two types: Industrial and Domestic sources.

Major pollutants of air

Pollutants	Primary sources	Significant Effects
SO_2	Vehicular combustion, fossil burning	Acid rain, irritation in eyes, premature falling of leaves
CO and CO_2	Vehicular combustion, burning of fuels and hydrocarbons	Global warming, green house effect, CO has great affinity for hydrocarbons, haemoglobin and forms carboxy haemoglobin
Smoke, fly ash and soot	Thermal power stations	Respiratory diseases.
Lead and mercury	Autoexhaust from gasoline (petrol), paints, storage batteries. Fossil fuel like coal burning.	Affects the nervous system and circulatory system causing nerve fuel burning and brain damage
CFCs (Chloro fluoro Carbon)	Refrigerants and aerosols	Kidney damage and ozone depletion.

Major pollutants of water

Pollutants	Primary sources	Significant Effects
Pesticides and insecticides	Improper use in agriculture like DDT, BHC, mosquito repellants	Toxic to fishes, predatory birds and mammals
Plastics	Homes and industries	Kills fishes and animals. Persists in the environment because of non-biodegrabality.
Chlorine compounds	Water disinfection with chlorine, paper industries and bleaching powder	Fatal for plankton (organisms floating on the surface of water), foul taste and odour, can cause Cancer in humans.
Lead paints	Leaded gasoline	Toxic to organisms
Mercury	Natural evaporation and dissolved industrial wastes, fungicides	Highly toxic to humans

Acids Mine drainage, industrial wastes	Mine drainage, industrial wastes	Kills organisms
Sediments	Natural errosion, run off from factories mining and construction activities, fertilizer and other	Reduces ability of water to assimilate oxygen.

Radioactive Pollution

Radioactive Pollution can be defined as the release of radioactive substances or high-energy particles into the air, water, or earth as a result of human activity, either by accident or by design. The sources of such waste include: (1) nuclear weapon testing or detonation; (2) the nuclear fuel cycle, including the mining, separation, and production of nuclear materials for use in nuclear power plants or nuclear bombs; (3) accidental release of radioactive material from nuclear power plants.

Some worst environmental disasters

S. No.	Name of the disaster	Reason for occurrence	Effect of the disaster
1.	The Great Smog of London	A smog covered London for 5 days in 1952. Cold weather, combined with windless conditions collected airborne pollutants from the use of coal to form a thick layer of smog over the city.	Thousands died and a hundred thousand fell ill because of a blanket of smog. An estimated 12,000 premature deaths have been attributed to this smog.
2.	Minamata disease (1956)	Industrial poisoning of Minamata Bay in Japan. Large amounts of mercury and other heavy metals were released into the waste water.	Large amounts of mercury and other heavy metals found their way into the fish and shellfish that comprised a large part of the local diet. Thousands of residents of the Minamata have slowly suffered over the decades and died from a disease-termed as Minamata disease.
3.	Bhopal Gas Leak (1983)	Toxic gases (Methyl iso-cyanide-CH_3NC) leaked from the Union Carbide (now Dow Chemical) pesticide plant in Bhopal, India	The harmful fumes spread into the sleeping city and people woke with burning eyes and lungs. Thousands died within days. Years later also, pollutants seeping out of the plant site into groundwater have caused cancer, growth retardation and dizziness.
4.	Exxon Valdez Oil Spill (1989)	Sinking/Crash of Oil Vessel the Exxon Valdez oil on Bligh Reef in the pristine waters of Alaska's Prince William Sound. The 10.8 million gallon of oil began to spew forth into the cold waters. It eventually spread almost 500 miles from the original crash site.	The spilled oil spread thousands of miles of coastline. Hundreds of thousands of birds, fish, seals, otters and other animals would perished by the spilled oil , despite the mobilization of more than 11,000 people and 1,000 boats as part of the cleanup. One of the largest man-made environmental disasters.
5.	Tokaimura Nuclear Plant (1999)	Japan's worst nuclear accident happened in a facility northeast of Tokyo.	Two ended up dying, and hundreds were exposed to various levels of radiation.
6.	Baia Mare Cyanide Spill (2000)	Cyanide-contaminated water leaked out from a dam, leaking out 100 tonnes of cyanide in to Baia Mare lake in Romania. It has been considered as the second fatal environmental next to Chernobyl in Russia which has been discussed already.	An incredible amount of fish and aquatic plants were killed and up to 100 people were hospitalized after eating contaminated fish.
7.	Fukushima Daiichi nuclear disaster (2011)	Massive Tsunami waves traveling at several hundred miles an hour caused extreme damage to the plant's cooling and venting systems which were integral to controlling the temperature in each reactor.	Damaging of the plant's active reactors and loss of backup electrical power led to overheating, meltdowns, and evacuations. This caused an immediate release of radioactivity into the local area. After a month of assessing the damage to the local population, the Japanese government declared a 20-kilometer restricted zone. The residents were evacuated and relocated. The government ordered all six reactors to be decommissioned, and they were completely shut down one year later.

> *Dioxin* is a general term that describes a group of hundreds of chemicals that are highly persistent in the environment. The most toxic compound is 2,3,7,8-tetrachlorodibenzo-p-dioxin or TCDD. Dioxin and furan are some of the most toxic compounds.

Dissolved Oxygen (DO)

Oxygen dissolved in water is vital for aquatic life. The optimum value for dissolved oxygen in good quality water is 4-8mg/L. It is consumed by oxidation of organic matter/ reducing agent etc. present in water. Water which has DO value less than 4 mg/L is termed as polluted and is unfit for human or aquatic animal consumptions.

Chemical Oxygen Demand (COD)

It is an index of the organic content of water, since the most common substance oxidized by the dissolved oxygen in water is organic matter, from a biological origin, such as dead plants etc.

Biological Oxygen Demand (BOD)

The capacity of the organic matter in the sample of natural water to consume oxygen is called its BOD. It is determined experimentally by determining the dissolved oxygen (DO) at the beginning and at the end of a 5-day period in a sealed sample. The BOD gives the measure of oxygen utilized or consumed in the period as a result of oxidation of dissolved organic matter present in the water sample.

Threshold Limit Value (TLV)

This value indicates the permissible level of a toxic pollutant in atmosphere to which a healthy industrial worker can be exposed during an eight-hour day without any adverse effect.

Smog

The word smog is derived from smoke and fog. There are two types of smog: classical and photochemical smog. Classical smog occurs in cool humid climate. It is a mixture of smoke, fog and sulphur dioxide. It is also called reducing smog. Whereas photochemical smog occurs in warm and dry sunny climate. It has high concentration of oxidizing agents and therefore, it is also called as oxidizing smog.

Biomagnification

This refers to increase in concentration of the toxicant at successive trophic levels. This happens because a toxic substance accumulated by an organisation can not be mitobolised or excreted, and is thus passed on to the next higher trophic level. Biomagnification happens in the aquatic food chain. This is well known for mercury and DDT.

Eutrophication

The process in which nutrient enriched water bodies support a dense plant population, which kills animal life by depriving it of oxygen and results in subsequent loss of biodiversity, is known as Eutrophication.

> Photochemical smog mainly contains ozone, nitric oxide, acrolein, formaldehyde and peroxyacetyl nitrate (PAN). These cause serious health problems. In order to stop photochemical smog, catalytic converter are used now-a-days in cars so that release of NO_2 and hydrocarbons are controlled.

MULTIPLE CHOICE QUESTIONS

1. Which of the following is not a synthetic fibre:
   (a) Angora
   (b) Rayon
   (c) Nylon
   (d) Polyester

2. Which one of the following is not contained in Portland cement ? **[NDA]**
   (a) $Ca_3Al_2O_6$
   (b) Ca_3SiO_5
   (c) Ca_2SiO_4
   (d) $Ca_3(PO_4)_2$

3. Which one of the following acids is used for etching glass? **[NDA]**
   (a) H_2SO_4
   (b) HNO_3
   (c) HF
   (d) HCl

4. What is the reason for white cement to be white? **[NDA]**
   (a) It does not contain carbon
   (b) It does not contain silicon
   (c) It does not contain iron
   (d) It does not contain calcium

5. What is the purpose of adding plasticizers in paint manufacturing process? **[NDA]**
   (a) They act as a film-forming constituent
   (b) They reduce the viscosity
   (c) They prevent the polymerization and condensation
   (d) They provide elasticity to the film and minimize its cracking

6. Which fertilizer is assimilated directly by the plant? **[NDA]**
   (a) Super phosphate
   (b) Nitrolim
   (c) Muriate of Potash
   (d) Humus

7. Which raw material is used in the preparation of soft glass? **[NDA]**
   (a) K_2CO_3, SiO_2, $CaCO_3$
   (b) K_2CO_3, SiO_2, $PbCO_3$
   (c) Na_2CO_3, SiO_2, $CaCO_3$
   (d) Na_2CO_3, SiO_2, PbO

8. Which of the following chemicals is used in foam fire extinguishers? **[NDA]**
   (a) Aluminium sulphate
   (b) Copper sulphate
   (c) Cobalt sulphate
   (d) Nickel sulphate

9. What is the composition of nitrolim – a chemical fertilizer? **[NDA]**
   (a) Nitrogen and limestone
   (b) Calcium carbide and nitrogen
   (c) Calcium carbide and carbon
   (d) None of the above

10. What is a mixture of potassium nitrate, powdered charcoal and sulphur called? **[NDA]**
    (a) Glass
    (b) Cement
    (c) Paint
    (d) Gun power

11. Flint glass is obtained from which of the following? **[NDA]**
    (a) Zinc and barium borosilicate
    (b) Sand, red lead and potassium carbonate
    (c) Sodium aluminum borosilicate
    (d) Pure silica and zinc oxide

12. Which one of the following correctly defines the state of glass? **[NDA]**
    (a) Crystalline solid
    (b) Super cooled liquid
    (c) Condensed gas
    (d) Liquid crystal

13. Which one of the following chemicals is used in beauty parlours for hair-setting? **[NDA]**
    (a) Sulphur based
    (b) Phosphorus based
    (c) Silicon based
    (d) Iron based

14. The major component used in preparation of different types of glasses is **[NDA]**
    (a) Silica
    (b) Sodium borate
    (c) Calcium silicate
    (d) Sodium silicate

15. Which one of the following substances is used in the manufacture of safety matches?
    (a) Red phosphorus **[CDS]**
    (b) White phosphorus
    (c) Phosphorus trioxide (P_2O_3)
    (d) Black phosphorus

16. Which one of the following is used as a mordant in dyeing and tanning industry? **[CDS]**
    (a) Magnesium oxide
    (b) Magnesium carbonate
    (c) Magnesium chloride
    (d) Magnesium sulphate

17. Which one of the following polymeric materials is used for making bullet proof jacket? **[CDS]**
    (a) Nylon-6, 6
    (b) Rayon
    (c) Kevlar
    (d) Dacron

18. The polymeric fibre used as a substitute for wool in making synthetic blankets, sweaters, etc., is **[CDS]**
    (a) nylon
    (b) teflon
    (c) orlon
    (d) bakelite

19. The chemical used as a 'fixer' in photography is
    (a) Sodium sulphate **[IAS Prelim]**
    (b) Sodium thiosulphate
    (c) Ammonium persulphate
    (d) Borax

20. **Statement I:** Coal-based thermal power stations contribute to acid-rain.
    Statement II: Oxides of carbon are emitted when coal burns. **[IAS Prelim]**
    (a) Both Statement I and Statement II are individually true and Statement II is the correct explanation of Statement I
    (b) Both Statement I and Statement II are individually true but Statement II is not the correct explanation of Statement I
    (c) Statement I is true but Statement II is false
    (d) Statement I is false but Statement II is true

21. Salts of which of the following elements provide colours to fireworks? **[IAS Prelim]**
    (a) Zinc and sulphur
    (b) Potassium and mercury
    (c) Strontium and barium
    (d) Chromium and nickel

22. **Statement I:** Phenyl is used as a household germicide.
    Statement II: Phenyl is phenol derivative and phenol is an effective germicide. **[IAS Prelim]**
    (a) Both Statement I and Statement II are true and Statement II is the correct explanation of Statement I

(b) Both Statement I and Statement II are true but Statement II is NOT the correct explanation of Statement I

(c) Statement I is true but Statement II is false

(d) Statement I is false but Statement II is true

23. Consider the following chemicals: **[IAS Prelim]**
1. Benzene
2. Carbon tetrachloride
3. Sodium carbonate
4. Trichloroethylene

Which of the above/is are used as dry cleaning chemical?

(a) 1 only   (b) 2 only

(c) 1, 2 and 4 only   (d) 1, 2, 3 and 4

24. Which one of the following is another name of RDX? **[IAS Prelim]**

(a) Cyanohydrin   (b) Dextran

(c) Cyclohexane   (d) Cyclonite

25. Which one of the following is used as an explosive? **[IAS Prelim]**

(a) Phosphorus trichloride   (b) Mercuric oxide

(c) Graphite   (d) Nitroglycerine

26. It is said, the Tajmahal may be destroyed due to –

(a) flood in Yamuna river

(b) decomposition of marble as a result of high temperature

(c) air pollutants released from oil refinery of Mathura

(d) all the above

27. Minimata disease is a pollution-related disease, which results from –

(a) release of human organic waste into drinking water

(b) release of industrial waste mercury into fishing water

(c) accumulation of arsenic into atmosphere

(d) oil spills into sea

28. Which one of the following is associated with the formation of brown air in traffic congested cities? **[CDS]**

(a) Sulphur dioxide   (b) Nitrogen oxide

(c) Carbon dioxide   (d) Carbon monoxide

29. From which one among the following water sources, the water is likely to be contaminated with fluoride? **[CDS]**

(a) Ground water   (b) River water

(c) Pond water   (d) Rain water

30. According to a group of scientists, aeroplanes may be ejecting significant amounts of black carbon (BC) and this may be depleting the ozone layer:

In this context consider the following statements:

1. Black carbon cannot be produced naturally.
2. It is known to be more potent than carbon dioxide in whetting global warming.
3. Black carbon is emitted directly into the atmosphere in the form of fine particles (PM 2.5)

Select the correct statement/statements using the codes given below:

(a) 1 and 2 only   (b) 2 and 3 only

(c) 1 and 3 only   (d) 3 only

31. The use of microorganisms (bacteria and fungi) to degrade the environmental contaminants into less toxic forms is known as

(a) Bio-magnification   (b) Bio-remediation

(c) Both (a) and (b)   (d) None of the above

32. Which one of the following is a cause of acid rains? **[NDA - 2017-II]**

(a) Ozone   (b) Ammonia

(c) Sulphur dioxide   (d) Carbon monoxide

33. Which one of the following is NOT true for bleaching powder? **[NDA - 2018-I]**

(a) It is used as a reducing agent in chemical industries

(b) It is used for bleaching wood pulp in paper factories

(c) It is used for disinfecting drinking water

(d) It is used for bleaching linen in textile industry

34. Which one of the following is the number of water molecules that share with two formula unit $CaSO_4$ in plaster of Paris? **[NDA - 2018-I]**

(a) One   (b) Two

(c) Five   (d) Ten

35. Which one of the following elements is needed in the human body to transfer electrical signals by nerve cells? **[NDA - 2018-I]**

(a) Lithium   (b) Sodium

(c) Rubidium   (d) Caesium

36. Which one of the following is called syngas? **[NDA - 2018-II]**

(a) $C(s) + H_2O(g)$ (b) $CO(g) + H_2O(g)$

(c) $CO(g) + H_2(g)$ (d) $NO_2(g) + H_2(g)$

37. Which one of the following is called dry ice? **[NDA - 2018-II]**

(a) Solid carbon dioxide   (b) Liquid carbon dioxide

(c) Liquid nitrogen   (d) Liquid ammonia

38. Which one of the following is not used as fertilizer? **[NDA - 2018-II]**

(a) Ammonium nitrate   (b) Ammonium sulphide

(c) Ammonium phosphate   (d) Ammonium sulphate

39. Which one of the following is the chemical formula of gypsum? **[NDA - 2018-II]**

(a) $CaSO_4 . 2H_2O$ (b) Ca_2SiO_4

(c) $2CaSO_4 . H_2O$ (d) $CaSO_4$

40. Which one of the following greenhouse gases is in largest concentration in the atmosphere? **[NDA - 2018-II]**

(a) Chlorofluorocarbon   (b) Nitrous oxide

(c) Carbon dioxide   (d) Methane

ANSWER KEY															
1	(a)	**2**	(d)	**3**	(c)	**4**	(c)	**5**	(d)	**6**	(c)	**7**	(c)	**8**	(a)
9	(d)	**10**	(d)	**11**	(b)	**12**	(b)	**13**	(c)	**14**	(a)	**15**	(a)	**16**	(a)
17	(c)	**18**	(c)	**19**	(b)	**20**	(b)	**21**	(c)	**22**	(a)	**23**	(c)	**24**	(d)
25	(d)	**26**	(c)	**27**	(b)	**28**	(b)	**29**	(b)	**30**	(d)	**31**	(b)	**32**	(c)
33	(a)	**34**	(a)	**35**	(b)	**36**	(c)	**37**	(a)	**38**	(b)	**39**	(a)	**40**	(c)

APPENDIX

CHEMICALS OF COMMON USE

Common name and chemical name of important compounds/elements

S. No.	Common Name	Chemical Name	Chemical Formula
1.	Potash alum	Potassium aluminium sulphate	$K_2SO_4Al_2(SO_4)_3$
2.	Baking Soda	Sodium bicarbonate	$NaHCO_3$
3.	Bleaching Powder	Calcium chlorohypochlorite	$CaOCl_2$
4.	Caustic soda	Sodium hydroxide	$NaOH$
5.	Blue vitriol	Copper sulphate	$CuSO_5 \cdot 5H_2O$
6.	Chalk	Calcium carbonate	$CaCO_3$
7.	Borax	Sodium tetraborate	$Na_2B_4O_7 \cdot 10H_2O$
8.	Galena	Lead sulphide	PbS
9.	Gypsum	Calcium Sulphate	$CaSO_4 \cdot 5H_2O$
10.	Green Vitriol	Ferrous sulphate	$FeSO_4$
11.	Formalin	23% solution of formaldehyde	$HCHO$
12.	Dry ice	Solid carbon dioxide	CO_2
13.	Brine or common salt or rock salt	Sodium chloride	$NaCl$
14.	White vitriol	Zinc sulphate	$ZnSO_4.7H_2O$
15.	Caustic potash	Potassium hydroxide	KOH
16.	Chile salt petre	Sodium nitrate	$NaNO_3$
17.	Carbolic acid	Phenol	C_6H_5OH
18.	Alcohol	Ethyl Alcohol	C_2H_5OH
19.	Bauxite	Hydrated Alumina	$Al_2O_3 \cdot 2H_2O$
20.	Washing soda	Sodium carbonate	$Na_2CO_3 \cdot 10H_2O$
21.	Acid salt	Hydrochloric acid	HCl
22.	Salt petre	Potassium nitrate	KNO_3
23.	Litharge	Lead oxide	PbO
24.	Laughing gas	Nitrous oxide	N_2O
25.	Lime water	Calcium hydroxide	$Ca(OH)_2$
26.	Lunar caustic	Silver nitrate	$Ag\,NO_3$
27.	Lime	Calcium oxide	CaO
28.	Minium or Red lead	Triplumbic tetroxide	Pb_3O_4
29.	Oil of vitriol	Sulphuric acid	H_2SO_4
30.	Limestone	Calcium carbonate	$CaCO_3$
31.	Lye	Sodium hydroxide	$NaOH$
32.	Sal ammoniac salt	Ammonium chloride	NH_4Cl
33.	Slate	Silica aluminium oxide	$Al_2O_3 \cdot 2SiO_2 \cdot 2H_2O$
34.	Silica	Silicon dioxide	SiO_2
35.	T.N.T.	Trinitro toluene	$C_6H_2CH_3(NO_2)_3$
36.	Vermillion	Mercuric sulphide	HgS

37.	Vinegar	Dilute solution of acetic acid	CH_3COOH
38.	White lead	Basic lead carbonate	$2PbCO_3 \cdot Pb(OH)_2$
39.	Hypo	Sodium thiosulphate	$Na_2S_2O_3 \cdot 5H_2O$
40.	Calomel	Mercuric chloride	Hg_2Cl_2
41.	Brimstone	Sulphur	S
42.	Marble	Calcium carbonate	$CaCO_3$
43.	Quartz	Silicon dioxide	SiO_2
44.	Quick Silver	Mercury	Hg
45.	Fool's gold	Iron disulphide	FeS_2
46.	Muriatic acid	Hydrochloric acid	HCl
47.	Freons	Chlorofluorocarbons (CFCs)	CCl_2F_2

NOBEL PRIZES IN CHEMISTRY (1901-2018)

Year	Scientist	Country	Contribution
1901	Jacobus Henricus van 't Hoff	Netherlands	Laws of chemical dynamics and osmotic pressure in solutions
1902	Hermann Emil Fischer	Germany	work on sugar and purine syntheses
1903	Svante August Arrhenius	Sweden	electrolytic theory of dissociation
1904	Sir William Ramsay	United Kingdom	Discovery of the inert gaseous elements in air, and determination of their place in the periodic system
1905	Johann Friedrich Wilhelm Adolf von Baeyer	Germany	Organic dyes and hydroaromatic compounds
1906	Henri Moissan	France	Investigation and isolation of fluorine, and for electric furnace
1907	Eduard Buchner	Germany	Biochemical researches and discovery of cell-free fermentation
1908	Ernest Rutherford	United Kingdom	Investigations into the disintegration of the elements, and the chemistry of radioactive substances
1909	Wilhelm Ostwald	Germany	Work on catalysis and investigations into the fundamental principles governing chemical equilibria and rates of reaction
1910	Otto Wallach	Germany	work on the alicyclic compounds
1911	Maria Skłodowska-Curie	France	Discovery of radium and polonium
1912	Victor Grignard	France	Discovery of Grignard reagent
	Paul Sabatier	France	Method of hydrogenating organic compounds in the presence of finely disintegrated metals
1913	Alfred Werner	Switzerland	Work on linkage of atoms in molecules
1914	Theodore William Richards	USA	Determinations of atomic weight of a large number of chemical elements
1915	Richard Martin Willstätter	Germany	Work on plant pigments
1918	Fritz Haber	Germany	Synthesis of ammonia from its elements
1920	Walther Hermann Nernst	Germany	Thermochemistry
1921	Frederick Soddy	United Kingdom	Radioactive substances, and nature of isotopes
1922	Francis William Aston	United Kingdom	Isotopes and enunciation of the whole-number rule
1923	Fritz Pregl	Austria	Micro-analysis of organic substances
1925	Richard Adolf Zsigmondy	Germany	Heterogeneous nature of colloid solutions
1926	Theodor Svedberg	Sweden	Disperse systems
1927	Heinrich Otto Wieland	Germany	Bile acids
1928	Adolf Otto Reinhold Windaus	Germany	constitution of sterols and their connection with vitamins

Year	Scientist	Country	Contribution
1929	Arthur Harden	United Kingdom	Sugar Fermentation
	Hans Karl August Simon von Euler-Chelpin	Sweden	
1930	Hans Fischer	Germany	Constitution of haemin and chlorophyll
1931	Carl Bosch	Germany	Development of chemical high pressure methods
	Friedrich Bergius	Germany	
1932	Irving Langmuir	USA	Discoveries and investigations in surface chemistry
1934	Harold Clayton Urey	USA	Discovery of heavy hydrogen
1935	Frédéric Joliot	France	their synthesis of new radioactive elements
	Irène Joliot-Curie	France	
1936	Petrus (Peter) Josephus Wilhelmus Debye	Netherlands	Dipole moments and the diffraction of X-rays and electrons in gases
1937	Walter Norman Haworth	United Kingdom	Work on carbohydrates and vitamin C
	Paul Karrer	Switzerland	Work on carotenoids, flavins and vitamins A and B_2
1938	Richard Kuhn	Germany	work on carotenoids and vitamins
1939	Adolf Friedrich Johann Butenandt	Germany	work on sex hormones
	Leopold Ruzicka	Switzerland	work on polymethylenes and higher terpenes
1943	George de Hevesy	Germany	work on the use of isotopes as tracers in the study of chemical processes
1944	Otto Hahn	Germany	Discovery of the fission of heavy nuclei
1945	Artturi Ilmari Virtanen	Finland	Fodder preservation method
1946	James Batcheller Sumner	USA	Enzyme crystallization
	John Howard Northrop	USA	preparation of enzymes and virus proteins in a pure form
	Wendell Meredith Stanley	USA	
1947	Sir Robert Robinson	United Kingdom	Plant products /alkaloids
1948	Arne Wilhelm Kaurin Tiselius	Sweden	Electrophoresis and adsorption analysis, serum proteins
1949	William Francis Giauque	USA	Chemical thermodynamics at extremely low temperatures
1950	Otto Paul Hermann Diels	West Germany	Diene synthesis
	Kurt Alder	West Germany	
1951	Edwin Mattison McMillan	USA	Chemistry of transuranium elements
	Glenn Theodore Seaborg	USA	
1952	Archer John Porter Martin	United Kingdom	Partition chromatography
	Richard Laurence Millington Synge	United Kingdom	
1953	Hermann Staudinger	West Germany	discoveries in the field of macromolecular chemistry
1954	Linus Pauling	USA	research into the nature of the chemical bond and its application to the elucidation of the structure of complex substances
1955	Vincent du Vigneaud	USA	work on biochemically important sulphur compounds, especially for the first synthesis of a polypeptide hormone
1956	Sir Cyril Norman Hinshelwood	United Kingdom	for their researches into the mechanism of chemical reactions
	Nikolay Nikolaevich Semenov	Soviet Union	
1957	Lord (Alexander R) Todd	United Kingdom	work on nucleotides and nucleotide co-enzymes
1958	Frederick Sanger	United Kingdom	work on the structure of proteins, especially that of insulin
1959	Jaroslav Heyrovský	Czechoslovakia	discovery and development of the polarographic methods of analysis

Year	Scientist	Country	Contribution
1960	Willard Frank Libby	USA	method to use carbon-14 for age determination in archaeology, geology, geophysics, and other branches of science
1961	Melvin Calvin	USA	research on the carbon dioxide assimilation in plants
1962	Max Ferdinand Perutz	United Kingdom	for their studies of the structures of globular proteins
	John Cowdery Kendrew	United Kingdom	
1963	Karl Ziegler	West Germany	for their discoveries in the field of the chemistry and technology of high polymers
	Giulio Natta	Italy	
1964	Dorothy Crowfoot Hodgkin	United Kingdom	for her determinations by X-ray techniques of the structures of important biochemical substances
1965	Robert Burns Woodward	USA	outstanding achievements in the art of organic synthesis
1966	Robert S Mulliken	USA	fundamental work concerning chemical bonds and the electronic structure of molecules by the molecular orbital method
1967	Manfred Eigen	West Germany	for their studies of extremely fast chemical reactions, effected by disturbing the equilibrium by means of very short pulses of energy
	Ronald George Wreyford Norrish	United Kingdom	
	George Porter	United Kingdom	
1968	Lars Onsager	USA	for the discovery of the reciprocal relations bearing his name, which are fundamental for the thermodynamics of irreversible processes
1969	Derek H R Barton	United Kingdom	for their contributions to the development of the concept of conformation and its application in chemistry
	Odd Hassel	Norway	
1970	Luis F Leloir	Argentina	discovery of sugar nucleotides and their role in the biosynthesis of carbohydrates
1971	Gerhard Herzberg	Canada West Germany	contributions to the knowledge of electronic structure and geometry of molecules, particularly free radicals
1972	Christian B Anfinsen	USA	work on ribonuclease, especially concerning the connection between the amino acid sequence and the biologically active conformation
	Stanford Moore	USA	for their contribution to the understanding of the connection between chemical structure and catalytic activity of the active centre of the ribonuclease molecule
	William H Stein	USA	
1973	Ernst Otto Fischer	West Germany	for their pioneering work, performed independently, on the chemistry of the organometallic, so called sandwich compounds
	Geoffrey Wilkinson	United Kingdom	
1974	Paul J Flory	USA	fundamental work, both theoretical and experimental, in the physical chemistry of macromolecules
1975	John Warcup Cornforth	United Kingdom	work on the stereochemistry of enzyme-catalyzed reactions
	Vladimir Prelog	Switzerland	research into the stereochemistry of organic molecules and reactions
1976	William N Lipscomb	USA	tudies on the structure of boranes illuminating problems of chemical bonding
1977	Ilya Prigogine	Belgium	contributions to non-equilibrium thermodynamics, particularly the theory of dissipative structures
1978	Peter D Mitchell	United Kingdom	contribution to the understanding of biological energy transfer through the formulation of the chemiosmotic theory
1979	Herbert C Brown	USA	for their development of the use of boron- and phosphorus-containing compounds, respectively, into important reagents in organic synthesis
	Georg Wittig	West Germany	
1980	Paul Berg	USA	fundamental studies of the biochemistry of nucleic acids, with particular regard to recombinant-DNA
	Walter Gilbert	USA	for their contributions concerning the determination of base sequences in nucleic acids
	Frederick Sanger	United Kingdom	
1981	Kenichi Fukui	Japan	for their theories, developed independently, concerning the course of chemical reactions
	Roald Hoffmann	USA	

Year	Scientist	Country	Contribution
1982	Aaron Klug	United Kingdom	development of crystallographic electron microscopy and his structural elucidation of biologically important nucleic acid-protein complexes
1983	Henry Taube	USA	work on the mechanisms of electron transfer reactions, especially in metal complexes
1984	Robert Bruce Merrifield	USA	development of methodology for chemical synthesis on a solid matrix
1985	Herbert A Hauptman	USA	for their outstanding achievements in developing direct methods for the determination of crystal structures
	Jerome Karle	USA	
1986	Dudley R Herschbach	USA	for their contributions concerning the dynamics of chemical elementary processes
	Yuan T Lee	USA	
	John C Polanyi	Canada	
1987	Donald J Cram	USA	for their development and use of molecules with structure-specific interactions of high selectivity
	Jean-Marie Lehn	France	
	Charles J Pedersen	USA	
1988	Johann Deisenhofer	West Germany	3-D structure of photosynthetic reaction centre
	Robert Huber	West Germany	
	Hartmut Michel	West Germany	
1989	Sidney Altman	USA	Catalytic properties of RNA
	Thomas Cech	USA	
1990	Elias James Corey	USA	Organic synthesis
1991	Richard R Ernst	Switzerland	NMR Spectroscopy
1992	Rudolph A Marcus	USA	Electron transfer reactions
1993	Kary B Mullis	USA	for contributions to the developments of methods within DNA-based chemistry & invention of the polymerase chain reaction (PCR) method
	Michael Smith	Canada	Site-directed mutagenesis
1994	George A Olah	USA	Carbocation chemistry
1995	Paul J Crutzen	Netherlands	for their work in atmospheric chemistry, particularly concerning the formation and decomposition of ozone
	Mario J Molina	Mexico	
	F Sherwood Rowland	USA	
1996	Robert F Curl Jr	USA	for their discovery of fullerenes
	Sir Harold W Kroto	United Kingdom	
	Richard E Smalley	USA	
1997	Paul D Boyer	USA	for their elucidation of the enzymatic mechanism underlying the synthesis of adenosine triphosphate (ATP)
	John E Walker	United Kingdom	
	Jens C Skou	Denmark	for the first discovery of an ion-transporting enzyme, Na^+, K^+-ATPase
1998	Walter Kohn	USA	development of the density-functional theory
	John A Pople	United Kingdom	development of computational methods in quantum chemistry
1999	Ahmed Zewail	USA	studies of the transition states of chemical reactions using femtosecond spectroscopy
2000	Alan J Heeger	USA	for their discovery and development of conductive polymers
	Alan G MacDiarmid	USA	
	Hideki Shirakawa	Japan	
2001	William S Knowles	USA	for their work on chirally catalysed hydrogenation reactions
	Ryōji Noyori	Japan	
	K Barry Sharpless	USA	work on chirally catalysed oxidation reactions

Year	Scientist	Country	Contribution
2002	John B Fenn	USA	for the development of methods for identification and structure analyses of biological macromolecules [] for their development of soft desorption ionisation methods for mass spectrometric analyses of biological macromolecules
	Koichi Tanaka	Japan	
	Kurt Wüthrich	Switzerland	for the development of methods for identification and structure analyses of biological macromolecules [] development of nuclear magnetic resonance spectroscopy for determining the three-dimensional structure of biological macromolecules in solution
2003	Peter Agre	USA	for discoveries concerning channels in cell membranes [] for the discovery of water channels
	Roderick MacKinnon	USA	for discoveries concerning channels in cell membranes [] for structural and mechanistic studies of ion channels
2004	Aaron Ciechanover	Israel	for the discovery of ubiquitin-mediated protein degradation
	Avram Hershko	Israel	
	Irwin Rose	USA	
2005	Yves Chauvin	France	for the development of the metathesis method in organic synthesis
	Robert H Grubbs	USA	
	Richard R Schrock	USA	
2006	Roger D Kornberg	USA	studies of the molecular basis of eukaryotic transcription
2007	Gerhard Ertl	Germany	for his studies of chemical processes on solid surfaces
2008	Osamu Shimomura	Japan	Discovery and development of the green fluorescent protein, GFP
	Martin Chalfie	USA	
	Roger Y Tsien	USA	
2009	Venkatraman Ramakrishnan	United Kingdom	Studies of the structure and function of the ribosome
	Thomas A Steitz	USA	
	Ada E Yonath	Israel	
2010	Richard F Heck	USA	Palladium-catalyzed cross couplings in organic synthesis
	Ei-ichi Negishi	Japan	
	Akira Suzuki	Japan	
2011	Dan Shechtman	Israel	Discovery of quasicrystals
2012	Robert Lefkowitz	USA	Studies of G-protein-coupled receptors
	Brian Kobilka	USA	
2013	Martin Karplus	USA	Development of multiscale models for complex chemical systems
	Michael Levitt	USA	
	Arieh Warshel	USA	
2014	Eric Betzig	USA	Development of super-resolved fluorescence microscopy
	Stefan W Hell	Germany	
	William E Moerner	USA	
2015	Tomas Lindahl	United Kingdom	Mechanistic studies of DNA repair
	Paul L Modrich	USA	
	Aziz Sancar	USA	
2016	Jean-Pierre Sauvage	France	Design and synthesis of molecular machines
	Fraser Stoddart	USA	
	Ben Feringa	Netherlands	
2017	Jacques Dubochet	Switzerland	cryo-electron microscopy for the high-resolution structure determination of bio-molecules in solution
	Joachim Frank	USA	
	Richard Henderson	United Kingdom	
2018	Frances H. Arnold	USA	for the directed evolution of the enzymes
	George P. Smith	USA	for the phage display of peptides and antibodies
	Sir Gregory P. Winter	United Kingdom	

Chapter 1

CLASSIFICATION/ CELL & CELLULAR DIVISION

BIOLOGICAL CLASSIFICATION

Biological classification is the scientific procedure of arranging organisms into groups and subgroups on the basis of their similarities and dissimilarities and placing the groups in a hierarchy of categories.

The purpose of biological classification is to organize the vast number of known plants and animals into groups that could be named, remembered and studied.

NEED FOR BIOLOGICAL CLASSIFICATION

Classification is Needed to

* help in establishing relationship between different organisms and to know about their evolution.
* help in the identification of organisms.
* study one or two organisms of one particular group and give the sufficient information of that group. It gives an idea of whole range of diversity found in organisms.
* it gives an idea of the evolution of various groups of organisms.

Systematics

Systematics is the study of the units of biodiversity. It is the study of the diversification of organisms and their relationship among living things through time. It includes the following parts:

* *Identification:* It is a process of finding the correct name and place of an organism in a system of classification.
* *Classification:* It is the arrangement of an organism in a particular group on the basis of their similarities and dissimilarities.
* *Nomenclature:* It is a system of providing proper and distinct name to one particular organism which helps in recognizing that organism.
* *Taxonomy:* It is a science dealing with the description, identification, naming and classification of organism.

Classification of Organisms

It is the arrangement of organisms into taxonomic group saccording to their similarities and dissimilarties. System of classification is an attempt to organize different organisms into different categories that we can use to study.

Hierarchy in Classification

Hierarchy in classification involves many steps. Each step represents a rank or category. All categories or steps together constitute the taxonomic hierarchy.

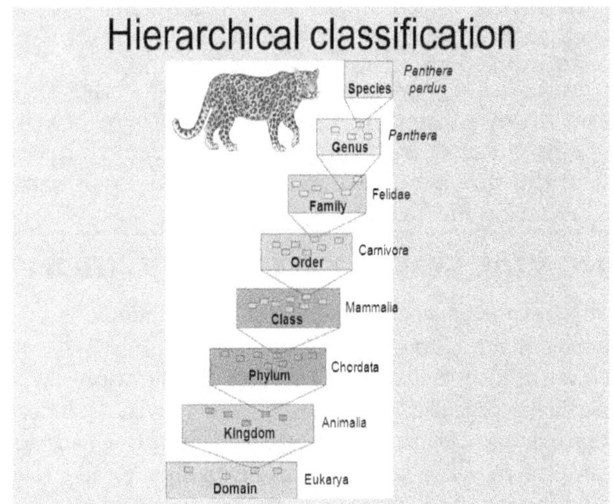

Species

The smallest taxon is species. At the species level organisms look alike and are able to breed with one another.

Genus

The next largest taxon is genus. At the genus level, there is a group of similar species that are closely related.

Family

A group of two or more genera with common characteristics make a family. For example, lion (*Panthera leo*), tiger (*Panthera tigris)* and the domestic cat(*Felis domesticus*) make the family **Felidae**.

Order

A group of related families make an order. For example the family of cat (Felidae) and the family of dogs, foxes, etc. (Canidae) is grouped under the Carnivora.

Class

Related orders make a class. For example several orders like those of the tigers, cats, dogs, monkey, bats and human belong to class *Mammalia*.

Phylum

A phylum is the largest category with related classes grouped together. For example the classes of mammals, birds, reptiles, amphibians and fishes together constitute the phylum *Chordata*. In plants, the corresponding category is named division.

Kingdom

Kingdom is the largest group of organisms differentiated on very general similarities. For example, plant and animal kingdom. The plant kingdom comprises all kinds of plants while animal kingdom comprises all kinds of animals.

- *Carolus Linnaeus* was a Swedish naturalist also known as the father of Taxonomy as he developed a way to name and organize species that we still use today. He wrote a book named *'Systema Naturae'* in which he describes the system of classification of nature. Two most important contribution of Linnaeus are:
  (i) Hierarchical Classification System
  (ii) System of Binomial Classification
- *Aristotle*, also known as father of zoology classified animals on the basis of habitat into aquatic, terrestrial and aerial animals.
- *Theopharastus*, also known as father of botany divided plants on the basis of form texture and habitat into four types as trees, shrubs, undershrubs and herbs. He wrote a book named *'Historia Plantarum'*.

BINOMIAL SYSTEM OF CLASSIFICATION

Biologists have devised a technique for identification naming and grouping of various organisms.

There is a need to standardize the naming of living organisms such as particular organism. *Carl Von Linnaeus* devised a binomial system of nomenclature in which an organism is given two names.

- A *Generic name* which it shares with other closely related organisms which has features similar enough to place them in the same group.
- A *specific name* which distinguishes the organism from all other species. No other organism can have the same combination of genus and species.

FIVE KINGDOM CLASSIFICATION

This type of classification was proposed by R.H. Whittaker. The five kingdom proposed by Whittaker are *Monera, Protista, Fungi, Plantae, Animalia.*

Kingdom Monera

- Monerans are single cell which may or may not move. It consists of primitive type of organism which includes *bacteria, cyanobacteria, archaebacteria* and *mycoplasma*. They can live in both living and non living environment.
- They can also survive in harsh and extreme climatic conditions like in hot springs, acidic soils etc.
- These are classified in 4 groups :– cyanobacteria, Archaebacteria, Bacteria and Mycoplasma.

- These are detected on the basis of Gram staining. Gram (+) thick Peptidoglycan cell wall. Gram (–) no cell wall/thin cell wall.

Economic importance of bacteria

- *Saprophytic* bacteria causes decay and decomposition of organic matter (dead plants and animals) clean the environment and release minerals in the soil.
- *Antibiotics* are the chemicals released by the bacteria which render the growth of other microorganisms.
- Some bacteria are also involved in gobar gas plant and manure formation. In gobar gas plant bacteria are used to convert animal dung and other organic wastes into manure along with the fuel gas. Biogas consists of methane (50-75%), CO_2 (25-50%), H_2S (0-3%), N_2 (0-10%) and O_2 (0-0.5%).

Streptomycin	— *Streptomyces griseus*
Chloramphenicol	— *S. venezuelae*
Tetracyclines	— *S. aureofaciens*
Terramycin	— *S. ramosus*
Erythromycin	— *S. erythreus*
Bacitracin	— *Bacillus Licheniformis*
Riboflavin	— *Clostridium butylicum*
Cobalamin (Vit B_{12})	— *Bacillus megatherium*
Vitamin C	— *Escherichia coli*

- *Nitrogen Fixation:* Some bacteria are free living which are able to pick nitrogen from the air and soil and0 convert it into organic nitrogen in the form of amino acid. E.g., *Azotobactor, Beijerinckia, Clostridium,* etc. On the other part some are symbiotic which forms nodules in the root of the plant. e.g., *Rhizobium*.

Kingdom Protista

Protista are considered as a diverse group of eukaryotic organism. Protists can be unicellular or multicellular and also exists in colonial form. They do not have specialized tissue organization. Protists live in water, in moist terrestrial habitats, and as parasites and other symbionts in the bodies of multicellular eukaroytes.

These are classified into 3 groups –: protistan algal, slime molds, protozoan protists.

Protozoan diseases	
Causative agent	**Diseases**
• *Trypanosoma gambiense*	– Central african sleeping sickness
• *Giardia Lambia*	– Giardiasis
• *Leishmania donovani*	– Kala-Azar
• *Dermal leishmaniasis*	– Leishmania tropica
• *Plasmodium vivax*	– Malaria
• *Entamoeba histolytica*	– Amoebic dysentery
• *Entamoeba gingivalis*	– Pyorrhoea

Economic Importance of Diatoms

- Diatoms are important sources of food to aquatic animals.
- The oils extracted from some fishes and whales are actually

produced by diatoms.

- Diatoms are employed as a cleaning agent in tooth pastes and metal polishes, added to paints for enhancing night visibility, are also employed as insulation material in refrigerators, boilers and furnaces.
- Diatomaceous earth is used to make sound proof rooms.

Kingdom Fungi

Fungi are basically multi-cellular. *Yeast* is an exception in being unicellular. The cell wall is generally composed of chitin (a nitrogen containing carbohydrate). They do not contain chlorophyll and hence are heterotrophic. Most of them are decomposers, hence fungi are also known as kingdom of multi-cellular decomposers. They may be saprophytic (depend on dead or decaying organic matter for their food) or may be parasitic (depend on living organisms for their food). Kingdom is classified on the basis of Morphology of reproductive structures, which exhibits more variation.

These are classified into 4 groups . Deuteromycetes, Oomycetes, Zygomycetes, Ascomycetes and Basidiomycetes.

> *Lichens* are dual organisms that are formed by permanent symbiotic association between an algae and a fungus. They co-exist for mutual benefit. This type of relationship is known as *symbiosis*. The alga manufactures food for itself and for the fungus. Fungus provides protection to algae and helps in fixation and absorption of water and minerals. Lichens act as Pollution indicator.

Importance of Lichen

- Lichens grows in a dry naked rocks, mountain, barren earth. It makes the way for growth of grasses and mosses.
- These are used as a food in tundra for reindeer, caribou, musk, etc., and also used as food article in iceland, sweden and Norway.

- These are used as dyes or biological stain obtained from *Rocella tinctoria*.
- These are used as perfumes obtained from species *Ramalina* and *Evernia*.
- Important bioindicators for Pollution

> Mycorrhizae are the type of symbiotic association between fungus with the root of higher plants, in which both the organism are mutually benefited, these fungus secretes antimicrobial substances, that protects the plant root from harmful pathogens, fungus helps plants to absorb water and important nutrients from the soil. Fungus also derives nutrient from the roots.
> e g. pinus, birch, etc.

Disease caused by fungi in Humans

Allergies	– *Alternaria, phoma, Trichoderma, Aspergillus,* etc.
Ear infection	– *Aspergillus flavus*
Valley fever	– *Coccidioidomycosis*
Neurites	– *Mucor pusillus*
Candidiasis	– *Candida albicans*

Kingdom Plantae

They are multicellular eukaryotes. All plants contain plastids. Plastids are double membrane organelle that possesses photosynthetic pigments. They are called *chloroplast*. They are usually *autotrophic*. Chloroplast contains a green colour pigment called *chlorophyll* and prepares own food by the process of photosynthesis. Cells have cell wall made up of cellulose.

Kingdom plantae shows a lot of diversity, because of which, it has been divided into four divisions: Algae, Bryophyta, Pteridophyta, and Spermatophyta (Gymnosperms and Angiosperms).

These are classified into 4 groups –:

Algal	**Bryophyta**	**Pteridophyta**	**Spermatophyta**
Red, Green, Brown	Liverwort Hornwort	Equisetum selaginella	Gymnosperms Angiosperms

Kingdom Animalia

There are diverse group of animals in the whole world they lives in different habitats. All animals are multicellular except protozoa, these are eukaryotic, lacks cell wall, heterotrophic, have power of locomotion and shows increased sensitivity through the nervous system. On the basis of presence and absence of vertebrate column. Animal Kingdom are broadly divided into vertebrates and invertebrates. Inverbrates consists 8-phylums named Porifera, Cnidaria, Platyhelmintus, Aschelminthus, Anellida, Arthropoda, Molluscs and Enchinodermata. Vertebrates or phylum chordata consists 3-subphylums, Urochordata, Cephalochordata and Vertebrata.

(Animal classification with characteristic features)

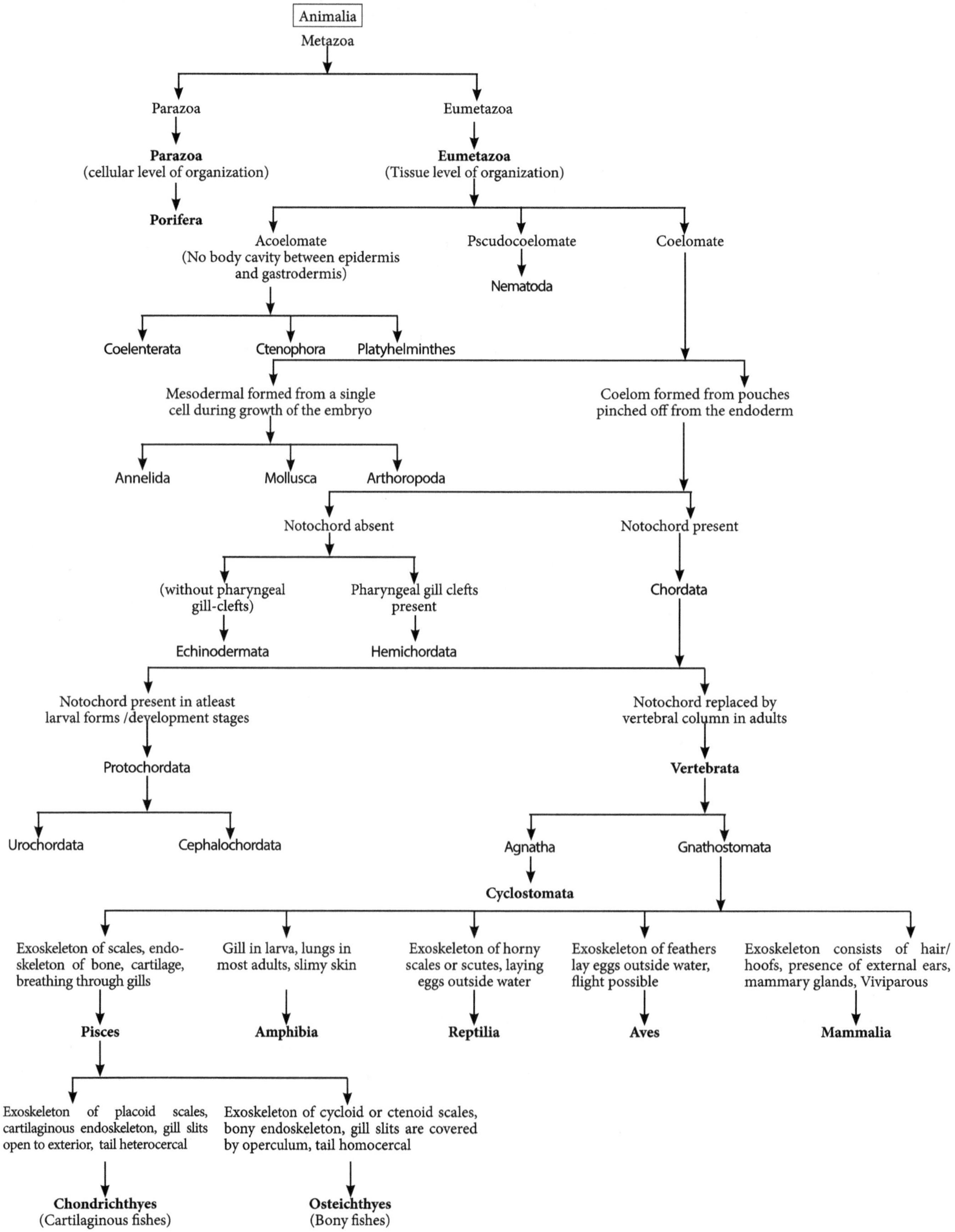

Animalia

Metazoa

Parazoa — Eumetazoa

Parazoa (cellular level of organization)

Porifera

Eumetazoa (Tissue level of organization)

Acoelomate (No body cavity between epidermis and gastrodermis) — Pscudocoelomate — Coelomate

Nematoda

Coelenterata — Ctenophora — Platyhelminthes

Mesodermal formed from a single cell during growth of the embryo

Coelom formed from pouches pinched off from the endoderm

Annelida — Mollusca — Arthoropoda

Notochord absent — Notochord present

Chordata

(without pharyngeal gill-clefts) — Pharyngeal gill clefts present

Echinodermata — Hemichordata

Notochord present in atleast larval forms /development stages

Notochord replaced by vertebral column in adults

Protochordata

Vertebrata

Urochordata — Cephalochordata

Agnatha — Gnathostomata

Cyclostomata

Exoskeleton of scales, endo-skeleton of bone, cartilage, breathing through gills → **Pisces**

Gill in larva, lungs in most adults, slimy skin → **Amphibia**

Exoskeleton of horny scales or scutes, laying eggs outside water → **Reptilia**

Exoskeleton of feathers lay eggs outside water, flight possible → **Aves**

Exoskeleton consists of hair/hoofs, presence of external ears, mammary glands, Viviparous → **Mammalia**

Exoskeleton of placoid scales, cartilaginous endoskeleton, gill slits open to exterior, tail heterocercal → **Chondrichthyes** (Cartilaginous fishes)

Exoskeleton of cycloid or ctenoid scales, bony endoskeleton, gill slits are covered by operculum, tail homocercal → **Osteichthyes** (Bony fishes)

CELL : FUNDAMENTAL UNIT OF LIFE

Cell is a structural and functional unit of life. In 1665, *Robert Hooke*, an English scientist, saw cells for the first time in a thin slice of cork with its microscope. He observed and described the cells as *"Honey comb"* like structures. He named the box-like compartments as *cellulae* or *cells*. The term "cell" is derived from a Latin word *cella* which means little room or hollow space.

In 1674, *Van Leeuwenhoek*, a Dutch Scientist, studied living cells for the first time with the help of an improved microscope.

CELL THEORY

- In 1838, two biologists, *J.M Schleiden and T.Schwann* proposed the **"Cell Theory"**.
- In 1855, *Rudolf Virchow*, a German pathologist proposed that all cells arise from pre-existing cells. He stated this in Latin as "Omnis cellula-e- cellula".
- Smaller Organisms, like bacteria are unicellular and larger organisms are made up of many cells, and are celled multicellular organism.

Cell theory

i. All living organisms are composed of one or more cells
ii. The cell is the basic unit of life.
iii. Cells develop from pre-existing cells. *Virus is an exception to cell theory.*

	Prokaryotic cell	Eukaryotic cell
1.	Primitive Organization	Advanced organization
2.	Unorganized nucleus is present. Hereditary material lies freely in cytoplasm.	Well developed organized nucleus is present. Hereditary material present in nucleus covered by nuclear membrane.
3.	Membrane bound organelles like ribosomes, nucleus, endoplasmic-reticulum, golgi body, mitochondria, lysosomes, vacuoles etc are absent.	Membrane bound organelles are present.
4.	DNA is naked.	DNA is associated with histone proteins.
5.	Site of translation and transcription is cytoplasm e.g.- Bacteria etc.	Site of translation is cytoplasm and transcription is nucleus ex-plants, animals, fungi.
6.	Endocytosis and exocytosis does not take place.	Endocytosis and exocytosis takes place in protists and animal cell.

CELL STRUCTURE

Cell Wall

Bacterial cell wall is made up of peptidoglycans. The archean cell wall is made up glycoproteins and polysaccharides. The plant cell wall is mainly composed of cellulose, hemi-cellulose glycoproteins, pectins and lignin. Animal cell lacks cell wall.

Plant Cell Wall

Plant cell walls are primarily made up of cellulose which is the most abundant micro molecule on the earth. Plant cell wall consists of three layers, the *primary cell wall, secondary cell wall* and *middle lamella.*

The middle lamella:

- It is a first, thin, amorphous sticky layer, which get deposited during cytokinesis.
- This layer is present in two adjacent cells, which are rich in Pectin.
- It consists calcium and magnesium pectates, these pectic compounds are partially solubilised to make the ripen fruits soft.

Primary cell wall (0.1-3 μm)

- It is formed inner to the middle lamella and are thin, flexible and extensive. ex-cells of cortex, pith, etc. It contains cellulose microfibril.

- Microfibril embedded in primary cell wall provides high tensile strength to the wall.

Secondary cell wall (3-19 μm)

- It is formed between the plasma - membrane and primary wall. Lignin, suberin, cutin, etc are deposited in the wall.
- These layers are thicker and provides mechanical strength to the cell. Xylan is present is this layer.

> - The smallest cell found is a mycoplasma cell, which is about 0.1 micron in diameter.
> - The longest cells are the nerve cells, measuring about a metre in length.
> - The largest cells are represented by eggs of Ostrich, which is about 170-135 mm.

Cell Membrane/Plasma Membrane

- Plasma membrane is a living, selectively permeable membrane. It allows some selected materials to move in and out of the cell, and prevents the entry and exit of the other substances.

  The plasma membrane is made up of a bilayer of lipids and proteins. Small carbohydrates are attached at places to outer surface of lipids and proteins.

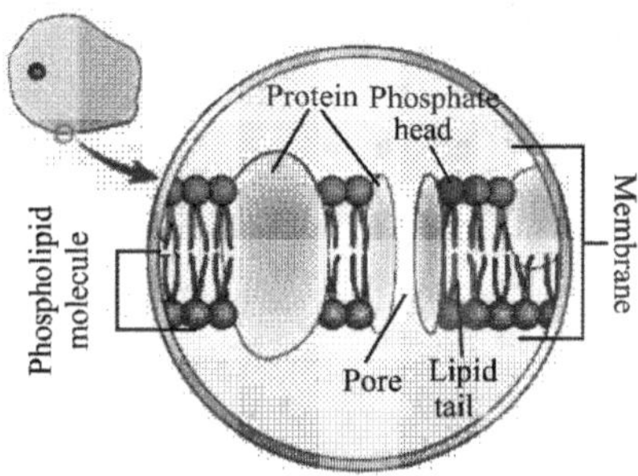

Fig. Plasma membrane

Fluid Mosaic Model

- Fluid Mosaic Model proposed by *Singer and Nicholson* and is widely accepted model of plasma membrane.
- The cell membrane is composed of lipid bilayer of phospholipid molecules into which variety of globular proteins are embedded.
- Each phospholipid molecule has two ends- an *outer head hydrophilic* (water attracting) and the *inner tail hydrophobic* (water repelling).

Plant-cell	Animal-cell
Larger	Smaller
cell wall present	Cell wall absent
Plastids present	Plastids absent
Large one vacuole	Small vacuoles
Golgi body is present in the form of dictyosomes.	Golgi body is well developed
Nucleus lies in the peripheral cytoplasm.	Nucleus lies in centre
Centrosome and centrioles are absent	Centrosome with centrioles are present.
Cannot change shape	Can change shape
Lysosome absent	Lysosomes Present
Chloroplast present	Chloroplast absent
Ribosomes present	Ribosomes present
ER present	ER present
Cell wall and plasma membrane both are present	Only plasma membrane present
Microtubules or microfilaments are Present	Present
Cytoplasm present	Present

Function of cell membrane

- It provides definite shape to the cell and acts as a mechanical barrier between external and internal environment of the cells.
- It regulates the movement of molecules in and out of cell.
- The flexibility of membrane helps the cell to engulf food and other substances from its external environment by endocytosis.

CYTOPLASM

It is living portion or protoplasm of cell that comprises jelly like Substance called *cytosol* and organelles with nucleus. It is present in both plant and animal cell. It includes, ER, Golgi bodies, plastids, lysosomes, peroxisomes, ribosomes, Mitochondria, and Centrosomes.

Endoplasmic Reticulum

Endoplasmic reticulum is a complex network of membrane bound structure which runs through the cytoplasm. Cisternae are spaces within the folds of the ER membranes. It is connected to both the outer nuclear membrane as well as cell membrane. The ER membrane has the same structure as the plasma membrane but ribosomes do not have membranes.

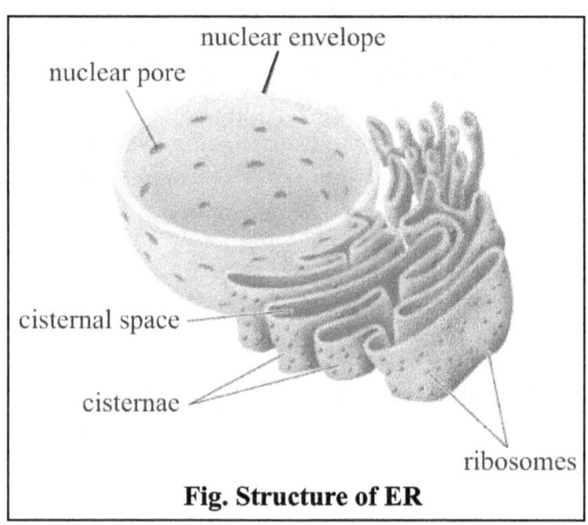

Fig. Structure of ER

- *Depending on presence or absence of ribosome on the surface of ER, it is divided into two types:*
  (i) *Rough Endoplasmic reticulum (RER):* It is lined with ribosomes and is rough in appearance, hence, named as rough endoplasmic reticulum. It is the site of protein synthesis.
  (ii) *Smooth Endoplasmic reticulum (SER):* It contains no ribosomes and hence is smooth in appearance. It helps in lipid and steroid synthesis.

Functions of endoplasmic reticulum:

- Endoplasmic reticulum helps in intracellular and intercellular transport of materials. It is the "*transport system*" of the cell. It transports chemicals between cells and within cells.
- RER is the site of protein and enzyme synthesis. It conjugates with golgi body and helps in the formation of lysosomes.
- SER helps in lipid synthesis and detoxifying many drugs and poisons.
- Proteins and lipids synthesized on ER are used for making cell membrane, through membrane biogenesis.

Golgi Bodies

Golgi body consists of smooth, flattened, membrane bound, sac-like structures called cisternae. The cisternae are stacked together; placed one above another in parallel rows. *Golgi body is a single complex in animal cells while in plant cells, it is formed of separate units called dictyosomes.* Membranes of Golgi body may develop connections with membranes of ER to form complex called extramembrane system.

Functions of golgi body

- It is involved in the synthesis, repair of cell membrane, formation of lysosomes and peroxisomes.
- Secretion is the major function of Golgi apparatus. All types of substances that are secreted and excreted are packed in vesicles by Golgi bodies for passage to the outside. It is the *secretory organelle* of the cell.
- It also takes part in storage, modification and packaging of various biochemical products produced by different components of the cell.

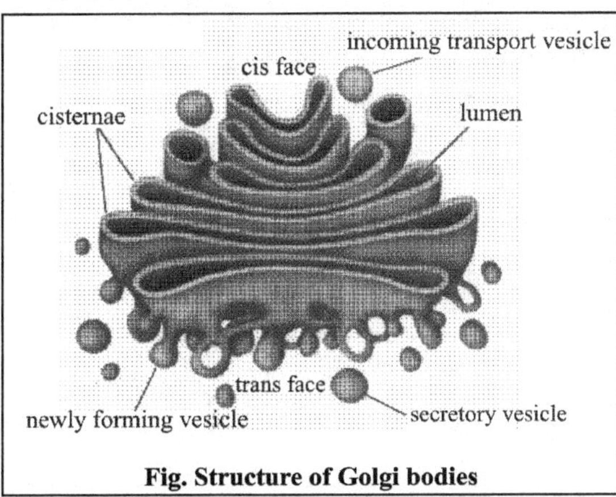

Fig. Structure of Golgi bodies

Lysosomes

Lysosomes are small, spherical vesicle covered by a single membrane. It is scattered all over the cytoplasm. It contains powerful digestive enzymes (about 40 in number) that are capable of breaking down the organic material. Thus, lysosome serves as an intracellular digestive system, and is called *digestive bags*. These are also known as suicidal bags.

Functions of lysosomes:

- Lysosome helps in intracellular digestion of food particles as they are rich in various digestive enzymes.
- They helps in destruction of foreign particles, as in white blood cell, and also help in cleaning up the cell by digesting damaged materials of the cell, therefore known as cellular scavengers.

Vacuoles

Vacuoles are membrane bound fluid-filled cavities or sacs present in the cytoplasm. They are surrounded by a membrane called tonoplast. The vacuole is filled with a liquid called *"cell sap"* that contains dissolved salts and sugars.

Functions of vacuoles

- *In plant cells* Vacuoles help to provide turgidity and rigidity to the cell.
- It acts as a store house of pigments and waste products. It also stores useful minerals and salts.

Mitochondria

Mitochondria are rod shaped cell organelles surrounded by a double membrane. The outer membrane is smooth and porous while the inner membrane is folded into large number of finger like structures called cristae. *Cristae* increase the surface area of the inner membrane, which provides more surface area for the metabolic reactions to take place. The fluid inside the mitochondria is called the *matrix*.

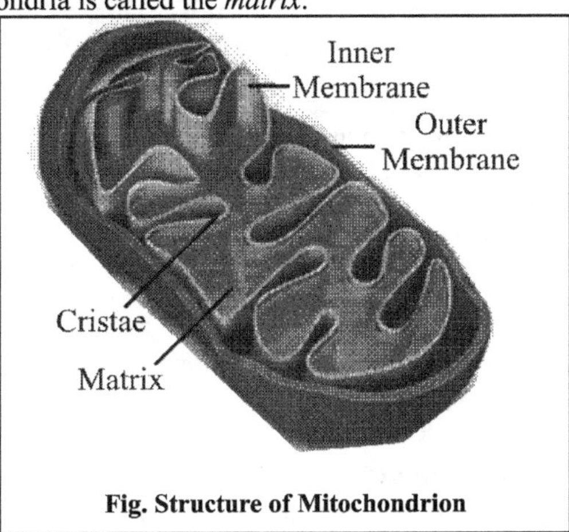

Fig. Structure of Mitochondrion

Function of Mitochondria

Mitochondria are commonly known as *"Powerhouse of the cell"*. They contain enzymes necessary for the total oxidation of food and for the release of large amount of energy in the form of ATP molecules. The energy stored in this ATP is used for synthesis of new products and other metabolic process.

- It also stores calcium when required during cell signaling, generation of heat, mediation of cell growth and death.

Plastids

- Plastids are semi-autonomous organelles having DNA, RNA, ribosomes and double membrane envelope. These are largest cell organelles in plant cell.
- Leucoplasts: They are colourless plastids which generally occur near the nucleus in non-green cells and possess internal lamellae. They mainly store food materials and occur in the cells not exposed to sunlight, e.g., seeds, underground stems, roots, tubers, rhizomes etc.
- These are of three types
  - **(i)** *Amyloplast:* Synthesize and store starch grains.
  - **(ii)** *Elaioplast (Lipidoplast, Oleoplast) :* They store lipids and oils.
  - **(iii)** *Aleuroplast (Proteinoplast):* Store proteins.
- *Chromoplasts:* Coloured plastids other than green are known as chromoplasts. These plastids are red, orange, yellow etc. coloured due to the presence at carotenoid. These are present in petals and fruits.
- *Chloroplast:* Chloroplasts are green coloured plastids due to the presence of chlorophyll. They occur abundantly in green leaves and green parts of the shoot. They trap the solar energy which is used for manufacturing food. So, they are the *sites of photosynthesis*.
- It is double membrane structure. Both membranes are smooth. The inner membrane is less permeable than outer but rich in proteins especially carrier proteins.

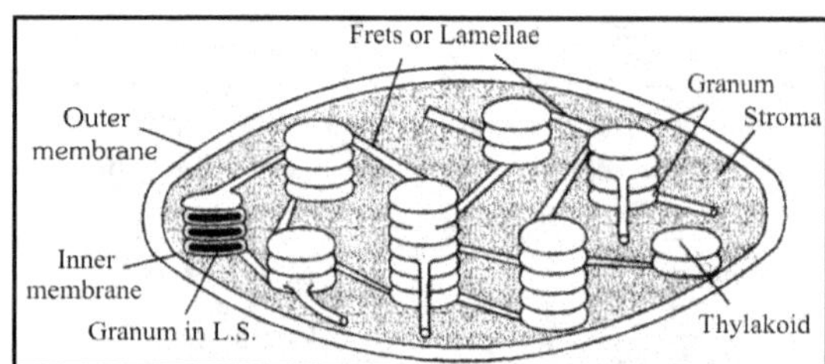

- The inter-membrane space is called the *periplastidial space.* Inner to membranes, matrix is present, which is divided into two parts–

  Grana: Inner plastidial membrane of the chloroplast is invaginated to form a series of parallel membranous sheets, called *lamellae,* which form a number of oval - shaped closed sacs, called *thylakoids.*

  Stroma: It is transparent, proteinaceous and watery substance. Dark reaction of photosynthesis occurs in this portions.

Functions of Plastids

- It is the site of photosynthesis, (light and dark reactions).
- Photolysis of water, reduction of NADP to $NADPH_2$ take place in granum.
- Photophosphorylation through cytochrome $b_6 f$ plastocyanin and plastoquinone etc.
- They store starch or factory of synthesis of sugars.

Ribosomes

- The ribosomes are smallest known electron microscopic without membrane, ribonucleo-protein particles attached either on RER or floating freely in the cytoplasm and are the sites of protein synthesis.
- It has two subunits, one is small and another is large. Small submit reads RNA and large subunits joins amino acids to form a long polypeptide chain through which protein synthesis takes place. 70S ribosomes are found in prokaryotes, mitochondria and plastids of eukaryotes while 80S ribosomes are found in cytoplasm of eukargotes.

Functions of ribosomes

- Ribosomes are also called protein factories of the cell.
- Enzyme peptidyl transferase occurs in large subunit of ribosome which helps in protein synthesis.

Cytoskeleton

In eukaryotic cell, a framework of fibrous protein elements became necessary to support the extensive system of membranes. These elements collectively form cytoskeleton of the cell. There are of three types- Microtubules, Microfilaments and intermediate filaments.

Microtubules

The microtubules are electron-microscopic structures found only in the eukaryotic cellular structures like cilia, flagella, centriole, basal-body, astral fibres, spindle fibres. These are mainly formed of tubulin protein.

Functions of microtubules

- These form a part of cytoskeleton and help in cell-shape and mechanical support.
- The microtubules of cilia and flagella help in locomotion and feeding.

Microfilaments

These are microscopic, long, narrow, cylindrical, non-contractile and proteins structures found only in the eukaryotic cytoplasm. These are present in the microvilli, muscle fibres (called myofilaments) etc. But these are absent in prokaryotes. These are mainly formed of actin-protein (contractile).

Functions microfilaments

- The microfilaments forms a part of cytoskeleton and change the cell shape during development, motility and division.
- The microfilaments bring about directed movements of particles and organelles along them in the cell.

Intermediate Filaments

They are supportive elements in the cytoplasm of the eukaryotic cells. They are missing in mammalian RBCs. The IFs are somewhat larger than the microfilaments and are about 10nm thick. They are solid, unbranched and composed of nonmotile structural proteins, such as keratin, desmin, vimentin.

Functions of intermediate filaments

- They form a part of cytoskeleton that supports the fluid cytosol.
- It maintains the shape of the cell.
- They provide support to myofibrils, which is essential for their *contraction.*

  Cilia (sing.: cilium) and *flagella* (sing.: flagellum) – (9+2) Pattern are hair-like outgrowths of the cell membrane.

Functions

- They help in locomotion, respiration, cleaning, circulation, feeding, etc.
- They show sensitivity to changes in light, temperature and contact.

CILIA AND FLAGELLA

Centrosome and Centriole

Centrosome is an organelle usually containing *two cylindrical structures* called *centrioles.* They are surrounded by amorphous pericentriolar materials. Both the centrioles in a centrosome lie perpendicular to each other in which each has an organisation like the cartwheel. They are made up of nine evenly spaced peripheral fibrils of tubulin.

Functions of centrosome

- The centrioles help in organising the spindle fibres and astral rays during cell division.
- They provide basal bodies which give rise to cilia and flagella.

Nucleus

Nucleus is the prominent, spherical structure found at the center of the cell. It is the largest organelle present in cell. Basically, nucleus is the controlling centre of all cell activities and hence, it has been described as the *brain of the cell.*

In *plant cell,* nucleus lies towards the periphery due to the presence of large central vacuole while in *animal cell,* nucleus lies in the central position.

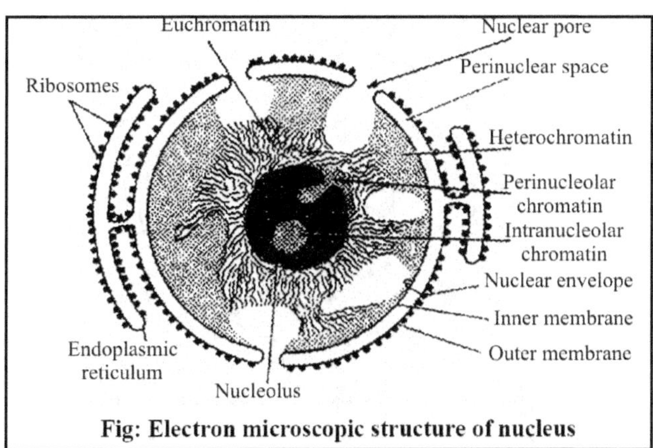

Fig: Electron microscopic structure of nucleus

Nuclear envelope or membrane

Nuclear membrane or nuclear envelope, consists of two parallel membranes inner and outer with a space between 10 to 50 nm called the *perinuclear space,* forms a barrier between the materials present inside the nucleus and that of the cytoplasm. The outer membrane usually remains continuous with the endoplasmic reticulum and also bears ribosomes on it.

Functions:

- It allows the passage of inorganic ions, small organic molecules, ribosomal subunits, RNAs and proteins through nuclear pores.
- It maintains the shape of the nucleus.

The nucleolus

Nucleolus is a conspicuous, darkly stained spherical body found in nucleoplasm. It is composed of large amount of ribosomal proteins and ribosomal RNA. It is generally associated with nucleolar organizer region (NOR) of the nucleolar chromosomes.

Functions of nucleolus

- It is seat of biogenesis of rRNA and also stores rRNA.
- It plays important role in spindle formation during cell division.

Nucleoplasm:

- It is transparent, homogenous, semifluid, colloidal, ground substance present inside the nuclear membrane.
- Function the nucleoplasm helps in maintaining the shape of nucleus formation of spindle protein of NAD, ATP, DNA, RNAs and ribosomal subunits.

Nuclear matrix:

- It is a fine network of proteinaceous fibrils that traverses the whole nucleus.

Function of nuclear matrix

- It helps in maintaining shape of nucleus.
- It provides anchorage to chromatin.

Chromosomes

- These are thread like structures which uniformly distributed in the nucleoplasm. They are observed only in the "interphase stage". Chromatin contains DNA and some basic proteins called histones, some non-histone proteins and also RNA.

Functions of Chromatin

- Chromatin stores genetic information and forms chromosomes for equitable distribution of genetic information during cell division and reproduction.
- They are DNA-protein hereditary structures which are formed by condensation of chromatin fibres for equitable distribution during cell division and reproduction.

> ### Giant Chromosome
> It was discovered by E.G. Balbiani in 1881. These are Commonly present in salivary glands of insect, hence known as salivary chromosomes. Its length is 2000mm.
>
> ### Lamp brush chromosome
> It was discovered by *Flemming* in 1882. It is larger in compared to giant chromosome. These are visible in diplotene stage of most animal oocytes, spermatocytes. and giant nucleus of unicellular algae i.e Acetabularia.

Microbodies

- Many membrane bound minute vesicles called microbodies that contain various enzymes, are present in both plant and animal cells.

Peroxisomes (Uricosomes)

- These were called peroxisomes because these contain peroxide producing enzymes (oxidases) and peroxide destroying enzymes (*catalases*).
- These are found in photosynthetic cells of plants. In animals peroxisomes are found in vertebrates (cells of liver, kidney), brain, small intestine, testis and adrenal cortex), invertebrates and protozoans, *e.g., Paramecium.*
- Their membrane is permeable to amino acids, uric acids, etc. They contain four enzymes of H_2O_2 metabolism. The enzymes *urate oxidase, d-amino oxidase, α-hydroxy acid oxidase* produce H_2O_2 whereas the *catalases* plays a significant protective role by degrading H_2O_2 because H_2O_2 is toxic for cells.

Glyoxysomes

- These are found in fungi, some protists and germinating fatty seeds where insoluble lipid food reserves must be turned into soluble sugars. These are absent in animal cell.
- They contain enzymes of metabolism of glycolic acid *via* glyoxylate cycle and bounded by a unit membrane. These also contain enzymes for β-oxidation of fatty acids, produce acetyl CoA. It is metabolised in glyoxylate cycle to produced carbohydrates.

CELL DIVISION

- *Rudolf Virchow* (1855) observed that new cells always develop from pre-existing cells. He also produced *cell lineage theory or law of cell lineage* and *doctrine of genetic continuity.*
- In *unicellular organisms,* cell division is the means of reproduction by which the mother cell produces two or more new cells. In *multicellular organisms* also, new individual develop from a single cell.

CELL CYCLE

- Cell division is a biological process in all living organisms in which mother cell divides into two daughter nuclei.
- Although cell growth (in terms of cytoplasmic increase) is a continuous process, DNA synthesis occurs only during one specific stage in the cell cycle. The replicated chromosomes (DNA) are then distributed to daughter nuclei by a complex series of events during cell division. These events are themselves under genetic control.
- The sequence of events which occur during cell growth and cell division are collectively called *cell cycle*.
  It was introduced by Howard and pole in 1953.

Phases of Cell Cycle

The period required to complete one cell cycle (from beginning of one cell division to the beginning of next) is called generation time. It is 24 hours in human cells and 90 minutes in yeast. Cell cycle is simpler in prokaryotes and more complex in eukaryotes.

The cell cycle is divided into two basic phases:
- Interphase
- M Phase (Mitosis phase)/Dividing phase

Interphase

- It is the period between the end of one cell division to the beginning of next cell division.
- It is highly metabolically active phase, in which cell prepares itself for next cell division.

Interphase is Completed into Three Successive Stages

- *G1 phase/Post mitotic/Pre-DNA synthetic phase/gap-I:*
- G1 phase corresponds to the interval between mitosis and initiation of DNA replication.

Following events take place during this phase
(i) Intensive cellular synthesis.
(ii) Synthesis of rRNA, mRNA ribosomes and proteins.
(iii) Metabolic rate is high.
(iv) Cell size increases.
(v) Synthesis of enzymes, amino acids, nucleotides etc. but there is no change in DNA amount.

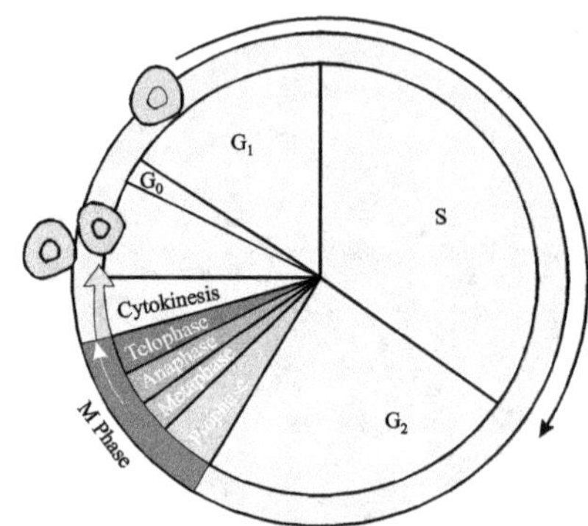

Fig: A diagrammatic view of Cell Cycle

- **S-phase/Synthetic phase**
  S or synthesis phase marks the period during which DNA synthesis or replication takes place.

Following events take place during this phase
(i) DNA replicates and its amount becomes double. If the initial amount of DNA is denoted as 2C then it increases to 4C.
(ii) Synthesis of histone proteins and NHC (non-histone chromosomal proteins).
(iii) Duplication of centriole in the cytoplasm.
- *G2-phase/Pre mitotic/Post synthetic phase/Gap-II*
  Following events take place during this phase
(i) Mitotic spindle protein (tubulin) synthesis begins.
(ii) Chromosome condensation factor appears.
(iii) Synthesis of 3 types of RNA, NHC proteins, and ATP molecule.
(iv) Repair of damaged DNA occurs.
- The cells that do not divide further exit G1 phase to enter an inactive stage called *quiescent stage (G_0)* of the cell cycle. Cells in this stage remain metabolically active but no longer proliferate unless called on to do so depending on the requirement of the organism.

Cell Cycle Regulators

Leland Hortwell, Tim Hunt and Paul Nurse received the 2001 Nobel Prize in Physiology for discovery of cell cycle regulators (CDK/Cyclins/Check points).

Cell division

Amitosis	Mitosis	Meiosis
• Amitosis is also called as direct cell division. • In this division there is no differentiation of chromosomes and spindle. The nuclear envelope does not degenerate. The nucleus elongates and constricts in the middle to form two daughter nuclei. This is followed by a centripetal constriction of the cytoplasm to form two daughter cells.	• Mitosis is also called indirect cell division or somatic cell division or equational division. • In this, mature somatic cell divides in such a way that chromosomes number is kept constant in daughter cells equal to those in parent cell. • The growing regions of plants have meristematic cells (e.g. these cells are found in apical portion of root and stem and in the expanding leaf) in which mitosis takes place.	• It is a division that occurs in a mature diploid reproductive cell (2x) in which nucleus divides twice but chromosome (DNA) replicates only once to form four haploid cells, each having half the number of chromosomes present in the parent cell. As it causes reduction in the number of chromosomes, it is known as *reduction division*.

MITOSIS

Prophase

It is the longest phase of karyokinesis.

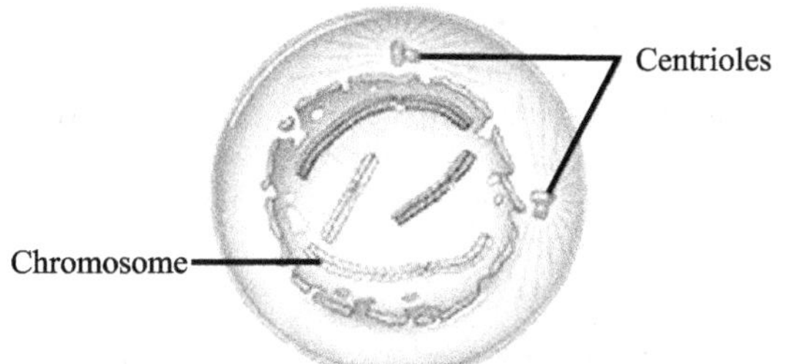

Fig.: Prophase

- Chromatin fibres thicken and shorten to form chromosomes which may overlap each other and appears like a ball of wool.
- Each chromosome divides longitudinally into 2 chromatids which remain attached to centromere.
- Nuclear membrane starts disintegrating except in dinoflagellates.
- Nucleolus starts disintegrating.
- Spindle formation begins.

Prometaphase

- The degeneration of nuclear envelop and membrane vesicles are formed.
- Emergence of kinetochores starts and spindle reaches to the chromosomes and get attached to the kinetochore.

Metaphase

- Chromosomes become maximally distinct i.e., size can be measured.

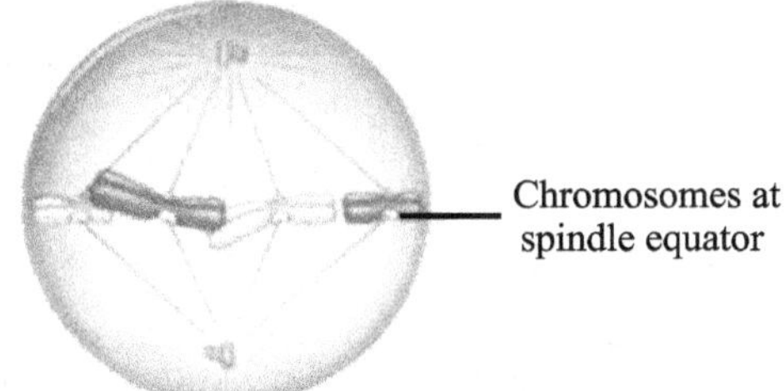

Fig.: Metapase

- Chromosomes move towards equatorial plane of spindles called congression and become arranged with their arms directed towards pole and centromere towards equator.
- Spindle fibres attach to kinetochores.
- Metaphase is the best stage for studying chromosome morphology (structure, size, number) and cancer studies.

Anaphase

- Centromere splits from the middle and two chromatids gets separated.

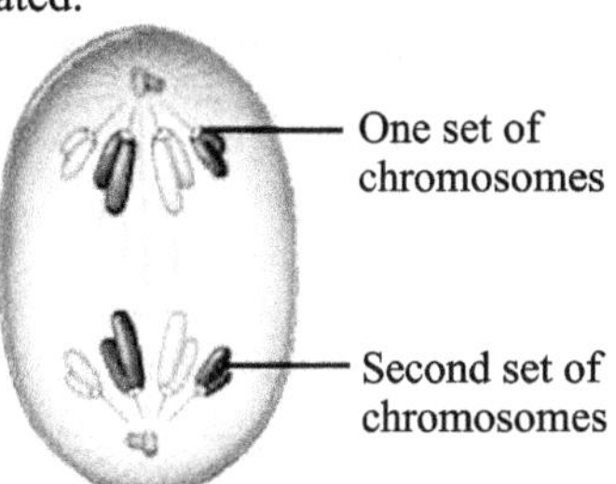

Fig.: Anaphase

- Both the chromatids move towards opposite poles due to repulsive force called anaphasic movement.
- The centromere faces towards equator.
- Shape of chromosome is best studied at anaphase.

Telophase

- Chromosomes reached on poles by the spindle fibers and form two groups.
- Chromosomes begin to uncoil and form chromatin net.
- The nuclear membrane and nucleolus reappear.

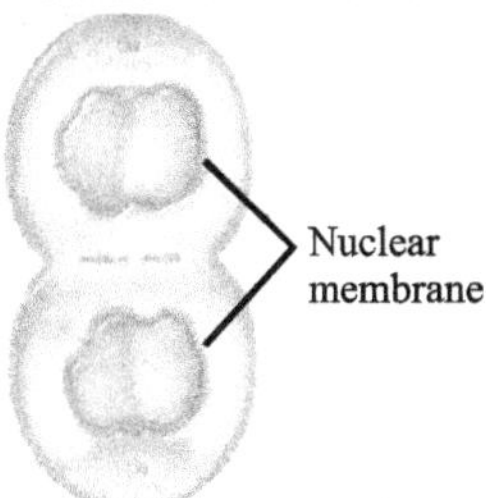

Fig. Anaphase

- In animal cells, astral rays and spindle fibres completely disappear in telophase. The two centriole pairs organise themselves into centrosomes.
- Golgi complex and ER etc., reform.

Cytokinesis

- Cytokinesis is division of cell having undergone karyokinesis to produce two daughter cells each with a daughter nucleus. It begins in mid-anaphase and is generally completed alongwith the completion of telophase.

ENDOMITOSIS

- *Endomitosis*: Chromosomes and their DNA duplicate but fails to separate which lead to polyploidy e.g., in liver of man, both diploid (2n) and polyploid cells have been reported. It is also called endoduplication and endopolyploidy.

S. No.	Animal cell cytokinesis	Plant cell cytokinesis
1.	Centrioles present at spindle poles.	Centrioles lacking at spindle poles.
2.	Asters are formed (amphiastral).	No asters are formed (anastral).
3.	Cytokinesis by furrowing of cytoplasm.	Cytokinesis mostly by cell plate formation.
4.	Furrow extends centripetally.	Cell plate grows centrifugally.
5.	Occurs nearly in all tissues.	Occurs mainly at meristems.
6.	Cell becomes rounded and its cytoplasm more viscous at the time of mitosis.	Cell does not change form or nature at the time of mitosis.

MEIOSIS

- It is a process in which, a single cell twice to produce four daughter cells.
- Occurs in reproductive cells, in which cell have a half number of chromosomes present in parent cell.
- It occurs only in reproductive cells.

Meiosis I	Meiosis II
Prophase I	Prophase II
Metaphase I	Metaphase II
Anaphase I	Anaphase II
Telophase I	Telophase II

Meiosis I

It results in the formation of two haploid cells from one diploid cell. The daughter cells are, therefore, haploid but with 2n DNA content. It is divided into four phases i.e., prophase, metaphase, anaphase, telophase.

Prophase-I: It is longest phase of karyokinesis of meiosis. It is again divisible into five subphases i.e., *leptotene, zygotene, pachytene, diplotene and diakinesis.*

(i)   Leptotene/Leptonema
Chromosomes are long thread like with chromomeres (i.e. linear series of darkly stained swollen areas) on it. *homologous chromosomes* derived from different parents either paternal or maternal.

(ii)   Zygotene/Zygonema
Pairing or "Synapsis" of homologous chromosomes takes place in this stage.

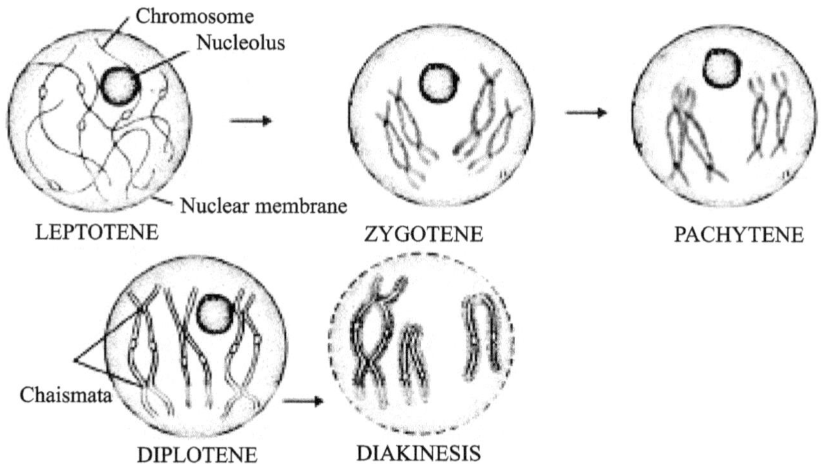

Paired chromosomes are called bivalents, which by further molecular packing and spiralization becomes shorter and thicker.

(iii)   Pachytene/Pachynema
Crossing over takes place by breakage and reunion of chromatid segments. Breakage called *nicking*, is assisted by an enzyme *endonuclease* and reunion termed *annealing* is added by an enzyme *ligase.*

(iv)   Diplotene/Diplonema
In this stage the paired chromosomes begin to separate **(desynapsis);** terminalisation starts.
It is formed at the place of crossing over between non-sister chromatids.
Homologous chromosomes move apart; they remain attached to one another at specific points called *chiasmata.*

(v)   Diakinesis
Terminalization of chiasmata. Nuclear membrane and nucleolus degenerates. Chromosome recondense and tetrad moves to the metaphase plate. Formation of spindle. When the diakinesis of prophase-I is completed then cell enters into the metaphase-I.

Metaphase-I

Chromosomes allign on the equator. Bivalents arrange themselves in two parallel equatorial or metaphasic plates.

Anaphase-I

In involves separation of homologous chromosomes which start moving towards opposite poles so each tetrad is divided into two daughter dyads. So anaphase-I involves the reduction of chromosome number, this is called *disjunction.*

Telophase-I

Two daughter nuclei are formed but the chromosome number is half of the chromosome number of mother cell. Nuclear membrane reappears and after telophase I cytokinesis may or may not occur.

Significance of meiosis-I

- It separates the homologous chromosomes to reduce the chromosome number to the haploid state, a necessity for sexual reproduction.
- It introduces variation by forming new gene combinations through crossing over and random assortment of paternal and maternal chromosomes.

Meiosis-II

It is also called equational or homotypical division because the number of chromosomes remains same as after meiosis-I. It involves the separation of two chromatids of each chromosome and their movement to separate cells. It is divided in four phases i.e., Prophase-II, Metaphase-II, Anaphase-II and Telophase-II.

Significance of Meiosis-II

- Constancy of chromosomes number in successive generation is brought by this process.
- It helps in introducing variations and mutations.
- It maintains the amount of genetic material.
- The four daughter cells will have different types of dramatids.

MULTIPLE CHOICE QUESTIONS

1. An important character of chordata is presence of
   (a) dorsal notochord
   (b) dorsal hollow nerve cord
   (c) post-anal tail
   (d) all the above

2. Venus fly trap is a
   (a) Bryophyta   (b) Pteridophyta
   (c) Gymnosperm   (d) Angiosperm

3.
	Column-I	Column-II
A.	The name of the genus begins with a letter.	P. underlined
B.	The name of the species begin with a letter.	Q. small
C.	When printed the scientific name is in a letter.	R. italics
D.	When written by hand the scientific name is a letter.	S. capitals

   (a) A-Q; B-R; C-S; D-P
   (b) A-P; B-Q; C-R; D-S
   (c) A-S; B-R; C-Q; D-P
   (d) A-S; B-Q; C-R; D-P

4. Largest group in Animal Kingdom is
   (a) Mollusca   (b) Amphibia
   (c) Arthropods   (d) Reptilia

5. Pollination takes place in
   (a) Gymnosperms   (b) Pteridophyta
   (c) Both (a) & (b)   (d) None of these

6. Which of the followings are correct order of hierarchy?
   (a) Kingdom, division, phylum, genus and species
   (b) Phylum, division, genus and class
   (c) Kingdom, genus, class, phylum and division
   (d) Phylum, kingdom, genus, species and class

7. Which one of the following is responsible for converting milk into curd? **[CDS]**
   (a) Fungi   (b) Bacteria
   (c) Virus   (d) None of these

8. Bryophytes are photosynthetic but do not have vascular tissue and true roots. This feature enables them to resemble with which of the following? **[CDS]**
   (a) Fungi   (b) Algae
   (c) Pteridophytes   (d) Angiosperms

9. Which one of the following is a freeliving bacterium that helps in nitrogen fixation in soil? **[CDS]**
   (a) Azotobacter   (b) Anabaena
   (c) Azolla   (d) Nostoc

10. Which one among the following groups of animals maintains constant body temperature in changing environmental conditions? **[CDS]**
    (a) Birds   (b) Fishes
    (c) Amphibians   (d) Reptiles

11. Among the following animals, choose the one having three pairs of legs. **[CDS]**
    (a) Spider   (b) Scorpion
    (c) Bug   (d) Mite

12. Rough endoplasmic reticulum is concerned with
    (a) Protein synthesis (b) Fat synthesis
    (c) Respiration   (d) Photosynthesis

13. Nucleolus is
    (a) rounded structure found in cytoplasm near nucleus.
    (b) rounded structure inside nucleus and having rRNA.
    (c) rod-shaped structure in cytoplasm near the nucleus.
    (d) none of the above.

14. Silver nitrate solution is used to study
    (a) endoplasmic reticulum
    (b) Golgi apparatus
    (c) nucleus
    (d) mitochondria

15. As per the cladistic taxonomy, Archosaurs are a group of diapsid amniotes which include extinct dinosaurs. The living representatives of the group consist of
    (a) Anurans and Aves
    (b) Aves and Crocodilia
    (c) Aves and Agnatha
    (d) Osteichthyes and Squamata

16. In *Drosophila melanogaster* males, homologous chromosomes pair and segregate during meiosis but crossing over does not occur. At which stage of meiosis does segregation of 2 alleles of a gene take place in these individuals?
    (a) Zygotene   (b) Diakinesis
    (c) Anaphase I   (d) Anaphase II

17. Which of the following group is present in animal cells? **[NDA]**
    (a) Mitochondria, Cell membrane, Cell wall, Cytoplasm
    (b) Chloroplasts, Cytoplasm, Vacuole, Nucleus
    (c) Nucleus, Cell membrane, Mitochondria, Cytoplasm
    (d) Vacuole, Cell membrane, Nucleus, Mitochondria

18. Which organelle in the cell, other than nucleus, contains DNA? **[NDA]**
    (a) Endoplasmic reticulum
    (b) Golgi apparatus
    (c) Lysosome
    (d) Mitochondria

19. Which of the following parts are found in both plant and animal cells? **[CDS]**
    (a) Cell membrane, Chloroplast, Vacuole
    (b) Cell wall, Nucleus, Vacuole
    (c) Cell membrane, Cytoplasm, Nucleus
    (d) Cell wall, Chloroplast, Cytoplasm

20. Which one among the following statements is correct? **[CDS]**
    (a) Prokaryotic cells possess nucleus.
    (b) Cell membrane is present both in plant and animal cells.
    (c) Mitochondria and chloroplasts are not found in eukaryotic cells.
    (d) Ribosomes are present in eukaryotic cells only.

21. What part of the cell serves as the intracellular highway?
   - (a)　Endoplasmic reticulum
   - (b)　Golgi apparatus
   - (c)　Cell membrane
   - (d)　Mitochondria

22. Which of the following is a part of endomembrane system of eukaryotic cell?
   - (a)　Peroxisomes
   - (b)　Chloroplasts
   - (c)　Mitochondria
   - (d)　Golgi complexes

23. Mitochondria supply most of the necessary biological energy by
   - (a)　Breaking down of sugar
   - (b)　Oxidizing substrates of TCA cycle
   - (c)　Reducing NADP
   - (d)　Breaking down of protein

24. 70S type of ribosomes is found in
   - (a)　Prokaryotic cells
   - (b)　Prokaryotic cells, chloroplasts and mitochondria
   - (c)　Mitochondria
   - (d)　Nucleus, mitochondria

25. Crossing over occurs during
   - (a)　leptotene
   - (b)　pachytene
   - (c)　diplotene
   - (d)　diakinesis

26. Recombination involves
   - (a)　crossing over
   - (b)　chromosome duplication
   - (c)　spindle formation
   - (d)　cytokinesis

27. Chiasmata are first seen in
   - (a)　leptotene
   - (b)　zygotene
   - (c)　pachytene
   - (d)　diplotene

28. Terminalization occurs during
   - (a)　mitosis
   - (b)　diakinesis
   - (c)　meiosis II
   - (d)　cytokinesis

29. In cell cycle, DNA replication takes place in
   - (a)　G1 phase
   - (b)　G2 phase
   - (c)　Mitotic metaphase
   - (d)　S phase

30. Which phase of cell cycle is known as quiescent stage?
   - (a)　M phase
   - (b)　G0 phase
   - (c)　G1 phase
   - (d)　S phase

31. Which of the following phase follows S and G2 phases of interphase?
   - (a)　Prophase
   - (b)　Metaphase
   - (c)　Anaphase
   - (d)　Telophase

32. The living content of cell is called protoplasm. It is composed of:　　　　　　　　　　　**[CDS 2016-I]**
   - (a)　Cytoplasm only
   - (b)　Cytoplasm and nucleoplasm
   - (c)　Nucleoplasm only
   - (d)　Cytoplasm, nucleoplasm and other organelles

33. Match List-I with List-II and select the correct answer using the code given below the Lists :　　**[CDS 2017-II]**

List-I (Cell Organelle)		List-II (Function)
A.	Mitochondria	1. Photosynthesis
B.	Chloroplast	2. Protein synthesis
C.	Ribosomes	3. Intracellular digestion
D.	Lysosomes	4. ATP formation

Codes:

	A	B	C	D
(a)	3	1	2	4
(b)	3	2	1	4
(c)	4	1	2	3
(d)	4	2	1	3

34. A protein is synthesized in the endoplasmic reticulum bound ribosomes and it targets to the inner thylakoid space of chloroplast. How many double-layered membrane layers it has to pass to reach its destination?　　**[CDS 2018-I]**
   - (a)　2
   - (b)　3
   - (c)　4
   - (d)　5

35. Lysosome is formed from which of the following cell organelles?　　　　　　　　　　　**[CDS 2018-I]**
   - (a)　Nucleus
   - (b)　Endoplasmic reticulum
   - (c)　Golgi bodies
   - (d)　Ribosomes

36. Which one of the following pairs about organ/part that helps in locomotion is not correctly matched?　　**[CDS 2018-I]**
   - (a)　Euglena　　　:　　Flagellum
   - (b)　Paramecium　:　　Cilia
   - (c)　Nereis　　　 :　　Pseudopodia
   - (d)　Starfish　　　:　　Tubefeet

37. Which one of the following is a true fish as per the biological system of classification?　　**[CDS 2018-I]**
   - (a)　Silver fish
   - (b)　Jelly fish
   - (c)　Cuttle fish
   - (d)　Flying fish

38. Cell wall of any fungus is different from plants in having　　　　　　　　　　　　　**[NDA 2017-I]**
   - (a)　cellulose
   - (b)　chitin
   - (c)　cholesterol
   - (d)　glycogen

39. Which one of the following is an organelle that is NOT found in prokaryotic cells?　　**[NDA 2018-I]**
   - (a)　Cell wall
   - (b)　Mitochondria
   - (c)　Plasma membrane
   - (d)　Ribosome

40. Which one of the following is the correct sequence of levels of hierarchy of classification of organisms from higher to lower?　　**[NDA 2018-I]**
   - (a)　Phylum – Class – Order – Family – Genus
   - (b)　Phylum – Class – Family – Order – Genus
   - (c)　Family – Order – Class – Species – Genus
   - (d)　Class – Family – Order – Species – Genus

41. Which one of the following statements about classification of plants is correct? **[NDA 2018-I]**
   (a) Thallophytes have well differentiated body design
   (b) *Funaria* is a fungus
   (c) All Pteridophytes are Phanerogams
   (d) Vascular system is not found among Bryophytes

42. Who among the following first discovered cell? **[NDA 2018-I]**
   (a) Robert Brown   (b) Robert Hooke
   (c) Leeuwenhoek   (d) Rudolf Virchow

Directions : The following item consist of two statements, Statement I and Statement II. Examine these two statements carefully and select the correct answer using the code given below.

code:
(a) Both the statements are individually true and Statement II is the correct explanation of Statement I
(b) Both the statements are individually true but Statement II is not the correct explanation of Statement I
(c) Statement is the true but Statement II is false
(d) Statement I is false but Statement II is true

43. **Statement I :** **[NDA 2018-II]**
Phytoplankton produce most of the organic carbon in the ocean.

Statement II :
Algae are produced in the cold water biome.

44. Which one of the following groups of cellular organelles contains DNA? **[NDA 2018-II]**
   (a) Mitochondria, nucleus, chloroplast
   (b) Mitochondria, Golgi bodies, nucleus
   (c) Mitochondria, plasma membrane, nucleus
   (d) Chloroplast, nucleus, ribosomes

45. One of the additional functions of Smooth Endoplasmic Reticulum (SER) is **[NDA 2018-II]**
   (a) protein synthesis
   (b) lipid synthesis
   (c) storage of biomolecules
   (d) detoxification of toxic substances

46. Which of the following kingdoms has/have only unicellular organisms? **[NDA 2018-II]**
   (a) Monera only
   (b) Protista only
   (c) Monera and Protista both
   (d) Protista and Fungi both

ANSWER KEY																			
1.	(d)	**2.**	(d)	**3.**	(d)	4.	**(c)**	5.	(a)	**6.**	(a)	**7.**	(b)	**8.**	(b)	9.	(a)	**10.**	(a)
11.	(c)	**12.**	(a)	**13.**	(b)	14.	**(b)**	15.	(b)	**16.**	(c)	**17.**	(c)	**18.**	(d)	**19.**	(c)	**20.**	(b)
21.	(a)	**22.**	(d)	**23.**	(b)	24.	**(b)**	25.	(b)	**26.**	(a)	**27.**	(d)	**28.**	(b)	**29.**	(d)	**30.**	(b)
31.	(a)	**32.**	(d)	**33.**	(c)	34.	**(b)**	35.	(c)	**36.**	(c)	**37.**	(d)	38	(b)	39	(b)	40	(a)
41	(d)	42	(b)	43	(b)	44	**(a)**	45	(b)	46	(c)								

Chapter 2

GENETICS

GENETICS

Heredity is the transmission of genetic characters from parent to offsprings. Individuals of same species have some differences, these are called variation.

MENDEL'S FINDINGS

1. **Mendel's Law of Dominance and Recessive**
   - Each of the f_1 generation plant shows inheritance of Y allele from one parent and a G allele from the other. When the f_1 plants breed, each has equal chance of passing on either Y or G allele to each offspring.
   - In all the seven traits that Mendel examined, one form appeared dominant over the other i.e., it marked the presence of the other allele, e.g.

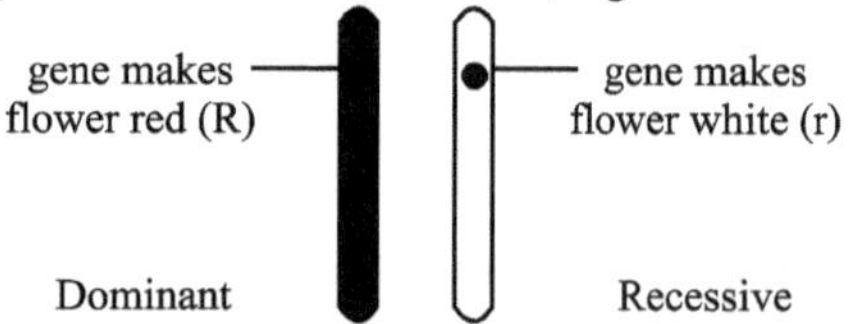

BASIC TERMS USED IN INHERITANCE STUDIES

- **Allele:** It is an alternative form of a gene which are located on same position (loci) on the homologous chromosome. Term allele was coined by Bateson.
- **Homozygous:** A zygote is formed by fusion of two gametes having identical factors is called homozygote and organism developed from this zygote is called homozygous.
  Ex. TT, RR, tt.
- **Heterozygous:** A zygote is formed by fusion of two different types of gamete carrying different factors is called heterozygote (Tt, Rr) and individual developed from such zygote is called heterozygous.
- **Hemizygous:** If individual contains only one gene of a pair then individual is said to be hemizygous. Male individual is always hemizygous for sex linked gene.
- **Phenotype:** It is the external and morphological appearances of an organism for a particular character.
- **Genotype:** It is the genetic constitution or genetic make-up of an organism for a particular character.
- **Back cross:** A back cross is a cross in which F_1 individuals are crossed with any of their parents.
- **Test cross:** When F_1 progeny is crossed with recessive parent then it is called test cross.

- **Monohybrid test cross:** The progeny obtained from the monohybrid test cross are in equal proportion, means 50% is dominant phenotype and 50% is recessive phenotype.

  It can be represented in symbolic forms as follows.
  F_1 progeny (hybrid) × Recessive parent

	t
T	Tt
t	tt

  Monohybrid test cross ratio = 1 : 1
- **Dihybrid test cross:** The progeny is obtained from dihybrid test cross are of four types and each of them is 25%.

2. **Law of Segregation:** According to this law, for any particular trait, the pair of alleles of each parent separate and only one allele passes from each parent to an offspring. Allele in a parent's pair of allele is inherited as a matter of chance (we now know segregation of alleles occurs during the process of meiosis).

3. **Law of Independent Assortment:** This is also known as 'Inheritance law'. According to this law, different pairs of alleles are passed to offspring independently of each other.

PARENTAL CROSS

Gametes from Hybrid 1

	Round – yellow seeds	Wrinkled–green seeds	Parental Phenotype
	RRYY	rryy	Parental Genotype
	RY RY	ry ry	Gametes

| | Rr Yy | Rr Yy | Rr Yy | Rr Yy | f_1 generation Genotype |
| | Round–yellow | Round–yellow | Round–yellow | Round–yellow | f_1 generation Phenotype |

	RY	Ry	rY	ry
RY	RRYY Round–yellow	RRYy Round–yellow	RrYY Round–yellow	RrYy Round–yellow
Ry	RRYy Round–yellow	Rryy Round–green	RrYy Round–yellow	Rryy Round–green
rY	RrYY Round–yellow	RrYy Round–yellow	rrYY wrinkled yellow	rrYy wrinkled yellow
ry	RrYy Round–yellow	Rryy Round–green	rrYy wrinkled yellow	rryy wrinkled green

Punnett Square

Exceptions of Conclusions of Mendel

Exception of Dominance
There are two exceptions of law of dominance–
(i)   Incomplete dominance
(ii) Co-dominance

LINKAGE

- Linkage is the phenomenon of certain genes staying together during inheritance through generations without any change or separation. This is due to their location on the same chromosomes.
- Linkage was first time seen by *Bateson and Punnett* in *Lathyrus odoratus* and gave coupling and repulsion phenomenon. But they did not explain the phenomenon of linkage.
- Sex linkage was first discovered by Morgan in *Drosophila* and coined the term linkage. He *proposed the theory of linkage.*

Sex Linkage

When the genes of vegetative/somatic characters are present on sex-chromosome, it is termed as *sex linked gene* and such phenomenon is known as *sex-linkage.*

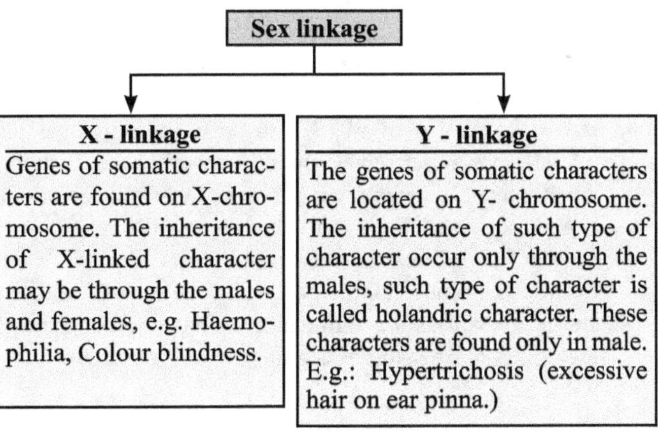

X - linkage	Y - linkage
Genes of somatic characters are found on X-chromosome. The inheritance of X-linked character may be through the males and females, e.g. Haemophilia, Colour blindness.	The genes of somatic characters are located on Y- chromosome. The inheritance of such type of character occur only through the males, such type of character is called holandric character. These characters are found only in male. E.g.: Hypertrichosis (excessive hair on ear pinna.)

GENES

Genes are responsible for the characteristics features (or traits) of organism-plant or animals. The characteristics or traits of parents are transmitted to their progeny (off springs) through genes present on their chromosomes during the process of sexual reproduction.

- Genes are arranged linearly along long chains of DNA sequence, called chromosomes. The DNA of the chromosome is associated with proteins that organise, compact and control the access to the DNA, forming a material called chromatin. In eukaryotes, chromatin is composed of nucleosomes – segments of DNA wound around histone protein. The full set of hereditary material in an organism i.e., the combined DNA sequences of all chromosomes is called genome.

Lethal Gene

- Gene which causes death of individual in early stage when it comes in homozygous condition is called lethal gene.
- It may be dominant or recessive both, but mostly recessive for lethality. Lethal gene was discovered by L. Cuenot in coat colour of mice.

MULTIPLE ALLELE

- More than 2 alternative forms of same gene is called as multiple allele. Multiple allele is formed due to mutation and located on same locus of homologous chromosome.

Example of multiple allele
- ABO blood group: ABO blood groups are determined by allele I^A, allele I^B, allele I^D

IA = dominant
IB = dominant
ID = recessive
Possible phenotypes - A, B, AB, O

Blood group	Genotype	Antigen or agglutinogen	Antibody or agglutinin
A	I^AI^A, I^AI^O	A	b
B	I^BI^B, I^BI^O	B	a
AB	I^AI^B	A & B	None
O	I^OI^O	None	a & b

SEX DETERMINATION

- Sex determination is a biological system that determines the development of sexual characters in an organism. Most sexual organisms have two sexes: Males and females.
- In a human, the sexual chromosomes complement is 46, 44 of which are autosomes while 2 distinct chromosomes are the sex chromosomes, which determine the sex of an organism and various sex-linked characteristics.
- In humans, sex is predetermined in the male gamete. The egg gamete mother cell is said to be homogametic because all its cells possess the XX sex chromosomes, sperms are said to be heterogametic because around half of them contain the X-chromosome and others possess the Y-chromosome to complement the first X-chromosome.

Deoxyribose Nucleic Acid (DNA)

- Deoxyribose nucleic acid (DNA) carries the genetic information. It is a constitute of chromosome.
- Structure of DNA was worked out by X-ray diffraction studies. A double helix model by DNA was proposed by Watson and Crick in 1953. Rosalind Franklin and Maurice Wilkins contributed significantly to this study. They suggested that:
(i)   Each DNA molecule consists of two polynucleotide chains.

(ii) The chains are helically coiled around a common axis.

(iii) DNA molecule has a diameter of 20 Å are complete turn of helix is 3.4 Å. So there are 10 bases per turn of helix.

(iv) Each DNA chain is complementary chain to the second chain.

- Deoxyribose and a nitrogeneous base together form a nucleoside. A nucleoside and a phosphate together form a nucleotide.

  Nucleoside = Deoxyribose + Nitrogenous base

  Nucleotide = Deoxyribose + Nitrogenous base + Phosphate

- Deoxyribose is pentose sugar with five carbon atoms, four of the given carbon atoms plus a single atom of oxygen for a five numbered ring.

GENETIC DISORDERS

- **Genetic disorder** is a disease caused by abnormality in an individual's DNA.

- Genetic disorder may be grouped into two categories- *Mendelian disorders and chromosomal disorders.*

- *Mendelian disorders* are chiefly determined by alteration or mutation in the single gene. eg. haemophilia, cystic fibrosis, sickle cell anaemia, thalassemia, colour blindness, phenylketonuria, etc.

(i) *Haemophilia* is an inherited disorder of blood in which essential clotting factors are either partly or completely missing.

(ii) In *sickle-cell anaemia;*. glutamic acid (glutamine) is replaced by valine at the sixth position in β chain of haemoglobin. In this disease red blood cells become sickle shaped as compared to normal one.

- The *chromosomal disorders* are caused due to absence or excess or abnormal arrangement of one or more chromosomes. Failure of segregation of chromatids during cell division cycle results in the gain or loss of a chromosome(s), called aneuploidy.

- Types of *chromosomal disorders* are Patau Syndrome, Edward's syndrome, *Down's Syndrome, Klinefelter's Syndrome* and *Turner's Syndrome.*

Patau's syndrome is a serious rare genetic disorder caused by having an additional copy of chromosome 13 in body's cells. It's also known as trisomy 13. Babies with Patau's syndrome grow slowly in the womb and have a low birth weight, along with a number of other serious medical problems. Patau's syndrome affects about 1 in every 5,000 births. The risk of having a baby with the syndrome increases with the mother's age.

Edwards' syndrome is another serious genetic condition also known as trisomy 18. It is caused due to presence of additional copy of chromosome 18 in body's cells and is responsible for severe medical problems like physical and mental disabilities. Most babies with Edwards' syndrome will die before or shortly after being born.

- *Down's Syndrome* is caused by the presence of an additional copy of the chromosome number 21 (trisomy 21). The affected individual is short statured with small round head, furrowed tongue and partially open mouth. Palm is broad with characteristic palm crease. Physical, psychomotor and mental development is retarded.

- *Klinefelter's Syndrome* is caused due to the presence of an additional copy of X-chromosome resulting into a karyotype of 47, XXY. Such an individual has overall masculine development, however, the feminine development (development of breast, i.e., Gynaecomastia) is also expressed. Such individuals are sterile.

- *Turner's Syndrome* is caused due to the absence of one of the X chromosome, i.e., 45 with XO, such females are sterile as ovaries are rudimentary besides other features including lack of other secondary sexual characters.

MULTIPLE CHOICE QUESTIONS

1. Which one of the following is a hereditary disease ?
   (a) Cataract   (b) Haemophilia   **[NDA]**
   (c) Pellagra   (d) Osteoporosis

2. Which one of the following statements is correct?
   Cretinism is a human disorder which is due to the under secretion of: **[NDA]**
   (a) Adrenalin hormone   (b) Cortisone hormone
   (c) Glucagon hormone   (d) Thyroxin hormone

3. Which one of the following is **not** a genetic disorder?
   [NDA]
   (a) Colour blindness   (b) Down's syndrome
   (c) Haemophilia   (d) Xerophthalmia

4. Which one of the following genetic diseases is sex-linked?
   [IAS Prelim]
   (a) Royal haemophilia   (b) Tay-Sachs disease
   (c) Cystic fibrosis   (d) Hypertension

5. A mother of blood group O has a group O child. What could be the blood group of father of the child?   **[CDS]**
   (a) Only O   (b) A or B or O
   (c) A or B   (d) Only AB

6. Between which one of the following sets of blood groups, is the blood transfusion possible?   **[CDS]**
   (a) A and O   (b) B and A
   (c) A and AB   (d) AB and O

7. Which one among the following is not correct about Down's syndrome?   **[CDS]**
   (a) It is a genetic disorder
   (b) Effected individual has early ageing
   (c) Effected person has mental retardation
   (d) Effected person has furrowed tongue with open mouth

8. Haemophilia is a genetic disorder which lead to   **[IAS]**
   (a) decrease in hamemoglobin level
   (b) rheumatic heart disease
   (c) decrease in WBC
   (d) non-clotting of blood

9. Which one of the following techniques can be used to establish the paternity of a child?   **[IAS]**
   (a) Protein analysis
   (b) Quantitative analysis of DNA
   (c) Chromosome counting
   (d) DNA fingerprinting

10. Which one of the following genetic disease is sex-linked?
    [IAS]
    (a) Royal haemophilia   (b) Tay-Sachs disease
    (c) Cystic fibrosis   (d) Hypertension

11. **Assertion (A):** In human beings, the female play a major role in determining the sex of the offspring.
    Reason (R): Women have two X-chromosomes.   **[IAS]**
    (a) Both A and R are true and R is the correct explanation of A
    (b) Both A and R are true, but R is not a correct explanation of A
    (c) A is true, but R is false
    (d) A is false, but R is true

12. Hereditary characteristics are passed on from parents to offspring chiefly through
    (a) gametes   (b) enzymes
    (c) genes   (d) centrosomes

13. Consider the following statements:
    A. Sex is determined by different factors in various species.
    B. Exchange of genetic material takes place in asexual reproduction.
    Which of these statement(s) is/are correct?
    (a) A only   (b) B only
    (c) Both A and B   (d) Neither A nor B

14. From heredity point of view which marriage is not suitable
    (a) Man Rh (–) and Woman Rh (+)
    (b) Both Rh (+)
    (c) Both Rh (–)
    (d) Man Rh (+) and Woman Rh (–)

15. In animals sex determination is due to
    (a) X-chromosome   (b) Y-chromosome
    (c) A-chromosome   (d) B-chromosome

16. A complete set of chromosomes inherited as a unit from one parent, is known as
    (a) Karyotype   (b) Gene pool
    (c) Genome   (d) Genotype

17. The ratio of phenotypes in F_2 of a monohybrid cross is
    (a) 3 : 1   (b) 1 : 2 : 1
    (c) 9 : 3 : 3 : 1   (d) 2 : 1

18. Sickle cell anaemia is
    (a) caused by substitution of valine by glutamic acid in the beta globin chain of haemoglobin.
    (b) caused by a change in a single base pair of DNA.
    (c) characterized by elongated sickle like RBCs with a nucleus.
    (d) an autosomal linked dominant trait.

19. Mutations can be induced with
    (a) infrared radiations   (b) IAA
    (c) ethylene   (d) gamma radiations

20.

	Column-I		Column-II
A.	ABO blood groups	I.	Dihybrid cross
B.	Law of segregation	II.	Monohybrid
	cross		
C.	Law of Independent	III.	Base pairs
	assortment		substitution
D.	Gene mutation	IV.	Multiple allelism

- (a) A – II; B – I; C – IV; D – III
- (b) A – IV; B – I; C – II; D – III
- (c) A – IV; B – II; C – I; D – III
- (d) A – II; B – III; C – IV; D – I

21.

	Column -I		Column -II
A.	Incomplete dominance	I.	*Drosophila*
B.	Mendelian disorder	II.	*Antirrhinum* sp.
C.	Transforming principle	III.	Griffith
D.	Dihybrid cross	IV.	Haemophilia

- (a) A – I; B – IV; C – III; D – II
- (b) A – IV; B – II; C – III; D – I
- (c) A – II; B – III; C – IV; D – I
- (d) A – II; B – IV; C – III; D – I

22. A recessive inherited disease is expressed only in individuals of blood group O and not expressed in blood groups A, B or AB. Alleles controlling the disease and blood group are independently inherited. A normal woman with blood group A and her normal husband with blood group B already had one child with the disease. The woman is pregnant for second time. What is the probability that the second child will also have the disease?

- (a) 1/2
- (b) 1/4
- (c) 1/16
- (d) 1/64

23. Who among the following shared the Nobel Prize in 1962 along with Francis Crick and James Watson for their discoveries concerning the molecular structure of nucleic acids?   **[NDA 2017-II]**

- (a) Erwin Chargaff
- (b) Maurice Hugh Frederick Wilkins
- (c) Rosalind Franklin
- (d) Phoebus Levene

ANSWER KEY

1.	(b)	2.	(d)	3.	(d)	4.	(a)	5.	(b)	6.	(c)	7.	(b)	8.	(d)
9.	(d)	10.	(a)	11.	(d)	12.	(a)	13.	(a)	14.	(d)	15.	(d)	16.	(c)
17.	(a)	18.	(b)	19.	(d)	20.	(c)	21.	(d)	22.	(c)	23	(b)		

Chapter 3

EVOLUTION AND ECOLOGICAL BIODIVERSITY

EVOLUTION

The branch of life science for the study of 'origin of life' and evolution of different forms of life on earth was called **bioevolution or evolutionary biology** by Mayer, (1970). The word evolution means to unfold or unroll or to reveal hidden potentialities. Evolution simply means an orderly change from one condition to another. Evolution is slow but continuous process which never stop.

ORIGIN OF LIFE

- Origin of life is the process by which living organisms developed from inanimate matter which is generally thought to have occurred on Earth between 3800 - 4200 millions years ago. There are several theories about the origin of life, like big bang theory, theory of special creation, theory of eternity, cosmozoic theory etc.

Chemosynthetic Theory of Origin of Life

The widely accepted theory is the Chemosynthetic theory of origin of life proposed by **A.I. Oparin.** It states that life has originated on earth through a series of combinations of chemical substances in the distant past. All these processes took place in water.

- The early atmosphere contained ammonia (NH_3), water vapour (H_2O), hydrogen (H_2), methane (CH_4). At that time there was no free oxygen.

Miller and Urey Experiment

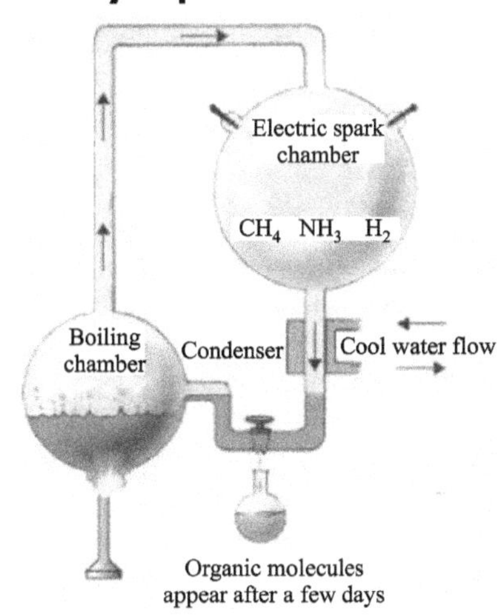

Organic molecules appear after a few days

CHEMICAL EVOLUTION AND ORGANIC EVOLUTION

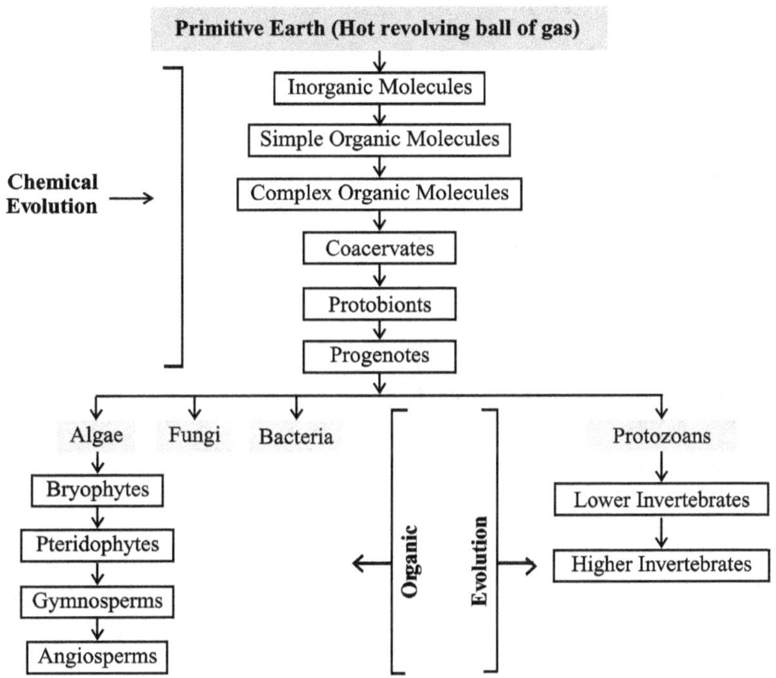

Comparative Anatomy and Morphology

- Different animals and plants show dissimilarities in their structure but in some characters they show similarity. These similarities provide one of the most concluding evidence of organic evolution.
- Similarities are of two types : **homology** and **analogy**.

Let us discuss some of the important sources that provide evidences for evolution.

- **Homologous organs:** Homologous organs are similar in origin (or are embryologically similar) but perform different functions.

  For example, the forelimbs of humans and the wings of birds look different externally but their skeletal structure is similar.

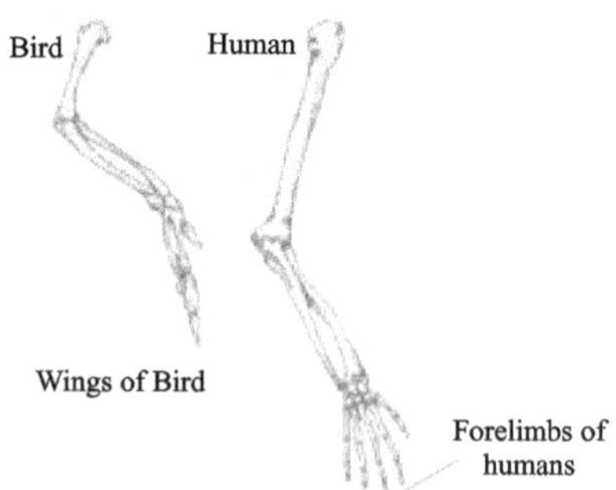

Homologous Organs: (a) Wings of bird and (b) Forelimbs of humans

- **Analogous organs**: Analogous organs have different origin but perform similar functions.

  For example, the wings of a bird and a bat are similar in function but this similarity does not mean that these animals are more closely related.

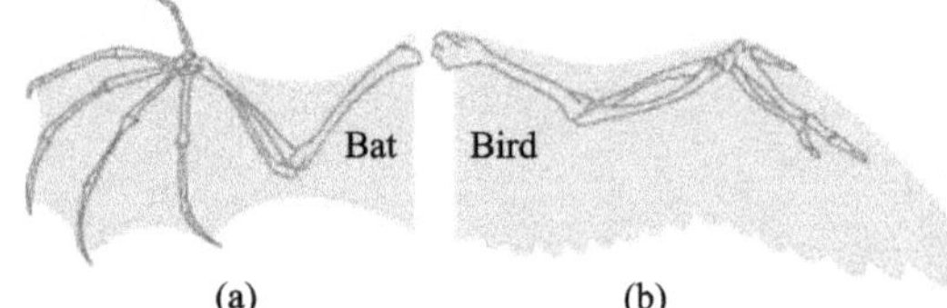

Analogous Organs: (a) Wings of bat and (b) Wing of a bird

Vestigial organs

- The organs which are present in reduced form and do not perform any function in the body but correspond to the fully developed functional organs of related animals are called **vestigial organs**.
- Human body possess about **180 vestigial organs**.

  Some of these are - nictating membrane, muscles of pinna (auricular muscles), vermiform appendix, coccyx, canine teeth, third molars (wisdom teeth), segmental muscles of abdomen, caecum, body hairs, nipples in male and ear pinna.

Theories of Organic Evolution

- Four main theories to explain theories of evolution are-
  - (i) Lamarckism
  - (ii) Darwinism
  - (iii) Mutation theory
  - (iv) Modern concept of evolution (synthetic theory)

Lamarckism

- *Theory of inheritance of acquired characters* is the first theory of organic evolution proposed by *Jean Baptiste de Lamarck* (1744-1829). Lamarck coined the terms
- It states about the internal vital forces, effect of environment and new needs, use and disuse of organs and inheritance of aquired characters. These aquired characters are passed from one generation to another which results in new species.
- Examples in support of Lamarckism are

  Long neck and high fore limb of Giraffe, Aquatic birds stretched their toes and developed web, Snakes lost their legs, Deers became good runners by the development of strong limbs and streamlined body and retractile claws of carnivorous animals.

Darwinism

- "Darwinism" or "The theory of Natural Selection" was proposed jointly by *Charles Darwin* and *A.R. Wallace*. This theory was explained by Darwin in his book 'On the origin of species by the means of Natural Selection' (1859).
- Darwin was influenced by two books–
  - (i) "Principles of Population" by Malthus.
  - (ii) "Principles of Geology" by Charls Lyell.

Main features of theory of Natural Selection

- **Over production**
  - – All organisms have capability to produce enormous number of offspring, organisms multiply in geometric ratio.
  - – examples
  - (i) Plants produce thousands of seeds.
  - (ii) Insects lay hundreds of egg.
  - (iii) One pair of elephant gives rise to about six offspring and if all survived in 750 years a single pair would produce about 19 million elephants. Thus, some organisms produce more offspring and other produce fewer offspring. This is called differential reproduction.

Mutation Theory

- The mutation theory was put forward in 1901 by **Hugo de Vries**.
- The plant on which Hugo de Vries had experimented was *Oenothera Lamarckiana*.
- Role of mutations in evolution are genetic variations.
- Mutations are discontinuous variation called **sports** by **Darwin** and **saltatory variation** by **Bateson**.
- *Features of mutation theory are-*
  - (i) It forms the raw material for mutation.
  - (ii) It appears suddenly and produce their effect immediately.
  - (iii) Mutations are markedly different from the parents and there are no intermediate stages between the two.
  - (iv) Mutations can **appear in all directions.**

HUMAN EVOLUTION

Evolution of man probably took place in *Central Africa*. Human evolution states that humans develops from primates or ape like ancestors. *Anthropology* is the study of human evolution and culture. It deals with the fossils of pre-historic and living man.

Homo erectus was the first human to leave Africa and move to Europe and Asia. It had a sloping forehead, flattish face and brain size between 850-1100 ml. These humans exploited more habitats than their ancestors. They were first to use fire.

Homo neanderthals were the first humans to have adopted to life in cold climates of Europe and Asia. They had strong physique and large brain. They more clothes, made a range of tools and used fire to keep warm. They were the first humans to bury their dead.

Homo sapiens or the "modern human" first evolved in Africa. They had a large brain, were considerably intelligent and had developed the ability to use language. Modern man took control of their surroundings as they developed agriculture, societies and technology.

> • Carolus linnaeus coined the term 'Homo Sapiens'.

ECOLOGY AND BIODIVERSITY

The term "ecology" was coined in 1866 by German scientist **Ernst Haeckel**. It is study of biota, environment and their interaction. Ecology also provides information about the benefits of ecosystems and how we can use Earth's resources in ways that leave the the environment healthy for future generations. Ecology can studied in following head.

Chronology of Human Evolution

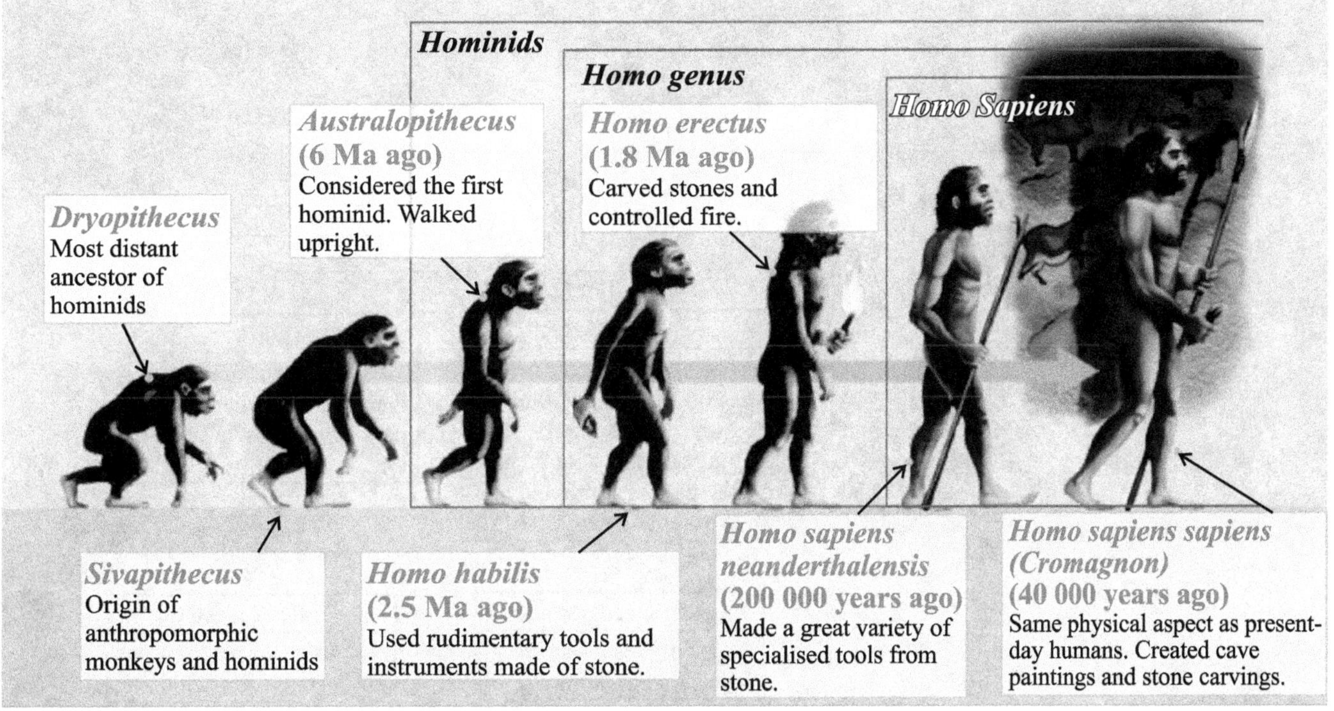

Taxonomic position of human with evolutionary history	
Class	– Mammalia
Sub class	– Eutheria
Order	– Primates (65 million years ago)
Sub order	– Anthropoidea (36 millions years ago)
Super family	– Hominoidea (24 millions years ago)
Family	– Hominidae (4 million years ago)
Genus	– Homo (2 million years ago)
Species	– *Sapiens* (< 1 million years ago)
Sub species	– *Sapiens* (10,000 years ago)

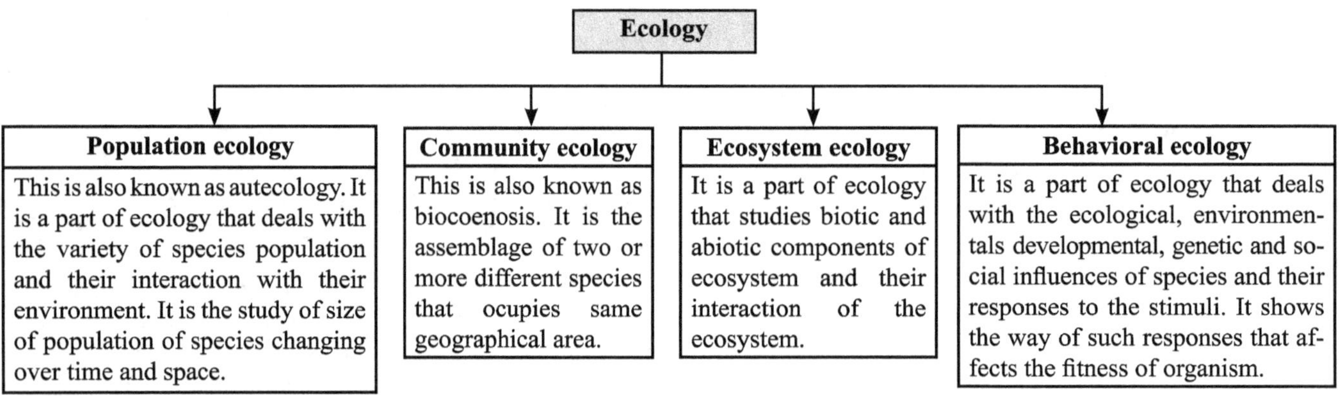

ECOSYSTEM

*   The term 'ecosystem' was proposed by a British ecologist **A.G. Tansley (1953)**. It represent the basic fundamental, functional unit of ecology which comprises of the biotic community together with its abiotic (non-living) environment. Ecosystem simply means 'ecological systems'. Ecology is the study of ecosystems.
*   Ecosystem is the functional unit of nature where living organisms interact with each other and with their environment.

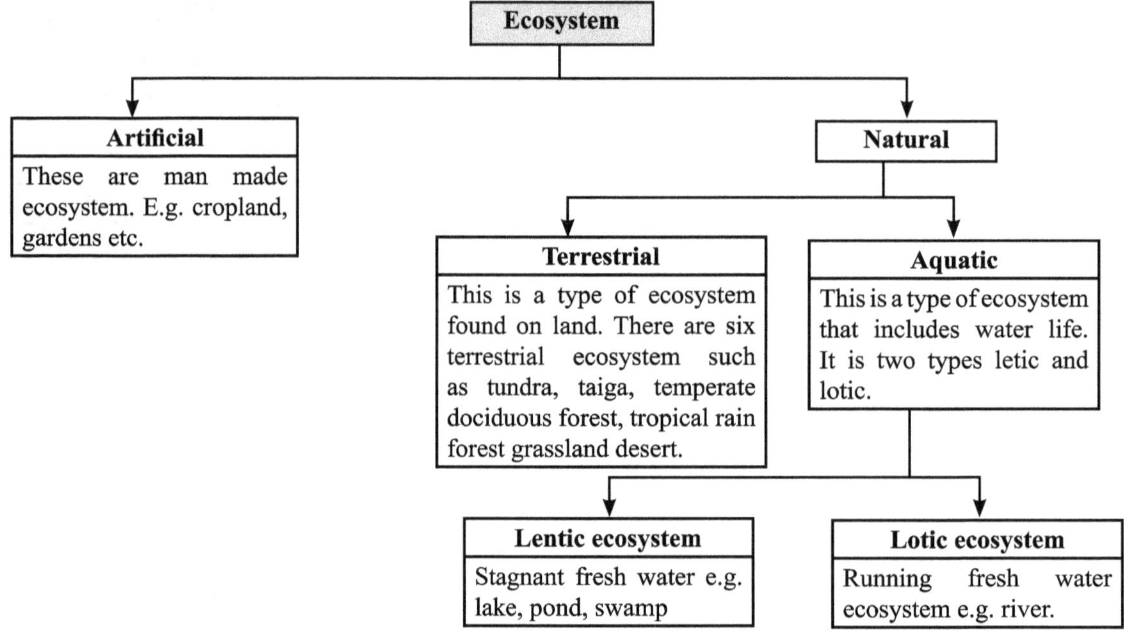

*   Ecosystem is normally an **open system** because there is a continuous and variable entry and loss of energy and materials. Ecosystem is known by different terms *i.e.*, biogeocoenosis or geobiocoenosis or microcosm or ecosom or biosystem etc., the whole earth can be called biosphere or ecosphere.

Components of Ecosystem

*   Ecosystem is composed of a variety of abiotic (non-living) and biotic (living organisms) components that function in an interrelated fashion.

Structure and Function of Ecosystem

*   *The structure of an ecosystem can be expressed by the following terms –*

*   *Species compositor:* Plant and animal species found in an ecosystem.
*   *Stratification:* Vertical layers of plants.
*   *Standing crop:* Amount of biomass.
*   *Standing state:* Amount of inorganic substances.
*   The proper functioning of an ecosystem takes place through the following processes:
*   *Productivity*
*   *Decomposition*
*   *Relationship of producers and consumers*
*   *Flow of energy through different trophic levels, and*
*   *Cycling of nutrients.*

Decomposition

- *Decomposition* is the breakdown of complex organic compounds of dead bodies of plants and animals into simpler inorganic compounds like CO_2, water & various nutrients.
- The organisms carrying out decomposition are called *decomposers*. It includes *micro-organisms* (bacteria and fungi), *detritivores* (earthworm) and some *parasites*.

Process of Decomposition

- *Decomposition is physical as well as chemical in nature and consists of the following processes:*

(i) Fragmentation
It is the formation of smaller pieces of dead organic matter or detritus by detritivores. Due to fragmentation, the surface area of detritus particles is greatly increased.

(ii) Catabolism
Chemical conversion of detritus into simpler inorganic substances with the help of bacterial and fungal enzymes is called catabolism.

(iii) Leaching
Water soluble substances (formed as a result of decomposition) are leached to deeper layers of soil.

(iv) Humification
If decomposition leads to the formation of colloidal organic matter (humus), the process is called **humification**. Humus is highly resistant to microbial action and undergoes extremely slow decomposition. It serves as a reservoir of nutrients.

(v) Mineralisation
Formation of simpler inorganic substances (like CO_2, water and minerals) is termed **mineralisation**.

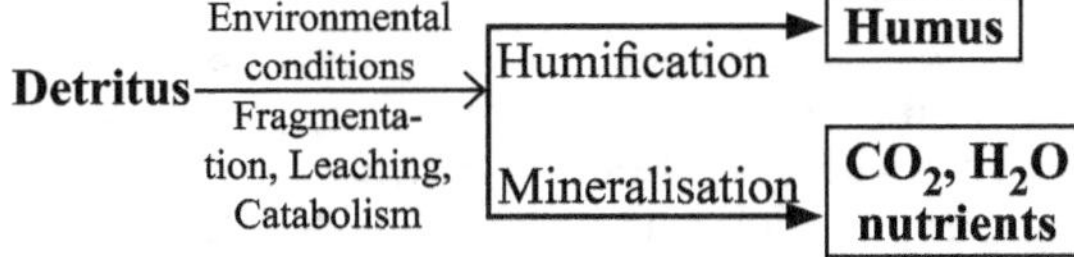

FOOD CHAIN

- *Food chain* is an order or sequence of different organisms which are arranged in a way that the food is passed from one type of organism to other organisms such that the organisms of one order or trophic level are the food of the organisms of next order.

Types of food chains

The food chains are of two types, namely:

(i) *Grazing food chain :* This food chain starts from plants, goes through herbivores and ends in carnivores. ex- Plant → Herbivores → Primary Carnivores → Sec. Carnivores. This type of food chain depends on the autotrophs which capture the energy from solar radiation.

(ii) *Detritus food chain :* It starts from dead organic matter and ends in inorganic compounds. There are certain groups of organisms which feed exclusively on the dead bodies of animals and plants. These organisms are called **detritivores**. The detritivores include algae, bacteria, fungi, protozoans, insects, millipedes, centipedes, crustaceans, mussels, clams, annelid worms, nematodes, ducks, etc.

FOOD WEB

- *Food web* refers to a group of inter-related food chains in a particular community. Under natural conditions, the linear arrangement of food chain hardly occurs & these remain indeed inter-connected with each other through different types of organisms at different trophic level.
- Food webs are very important in maintaining equilibrium (homeostasis) of ecosystem.
  Example : In a grassland ecosystem
  - *Grass → Grasshopper → Hawk*
  - *Grass → Grasshopper → Lizard → Hawk*
  - *Grass → Rabbit → Hawk*
  - *Grass → Mouse → Hawk*
  - *Grass → Mouse → Snake → Hawk*

ECOLOGICAL PYRAMIDS

- The pyramidal representation of trophic levels of different organisms based on their ecological position is called Ecological pyramids.
- Three ecological pyramids which are studied are – **pyramid of number, pyramid of biomass and pyramid of energy**.

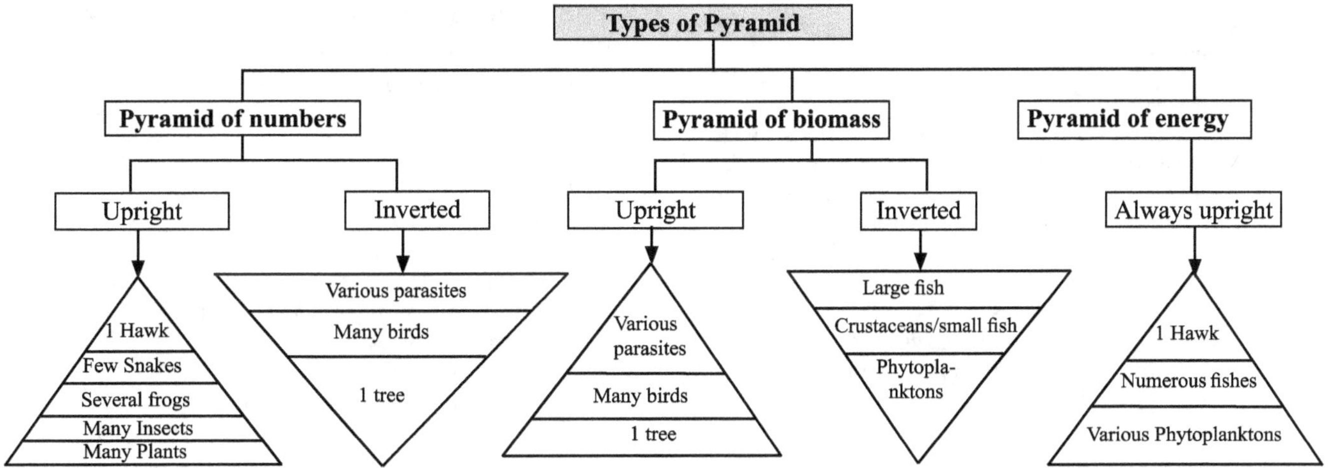

ECOLOGICAL SUCCESSION

- Ecological succession is the successive development of different biotic communities at the same site. The communities develop one after another till the development of a community which is near equilibrium with the environmental conditions. This is called **climax community**.
- Climax community is the stable perpetuating and final biotic community that develops at the end of biotic succession. It has maximum diversity & niche specialization.
- The first biotic community which invades a base area is called **pioneer community**. It is characterized by high growth rate and short life span.
- The transitional communities which develop during the ecological succession or in between the pioneer and climax community are called **seral communities**.

> ### Sere
> The entire sequence of communities that successively change in a given area are known as Sere/s.

Types of Succession

- Succession is of *two types* : Primary and Secondary.
- *Primary succession* : It is the ecological succession occurring in an area where no organisms are found, like bare rocks.
- *Secondary succession* : This type of succession takes place in those areas where all the previous biotic communities have been destroyed, e.g.- burned forests, flooded fields.

Hydrach/Hydrosere Succession

- Hydrosere is a sequence of communities that reflects the developmental stages in a plant succession, which commences on soil, submerged by fresh water.
- *Hydrach succession* takes place in wetter areas like ponds, lakes etc. and the successional series progress from hydric to the mesic conditions.

Xerarch Succession

- Xerarch succession starts in dry areas & the series progress from xeric to mesic conditions.
- Stages in xerarch occurring on bare rock is called **lithosere.**
- Pioneer of this succession depends on climate. In tropical areas the pioneers are cyanobacteria or blue green algae. In temperate areas, they are crustose lichens.
- The ecological succession on bare rocks includes the development of following communities –
  Crustose lichens → foliose lichens → mosses → grasses → shrubs → trees.

NUTRIENT CYCLING

- These are the cyclic events by which various nutrients which are essential for the living organisms are transferred from one form to other. During these cycles, the nutrients pass from the biotic components to the abiotic components and vice-versa,; hence these are also called *biogeochemical cycles*.
- *Two types* of nutrient cycles are –
  (i) *Gaseous cycles* (nitrogen, oxygen, carbon cycles)
  (ii) *Sedimentary cycles* (phosphorus, sulphur cycles)
- In gaseous cycle, the main reservoirs of chemicals are the atmosphere and ocean.
- In sedimentary cycles, the main reservoirs are soils and rocks.

Carbon Cycle

- Discovered by Joseph priestley and Antoine Lavoisier
- Carbon is present in carbohydrates, proteins and fats.
- Carbon is taken up by green plants as CO_2 for photosynthesis.
- Carbon is present as CO_2 in atmosphere, as graphite and carbonates in rocks and also in fossil fuels (coal, petroleum).
- Ocean are big reservoirs of carbon.
- Carbon is released as CO_2 in atmosphere during –
  (i) respiration of plants and animals
  (ii) burning of fossil fuels
- Carbon is also released in atmosphere as methane by rice fields and marshes.

Phosphorus Cycle

- Phosphorus is an important element for living beings.
- The cycling of phosphorus between biotic & abiotic components of the environment represent phosphorus cycle.
- Phosphorus is present in biomembranes (as phospholipids). nucleic acids (as phosphoric acid). nucleotides (as AMP, ADP, ATP etc) and bones and teeth (as hydroxyapetite).
- Consumers obtain phosphorus directly or indirectly from plants.
- Phosphorus is also present in phosphatic rocks.
- Phosphorus is released during the decomposition of plant and animal remains.
- The released phosphorus may reach the deeper layers of soil and gets deposited as phosphate rocks.
- Phosphorus containing rocks are mined for manufacture of fertilizers, which provide an additional supply of an organic phosphates to the abiotic environment.

NITROGEN CYCLE

- *Nitrogen cycle* is a cyclic process that involves conversion of elemental nitrogen of atmosphere into simple molecules that enter living beings forming complex molecules. Then these complex molecules are broken down to release nitrogen back into the atmosphere.
- Earth's atmosphere has about 78% of nitrogen gas. It forms essential constituents of all living organisms and is essential for many biological processes. It is present in all amino acid, nucleic acid and vitamins.

> ### Broadly, the nitrogen cycle in the biosphere involves five main steps:
> *Atmospheric nitrogen → Nitrogen fixation → Nitrogen assimilation → Ammonification → Nitrification → Denitrification*

- *Plants cannot absorb nitrogen from the atmosphere. So, how is atmospheric nitrogen then utilized by plants?* It is through nitrogen fixation.
  (i) *Nitrogen fixation:* It is the process of converting atmospheric nitrogen into usable forms like nitrates. It is of three types:
  - *Biological nitrogen fixation:* Certain bacteria and blue-green algae can fix atmospheric nitrogen directly into ammonia that combines with organic acids to form amino acids.

- *Atmospheric nitrogen fixation:* During lightning and thunder, the high temperature and pressure in the air convert atmospheric nitrogen into oxides of nitrogen that can dissolve in water to produce nitric and nitrous acids. The nitrogen oxide then dissolve in rain water and pass down as nitrites and nitrates.

(ii) *Nitrogen assimilation:* Nitrogen assimilation is carried out by plants. Plants cannot absorb nitrogen in its elemental form. It has to be first converted into nitrates for the use of plants by the process of nitrogen fixation. The atmospheric nitrogen after nitrogen fixation gets converted into nitrates which are then absorbed by plants. Nitrate first changes into ammonium state. Ammonium ions combine with organic acids to form amino acids. Amino acids give rise to proteins and nucleotides, which in turn produce nucleic acids.

   Animals take organic nitrogen directly or indirectly from plants.

(iii) *Ammonification:* It is the process of conversion of complex organic compounds like proteins into ammonia, in the presence of ammonifying bacteria or putrefying bacteria.

(iv) *Nitrification:* It is the process of conversion of ammonia into nitrites and nitrates. Nitrification is brought about by nitrifying bacteria such as *Nitrosomonas* and *Nitrobacter.*

(v) *Denitrification:* It is the process of conversion of nitrate salts present in the soil and water to gaseous nitrogen which escapes into atmosphere. It takes place with the help of bacteria called *Pseudomonas* present in water logged soils. Denitrification reduces soil fertility.

Water Cycle (Also known as hydrological cycle)

Water cycle is the cyclic process of water between various components of biosphere especially evaporation of water from sea, falling on land and then flowing back into sea by rivers. Water is not evenly distributed throughout the surface of the earth. Major percentage of the total water on the earth is chemically bound to rocks and does not cycle. Out of the remaining, nearly 97.3% is in the oceans and 2.1% exists as polar ice caps. Thus only 0.6% is present as fresh water (in the form of atmospheric water vapors, ground and soil water). The ice caps and the water deep in the oceans form the reservoir.

Sulphur Cycle

- Sulphur is the tenth abundant non metallic element, which is brittle, tasteless and odorless. It is a component of litamin, protein and hormones and plays very important role in both climate and ecosystem.

- Its cycle begins with weathering of rocks, due to which sulphur is released in air and converted into sulphate (SO_4). Later it is taken up by plants, and microorganisms and converted into organic forms, which is consumed by animals and moves into food chain. Dead and decayed organism after decomposition again releases sulphur in atmosphere.

BIODIVERSITY

Biodiversity means diversity or heterogeneity at all levels of biological organization, i.e., from macromolecules of the cells to the Biomass. The term Biodiversity was popularized by the sociologist- Edward Wilson.

- The important levels of biodiversity are: *Genetic diversity, Species diversity and Ecological diversity*

Genetic Diversity

- It is the diversity at genetic level, or at subspecies level, i.e. below species level, in a single species.
- For example there are about 1000 varieties of mango (*Mangifera indica*) and 50,000 strains of rice.
- The genetic diversity helps the population to adapt.
- The low diversity leads to uniformity.
- The genetic variability is therefore, considered to be the raw material for speciation.

Species Diversity

The measurement of species diversity is its richness, i.e. the number of species per unit area. The greater is the species richness the more will be the species diversity.

Ecological Diversity

It is the diversity at community level. It can be of 3-types

Alpha (α) diversity

It is the diversity of organisms within the *same community or habitat.*

Beta (β) diversity

It is the diversity *between communities or different habitats.* Higher the heterogenecity in the altitude, Humidity and Temperature of a region, the greater will be the dissimilarity between communities, and higher will be the β diversity.

Gamma (γ) diversity

It is the diversity of organisms over the *entire geographical area*, covering several ecosystems or habitats and various trophic levels and food webs. Such diversity is most stable and productive.

Loss of Biodiversity

- There is continuous loss of the Earth's treasure of species. For example, the colonization of tropical pacific Islands by

- human has led to extinction of more than 2000 species of native birds.
- The Red list of IUCN documented the extinction of 784 species in last 500 years. The last 20 years witnessed the disappearance of 27 species.
- Some important examples of recent extinctions are. *Dodo* (Mauritius), *Quagga* (Africa), *Thylacine* (Australia), *Steller Sea-cow* (Russia), and subspecies of Tiger, like *bali, javan* and *caspian*.

Causes of Loss of Biodiversity

The accelerated rate of species-extinction is largely due to human activities. There are 4-major causes, called **'The Evil Quartet'**, for the loss of biodiversity are: Habitat loss and fragmentation, Overexploitation, Invasion of Alien or exotic species and Co-extinctions

Habitat loss and fragmentation

- The cutting trees, burning of forest, construction of mines, dams, harbors, industries and buildings for human settlement has also affected the biodiversity.
- The Habitat destruction is the primary and major reason for the loss of biodiversity.

Overexploitation

- Many species – extinction, like that of Stellar sea-cow and Passenger pigeon, in last 500 years, are due to overexploitation by humans.
- Ever–increasing need of organism for food and shelter leads to overexploitation.
- It includes as overharvesting, overhunting, overfishing etc.

Invasion of Alien or exotic species

When alien species are introduced into an explored area, some of the species turn invasive and cause decline or extinction of indigenous species. For example –

- Introduction of *Nile perch* into lake Victoria (E. Africa) led to the extinction of more than 200 species of Cichlid fish in the lake.
- Introduction of weed species, like *Carrot grass (Parthenium)*, Lantana and *water hyacinth (Eicchornia)* has posed threat to the native species and damage to environment.

Prosopis juliflora has become an invasive species/weeds in several countries including India, Kenya, Ethiopia, USA (SW states). Several Indian states like – Tamil Nadu, Delhi are taking steps to wipe out this Mexican weed.

Co-extinctions

- Whenever a plant or animal species becomes extinct, its obligatory-associated species also become extinct.

CONSERVATION OF BIODIVERSITY

Conservation means management of human-use of the biosphere so that it may yield greatest long term (sustainable) benefits for the present generation by maintaining its potential to meet the needs and aspiration of future generations.

The **Conservation of biodiversity** can be *in situ* (on site) or *ex situ* (off site)–

In Situ Conservation

- In such conservation the endangered species are protected in their natural habitat with entire ecosystem.
- The conservationists, on global basis, have identified certain ***Biodiversity Hot Spots*** (with high level of species richness and high degree of endemism).
- The hot spots are also the regions of accelerated habitat loss. The number of such hot spots is now 34. These hot spots cover only 1 to 2 percent of earth's land area, but according to one estimate, the strict protection in them can reduce the on-going mass extinction by almost 30%.
- The 3-biodiversity hot spots of India, that cover rich-biodiversity regions, are : Western Ghat, Himalaya and Indo-Burma
- The *in situ* conservation, in India, is done through – *Biosphere reserves, National Parks, wildlife sanctuaries* and several *Sacred Groves* or the tracts of forests.

Biosphere reserves

They represent natural biomes which contain unique biological communities. They include land as well as coastal environment. Biosphere reserves were created under MAB (Man and Biosphere) programme of *UNESCO* in 1971. There are 3-zones in a biosphere reserve.

- *Core (natural) zone* - It is inner most zone which is legally protected and completely undisturbed from human interference,
- *Buffer zone* - In this zone limited human activity is allowed for research and education purposes.
- *Transition (manipulation) zone* - It is the outermost zone of biosphere reserve in which large number of human activities are permitted, eg. Cultivation, domestication, harvesting of natural product, grazing, forestry, settlement and recreation etc. In this zone the traditional life style of tribals is protected with their livestock.

Functions of biosphere reserves

- For conservation of landscape, ecosystem and genetic resources.
- For economic development.
- For scientific research, education and for exchange of information at national and global level.

Biosphere Reserves in India

	Site	State/s	Year	Type
1.	Nilgiri	Karnataka, Kerala and Tamil Nadu	1986	Western Ghats
2.	Nanda Devi	Uttarakhand	1988	Western Himalayas
3.	Nokrek	Meghalaya	1988	East Himalayas
4.	Manas	Assam	1989	East Himalayas
5.	Sunderbans	West Bengal	1989	Gangetic Delta
6.	Gulf of Mannar	Tamil Nadu	1989	Coast
7.	Great Nicobar	Andaman and Nicobar Islands	1989	Islands
8.	Simlipal	Odisha	1994	Deccan Peninsula
9.	Dibru-Saikhowa	Assam	1997	East Himalayas
10.	Dihang Dibang	Arunachal Pradesh	1998	East Himalayas
11.	Pachmarhi	Madhya Pradesh	1999	Semi-Arid
12.	Khangchendzonga	Sikkim	2000	East Himalayas
13.	Agasthyamalai	Kerala and Tamil Nadu	2001	Western Ghats
14.	Achanakamar Amarkantak	Madhya Pradesh and Chhattisgarh	2005	Maikala Hills
15.	Great Rann of Kutch	Gujarat	2008	Desert
16.	Cold desert	Himachal Pradesh	2009	Western Himalayas
17.	Seshachalam Hills	Andhra Pradesh	2010	Eastern Ghats
18.	Panna	Madhya Pradesh	2011	

National Parks

They are reserved for the betterment of wild life, both *fauna and flora*. In national parks private ownership is not allowed. The grazing, cultivation, forestry etc. is also not permitted. The first national park of the world, Yellow stone, in U.S.A., was founded in 1872.

Important state wise national parks of India are –

National Parks in India

S.No.	Places	National Parks
1.	Assam	Kaziranga, Manas, Nameri, Dibru-Saikhowa, Orang
2.	Andhra Pradesh	Mahaveer Harina Vanasthali, Mrugavani,Papikonda, Rajiv Gandhi, Sri Venkateswara, Kasu Brahmananda Reddy
3.	Arunachal Pradesh	Mouling, Namdapha
4.	Bihar	Valmiki
5.	Chhattisgarh	Indravati, Guru Ghasi Das (Sanjay), Kangerghati
6.	Goa	Mollem (Bhagwan Mahavir)
7.	Gujarat	Gir, Bansda, Blackbuck, Marine (Gulf of Kachchh)
8.	Haryana	Kalesar, Sultanpur
9.	Himachal Pradesh	Great Himalayan, Inderkilla, Khirganga, Pin Valley, Simbalbara
10.	Jammu and Kashmir	Dachigam, City Forest (Salim Ali), Kishtwar, Hemis
11.	Jharkhand	Betla
12.	Karnataka	Bandipur, Bannerghatta, Kudremukh, Nagarhole (Rajiv Gandhi), Anshi, Rajiv Gandhi (Nagarahole)
13.	Kerala	Anamudi, Eravikulam, Mathikettan Shola, Periyar, Silent Valley
14.	Madhya Pradesh	Bandhavgarh, Fossil, Kanha, Madhav, Panna, Pench (Priyadarshini), Sanjay, Sapura, Van Vihar
15.	Maharashtra	Chandoli, Gugamal, Nawegaon, Sanjay Gandhi (Borivilli), Pench (Maha.side), Tadoba

16.	Manipur	Keibul-Lamjao
17.	Meghalaya	Balphakram, Nokrek Ridge
18.	Mizoram	Phawngpui Blue Mountain, Murlen
19.	Nagaland	Intanki
20.	Odisha	Bhitarkanika, Simlipal
21.	Rajasthan	Desert, Keoladeo Ghana, Ranthambhore, Sariska
22.	Sikkim	Khangchendzonga
23.	Tamil Nadu	Guindy, Indira Gandhi (Annamalai), Mudumalai, Mukurthi, Gulf of Mannar Marine National Park
24.	Tripura	Bison (previously known as Rajbari National Park), Clouded Leopard
25.	Uttar Pradesh	Dudhwa
26.	Uttarakhand	Corbett, Rajaji, Gangotri, Nanda Devi, Govind, Valley of Flowers
27.	West Bengal	Buxa, Gorumara, Neora Valley, Singalila, Sunderban
28.	Andaman & Nicobar Islands	Galathea Bay, Campbell Bay, Mahatama Gandhi Marine (Wandoor), North Button Island Middle Button Island, South Button Island, Mount Harriett, Rani Jhansi Marine, Saddle Peak .

Wildlife sanctuaries

A sanctuary is a protected area which is reserved for the conservation of only animal and controlled human activities is permitted as long as they do not interfere with well-being of animals. It is defined as an area declared, whether under sec. [26(A)] or sec 38, or deemed, under sub section (3) of Sec.66 to be declared, as a wildlife sanctuary. It is an area which is of adequate ecological, faunal, floral, geomorphological, natural or zoological significance.

Some of the Wildlife sanctuaries of India are listed below

S.No.	Places	Wild Sanctuaries
1	Assam	Nambor Doigrung, Garampani, Lawkhowa, Pani-Dihing, Porbitora
2	Andhra Pradesh	Rollapadu, Pulicat, Nellapattu, Kolleru, Koundinya
3	Arunachal Pradesh	Kamlang, Kane, Mehao, Pakhui (Pakke), Yordi-Rabe Supse
4.	Bihar	Kusheshwar Asthan, Nagi, Nakti, Kanwarjheel, Gautam Buddha
5.	Chhattisgarh	Barnawapar, Badalkhol, Semarsot, Sitandi, Udanti
6.	Goa	Cotigaon, Madei, Bondla, Netravali, Chorao Island (Dr. Salim Ali)
7.	Gujarat	Balaram Amji, Girnar, Barda, Jessore, Khijadia
8.	Haryana	Nahar, Chhichila, Bhindawas, Kalesar, Abubshehar
9.	Himachal Pradesh	Chail, Dhauladhar, Kais, Daranghati, Chandratal, Shikari Devi
10.	Jammu and Kashmir	Hirapora, Hokersar, Baltal-Thajwas, Nandni, Lachipora
11.	Jharkhand	Dalma, Koderma, Lawalong, Hazaribagh, Parasnath
12.	Karnataka	Bhadra, Attiveri, Adichunchunagiri, Brahmagiri, Chincholi
13.	Kerala	Chimmony, chinnar, Idukki, Parambikulam, Neyyar
14.	Madhya Pradesh	Bori, Gandhi Sagar, Karera, Bagdara, Kuno
15.	Maharashtra	Amba Barwa, Bhamragarh, Chaprala, Dhyanganga, Katepurna
16	Manipur	Khongjaingamba Ching, Yangoupokpi-Lokchao
17.	Meghalaya	Nongkhyllem, Baghmara, Narpuh, Siju
18.	Mizoram	Khawnglung, Dampa, Ngengpui, Tawi, Tokalo
19.	Nagaland	Puliebadze, Rangapahar, Fakim
20.	Odisha	Chandaka Dampara, Balukhand Konark, Badrama, Karlapat, Kotagarh

21.	Rajasthan	Bassi, Darrah, Jaisamand, Kesarbagh, Sitamata, Shergarh
22.	Sikkim	Barsey, Kyongnosla Alpine, Fambong, Kitam, Pangolakha
23.	Tamil Nadu	Karaikilli, Kanyakumari, Kalakad, Gangaikondam, Satyamangalam
24.	Tripura	Gumti, Rowa, Trishna, Sepahijala
25.	Uttar Pradesh	Chandraprabha, Bakhira, Katerniaghat, Lakh Bahosi, Patna
26.	Uttarakhand	Sonanadi, Govind Pashu Vihar, Binsar, Nandhaur, Kedarnath, Askot
27.	West Bengal	Bibhuti Bhusan, Chapramari, Ballavpur, Haliday, Senchal
28.	Andaman & Nicobar Islands	Arial, Bamboo, Barren, Belle Island, Bingham Island
29.	Chandigarh	City Birds, Sukhna Lake
30.	Dadra & Nagar Haveli	Dadra Nagar Haveli
31.	Daman and Diu	Fudam
32	Punjab	Bir Aishvan, Bir Bhadson, Bir Dosanjh, Kathlaur Kushlian, Nangal
33	Telangana	Pranahita (Joint area with Andhra Pradesh), Pakhal, Manjeera, Pocharam, Nagarjuna Sagar
34.	Puducherry	Oussudu
35.	Delhi	Asola Bhati (Indira Priyadarshini)
36.	Lakshadweep	Pitti Bird Sanctuary

Ex situ Conservation

In such type of conservation the threatened animals and plants are taken out of their natural habitat and are protected in special parks or areas like, *Zoological parks, Wild life safari parks* and *Botanical gardens* etc. The ex situ conservation also includes
- *Cryopreservation* of gametes of threatened species in viable and fertile form.
- Fertilization of eggs *in vitro* and propagation of plants through *'Tissue culture methods'*
- Preservation of seeds through *Seed banks*

MULTIPLE CHOICE QUESTIONS

1. Fossils are
   (a) remains of deadly plants and animals that are extinct
   (b) remains of plants and animals that are still surviving
   (c) both (a) & (b)
   (d) none of the above

2. Speciation is
   (a) making of independent species
   (b) macro evolution
   (c) new environmental ways for existence
   (d) all of the above

3. The scientific name for the maximum modern man among these is
   (a) Homosapiens   (b) Human species
   (c) Neanderthalensis   (d) Homo sapiens

4. Modern man evolved from
   (a) Java man   (b) Peking man
   (c) Neanderthal man   (d) cro-magnon man

5. The book 'Origin of Species' was written by
   (a) Darwin   (b) Lamarck
   (c) Mendel   (d) de Vries

6. **Column-I**   **Column-II**
   A. Wing of a bat and   P. Darwin
        wing of a bird
   B. Dihybrid ratio   Q. Mendel
   C. Natural selection   R. Analogous organ
   D. Arm of a man and   S. Homologous organs
        wing of a bird
   (a) A -S; B - P; C - Q; D - R
   (b) A - R; B - Q; C - P; D - S
   (c) A -R; B -Q; C - P; D- S
   (d) A - S; B - P; C-P; D-Q

7. Consider the following statements :
   A. Life can originate on earth from pre-existing life only.
   B. The atmosphere of the primitive earth was reducing.
   Which of these statement(s) is/are correct ?
   (a) A only   (b) B only
   (c) Both A and B   (d) Neither A nor B

8. Given below are names of some of the National Parks of India and their key protected animals.

	Name of the National Park		Key protected animal
A	Dibru-Saikhowa National Park, Assam	(i)	Indian Rhinoceros
B	Jaldapara National Park, West Bengal	(ii)	Hangul
C	Mukurthi National Park, Tamil Nadu	(iii)	Feral Horse
D	Dachigam National Park, Jammu and Kashmir	(iv)	Asiatic Lion
E	Gir Forest National Park, Gujarat	(v)	Nilgiri Tahr

Based on the table given above, which of the following options represents the correct match?
(a) A-(iii): B-(i); C-(iv); D-(ii); E-(v)
(b) A-(i): B-(ii); C-(v); D-(iii); E-(iv)
(c) A-(i): B-(ii); C-(iii); D-(iv); E-(v)
(d) A-(iii): B-(i); C-(v); D-(ii); E-(iv)

9. Vestigial organs are those present in the living beings without functions gives and mark the correct option for vestigial organs in humans
   (a) Vermifrom appendix
   (b) mammary glands of male
   (c) nictitating membrane in eyes
   (d) all of the above

10. In evolution which animals class is between entirely water living to land
    (a) fishes and reptiles
    (b) fishes & reptiles
    (b) reptiles and Amphibian
    (d) reptiles and birds

11. To which of the following types of animals are Salamanders closely related?   **[NDA]**
    (a) Dolphins and Whales
    (b) Frogs and Toads
    (c) Prawns and Crabs
    (d) Seals and Walruses

12. In terms of the evolution of organisms, which one among the following is the most advanced?   **[NDA]**
    (a) Bat   (b) Pigeon
    (c) Shark   (d) Vulture

13. Analogous organs are
    (a) different in origin but perform similar functions.
    (b) common in origin and perform common functions.
    (c) common in origin but perform different functions.
    (d) different in origin and perform different functions.

14. The term 'Survival of Fittest' was used by
    (a) Charles Darwin   (b) Herbert Spencer
    (c) Jean Baptiste   (d) Hugo de Vries

15. **Column-I**   **Column-II**
    (Name of the Scientist) **(Contributions)**
    A. Charles Darwin   I. Mutation theory
    B. Lamarck   II. Germ plasm theory
    C. Hugo de Vries   III. Philosophie Zoologique
    D. Ernst Haeckel   IV. The Origin of species
    E. August Weismann   V. Biogenetic law
                            VI. Essay on population
    (a) A – IV; B – III; C – I; D – V; E – II
    (b) A – IV; B – III; C – V; D – I; E – VI
    (c) A – IV; B – VI; C – V; D – III; E – I
    (d) A – II; B – III; C – I; D – V; E – II

16. What was the most significant trend in the evolution of modern man (*Homo sapiens*) from his ancestors?
  (a) Shortening of jaws
  (b) Binocular vision
  (c) Increasing cranial capacity
  (d) Upright posture.

17. In the context of diversity patterns of species, which one of the following statements is **INCORRECT?**
  (a) Alpha diversity is diversity within a single community
  (b) Beta diversity is a measure of the change in species composition from one community or habitat to another
  (c) Alpha diversity is the regional diversity found among range of communities in a geographical region
  (d) Gamma diversity is the regional diversity found among range of communities/habitats in a geographical region

18. A biogeographic region with significant reservoir of biodiversity that is under threat from humans is called as **[NDA]**
  (a) bioendangered region
  (b) biodiversity hotspot
  (c) biodiversity reservoir
  (d) environmentally endangered region

19. Which one of the following processes of weathering belongs to both mechanical and chemical weathering? **[NDA]**
  (a) Crystallization (b) Exfoliation
  (c) Hydration (d) Carbonation

20. In the context of ecology and environment, what does the Red Data Book pertain to? **[CDS]**
  (a) Details of harmful levels of various pollutants
  (b) A complete list of all endangered plants and animals
  (c) A description of the consequences of nuclear holocaust
  (d) A description of the sociological and psychological consequence of genetically modified plants and animals

21. Which of the following is not a bird? **[CDS]**
  (a) Bat (b) Emu
  (c) Kiwi (d) Ostrich

22. The branches of this tree root themselves like new trees over a large area. The roots then give rise to more trunks and branches. Because of this characteristic and its longevity, this tree is considered immortal and is an integral part of the myths and legends of India. Which tree is this? **[CDS]**
  (a) Banyan (b) Neem
  (c) Tamarind(Imli) (d) Peepal

23. Which one of the following is not a feature of eutrophic lakes? **[CDS]**
  (a) Blooms are frequent in eutrophic lakes
  (b) Plant nutrient flux is high
  (c) Primary productivity is low
  (d) Dominated by blue green algae

24. Polar bears are carnivores and prey on many arctic birds and fishes. However, under natural conditions, no one found polar bears predating any penguin. This is because **[CDS]**
  (a) penguins have chemical substance in their muscles which is toxic to polar bears
  (b) penguins are gregarious and always move in groups. Therefore, a polar bear cannot approach them
  (c) polar bears and penguins never coexist under natural conditions. The former lives in the North Pole while the latter lives in the South Pole
  (d) None of these

25.

	List-I	**List-II**
	(Indian wild life species)	**(Scientific names)**
A.	Asiatic wild ass	1. *Boselaphus tragocamelus*
B.	Barasingha	2. *Cervus duvauceli*
C.	Chinkara	3. *Equus hemionus*
D.	Nilgai	4. *Gazella gazella*

  (a) A – 2; B – 3; C – 1; D – 4 **[IAS Prelim]**
  (b) A – 3; B – 2; C – 4; D – 1
  (c) A – 2; B – 3; C – 4; D – 1
  (d) A – 3; B – 2; C – 1; D – 4

26. With reference to soil conservation, consider the following practices : **[IAS Prelim]**
  1. Crop rotation 2. Sand fences
  3. Terracing 4. Wind breaks
  Which of the above are considered appropriate methods for soil conservation in India.
  (a) 1, 2, and 3 only (b) 2 and 4 only
  (c) 1, 3 and 4 only (d) 1, 2, 3 and 4

27. All producers are
  (a) Food making organisms
  (b) Make food in the presence of sunlight with chlorophyll
  (c) All autotrophs
  (d) All the above

28. Which one of these is not a food chain
  (a) Trees → Deer → Lion
  (b) Plants → Man → Anaconda
  (c) Plants → Insects → Frog → Snake → Kite
  (d) Small → plants → Crabs → Fish → Swan → bird

29. The accumulation of non-biodegradable substances in a food chain in increasing amount at each higher trophic level is known as:
  (a) Accumulation (b) Eutrophication
  (c) Pollution (d) Bio magnification

30. Flow of energy in an ecosystem is always
  (a) Unidirectional
  (b) Bidirectional
  (c) Multi directional
  (d) No specific direction

31. Consider the following statements :
   A. Earth is kept warm due to green house flux.
   B. The reproduction and other activities of living organisms are affected by the abiotic components of ecosystem.
   C. Ecology is the scientific study of the interaction of organisms with each other and the environment.
   Which of these statement(s) is/are correct ?
   (a) A and B   (b) B and C
   (c) A, B and C   (d) None of these

32. Why is a plant called *Prosopis juliflora* often mentioned in news ?   **[UPSC 2018]**
   (a) Its extract is widely used in cosmetics.
   (b) It tends to reduce the biodiversity in the area in which it grows.
   (c) Its extract is used in the synthesis of pesticides.
   (d) None of the above

33. The term "sixth mass extinction/sixth extinction" is often mentioned in the news in the context of the discussion of   **[UPSC 2018]**
   (a) Widespread monoculture practices in agriculture and large-scale commercial farming with indiscriminate use of chemicals in many parts of the world that may result in the loss of good native ecosystems.
   (b) Fears of a possible collision of a meteorite with the Earth in the near future in the manner it happened 65 million years ago that caused the mass extinction of many species including those of dinosaurs.
   (c) Large scale cultivation of genetically modified crops in many parts of the world and promoting their cultivation in other parts of the world which may cause the disappearance of good native crop plants and the loss of food biodiversity.
   (d) Mankind's over-exploitation/misuse of natural resources, fragmentation/loss of natural habitats, destruction of ecosystems, pollution and global climate change.

34. In which one of the following States is Pakhui Wildlife Sanctuary located?   **[UPSC 2018]**
   (a) Arunachal Pradesh
   (b) Manipur
   (c) Meghalaya
   (d) Nagaland

35. Statement I: **[CDS 2018]**
   Bioaccumulation is a process of progressive accumulation of heavy metals and pesticides in an organism.
   Statement II:
   Large fishes of the pond are found to have higher concentration of pesticides than planktons of the same pond.

36. A biological community in its environment such as a pond, an ocean, a forest, even an aquarium is known as   **[CDS 2017-II]**
   (a) biome
   (b) community
   (c) abiotic environment
   (d) ecosystem

37. Which one of the following is most sensitive to environmental change?   **[CDS 2018]**
   (a) Amphibian   (b) Reptile
   (c) Mammal   (d) Insect

38. Which one of the following group of organisms forms a food chain?   **[NDA 2018-I]**
   (a) Grass, human and fish
   (b) Grass, goat and human
   (c) Tree, tree cutter and tiger
   (d) Goat, cow and human

39. Consider the following Wildlife Sanctuaries of India: **[NDA 2018-II]**
   1. Shikari Devi
   2. Bhadra
   3. Simplipal
   4. Pachmarhi
   Which one of the following is the correct order of the above Wildlife Sanctuaries in terms of their location from south to north?
   (a) 1-2-3-4   (b) 2-4-3-1
   (c) 2-3-4-1   (d) 3-1-2-4

ANSWER KEY															
1.	(c)	**2.**	(d)	**3.**	(d)	**4.**	(d)	**5.**	(a)	**6.**	(b)	**7.**	(c)	**8.**	(d)
9.	(d)	**10.**	(c)	**11.**	(b)	**12.**	(a)	**13.**	(a)	**14.**	(b)	**15.**	(a)	**16.**	(c)
17.	(c)	**18.**	(b)	**19.**	(b)	**20.**	(a)	**21.**	(a)	**22.**	(c)	**23.**	(c)	**24.**	(a)
25.	(b)	**26.**	(d)	**27.**	(d)	**28.**	(b)	**29.**	(d)	**30.**	(a)	**31.**	(c)	**32.**	(b)
33.	(d)	**34.**	(a)	**35.**	(b)	**36.**	(a)	**37.**	(a)	**38.**	(b)	**39.**	(b)		

Chapter 4

TISSUE, PHYSIOLOGY OF PLANTS AND ANIMALS

TISSUE

Tissue is a group of cells with common origin, structure and function that work together to perform a particular function. For example, Blood, bone, cartilage are some examples of animal tissues while xylem, phloem, parenchyma etc are different types of tissues found in plants. *The study of tissue is called histology. The term was coined by Meyer.*

PLANT TISSUES

On the basis of their ability to divide, plant tissues are divided into two types:

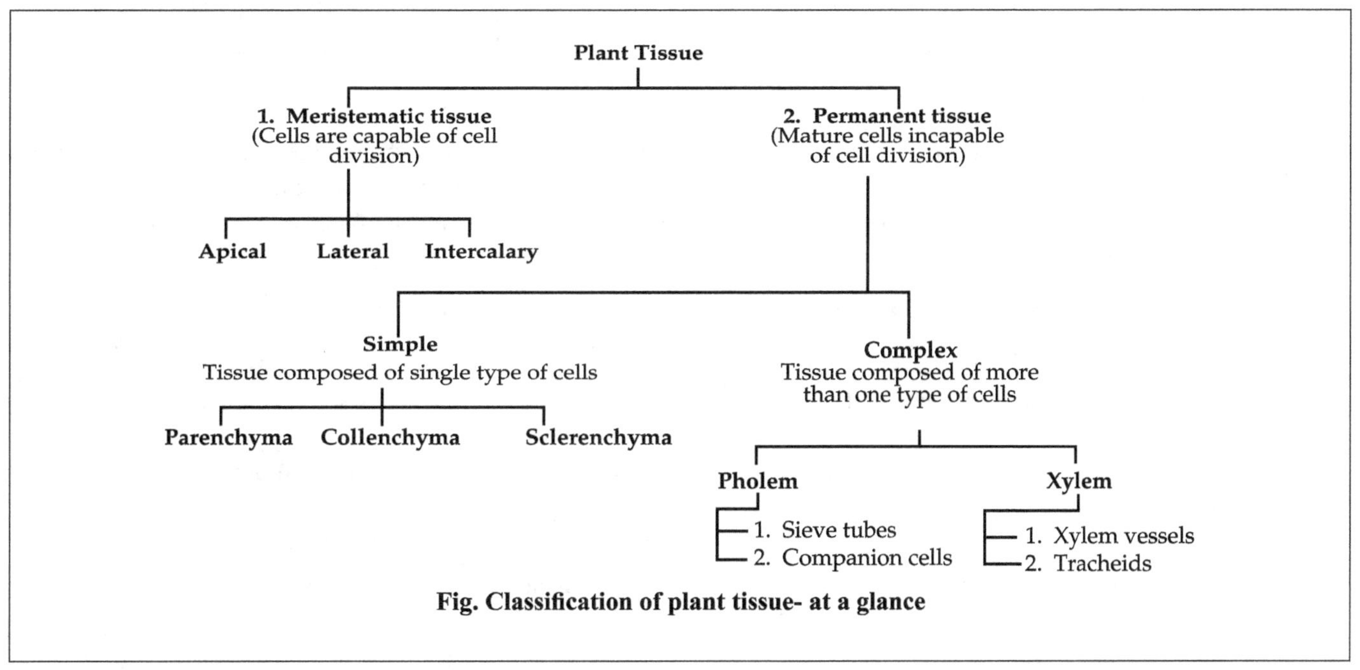

Fig. Classification of plant tissue- at a glance

Meristematic Tissues

- Meristematic tissues are thin-walled compactly arranged, immature cells that keep on dividing continuously. The new cells produced are initially Meristematic. Slowly, they grow, differentiate and mature into permanent tissues.

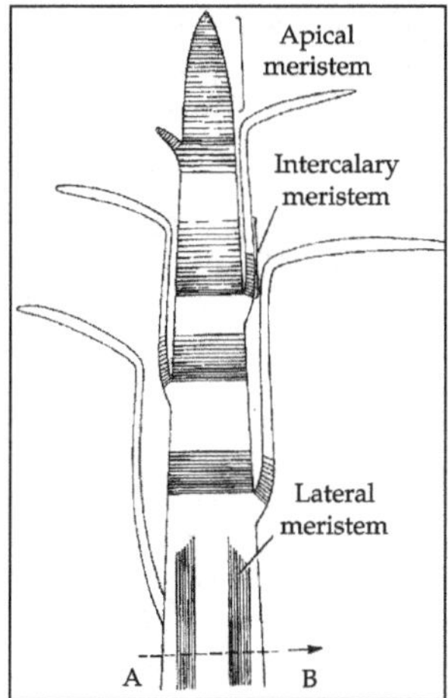

- The meristematic cells are spherical, or polygonal in shape and the cells are compactly arranged without inter-cellular spaces. The cell wall is thin, elastic and is made of cellulose. Each cell has abundant cytoplasm and prominent nuclei. These cells are always living.

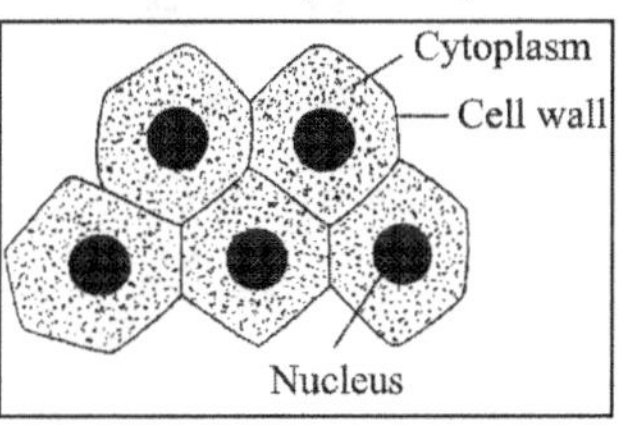

Classification of meristematic tissue

On the basis of origin and development		
Promeristem	**Primary meristem**	**Secondary meristem**
• Represents primary stages of meristematic cells • Present at the tip of radicle and plumule	• Originate from promeristem that continue to divide to form different tissues. • Always in active state of division and give rise to primary permanent tissues for growth in length as well as width e.g., apical meristems, intercalary meristems, lateral meristems (intra-fascicular cambium in the vascular bundle of dicot stem).	• Developed from primary permanent tissue. They are developed at a later stage by differentiation and acquire power of division. e.g., interfascicular cambium in stem, cambium in roots and also cork cambium (phellogen).

On the basis of function		
Protoderm	**Periblem**	**Procambium**
• It is the outermost layer meant for producing the single layered epidermis, hairs, velamen, stomata i.e., epidermal tissue system.	• It produces hypodermis, cortex and endodermis or ground tissue system.	• It is the innermost part of the meristem. It gives rise to the stele which comprises primary vascular tissues and ground tissues like pith, medullary rays and the pericycle.

PERMANENT TISSUE

Permanent tissues are tissues that have lost the ability to divide, and have attained a definite form and size. They are actually derived from Meristematic cells. Different type of permanent tissues is formed due to differences in their specialization. Differentiation is the process whereby cells take up a definite shape, size, structure and function. These tissues are divided into simple, Complex and special.

Table : Difference between Meristematic tissue and Permanent tissue

Sl No.	Meristematic Tissue	Permanent Tissue
1.	Meristematic tissues are composed of cells that divide continuously.	Permanent tissues are composed of cells that are derived from Meristematic tissue.
2.	Cells are small, undifferentiated and isodiametric in shape.	Cells are large, differentiated with different shapes.
3.	Cell wall is thin and living.	Cell wall may be thin (living) or thick (dead).
4.	Cells are compactly arranged without inter-cellular spaces.	Intercellular spaces are often present.
5.	Nucleus is large and prominent.	Nucleus is less conspicuous.
6.	Cells of Meristematic tissue take part in growth.	Permanent tissue provides protection, support, conduction of substances, storage, photosynthesis etc.

Simple Tissue

It is made up of only one kind of cells forming a uniform mass. The cells are similar in structure, origin and function. *Simple permanent tissues are of three types: Parenchyma, Collenchyma and Sclerenchyma*

Parenchyma	Collenchyma	Sclerenchyma
Parenchyma: Parenchyma is widely distributed in plant body such as stem, roots, leaves and flower. • They are found in the cortex of root, ground tissue in stems and mesophyll of leaves, cells are isodiametric. • It may contain chlorophyll Parenchyma containing chlorophyll is called *chlorenchyma*. It is the site of photosynthesis. • Parenchyma that encloses large air cavities is known as *aerenchyma*. Aerenchyma provides buoyancy to aquatic plants.	*Collenchyma*: Collenchyma is a strong and flexible tissue that provides flexibility to soft aerial parts. • Collenchyma provides mechanical support, flexibility to soft aerial parts so that they can bend without breaking and may contain chloroplasts and thus take part in photosynthesis.	*Sclerenchyma*: It is found in and around the vascular tissue, under the skin *i.e.* the epidermis in dicot stems. • Cells are long, narrow, thick and lignified usually pointed at both ends. The cell wall is evenly thickened with lignin. Lignin is a water proof material. • It gives mechanical support to the plant by giving rigidity, flexibility and elasticity to the plant body.

Complex Tissue

Complex tissue is made up of more than one type of cells that work together to perform a particular function. *Complex tissues are of two types: Xylem and Phloem.*

Table : Difference between xylem and Phloem

Xylem	Phloem
Xylem helps in conduction of water and minerals.	Phloem helps in conduction of food materials and organic solutes.
The flow of material is mostly unidirectional.	The flow of material is bidirectional.
Xylem consists of tracheids, vessels, xylem parenchyma and xylem fibres.	Phloem consists of sieve tubes, companion cells, phloem parenchyma and phloem fibers.
Conducting elements of xylem are tracheids and vessels.	Conducting element of phloem is sieve tubes.
Out of four element of xylem, only xylem parenchyma is living, rest three are dead.	Out of four elements of phloem, only phloem fibres are dead, rest three are living.

They are scattered throughout the ground tissue of the plant and contain stored organic matter in the form of starch, rubber, tannins, alkaloids, mucilage enzymes, protein, etc.

TISSUE SYSTEM

In higher plants several tissue work together in form of a unit to perform particular function. These tissue have the same origin and form a system which is called tissue system. On the basis of division of labour, tissue categorised by sachs into three different system-epidermal, grand and vascular tissue system.

Stomata

• Stomata are tiny pores that are found on the epidermis of leaves, stem and some fruits and are absent in roots.
• Stomata helps in gaseous exchange at the time of respiration and photosynthesis.
• These are composed of two bean-shaped epidermal cell called *guard cells* which encloses stomatal pore.
• In grasses, guard cells are dumb bell shape. In dicot leaves, stomata are scattered whereas in monocots, these are arranged in rows.
• In xerophytes, stomata are of sunken type so as to reduce water loss by transpiration.

Vascular Bundles

- Xylem and phloem are collectively termed as vascular bundles.
- On the basis of arrangement of different parts, vascular bundles are divided into three categories; *radial vascular bundles, conjoint vascular bundles and concentric vascular bundles.*

Secondary Growth

- Increase in the circumference/girth of the plant organs due to the formation of secondary tissue in stelar and extra stelar region, is called as secondary growth.

- Normally secondary growth takes place in roots and stem of dicotyledons as Gymnosperms.

ANIMAL TISSUES

The working of animal body is coordinated by tissues and organs present in their body.

On the basis of structure and function, animal tissues are divided into four types

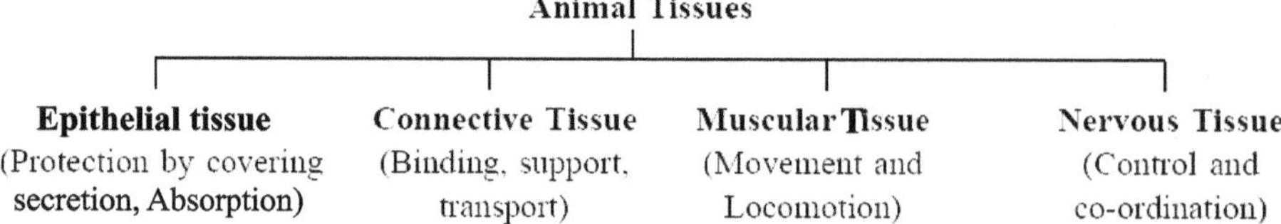

Epithelial Tissue

- Epithelial Tissue is the simplest animal tissue that forms the continuous sheet of closely packed cells that covers all external and internal surface of the animal body. Thus, it is also known as *covering tissue.*

Functions

- It protects the underlying tissues against mechanical injury, dehydration and against infection by micro-organisms.
- Epithelium lining is present in the lung alveoli allows exchange of gases between blood and alveolar air and also present in the uriniferous tubules that helps in ultrafiltration, secretion and reabsorption to produce urine.

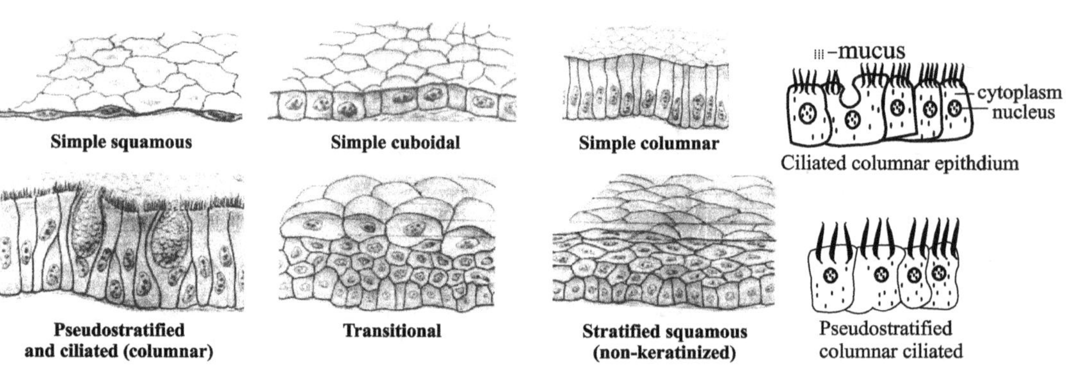

Compound Epithelium	
Transitional epithelium	**Stratified epithelium**
It is 2-6 cells thick. *Basement membrane is absent and* occurs in the areas where stretching is required *eg.* Epithelium of Urinary bladder, Ureter and Pelvis.	This epithelial layer is more than 6 cells thick. Basement membrane is present but single. The name of the epithelium is according to the 'cells' of the top layer. It is of 3-types **Stratified Squamous Epithelium** is the most common stratified epithelium. The cells of the top layer are squamous. Such epithelium occurs in the region where protection is required, or where there is sufficient wear and tear of the tissue. *eg.* Buccal cavity (cheek epithelium), skin, pharynx, oesophagus, vaginal epithelium, urethra, conjunctiva and cornea. **Stratified Cuboidal Epithelium** is present in the ducts of mammary glands and sweat glands. **Stratified Columnar Epithelium** It mainly occurs in the embryonic tissue and is poorly developed in adults.

Glandular Epithelium

They are epithelial in origin and therefore, may develop from any of the 3-germ layers.

They can be **Exocrine** or **Endocrine** type ; **Unicellular** (ex. Goblet glands) or **multicellular** type.

Connective Tissue

It is mesodermal in origin. It binds and supports body parts. The cells are loosely arranged, i.e. the intercellular matrix is well developed and Basement membrane is absent. It is nourished with the blood / lymph.

The study of bones is called **Osteology** and the study of cartilage is called **Chondrology**.

	BONES	CARTILAGE
1.	Outer covering (white fibrous connective tissue) of bones is called periosteum	Outer covering (white fibrous connective tissue) of cartilage is called perichondrium.
2.	Bone forming cells are called osteoblasts	Cartilage forming cells are called chondroblasts.
3.	Bone Protein is 'Ossein'	Cartilage protein is 'Chondrin'. (The sugar in cartilage is chondriotin sulphate)
4.	Osteocytes (bone cells) are solitary	Chondrocytes (cartilage cells) are in groups of 2's or 3's
5.	Osteocytes are arranged on lamellae	Chondrocytes are scattered in matrix.

BLOOD -
- Study of blood is called Haematology
- Blood is 8% of the body weight (4 litre in a person of 50 kg.)
- Osmotic pressure is equivalent to 7-8 atmospheric pressure . pH 7.4 (slightly alkaline)
- Specific Gravity - 1.003 (slightly heavier than water)
- Viscosity - 3-5 times than that of water.

Muscular Tissue

Muscular tissue is a contractile tissue that occupies more than 40% of total weight of the body.

Types of Muscle Fibres

On the basis of their location, structure and function, there are three types of muscle fibres.

Sl No	Striated muscle fibres	Smooth muscle fibres	Cardiac muscle fibres
On the basis of structure			
1.	Cells are long and cylindrical in shape.	Cells are elongated and spindle shaped.	Cells are small and cylindrical
2.	Cells are unbranched.	Cells are unbranched.	Cells are branched.
3.	Fibres have blunt ends.	Fibres have pointed ends.	Fibres have broad ends.
4.	Cells are multinucleated.	Cells are uni-nucleated.	Cells are uni-nucleated.
On the basis of location			
9.	They are found in limbs, hands, feet, tongue, pharynx etc.	They are found in urinogenital tracts, digestive tract, lungs, iris, blood vessel etc.	They are found only in the wall of heart.
On the basis of function			
10.	They are able to perform fast and powerful contractions. Hence, get fatigued soon.	They perform slow but prolonged contractions.	They perform powerful and rhythmic contraction and get fatigued seldom.

Nervous Tissue

Nervous tissue is specialized to transmit messages in our body. They can receive, integrate and transmit stimuli to various parts of the body. It is devoid of matrix. Its cell is surrounded by a special connective tissue cell. *Nervous tissue contains two types of cells Neuron and neuroglial cells.*

- **Neuron:** It is the functional unit of nervous tissue. It is also known as nerve cells. They are the longest cells of the body reaching upto a metre in length. *Each neuron is made of three parts:*
- **Cell body (Cyton):** is a broader nucleated part of neuron. Its cytoplasm is called Neuroplasm. Neuroplasm contains two special structure called *neurofibrils* and *Nissl granules. Neurofibrils* are fine fibrils involved in transmission of impulses.
- *Nissl granules* are ribosome containing structures. They are made up of RNA and protein.

- Axon is a single, long, fibre like process generally arising singly from the cell body of a neuron. It is devoid of Nissl granules. However, it contains neurofibrils.
- Axon is surrounded by a sheath called neurolemma of a special connective tissue called Schwann cells.
- Each such junction is called synapse. Synapse is meant for transmission of impulse from one neuron to another. Axon carries impulses towards the cell body.

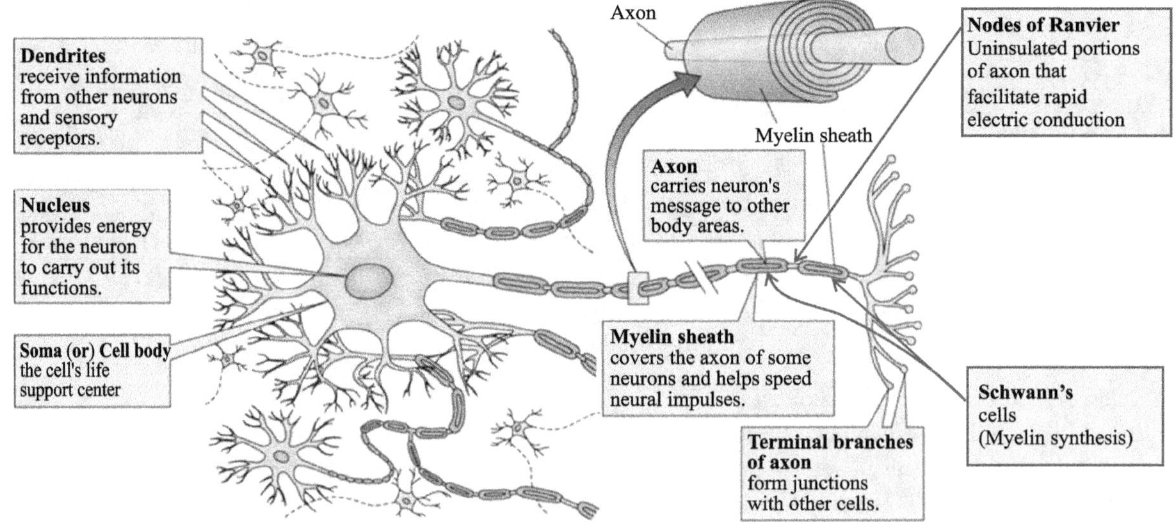

Fig. Structure of neuron

PHYSIOLOGY OF PLANTS

Morphology is the branch of biology which deals with the study of form, structure and relative position of different organs. Physiology is the branch of science that deals with the study of different functions of organs.

- **Plant morphology** refers to the study of external form and structure of plants.

FLOWERING PLANTS (ANGIOSPERMS)

- These are seed bearing plants in which seeds are always enclosed in an ovary inside the fruits and the sporophylls are organized into flowers.
- These plants have been classified into *monocots* and *dicots*.

Herbs : These are the plant, lacking a permanent woody stem and generally dies back at the end of each growing season. e.g., Whean Hen bone, Canna etc.

Shrubs : These are the woody plant which is smaller than a tree and has several main stem arising at or near the ground. e.g., Jasmine rose etc.

Tree: A woody perennial plant having a single usually elongate main stem generally with few or no branches. e.g., Palm, Pinus, Castuarina, Dalbergia, etc.

Creepers: A weak plant that grows along the ground, walls or trees. e.g., grass.

Climbers: They have week stem which help plant to climb up trees and other tall object. e.g., Grape vine etc.

Lianas: These are the woody climbinig plant that hangs from trees, especially in tropical rain forest. e.g., Hiptage, Phanera, etc.

Epiphytes: These are the plant that grow above the ground, supported non parasitically by another plant. e.g., Vanda, etc.

Root System

Characteristics

- Root is the descending, nongreen, underground part lacking nodes, internodes, leaves and buds.
- It is responsible for nutrition and support.
- Radicle comes out/arise from the seed coat in the form of soft structure and move toward the soil. It develops and forms *primary root.*

Root

Tap root	Adventitious root
It develops from radicle which is made up of one main branch and other sub-branches. It also forms lateral branches (called secondary roots) which further divide to form tertiary roots. Tap roots, with the secondary and tertiary roots form tap root system. It is the characteristic of dicot plants.	In some plants after sometime the growth of tap root stops and then roots develops from other part of plant which are branched or unbranched, fibrous or storage, are known as *adventitious roots.* These are mainly found in monocots and can be grouped into 3 types on the basis of their appearance - roots arising from the base of the stem, e.g. Triticum. - roots arising from leaves, e.g. Bryophyllum. - roots developing from nodes and internodes of the stem.

Regions

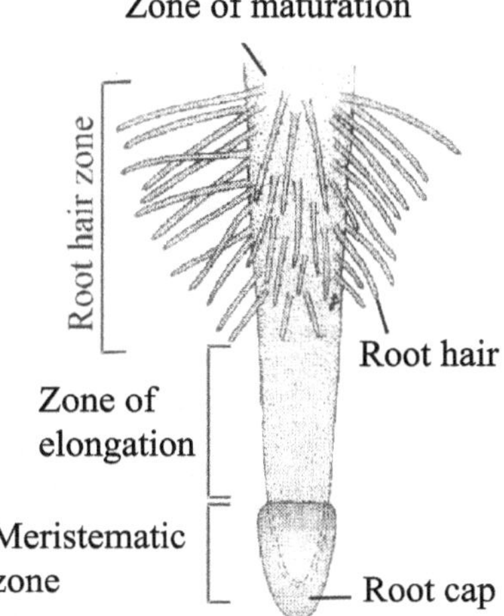

Fig. : Zones or regions of a typical root

Modification of roots:

Tap and adventitious roots are modified in different forms to perform special functions and called as modified roots.

Modification of Tap root	Modification of Adventitious root
Taproot are modified for food storage and respiration **Fusiform roots:** eg. - Radish. **Tuberous roots:** eg. *Mirabilis.* **Nodulated roots:** eg. Plants of leguminosae family (Papilionateae) - Pea. **Modified tap root for respiration are pneumatophores:** The plants, which grow in this region have some branches of tap root that grow vertically upward and comes on surface of soil. These roots are called **pneumatophores.** They have minute pores called **pneumathodes or lenticels** by which air enter inside the plant and get oxygen for respiration. Eg. *Rhizophora,* Mangrove, *Heritiera.*	Adventitious roots can be modified on the basis of functions like **fleshy for storage** (eg moniliform, annulated, tuberous, fasciculated, palmate, nodulose), **mechanical support** and for **vital functions.** *Tuberous adventitious root :* eg. Sweet potato. **Fasciculated roots :** eg. *Asparagus, Dahlia.* **Stilt roots :** eg. Maize, Sugarcane, *Pandanus* (screwpine). **Prop root or pillar roots :** eg. Banyan. **Buttress root :** eg. *Terminalia.* **Climbing roots :** eg. Money plant (pothos), *Monstera* (Betel), Black pepper. **Respiratory root :** eg. *Avicennia, Jussiaea.* **Foliar root or Epiphyllous root :** eg. *Bryophyllum, Begonia.* **Sucking or haustorial roots or Parasitic roots :** eg. *Dendrophthoe, Cuscuta, Viscum.* **Annulated roots :** e.g. *Ipecac.*

Functions of Root:
- It helps in the absorption of water and in organic nutreint from the soil.
- It anchors the plant body and support it
- It is a storage of food and nutrients.

Economic importance
(i) Sugar beet is edible root, which is an important source of sugar.
(ii) Birth control pills compounds area derived from yam roots.
(iii) Various medicines like ginseng, aconite, ipecac, gentian are made from roots

Stem
Characteristics
- It is the ascending part of plant, which develops from the plumule of embryo.
- These are differentiated into nodes and internodes and nodes posses leaves.
- It carries terminal bud for growth in length.
- These are capable of doing photosynthesis.
- When it get matured, it carries flowers and fruits.
- These are positively phototropic, negatively geotropic and negatively hydrotropic.

Functions of stem
- It supports plants and holds leaves flower and buds.
- It also connects the passage of roots to leaves and help in transport of water. minerals, sugar, etc to different part of plant.
- Due of modification of stem in thorn, it reduces transpiration

Economic importance of stem
(i) Stems like sugarcane are the source of sugar.
(ii) Stems like asparagus, bamboo, etc. are vegetables, cinnamon used as a spice is derived from the bark of the tree.
(iii) Medicines are obtained like quinine, Camphor, etc.

Leaf

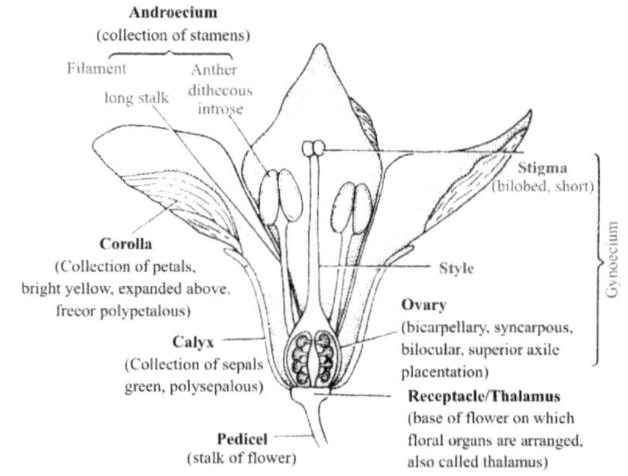

Fig. : Parts of a leaf

```
                    LEAF
```

Simple	Compound
It is a leaf which may be incised to any depth, but not down to the midrib or petiole. eg. mango, guava, papaya etc.	It is a leaf in which the leaf blade is incised up to the midrib or petiole, thus dividing it into several small parts, known as leaflets.

Modification of leaves

- When leaf is modified in different structure. It is called modification of leaves. eg – leaf tendrils, leaf spine etc.
- **Leaf tendril:** The whole leaf is modified into a wire like structure which is called leaf tendril. eg. *Lathyrus aphaca* (wild pea).

- **Leaf spine:** Leaves or any part of leaflet are modified into pointed spine. (eg. *Opuntia, Aloe, Argemone.*) either to escape transpiration or for protection.
- **Leaf scale:** Leaves become thin, dry and form a membrane or paper like structure and serve to protect axillary buds as in *Ficus* and *Tamarix, Ruscus* or store food and water as in onion.

FLOWER

Flower is a specialized branch of limited growth which bears floral leaves that carry on sexual reproduction and give rise to seeds and fruits. The study of flower as called *anthology*. The part. In a flower, 4 types of floral leaves are found. These are - sepal, petal, stamen and carpel.

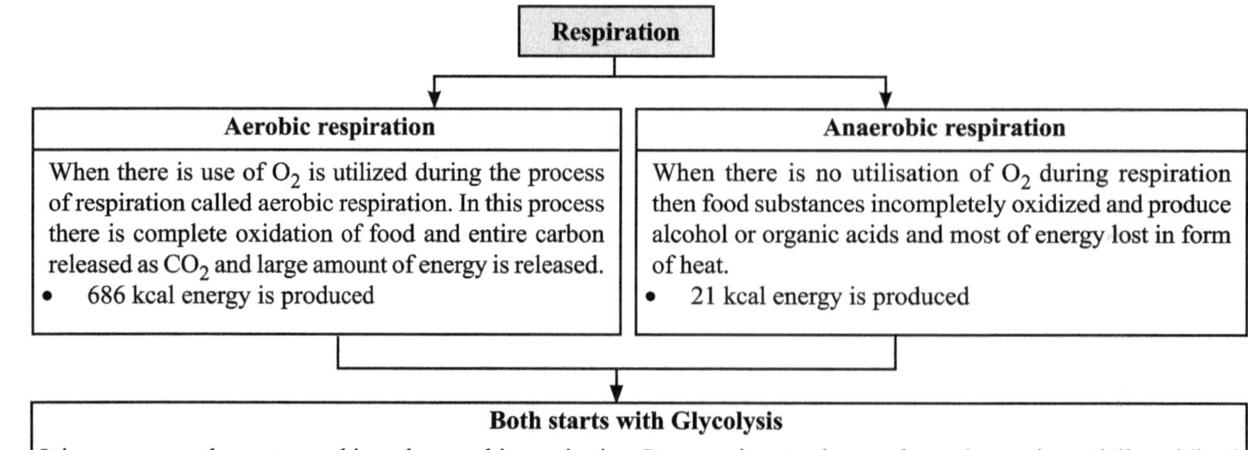

Fig. : Parts of a flower

Flower			
Calyx	**Corolla**	**Androecium**	**Gynoecium**
It is the outermost whorl of flower. cach whorl of flower us known as sepal. Sometimes it get modified into spine (Trapa), hairy structure (sunflower), etc.	It is a second whorl of the flower and each members is known as petals. It may be Polypetlous and gamopetalous.	It is a male reproductive part of flower, It consists stamen, which is differentiated into anther and filament.	It is a female reproductive part of flower It comprises stigma, style and ovary.

RESPIRATION IN PLANTS

Cellular Respiration

Cellular respiration is an enzyme catalyzed process involving biological oxidation of food materials in a living cell. The process utilizes molecular O_2, producing CO_2 and H_2O and releasing energy in gradual steps and storing it in biologically useful forms, **generally ATP**.

So respiration is **catabolic, exothermic** and **oxidative** process.

$$\underset{\text{glucose}}{C_6H_{12}O_6} + \underset{\text{oxygen}}{6O_2} \xrightarrow{\text{enzymes}} \underset{\text{carbon-dioxide}}{6CO_2} + \underset{\text{water}}{6H_2O} + \underset{\text{(ATP)}}{\text{energy}}$$

```
                Respiration
```

Aerobic respiration	Anaerobic respiration
When there is use of O_2 is utilized during the process of respiration called aerobic respiration. In this process there is complete oxidation of food and entire carbon released as CO_2 and large amount of energy is released. • 686 kcal energy is produced	When there is no utilisation of O_2 during respiration then food substances incompletely oxidized and produce alcohol or organic acids and most of energy lost in form of heat. • 21 kcal energy is produced

Both starts with Glycolysis
It is common pathway to aerobic and anaerobic respiration. It occurs in cytoplasm, where glucose is partially oxidized 2mol - of pyruvic acid. It was given by Gustav Embden, Otto Meyerhof and Jakub Parnas, hence known as EMP pathway.

RESPIRATORY QUOTIENT (R.Q.)

The ratio of the volume of CO_2 released to the volume of O_2 taken in respiration is called Respiratory Quotient (R.Q.)

$$R.Q. = \frac{\text{Volume of } CO_2 \text{ evolved}}{\text{Volume of } O_2 \text{ absorbed}}$$

TRANSPORT IN PLANTS

Plants need to move molecules over very long distances, much more than animals do; they also do not have a circulatory system in place. In a flowering plant the substances that are transported includes water, mineral nutrients, organic nutrients and plant growth regulators.

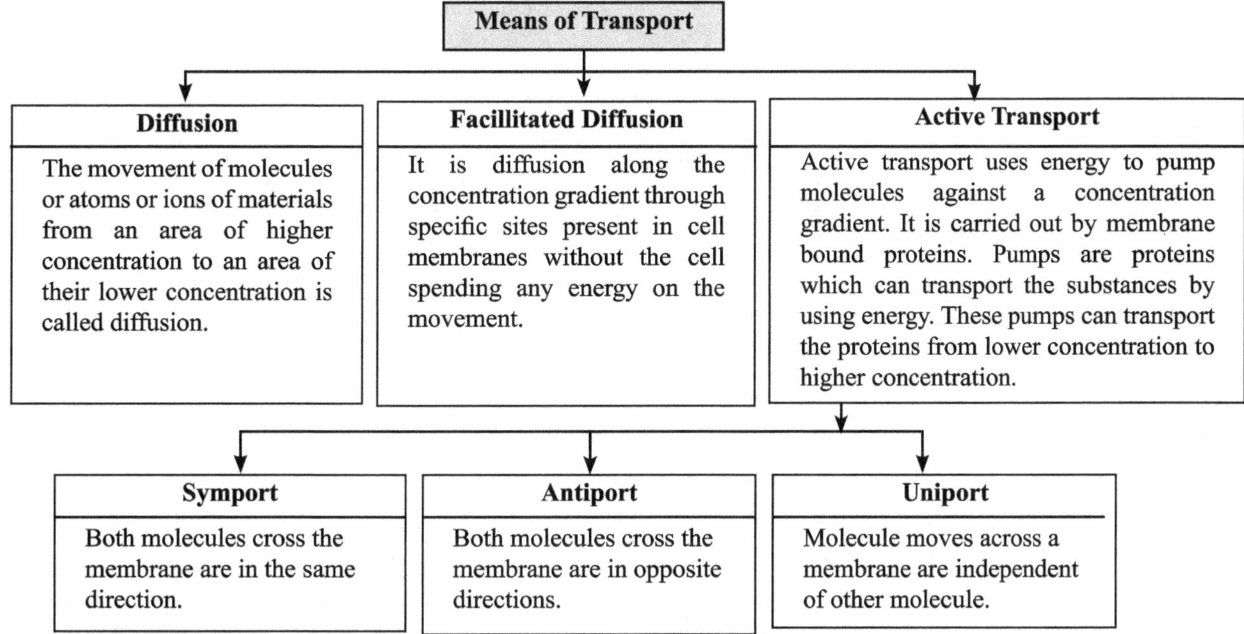

Plant-water Relations

Water is essential for all physiological activities of plants. It acts as an excellent solvent and help in the uptake and distribution of mineral nutrients and other solutes and also useful for maintaining the turgidity of cells which is essential for cell enlargement, growth & development.

Osmosis

It is a *type of diffusion* in which water molecules diffuse from the region of *higher chemical potential* (or concentration) to its region of *lower chemical potential* (concentration) *across a permeable membrane.*

Plasmolysis

The behaviour of the plant cells (or tissues) with regard to water movement depends on the surrounding solution. The shrinkage of the protoplast of a living cell from its cell wall due to exosmosis under the influence of a hypertonic solution is called **plasmolysis**.

Solution		
Isotonic	**Hypotonic**	**Hypertonic**
If the solution in which a cell is placed, has equal osmotic concentration to that of cell sap, the outer solution is called isotonic solution.	If the osmotic concentration of outer solution is less than that of the cell sap, the outer solution is called hypotonic solution. If a cell is placed in such solution endosmosis takes place and cell swells up, e.g., swelling of dried grape (Resins).	If the osmotic concentration of a solution is higher than that of the other (cell sap) solution, is known as hypertonic solution.

Deplasmolysis

The swelling up of a plasmolysed protoplast due to endosmosis under the influence of a hypotonic solution or water is called **deplasmolysis.**

Imbibition

It is a special type of diffusion when water is absorbed by solids - colloids - causing them to enormously increase in volume.

- The classical examples are seeds and dry wood.
- The *various factors* which influencing the rate of imbibitions are *nature of imbibant, surface area of imbibant, temperature, degree of dryness of imbibant, concentration of solutes, pH of imbibant* etc.

Ascent of sap

- The upward movement of absorbed water against the gravitational force upto top parts of plants is called as *ascent of sap*. Xylem is water conducting tissue in plants.
  Cohesion and tension theory by Dixon and Joly (1894), etc. is the most accepter theory.

Transpiration

- Loss of water in vapour form, from the aerial parts(organs) of living plants is known as *transpiration*. The *minimum transpiration* is found in *succulent xerophytes* and *no transpiration* in *submerged hydrophytes. Maximum* transpiration is found in *mesophytes*.

Guttation

* Loss of water from the aerial parts or leaves of the plant in the form of water droplets is called guttation. Normally, guttation process is found in hearbaceous plants like Grasses.

PLANT GROWTH REGULATORS

Plant hormone is a chemical substance which may be translocated to another region, for regulating one or more physiological reactions when present in low concentration.

* All phytohormones are growth regulators but **all growth regulators are not phytohormones**.
* Plant growth regulators are **grouped into two categories** based on the nature of their actions :
Plant growth promoters, *e.g.*, auxins, cytokinins, gibberellins. They promote growth activities like cell division, cell enlargement, flowering, fruiting and seed formation, etc.
Plant growth inhibitors, *e.g.*, abscisic acid (ABA) and ethylene. They play an important role in plant response to wounds and stresses of biotic and abiotic origin and are involved in growth inhibiting activities such as dormancy and abscission.

Plant hormones and their functions		
Plant hormones	**Site of production**	**Functions**
Auxin	Embryo of seed, meristerms of apical buds, young leaves	Stimulates stem elongation (low concentration only), root growth, cell differentiation, and branching; regulates development of fruit; enhances apical dominance; functions in phototropism and gravitropism; promotes xylem differentiation; retards leaf abscission.
Cytokinins	Synthesized in roots and transported to other organs	Affect root growth and differentiation; stimulate cell division and growth; stimulate germination; delay senescence.
Gibberellins	Meristerms of apical buds and roots, young leaves, embryo	Promote seed and bud germination, stem elongation, and leaf growth; stimulate flowering and development of fruit; affect root growth and differentiation.
Abscisic acid	Leaves, stems, roots, green fruit	Inhibits growth; closes stomata during water stress; promotes seed dormancy.
Ethylene	Tissues of ripening fruit, nodes of stems, aging leaves and flowers.	Promotes fruit ripening, opposes some auxin effects; promotes or inhibits growth and development of roots, leaves, and flowers, depending on species.

Plant Disease		
Diseases	**Causative agent**	**Symptoms**
Branchy top of Banana	*Banana Virus- 1*	Newly formed leaves becomes narrow.
Necrosis (potato)	*Potato virus-X(PVX)*	Leaves become dwarf and sharp spots are present
Potato mosaic	*Potato virus-X*	Leaves become dward and exhibits dark spots.
Tobacco Mosaic	*Tobacco Mosaic Virus (TMV)*	Stunted growth of leaves, Mottle appearance and leaves shrinks
Yellow vein Mosaic (Bhindi)	*Begmovirus or (YVM)*	yellowing of veins leaf become chlorotic
• Fungal		
Early blight	*Alternaria solani*	Concentric rings are present on leaves and it becomes brown, angular, have necrotic spots on the leaves.
Late blight Potato/Tomato	*Phytopthora infestans*	appearance of brown lesions on leaves and stem.
Rust of wheat	*Puccinia graminis*	appearance of red brown rust on stem and leaves.
Loose smut of wheat	*Ustilago tritci*	Infloresence is affected and shows early burst of fruits wall.

Red rot (Sugarcane)	*Colletotrichum falcatum went, Glomerella cingulata*	Leaf dries and exhibits brown or reddish nodal region

• Bacterial

Citrus canker	*Xanthomonas axonopodis pvcitri, Xanthomonas axonopodis PV aurantifolis*	appearance of lesion in leaves, stem and fruit in lemon plant.
Ring disease (wilt of potato)	*Pseudomonas solanacearum*	appearance of share brown ring in xylem of vascular system and collapsing of vascular system occurs.
Bacterial leaf spot	*Xanthomonas campestris*	appearance of translucent spots, then large brown to black circular area.

PHYSIOLOGY IN HUMANS

Physiology is a branch of science which deals with normal functions takes place throughout the living system. A living body comprises different system which are separate, but interconnected to each other. It includes Digestion, Respiration, Circulation, Neural and chemical control and co-ordination, excreation and their related disorders. It deals with all metabolic and catabolic processes occurs in the living body. *The process of conversion of complex food substances to simple absorbable forms is called digestion.*

DIGESTIVE SYSTEM IN HUMANS

The digestion in vertebrates occurs in the digestive tract or alimentary canal. The various parts involved in digestion can be broadly divided in two groups -

- **Digestive tract or alimentary canal**
- **Accessory digestive glands**

Alimentary Canal

- The alimentary canal is a long coiled tube having muscular wall & glandular epithelium extending from mouth to anus.
- The human digestive system consists of 9 metre long alimentary canal and several digestive glands which pour their secretion into the canal. The alimentary canal is a long tube with muscular wall, glandular epithelial lining and varying diameter.

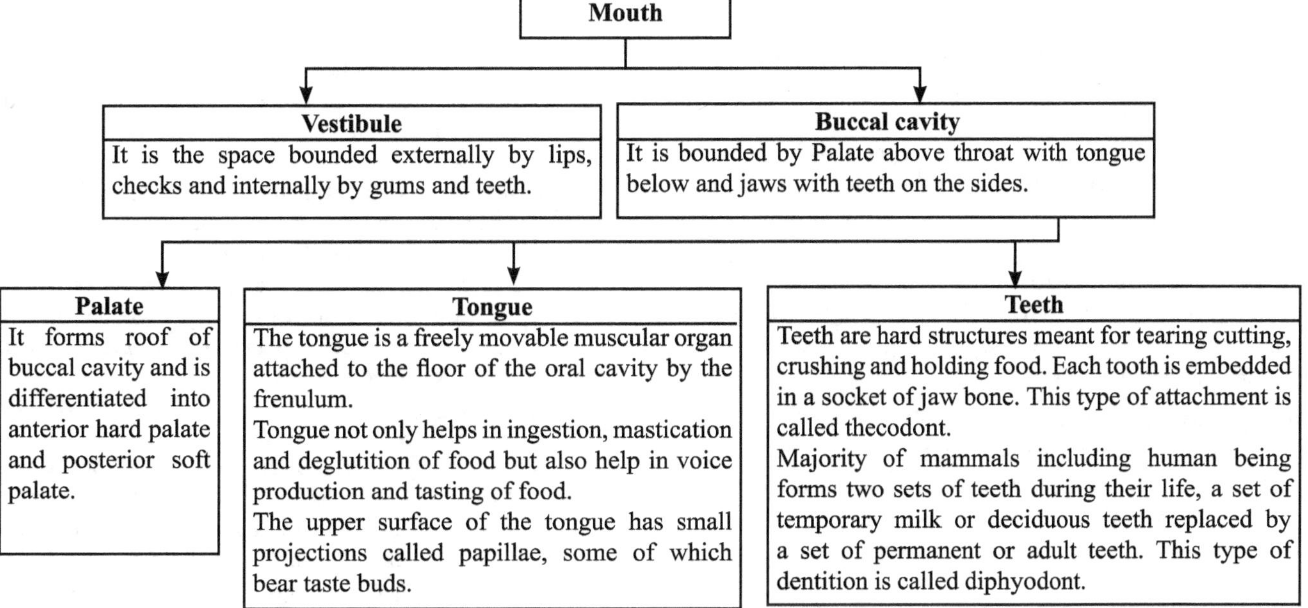

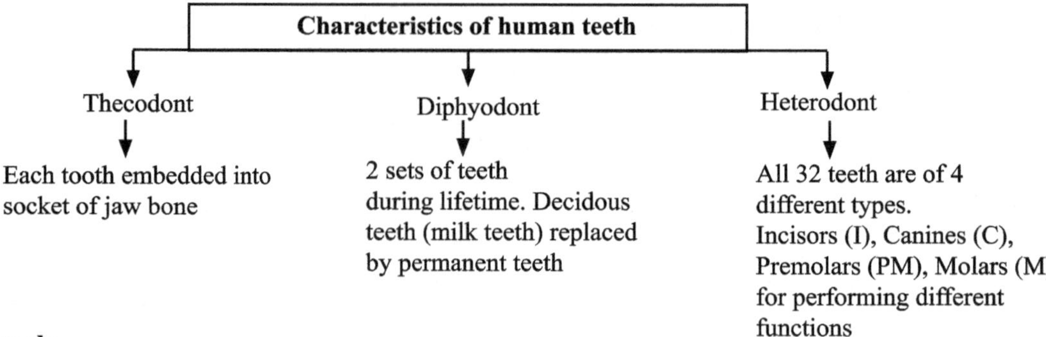

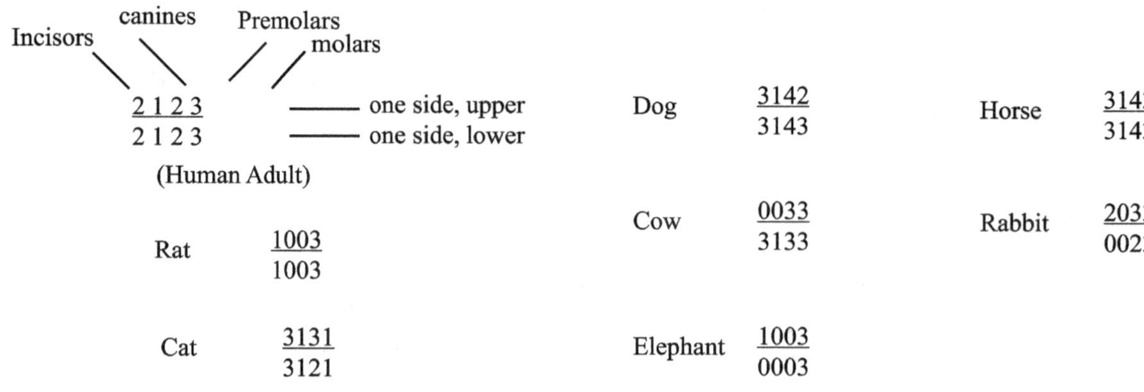

			Dog	3142 / 3143	Horse 3143 / 3143
Rat	1003 / 1003		Cow	0033 / 3133	Rabbit 2033 / 0023
Cat	3131 / 3121		Elephant	1003 / 0003	

Pharynx

It is a 12 cm funnel shaped passage from buccal cavity to esophagus. It is a common passage for both food and air. A flap, epiglottis closes over the trachea when food is swallowed to prevent choking.

Oesophagus

- The oesophagus is a thin, long tube (25 cm) which extends posteriorly passing through the neck, thorax and diaphragm and leads to a 'J' shaped bag like structure called stomach.
- A muscular sphincter (gastro-oesophageal) regulates the opening of oesophagus into the stomach.

Stomach

It is differentiated into three main parts, i.e. fundic stomach, body of stomach and pyloric stomach. The fundic as well as body of the stomach are for digestion and contain gastric glands (simple, branched and tubular type).

These glands contain three types of cells.

(i) *Mucus cells* – These secrete mucus which acts as a lubricant. Mucus also prevents the digestion of stomach by proteolytic enzymes, and injury to stomach, by acid.

(ii) *Oxyntic (parietal) cells* – These secrete HCl and *Castle's intrinsic factor.*

(iii) *Peptic/zymogen/chief cells* – These secrete digestive enzymes.

Functions of HCl

- It inactivates ptyalin and maintains pH 1-2 (strongly acidic)
- It is germicidal and kills microbes.
- It activates pro-enzymes.

The secretion of HCl is stimulated by histamine, acetylcholine and gastrin.

Small Intestine

The small intestine is coiled and narrow tube which can be distinctly divided into three regions i.e. Duodenum, Jejunum and Ileum.

(i) *Duodenum :*
- It is the proximal part of small intestine.
- It is a U-shaped structure, starts from pyloric end of the stomach and receives the secretion of common duct which brings secretion of liver and pancreas.

(ii) *Jejunum :* It is 2.4 metre long and bears finger likes projections called **villi** which increase the surface area of the inner lining of intestine.

(iii) *Ileum :* It is 2.4 metre long with **club-shaped villi.** Its lower end forms a **Merkel's diverticulum.** The opening of ileum in caecum (large intestine) called **ileocaecal orifice.**

Large Intestine

- It is roughly 1.5 meters long with three parts: the **cecum** at the junction of small intestines, the **colon**, and the **rectum**.
- The colon itself has four parts: *ascending colon, transverse colon, descending colon* and the *sigmoid colon.*
- Food products that cannot go though the villi, such as cellulose (dietary fibre), are mixed with other waste products and become hard and concentrated faeces.

Digestion in Man

- Digestion in man starts from his mouth. In mouth food gets mixed up with saliva secreted by salivary glands. Saliva contains enzymes ptyalin which break starch into single carbohydrates maltose.

- In stomach food is churned by the action of muscles of the stomach. The food gets mixed with the gastric juice which contains dil. HCl and two enzymes namely *renin* and *pepsin*. HCl soften food, kill bacteria present in the food. It provides acidic medium for the enzymes present in the gastric juice to act.

  Renin enzyme present in infants or curdles milk. Pepsin break proteins into proteoses and peptones.
- In duodenum bile juice and pancreatic juice mixed into the churned food. Bile juice emulsified the fat. Pancreatic juice consist of three enzymes.
  - (i) *Trypsin* breaks proteins, peptones and peptides into amino acids.
  - (ii) *Amylase* breaks starch into sugar.
  - (iii) *Lipase* breaks patsineo acids and glycerol.
- From the duodenum food slowly moves towards ileum, where it gets mixed with intestinal juice secreted by intestinal glands. Intestinal juice consists of amylotic, protolytic and lipolytic enzymes.
- Absorption of the digested food occurs through the villi of small intestine.
- The undigested food is collected as faeces in the rectum, rectal wall absorbs water from it and the faecal matter is egested out through anus.

NUTRITIONAL AND DIGESTIVE DISORDERS

- *Jaundice:* The liver is affected, skin and eyes turn yellow due to the deposit of bile pigments.
- During jaundice or hepatitis the bilirubin (a toxic chemical) is not excreted out and gets deposited in the body tissues.
- *Vomiting* is the ejection of stomach contents through the mouth.
- The abnormal frequency of bowel movement and increased liquidity of the faecal discharge is known as diarrhoea. It reduces the absorption of food.
- **Indigestion** is a condition in which the food is not properly digested leading to a feeling of fullness. The causes of indigestion are inadequate enzyme secretion, anxiety, food poisoning, over eating, and spicy food.

RESPIRATORY SYSTEM

Respiration is an oxidative process occurring within living cells by which the chemical energy of organic molecules is released in a series of metabolic steps involving the consumption of oxygen and liberation of carbon dioxide and water. As the process of respiration takes place inside the cells, it is also known as *cellular respiration.*

- Respiration is of 2-types — aerobic and anaerobic respiration

Respiration	
Aerobic respiration	**Anaerobic respiration**
• It is a process of cellular respiration that uses oxygen in order to break down respiratory substrate which then releases energy.	• It is a process of cellular respiration that takes place in absence of oxygen, there is incomplete breakdown of respiratory substrate and little energy is released.
• 38 molecules of ATP are released for every glucose molecule broken down.	• 2 molecules of ATP are released for break down of every glucose molecule.
• It takes place in the cytoplasm (glycolysis) and mitochondria (Krebs and Electron Transport Chain) of the cell.	• It takes place in the cytoplasm of the cell, mitochondria is not involved. The equation is:
• The equation of aerobic breakdown of glucose is:	

Aerobic:

$$\text{Glucose (6–Compound)} \xrightarrow{\text{In cytoplasm}} \text{Glucose} \longrightarrow \text{Pyvuric Acid (3–Compound)} \xrightarrow[\text{presence of } O_2]{\text{In mitochondria}} \text{Kreb's Cycle}$$

$$CO_2 + H_2O + 38\ ATP$$

Anaerobic:

$$\text{Glucose (6–Compound)} \xrightarrow{\text{In cytoplasm}} \text{Glucose} \longrightarrow \text{Pyvuric Acid (3–Compound)} \xrightarrow[\text{of muscle cells}]{\text{In cytoplasm}} \text{No oxygen}$$

$$\text{Lactic Acid (3–Compound)} + 2ATP$$

TYPES OF RESPIRATION AND RESPIRATORY ORGANS OF ANIMALS

Respiratory System in Human

The primary structure involved in respiratory system are lungs. Which are endodermal in origin. Its components are nasal passage, pharynx, larynx, trachea, bronchi, bronchioles and alveoli.

Mechanism of Breathing

The physical movements associated with the gaseous exchange are called breathing. They are controlled by the respiratory centre of medulla oblongata in the human brain. Thus, the breathing movements are involuntary to a large extent. However, we can control the rate of breathing and the extent of breathing but not for a long time. The respiratory centre is stimulated by the carbon dioxide concentration of the blood. There are two types of physical movements associated with the gaseous exchange.

Inspiration (or Inhalation)

Inspiration of air occurs when the volume of the thoracic cavity is increased. When the volume increases, the pressure in the thoracic cavity becomes lower than the outside atmospheric air. Hence atmospheric pressure forces air into the lungs through the nose and trachea.

Expiration (or Exhalation)

When the volume of thoracic cavity is reduced, the pressure of the air inside the thoracic cavity becomes greater than outside atmosphere. Hence, air from inside the lungs expelled through the trachea and nose to the outside to equalize the internal and external pressure.

DISORDERS OF RESPIRATORY SYSTEM

- *Asthma* is an allergic reaction that causes constriction of the bronchiole muscles, thereby reducing the air passage thus the amount of the air that can get to the alveoli.
- *Emphysema* it is a situation of short breath in which alveolar walls are damaged due to which respiratory surface is decreased. It is often caused by cigarette smoking.
- Occupational – Respiratory disorders
  (i) *Asbestosis* – Exposure to the fibrous minerals of asbestos
  (ii) *Bauxite fibrosis* – Exposure to bauxite fumes that contains aluminum and silica particles.
  (iii) *Siderosis* – due to the deposition of iron in tissue.
  (iv) *Byssinosis* – Also known as "brown lung disease" and caused due to exposure to cotton dust in inadequately ventilated environments.

> **Bronchitis :** It is caused by the permanent swelling in bronchi. As a result of bronchitis cough is caused and thick mucus with pus cells is spitted out. The patient experiences difficulty in breathing.

> **Tuberculosis (TB) :** It is caused by bacteria Mycobacterium tuberculosis.
> **Lung cancer :** It is believed that by excess smoking, lung cancer (carcinoma of lungs) is caused. The tissue increases limitlessly, which is called malignancy.

HUMAN CIRCULATORY SYSTEM

- Human circulatory system, also called the blood vascular system, consists of a muscular chambered heart, a network of closed branching blood vessels, blood and the fluid which is circulated. Circulatory system of human is of closed type.

Heart

- Heart is situated in the thoracic cavity between the lungs with its apex resting on the diaphragm.
- It is measured about 12 cm in length and 9 cm in breath. It weight in males (average 300 g) and (average 250 in females). It is enclosed in double walled membranous bag, pericardium, enclosing the pericardial fluid.

- Heart has four chambers, with two anterior auricles and two posterior ventricles.

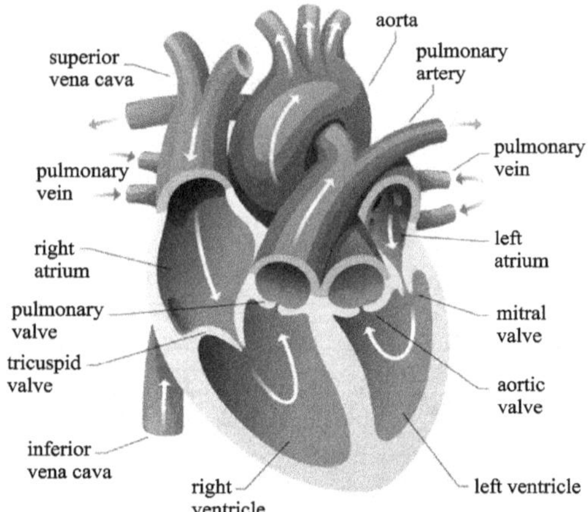

(Fig. Anatomy of human heart)

Rhythmicity of Heart

- Automatic rhythmicity of the heart is the ability to contract spontaneously and at a regular interval of time. A specialized tissue called nodal tissue are distributed throughout the heart. This tissue consists sino-atrial node (SAN) atrio ventricular node (AVN).
- Purkinje branches give rise to minute fibres throughout the ventricular musculature of the respective sides and are called **purkinje fibres.** Purkinje fibres along with right and left bundles are known as **bundle of HIS.**
- The SAN can generate the maximum number of action potentials, i.e., 70-75 min–1, and is responsible for initiating and maintaining the rhythmic contractile activity of the heart. Therefore, it is called the **pacemaker.**

Blood Pressure

The pressure exerted by the blood on the wall of the blood vessels in which it is present is called blood pressure.

- It is usually measured in brachial artery by an instrument called sphygmomanometer.

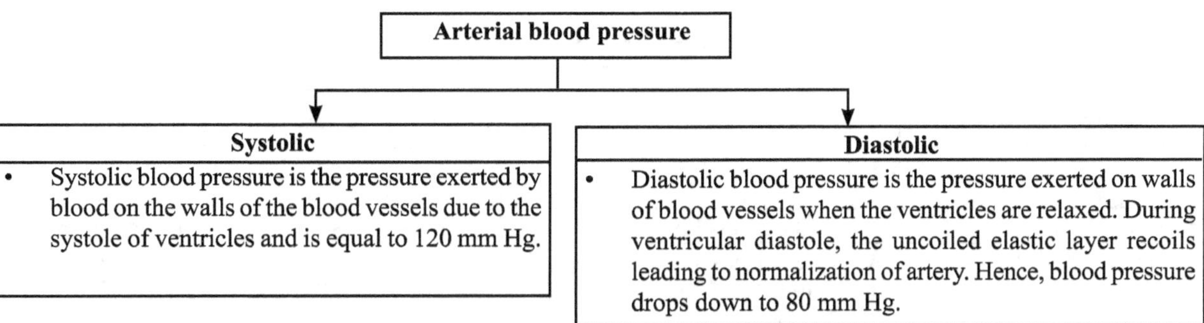

Systolic	Diastolic
• Systolic blood pressure is the pressure exerted by blood on the walls of the blood vessels due to the systole of ventricles and is equal to 120 mm Hg.	• Diastolic blood pressure is the pressure exerted on walls of blood vessels when the ventricles are relaxed. During ventricular diastole, the uncoiled elastic layer recoils leading to normalization of artery. Hence, blood pressure drops down to 80 mm Hg.

ELECTROCARDIOGRAM (ECG)

- The blood pressure in normal person is systolic/diastolic pressure i.e. 120/80 mm Hg.
- The instrument which records electrical activity of the heart muscles is called Electrocardiograph. The sketch obtained on the graph paper is called **electrocardiogram** (or ECG).
- The standard symbols used for ECG are PQRST, where P* represents atrial depolarisation; QRS* complex represents ventricular depolarisation and T* represents ventricular repolarisation. (P, R & T are deflection waves).

EXCRETORY SYSTEM

- Excretion is the essential process in all forms of life. In one celled organisms waste are discharged through the surface of the cell. The higher plants eliminates gases through the stomata or pores present on the leaf surface. Multicellular animals have special excretory organs.
- Ammonia, urea and uric acid are the major forms of nitrogenous wastes excreted by the animals.
- On the basis of main excretory products, animals can be divided into 3 groups – ammonotelic, ureotelic and uricotelic (described later).

Human Excretory System

Excretory system consists of a pair of kidneys, one pair of ureters, a urinary bladder and a urethra.

Kidneys

These are two bean- shaped purplish brown colored structures located in the back of the abdominal cavity. It is the main organ of excretion through which the nitrogenous waste are eliminated in the form of urine about 12 cm long, about 6 cm thick and weighs about 150 gm. Kidneys contain millions of nephron which filter 170 to 200 litres blood to produce 1-1.8 litres of urine daily.

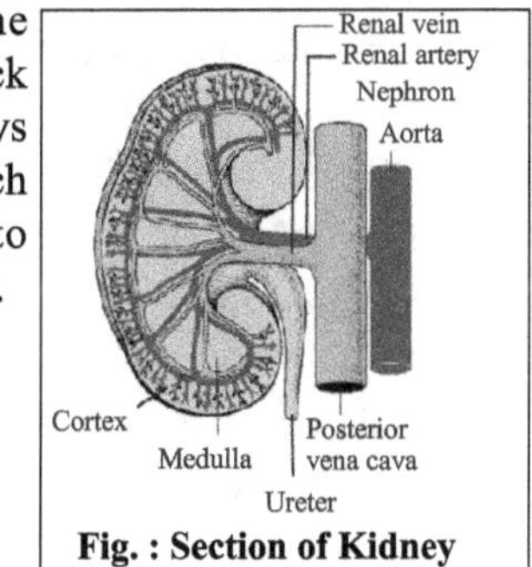

Fig. : Section of Kidney

Renal Arteries

Two renal arteries constantly transport blood to each of the kidneys.

Renal vein

Two renal veins return useful nutrients back into the bloods stream after filtering the unwanted materials in kidneys.

- Internally the kidney is divided into two zones–an outer **cortex** and an inner **medulla.**
- **Cortex** - is granular in appearance. Cortex contain malpighean corpuscles, proximal convoluted tubule and distal convoluted tubule.

Nephron

- Nephrons are the structural and functional units of kidneys. Nephron eliminates wastes from the body, regulate blood volume and pressure, control levels of electrolytes and metabolites and regulate blood pH.
- *There are two types of nephron according to their position in kidney - cortical and juxta medullary nephron.*

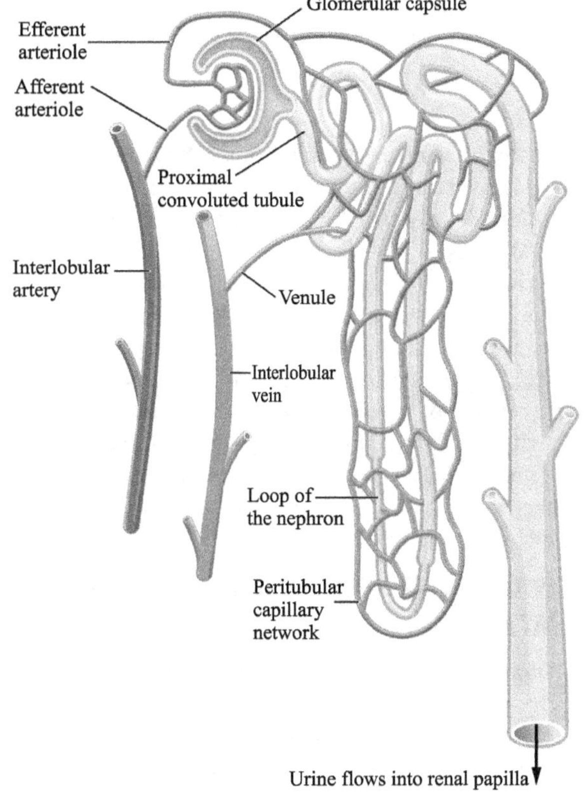

Fig. Anatomy of nephron

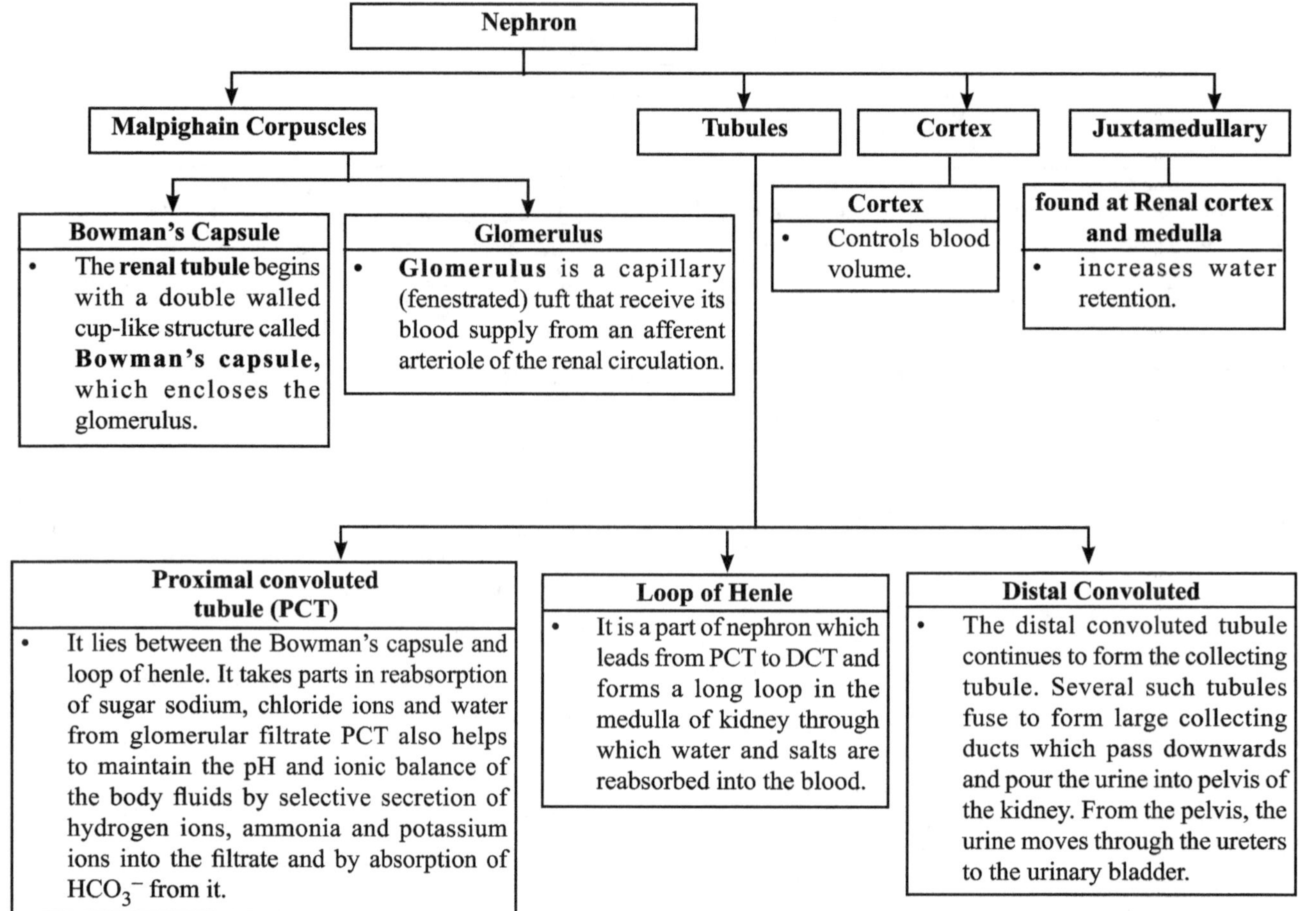

Dialysis

Urea is a toxic chemical. When it is not removed from the body, due to kidney disease, it gets accumulated in blood (**Uremia**) and can cause kidney failure. The urea can be removed from the blood by dialysis.

- **Peritoneal dialysis-**
  It is less costly but risky as there are chances of infection due to the permanent tube in the abdomen. A fluid (dialysate), containing sodium, chloride, bicarbonate and high percentage of glucose, is introduced into the abdominal cavity through a permanent- attached tube. The peritoneum of abdomen acts as a membrane and the exchange of substances occur with the blood. The fluid, containing urea, is removed periodically.

CONTROL AND COORDINATION IN ANIMALS

- Animals receive a variety of external information through specialised system or organ called **sense organs** or **receptors organ**. There are five sense organs present in the human beings eye, ear, nose tongue and skin.
- The receptors are a nerve cell or group of nerve cells which collect information about changes in the environment, in the form of stimuli.
- The receptors pass information to the brain by a type of nerve cells called sensory neurons.

DIVISION OF HUMAN NERVOUS SYSTEM

The human nervous system consists of : Central Nervous System (CNS) and Peripheral Nervous System (PNS)

Central Nervous System

It lies in the mid–dorsal region along the lontudinal axis of the body. It consists of two parts. *Brain and Spinal Cord.*

Brain

This is the highest coordinating centre in the body. It is situated in the head region, in the cranial cavity of the skull. It is soft, whitish organ which weighs 1.2–1.4 kg. It forms 98% of the weight of the whole CNS. Brain is surrounded by three protective membranes called The space between these meninges is filled with **cerebrospinal fluid** which protects the brain from mechanical shocks. Brain is divisible into three main regions : **Fore brain, Mid brain and Hind brain**

(i) Fore brain forms the greatest part of the brain. It consists of three regions:

Olfactory lobes are a pair of club–shaped small structures present below the cerebral hemisphere. Both lobes are widely separated. It is centre of smell.

Cerebral hemispheres or cerebrum: It forms the largest part of the brain. It cerebrum has two cerebral hemispheres which lie side by side and are separated by a deep cerebral fissure. The surface of cerebral hemisphere has grooves (sulci) and folds (gyri) to accomodate larger number of nerve cells.

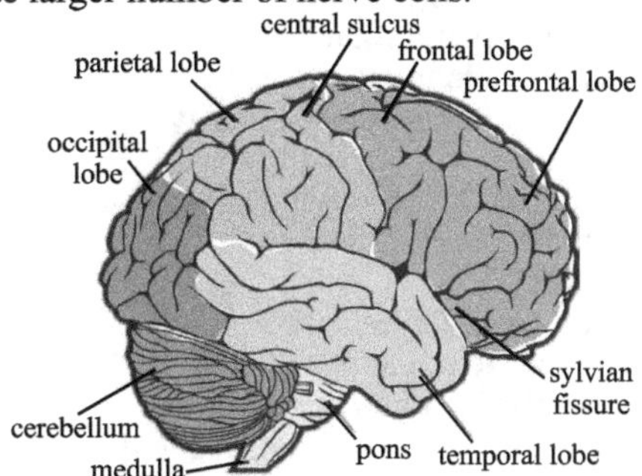

Fig. Human Brain

Diencephalon: It is smallest and unpaired part of brain. It lies on the lower side of cerebrum.

(ii)　Mid brain : It extends from the pons to the lower portion of the diencephalon. Mid brain is sub divided into Optic Lobes and Crura Cerebri

- **Optic lobes :** There are four round solid optic lobes called corpora quadrigemina. Anterior optic lobes are centre of vision and posterior lobes are for hearing.
- **Crura cerebri :** These are two ventral bands of nerves connecting diencephalon and medullaoblongata.

(iii)　Hind brain consists of three parts :

- **Cerebellum** is the second largest part of the brain. It maintains equilibrium posture and tones of muscles.
- **Pons :** It is located in the centre of brain below the cerebellum.
- **Medulla oblongata** is the posterior most part of the brain which lies below the cerebellum. It continues posteriorly into the spinal cord.

Spinal Cord

It lies in the mid–dorsal region along the longitudinal axis of the body. It is a slender, cylindrical structure, about 45 cm long, originating from medulla oblongata and extending downwards upto the lumber region. Spinal cord is also covered by three meninges, like the brain, in between which is the cerebrospinal fluid. It acts as a centre for reflex actions, thus, reduces brain's work. It also conducts sensory and motor impulses to and from the brain.

Function :-

- It transmits neural signals between the brain and the rest of the body.
- It controls numerous reflexes and central pattern generators.

HORMONES

Hormones are the intercellular messengers produced by ductless glands known as endocrine glands. These are released into the blood and transported to a distantly located target organ. Vertebrates produce a large number of hormones for coordination. The human endocrine system consists of following gland/organs and their products. (hormones).

Endocrine glands	Hormones	Type	Functions
Thyroid gland	– Thyroxine (T_4) and triiodothyronine (T_3) – Calcitonin	Amine Peptide	Stimulate and maintain metabolic process Lowers blood calcium level
Parathyroid glands	– Parathyroid hormone (PTH)	Peptide	Raises blood calcium level
Thymus	– Thymosin	Peptide	Stimulates T cell development
Adrenal gland Adrenal medulla Adrenal cortex	– Epinephrine and norepinephrine – Glucocorticoids Mineralocorticoids	Amine Steroid Steroid	Increase blood glucose; increase metabolic activities; constrict certain blood vessels Increase blood glucose Promote reabsorption of Na^+ and excretion of K^+ in kidneys.
Pancreas	– Insulin – Glucagon	Protein Protein	Lowers blood glucose Raises blood glucose
Testes	– Androgens	Steroid	Support sperm formation; promote development and maintenance of male secondary sex characteristics.
Ovaries	– Estrogens – Progesterone	Steroid Steroid	Stimulate uterine lining growth; promote development and maintenance of female secondary sex characteristics. Promotes uterine lining growth.

MULTIPLE CHOICE QUESTIONS

1. Meristematic tissues are found in
   (a) only stems of the plants
   (b) both roots and stems
   (c) in all growing tips of the plant body
   (d) only roots of the plants
2. The process of formation of blood corpuscles is called
   (a) haemopoiesis   (b) heamolysis
   (c) heamozoin   (d) None of these
3. Which tissue does lack blood supply and heals slowly ?
   (a) nervous   (b) muscle
   (c) cartilage   (d) bone
4. Nervous tissue is not found in
   (a) brain   (b) spinal cord
   (c) tendons   (d) nerves
5. The dead element present in the phloem is
   (a) companion cells
   (b) phloem fibres
   (c) phloem parenchyma
   (d) sieve tube
6. Girth of stem increases due to
   (a) apical meristem
   (b) lateral meristem
   (c) intercalary meristem
   (d) vertical meristem
7. The pH of blood is.
   (a) acidic   (b) Alkaline
   (c) Slightly alkaline   (d) None of the above
8. Which of the following tissues has dead cells?
   (a) Parenchyma   (b) Sclerenchyma
   (c) Collenchyma   (d) Epithelial tissue
9. The chief function of vessels in the plant body is
   (a) to translocate food material
   (b) to conduct water and mineral salts
   (c) to support living cells
   (d) all above
10. Various functions like photosynthesis, storage, excretion performed by _____________.
    (a) sclerenchyma   (b) parenchyma
    (c) collenchyma   (d) aerenchyma
11. Lignin is the important constituent in the cell wall of
    (a) phloem   (b) parenchyma
    (c) xylem   (d) cambium
12. Main function of lenticel is
    (a) transpiration   (b) guttation
    (c) gaseous exchange (d) both (a) & (c)
13. Cork is formed from
    (a) phellogen   (b) vascular cambium
    (c) phloem   (d) xylem
14. Which of the following statement(s) is/are correct about the ground tissue system?
    (i) All tissues except epidermis and vascular bundles constitute the ground tissue.
    (ii) It consists of xylem and phloem.
    (iii) In leaves, it consists of thin – walled chloroplast containing cells called mesophyll.

   (a) Only (i)
   (b) Both (i) and (iii)
   (c) Both (ii) and (iii)
   (d) All of these
15. Root hairs develop from
    (a) region of maturation
    (b) region of elongation
    (c) region of meristematic activity
    (d) root cap
16. Which one of the following process releases a carbon dioxide molecule?
    (a) Glycolysis
    (b) Lactic acid fermentation
    (c) Alcohol fermentation
    (d) Hydrolysis of glycogen
17. The plant hormone, Gibberellic Acid is generally NOT associated with
    (a) stem elongation
    (b) parthenocarpy
    (c) parthenogenesis
    (d) malt production
18. What is the effect of sudden increase in the levels of ATP and citrate on an erythrocyte undergoing glycolysis?
    (a) It inhibits glycolysis
    (b) It stimulates glycolysis
    (c) The rate of glycolysis remains unaltered
    (d) The rate of glycolysis increases gradually

19.

	Column-I		Column-II
A.	Auxin	I.	Fruit ripening
B.	Cytokinins	II.	Apical dominance
C.	Abscisic acid	III.	Antagonist to GAs
D.	Ethylene	IV.	Stomatal opening and closing
		V.	Growth of lateral buds

   (a) A-IV; B-V; C-III; D-I
   (b) A-II; B-IV; C-III, IV; D-I
   (c) A-II; B-V; C-III, IV; D-I
   (d) A-III, IV; B-V; C-II; D-I

20.

	Column - I		Column - II
A.	Isotonic	I.	External solution is more concentrated
B.	Hypotonic	II.	Shrinkage of protoplasm
C.	Hypertonic	III.	Solution is more dilute than the cytoplasm
D.	Plasmolysis	IV.	Two solutions have the same osmolarity

   (a) A – II; B – I; C – IV; D – III
   (b) A – IV; B – III; C – I; D – II
   (c) A – III; B – I; C – IV; D – II
   (d) A – II; B – III; C – IV; D – I

21. Cloves, used as a spice, are derived from which of the following plant parts?   **[CDS]**
    (a) Seeds   (b) Fruits
    (c) Flower buds   (d) Young leaves

22.

	List-I		List-II
A.	Fruit	1.	Ovule
B.	Seed	2.	Leaf
C.	Wood	3.	Stem
D.	Starch	4.	Ovary

(a) A-2; B-1; C-3; D- 4 **[IAS Prelim]**
(b) A-4; B-1; C-3; D-2
(c) A-2; B-3; C-1; D-4
(d) A-4; B-3; C-1; D-2

23. The involvement of which one of the following is essential in the control of blood sugar? **[NDA]**
(a) Adrenal (b) Pancreas
(c) Parathyroid (d) Spleen

24. Which one of the following pairs is not correctly matched: **[NDA]**
(a) Loop of Henle : Kidney
(b) Fallopian tube : Female reproductive system
(c) Epididymis : Male reproductive system
(d) Cowper's gland : Intestine

25. Which one of the following glands produces insulin in human body? **[NDA]**
(a) Liver (b) Pancreas
(c) Spleen (d) Pituitary

26. A surge of which hormone stimulates ovulation in human females? **[NDA]**
(a) Luteinizing hormone
(b) Estrogen
(c) Follicle stimulating hormone
(d) Progesterone

27. Which one of the following is an enzyme? **[NDA]**
(a) Gastrin (b) Keratin
(c) Trypsin (d) Vasopressin

28. Due to accumulation of which one of the following, joggers experience pain in their leg muscles after running? **[NDA]**
(a) Lactic acid (b) Acetic acid
(c) Malic acid (d) Citric acid

29. A typical human ribcage consists of how many ribs? **[NDA]**
(a) 12 (b) 14
(c) 16 (d) 24

30. Biological catalysts in living organisms are known as **[NDA]**
(a) hormones (b) vitamins
(c) steroids (d) enzymes

31. Cure to spinal injury is likely to emerge from **[NDA]**
(a) gene therapy (b) stem cell therapy
(c) xenograft (d) transfusion

32. Which one among the following statements about stomach is not correct? **[NDA]**
(a) Stomach acts as a temporary reservoir
(b) Stomach mixes food with gastric juice
(c) Stomach secretes lipase and amylase in gastric juice
(d) Rate of stomach emptying depends on the type of food

33. Which one among the following statements is correct? **[NDA]**
(a) All arteries carry oxygenated blood
(b) All veins carry oxygenated blood
(c) Except the pulmonary artery, all other arteries carry oxygenated blood
(d) Except the pulmonary vein, all other veins carry oxygenated blood

34. Which one among the following is the hardest part of our body ? **[NDA]**
(a) Skull bones of head
(b) Thumb nails
(c) Enamel of teeth
(d) Spinal vertebra

35. Plants contain a variety of sterols like stigmasterol, ergosterol, sitosterol etc. which very closely resemble cholesterol. These plant sterols are referred as: **[CDS 2018]**
(a) Phytosterols (b) Caleiferols
(c) Ergocaleiferols (d) Lumisterols

36. Which one of the following hormones contains peptide chain ? **[CDS 2018]**
(a) Oxytocin (b) Corticotropin
(c) Insulin (d) Cortisone

37. Which one of the following hormones is essential for the uptake of glucose by cells in the human body? **[CDS 2018]**
(a) GH (b) TSH
(c) Insulin (d) Cortisol

38. The mammalian heart is myogenic and it is regulated by nerves. The heartbeat originates from **[CDS 2018]**
(a) sinoatrial node (b) QRS wave
(c) T wave (d) hepatic portal system

39. The plant growth regulators are small, simple molecules of diverse chemical composition. They are **[CDS 2018]**
(a) carbohydrates, fats and proteins
(b) indole compounds, adenine derivatives, carotenoids and terpenes
(c) fatty acids, glucose and vitamins
(d) vitamin C, vitamin D and glucose

40. In which one of the following types of connective tissues in animals does fat get stored? **[CDS 2018]**
(a) Adipocyte (b) Chondrocyte
(c) Osteocyte (d) Reticulocyte

41. Kidney secretes an enzyme, which changes plasma protein angiotensinogen into angiotensin. The enzyme is **[NDA 2017-I]**
(a) Renin (b) Nitrogenase
(c) Hydrolase (d) Mono-oxygenase

42. Red blood cells (RBCs) have **[NDA 2017-I]**
(a) no nucleus, no mitochondria and no endoplasmic reticulum
(b) nucleus, mitochondria and endoplasmic reticulum
(c) nucleus, mitochondria but no endoplasmic reticulum
(d) no mitochondria but endoplasmic reticulum is present

43. Colour vision in human eyes is the function of photoreceptor cells named **[NDA 2017-I]**
(a) Rods (b) Cones
(c) Blind spot (d) Fovea

44. Tendons through which muscles are connected to bones are tightly compacted bundles of which one of the following long fibrous protein? **[NDA 2017-II]**
(a) Fibrin (b) Collagen
(c) Elastin (d) Cellulose

45. Melanin is the natural pigment that gives colour to human skin, hair and the iris. It provides protection against
[NDA 2017-II]
 (a) Ultraviolet radiation
 (b) Infrared radiation
 (c) X-ray radiation
 (d) Short wave radio radiation

46. Which one of the following parts of body does NOT take part in the process of breathing? **[NDA 2018-I]**
 (a) Bronchi   (b) Bowman's capsule
 (c) Diaphragm   (d) Trachea

47. Which one of the following statements about meristematic tissues in plants is correct? **[NDA 2018-I]**
 (a) These are dead tissues and form wood
 (b) They provide flexibility to plant due to their thickened walls
 (c) These are present in the bark of a tree only
 (d) Growth occurs in plants due to division of cells of these tissues

48. Which one of the following types of tissues will have contractile proteins? **[NDA 2018-I]**
 (a) Nervous tissue   (b) Muscle tissue
 (c) Bone tissue   (d) Blood tissue

49. If by an unknown accident the acid secreting cells of the stomach wall of an individual are damaged, digestion of which one of the following biomolecule will be affected to a greater extent? **[NDA 2018-I]**
 (a) Protein only
 (b) Lipid
 (c) Carbohydrate only
 (d) Protein and Carbohydrate

50. Damage to the apical meristem of a growing young plant will affect the **[NDA 2018-II]**
 (a) length of the plant
 (b) colour of the flower
 (c) colour of the leaves
 (d) taste of the fruits

51. The acidic semidigested food coming out of the stomach is neutralized by **[NDA 2018-II]**
 (a) pancreatic juice
 (b) duodenal secretion
 (c) large intestine secretion
 (d) bile juice

52. Th oxygenated blood from the lungs is received by the **[NDA 2018-II]**
 (a) left auricle   (b) left ventricle
 (c) right auricle   (d) right ventricle

53. The oxygen evolved during photo synthesis comes from splitting of **[NDA 2018-II]**
 (a) water   (b) carbon dioxide
 (c) oxygen   (d) light

54. Which one of the following depicts the correct circuit of a reflex arc? **[NDA 2018-II]**
 (a) Effector-sensory neuron-spinal cord-motor neuron-receptor
 (b) Receptor-sensory neuron-spinal cord-motor neuron-effector
 (c) Receptor-sensory neuron-brain-motor neuron-effector
 (d) Sensory neuron-receptor-brain-effector - motor neuron

ANSWER KEY																			
1.	(c)	2.	(a)	3.	(c)	4.	(c)	5.	(b)	6.	(b)	7.	(c)	8.	(b)	9.	(b)	10.	(b)
11.	(c)	12.	(a)	13.	(a)	14.	(b)	15.	(a)	16.	(c)	17	(c)	18	(a)	19.	(c)	20.	(b)
21.	(c)	22.	(b)	23.	(b)	24.	(d)	25.	(b)	26.	(a)	27.	(c)	28.	(a)	29.	(d)	30.	(d)
31.	(b)	32.	(d)	33.	(c)	34.	(c)	35.	(a)	36.	(c)	37.	(c)	38.	(a)	39.	(b)	40.	(a)
41.	(a)	42.	(a)	43.	(b)	44.	(b)	45.	(a)	46.	(b)	47.	(d)	48.	(b)	49.	(a)	50.	(a)
51.	(a)	52.	(a)	53.	(a)	54.	(b)												

Chapter 5

REPRODUCTION

REPRODUCTION

Reproduction is the process by which all living organism give rise to new organisms similar to themselves. It is essential for the survival of the species since all the living beings have a similar life span. Organism reproduces by two modes asexual and sexual reproduction.

Asexual Reproduction

Asexual reproduction produces offspring that are genetically identical to the parent because the offspring are all clones. The main process of asexual reproduction is mitosis. This type of reproduction is common among same single cell organisms for example, amoeba, etc. Many plants also reproduce asexually.

Sexual Reproduction

Sexual reproduction is a biological process that creates a new organism by combining the genetic material of two organisms in a process that starts with meiosis, a specialized type of cell division.

Difference between asexual and sexual reproduction

	Asexual reproduction	Sexual reproduction
1.	It occurs only in invertebrates and lower chordates.	It occurs almost in all types of animals.
2.	It is always uniparental.	It is usually biparental.
3.	Gametes are not formed.	Two types of gametes are formed.
4.	It involves only mitosis.	It involves both meiosis and mitosis.
5.	Daughter organisms are genetically identical to the parent.	Daughter organisms genetically differ from their parents.
6.	Since there is no variation, so it does not contribute to evolution of the species.	Because of variations, it contributes to the evolution of species.
7.	Occurs by fission, budding or fragmentation.	Occurs by the formation of haploid gametes which fuse to form a diploid zygote.
8.	It is a quick method of multiplication.	It is a slower method of multiplication.

REPRODUCTION IN PLANTS

In plants, asexual reproduction is of *3 types – agamospermy, spore formation and vegetative reproduction.*

Vegetative Propagation

Vegetative propagation or vegetative reproduction is the process of multiplication in which a portion of fragment of the plant body functions as propagules and develop into a new individual.

> **Artificial Vegetative Propagation**
> * Cutting - e.g sugarcane
> * Grafting - e.g grafted margo, roses, orange, seedless grapes, guava, apple and pear.

Underground stem

* Rhizome – Ginger, banana, turmeric, Lotus, Musa, etc.
* Corm – Gladiolus, colocasia, crocus, Alocasia, etc.
* Bulbs – Onion, garlic and lilies.
* Tubers – Potato, Helianthus tuberosus etc
* Suckers – Mint and chrysanthemum.

Creeper stem

* Runners – Cyndon, oxalis and centealla
* Stolon – Fragaria, vallisneria
* Offset – Pistia, Eichhornia, etc.
* Aerial stem - Opuntia.

Leaves – e.g. – Bryophyllum, Begonia, Streptocarpus, Saintpaulia

SEXUAL REPRODUCTION IN FLOWERING PLANT

Sexual reproduction is the process of development of new organisms through the formation and fusion of gametes. In flowering plants, stamens are male reproductive organs while carpels are female reproductive organs. Sexual reproduction can be summarised as :

Sexual reproduction

Pre Fertilization	Fertilization	Post-Fertilization
This process consists 2 - events : – Gametogenesis i.e formation of male gamete (Androecium), female gamete (gynoecium). Gamete transfer i.e pollengrains carries male gamete are transfered to stigma that leads to fertilization (Ovule have egg)	The process of fusion of gametes and formation of diploid zygote.	The events after zygoto formation . After this embryogenesis is takes place. The ovary develops into fruit, which develops a thick wall called pericarp which is protective in function.

Double Fertilization

fusion of female gametophyte with two male gametes.

Male Reproduction Unit

It includes

- Stamen – unit of male gamete, consists anther, connective and filament.
- Microsporangium – sporangium containing micropores.
- Microsporogenesis – Formation of micropores or pollen grains
- Pollen-grains – it consists male reproductive bodies of flower.

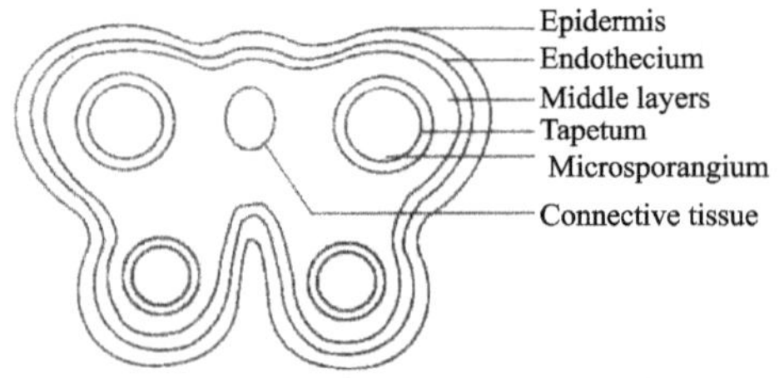

T. S. of young anther

Female Reproduction Unit

It includes

- Gynoecium/Pistil –Female reproductive part and carpet is a unit of gynoecium. Carpel consists three parts–stigma, style and ovary.
- Megasporangium (Ovule) – The integumented nucellus or megasporangium
- Megasporogenesis – The process of formation of megaspore mother cell.
- Embryo sac – Female gametophyte

Sexual Reproduction Cycle

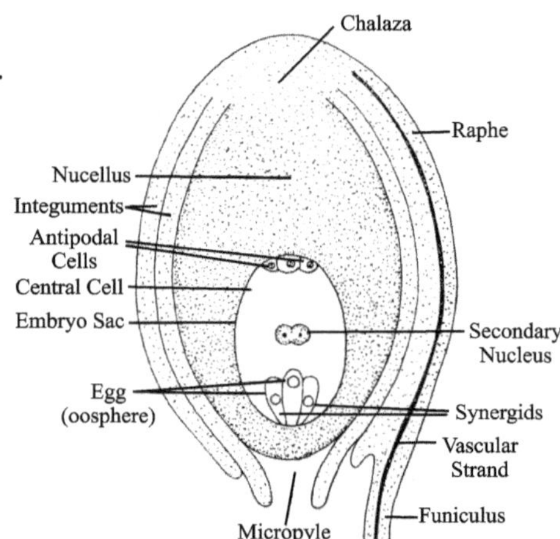

Structure of a typical ovule (anatropous ovule) prior to fertilization

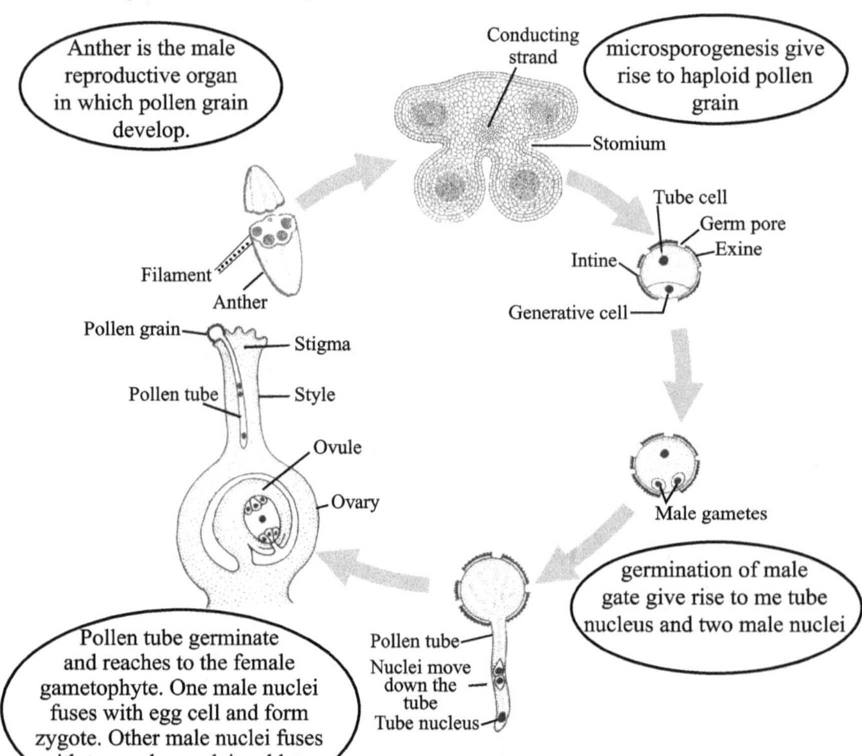

POLLINATION

The process of transfer of pollen grains form an anther to the stigma of the same flower or different flower is called *pollination*.

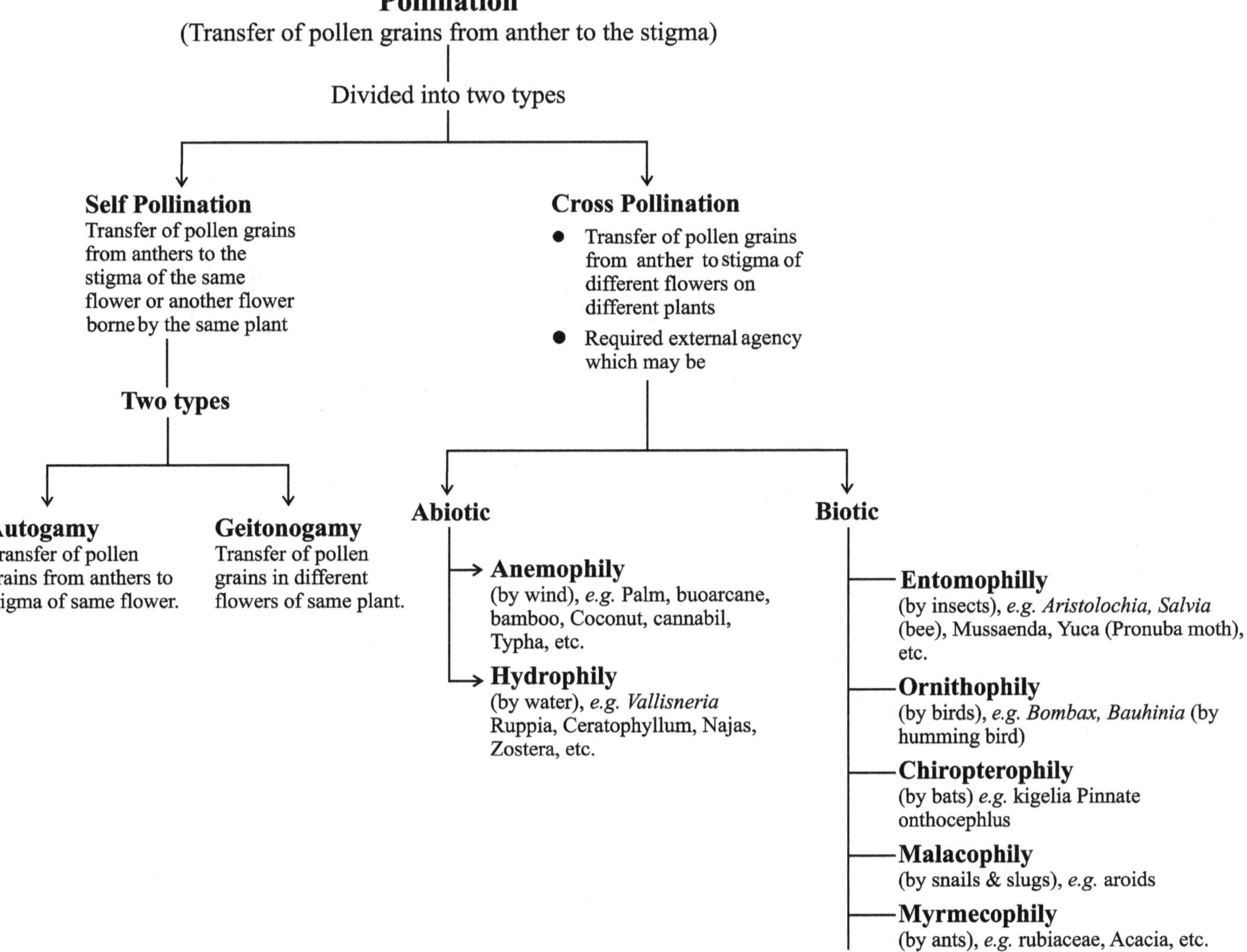

Post Fertilization Events

It involves development of endosperm, embryo, ovules and seeds

Endosperm – Endosperm is the nutritive tissue which provides nourishment to the embryo in seed plant. It also protects the embryo from mechanical injury. It may be completely consumed by developing embryo before it matures (e.g. beans and peas) or it may persist in the mature seed and used up during seed germination, e.g., coconut.

Embryo – The process of development of mature embryo from zygote or oospore is called embryogeny. Zygote starts dividing to produce embryo, together with the development of endosperm.

Seed – Seed is a fertilized ovule. It is the final product of fertilization in angiosperm and acts as a main propagative unit in plants. Ovules mature into seed and simultaneously ovary develops into a fruit.

- Transformation of various units of ovary during seed formation are.

(i)	Ovary wall	– Fruit wall
(ii)	Ovary	– Fruit
(iii)	Integuments	– Seed coats
(iv)	Outer	– Testa
(v)	Inner	– Tegmen
(vi)	Ovule	– Seed

- Apomixis is the production of seed without fertilization.
- The normal process of cell cycle involving meiosis and fertilization is called amphimixis.
- Polyembryony is the state of occurrence of more than one embryo in a seed, e.g. onion and groundnut.

- **Emasculation** – It is the process of removal of anther from the flower bud before the anther dehisces
- **Artificial hybridisation** – It is the process in which the desired pollen grains are taken out by emasculation and then pollinated on specific stigma.

FRUIT

Fruit is a mature ovary. The ovary wall thickens to become the **Pericarp**.

Most fruits are **simple fruits;** they are derived from an individual ovary, either simple or compound. Peaches and plums are good example of **simple fleshy fruits. Aggregate fruits (etaerio)** develop from the multicarpellary apocarpous ovary. The **composite fruits (multiple)** develop from the complete inflorescence.

If fruit is developed from the ovary only, the fruit is known as the **true fruit.** But sometimes some other floral parts take part in the formation of fruit, such fruits are known as **false fruits;** e.g., coconut, apple.

S.No.	(Fruit)	(Type)	(Edible Part)
A. Simple Fruit			
1.	Apple	Pome	Fleshy thalamus
2.	Almond	Drupe	Seed
3.	Banana	Berry	Mesocarp and endo-carp
4.	Coconut	Drupe	Endosperm, cotyledon and embryo
5.	Cashew	Nut	Cotyledons and fleshy pedicel
6.	Datepalm	Drupe	Pericarp
7.	Grape	Berry	Pericarp and Placenta
8.	Groundnut	Lomentum	Seeds (cotyledons)
9.	Guava	Berry	Pericarp and Placenta
10.	Litchi	Nut	Fleshy aril
11.	Mango	Drupe	Mesocarp
12.	Muskmelon	Pepo	Mesocarp and endo-carp
13.	Orange	Hespiridium	Endocarpic juicy hairs
14.	Pear	Pome	Fleshy thalamus
15.	Plum	Drupe	Epicarp and mesocarp
16.	Papaya	Berry	Mesocarp
17.	Pomegranate	Balausta	Juicy testa
18.	Tamarind	Lomentum	Mesocarp
19.	Raspberry	Etaerio of drupes	Mesocarp
20.	Tomato	Berry	Pericarp and placenta
21.	Watermelon/ Muskmelon	Pepo	Mesocarp and endo-carp
22.	Strawberry	Etaerio of achenes	Succulent Thalamus
23.	Wood apple	Amphisarca	Mesocarp and endo-carp
24.	Lotus	Etaerio of archens	Thalamus and seed
25.	Wheat, Rice, Barley	Caryopsis	Endosperm and em-bryo
26.	Fig	Syconus	Perianth, Fleshy Receptacle
27.	Walnut	Drupe	Cotyledons
28.	Jack fruit	Sorosis	Bracts, perianth and seeds
29.	Water chest-nut	Nut	Pericarp and aril
30.	Mulberry	Sorosis	Perianth, Mesocarp
31.	Pine apple	Sorosis	Peduncle, seeds and perianth

REPRODUCTION IN ANIMALS

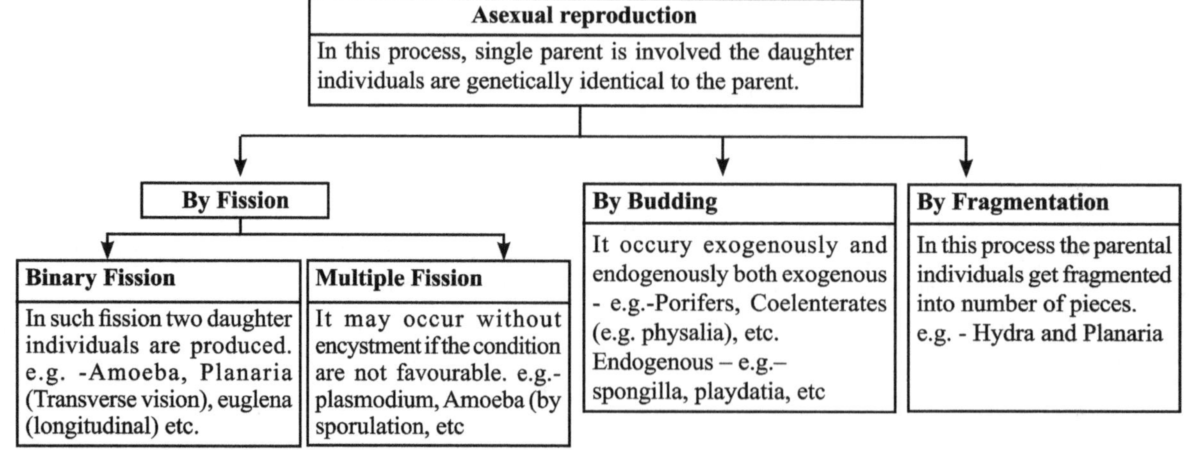

Cloning

It is the process used to create an exact copy of a cell, tissue or a complete organism. It was performed by Ian Wilmut and his colleagues at Roslin institute Edinburg, Scotland. They cloned sheep named "Dolly". she was born on 5th july 1996 and was the 1st mammal cloned from adult somatic cell. She died on 14th feb 2003 due to lung disease.

SEXUAL REPRODUCTION

- In this process Two parents are involved and Gametes formation occurs.

- The daughter individuals are genetically different from both the parents.

- The parental individuals may be unisexual (**dioecious**) or bisexual/ hermaphrodite (**monoecious**)

  e.g. Paramaecium, Plasmodium, Hydra, tape worm and earthworm.

Reproduction in Human

In human beings reproduction is much the same as for mammals specialized reproductive organs are located in their lower abdomen.

- Male system consists of glands called testes that make microscopic, tadpole - shaped sperm cell

- The female has glands called ovaries that make pin point - sized egg cell.

- Humans are sexually reproducing and viviparous.

- Rate of reproduction is slower in sexual reproduction.

- Human are unisexual. The reproductive system of each sex consists of many organs. The latter are distinguishable into primary and secondary sex organs. Besides these, there are some accessory sex characters.

Puberty is the name for the time when body beings to develop and change as move from kid to adult. Usually, puberty starts between ages 8 and 13 in girls and ages 9 and 15 in boys.

Male Reproductive System

- Its acessory or external sexual character are low pitch voice, beard, broad shoulder, Moustaches etc.

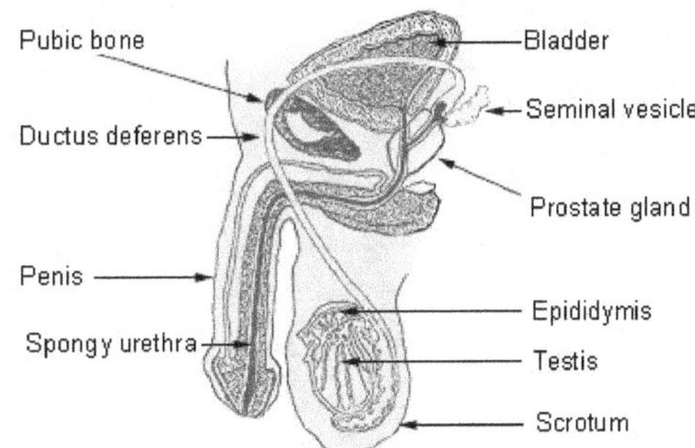

(Fig. Anatomy of male reproductive system)

Female Reproductive System

- Accessory or external sex characters of female are high pitched voice, smooth face, narrow shoulder, broad hips etc.

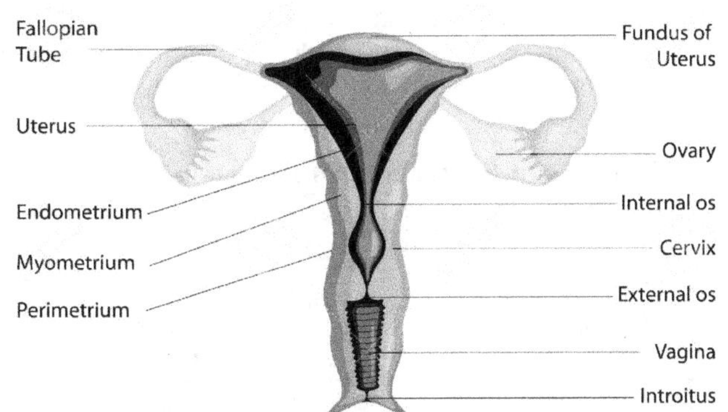

(Fig. Anatomy of female reproductive system)

REPRODUCTIVE HEALTH

- According to the World Health Organisation (WHO), reproductive health means a total well-being in all aspects of reproduction, i.e., physical, emotional, behavioural and social.

Table : Method of Birth control

S. No.	Method	Action
(1)	Vasectomy	Man's vasa deferentia are cut and tied permanently blocking sperm passage.
(2)	Tubectomy	a small part of the fallopian tube is removed or tied up through a small incision in the abdomen or through vagina.
(3)	Intrauterine device (IUD) non-medicated IUDs (e.g., Lippes loop), copper releasing IUDs (CuT, Cu7, Multiload 375) and the hormone releasing IUDs (Progestasert, LNG-20).	Small plastic or metal device placed in the uterus to -prevent implantation. Some contain copper, other release hormones.
(4)	Oral contraceptive e.g. – saheli. MalaD. etc.	Synthetic estrogens and progesterones prevent normal menstrural cycle; primarily prevent ovulation.
(5)	Male condom	Thin rubber sheath on erect penis collects ejaculated semen.
(6)	Female condom	Plastic pouch inserted into vagina catches semen.
(7)	Diaphargm	Soft rubber cup covers entrance to uterus, prevents sperm from reaching egg and holds spermicide.
(8)	Cervical cap	Miniature diaphragm covers cervix closely, prevents sperm from reaching egg and holds spermicide.

- **MTP** is used to get rid of unwanted pregnancies and where continuation of the pregnancy could be harmful or even fatal either to mother or to the foetus or both.

SEXUALLY TRANSMITTED DISEASES

- Diseases which are transmitted through sexual intercourse are collectively called sexually transmitted diseases (STD) or venereal diseases (VD) or reproductive tract infections (RTI).
- These disease are caused by a widerange of bacterial, viral, protozoan, fungal agents and ectoparasites.

Table : Some STDs and their pathogens

	Disease	Pathogen
	Bacterial	
1.	Syphilis	Treponema pallidum
2.	Gonorrhoea	Neisseria gonorrnoeae
3.	Chancroid	Haemophilus ducreyi
4.	Vaginitis	Gardnerella vaginalis
5.	Chlamydiasis	Chlamydia trachomatis
	Viral	
6.	Herpes genitalis	HSV-2 (DNA) virus
7.	Condyloma acuminatum	Papova (DNA) virus
8.	Molluscum contagiosum	Pox (DNA) virus
	Protozoan	
9.	Trichomoniasis	Trichomonas vaginalis

INFERTILITY

- Inability to conceive or produce children even after 2 years of unprotected sexual cohabitation is called infertility.
- Various methods are now available to help such couples.

The main ART-techniques includes:

In vitro fertilization (IVF)

Zygote intra fallopian transfer (ZIFT)

Intra cytoplasmic sperm injection (ICST).

Gamete intra fallopian transfer (GIFT).

Surrogacy or surrogate motherhood.

Gestational Surrogacy

Surrogacy is used for delivering a baby on behalf of other parent. In this procedure a woman carries and delivers a pregnancy for another couple. This woman, the surrogate mother, may be genetically unrelated to the child.

MULTIPLE CHOICE QUESTIONS

1. Pick out the mismatched pair in the following pairs:-
   A. Sperms → testes
   B. Eggs → ovaries
   C. Pollen → anther
   D. Ovule → somatic cell
   (a) A   (b) B
   (c) C   (d) D

2. Contraception (to avoid pregnancy) can be attained by.
   (a) use of condoms   (b) oral pills
   (c) copper-T   (d) all of these above

3. All are hormones except
   (a) Estrogen   (b) Testosterone
   (c) FSH   (d) Tocopherol

4. External fertilization takes place in
   (a) Crocodiles   (b) Frogs
   (c) Tortoise   (d) Amoeba

5. Fertilization is
   (a) Formation of seedling from seeds
   (b) Transfer of pollen to the carpel part
   (c) Fusion of sperm and ovum.
   (d) All the above

6. The development of off spring from any part of body is called
   (a) Asexual reproduction
   (b) Sexual reproduction
   (c) Vegetative reproduction
   (d) All the above

7. The migration of pollen grains to stigma is called as
   (a) Fertilization   (b) Pollination
   (c) Fusion   (d) Reproduction

8. The anther contains
   (a) Sepals.   (b) Ovules.
   (c) Carpel.   (d) Pollen grains.

9. When a seed matures into a seedling under favourable conditions it is called
   (a) Fertilization   (b) Reproduction
   (c) Pollination   (d) Germination

10. In sweet potato vegetative propagation takes place by
    (a) Root   (b) Stem
    (c) Leaves   (d) All of them

11. The process of development of organism like itself is called
    (a) Budding   (b) Flowering
    (c) Reproduction   (d) None of the above

12. Progesterone is secreted by
    (a) Corpus luteum   (b) Thyroid
    (c) Thymus   (d) Testes

13.
Column-I		**Column-II**
A.	Pollen & stigma	P. female part in plants
B.	Radicle in a cotyledon	Q. root
C.	Ovule	R. root
D.	Pcumule	S. male reproductive parts in a plant.

    (a) A-P ; B-Q ; C-R ; D-P
    (b) A-S ; B-Q ; C-R ; D-R
    (c) A-P ; B-Q ; C-S ; D-R
    (d) A-S ; B-P ; C-R ; D-Q

14. Orchids of the genus *Cryptostylis* are known to maintain reproductive isolation because their flowers look and smell like females of the wasps of genus *Lissopimpla*. When the male wasp visits and attempts to mate with the flower, the shape of anther and stigma allows correct placement and transfer of pollen to the wasp, which then transfers the pollen to species specific flower that it next attempts to mate with. This prezygotic barrier that prevents inter-species cross-pollination in *Cryptostylis* is best explained by:
    (a) behavioural isolation through mimicry
    (b) mechanical isolation through mimicry
    (c) temporal isolation
    (d) habitat isolation

15. Which is common method of multiplication of *Yeast* and *Hydra*.
    (a) Budding
    (b) Fragmentation
    (c) Binary fission
    (d) Vegetative reproduction

16. Callus formation in plants means
    (a) growth of cancer cells.
    (b) microorganism attack only.
    (c) a disease.
    (d) tissue culture technique.

17. The number of chromosomes in a female fertilized egg cell is
    (a) 44   (b) 21   (c) 23   (d) 46

18. Menstruation takes place as
    (a) The egg is fertilized and is nourished.
    (b) The egg is released from the ovaries and comes to the uterus.
    (c) The egg released is not fertilized, the lining becomes thick and breaks down.
    (d) None of the above.

19. Fertilization takes place in the
    (a) ovary sacs   (b) fallopian tube
    (c) urethra   (d) vagina

20. Ovulation in mammals is caused by
    (a) FSH and TSH   (b) FSH and LH
    (c) FSH and LTH   (d) LTH and LH

21. Cowper's glands are found in
    (a) male mammals   (b) female mammals
    (c) male amphibians   (d) female amphibians

22. Vegetative propagation refers to formation of new plants from
    (a) stem, roots and flowers
    (b) stem, roots and leaves
    (c) stem, flowers and fruits
    (d) stem, leaves and flowers

23. Cross pollination brings about .... recombination in new plants.
    (a) Genetic   (b) chromosomes
    (c) Genes   (d) chromatids
24. 'Saheli' a new oral contraceptive developed by
    (a) All Indian Institute of Medical Science
    (b) Central Drug Research Institute
    (c) Health Care Pvt. Ltd.
    (d) Bharat Immunologicals & Biologicals corp. Ltd.
25. IUDs stands for
    (a) Intra Uterine Devices
    (b) Internal Uterine Devices
    (c) Inseminated Uterine Devices
    (d) Injected Uterine Devices
26. The most important component of the oral contraceptive pills is
    (a) progesterone
    (b) growth hormone
    (c) thyroxine
    (d) luteinizing hormone
27. **Assertion (A) :** *Amoeba* reproduces by fission.
    Reason (R) : All unicellular organisms reproduce by asexual methods.   **[IAS Prelim]**
    (a) Both A and R are individually true and R is the correct explanation of A
    (b) Both A and R are individually true but R is not the correct explanation of A
    (c) A is true but R is false
    (d) A is false but R is true
28. Polar body is produced during the formation of –
    (a) Sperm   (b) Secondary oocyte
    (c) Oogonium   (d) Spermatocytes
29. Egg is liberated from ovary in
    (a) Secondary oocyte stage
    (b) Primary oocyte stage
    (c) Oogonial stage
    (d) Mature ovum stage
30. Which of the following statements are true for flowers?
    A. Flowers are always bisexual.
    B. They are the sexual reproductive organs.
    C. They are produced in all groups of plants.
    D. After fertilization they give rise to fruits.
    (a) A and D   (b) B and C
    (c) A and C   (d) B and D
31. Consider the following statements :
    A. Plants are divided into five groups: Thallophytes, Bryophytes, Pteridophytes, Gymnosperms and Angiosperms.
    B. Lichens are examples of liverworts.
    C. The algae are vascular plants.

D. Angiosperm is the least diversified form than any other plant groups.
Which of these statement(s) is/are correct ?
    (a) A, B and C   (2) B, C and D
    (c) A and D   (d) All are correct
32. According to which of the following organization "reproductive health means a total well-being in all aspects of reproduction"?
    (a) WHL   (b) UNESCO
    (c) WHO   (d) WWW
33. In a bisexual flower, if androecium and gynoecium mature at different times, the phenomenon is known as
                          [IAS Prelim]
    (a) dichogamy   (b) herkogamy
    (c) heterogamy   (d) monogamy
34. Which one of the following is monogamous?
                          [IAS Prelim]
    (a) Wolf   (b) Walrus
    (c) Seal   (d) Deer
35. In artificial insemination (AI) process. Which of the following is/are introduced into the uterus of the female?   **[CDS 2016-I]**
    (a) Egg only   (b) Fertilized egg
    (c) Sperm only   (d) Egg and sperm
36. The Germplasm is required for the propagation of plants and animals, Germplasm is the :   **[CDS 2016-I]**
    1. genetic resources
    2. seeds or tissues for breeding
    3. egg and sperm repository
    4. a germ cell's determining zone
    Select the correct answer using the code given below
    (a) 1 only   (b) 1, 2 and 3
    (c) 2 and 3 only   (d) 2 and 4
37. An irregular mode of reproduction resulting in the development of an embryo without fertilization is called
    1. Parthenogenesis   **[CDS 2016-II]**
    2. Apogamy
    3. Sporophytic budding
    Select the correct answer using the code given below.
    (a) 1 only   (b) 2 only
    (c) 2 and 3 only   (d) 1, 2 and 3
38. Syngamy results in formation of   **[CDS 2017-I]**
    (a) haploid zygote
    (b) diploid zygote
    (c) non-motile male gametes
    (d) motile male gametes
39. The colourful part of the Sunflower or Marigold plant is
                          [NDA 2017-I]
    (a) Flower   (b) Inflorescence
    (c) Fruit   (d) Seed

ANSWER KEY															
1.	(d)	**2.**	(d)	**3.**	(c)	**4.**	(b)	**5.**	(c)	**6.**	(a)	**7.**	(b)	**8.**	(d)
9.	(d)	**10.**	(a)	**11.**	(c)	**12.**	(a)	**13.**	(b)	**14.**	(b)	**15.**	(a)	**16.**	(d)
17.	(d)	**18.**	(c)	**19.**	(b)	**20.**	(a)	**21.**	(a)	**22.**	(b)	**23.**	(a)	**24.**	(b)
25.	(a)	**26.**	(a)	**27.**	(a)	**28.**	(b)	**29.**	(a)	**30.**	(d)	**31.**	(c)	**32.**	(c)
33.	(a)	**34.**	(d)	**35.**	(c)	**36.**	(b)	**37.**	(d)	**38.**	(b)	**39.**	(b)		

NUTRITION, HEALTH AND DISEASES

NUTRITION

Nutrition is the process of intake and utilisation of nutrients/food, by an organisms to get energy which is further used in various life processes. The substance that is needed to keep them living is called nutrient.

Nutrients are organic and inorganic substances which the organism obtains from its surroundings and uses it as a source of energy or for biosynthesis of its body constituents.

Organic nutrients - Carbohydrates, Proteins, Fats

Inorganic nutrients - Water, Carbon dioxide, Minerals (Iron, copper, zinc, etc.)

NUTRITION IN PLANTS

Various organisms live in different environmental conditions and they have different methods of obtaining nutrients from the environment. The method of obtaining food by the organism is called **mode of nutrition.** Depending on the mode of nutrition, all organisms can be classified into two major groups – **Autotrophic and Heterotrophic.**

Nutrition in Plants	
Autotrophic	**Heterotrophic**
Organisms which can make their own organic food from inorganic raw materials (carbondioxide and water) and remain independent of obtaining external source of organic compound are called **Autotrophs**. All green plants are autotrophs.	Plants are generally autotrophic but there some plants which are unable to manufacture their food, due to lack of chlorophyll like parasitic plants saprophytic and insectivorous plants or symbionts

- In addition to carbon, hydrogen and oxygen plants require a variety of mineral elements for their survival. Absorption of minerals and their utilization by plant is called **mineral nutrition.**
- The technique of growing plants in a nutrient solution is known as **hydroponics or soilless growth.**
- Aeroponics is a system of growing plants with their roots bathed in nutrient mist (a cloud of moisture in air).

Role of Micro and Macro Elements and Their Deficiency Symptoms

S. no.	Name of element (location)	Functions	Deficiency symptoms
1.	**Nitrogen** (NO_2^-, NO_3^- or NH_4^+)	Major constituent of proteins, nucleic acids, vitamins and minerals.	**Chlorosis** of leaves, stunting of plants, dormancy of lateral buds, inhibition of cell division etc.
2.	**Phosphorous** ($H_2PO_4^-$, or HPO_4^{2-})	Constituent of cell membrane, nucleic acids, nucleotides and some proteins.	Delay in seed germination, reduced growth, purple or red spots on leaves etc.
3.	**Potassium** (K^+)	Determine cation- anion balance in cell. Involved in protein synthesis, closing & opening of stomata.	**Scorched leaf tips,** shorter internodes, chlorosis in interveinal, loss of apical dominance, loss of cambial activity.
4.	**Calcium** Ca^{2+})	Activate certain enzymes and regulates metabolic activities. Used in synthesis of cell wall (middle lamella). Help to stabilize the structure of the chromosomes.	Stunted growth, necrosis (death of tissue) of meristematic regions, chlorosis along the margins of young leaves, **wither tip disease,** premature flower abscission, **blossoms end rots of tomato.**

5.	**Magnesium** (divalent Mg^{2+})	Activate enzymes in respiration, photo-synthesis, DNA and RNA synthesis.	Chlorosis between leaf veins, necrosis on older leaves. Premature leaf abscission, reduced growth.
6.	**Sulphur** (SO_4^{2-})	Constituent of amino acids like Cysteine and methionine and main constituent of several coenzymes, vitamins (thymine, Co-A and ferredoxin, biotin)	Chlorosis of younger leaves, stunted growth, anthocyanin accumulation, leaf curl, less juice content in citrus, **yellow disease of tea, marsh spots (peas).**
7.	**Iron** (Fe^{3+})	Constituent of ferredoxin and cytochromes. Involves in electron transfer. Activates catalase and Helps in formation of chlorophyll.	**Chlorosis**-initiates in intravenous regions and then in the complete leaf, growth reduced, inhibition of chloroplast formation.

PHOTOSYNTHESIS

Green plants are autotrophic in the sense that they synthesize their own organic food from inorganic raw materials. This is done by the process of **photosynthesis**.

$$6CO_2 + 12H_2O \xrightarrow[\text{Chlorophyll}]{\text{Light}} C_6H_{12}O_6 + 6H_2O + 6O_2$$

carbon dioxide   water   Glucose   water   oxygen

PHOTOSYNTHESIS IN HIGHER PLANTS

- In higher plants photosynthesis occurs particularly in specialized cells called mesophyll cells of leaves. These cells contain **chloroplast**, which is the actual sites for photosynthesis. It fixes CO_2 into carbohydrates.
- Chloroplasts are double membrane bound organelle. The space limited by the inner membrane of the chloroplast is called the **stroma**.
- A number of organised flattened membranous sacs (called the **thylakoids**) are present in the stroma. Thylakoids are arranged in stacks like the piles of coins called **grana**.

Photosynthetic Pigments

- **Pigments** are the organic molecules that absorb light of specific wavelengths in the visible region due to presence of conjugated double bonds in their structures.
- **Chlorophyll-*a***
  Chlorophyll *b*
  Chlorophyll *c*
  Carotenes – $C_{40}H_{56}$ and **Xanthophylls** – $C_{40}H_{56}O_2$.
- Chl-*a* and carotenes are universal pigment, which are found in all O_2 liberating cells. Chlorophylls are soluble only in organic solvents like ketones, ethers etc.
- **Carotenoids** absorb light energy and transfer it to *Chl a* and thus act as **accessory pigments**.

MECHANISM OF PHOTOSYNTHESIS

- **Photosynthesis is** an **oxidation-reduction** process in which water is oxidised to release O_2 and CO_2 is reduced to form starch and sugars.
- These are of two types
- (i) light Reaction
- (ii) Dark Reaction

Light reaction

It occurs in **grana fraction** of chloroplast and in this reaction are included those activities, which are dependent on light. Assimilatory powers (ATP and $NADPH_2$) are mainly produced in this light reaction.

Non-cyclic Photophosphorylation

- In light reaction, the formation of ATP from ADP in presence of light called **non-cyclic photophosphorylation**.
  The system is dominant in green plants. It involves both PS-I and PS-II.
- Flow of electrons is **unidirectional**. Here H_2O is utilized and O_2 evolution occurs. In this chain, high energy electrons released from 'P-680' do not return to 'P-680' but pass through pheophytin, plastoquinone, cytochrome b_6-*f* complex plastocyanin (Cu containing pigment) and then enter P-700. Because in this process high energy electrons released from 'P-680' do not return to 'P-680' and ATP (1 molecule) is formed, this is called **Noncyclic photophosphorylation. ATP is synthesized at only one step.**
- *This non-cyclic photophosphorylation* is also known as Z-scheme (because of shape of path of electron-flow) and this was given by Hill and Bendall (1960).

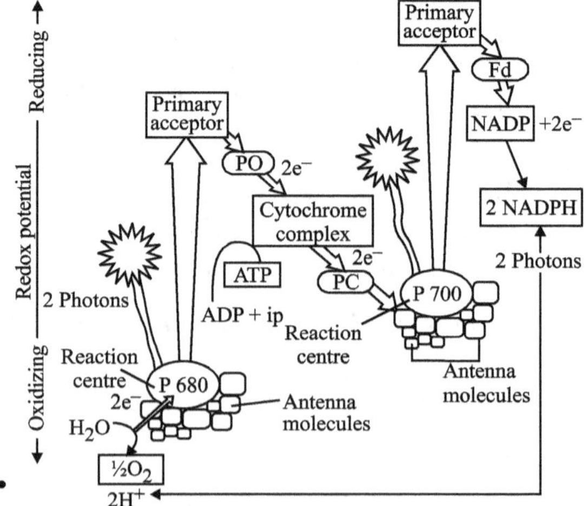

Non-cyclic photophosphorylation (z-scheme)

Cyclic Photophosphorylation

In this light reaction of photosynthesis, the formation of ATP from ADP and H_3PO_4 in the presence of light & chlorophyll *a* during the cyclic transfer of electrons is called *cyclic photophosphorylation*.

The system is *found dominantly in bacteria. It involves only PS I.*

Flow of electron is cyclic. If NADP is not available then this process will occur. When the photons activate PS I, a pair of electrons are raised to a higher energy level. They are captured by primary acceptor which passes them on to ferredoxin, plastoquinone, cytochrome complex, plastocyanin and finally back to reaction centre of PS I *i.e.*, P_{700}. At each step of electron transfer, the electrons lose potential energy. Their trip down hill is caused by the transport chain to pump H^+ across the thylakoid membrane.

Dark Reaction

Dark reaction is a thermochemical reaction. It takes place in the **stroma of the chloroplast.**

It is *also called CO_2 fixation or carbon assimilation.*

The dark reaction involves thermochemical reduction of CO_2 to form carbohydrates. This was first established by **Blackman (1905)**, hence it is also called **Blackman reaction.**

There are two main pathways for the biosynthetic or dark phase – *Calvin cycle* (C_3) and C_4 *(dicarboxylic acid) cycle.*

Calvin Cycle–(C_3 Cycle)

Carbon assimilation in C_3 plants were explained by **Melvin Calvin**

This is known as C_3 **cycle** because CO_2 reduction is cyclic process and first stable product in this cycle is a 3-C compound

(*i.e.*, 3-Phosphoglyceric acid or -PGA. Calvin cycle occurs in all photosynthetic plants whether they have C_3 or C_4 pathway.

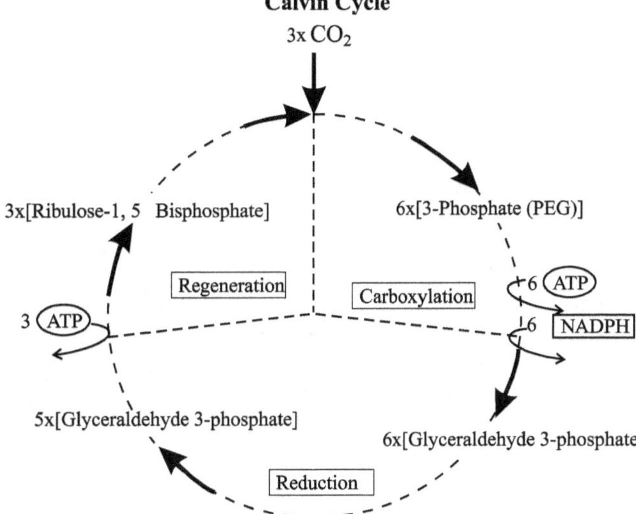

C_4 Cycle

- C_4 acid (dicarboxylic acid) is formed due to carboxylation. It was shown by **Kortschak *et al*** in sugarcane. **Kortschak and Hart** supplied CO_2 to the leaves of sugarcane, they found that the first stable product is a four carbon (C_4) compound oxaloacetic acid instead of 3-carbon atom compound. The detailed study of this cycle was introduced by **M.D. Hatch and C.R. Slack (1966).** So it is called as **"Hatch and Slack cycle".** The stable product in C_4 plant is a dicarboxylic substance. Hence, it is called **dicarboxylic acid cycle or DCA-cycle.**
- C_4 plants are **true xerophytic plants.** They are adapted for hot and dry climate. The important C_4 **plants** are **sugarcane, maize, sorghum,** *Cyperus rotundus, Digitaria brownii, Amaranthus,* etc.
- These plants have **"Kranz"** (German term meaning halo or wreath) **type of leaf anatomy.** The vascular bundles in C_4 leaves are surrounded by a layer of bundle sheath cells that contain large number of chloroplasts.

Table: Difference between C_3 and C_4 Plants

	C_3 Plants	C_4 Plants
1.	Photosynthesis occurs in mesophyll cells.	Photosynthesis occurs in mesophyll and bundle sheath cells.
2.	Kranz anatomy is absent.	Kranz anatomy is present.
3.	RuBP is the primary carbon dioxide acceptor.	PEP is the primary carbon dioxide acceptor.
4.	3-phosphoglyceric acid (3-PGA), a 3C-compound is the first stable product.	Oxaloacetic acid, a 4C-compound is the first stable product of photosynthesis.
5.	Chloroplast are of only one type, *i.e.*, granal.	Chloroplasts are dimorphic, *i.e.*, granal in the mesophyll cells and agranal in the bundle sheath cells.

NUTRITION IN ANIMALS

It is a biochemical process in which animals derives nutrients in the form of organic and inorganic substances for the proper maintenance and for all metabolic and catabolic activities occurs in the body.

Nutrition

Nutrition is divided into three types :

Holozoic

- Holozoic nutrition:- This literally means feeding like an animal. Holozoic nutrition is a mode of heterotrophic nutrition in which an organism takes the complex organic food material into its body by the process of ingestion, which is then digested, absorbed and assimilated in the body cells of the organism.
- Holozoic nutrition is of three types :
(i) Herbivores , (ii) Carnivores , (iii) Omnivores

Saprozoic

- Type of nutrition in which, animals derives nutrients from dead and decayed animals.
  e.g.-insects in drainage, on pickles, etc.

Parasitic

- Organism derives its food from the host cell
  e.g.- plasmodium (causes malaria in man), etc.

Macronutrients Can be Summarized in the Flow Chart give Below:

Macronutrients

Carbohydrate

- This is an energy yielding food nutrients and provides 17 KJ energy to the body.
- Classified into mono, di and polysaccharide food which are absorbed in the form of monosaccharides
- Sources – breads, beans, milk, .spaghetti, etc.

Proteins

- These are also known as building block of body and made up of its smaller unit amino acids.
- It gives 17KJ energy to the body.
- Deficiency causes kwashiorkor and Marasmus
- Sources - eggs, yogurt, fish, sea-food soya bean, milk, etc.

Water

- It maintains health and turgity of every cell, helps to eliminate the excreatory products in the form of sweat, urine, etc Prevents constipation, reduces the high risk of cystitis, moisturizes the skin, carry nutrients and acts as a shock absorber in eyes, spinal -cord and in amniotic sac.

Fats

- These are also energy yielding food nutrients, which provides 37KJ of energy.
- These are broken down into fatty acids and glycerol and then absorbed. It takes part in the transport of fat soluble vitamin A,D,E and K. Excessive intake causes heart diseases, obesity, etc.

Fiber or Roughage

- These are present in the form of soluble fibre and insoluble fiber
- Soluble fibers-legumes, oats, rye, nuts, etc.
- Insoluble fibers, whole grain, nuts and seeds etc.
- It cures gastrointestinal disorders.

VITAMINS

Vitamins are organic compounds essential in trace amounts to the health of animals. Vitamins can be water soluble or fat soluble.

Fat Soluble Vitamins: These vitamins are stored in the liver in the form of fat droplets.

Name	Source	Functions	Deficiency symptoms
Vitamin A (Retinol)	Carrot, tomato, papaya, mango, milk, eggs, cod-liver oil	Essential role for vision, growth, differentiation of epithelial tissue.	Night blindness, xerophthalmia poor growth, rough and dry skin.
Vitamin D It exists in two Forms **D_2 (Ergocalciferol) and D_3 (cholecalciferol).**	Cod liver oil. Skin can synthesize Vitamin D in the presence of sunlight.	It promotes growth of bones and teeth	Rickets in children and osteomalacia in adult.
Vitamin E (Tocopherol)	Wheat germ, green leafy vegetables. Fats of vegetable origin	Acts as good antioxidant, essential for normal functioning of reproductive organs	Reproductive failure, muscular dystrophy increased haemolysis leading to macrocytic anaemia
Vitamin K There are three derivatives of vitamin K.	Leafy vegetables, wheat germ, Vitamin K is synthesized by bacteria of large intestine.	Helps in blood clotting, prevention of excessive bleeding.	Faulty blood clotting.

Water soluble Vitamins

Water soluble vitamins travel freely through the body, and excess amounts usually are excreted by the kidneys. The body needs water soluble vitamins in frequent small doses. .

| **Vitamin B– Complex** **Vitamin B_1 (Thiamine)** | Whole grain, wheat germ, legumes, nuts, fish. | It acts as precursor of thiamine pyrophosphate (TPP) in TCA cycle (Kerbs Cycle) | **Beri beri** disease (B1) deficiency in alcoholics causes **Wernicke-Korsakoff syndrome** |
| **Vitamin B_2 (Riboflavin)** | Milk, cheese, meats, eggs, legumes, wheat germ mushrooms, green leafy vegetables. | It helps in RBCs production. It acts as FMN and FAD. FMN acts in ETC. however FAD acts in both TCA cycle and ETC. | Cheilosis (Painful inflammation) and cracking of the corners of mouth), Anaemia etc. |

Vitamin B$_3$ (Niacin)	Barley, liver maize, wheat	Plays a key role in skin, digestive system and mental health	Pellagra (skin pigmentation) degeneration of spinal cord)
Vitamin B$_5$ (Pantothenic acid)	Meat, Eggs, Green vegetables Legumes, Milk	Necessary for haematopoiesis, and metabolism	Fatigue, depression, Insomnia, Paresthesia
Vitamin B$_6$ (Pyridoxine)	Yeast, milk, egg yolk, rice, cereals and grams	Synthesis of glucose, aminoacids and neurotransmitters.	Anaemia
Vitamin B$_{12}$ (Cyanocobalamine)	Meat, fish, egg and curd	Formation of RBCs and maintenance of CNS	Pernicious anaemia (RBC deficient in haemoglobin)
Vitamin C (Ascorbic acid)	Cirtrus fruits (amla, guava, tomato etc).	Essential for the formation of RBCs and the production of antibodies.	Its deficiency causes **Scurvy**

HEALTH AND DISEASE

Anything that disturbs the proper functioning of cells, tissues and organs will result in the lack of proper activity of the body or unhealthy body. Thus, health is considered to be the state of perfect functioning of body and mind, unhindered by diseases.

A good health is a healthy body with a healthy mind and healthy attitude.

Health is a state of complete physical, mental and social well being, and not merely an absence of disease or infirmity (W.H.O - 1948). Any change from the normal state that causes discomfort or disability or impairs the health is called as **disease**.

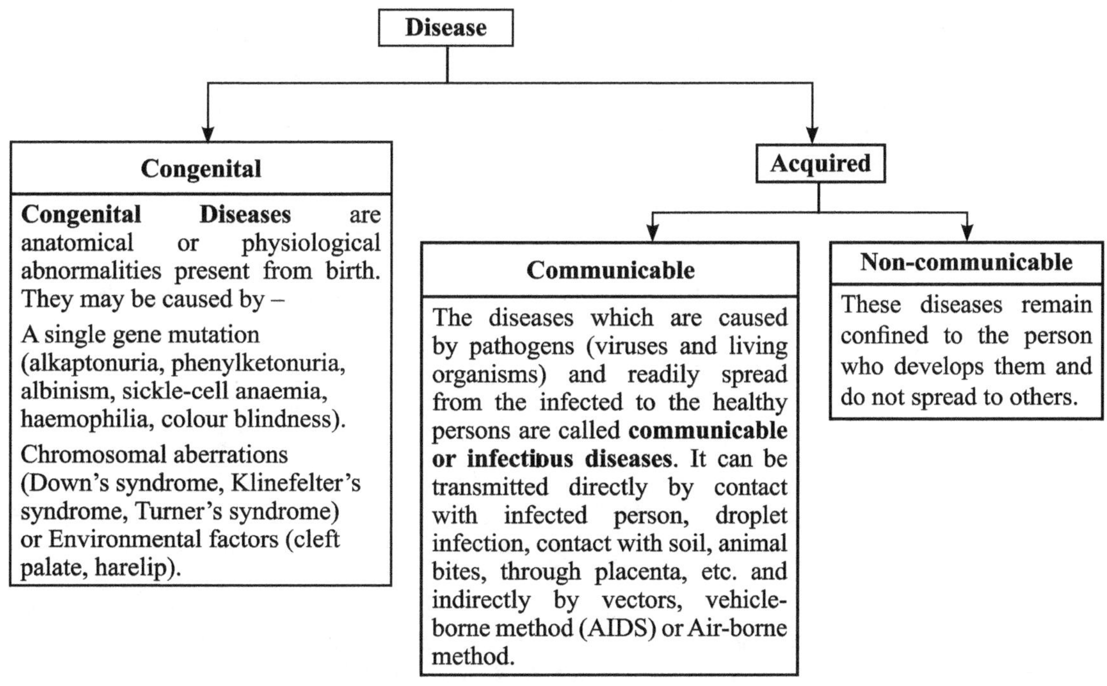

Communicable Disease

• Depending upon the type of causative agent communicable disease are the following types - bacterial, viral, rickettsial, spirochaetal, protozoan, fungal and helminthes etc.

Table : Bacterial Diseases in Human

S. No.	Disease	Pathogen	Main Symptoms
1.	Cholera (Haiza)	Comma shaped -*Vibrio comma* (*V.cholerae*)	Severe diarrhoea and vomiting
2.	Pneumonia	*Diplococcus or Streptococcus pneumoniae*	Sudden chill, chest pain, difficulty in breathing
3.	Typhoid	Rod like motile *Salmonella typhi*	Constant fever
4.	Tuberculosis	*Mycobacterium tuberculosis.*	Cough, bloody sputum, chest pain, loss of weight

Trachoma

Trachoma is the leading infectious cause of blindness across the world. It is responsible for the blindness or visual impairment of around 1.9 million people in 41 countries. Caused by the bacterium *Chlamydia trachomatis*, the infection is transmitted through contact with eye and nasal discharge of infected people. The bodily discharges can be transmitted directly from person to person and also spread through flies which have been in contact with the eyes and noses of infected people.

The Himalayan nation, Nepal becomes the first country in South-East Asia Region to eliminate Trachoma. The World Health Organization (WHO) has validated Nepal for having eliminated trachoma as a public health concern. Nepal joins a small number of countries and sixth in the sequence to have eliminated trachoma. Oman, Morocco, Mexico, Cambodia and Laos are other countries.

Viral Diseases

- Viral diseases are transmitted by contact fomite and droplet method. Types of viral disease are-influenza, small pox, etc.

Table : Viral Diseases in Humans

S.No.	Disease	Pathogen	Main Symptoms
1.	Influenza (Flu)	*Myxovirus Influenzae*	Nasal discharge, sneezing, coughing, fever, body ache
2.	Chicken pox	*Varicella zoster* (DNA virus)	Skin sores that open & emit fluid
3.	Poliomyelitis (polio) (Highly infectious disease of infants and children)	*Poliovirus*	Inflammation of nervous system, muscle shrinkage, limb paralysis
4.	Dengue	*Arbovirus (RNA)*	Mild conjunctivitis, high fever, backache, nausea vomiting etc.
5.	Hepatitis	*Infectious & serum hepatitis viruses (A, B, C, D & E)*	Jaundice due to damaged liver cells
	– Hepatitis A	*Hep. A virus*	Hepatic anorexia resulting in liver damage
	– Hepatitis B	*B Hep virus*	Swelling of liver cells

Nipah virus

Nipah virus (NiV) is a member of the family *Paramyxoviridae*. The Nipah virus infection is a newly emerging zoonosis that causes severe disease in both animals and humans. The natural hosts of the virus are fruit bats and Pigs act as the intermediate host. NiV was initially isolated and identified in 1999 during an outbreak of encephalitis and respiratory illness among pig farmers and people with close contact with pigs in Malaysia and Singapore.

A genetically distinct strain of NiV emerged in Bangladesh and periodic outbreaks have been reported in Bangladesh from 2001. India has reported outbreaks of NiV; most recently in Kerala, May 2018 (mostly from Kozhikode district). Previously it was reported in Siliguri (2001) and Nadia (2007).

Protozoan disease

	Disease	Causative agent	Symptom
1	Malaria	*Plasmodium* (female *anopheles* as vector)	It results in anaemia, toxaemia and splenomegaly. **Antimalarial drugs** are quinine, chloroquine etc. *Dalaprim* drug kills the parasitic stages present in both liver cells and RBC's of blood.
2	Amoebiasis	*Entamoeba histolytica*	It is characterized by abdominal pain alternating diarrhoea and constipation etc Entamoeba secretes cytolysin that erodes the mucous membrane of intestine.

Table : Sexually Transmitted Diseases (STD) in Human

S. No.	Disease	Causative organism	Symptoms-Treatment
1.	AIDS	*Retrovirus – HIV*	Enlarged lymph nodes, long fever, weight loss
2.	Genital Herpes	*Herpes simplex virus*	Painful ulcer on genitals
3.	Genital warts	*Human papilloma virus (HPVs)*	Tumor of the vulva, vagina, anus and penis
4.	Syphilis	*Treponema pallidum*	Cancer and skin eruption – Benzene and Penicillin

Non-Communicable Diseases (NCD)

The main non-communicable diseases are *diabetes, inflammatory diseases of joints* such as arthritis, gout, cardiovascular diseases and cancer.

Diabetes Mellitus

Diabetes is characterized by chronic hyperglycemia which is excessive concentration of glucose in the blood. It primarily occurs as a result of relative or complete lack of insulin secretion by the β cells of islets of Langerhans in pancreas.

Arthritis

Arthritis is any inflammatory condition of the joints characterized by pain and swelling.

Arthritis

Rheumatoid arthritis	Osteoarthritis	Gout
It is characterized by inflammation of the synovial membrane. It is kind of rheumatoid arthritis that occurs in younger **people** is **Still's disease**, and usually starts in the small joints in the hand and progress to other body joints.	It is a common disease among the elderly persons resulting from erosion of articular cartilage. In osteoarthritis, the secretion of lubricating synovial fluid between the bones at the joint stops.	Gout results from accumulation of uric acid crystals in the synovial joints. It is a disease associated with an inborn error of uric acid metabolism that increases production or interferes with the excretion of uric acid.

Cardiovascular Diseases

- Cardiovascular diseases refer to a number of diseases associated with the blood vascular system.
- Some major cardiovascular diseases are **rheumatic heart disease, hypertensive heart disease** and **coronary heart disease.**

Cause of Death across world

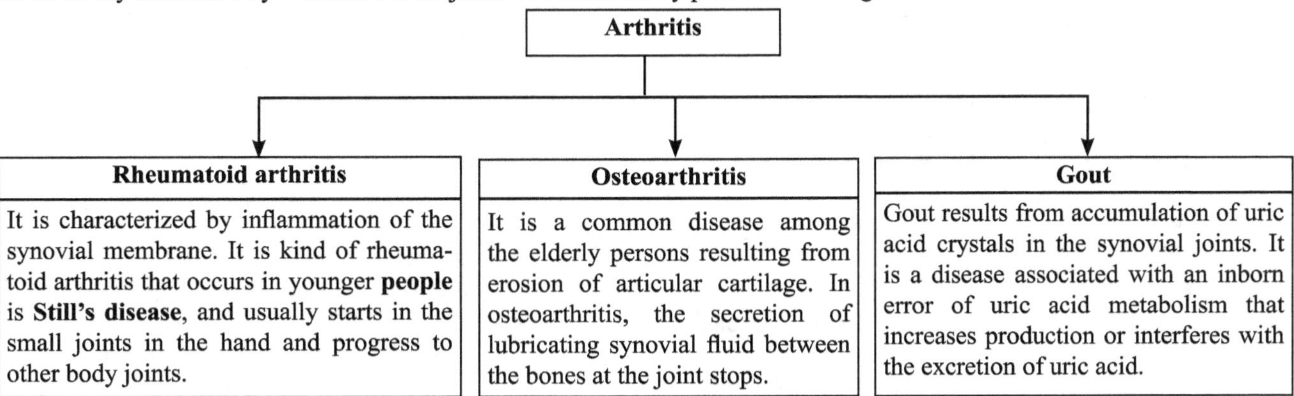

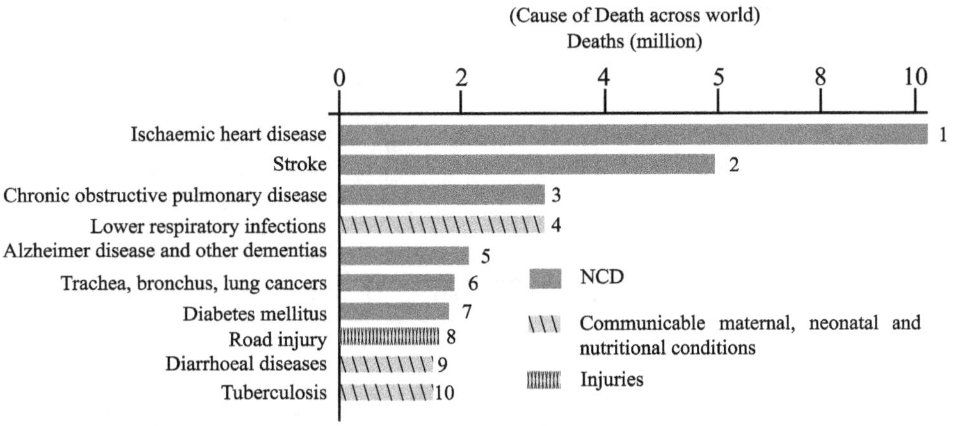

Source : Gobal Health estimates 2016: Deaths by Cause. Age. Sex. by Country and by Region, 2000-2016. Geneva. World Health Organisation. 2018

CANCER

Cancer is an abnormal and uncontrolled division of cells, known as cancer cells, that invade and destroy the surrounding tissues. **Neoplasm** (called **tumor**) is a new abnormal tissue which is capable of continued growth. Tumors may be **benign** and **malignant**.

Tumor	
Benign	**Malignant**
Benign tumor is a large localized mass of abnormal tissue enclosed in connective tissue which does not invade adjacent tissue.	**Malignant tumor** is not encapsulated and is capable of invading adjacent tissues and distant sites.

Symptoms of Cancer

- Thickening or lump in the breast or any other part of the body.
- Changes in bowel or bladder habits.
- Indigestion of difficulty in swallowing.
- Unexplained changes in weight.

Causes of Cancer

- **Chemical** or **physical agents** that can cause cancer are known as **carcinogen**.
  Depending on their mode action, carcinogens fall into the following main categories:
  (i) Agents that can cause alterations in the genetic material (DNA), resulting in oncogenic transformation.
  (ii) Agents that promote the proliferation of cells, which have already undergone genetic alterations responsible for oncogenic transformation. These agents are called **tumour promoter**, *e.g.* some growth factors and hormone.
  (iii) Cancer causing DNA and RNA viruses (tumour viruses) have been shown to be associated with oncogenic transformation.

Treatment

- Surgery : By removing the entire cancerous tissue and infected lymph nodes.
- Radiation: Cobalt therapy (Co-60), X-rays radiations are given. These radiations destroy the rapidly dividing cells.
- Chemotherapy: Anti-cancerous drugs
  like: Vincristine and Vinblastine obtained from
  Catharanthus roseus (*vinca rosea*)
- Most of cancer are treated by combination therapy of surgery, radiation and anti cancerous drug.

AIDS

- AIDS (Acquired Immuno Deficiency Syndrome) is a chronic life threatening disorder which damages the human body's immune system. It is **caused by HIV** (human immuno-deficiency virus) which belong to retrovirus (group of RNA virus) The HIV can only survive in body fluids like blood, semen, vaginal secretion etc.

- HIV is transmitted through body fluids by- Sexual contact blood contact and by mother to child by placenta,
- HIV is not transmitted through - ordinary contact (hugging, dancing, talking, touching etc.) with someone who has HIV or AIDS; sweat, tears or saliva etc. The major cell affected by HIV is the *helper-T-lymphocyte or* $T_{Helper cells}$

Investigation

- Screening test is Enzyme Linked Immuno sorbent assay (E.L.I.S.A.) .
- Confirmatory tests : **Western blot test** Detects antibodies (proteins) in patient's serum.

Treatment

- Drugs used are -
  - AZT (Azidothymidine) or Zidowdine
  - DDI (Dideoxyinosine)
  - Foscarnet
  These drugs inhibit the enzyme of HIV.
- Highly active antiretroviral therapy (HAART) is a combination of three or more antiretroviral agents (called triple therapy or HAART), which has been highly effective in reducing the number of HIV particles in the blood stream and as a result increase the CD4 count.

IMMUNE SYSTEM

- System which protect the body from disease is called **immune system**.
- The immune system consisting several organs as well as WBC in blood and lymph has the job of fighting off invading pathogens and preventing growth and spread of cancers.
- Lymphoid organs are those organs where origin and maturation and proliferation of lymphocyte occur.
- The **primary lymphoid organs** are **bone marrow** and **thymus**.
- **Bone marrow** manufactures the billions of WBC needed by the body every day. Some newly produced WBC remain in the bone marrow to mature and specialize and while others travel to the **thymus** to mature.

Acquired Immunity

- It is the resistance that an individual acquires during life. This is generated in response to an exposure to the microoganism in question. This type of immunity is found only in vertebrates. It is also called **adaptive or specific immunity**. This immunity is acquired after birth by experience and recognises and selectively eliminate the pathogen.

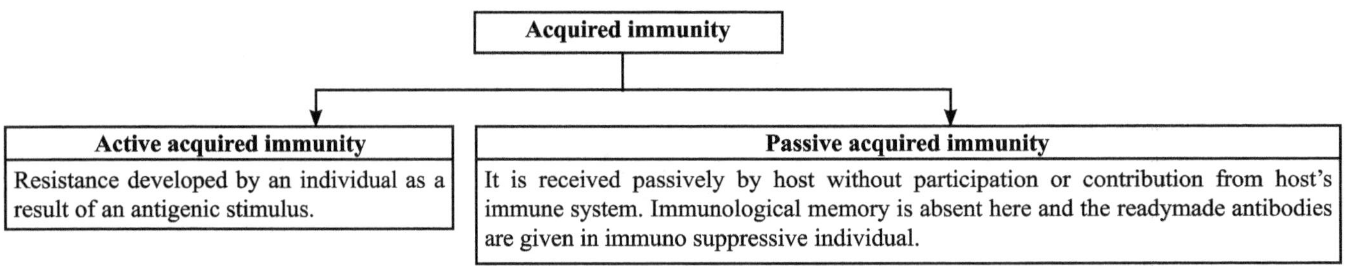

Acquired immunity	
Active acquired immunity	**Passive acquired immunity**
Resistance developed by an individual as a result of an antigenic stimulus.	It is received passively by host without participation or contribution from host's immune system. Immunological memory is absent here and the readymade antibodies are given in immuno suppressive individual.

Antibodies: These are complex glycoproteins made up of polypeptide chains.

S. No.	Group of Antibodies	Main Characters and occurrence	Functions
1.	IgA	The primary antibodies present in colostrum, present in saliva, mucus and other secretions.	Protection of mucous membranes and outer surface of body and protection from inhaled ingested pathogens.
2.	IgD	Present in trace amount on the surface of lymphocytes in blood.	Activation of B-lymphocytes and development and maturation of immune reactions.
3.	IgE	Present in very small quantities, show specific linkage with mast cells and basophils.	Stimulation of mast cells. Related to allergic reactions and protection from parasites.
4.	IgG	Most abundantly found antibodies, main immunoglobulin of blood and interstitial fluid which has capacity to pass through placenta.	Stimulate the complementary system, provide immune power to human embryo and specific linkage with phagocytic cells for phagocytosis.
5.	IgM	Oldest and first antibody generated in response to antigens, present in blood plasma (80%) and interstitial fluids and largest sized immunoglobulin with pentameric form, M.W.	First line of defence against bacteria, perfection of agglutination, related to complement system.

Mission Indradhanush

Government of India has launched Mission Indradhanush to immunise all children under the age of 2 years against 7 vaccine-preventable diseases. Expecting mothers are also included in this national mission. Mission Indradhanush aims to cover all those children by 2020 who are either unvaccinated, or are partially vaccinated against 7 diseases (Diphtheria, whooping cough, tetanus, polio, tuberculosis, measles and hepatitis B)

Table : Some Important Vaccines

S. No.	Name of Vaccine	Used for treatment of
1.	B.C.G.	Tuberculosis
2.	Cholera vaccine	Cholera
3.	Oral Polio Vaccine (OPV)/IPV Injectable Polio vaccine	Polio
4.	Tetanus toxoid (TT)	Tetanus
5.	$DTP/DT_aP/DT_wP$	Diptheria, Tetanus and Whooping cough
6.	PCV (Pneumococcal Conjugate Vaccine)	Pneumonia
7.	MMR1/MR	Measles
8.	Hep A/ Hep B	Hepatitis A/Hepatitis B
9.	Varicella Zoster Vaccine	ChickenPox
10.	Rotavirus Vaccine (RV)	Diarrhoea

MULTIPLE CHOICE QUESTIONS

1. The site of photosynthesis in plants is
   - (a) mitochondria
   - (b) chloroplasts
   - (c) leucoplasts
   - (d) dictyosomes

2. Autotrophic nutrition occurs in
   - (a) fungi
   - (b) plants
   - (c) some protists and prokaryotes
   - (d) Both (b) and (c)

3. Which one of the following is NOT a bacterial disease?
   - (a) Tuberculosis
   - (b) Typhoid
   - (c) Tetanus
   - (d) Small Pox

4. Select the statement which does not occur during the process of photosynthesis.
   - A. Absorption of light energy by chlorophyll.
   - B. Conversion of chemical energy to light energy and splitting of water molecules into hydrogen and oxygen.
   - C. Oxidation of carbon dioxide to carbohydrates.
   - (a) A and B
   - (b) A and C
   - (c) B and C
   - (d) All of the above

5.
Column-I		Column-II	
A.	parasites	P.	fungi
B.	saprophytes	Q.	Humans
C.	Autotrophs	R.	Leech
D.	Holozoic	S.	Algae.
   - (a) A-P ; B-Q ; C-R ; D-S
   - (b) A-R ; B-P ; C-S ; D-Q
   - (c) A-P ; B-R ; C-Q ; D-S
   - (d) A-R ; B-S ; C-P ; D-Q

6. Which of the following is a micronutrient element-
   - (a) Mg
   - (b) K
   - (c) Ca
   - (d) Zn

7. Erythropoesis may be stimulated by the deficiency of
   - (a) Iron
   - (b) Oxygen
   - (c) Protein
   - (d) None of the above

8. Exchange of gases in leaf occurs through
   - (a) tentacles
   - (b) skin of the leaf
   - (c) stomata
   - (d) root hair

9. Which mineral is obtained from the atmosphere?
   - (a) Potassium
   - (b) Iron
   - (c) Magnesium
   - (d) Nitrogen

10. Photosynthesis is an important mode of autotrophic nutrition. The event which does not occur in photosynthesis is
    - (a) Conversion of light energy to chemical energy
    - (b) Reduction of carbon dioxide to carbohydrate
    - (c) Oxidation of carbon to carbondioxide
    - (d) Absorption of light energy by chlorophyll

11. Hydroponics refers to the plant development
    - (a) without soil.
    - (b) in saline soil.
    - (c) in water without soil.
    - (d) without soil with alkaline pH.

12. Which of the following is not caused by deficiency of mineral nutrition?
    - (a) Necrosis
    - (b) Chlorosis
    - (c) Etiolation
    - (d) Shortening of internodes

13. Boron in green plants assists in
    - (a) sugar transport
    - (b) activation of enzymes
    - (c) acting as enzyme cofactor
    - (d) photosynthesis

14. Which of the following elements are constituents of protein?
    - (a) Nitrogen and phosphorus
    - (b) Nitrogen and chlorine
    - (c) Phosphorus and boron
    - (d) Chlorine and potassium

15. Nitrogen fixation is a process of
    - (a) converting nitrogen in the air to form a usable form by plants.
    - (b) recycling nitrogen from organic matter in the soil.
    - (c) absorbing nitrogen from the soil.
    - (d) conversion of NO_3 to N_2 .

16. Which of the following statements is not correct about macro- nutrients?
    - (a) These are present in plant tissues in excess of 100 m mole per kg of dry matter.
    - (b) These include C, H, O, N, P, S, K, Ca, Mg.
    - (c) Some elements attained from CO_2 and H_2O while the others are absorbed from the soil.
    - (d) C, H & O are mainly obtained from CO_2 and H_2O.

17.
Column-I (Minerals)	Column-II (Functions)
A. K	I. Stomatal opening
B. Mo	II. Constituent of cell membrane
C. P	III. Photolysis of water
D. Mn	IV. Free ion
	V. Component of nitrogenase and nitrate reductase

	A	B	C	D
(a)	I, IV	V	II	III
(b)	I, V	IV	III	II
(c)	I , V	IV	II	III
(d)	IV	I	III	II, V

18.
Column -I		Column-II	
A.	Zinc	I.	Chlorophyll
B.	Sulphur	II.	IAA
C.	Magnesium	III.	Nitrate reductase
D.	Molybdenum	IV.	Cysteine
    - (a) A – I, B – II, C – III, D – IV
    - (b) A – III, B – IV, C – I, D – II
    - (c) A – III, B – I, C – II, D – IV
    - (d) A – II, B – IV, C – I, D – III

19. The malignant tertian malaria is caused by
    (a) *Plasmodium vivax*
    (b) *Plasmodium falciparum*
    (c) *Plasmodium ovale*
    (d) *Plasmodium malaria*
20. 'Black death' is related with
    (a) plague
    (b) cancer
    (c) tuberculosis
    (d) measles
21.
Column-I		Column-II
(Drug/Cure)		(Diseases)
A.	Streptomycin	P. Viral Disease
B.	Chloroquine	Q. Diabetes Mellitus
C.	Penicillin	R. Disease caused by Bacteria
D.	Insulin	S. Malaria

    (a) A-R; B-S; C-P; D-Q
    (b) A-R; B-S; C-Q; D-P
    (c) A-R; B-Q; C-P; D-S
    (d) A-P; B-Q; C-R; D-S
22.
Column-I		Column-II
A.	Small pox	P. Bacteria
B.	Cholera	Q. Virus
C.	Malaria	R. Deficiency of minerals
D.	Anaemia	S. Female mosquito

    (a) A-S; B-Q; C-R; D-P
    (b) A-Q; B-P; C-S; D-R
    (c) A-S; B-R; C-Q; D-P
    (d) A-R; B-S; C-P; D-Q
23. DPT vaccine stands for
    (a) diphtheria, polio and tuberculosis
    (b) diphtheria, pertussis and tuberculosis
    (c) diphtheria, polio and tetanus
    (d) diphtheria, pertussis and tetanus
24. Which Vector Spread the yellow fever disease?
    (a) *Musca sp*   (b) *Anopheles sp*
    (c) *Culex sp*   (d) *Aedes aegypti*
25. Which of the following is an air-borne disease?
    (a) Tuberculosis   (b) Cholera
    (c) Jaundice   (d) Brain fever
26. Which of the following is a communicable disease?
    (a) Phenylketoneuria (b) Cancer
    (c) Rabies   (d) Alkaptonuria
27. Which of the following disease is confirmed by 'widal test'?
    (a) Tuberculosis   (b) Typhoid
    (c) Plague   (d) Tetanus
28. "Athlete's Foot" is a disease' caused by   [IAS Prelim]
    (a) Bacteria   (b) Fungus
    (c) Protozoan   (d) Nematode
29. According to the World Health Organisation (WHO), the disease which causes the death of the largest number of people today is   [IAS Prelim]
    (a) AIDS   (b) Tuberculosis
    (c) Malaria   (d) Ebola

30. Which of the following are associated with *Diabetes mellitus*, a common disease in adults ?   [IAS Prelim]
    1. Higher sugar level in blood
    2. Lower sugar level in blood
    3. Lower insulin level in blood
    4. Higher insulin level in blood
    Select the correct answer by using the codes given below:
    Codes:
    (a) 2 and 4   (b) 1 and 2
    (c) 2 and 3   (d) 1 and 3
31. Consider the following statements.   [IAS Prelim]
    AIDS -is transmitted
    1. By sexual intercourse
    2. By blood transfusion
    3. By mosquitoes and other blood sucking insects
    4. Across the placenta
    (a) 1, 2 and 3 are correct
    (b) 1, 2 and 4 are correct
    (c) 1, 3 and 4 are correct
    (d) 1 and 3 are correct
32. People drinking water from a shallow hand pump, are likely to suffer from all of the following diseases except   [IAS Prelim]
    (a) Cholera   (b) Typhoid
    (c) Jaundice   (d) Fluorosis
33. Antigen is a substance which   [IAS Prelim]
    (a) lowers body temperatures
    (b) destroys harmful bacteria
    (c) triggers the immune system
    (d) is used as an antidote to poison
34.
List- I		List-II	[IAS Prelim]
A.	Atropine	1. Local anaesthesia	
B.	Ether	2. Heart trouble	
C.	Nitroglycerine	3. Dilation of pupil	
D.	Pyrethrin	4. Mosquito control	

    Codes :
    (a) A – 1; B – 3; C – 2; D – 4
    (b) A – 1; B – 3; C – 4; D – 2
    (c) A – 3; B – 1; C – 4; D – 2
    (d) A – 3; B – 1; C – 2; D – 4
35. Which one of the following vitamins has a role in blood clotting ?   [CDS 2016-I]
    (a) Vitamin A   (b) Vitamin B
    (c) Vitamin D   (d) Vitamin K
36. Vitamin B_{12} deficiency causes pernicious anemia, Animals cannot synthesize vitamin B_{12}. Humans must obtain all their vitamin B_{12} from their diet. The complexing metal ion in vitamin B_{12} is :   [CDS 2016-I]
    (a) Mg^{2+} (Magnesium ion)
    (b) Fe^{2+} (Iron ion)
    (c) Co^{3+} (Cobalt ion)
    (d) Zn^{2+} (Zinc ion)
37. Which of the following pairs of vitamin and disease is / are correctly matched ?   [CDS 2016-I]

1.	Vitamin A	A	Rickets
2.	Vitamin B1	B	Beribri
3.	Vitamin C	C	Scurvy

Select the correct answer using the code given below:
(a)　2 only　　　　　　　(b)　2 and 3 only
(c)　1 and 3 only　　　　(d)　1, 2 and 3

38. Dengue virus is known to cause low platelet count in blood of patient by : **[CDS 2016-I]**
1. interfering in the process of platelet production in bone marrow
2. infecting endothelial cells
3. binding with platelets
4. accumulating platelets in intestine
Select the correct answer using the code given below:
(a)　1 and 2 only　　　　(b)　1 and 3 only
(c)　3 and 4　　　　　　(d)　1, 2 and 3

39. The HIV virus weakens the immunity of a person because it destroys **[CDS 2016-II]**
(a)　mast cells　　　　　(b)　platelets
(c)　erythrocytes　　　　(d)　lymphocytes

40. Deficiency of fluoride leads to which one of the following health problems? **[CDS 2016-II]**
(a)　Tooth caries　　　　(b)　Mottling of tooth
(c)　Bending of bones　(d)　Stiffening of joints

41. The elemental composition of an adult human body by mass is **[CDS 2016-II]**
(a)　$C > O > H > N$　　(b)　$O > C > H > N$
(c)　$N > C > H > O$　　(d)　$N > C > O > H$

42. Bleeding of gums, falling of teeth, fragile bones and delayed wound healing occur due to the deficiency of which one of the following vitamins? **[CDS 2017-I]**
(a)　Vitamin C　　　　　(b)　Vitamin K
(c)　Vitamin D　　　　　(d)　Vitamin B

43. Which one of the following elements is involved in the control of water content of the blood? **[CDS 2018-I]**
(a)　Potassium　　　　　(b)　Lithium
(c)　Rubidium　　　　　(d)　Caesium

44. Which one of the following elements is essential for the formation of chlorophyll in green plants? **[CDS 2018-I]**
(a)　Calcium　　　　　　(b)　Iron
(c)　Magnesium　　　　(d)　Potassium

45. Sleeping sickness is a parasitic disease of humans and other animals. It is caused by **[NDA 2017-I]**
(a)　*Histomonas*　　　　(b)　*Trypanosoma*
(c)　*Angomonae*　　　　(d)　*Naegleria*

46. Dengue virus causes high fever, rashes and reduces the number of a particular type of blood cells. Those blood cells are **[NDA 2017-I]**
(a)　Monocytes　　　　　(b)　Platelets
(c)　Eosinophils　　　　(d)　Neutrophils

47. Which one of the following statements is NOT correct? **[NDA 2017-I]**
(a)　All proteins are enzymes
(b)　Mostly enzymes are proteins
(c)　All fats are energy rich compounds
(d)　Glucose is a common carbohydrate

48. Sugarcane is one of the important cash crops in India. It is grown to obtain **[NDA 2017-I]**
(a)　Starch　　　　　　　(b)　Glucose
(c)　Fructose　　　　　　(d)　Sucrose

49. Which one of the following is the scientific name of the causal organism of elephantiasis ? **[NDA 2017-II]**
(a)　*Ascaris lumbricoides*
(b)　*Culex pipiens*
(c)　*Wuchereria bancrofti*
(d)　*Fasciola hepatica*

50. Intake of which one of the following food components should be minimized by patients having Gouty Arthritis due to elevated serum uric acid level ? **[NDA 2017-II]**
(a)　Food fibres　　　　　(b)　Nucleic acids
(c)　Lipids　　　　　　　(d)　Carbohydrates

51. Which one of the following vitamins has a role in blood clotting? **[NDA 2017-II]**
(a)　Vitamin A　　　　　(b)　Vitamin D
(c)　Vitamin E　　　　　(d)　Vitamin K

52. The term 'Probiotic' is applied to **[NDA 2017-II]**
(a)　Organic food
(b)　Antacid
(c)　Antibiotic
(d)　Live microbial food supplement

53. Which one of the following microbes causes acidification and curding of milk? **[NDA 2017-II]**
(a)　Lactic Acid *Bacillus*
(b)　*Clostridium botulinum*
(c)　*Vibrio cholerae*
(d)　*Saccharomyces cerevisiae*

54. AIDS is caused by a virus whose genetic material is **[NDA 2018-I]**
(a)　single stranded circular DNA
(b)　double stranded DNA
(c)　single stranded RNA
(d)　double stranded RNA

55. Which one of the following is a waterborne disease? **[NDA 2018-II]**
(a)　Jaundice　　　　　　(b)　Tuberculosis
(c)　Rabies　　　　　　　(d)　Arthritis

ANSWER KEY															
1.	(b)	**2.**	(d)	**3.**	(d)	**4.**	(c)	**5.**	(b)	**6.**	(d)	**7.**	(b)	**8.**	(c)
9.	(d)	**10.**	(c)	**11.**	(c)	**12.**	(c)	**13.**	(a)	**14.**	(a)	**15.**	(a)	**16.**	(a)
17.	(a)	**18.**	(d)	**19.**	(b)	**20.**	(a)	**21.**	(a)	**22.**	(b)	**23.**	(d)	**24.**	(d)
25.	(a)	**26.**	(c)	**27.**	(b)	**28.**	(b)	**29.**	(b)	**30.**	(d)	**31.**	(b)	**32.**	(d)
33.	(c)	**34.**	(b)	**35.**	(d)	**36.**	(c)	**37.**	(b)	**38.**	(d)	**39.**	(d)	**40.**	(a)
41.	(b)	**42.**	(a)	**43.**	(a)	**44.**	(c)	**45.**	(b)	**46.**	(b)	**47.**	(a)	**48.**	(d)
49.	(c)	**50.**	(b)	**51.**	(d)	**52.**	(d)	**53.**	(a)	**54.**	(c)	**55.**	(a)		

[APPENDIX]
Nobel Prizes in Physiology/Medicine (1901-2018)

Year	Scientist	Country	Contribution
1901	Emil Adolf von Behring	Germany	Serum therapy
1902	Sir Ronald Ross	UK	Malaria pathogen
1903	Niels Ryberg Finsen	Denmark	Treatment of diseases/lupus vulgaris, with concentrated light radiation
1904	Ivan Petrovich Pavlov	Russia	Physiology of digestion
1905	Robert Koch	Germany	Tuberculosis
1906	Camillo Golgi	Italy	Structure of the Nervous System
	Santiago Ramón y Cajal	Spain	
1907	Charles Louis Alphonse Laveran	France	Protozoan pathogens
1908	Ilya Ilyich Mechnikov	Russia	Immunity
	Paul Ehrlich	Germany	
1909	Emil Theodor Kocher	Switzerland	Thyroid gland
1910	Albrecht Kossel	Germany	Cellular chemistry involving proteins and nucleic substances
1911	Allvar Gullstrand	Sweden	Dioptrics of eye
1912	Alexis Carrel	France	Transplantation of blood vessels and organs
1913	Charles Richet	France	Anaphylaxis
1914	Robert Bárány	Austria	Physiology and pathology of vestibular apparatus
1919	Jules Bordet	Belgium	Immunity
1920	Schack August Steenberg Krogh	Denmark	Capillary motor regulating mechanism
1922	Archibald Vivian Hill	UK	Heat production in the muscle
	Otto Fritz Meyerhof	Germany	Relationship between O_2 consumption and the metabolism of lactic acid in the muscle
1923	Sir Frederick Grant Banting	Canada	Insulin
	John James Rickard Macleod	UK	
1924	Willem Einthoven	Netherlands	Mechanism of ECG
1926	Johannes Andreas Grib Fibiger	Denmark	Spiroptera Carcinoma
1927	Julius Wagner-Jauregg	Austria	Therapeutic value of malaria inoculation in the treatment of dementia paralytica
1928	Charles Jules Henri Nicolle	France	Typhus
1929	Christiaan Eijkman	Netherlands	Antineuritic Vitamin
	Sir Frederick Gowland Hopkins	UK	Growth stimulating vitamins
1930	Karl Landsteiner	Austria	Human blood groups
1931	Otto Heinrich Warburg	Germany	Nature and mode of action of the respiratory enzyme
1932	Sir Charles Scott Sherrington	UK	Functions of neurons
	Edgar Douglas Adrian	UK	
1933	Thomas Hunt Morgan	USA	Chromosome in heredity
1934	George Hoyt Whipple	USA	Liver therapy in anaemia
	George Richards Minot	USA	
	William Parry Murphy	USA	
1935	Hans Spemann	Germany	Organizer effect in embryonic development
1936	Sir Henry Hallett Dale	UK	Chemical transmission of nerve impulses
	Otto Loewi	Austria	
1937	Albert Szent-Györgyi von Nagy-rapolt	Hungary	vitamin C and catalysis of fumaric acid
1938	Corneille Jean François Heymans	Belgium	Sinus and aortic mechanisms in the regulation of respiration
1939	Gerhard Domagk	Germany	Antibacterial effects of prontosil/ sulfamidochrysoidine
1943	Carl Peter Henrik Dam	Denmark	Discovery of vitamin K
	Edward Adelbert Doisy	USA	Chemical nature of vitamin K
1944	Joseph Erlanger	USA	Differentiated functions of single nerve fibres
	Herbert Spencer Gasser	USA	
1945	Sir Alexander Fleming	UK	Discovery of penicillin and its antibacterial effect
	Sir Ernst Boris Chain	UK	
	Howard Walter Florey	Australia	
1946	Hermann Joseph Muller	USA	Production of mutations by X-ray irradiation

Year	Scientist	Country	Contribution
1947	Carl Ferdinand Cori	USA	Catalytic conversion of glycogen
	Gerty Theresa Cori, née Radnitz	USA	
	Bernardo Alberto Houssay	Argentina	hormone of the anterior pituitary lobe and Sugar metabolism
1948	Paul Hermann Müller	Switzerland	DDT as a contact poison against several arthropods
1949	Walter Rudolf Hess	Switzerland	Functional organization of interbrain as a coordinator of the activities of the internal organs
	António Caetano Egas Moniz	Portugal	Therapeutic value of leucotomy (lobotomy) in certain psychoses
1950	Philip Showalter Hench	USA	Hormones of the adrenal cortex
	Edward Calvin Kendall	USA	
	Tadeusz Reichstein	Switzerland	
1951	Max Theiler	South Africa	Yellow fever
1952	Selman Abraham Waksman	USA	Streptomycin and tuberculosis
1953	Sir Hans Adolf Krebs	UK	Citric acid cycle
	Fritz Albert Lipmann	USA	Discovery of co-enzyme A/role in intermediary metabolism"
1954	John Franklin Enders	USA	Cultures of Polio Viruses in various tissues
	Frederick Chapman Robbins	USA	
	Thomas Huckle Weller	USA	
1955	Axel Hugo Theodor Theorell	Sweden	Nature and mode of action of oxidation enzymes
1956	André Frédéric Cournand	USA	Heart catheterization and pathological changes in the circulatory system
	Werner Forssmann	West Germany	
	Dickinson W. Richards	USA	
1957	Daniel Bovet	Italy	Synthetic compounds and their action on the vascular system and the skeletal muscles
1958	George Wells Beadle	USA	Genes action/regulation
	Edward Lawrie Tatum	USA	
	Joshua Lederberg	USA	Genetic recombination and organization of bacterial genetic material
1959	Arthur Kornberg	USA	Biological synthesis of RNA/DNA
	Severo Ochoa	USA	
1960	Sir Frank Macfarlane Burnet	Australia	Discovery of acquired immunological tolerance
	Sir Peter Brian Medawar	Brazil, UK	
1961	Georg von Békésy	USA	Physical mechanism of stimulation within the cochlea
1962	Francis Harry Compton Crick	UK	Molecular structure of nucleic acids and its role
	James Dewey Watson	USA	
	Maurice Hugh Frederick Wilkins	New Zealand, UK	
1963	Sir John Carew Eccles	Australia	Ionic mechanisms involved in excitation and inhibition of nerve cell membrane
	Sir Alan Lloyd Hodgkin	UK	
	Sir Andrew Fielding Huxley	UK	
1964	Konrad Bloch	USA	Mechanism and regulation of the cholesterol and fatty acid metabolism
	Feodor Lynen	West Germany	
1965	François Jacob	France	Genetic control of enzyme and virus synthesis
	André Lwoff	France	
	Jacques Monod	France	
1966	Peyton Rous	USA	Tumor-inducing viruses
	Charles Brenton Huggins	USA	Hormonal treatment of prostatic cancer
1967	Ragnar Granit	Sweden	Primary physiological and chemical visual processes in the eye
	Haldan Keffer Hartline	USA	
	George Wald	USA	
1968	Robert W. Holley	USA	Interpretation of genetic code and its role in protein synthesis
	Har Gobind Khorana	USA	
	Marshall W. Nirenberg	USA	
1969	Max Delbrück	USA	Replication mechanism and genetic structure of viruses
	Alfred D. Hershey	USA	
	Salvador E. Luria	USA	
1970	Julius Axelrod	USA	Humoral transmittors in nerve terminals
	Ulf von Euler	Sweden	
	Sir Bernard Katz	UK	

Year	Scientist	Country	Contribution
1971	Earl W. Sutherland, Jr.	USA	Mechanisms of the action of hormones
1972	Gerald M. Edelman	USA	Discoveries concerning the chemical structure of antibodies
	Rodney R. Porter	UK	
1973	Karl von Frisch	West Germany	Organization and elicitation of individual and social behaviour patterns
	Konrad Lorenz	Austria	
	Nikolaas Tinbergen	Netherlands	
1974	Albert Claude	Belgium	Structural and functional organization of the cell
	Christian de Duve	Belgium	
	George E. Palade	Romania	
1975	David Baltimore	USA	Interaction between tumor viruses and cellular genetic material
	Renato Dulbecco	UK, (USA)	
	Howard Martin Temin	USA	
1976	Baruch S. Blumberg	USA	Mechanisms for origin and dissemination of infectious diseases
	D. Carleton Gajdusek	USA	
1977	Roger Guillemin	USA	Brain and Peptide hormone production
	Andrew V. Schally	USA	
	Rosalyn Yalow	USA	Radioimmunoassays (RIA) of peptide hormones
1978	Werner Arber	Switzerland	Restriction endonucleases and their application in molecular genetics
	Daniel Nathans	USA	
	Hamilton O. Smith	USA	
1979	Allan M. Cormack	South Africa	Development of computer assisted tomography (CAT)
	Sir Godfrey N. Hounsfield	UK	
1980	Baruj Benacerraf	Venezuela	MHC/HLA and regulation of immunological reactions
	Jean Dausset	France	
	George D. Snell	USA	
1981	Roger W. Sperry	USA	Functional specialization of cerebral hemispheres
	David H. Hubel	Canada	Information processing in the visual system
	Torsten N. Wiesel	Sweden	
1982	Sune K. Bergström	Sweden	Prostaglandins and related biologically active substances
	Bengt I. Samuelsson	Sweden	
	Sir John R. Vane	UK	
1983	Barbara McClintock	USA	Discovery of mobile genetic elements/jumping genes
1984	Niels K. Jerne	Denmark	Control of immune system and principle for production of monoclonal antibodies
	Georges J.F. Köhler	West Germany	
	César Milstein	UK	
1985	Michael S. Brown	USA	Regulation of Cholesterol metabolism
	Joseph L. Goldstein	USA	
1986	Stanley Cohen	USA	Discoveries of Growth factors
	Rita Levi-Montalcini	Italy	
1987	Susumu Tonegawa	Japan	Genetic principle for generation of antibody diversity
1988	Sir James W. Black	UK	Important principles for drug treatment
	Gertrude B. Elion	USA	
	George H. Hitchings	USA	
1989	J. Michael Bishop	USA	Cellular origin of retroviral oncogenes
	Harold E. Varmus	USA	
1990	Joseph E. Murray	USA	Organ and cell transplantation in the treatment of human diseases
	E. Donnall Thomas	USA	
1991	Erwin Neher	Germany	Function of single ion channels in cells
	Bert Sakmann	Germany	
1992	Edmond H. Fischer	USA	Reversible protein phosphorylation as biological regulatory mechanism
	Edwin G. Krebs	USA	
1993	Sir Richard J. Roberts	UK	Discoveries of split genes
	Phillip A. Sharp	USA	
1994	Alfred G. Gilman	USA	Discovery of G-proteins and their role in signal transduction
	Martin Rodbell	USA	

Year	Scientist	Country	Contribution
1995	Edward B. Lewis	USA	Genetic control of early embryonic development
	Christiane Nüsslein-Volhard	Germany	
	Eric F. Wieschaus	USA	
1996	Peter C. Doherty	Australia	Specificity of cell mediated immune defence
	Rolf M. Zinkernagel	Switzerland	
1997	Stanley B. Prusiner	USA	Discovery of Prions/infectious proteins
1998	Robert F. Furchgott	USA	NO as signaling molecule in the cardiovascular system
	Louis J. Ignarro	USA	
	Ferid Murad	USA	
1999	Günter Blobel	USA	Intrinsic signals directing protein transport and localization
2000	Arvid Carlsson	Sweden	Signal transduction in nervous system
	Paul Greengard	USA	
	Eric R. Kandel	USA	
2001	Leland H. Hartwell	USA	Key regulators (CDK/ Cyclins/Check points) of Cell cycle
	Sir Tim Hunt	UK	
	Sir Paul M. Nurse	UK	
2002	Sydney Brenner	South Africa	Genetic regulation of organ development and programmed cell death
	H. Robert Horvitz	USA	
	Sir John E. Sulston	UK	
2003	Paul Lauterbur	USA	Magnetic Resonance Imaging (MRI)
	Sir Peter Mansfield	UK	
2004	Richard Axel	USA	Odorant receptors and organization of olfactory system
	Linda B. Buck	USA	
2005	Barry J. Marshall	Australia	*Helicobacter pylori* and its role in gastritis/peptic ulcer
	J. Robin Warren	Australia	
2006	Andrew Z. Fire	USA	Gene silencing by RNA interference (RNAi) through double-stranded RNA
	Craig C. Mello	USA	
2007	Mario R. Capecchi	USA, Italy	Specific gene modifications in mice through embryonic stem cells
	Sir Martin J. Evans	UK	
	Oliver Smithies	USA	
2008	Harald zur Hausen	Germany	Human Papilloma viruses and cervical cancer
	Françoise Barré-Sinoussi	France	Discovery of human immunodeficiency virus (HIV)
	Luc Montagnier	France	
2009	Elizabeth H. Blackburn	USA	Telomeres and telomerase
	Carol W. Greider	USA	
	Jack W. Szostak	USA	
2010	Sir Robert G. Edwards	UK	Development of *in vitro* fertilization
2011	Bruce A. Beutler	USA	Activation of innate immunity
	Jules A. Hoffmann	France	
	Ralph M. Steinman	Canada	Discovery of dendritic cell and its role in adaptive immunity
2012	Sir John B. Gurdon	UK	Mature cells can be reprogrammed to become pluripotent
	Shinya Yamanaka	Japan	
2013	James E. Rothman	USA	Machinery regulating vesicle traffic in cells
	Randy W. Schekman	USA	
	Thomas C. Südhof	USA	
2014	John O'Keefe	UK	Discoveries of cells that constitute a positioning system in the brain/Inner GPS
	May-Britt Moser	Norway	
	Edvard I. Moser	Norway	
2015	William C. Campbell	USA	Novel therapy against infections caused by roundworm parasites
	Satoshi Ōmura	Japan	
	Tu Youyou	China	Novel therapy against Malaria
2016	Yoshinori Ohsumi	Japan	Mechanisms for autophagy
2017	Jeffrey C. Hall	USA	Molecular mechanisms controlling circadian rhythm
	Michael Rosbash	USA	
	Michael W. Young	USA	
2018	James P. Allison	USA	For discovery of cancer therapy by Inhibition of negative immune regulation
	Tasuku Honjo	Japan	

Chapter 1

COMPUTER AND TECHNOLOGY

The word computer originated from the English word compute, which means to do calculation. The new definition of the computer can be" defined as an electronic device through which different kinds of informations are processed on the basis of definite set of instructions called program and with this device both mathematical and non –mathematical informations can be processed.

COMPUTER GENERATIONS

Till today five generations of computers have been developed.

HISTORY

Abacus is considered as first calculating device, which was originated in China during 16th century. But first calculating machine was invented by Blaise Pascal in 1642, which was named as *Pascalene*. Later in 1833 *Charles Babbage* made an automatic calculator. He is also known as *father of modern computer*.

Computer Generations

Generation	Period	Main Electronic Component	Main Computers
I	1951-1958	Electronic tube/Vaccum tubes	EDSAC, EDVAC, UNIVAC
II	1959-64	Transistor	IBM-700, IBM-1401, IBM-1620, CDC-1604, CDC-3600 ATLAS, ICL-1901
III	1965-1971	Integrated circuit (IC)	IBM-360,IBM-370,NCR-395,CDC-1700, ICL-2903
IV	1971-2010	Large Integrated Circuits, Microprocessor VLSI	APPLE, DCM
V	2010 onwards	Based on AI	Self-decision Computer

Fifth Generation (2010 to Present)

Artificial Intelligence

Fifth generation computing devices, based on artificial intelligence, are still in development, though there are some applications, such as voice recognition, that are being used today. The goal of fifth-generation computing is to develop devices that respond to natural language input and are capable of learning and self-organization.

TYPES OF COMPUTER

Computers are classified on the basis of its size and its uses.

On the Basis of Size

Micro computers: In such computers ALU are based in same chip.

Personal computers: It is single user system which is used in offices, workshops, business etc.

Mini computers: It is power full than micro computer. It can be used by many users at same time. Its processing speed is very fast.

Main frame computers: These are larger in size and fabricated in steel frames. They can process an ample amount of data very rapidly. Banks, educational institute and insurance company mainly use this type of computer.

Super computers: These are the most powerful computers, which can process extremely complex data very quickly and its storage capacity is also very large. It is the costliest and fastest working computer. Super computers are used in weather forecasting, space research, computerized nuclear tests, satellite launching, etc.

The super computer developed in India are Flo Solver. (developed by NAL, Bangalore), Multi Micro (developed by IISc, Bangalore), Param -10,000 (by C-DAC Pune), Mach (by IIT, Mumbai)

On the Basis of Uses

(i) **Digital computer:** These computers do calculations digitally by alegebric addition. The special feature of these computers is accurate numerical calculations. These are used mainly in banking.

(ii) **Analog computers:** It measures temperature, length, pressure, etc. (all physical quantities) and converts it into numerical values. These are used in scientific and engineering works.

(iii) Hybrid computers: In hybrid computers digital and analogue both types of computers are utilized. These are used in automatic operating devices like a versatile robot, in factories and machines etc.

COMPONENTS OF A COMPUTER

Input Unit

It receives data and instructions from the user.
It sends converted instructions to CPU for processing

CPU (Central Processing Unit)

It contrals all the parts of computer processing
It performs processing works of computer.

The CPU consists of three components are:

1. ALU (Arithmetic and Logic Unit)

It performs all arithmetic and logic operations.

2. Control Unit

It controls the transfer of data from the input device to memory and from memory to ALU. It also transfers the results from memory to output unit.

3. Memory

It holds the received data from input device temporarily/permanently.
Example: RAM (Random Access Memory) & ROM (Read only Memory)

Output Unit

It recives processed data from CUP.
It converts the output into simple language and displays result on the screen.

HARDWARE

All the components and mechanical equipments that we can touch are known as hardware.

Input Devices

The devices which are used to give instructions and data to the computer are called input device. Some of main input devices are:
Scanner, Touch screen, Optical Character Reader
Magnetic Ink character Reader(MICR), Bar code Reader, Optical Mark-Reader (OMR), Voice input device, etc.

Output Devices

These are the devices through which computer gives output. Some of the main output devices are monitor, printer, projector, sound card, speaker, video card etc.

INFORMATION TECHNOLOGY

Information technology (also referred to as IT) is the application of computers and telecommunications equipment to *store, retrieve, transmit* and *manipulate data,* often in the context of a business or other enterprise. Several industries are associated with information technology, such as computer hardware software, electronics, semiconductors, internet, telecom equipment, e-commerce and computer services.

Application

Information Technology has applications in almost all aspects of our life. Some of the important ones are:
Science and Engineering, Business & Commerce, Education, Governance, Medicine, Entertainment, Geographic information system (GIS), E-Banking, Core Banking, Electronic Clearing Service *(ECS),* Multi-application Smart Cards, etc.

STORAGE DEVICES

Storage devices are also called storage media. It is a hardware device that can hold information. Two main storage devices are used in computers.
*   The primary storage device also known as RAM,
*   The secondary storage device such as a computer hard drive. Secondary storage can be either internal or external storage.
Storage device is required by the computer to save any settings or additional information.

TYPE OF SECONDARY STORAGE DEVICES

Different types of storage devices Includes:

Magnetic Disks, Optical Disks, Magnetic Tape , Floppy Diskette CD-ROM disc, CD-R and CD-RW disc, Recordable DVD Drives, Jump drive and USB Flash Drive, Hard Drive, Memory Card, Memory Stick, Zip Diskette, Blue Ray Disk, etc.

INFORMATION & COMMUNICATIONS TECHNOLOGY (ICT)

ICT refers to all the technology used to handle telecommunications, broadcast media, intelligent building management systems, audiovisual processing and transmission systems, and network-based control and monitoring functions.

COMPUTER TECHNOLOGY

Computer technology is the activity of designing and constructing and programming computers.

The first major development in computer technology was in 1946, with a vacuum tube-based computer model that was produced to aid in military efforts. Since the invention of computers and the internet, technology including operating systems, platforms, hardware and software has rapidly advanced.

Type of computer technology

They are some computer technology includes:

An Embedded Systems, Microcomputer, Workstation, Mini-computer, Supercomputer, A Parallel Processing System, etc.

COMPUTER SOFTWARE

Computer Programs are called as Computer software, or just software. A computer Software is set of programs that guides the hardware through its job.

Types of Software

Computer softwares are mainly divided into two parts:
(a) System Software   (b) Application Software

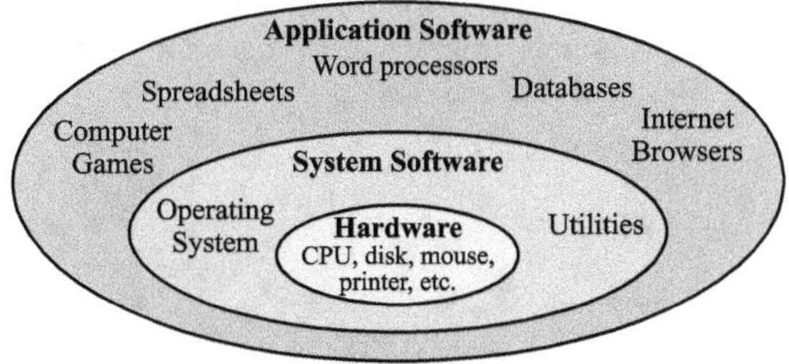

(A) SYSTEM SOFTWARE

System software is the software which manages and controls the hardware components and allows interaction between the hardware and the other different types of software.

System software can be separated into two different categories: **Operating systems and Utility software.**

Operating System

A program that acts as an intermediary between a user of a computer and the computer hardware is called an operating system. Application programs usually require an operating system to function.

Ex: UNIX, MS-DOS, WINDOWS, 98/2000/XP/7/8/10.

Functions of an operating system –

The basic functions of an operating system are:
I.   Booting the computer
II. Performs basic computer tasks e.g. managing the various peripheral devices e.g. mouse, keyboard
III. Provides a user interface, e.g. command line, graphical user interface (GUI)
IV. Handles system resources such as computer's memory and sharing of the central processing unit (CPU) time by various applications or peripheral devices
V.   Provides file management which refers to the way that the operating system manipulates, stores, retrieves and saves data.

There are different types of operating system to support the computer system. Includes:

Single-user, Single Task Operating System, Single-user, Multitasking Operating System, Multi-user Operating System, Real Time Operating System, Time-sharing Operating System, Distributed Operating System, Network Operating System, Stand-alone Operating System, Embedded Operating System, Mobile Operating System, Microsoft Windows operating system, Linux Operating System, MS DOS (Microsoft Disk Operating System), etc.

(B) APPLICATION SOFTWARE

Application Software are designed to achieve a complete task or a set of tasks. Application software consists of the programs for performing varied tasks particular to the machine's utilization. There are various examples of application software that include MS Word, MS Excel, a console game, database systems, desktop publishing systems, program development software, a library management system, graphics software, etc.

PROGRAMMING LANGUAGES

A programming language is a set of commands, instructions, and other syntax use to create a software program. Languages that programmers use to write code are called "high-level languages." This code can be compiled into a "low-level language," which is recognized directly by the computer hardware.

(a) **Low Level Languages**

Low level computer languages are machine codes or close to it. Computer cannot understand instructions given in high level languages or in English. It can only understand and execute instructions given in the form of machine language i.e. language of 0 and 1.

Example: Machine & Assembly language

(b) **High-Level Language**

High-level programming languages allowed the specification of writing a program closer to those used by human beings. With the advent of high level languages ,programming became far easier, less error-prone and also removed the programmer from having to know the details of the internal structure of a particular computer. Fortran II was one of the first high level language introduced in 1957.

Many high level languages were developed since Fortran II among the most widely used have been:

Language	Application Area	Developer
FORTRAN (Formula Translation)	Engineering & Scientific Applications	IBM in 1957
LISP (List Processing)	Artificial Intelligence	John Mc carthy in 1958
COBOL(Common Business Oriented Language)	Business applications	Grace Hopper in 1959
PASCAL	General use and as a teaching tool	Niklaus wirth in 1972
C & C++	General Purpose - currently most popular	C, Dennis Ritchie in 1972 C++ Bjarne Stroustrup in 1983.
JAVA	General Purpose - Internet Oriented Programming	James gosling in 1995

COMPUTER NETWORK

A computer Network is a group of computer systems and other computing hardware devices that are linked together through communication channels to facilitate communication and resource-sharing among a wide range of users.

TYPES OF COMPUTER NETWORKS

There are many types of Computer Networks includes:

1. **Personal Area Network (PAN):** It is smallest network which and very personal to a user. This may include Bluetooth enabled devices or infra-red enabled devices. PAN has connectivity range up to 10 meters.
2. **Local Area Network (LAN):** It is operated inside a building and under single administrative system. For e.gs. offices, schools, college/universities etc. Number of systems may vary from as least as two to as much as 16 million. Resources like Printers, File Servers, Scanners and internet is easy sharable among computers.
3. **Metropolitan Area Network (MAN):** It, generally expands throughout a city such as cable TV network. It can be in form of Ethernet, Token-ring, ATM or FDDI.
4. **Wide Area Network (WAN):** It covers a wide area which may span across provinces and even a whole country. Generally, telecommunication networks are Wide Area Network. These networks provides connectivity to MANs and LANs.
5. **Virtual Private Network (VPN):** It is constructed by using public wires usually the Internet to connect to a private network, such as a company›s internal network.
6. **Internetwork:** A network of networks is called internetwork, or simply Internet or net. It is the largest network in existence on this planet. Internet hugely connects all WANs and it can have connection to LANs and Home networks. Internet uses TCP/IP protocol suite and uses IP as its addressing protocol. Present day, Internet is widely implemented using IPv4. Because of shortage of address spaces, it is gradually migrating from IPv4 to IPv6.

INTERNET

Internet, also called the Net, is an electronic communication device. It is one of the largest networks that links millions or trillions of computers all over the world. You can access this network via communication devices and media such as, modems, cables, telephone lines and satellites.No one knows exactly how many computers are connected to the Internet. It is certain, however, that these numbers are in millions and are increasing at a rapid rate.

A networking project called ARPA or Advanced Research Projects Agency was launched, which was to work as a network that would allow scientists and military personnel to exchange information in a war scenario without disruption in communications. This network, called ARPANET, became functional in September 1969, linking scientific and academic researchers in the United States. By 1984, ARPANET had more than 1,000 individual computers linked as hosts. Internet, the outgrowth of ARPANET today attracts hundreds of millions of hosts.

INTERNET ADDRESSES

Because the Internet is a global network of computers each computer connected to the Internet **must** have a unique address. Internet addresses are in the form **bbbb.bbbb.bbbb.bbbb** where bbbb must be a number from 0 - 255. This address is known as an Internet Protocol (IP) address.

Diagram

DOMAIN NAME SYSTEM

The Domain Name System (DNS) is a hierarchical decentralized naming system for computers, services, or any resource connected to the Internet or a private network. It associates various information with domain names assigned to each of the participating entities. Most prominently, it translates more readily memorized domain names to the numerical IP addresses needed for the purpose of locating and identifying computer services and devices with the underlying network protocols. By providing a worldwide, distributed directory service, the Domain Name System is an essential component of the functionality of the Internet, and has been in use since the 1980s.

INTRANETS AND EXTRANETS

Intranets

Intranets typically start by publishing web pages about company events, health and safety policies, and staff newsletters. Popular applications follow, such as forms to reclaim expenses or request holidays. All these help eliminate paperwork and speed up workflows.

The intranet is protected from the global internet by firewalls and by the need to log on with a secure password. Staff working outside the organization may be able to access the intranet by using a VPN (virtual private network). This means all communications between the intranet and the user's personal computer are encrypted.

Extranets

Extranets take this process a step further, by providing access to people who work for different organizations. For example, a company could provide access to a supplier for online ordering, order tracking and inventory management.

An extranet should be more efficient because everyone has access to the same data in the same format. Because all extranet communications can be encrypted over a VPN, it should also be more secure than sending data over the public internet.

Application of The Internet

There are some application of internet given below.

E-mail (electronic mail)

Information fatch

Entertainment

Programs creation

Online discussion groups
On-line shopping
Chat

NETWORK DEVICES

Node

A network is a collection of computers or other devices, commonly called **nodes**, that are able to communicate with each other.

HUB

The most common type of network is the Ethernet network where all nodes are connected to a central device. In its simplest form this central node is called a **hub**.

Switch

A commonly used solution today is a **switch**. A switch still connects all nodes to each other, like a hub, but is more intelligent in which messages are passed on to which node.

Segments and Bridges

A large network can be divided into multiple parts which are called **segments**. Nodes on different segments cannot directly communicate with each other. To make this possible, a **bridge** is added between the segments.

Router

A router is connected between two networks and passes packets between them choosing the shortest path and deliver high security, reliable service to the user.

Gateway

A gateway is the same as a router, except in that it also translates between one network system or protocol and another. It router the traffic from a work station to the outside network that serving the web pages.

Firewell

A firewall act as a barrier between a trusted network and untrusted network. It control access to the resources of a network through a passive control model.

INTERNET GOVERNANCE

Internet governance is the development and application by Governments, the private sector and civil society, in their respective roles, of shared principles, norms, rules, decision-making procedures, and programmers that shape the evolution and use of the Internet

Internet governance should not be confused with E-Governance, which refers to governments' use of technology to carry out their governing duties.

COMPUTER SECURITY

Computer security (also known as cyber security or IT security) is information security as applied to computing devices such as computers and smart phones, as well as computer networks such as private and public networks, including the whole Internet.

The Basic Components of Computer Security

- **Confidentiality**
- **Integrity**
- **Availability**
- **Access Control System**
- **Transport Layer Security**

COMPUTER VIRUSES

A computer virus or worm is program that replicates itself on its own by inserting copies of itself into other programs or documents. It can spread by email also. These viruses or worms are malicious programs that aredesigned to infect and gain control over a computer without the owner's knowledge.

Top Sources of Computer Virus Attack

The top sources of virus attacks are highlighted below:
- **Downloadable Programs**
- **Illegal Software**
- **Email Attachments**
- **Using Internet**
- **Booting from Unknown CD**
- **Using Pendrive/USB Flash drive**
- **Not running the latest updates**

RANSOMWARES

A type of malicious software designed to block access to a computer system until a sum of money is paid.

WannaCry Ransomware

WannaCry is a file-encrypting virus/ransomware which is active since 2017 and is designed to encrypt data on the victimized computer using RSA algorithms. It can be easily recognized by .wncry, .wncryt, or .wcry extensions at the end of the corrupted file-names. Victims of Wanna Cry receive Please Read Me!.txt or @Please_Read_Me@.txt files which serve as ransom notes and opens Wanna Decrypt0r window to display key information.

Petya Ransomware

Similar to WannaCry, Petya uses the EternalBlue exploit as one of the means to propagate itself. However, it also uses classic SMB network spreading techniques, meaning that it can spread within organizations, even if they have patched against EternalBlue.

CryptoWall

CryptoWall is another ransomwares attacking on Windows. Since 2014 it has affected several websites.

Some of the major Ransomwares include Fusob, BadRabbit, SamSam, CryptoLocker, Reveton

Solutions to Computer Security Threats

Some safeguards or solutions to protect a computer system from accidental access. These are.

- Install Anti-Virus Software
- Employ a firewall to protect networks
- Filter all email traffic
- Scan Internet Downloads
- Implement a vulnerability management program
- Develop an Information Security Policy
- Password Protection
- Security Certificate

CYBERCRIME

Cybercrime is a fast-growing area of crime. Cyber crime encompasses any criminal act dealing with computers and networks (called hacking). More and more criminals are exploiting the speed, convenience and anonymity of the Internet to commit a diverse range of criminal activities that know no borders, either physical or virtual, cause serious harm and pose very real threats to victims worldwide. Some technique are used to reduce the cyber crime.

(i) Biometric technology.
(ii) Biometric passport.
(iii) Policing cyber crime.
(iv) Data encryption.
(v) Digital signature.

IT INDUSTRY IN INDIA

The IT industry in India is a key part of the country's economy. In 2013, information technology and its various subsectors represented 8 percent of the nation's overall GDP, making it the fifth largest industry in India. In the 2014/15 financial year alone, the IT industry in India generated an annual revenue of around 120 billion U.S. dollars, a significant increase from around 60 billion U.S. dollars in 2008/09. Of this revenue in 2015. The majority, 98.1 billion U.S. dollars, was generated in exports while domestic revenue totaled more than 20 billion U.S. dollars. The revenue of Indian IT industry approx 160 billion U.S. dollars in 2016.

Evaluation of Indian IT Industry

The IT industry in India came into existence in the year 1974. It was the time when mainframe manufacturer Burroughs asked Tata Consultancy Services (TCS) to export programmers for installing system software for a U.S. client. Import tariffs were high (135% on hardware and 100% on software) and software was not considered an "industry", so that exporters were ineligible for bank finance. Government policy towards IT sector changed when Rajiv Gandhi became Prime Minister in 1984. His New Computer Policy (NCP-1984) consisted of a package of reduced import tariffs on hardware and software.

The industry structure in the IT sector has four major categories:

- IT Software,
- IT services,
- BPO & IT enabled services,
- Hardware

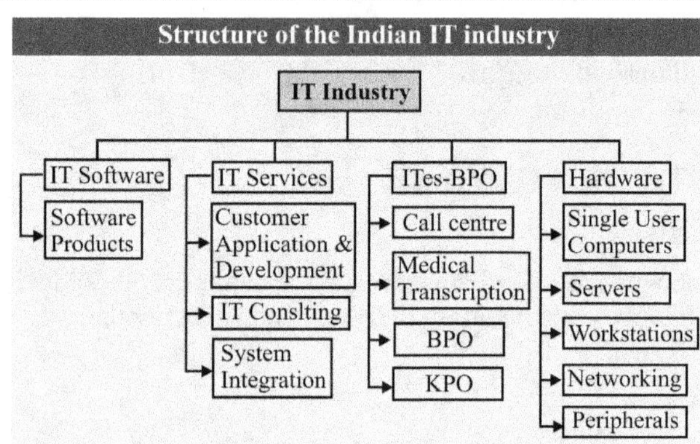

Computer Hardware Industry in India

The computer hardware market consists of the following segments: computers, peripherals and devices, and storage devices.

- The Indian computer hardware market had total revenues of $4.8bn in 2014, representing a compound annual growth rate (CAGR) of 16.3% between 2010 and 2014 after that total revenues of computer hardware $15.8 bn in 2015.

IT Enabled Services

India is regarded as the back office of the world owing mainly to its IT and ITES industry. The sector in India grew at a Compound Annual Growth rate (CAGR) of 15 % over 2010-15, which is 3-4 times higher than the global IT-ITES spend, and is estimated to expand at a CAGR of 9.5% to US$ 300 bn by 2020. India is also the world's largest sourcing destination for the information technology (IT) industry, accounting for approximately 67% of the US$ 124-130 bn market.

IT AND GOVERNMENT IN INDIA

Indian Government Department of Information Technology

Department of Information Technology was set up in year 2000 to implement the Information Technology (IT) Policy of Govt. of National Capital Territory of Delhi. Department of Information Technology is working to put technology to its highest and best use throughout Delhi Government Department/Autonomous Bodies to improve the administration of State programs and services.

E-Governance

The "e" in e-Governance stands for 'electronic'. Thus, e-Governance is basically associated with carrying out the functions and achieving the results of governance through the utilization of ICT (Information and Communications Technology).

National Informatics Centre (NIC)

National Informatics Centre (NIC) was established in 1976, and has since emerged as a "prime builder" of e-Government/e-Governance applications up to the grassroots level as well as a promoter of digital opportunities for sustainable development. NIC, through its ICT Network, "NICNET", has institutional linkages with all the Ministries /Departments of the Central

Government, 36 State Governments/ Union Territories, and about 688 District administrations of India. NIC has been instrumental in steering e-Government/e-Governance applications in government ministries/departments at the Centre, States, Districts and Blocks, facilitating improvement in government services, wider transparency, promoting decentralized planning and management, resulting in better efficiency and accountability to the people of India.

DIGITAL INDIA

The Digital India programmed is a flag-ship programmed of the Government of India with a vision to transform India into a digitally empowered society and knowledge economy.

Some Recent Indian Digital Initiatives

Top 10 digital initiatives taken by the Indian government are:

Digital Locker, Digital Life Certificates, Digital Boost to MGNREGA, Twitter Samvad, Madad (Help), SMS-Based Cyclone Warning System, Online Facility for Firms to File Single Return, Online facility to Issue PAN Card in 48 hours, eMoney, pragati.

SOME RECENT ADVANCEMENTS

Blockchain Technology & Cryptocurrencies

Blockchain Technology involves holding of Information on a blockchain as a shared and continually reconciled database. The database is neither stored in any single location nor centralized version of this information exists. It is hosted by millions of computers simultaneously and the data is accessible to anyone on the internet.

The blockchain network lives in a state of consensus and undergoes a kind of self-auditing ecosystem of a digital value. The network reconciles every transaction that happens in ten-minute intervals. Each group of these transactions is referred to as a "block" and hence the name BlockChain Technology.

Cryptocurrencies works on the Blockchian technology. A cryptocurrency(e.g. bitcoins) is a digital/ virtual currency designed to work as a medium of exchange. It uses cryptography to secure and verify transactions as well as to control the creation of new units of a particular cryptocurrency. It is part of peer-to-peer electronic cash system which is completely decentralized since there is no involvement of central controlling authority.

Internet of Things (IoT)

The internet of things (IoT) is a concept that describes the idea of everyday physical objects being connected to the internet. In IoT, the connected devices should be able to identify themselves to other devices. It describes a world where just about anything can be connected and communicates in an intelligent fashion.

This is the concept of basically connecting any device with an ON and OFF switch to the Internet or to each other. This includes everything from cell phones, Air-conditioner, Television, Music system, smart door and lights, washing machines, geysers, etc.

3-D PRINTING

3D printing is a digital manufacturing process that makes it possible to create a physical object from a 3D file. 3D printing works on additive manufacturing, because 3D printing adds layer after layers. The technology involves Stereolithography process to produce 3D models.

3-Dimensional printing begins with a digital file derived from computer aided design (CAD). After CAD the file is exported as a standard tessellation language (STL) file, featuring triangulated surfaces and vertices. The STL file is then sliced into hundreds to thousands of 2-D layers. A 3D printer then reads the 2-D layers as building blocks which it layers one atop the other, thus forming a 3-D object. All design files, regardless of the 3D printing technology, are sliced into layers before printing. Layer thickness – the size of each individual layer of the sliced design – is determined partly by technology, partly by material, and partly by desired resolution and your project timeline; thicker layers equates to faster builds, thinner layers equate to finer resolution, less visible layer lines and therefore less intensive post-processing work . After a part is sliced, it is oriented for build.

EDGE TPU AND CLOUD IoT EDGE

The multinational technology giant Google has announced to launch two new products Edge TPU and Cloud IoT Edge.

The Edge TPU is a hardware product based on Google's own Tensor Processing Unit (TPU) deep-learning acceleration technology. It will be part of artificial intelligence components for Internet of Things (IoT). As per information provided by Google, Edge TPU is Google's purpose-built ASIC (Application Specific Integrated Circuit) chip designed to run Tensor Flow Lite ML models at the edge.

Additionally the company has announced launch of Cloud IoT Edge which will be an expansion to Google Cloud that allows machine learning models built on the full-fat cloud-based TPUs to be executed on the Edge TPU along with GPU- and CPU-based accelerators running on Android/ Linux-based operating systems.

The Edge TPU is based on an NXP Semiconductors system-on-chip processor. It will initially be launched as part of a Raspberry Pi-like system-on-module (SOM) development kit. The bare TPU chip itself, meanwhile, is due to appear in products from companies including Nokia, NXP, and Trax, among others named as partners in the programme.

Radio Frequency Identification (RFID)

Radio frequency identification (RFID) is a system that transmits the identity in the form of a unique serial number of an object or person wirelessly, using radio waves. It's grouped under the broad category of automatic identification technologies. Auto-ID technologies include bar codes, optical character readers and other related technologies. The auto-ID technologies have been used to reduce the amount of time and labor needed to input data manually and to improve data accuracy.

The purpose of an RFID system is to enable data to be transmitted by a mobile device, called a tag, which is read by an RFID reader and processed according to the needs of a particular application. The data transmitted by the tag may provide identification or location information, or specifics about the product tagged. RFID applications are growing attention because of its ability to track moving objects

RFID is designed to enable readers to capture data on tags and transmit it to a computer system—without needing a person to be involved. An RFID system may consist of several components: tags, tag readers, edge servers, middleware, and application software.

An RFID tag or transponder consists of a chip and an antenna. The microchip contains memory and logic circuits to receive and send data back to the reader. Each tag contains an identification number, data identifying the issuing agency, other specific tag description etc.

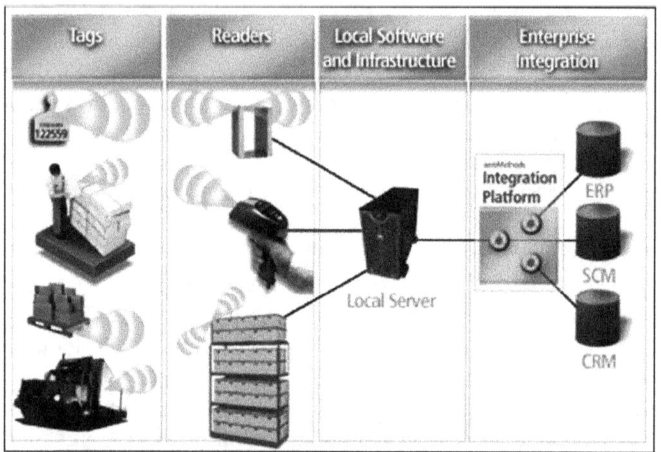

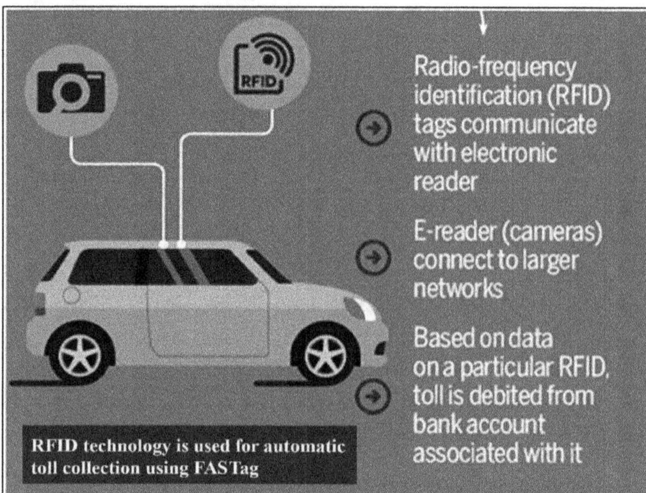

Fig. Working of RFID technology and its application

FASTag and RFID

FASTag is a simple to use; reloadable tag which enables automatic deduction of toll charges and lets you pass through the toll plaza without stopping for the cash transaction. FASTag is linked to a prepaid account from which the applicable toll amount is deducted. The tag employs Radio-frequency Identification (RFID) technology and is affixed on the vehicle's windscreen after the tag account is active. FASTag is a perfect solution for a hassle free trip on national highways.

COMPUTER TERMINOLOGY

There are some important computer terminology includes:

Analog Computer: A computer in which numerical data are represented by measurable physical variables, such as electrical.

Antivirus: Computer antivirus refers to a software program that can protect your computer from unwanted viruses and remove any that penetrate your computer's defenses.

Artificial Intelligence: Artificial intelligence (AI) is the intelligence of machines and the branch of computer science that aims to create it. AI textbooks define the field as "the study and design of intelligent agents" where an intelligent agent is a system that perceives its environment and takes actions that maximize its chances of success.

ASCII (American Standard Code for Information Interchange): ASCII, a code for information exchange between computers made by different companies; a string of 7 binary digits represents each character; used in most microcomputers.

Android: It is linux based operating system designed primarily for touch screen mobile devices such as smartphones and tablets computers.

Biometric Device: Biometrics (biometric authentication) consists of methods for uniquely recognizing humans based upon one or more intrinsic physical or behavioral traits.

Bluetooth: Bluetooth is a proprietary open wireless technology standard for exchanging data over short distances (using short wavelength radio transmissions in the ISM band from 2400-2480 MHz) between fixed and mobile devices, creating personal area networks (PANs) with high levels of security.

Booting: To boot (as a verb; also "to boot up") a computer is to load an operating system into the computer's main memory or random access memory (RAM).

Bit. A contraction of the term binary digit. The bit is the basic unit of digital data. It may be in one of two states, logic 1 or logic 0.

Compressed File: Computer files that have been reduced in size by a compression program. Such programs are available for all computer systems.

Cookie. A packet of information that travels between a browser and web server.

CD ROM (Compact Disk- Read Only Memory): a type of optical disk capable of storing large amounts of data — up to 1GB, although the most common size is 700 MB (megabytes).

Digital Computer: A reference to any system based on discrete data, such as the binary nature of computers.

Digital Video/ Versatile Disk (DVD): The successor technology to the CD-ROM, that can store up to 10 gigabytes or more.

Downloading : Retrieving a file or group of files from the Internet so that they can be stored on a local hard drive.

Error: A discrepancy between a computed, observed, or measured value or condition and the true, specified, or theoretically correct value or condition.

Electronic Mail: When a message is sent, the message is sent first to the SMTP server, which acts as an "outbox" for users. The message is then relayed to the appropriate mail server, which can be found listed after the @ symbol in the recipient's E-mail address. The message then waits on that server until the recipient accesses the message.

Fault: An incorrect step, process, or data definition in a computer program which causes the program to perform in an unintended or unanticipated manner.

Fiber optics: Communications systems that use optical fibers for transmission.

Gigahertz: One gigahertz is equivalent to 1000 megahertz, or 1,000,000,000 hertz.

Hacker: An individual with vast experience with security protocols who attempts to illegally access secure servers in an attempt to download private information, damage systems, or act in some other way to "free information".

HTTP: Acronym for «Hypertext Transfer Protocol» The protocol that forms the basis of World Wide Web technology. HTTP is the set of rules governing the software that transports hyperlinked files along the Internet.

Internet: Internet is the largest wide area network in the world which links millions of computers. Through internet information can be shared, business can be conducted and research can be done.

Intranet: An Internet-like network whose scope is restricted to the networks within a particular organization.

JPEG (Joint Photographic Experts Group) : A bit-mapped file format that compresses image size.

Kernel: It is a fundamental part pf program, such as an operating system, that resides in a memory at all times.

Keyboard: is one of computer components which used to input data to a computer. It is called an input device.

LCD: Acronym for "Liquid Crystal Display". It is the technology used for displays in notebooks and monitors for computers.

Linux: An open source spinoff of the UNIX operating system that runs on a number of hardware platforms and is made available for free over the Internet.

Motherboard : is the core of a computer system. It is the circuit board where all other parts connect. It communicates and controls the overall system. No motherboard means no computer system.

MP3: this stands for "MPEG I Audio Layer- 3" and is a digital. compressed music file (their file names always end with an mp3 extension). MP3 files are often downloaded or exchanged between people online.

Microprocessor: A computer on a single chip. The central processing component of a microcomputer.

Nibble: Half a byte, or four bits.

Node: A junction or connection point in a network, e.g. a terminal or a computer.

Online: Pertaining to data and/or hardware devices accessible to and under the control of a networked computer system.

Operating System or Platform: Operating systems create an environment in which a user and hardware interact to each other. These terms refer to the software that your computer uses to operate (otherwise known as your OS) and not to a manufacturer or company. Windows 2000, Windows XP, and OSX (Mac) are common platforms.

Programming: The act of writing a computer program.

Pixel: In computer graphics, the smallest element of a display surface that can be assigned independent characteristics.

Query: A request for information from a database.

Routing. The process of choosing the best path throughout the LAN.

Search Engine: A tool used which matches key words you enter with titles and description on the Internet. It then displays the matches allowing you to easily locate a subject. Similar to a card catalog, but not as efficient. Common search engines are Webcrawler, Yahoo, Alta Vista, Infoseek, Google and Lycos.

Surfing: The random, aimless exploration of web pages achieved through following links that look interesting within a document

Testing: The process of operating a system or component under specified conditions, observing or recording the results, and making an evaluation of some aspect of the system or component.

USB: Acronym for "Universal Serial Bus". This is a style of port connection that is used by many peripheral devices such as Palm Pilots, phones, scanners, printers etc. This type of connection is much faster than more traditional kinds of connections such as serial and parallel ports.

URL: Acronym for "Universal Resource Locator" The specific path to a World Wide Web file, including filename and extension.

Virus: A virus is a program that will seek to duplicate itself in memory and on disks, but in a subtle way that will not immediately be noticed. A computer on the same network as an infected computer or that uses an infected disk (even a floppy) or that downloads and runs an infected program can itself become infected.

World Wide Web or WWW: This is the part of the Internet that you acces. The World Wide Web is so named because each page in the WWW has links to other pages, which have links to other pages, and so on, creating what could visually be seen as a web-like network of links.

XML: Stands for "Extensible Markup Language." technically it should be EML. XML is used to define documents with a standard format that can be read by any XML-compatible application. The language can be used with HTML pages, but XML itself is not a markup language. Instead, it is a "meta-language" that can be used to create markup languages for specific applications. For example, it can describe items that may be accessed when a Web page loads. Basically, XML allows you to create a database of information without having an actual database. While it is commonly used in Web applications, many other programs can use XML documents as well.

YOBIBYTE: A yobi-byte is a unit of data storage that equals 2 to the 80th power, or 1,208,925,819,614,629,174,706,176 bytes.

ZIP: A ZIP file (ZIP) is a "zipped" or compressed file.

MULTIPLE CHOICE QUESTIONS

1. **Assertion (A):** Information technology is fast becoming a very important field of activity in India.

   Reason (R): Software is one of the major exports of the country and India has a very strong base in hardware.

   [IAS Prelim]

   Codes:
   (a) Both A and R are true and R is the correct explanation of A
   (b) Both A and R are true but R is not a correct explanation of A
   (c) A is true but R is false
   (d) A is false but R is true

2. The memory of a computer is commonly expressed in terms of kilobytes or megabytes. A byte is made up of:

   [IAS Prelim]
   (a) eight binary digits
   (b) eight decimal digits
   (c) two binary digits
   (d) two decimal digits

3. Consider the following statements: **[IAS Prelim]**
   1. Smart card is a plastic card with an embedded microchip.
   2. Digital technology is primarily used with new physical communication medium such as satellite and fibre optics transmission.
   3. A digital library is a collection of documents in an organized electronic form available on the internet only.

   Which of the statements given above is/are correct?
   (a) 3 only   (b) 1 and 2
   (c) 2 and 3   (d) 1, 2 and 3

4. Consider the following: **[IAS Prelim]**
   1. Bluetooth device 2. Cordless phone
   3. Microwave oven 4. Wi-Fi device

   Which of the above can operate between 2.4 and 2.5 GHz range of radio frequency band?
   (a) 1 and 2 only   (b) 3 and 4 only
   (c) 1, 2 and 4 only   (d) 1, 2, 3 and 4

5. Which among the following do/does not belong/belongs to the GSM family of wireless technologies? **[IAS Prelim]**
   (a) EDGE   (b) LTE
   (c) DSL   (d) Both EDGE and LTE

6. What is the difference between Blue-tooth and Wi-Fi devices? **[IAS Prelim]**
   (a) Bluetooth uses 2.4 GHz radio frequency band, whereas Wi-Fi can use 2.4 GHz or 5 GHz frequency band
   (b) Bluetooth is used for Wireless Local Area Networks (WLAN) only, whereas Wi-Fi is used for wireless wide area networks (WWAN) only
   (c) When information is transmitted between two devices using Bluetooth technology, the devices have to be in the line of sight of each other, but when Wi-Fi technology is used the devices need not be in the line of sight of each other
   (d) The statements (a) and (b) given above are correct in this context

7. A new optical disc format known as the Blu-ray Disc (BD) is becoming popular. In what way is it different from the traditional DVD ? **[IAS Prelim]**
   1. DVD supports Standard Definition video while BD supports high definition video
   2. Compared to a DVD, the BD format has several times more storage capacity
   3. Thickness of BD is 2.4 mm while that of DVD is 1.2 mm.

   Which of the statements given above is/are correct?
   (a) 1 only   (b) 1 and 2 only
   (c) 2 and 3 only   (d) 1, 2 and 3

8. What is "Virtual Private Network"? **[IAS Prelim]**
   (a) It is a private computer network of an organization where the remote users can transmit encrypted information through the server of the organization.
   (b) It is a computer network across a public internet that provides users access to their organization's network while maintaining the security of the information transmitted.
   (c) It is a computer network in which users can access a shared pool of computing resources through a service provider.
   (d) None of the statements (a), (b) and (c) given above is correct description of Virtual Private Network.

9. With reference to 'Near Field Communication (NFC) Technology', which of the following statements is/are correct? **[IAS Prelim]**
   1. It is a contactless communication technology that uses electromagnetic radio fields.
   2. NFC is designed for use by devices which can be at a distance of even a metre from each other
   3. NFC can use encryption when sending sensitive information.

   Select the correct answer using the code given below.
   (a) 1 and 2 only   (b) 3 Only
   (c) 1 and 3 only   (d) 1, 2 and 3

10. Apple Computers of USA has launched a touch pad which allows a user to operate desktop computer with finger gestures, eliminating the need for a mouse. What is the name of the device? **[IAS Prelim]**
    (a) Mirror image pad (b) Virtual pad
    (c) Fingertrip track pad (d) Magic track pad

11. Which one among the following is the fastest Indian Supercomputer recently developed by ISRO? **[IAS Prelim]**
   (a) Aakash A-1
   (b) Saga 220
   (c) Jaguar-Cray
   (d) Tianhe-IA

12. Which of the following devices can be used to directly image printed text?
   (a) OCR
   (b) OMR
   (c) MICR
   (d) All ofabove

13. Which programming languages are classified as low level languages?
   (a) BASIC, COBOL, FORTRAN
   (b) Prolog
   (c) C, C+
   (d) Assembly languages

14. FORTRAN is
   (a) File Translation
   (b) Format Translation
   (c) Formula Translation
   (d) Flopy Translation

15. What type of computers are client computers (most of the time) in a client-server system?
   (a) Mainframe
   (b) Mini-computer
   (c) Microcomputer
   (d) PDA

16. Consider the following statements regarding pan-India mobile tele network
   1. The Pan-India mobile tele-network was launched in Coimbatore.
   2. The aim of the initiative is to strengthen the spice farming community with the help of latest technologies.
   3. The purpose of the scheme is to get in direct touch with the spice farmers of the state who are the core section of the society.

   Correct statement is/are:
   (a) 1 and 2
   (b) 1 and 3
   (c) 2 and 3
   (d) All of the above

17. Consider the following guiding principles and objectives that would underpin the public-private partnership (PPP) in cyber security has been identified by JWC and select incorrect one.
   1. Given the diverse stakeholders in cyber security, institutional mechanisms should be set up to promote convergence of efforts both in public and private domains.
   2. Use existing institutions and organizations to the extent possible in both private sector and government and create new institutions where required to enhance cyber security.
   3. Identify areas where public sector can build capacities for cyber security.
   4. Put in place appropriate policy and legal frameworks to ensure compliance with cyber security efforts.
   (a) 1 only
   (b) 2 only
   (c) 3 only
   (d) 4 only

18. A packet whose destination is outside the local TCP/IP network segment is sent to______.
   (a) File server
   (b) DNS server
   (c) DHCP server
   (d) Default gateway

19. Match the following Layers and Protocols for a user browing with SSL:
   A. Application of layer   i. TCP
   B. Transport layer   ii. IP
   C. Network layer   iii. PPP
   D. Datalink layer   iv. HTTP

   Codes:

	a	b	c	d
(a)	iv	i	ii	iii
(b)	iii	ii	i	iv
(c)	ii	iii	iv	i
(d)	iii	i	iv	ii

20. What do you call the programs that are used to find out possible faults and their causes?
   (a) Operating system extensions
   (b) Cookies
   (c) Diagnostic software
   (d) Boot diskettes

21. Consider the following statements
   1. International Organization for Standardization is the world's leading organization for the preparation and publication of International Standards for all electrical, electronic and related technologies.
   2. International Telecommunication Union allocate global radio spectrum and satellite orbits, develop the technical standards that ensure networks and technologies seamlessly interconnect, and strive to improve access to ICTs to underserved communities worldwide.

   Correct statement is/are
   (a) 1 only
   (b) 2 only
   (c) Both 1 and 2
   (d) None of above

22. Identify the correct statement(s):
   1. Tianhe is a Chinese Supercomputer.
   2. SAGA 220 is the supercomputer of ISRO.
   (a) 1 only
   (b) 2 only
   (c) Both 1 and 2
   (d) None

23. Consider the following statement:
   1. Musical Instrument Digital Interface (MIDI) ports connected special types of music instruments to sound cards
   2. Software you can use to create a budget is called utility software.
   3. CPU consists of the development of the computer programme.

   Correct statement is /are
   (a) 1, 2 and 3
   (b) 1 and 2
   (c) 1 and 3
   (d) 1 only

24. What is "Virtual Private Network" ? **[IAS Prelim 2011-I]**
    (a) It is a private computer network of an organization where the remote users can transmit encrypted information through the server of the organization.
    (b) It is a computer network across a public internet that provides users access to their organization's network while maintaining the security of the information transmitted.
    (c) It is a computer network in which users can access a shared pool of computing resources through a service provider.
    (d) None of the statements (a), (b) and (c) given above is correct description of Virtual Private Network.

25. "Project Brainwave" deep Learning acceleration platform for real-time Artificial Intelligence has been launched by,
    (a) Google   (b) Microsoft
    (c) IBM   (d) Apple

26. Which of the following is not a cyber security initiative?
    (a) Budapest Convention on Cyber Crime
    (b) National Computer Saksharta Mission
    (c) Cyber Surakshit Bharat Initiative
    (d) Global Centre for Cyber Security

27. What is BRABO?
    (a) First 'Made in India' Industrial Robot manufactured by TAL manufacturing solutions.
    (b) Brazil's first ever robot for manufacturing solutions by Mabru Automation .
    (c) All electric Industrial Robot manufactured by Staubli.
    (d) High-precision, High-speed compact robot manufacturing by Epson.

28. The technical body which is responsible for prevention of cyber attacks on governmental institutions/entities,
    (a) MeitY   (b) CERT-In
    (c) NTRO   (d) NIC-CERT

29. Which one of the following Ministries has launched a new programme on Interdisciplinary Cyber Physical systems (ICPS) to foster and promote R&D?   **[NDA (II) 2017]**
    (a) Ministry of Earth Sciences
    (b) Ministry of science and Technology
    (c) Ministry of Information and Broadcasting
    (d) Ministry of New and Renewable Energy

ANSWER KEY

1	(c)	2	(a)	3	(b)	4	(d)	5	(c)	6	(a)	7	(b)	8	(b)
9	(c)	10	(d)	11	(b)	12	(a)	13	(d)	14	(c)	15	(c)	16	(d)
17	(c)	18	(d)	19	(a)	20	(c)	21	(b)	22	(c)	23	(d)	24	(a)
25	(b)	26	(b)	27	(a)	28	(d)	29	(b)						

Chapter 2

COMMUNICATION TECHNOLOGY

Communication is the transfer of information from one place to another and some means of ensuring that what is sent is also received. Technology increases the ways in which information can be communicated, the speed of transmission, and the total volume that can be handled at any one time.

RECENT COMMUNICATION TECHNOLOGY

5G (Fifth Generation)

As the next step in the continuous innovation and evolution of the mobile industry, 5G will not only be about a new air interface with faster speeds, but it will also address network congestion, energy efficiency, cost, reliability, and connection to billions of people and devices.

Cognitive Networks, Big Data

Communication systems handle volumes of data generated by embedded devices, mobile users, enterprises, contextual information, network protocols, location information and such. It is a vast amount of information: A global IP backbone generates over 20 billion records per day, amounting to over 1 TB per day! Processing and analyzing this "big data" and presenting insights in a timely fashion are becoming a reality with advanced analytics to understand the environment, to interpret events, and to act on them.

Cyber Security

2014 was most remarkable for demonstrating that everything connected to the Internet can, and will be hacked. On daily basis we heard of retailers (Target, Home Depot, Neiman Marcus), financial institutions (Chase), technology companies (Snapchat, eBay, Sony) being hacked. No one is cyber-safe, and the road to the future leads through new cybersecurity technologies beyond current perimeter firewall-like defenses.

Green Communications

It is being reported that communications technologies are responsible for about 2-4% of all of carbon footprint generated by human activity. This highlights the need to focus on managing these numbers, and Green communications is doing just that. The trend is tackling first mobile networks because of their high energy use. Basestations and switching centers could count for between 60% and 85% of the energy used by an entire communication system.

Smarter Smartphones, Connected Sensors

The indisputable rock-start of devices is the smartphone, and its future can't be brighter. In 2014 we saw that only a few days after the iPhone 6 was released, there are already articles being written about the next-generation iPhone 7. Size, shape, and capabilities of these ubiquitous communication devices continue evolving, and so are prices which, driven by cost and performance improvements in digital technologies, are falling rapidly. The average selling price of a smart-phone went down in 2014, and we expect this to continue in coming days with low-cost OEMs such as Xiaomi and Lenovo leading the trend.

Network Neutrality, Internet Governance

The Internet has been operating since its inception under "open" principles, i.e. an open standards-based network that treats all traffic in roughly the same way, i.e. no connection blocking, bandwidth transparency, universal connectivity, and best effort service. Can these principles be sustained in a new word of data-hungry applications and services? Is regulation needed to prevent traffic throttling, unfair raise of fees, and construction of preferential high-speed Internet lanes? In 2014, Network Neutrality (NetNeutrality) discussions covered these questions in the context of ISPs transit and peering, and CDNs. Governments and institutions around the world will continue working on it during days to come.

Molecular Communications

Molecular communication is an emerging paradigm where bio-nano-machines(e.g.,artificialcells,geneticallyengineeredcells)communicate to perform coordinated actions. Unlike traditional communication systems which utilize electromagnetic waves, molecular communications utilize biological molecules both as carriers and as information. The advantages provided by this "molecular" approach to communications are size, biocompatibility, and bio-stability.

MODERN TELECOMMUNICATION SYSTEM

Most modern day telecommunications systems are best described in terms of a network. There are six basic components to a telecommunications network.

1. Input and output devices, also referred to as 'terminals'.

These provide the starting and stopping points of all communication. A telephone is an example of a terminal. In computer networks, these devices are commonly referred to as 'nodes' and consist of computer and peripheral devices.

2. Telecommunication channels, which transmit and receive data.

This includes various types of cables and wireless radio frequencies.

3. **Telecommunication processors, which provide a number of control and support functions.**

For example, in many systems, data needs to be converted from analog to digital and back.

4. **Control software,** which is responsible for controlling the functionality and activities of the network.

5. **Messages represent the actual data that is being transmitted.**

In the case of a telephone network, the messages would consist of audio as well as data.

6. **Protocols specify how each type of telecommunication systems handles the messages.**

For example, GSM, CDMA, 3G and 4G are protocols for mobile phone communications, and TCP/IP is a protocol used for communications over the Internet.

INFORMATION COMMUNICATION TECHNOLOGY (ICT) APPLICATIONS

ICT applications, such as e-Government, e-commerce, e-Education, e-Health and e-Environ-ment, are seen as enablers for development, as they proivde an efficient channel to deliver a wide range of basic services in remote and rural areas. ICT applications can facilitate the achievements of millennium development targets, reducing poverty and improving health and environmental conditions in developing countries.

ICT applications can deliver basic services in a wide range of sectors including: health, agriculture, education, public administration, commerce, etc. ICT applications constitute one of the priority domains for ITU-D programme 2 (2010) and the ITU-D ICT Applications and Cyber-security Division. Improving social conditions and building an entry ramp into the information society are amongst the purposes of ITU's ICT Applications work Programme for Developing Countries.

NEAR FIELD COMMUNICATION TECHNOLOGY

Near field communication (NFC), is a form of contactless communication between devices like smart-phones or tablets. Contactless communication allows a user to wave the smart-phone over a NFC compatible device to send information without needing to touch the devices together or go through multiple steps setting up a connection. Fast and convenient, NFC technology is popular in parts of Europe and Asia, and is quickly spreading throughout the United States.

WIRE COMMUNICATION

Every telecommunications system involves the transmission of an information-bearing electro-magnetic signal through a physical medium that separates the transmitter from the receiver. All transmitted signals are to some extent degraded by the environment through which they propagate. Signal degradation can take many forms, but generally it falls into three types: noise, distortion, and attenuation (reduction in power).

Types of wires

There are many types of wires used in wire communication these are :

Single-wire Cable

In the early days of the telegraph, a single un-insulated iron wire, strung above ground, was used as a transmission line. Return conduction was provided through an earth ground. This arrangement, known as the single-wire line, was quite satisfactory for the low-frequency transmission requirements of manual telegraph signaling

Multi Pair Cable

In multi pair cable anywhere from a half-dozen to several thousand twisted-pair circuits are bundled into a common sheath. The twisted pair was developed in the late 19th century in order to reduce cross talk in multi pair cables.

Coaxial Cable

By enclosing a single conducting wire in a dielectric insulator and an outer conducting shell, an electrically shielded transmission circuit called coaxial cable is obtained.

Optical Fibre System

Like all other communication system, the primary objective of optical fiber communication system also is to transfer the signal containing information (voice, data, and video) from the source to the destination. The source provides information in the form of electrical signal to the transmitter. The electrical stage of the transmitter drives an optical source to produce modulated light wave carrier.

NETWORKING DEVICES

Networking hardware's are also known as computer networking devices, are physical devices which are required for communication and interaction between devices on a computer network. Specifically, they mediate data in a computer network.

Networking devices may include gateways, routers, network bridges, modems, cable modem, wireless access points, networking cables, line drivers, switches, hubs, and repeaters; and may also include hybrid network devices such as multilayer switches, protocol converters, bridge routers, proxy servers, firewalls, network address translators, multiplexers, network interface controllers, wireless network interface controllers, ISDN terminal adapters and other related hardware.

NANOTECHNOLOGY IN TELECOMMUNICATION

Nanotechnology is set to have a profound impact on telecommunications leading to easier convergence of related technologies, massive storage data, compact storage devices, and higher performance computing. Nanotechnology for Telecommunications covers research and developmental issues as well as future directions of MEMs and nanotechnology as they apply to telecommunications. It discusses the impact of nanotechnology on devices such as photonic crystals lasers, light emitters (LED), compact fluorescent lamp (CFL), sensors.

WIRELESS COMMUNICATIONS

Wireless communication is the transmission of information over a distance without help of wires, cables or any other forms of electrical conductors. The transmitted distance can be anywhere between a few meters (for example, a television's remote control) and thousands of kilo-meters (for example, radio communication).

THE RADIO-FREQUNCY SPECTRUM

The radio spectrum is the radio frequency (RF) portion of the electromagnetic spectrum.

Radio frequency bands are divided into 3 broad categories:

- Frequencies that are not usable for commercial purposes and are kept reserved for radio astronomy and Defence forces.
- Frequencies that are unlicensed and are open for personal or commercial use for free which includes 2.4GHz and 5GHz WiFi, Bluetooth, cordless phones, etc.
- Frequencies that are licenced by the government for purposes like telecommunication.

The frequency bands used for telecommunication worldwide follow an international convention where the ITU has identified 3 distinct 'International telecommunication regions' and each region have its own distinct set of frequency bands that it uses for telecom.

TELECOM SPECTRUM

In 2010, 3G and 4G telecom spectrum were auctioned in a highly competitive bidding. The winners were awarded spectrum in September, and Tata Docomo was the first private operator to launch 3G services in India. The Government earned US$16 billion in 2016 from the 3G spectrum auction and the broadband wireless spectrum auction generated a revenue of US$9.0 billion in 2016 for a total revenue of US$25 billion in 2016 from both auctions.

MOBILE NETWORK

A mobile network is a communication network where the last link is wireless. The network is distributed over land areas called cells, each served by at least one fixed-location transceiver, known as a cell site or base station. This base station provides the cell with the network coverage which can be used for transmission of voice, data and others.

Cell Signal Encoding

To distinguish signals from several different trans-mitters, time division multiple access (TDMA), frequency division multiple access (FDMA), code division multiple access (CDMA), and Global System for Mobile communication (GSM) were developed. First we understand three different access technologies. FDMA, TDMA and CDMA.

Suppose you have got 100 people to sing and you want to record them singing without any interference. You can do it in three ways.

First way: All the 100 people are allocated different rooms and they can sing at same time and get recording done without interference. This technique is called FDMA. Frequency Division Multiple Access.

Second way: All the 100 people stay in the same room and sing one after another in queue. This way everyone will be recorded without interference because they are not singing simultaneously. This is TDMA. Time Division Multiple Access.

Third way: All the 100 people sing simultaneously and in the same room. But, they sing in different languages so that they can be identified later without any interference. This is CDMA. Code Division Multiple Access.

Now that you have understood these three techniques, the most important difference between GSM and CDMA will become clear easily.

GSM is combination of FDMA and TDMA

Meaning, the 100 people who want to communicate can be divided into five groups of 20 each in different rooms where they can communicate one after another in a queue.

CDMA is Just as the Name Suggests CDMA Access Technology

All the 100 people will communicate simultaneously in same room, but each person will have a unique code to differentiate that person from others.

Difference Between GSM/CDMA

Features	GSM	CDMA
Stands For	Global System for Mobile communication	Code Division Multiple Access
Evolution	1990	1995
Presence	Europe, Asia and Middle East	US and Asian Countries
Handset Compatibility	850/900/1800/1900 MHz	850/1900 MHz
Switching B/W Service Providers	Simply Change Your SIM Card	Handset Needs To Be Changed
Handset Availability	Wide Range of Handsets Available In The Market	A Limited Range of Handsets Support CDMA
Voice Quality	Fluctuates From Time To Time	Comparatively Better Voice Quality
Data Transfer Speed	Lower Data Speed	BREW Facilitates Faster Data Transfer
International Roaming	Easy and Convenient	Hardly Any CDMA Network Provider Offers International Roaming
International Usage	Easy to use	Difficult to use

GENERATION OF INTERNET TECHNOLOGY:

The "G" in wireless networks refers to the "generation" of the underlying wireless network technology.

Technically generations are defined as follows:

1G networks (NMT, C-Nets, AMPS, TACS) are considered to be the first analog cellular systems, which started early 1980s. There were radio telephone systems even before that. 1G networks were conceived and designed purely for voice calls with almost no consideration of data services.

2G networks (GSM, CDMAOne, D-AMPS) are the first digital cellular systems launched early 1990s, offering improved sound quality, better security and higher total capacity. GSM supports circuit-switched data (CSD), allowing users to place dial-up data calls digitally, so that the network's switching station receives actual ones and zeroes rather than the screech of an analog modem.

2.5G networks (GPRS, CDMA2000 1x) are the enhanced versions of 2G networks with theoretical data rates up to about 144kbit/s. GPRS offered the first always-on data service.

3G networks (UMTS FDD and TDD, CDMA2000 1x EVDO, CDMA2000 3x, TD-SCDMA, Arib WCDMA, EDGE, IMT-2000 DECT) are newer cellular networks that have data rates of 384kbit/s and more.

The UN's International Telecommunications Union IMT-2000 standard requires stationary speeds of 2Mbps and mobile speeds of 384kbps for a "true" 3G.

4G technology refers to the fourth generation of mobile phone communication standards. LTE and WiMAX are marketed as parts of this generation, even though they fall short of the actual standard.

The term "4G" references to the speed standard in wireless connectivity.

4G technology is meant to provide what is known as "ultra-broadband" access for mobile devices, and the International Telecommunications Union-Radio communications sector (ITU-R) created a set of standards that networks must meet in order to be considered 4G, known as the International Mobile Telecommunications Advanced (IMT-Advanced) specification.

4G Standards

First, 4G networks must be based on an all Internet protocol (IP) packet switching instead of circuit-switched technology, and use multi-carrier transmission methods or other frequency-domain equalization (FDE) methods instead of current spread spectrum radio technology. In addition, peak data rates for 4G networks must be close to 100 megabit per second for a user on a highly mobile network and 1 gigabit per second for a user with local wireless access or a nomadic connection.

5G

5G stands for the fifth generation of wireless technologies and it will be faster than 4G. That is a no-brainer but how much faster is the question. The details are a bit sketchy at this point but the speeds are supposed to be upwards of 1 to 10Gbps compare to the 4G standards which are 100Mbps up to 1Gbps. But will those speeds ever be realized is another question that we will find out sometime around the year 2020. That is the expected date of the rollout.

TELECOMMUNICATION

Telecommunication is the transmission of signs, signals, messages, writings, images and sounds or intelligence of any nature by wire, radio, optical or other electromagnetic systems. Telecommunication occurs when the exchange of information between communication participants includes the use of technology. It is transmitted either electrically over physical media, such as cables, or via electromagnetic radiation, etc.

HISTORY OF INNOVATIONS IN TELECOMMUNICATION

Pre-1902 – Cable telegraph

1902 – First wireless telegraph station established between Sagar Island and Sand-head.

1907 – First Central Battery of telephones introduced in Kanpur.

1913–1914 – First Automatic Exchange installed in Shimla.

1927 – Radio-telegraph system between the UK and India, with Imperial Wireless Chain beam stations at Khadki and Daund. Inaugurated by Lord Irwin on 23 July by exchanging greetings with King George V.

1933–Radiotelephone system inaugurated between the UK and India.

1953–12 channel carrier system introduced.

1960 – First subscriber trunk dialling route commissioned between Lucknow and Kanpur.

1975 – First PCM system commissioned between Mumbai City and Andheri telephone exchanges.

1976 – First digital microwave junction.

1979 – First optical fibre system for local junction commissioned at Pune.

1980 – First satellite earth station for domestic communications established at Sikandarabad, U.P..

1983 – First analogue Stored Programme Control exchange for trunk lines commissioned at Mumbai.

1984 – C-DOT established for indigenous development and production of digital exchanges.

1995 – First mobile telephone service started on non-commercial basis on 15 August 1995 in Delhi.

1995 – Internet Introduced in India starting with Laxmi Nagar, Delhi 15 August 1995.

TELECOMMUNICATION IN INDIA

India is currently the world's second-largest tele-communications market and has registered strong growth in the past decade and half. The Indian mobile economy is growing rapidly and will contribute substantially to India's Gross Domestic Product (GDP), according to report prepared by GSM Association (GSMA) in collaboration with the Boston Consulting Group (BCG).

India is expected to have over 180 million smart-phones by 2019, contributing around 13.5 % to the global smart-phone market.

According to a report by leading research firm Market Research Store, the Indian telecommunication services market will likely grow by 10.3 % year-on-year to reach US$ 103.9 billion by 2020.

According to the Ericsson Mobility Report India, smart-phone subscriptions in India is expected to increase four-fold to 810 million users by 2021, while the total smart-phone traffic is expected to grow seventeen-fold to 4.2 Exabyte's (EB) per month by 2021.

DIGITAL TELEVISION

Digital television (DTV) is the transmission of television signals using digital rather than conventional analog methods.

Digital television is not the same thing as HDTV (high-definition television). HDTV describes a new television format (including a new aspect ratio and pixel density), but not how the format will be transmitted.

Digital television can be either standard or high definition.

Advantages of DTV over analog TV include:

- Interactivity
- Superior audio quality
- Consistency of reception over varying distances
- Superior image resolution.
- Smaller bandwidth for a given image resolution
- Compatibility with computers and the Internet.

CABLE TELEVISION

Cable television is a system that distributes television signals by means of coaxial or fibre-optic cables. The term also includes systems that distribute signals solely via satellite. Cable-television systems originated in the United States in the late 1940s and were designed to improve reception of commercial network broadcasts in remote and hilly areas.

During the 1960s they were introduced in many large metropolitan areas where local television reception is degraded by the reflection of signals from tall buildings. Commonly known as community antenna television (CATV).

Since the mid-1970s there has been a proliferation of cable-television systems offering special services. Some of these systems can deliver 50 or more channels.

HDTV

HDTV (high definition television) is a television display technology that provides picture quality similar to 35 mm. movies with sound quality similar to that of today's compact disc. Some television stations have begun transmitting HDTV broadcasts to users on a limited number of channels.

HDTV generally uses digital rather than analog signal transmission. However, in Japan, the first analog HDTV program was broadcast on June 3, 1989.

DTV India

DTV India is an entertainment revolution that delivers LIVE TV on your android phone, PC, Tablet and other android based devices; anytime, anywhere absolutely free. With DTV, you can watch movies, television shows, sports, the latest news & updates, at your own time and convenience; even when you are away from home!

India's PAY TV

Indian cable and DTH operators rank as one among the top in the world in the number of subscribers in terms of Pay-TV or digital. The Media Partners Asia (MPA) – Media Route 26 India report released recently showed a list of India & global pay-TV operators in terms of the subscribers.

Direct To Home

In India, direct-to-home (DTH) Broadcasting Service refers to the distribution of multi channel TV programmers in Ku Band by using a satellite system by providing TV signals direct to subscribers' premises. For DTH connection the broadcasting company provides a set that comprises the dish and a receiving set. The company beams an encrypted signal that only the set installed in your household can receive and enable viewing.

Interactive TV (iTV)

Interactive TV (iTV) is any television with what is called a "return path". Information flows not only from broadcaster to viewer, but also back from viewer to broadcaster. Another feature common to all iTV systems is the ability to offer each TV set, or each viewer who uses that TV set, a different choice of content.

Digital cinema

Digital cinema refers to the use of digital technology to distribute or project motion pictures as opposed to the historical use of reels of motion picture film, such as 35 mm film. Whereas traditional film reels had to be shipped to movie theaters, a digital movie can be distributed to cinemas in a number of ways: over the Internet or dedicated satellite links or by sending hard drives or optical discs such as Blu-ray discs.

Digital Cinema is a complete system to deliver "cinema-quality" programs to "theaters" (including consumer homes) throughout the world using digital technology.

In digital cinema, resolutions are represented by the horizontal pixel count, usually 2K (2048×1080 or 2.2 megapixels) or 4K (4096×2160 or 8.8 megapixels).

CLOSED CIRCUIT TELEVISION (CCTV):

CCTV (closed-circuit television) is a TV system in which signals are not publicly distributed but are monitored, primarily for surveillance and security purposes.

MULTIPLE CHOICE QUESTIONS

1. Which of the following is/are the main part(s) of basic cellular system.
   (a) A mobile Unit
   (b) A cell Site
   (c) A mobile Telephone Switching Office
   (d) All of the above

2. Fading of the received radio signals in a mobile communication environment occurs because of .....
   (a) Direct propagation
   (b) Multipath Propagation
   (c) Bi-path Propagation
   (d) None of the above

3. The basic GSM is based on .... traffic channels.
   (a) connection oriented.
   (b) connection less.
   (c) packet switching.
   (d) circuit switching.

4. .... are typically characterized by very small cells, especially in densely populated areas.
   (a) 2G system.   (b) 3G system.
   (c) 2.5G system.   (d) 3.5G system.

5. A antenna which attempts to direct all its energy in a particular direction is called as a ....
   (a) Directional Antenna
   (b) One to One Antenna
   (c) Propagation Antenna
   (d) Single Direction Antenna

6. Speeds of laboratory fiber optic Local Area Networks are now in the range of
   (a) 1 Mbits/s.
   (b) 10 Mbits/s.
   (c) gigabits per second.
   (d) hundreds of megabits per second.

7. Which of the following happen to be the limitations of optical fiber?
   I.   The architecture of their couplers.
   II. Costs of implementing them.
   III. Modification of the software and hardware on existing systems.
   IV. The difficulty of installing the cables.
   (a) II and IV only.   (b) I, II and III only.
   (c) I, III and IV only. (d) I, II, III and IV.

8. What types of handover are supported in LTE?
   (a) Hard handover only
   (b) Hard and soft handovers
   (c) Hard, soft and softer handovers
   (d) Handover is not supported

9. Which of the following does not apply to nanotechnology?
   (a) It is a general-purpose technology.
   (b) It can be called Green technology.
   (c) Newtonian mechanics can describe it.
   (d) It involves rearrangement of atoms.

10. Which type of access used in GSM technology?
    (a) FDMA/TDMA   (b) CDMA
    (c) OFDMA   (d) None of the above

11. The type of Access technology which can enhance the battery life is
    (a) CDMA   (b) TDMA
    (c) OFDMA   (d) None of the above

12. The process of channel coding, Encryption, Multiplexing and modulation for Trans direction and reverse for reception are to be carried out by
    (a) BTS   (b) BSC
    (c) MSC   (d) MS

13. Which type of handoff used in CDMA?
    (a) Soft handoff
    (b) Hard handoff
    (c) Soft & hard handoff
    (d) None of the above

14. In 3G network, W-CDMA is also known as UMTS. The minimum spectrum allocation required for W-CDMA is ________.
    (a) 2 MHz   (b) 20 KHz
    (c) 5 KHz   (d) 5 MHz

15. __________ is a second-generation cellular phone system.
    (a) GSM   (b) D-AMPS
    (c) IS-95   (d) none of the above

16. Modulation refers to __________.
    (a) the distance between the uplink and downlink frequencies
    (b) the separation between adjacent carrier frequencies
    (c) the process of changing the characteristics of a carrier frequency
    (d) the number of cycles per unit of time

17. which of the following are not telephony services supported by GSM?
    (a) dual-tone multi-frequency
    (b) voice mail
    (c) fax mail
    (d) call waiting

18. Commonly used mode for 3G networks is
    (a) TDMA
    (b) FDMA
    (c) TDD (Time-division du-plexing)
    (d) FDD(Frequency-division du-plexing)

19. Communication in traditional cable TV network is
    (a) 180 degree direction
    (b) Omni directional
    (c) bidirectional
    (d) unidirectional

20. Coaxial cable has a bandwidth that ranges from
    (a) 5- 750MHz   (b) 10-300 MHz
    (c) 5-550 MHz   (d) 10-3000MHz

21. World's first hybrid 'Aeroboat' has been built by India under a joint venture with which country,
    (a) Japan   (b) France
    (c) Germany   (d) Russia

22. Read the following statements with reference to MIMO.
    1. It is a type of Antenna-free technology.
    2. It is a type of Video communications technology.
    Select the correct answer using the code given below.
    (a) 1 only   (b) 2 only
    (c) 1 and 2 only   (d) Neither 1 nor 2

23. With reference to 'Near Field Communication (NFC) Technology', which of the following statements is/are correct? **[IAS Prelim 2015]**
    1. It is a contactless communication technology that uses electromagnetic radio fields.
    2. NFC is designed for use by devices which can be at a distance of even a metre from each other
    3. NFC can use encryption when sending sensitive information.
    Select the correct answer using the code given below.
    (a) 1 and 2 only   (b) 3 Only
    (c) 1 and 3 only   (d) 1, 2 and 3

24. Consider the following statements: **[IAS Prelim 2016]**
The Mangalyaan launched by ISRO
    1. is also called the Mars Orbiter Mission
    2. made India the second country to have a spacecraft orbit the Mars after USA
    3. made India the only country to be successful in making its spacecraft orbit the Mars in its very first attempt

Which of the statements given above is/are correct?
    (a) 1 only   (b) 2 and 3 only
    (c) 1 and 3 only   (d) 1, 2 and 3

25. With reference to 'Astrosat', the astronomical observatory launched by India, which of the following statements is/are correct? **[IAS Prelim 2016]**
    1. Other than USA and Russia, India is the only country to have launched a similar observatory into space.
    2. Astrosat is a 2000 kg satellite placed in an orbit at 1650 km above the surface of the Earth.
    Select the correct answer using the code given below.
    (a) 1 only   (b) 2 only
    (c) Both 1 and 2   (d) Neither 1 nor 2

26. With reference to the Indian Regional Navigation Satellite System (IRNSS), consider the following statements : **[IAS Prelim 2018]**
    1. IRNSS has three satellites in geostationary and four satellites in geosynchronous orbits.
    2. IRNSS covers entire India and about 5500 sq. km beyond its borders.
    3. India will have its own satellite navigation system with full global coverage by the middle of 2019.
    Which of the statements given above is/are correct?
    (a) 1 only   (b) 1 and 2 only
    (c) 2 and 3 only   (d) None

27. In which of the following areas can GPS technology be used? **[IAS Prelim 2018]**
    1. Mobile phone operations
    2. Banking operations
    3. Controlling the power grids
    Select the correct answer using the code given below:
    (a) 1 only   (b) 2 and 3 only
    (c) 1 and 3 only   (d) 1, 2 and 3

ANSWER KEY															
1.	(d)	**2.**	(b)	**3.**	(a)	**4.**	(c)	**5.**	(a)	**6.**	(d)	**7.**	(c)	**8.**	(a)
9.	(c)	**10.**	(a)	**11.**	(b)	**12.**	(a)	**13.**	(a)	**14.**	(d)	**15.**	(a)	**16.**	(c)
17.	(d)	**18.**	(d)	**19.**	(d)	**20.**	(a)	**21.**	(d)	**22.**	(d)	**23.**	(b)	**24.**	(c)
25.	(d)	**26.**	(a)	**27.**	(d)										

DEFENCE TECHNOLOGY

India has been the recipient of transfers of defence technology predominantly through the licensed manufacture mode. The country is now one of the largest importers of defence materials in the world. It has also shown the indigenously developed techniques for better independent capabilities and for strategic purposes in this sector

DRDO

The responsibility of developing India's defence technology is assigned to the Defence Research and Development Organization (DRDO). The organization is the main body dedicated to research & development, monitoring, regulating, and administering of country's Defence Research and Development Program.

DRDO looks after diverse areas of defence technology such as aeronautical engineering, armaments, combat vehicles, electronic instrumentation, engineering systems, missiles, naval systems, advanced computing & simulation, life sciences, high altitude defence, development of special materials, laser systems etc.

Major achievements of DRDO

Some of the major achievements towards indigenous development/ joint collaboration of defence equipments and systems and also for the civilian purposes include production of surface to surface missile-Prithvi; Pilotless target craft-Lakshya, Supersonic BrahMos missile system, Light Combat Aircraft (LCA)-Tejas; Airborne Early Warning and Control (AEW&C) System;   Advanced Towed Artillery Gun System (ATAGS); Weapon Locating Radar (WLR)-Swati; High Speed Heavy Weight Ship Launched Torpedo –Varunastra ; Medium Power Radar- Arudhra-; Akash Weapon System; Sonar- Abhay; Hull Mounted Sonar (HUMSA); Advanced Indigenous Distress Sonar System (AIDSS); various types of ammunition for MBT Arjun; Anti Torpedo Decoys; Electro-Optical Fire Control System for Naval Ships; Electro-Optical Sensors for Airborne Platforms; Mountain Foot Bridge; Sub-munition warheads for Pinaka; Terrain Assessment System for trans-border deserts etc.

DEFENCE PUBLIC SECTOR UNDERTAKINGS

Additionally Defence Public Sector Undertakings (DPSUs) also play an important role for production and development of technologies and equipments for strategic purposes. These Public Sector Undertakings fall under the administrative control of the Department of Defence Production, Ministry of Defence.

Major Achievements of DPSUs

Some of the major achievements by Defence Public Sector Undertakings incude,

Production of Naval Offshore Patrol Vessels, Damage Control Simulator, Fuel Barge, Fast Patrol Vessel for the Indian Navy and Coast Guard (by Goa Shipyard Limited); Akash Weapon System for Army, Long Range Surface to Air Missile for the Indian Navy and test fired the Anti-Tank Guided Missile (by Bharat Dynamics Limited); Visakhapatnam Class Destroyers and commissioned the INS Kalvari, the Scorpene class Submarine (by Mazagon Dock Shipbuilders Limited); secure CDMA Cellular Network at Srinagar (Bharat Electronics Limited); Anti Submarines Warfare Corvette, Offshore Patrol Vessel, Water Jet Fast Attack Aircraft and Landing Craft Utility (by Garden Reach Shipbuilders & Engineers Limited)

India's Missile System: At a Glance

S. No.	Missile	Feature	Range
1	Astra Missile	All weather modes, Beyond Visual range, air-to-air Missile	A range of over 80 km in head on mode and 20 km in tail-chase mode.
2	Shaurya Missile	Canisterised Surface-to-surface missile.	600 km
3	Sagarika Missile (K-15)	Submarine-to-Surface Missile.	More than 700 km
4	Akash Missile	Medium range Surface-to-Air Missile.	25 km
5	Nag Missile	Third Generation-fire and forget-anti-tank guided missile.	4 to 6 km
6	Nirbhay Missile	Long range subsonic cruise missile.	1000 km

7	Dhanush Missile		The Ship-based Surface-to-surface ballistic missile.	300 to 350 km
8	BrahMos Missile (Joint Indo-Russia Venture) I/ II		Supersonic cruise missile (can be launched from ships, submarines, aricrafts and land)	290 - 450 km
9	(a)	Prithvi-I (Army version)	A single stage liquid-fuelled surface-to-surface missile.	150 km
	(b)	Prithivi-II (Air force version)	A single stage liquid-fuelled surface-to-surface missile. Developed In Nov 2006, by DRDO.	250 km
	(c)	Prithvi-III (Naval Version)	A two-stage surface-to-surface missile (first stage is solid fuelled and second stage is liquid fuelled).	350 km
10	(a)	Agni-I	Short range ballistic missile	700-800 km
	(b)	Agni-II	Medium range ballistic missile	2500 km
	(c)	Agni-III	Intermediate range ballistic missile	3500 km
	(d)	Agni-IV	Intermediate, range ballistic missile	4000 km
	(e)	Agni-V	Intercontinental ballistic missile	5500-5800 km
	(f)	Agni-VI	Intercontinental ballistic missile	8000-12000 km

Tanks in India

Type	Quantity (Estimated)	Origin	Description
Arjun MBT	248	India	The Indian Army ordered 124 'Arjun' Mk1 MBTs in 2000 and placed another order for additional 124 'Arjun' Mk1 MBTs and 124 'Arjun' Mk2 MBTs in 2010, after Arjun tank had conclusively outperformed the T-90. Indian Army is set to acquire 124 Arjun Mk2 tanks as a follow-on order, according to the Defence Minister.
T-90 BHISHMA	1,050	Russia	Procured in three separate orders. Two batches (310 tanks and knockdown kits in 2000 and a further 300 in 2006) were purchased from Russia. A further 1000 were to be produced locally by 2020. Of those, the first batch of 10 were delivered in August 2009.
T-72 AJEYA	2,414	Soviet Union Poland	Upgraded to advanced Ajeya Mk1 and MK2 standard mainly based on Polish PT-91 Twardy Tank features developed by DRDO

Indian sea-based nuclear-armed ballistic missiles

Name	Type	Maximum range (km)	Status
Dhanush	Short-range	350	Developed, but not deployed
Sagarika (K-15)	SLBM	700	Awaiting deployment on INS
K-4	SLBM3	500	Tested

Nuclear-powered submarines

Class	Type	Boats	Displacement	Note
Chakra (Akula II)-class	Attack Submarine (SSN)	INS Chakra (S71)	12,770 tonnes	Under a 10 year lease from Russia since 2012.
Arihant-class	Ballistic Missile submarine (SSBN)	INS Arihant (S73)	6,000 tonnes, surfaced	Commissioned in August 2016.

Aircraft carriers

Class	Type	Ships	Displacement	Description
Modified Kiev-class	Aircraft carrier	INS Vikramaditya (R33)	45,400 tonnes	STOBAR carrier.

Replenishment ships

Class	Type	Ships	Origin	Displacement
Deepak-class	Replenishment oiler	INS Deepak (A50) INS Shakti (A57)	Italy	27,500 tonnes
Jyoti-class	Replenishment oiler	INS Jyoti (A58)	Russia	35,900 tonnes
Aditya-class	Replenishment oiler & Repair ship	INS Aditya (A59)	India	24,612 tonnes

Research and survey ships

Class	Type	Ships	Origin	Displacement
Sagardhwani	Research vessel	INS Sagardhwani (A74)	India	2,050 tonnes
Sandhayak-class	Survey vessel	INS Nirupak (J14) INS Investigator (J15) INS Jamuna (J16) INS Sutlej (J17) INS Sandhayak (J18) INS Nirdeshak (J19) INS Darshak (J20) INS Sarvekshak (J22)	India	1,800 tonnes
Makar-class	Survey vessel	INS Makar (J31)	India	500 tonnes

BARAK-ANTI MISSILE

Barak-anti missile' is known as (LR-SAM), it is designed to defined against any type of airborne threat including aircraft helicopters Anti-ship missiles and combat jets out to a maximum range of 70 km to 90 km. India and Israel jointly developed Long Range Surface to Air Missile (LRSAM) Barak 8 was successfully test fired from INS Kolkata. The firing trial of the LR SAM has been jointly carried out by the Indian Navy, Defence Research and Development Organisation (DRDO) and Israel Aerospace Industries. This successful test marks a significant milestone in enhancing Indian Navy's Anti Air Warfare capability and also India-Israel relations.

SHAURYA MISSILE

It is a canister launched hypersonic surface-to-surface tactical missile developed by the Indian Defence Research and Development Organization (DRDO) for use by the Indian Armed Forces. It has a range of between 750 to 1,900 km (470 to 1,180 mi) and is capable of carrying a payload of one ton conventional or nuclear warhead. It gives the potential to strike in the short-intermediate range against any adversary.

Shaurya can reach a velocity of Mach 7.5 even at low altitudes. On 12 November 2008, the missile reached a velocity of Mach 5 as it crossed a distance of 300 km, with a surface temperature of 70° Celsius. The missile performed rolls to spread the heat uniformly on its surface. Flight time is between 500 seconds and 700 seconds.

DHRUV

The Advanced Light Helicopter (ALH), also known as 'Dhruv', is the first indigenously designed and manufactured helicopter by **HAL** Bangalore. Dhruv was designed against then **futuristic** benchmarks and its design and technology is indicative of this fact. At the time of inception in the early Eighties. There were several budding technological options in rotor blades, gear boxes, that promised large jumps in performance and other benefits.

The ALH is being employed for a variety of missions including Advanced Search and Rescue, Special Heli-Borne Operations, Armed Patrol, Sniper Ops, VVIP Carriage and Night SAR.

IndARC

IndARC is the India's first underwater moored observatory anchored in the Kongsfjorden fjord, half way between Norway (1100km away from Norway) and the North Pole at a depth of 192 metres. It has been deployed for the continuous monitoring of the oceanographic parameters from various depths in order to obtain significant inputs in the understanding of the Arctic climate and its possible link to tropical processes, specifically the Indian monsoon. IndARC was Designed and developed by scientists from the Earth System Science Organisation (ESSO), National Centre for Antarctic and Ocean Research (NCAOR), National Institute of Ocean Technology (NIOT) and Indian National Centre for Ocean Information Services (INCOIS).

NETRA

The Indian Airforce (IAF) has formally inducted the first ever indigenously built Airborne Early Warning and Control System (AEW&C) dubbed as NETRA. NETRA has been indigenously developed by the DRDO. It was made public at the Aero India exhibition held in Bengaluru, Karnataka on 14 Feb 2017. AEW&C are airborne radar systems mounted on a carrier jet for airborne surveillance system i.e. to spot and track aircraft, missiles, ships and vehicles and offer command and organize direct friendly forces.

INDIAN AIRCRAFT CARRIER

Indian Aircraft Carrier will use STOBAR (Short take off but arrested recovery) by using or sky-jump for take off, just like: INS Vikramaditya, INS Vishal, INS Virat, etc.

Russia has offered its nuclear aircraft carrier, dubbed "Storm," to India for purchase, a senior Indian Navy official said. The offer comes as India and the US discuss the transfer of technology for India's future nuclear aircraft carrier, the INS Vishal.

India plans to build its second homegrown aircraft carrier, INS Vishal, which will be nuclear-powered, 300 meters long, 70 meters wide and displace 65,000 tons.

INS Viraat: It is a centaur-class air-craft carrier in service with the Indian Navy.

INDIAN COST-GUARDSHIP (ICGS) AYUSH

Indian Coast Guard (ICG) has augmented its growing strength when vice admiral A R Larve, flag officer commanding-in-chief, Southern Naval Command, commissioned CGS Ayush, the final vessel in the series of twenty fast patrol vessels (FPVs) designed and built by the Cochin Shipyard Ltd (CSL). The 50-m-long ship having a maximum speed of 33 knots was delivered to the CG. It was made public at Kochi on 18 Feb 2017.

INSV TARINI

The main objective of INSV Tarini, It carries a suite of six sails including a main sail, head sails, downwind sails and storm sail genoa sails and stay sails, and it is the first all woman crew to take up such challenging task, It was inducted into the Indian navy at Goa on 18 feb 2017. Indian Navy's six women officers circumnavigated the globe on INSV Tarini during Navika sagar Parikrama.

AIRCRAFTS

C-130J: The aircraft is capable of performing paradrop, heavy drop, casuality evacuation and can also operate from short and semi prepared surfaces. C-130J is the heaviest aircraft to land at DBO in Aug 2013.

C-17: The aircraft is capable of carrying a payload of 40-70 tons up to a distance of 4200-9000 km in a single hop.

IL-76: A four engine heavy duty/long haul military transport aircraft of Russian origin with a max speed of 850 km/hr. It has a twin 23 mm cannon in tail turret and capacity to carry 225 paratroopers or 40 tones freight, wheeled or tracked armored vehicles.

AN-32: Twin engine turboprop, medium tactical transport air-craft of Russian origin with a crew of five and capacity to carry 39 paratroopers or max load of 6.7 tonnes. It has a max cruise speed of 530 km/hr.

EMBRAER: The main role of employment of this executive Jet Air craft is to convey VVIPs/VIPs to destinations within India and abroad. Air HQ Communication Squadron operates this aircrafts and it has maintained a flawless incident/accident free track record till date.

AVRO: Twin engine turboprop, military transport and freighter of British origin having a capacity of 48 paratroopers or 6 tonnes freight and max   cruise speed of 452 km/hr.

Dornier: Twin engine turboprop, logistic air support staff trans-port aircraft of German origin capable of carrying 19 passengers or 2057 kg freight.   It has a max speed of 428 km/hr.

Boeing 737-200: Twin engine turbofan, VIP passenger aircraft of American origin with total seating capacity of upto 60 passengers. It has a max cruise speed of 943 km/hr.

MI-25/MI-35: Twin engine turboshaft, assault and anti armour helicopter capable of carrying 8 men assault squad with four barrel 12.7 mm rotary gun in nose barbette and upto 1500 Kg of external ordnance including Scorpion anti-tank missiles. It has a max cruise speed of 310 km/hr.

MI-26: Twin engine turboshaft, military heavy lift helicopter of Russian origin with carrying capacity of 70 combat equipped troops or 20,000 kg payload. It has a max speed of 295 km/hr.

MI-17 V5: The Mi-17 V5 is a potent helicopter platform, equipped with modern avionics and glass cockpit instrumenta-tion. They are equipped with state-of-art navigational equipment, avionics, weather radar and are NVG-compatible.

LIST OF INDIAN MILITARY AIRCRAFTS

The following list of active Indian military aircraft is a list of military aircraft currently in service with the Indian Armed Forces. For a list of historical aircraft used by the Indian Military, see list of historical aircraft of the Indian Air Force.

Type	Origin	Role	Version	Number	Notes
SukhoiSu-30Mk	India & Russia	Multirole air superiority fighter	Su - 30 Mk1 Trainer	230	All aircraft to be upgraded to super sukhoiSu standards and introduced from 2020-21.
HAL Tejas	India	Multirole combat aircraft	Mk.1 Trainer	2 1	103 LCA (20 x Mk. 1 + 83 x Mk. 1-A) aircraft to be ac-quired. Final operational certification (FOC) scheduled for early-mid 2017, 2 Mk.1 aircraft inducted; SP-3 ready for induction. Full squadron of 20 Mk.1 aircraft to be introduced by 2018; improved Mk.1-A to be introduced from 2020-21.
HAL Rudra	India	Attack	ALH-WSI	7	Total of 38 on order.

HAL Light Combat Helicopter	India	Attack	LCH	3 proto-types	65 on order. 3 prototypes delivered.
HAL HJT-16 Kiran	India	Trainer	HJT-16 HJT-16II	81	To be phased out by 2017 and eventually be replaced by BAE Hawk (20 Hawks currently on order).
HAL Dhruv	India	Utility	Dhruv	66	65 more on order.
HAL Chetak	India	Utility	SA316B SA319	74	Being withdrawn from service and replaced by HAL Dhruv
HAL Cheetah	India	Utility	Cheetah	14	Hal Cheetah manufactured with HAL Turbomecca TM 333-2M2 Shakti engine.

GLOBAL DEFENCE TECHNOLOGY

TERMINAL HIGH ALTITUDE AREA DEFENSE (THAAD) SYSTEM

Terminal High Altitude Area Defense (THAAD) is a transportable system that intercepts ballistic missiles inside or outside the atmosphere during their final, or terminal, phase of flight. THAAD uses a one-stage hit-to-kill interceptor to destroy incoming ballistic missile targets. The system is able to intercept incoming missiles both inside and just outside of the Earth's atmosphere at a range of 200 kilometers, which mitigates the effects of weapons of mass destruction before they reach the ground. This ability to intercept makes THAAD an important part of layered missile defense concepts.

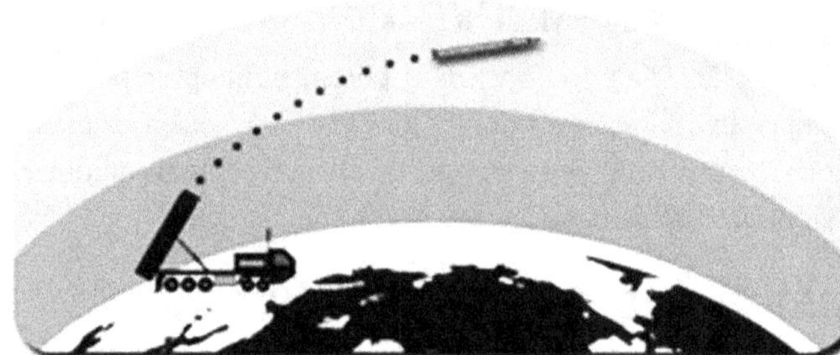

(Fig. THAAD System)

THAAD was developed after the experience of Iraq's Scud missile attacks during the Gulf War in 1991. The THAAD interceptor carries no warhead, but relies on its kinetic energy of impact to destroy the incoming missile. A kinetic energy hit minimizes the risk of exploding conventional-warhead ballistic missiles, and the warhead of nuclear-tipped ballistic missiles will not detonate on a kinetic-energy hit.

MULTIPLE CHOICE QUESTIONS

1. Consider the following statements: **[IAS Prelim]**

1. In November, 2006, DRDO successfully conducted the interception test using Prithvi-II missile.
2. Prithivi-II is a surface-to-surface missile and can be deployed to guard the metros against air attacks.

Which of the statements given above is/are correct?

(a) 1 only 　　　　(b) 2 only

(c) Both 1 and 2 　　(d) Neither 1 nor 2

2. What is the Galileo Project which has been in news recently? **[IAS Prelim]**

(a) An intercountry programme of missile shield developed by the United States of America

(b) A project developed by India with assistance from Canada

(c) An environmental protection project being developed by Japan

(d) A multi-satellite navigation project being developed by the European Union

3. In which one of the following did India buy the Barak anti-missile defence systems? **[IAS Prelim]**

(a) Israel 　　　　(b) France

(c) Russia 　　　　(d) USA

4. In which one of the following locations is the International Thermonuclear Experimental Reactor (ITER) project to be built? **[IAS Prelim]**

(a) Northern Spain 　(b) Southern France

(c) Eastern Germany 　(d) Southern Italy

5. In the context of the Indian defence, what is 'Dhruv'? **[IAS Prelim]**

(a) Aircraft-carrying warship

(b) Missile-carrying submarine

(c) Advanced light helicopter

(d) Intercontinental ballistic missile

6. In the context of Indian defence, consider the following statements: **[IAS Prelim]**

1. The Shaurya missile flies with a speed of more than 8 Mach.
2. The range of Shaurya missile is more than 1600 km.

Which of the statements given above is/are correct?

(a) 1 only 　　　　(b) 2 only

(c) Both 1 and 2 　　(d) Neither 1 nor 2

7. Consider the following statements: **[IAS Prelim]**

1. INS Sindhughosh is an aircraft carrier.
2. INS Viraat is a submarine.

Which of the statements given above is/are correct?

(a) 1 only 　　　　(b) 2 only

(c) Both 1 and 2 　　(d) Neither 1 nor 2

8. With reference to Agni-IV Missile, which of the following statements is/are correct? **[IAS Prelim]**

1. It is a surface-to-surface missile.
2. It is fuelled by liquid propellant only

3. It can deliver one-tonne nuclear warheads about 7500 km away

Select the correct answer using the code given below.

(a) 1 only 　　　　(b) 2 and 3 only

(c) 1 and 3 only 　　(d) 1, 2 and 3

9. The term 'IndARC', sometimes seen in the news, is the name of **[IAS Prelim]**

(a) an indigenously developed radar system inducted into Indian Defence

(b) India's satellite to provide services to the countries of Indian Ocean Rim

(c) a scientific establishment set up by India in Antarctic region

(d) India's underwater observatory to scienti-fically study the Arctic region

10. Consider the following Statements: -

1. BrahMos armed with su-30MKI would be a game changer in the India ocean because it has a range of 290 km and can also travel at a top speed of mach 2.8 barely 3-4 metres above the sea Surface, the missile cannot be intercepted by any known weapon system in the world.
2. BrahMos Acrospace, a joint venture between India and Russia has started designing a hypersonic version of the Brahmos missile Brahmos - II

Which of the above statement is / are correct?

(a) 1 only 　　　　(b) 2 only

(c) Both 1 and 2 　　(d) Neither 1 nor 2

11. Consider the following Statements:

1. Agni - II is a Surface - to - surface intermediate range missile that can carry nuclear weapons and has a range of more than 2000 km.
2. The missile re-entry vehicle is made with Carbon – Carbon Composits. To with stood very high temperatures of up to 3,000 degree Celsius.

Which of the above statements is/are correct?

(a) 1 only 　　　　(b) 2 only

(c) Both 1 and 2 　　(d) Neither 1 nor 2

12. Consider the following statements:

1. Medium range surface - to- surface prithvi-II ballistic missile is a single stage, liquid propelled missile, that is capable of striking targets at a maximum range of 350km.
2. The Prithvi is the first of the missiles developed under the country's Integrated Guided missile development programme. It has now two variants -Air force version (Prithvi-II) and Naval (Dhanush) both having a range of 350 km.

Which of the above statement is/are Correct?

(a) 1 only 　　　　(b) 2 only

(c) Both 1 and 2 　　(d) Neither 1 nor 2

13. Consider the following statements
1. Rustom I, a medium altitude and long- endurance Unmanned Aerial Vehichle (UAV).
2. Lakshy (UAV) -A drone that is remotely piloted by a ground control station provides aerial subtargets for live fire training.
3. Nishant (UAV) is a Surveillance aircraft primarily tasked with intelligence gathering over enemy territory.
4. All the above UAV are developed by the Hyderabad - based Aeronautical Development Establishment (ADE).

Which of the above statement is/are Correct?
(a) 1 only   (b) 2 only
(c) 1, 2 and 3   (d) 4 only

14. Which of the following pairs is/are correctly matched?
1. Kiran MK 11: Aerobatic aircraft
2. MI 35: Attack helicopter
3. Mirage 2000: Military transport aircraft

Select the correct answer using the code given below
(a) 1 only   (b) Both 1 and 2
(c) Both 2 and 3   (d) 1, 2 and 3

15. Consider the following statements regarding Sukhoi PAK FA T-50 aircraft.
1. It is a joint venture of USA and India.
2. It is a fifth generation fighter aircraft.
3. It has the ability to super cruise or operate at speeds beyond the sound.

Which of the statements given above is/are correct?
(a) 1 only   (b) 2 and 3
(c) 1 and 2   (d) 1, 2 and 3

16. The "Synthetic Aperture Radar" Technology is used in:
1. RISAT-1   2. RISAT-2
3. CARTOSAT   4. KALPANA
(a) 1 and 4   (b) 3 and 4
(c) 2 and 3   (d) 1 and 2

17. F-22 Raptor which is a fighter aircraft:
1. Belongs to fifth generation of fighter aircraft.
2. Is having hypersonic speed and advanced stealth technology.
3. Is manufactured by Boeing.
(a) 1 and 3   (b) 2 and 3
(c) 1 and 2   (d) All

18. Choose the correct statement(s).
1. The Agni-IV is a short Range Ballistic Missile with a range of 3,500 km.
2. The Agni-IV is capable of carrying five tonne of nuclear warhead.
3. Agni-V will be Intercontinental Ballistic Missile.
(a) 1 only   (b) 2 only
(c) 3 only   (d) None

19. Identify the correct statement(s):-
1. The anti-Ballistic missile system of India intercepted the agni missile.
2. INS-shivalik is India's first indigenous stealth warship.

(a) 1 only   (b) 2 only
(c) Both 1 and 2   (d) None

20. Which of the following pairs is/are correctly matched?
1. Director of Agni I & II : Dr. APJ Abdul Kalam
2. Director of Agni III : Avinash Chander
3. Director of Agni V : Tessy Thomas
(a) 1 and 2   (b) 2 and 3
(c) 1, 2 and 3   (d) None

21. Consider the following statements:
1. AURA (Autonomous Unmanned Research Aircraft) is an unmanned Combat Air Vehicle (UCAV) for the Indian Air Force.
2. It is designed and developed jointly by ADE and Defense Electronic Application Laboratory.

Which of the above statements is/are true?
(a) 1 only   (b) 2 only
(c) 1 and 2 both   (d) None

22. Consider the following statements:
1. The DRDO developed two variants of Prithvi Missile.
2. Prithvi II is equipped with features of manoeuvrability to deceive the enemy defence system.
3. Induction of Prithvi Missile enhances the capability of the Indian Army to attack multiple targets simultaneously.

Which of the statements given above is/are correct?
(a) 2 and 3   (b) 2 only
(c) 1 and 3   (d) 1, 2 and 3

23. Sukhoi-30 MKI Squadron is not stationed at
(a) Tezpur   (b) Pune
(c) Jamnagar   (d) Bareilly

24. The aircraft carrier Admiral Gorshkov procured by Indian from Russia is renamed as
(a) INS Virat   (b) INS Godavari
(c) INS Trishul   (d) INS Vikramaditya

25. Arihant is a
(a) Multi barrel rocket launcher
(b) Airborne Early Warning and Control System
(c) Unmanned Combat Aerial Vehicle
(d) Nuclear-powered ballistic missile submarine

26. Which one of the following pairs is not correctly matched?
(a) Arjun: Indigenously produced Main Battle Tank (MBT)
(b) Phalcon: Cruise missile supplied by Russia to India.
(c) Saras: Indigenously developed civilian passenger aircraft.
(d) Operation Seabird: New Indian naval base at Karwar.

27.

List I (Name of warhead)	List II (Type)
A. Tejas	1. Air-to-air missile
B. Arjun	2. Ship-based missile
C. Dhanush	3. Main battle tank
D. Astra	4. Light combat aircraft

Codes:

	A	B	C	D
(a)	4	3	2	1
(b)	1	2	3	4
(c)	4	2	3	1
(d)	1	3	2	4

28. Which among the following is/are Scorpene-class Submarines?

(i) INS Khanderi　　　　(ii) INS Kalvari

(iii) INS Ranvijay　　　　(iv) INS Karanj

Select the correct answer using the codes given below.

(a) (i) and (ii)　　　　(b) (i), (ii) and (iii)

(c) (i) and (iii)　　　　(d) (i), (ii) and (iv)

29. Select the correct statement about Free Space Optical Communication technology,

(a) Data is transmitted by propagation of different electromagnetic waves in vacuum.

(b) Data is transmitted by propagation of light waves in free space.

(c) Data is transmitted by propagation of light waves in free space using optical fibers.

(d) Data is transmitted by propagation of light waves in vacuum using free space optical fibers.

30. Which of the following missiles was/were developed under the Integrated Guided Missile Development Programme of DRDO?

1. BrahMos　　　　2. Trishul

3. Prahaar　　　　4. Nag

Select the correct answer using the codes given below:

(a) 1 and 3 only　　　(b) 2 and 4 only

(c) 1, 2 and 3 only　　(d) 2, 3 and 4 only

31. Recently, Stratgic forces command of Indian Army successfully test fired its indigenously built nuclear - capable missile Agni-V.

What is unique about Agni-V?

(i) It is an inter-continental surface to surface ballistic missile.

(ii) It is Hypersonic Cruise Missile

(iii) It is an Anti-Radiation Missile

Select the correct statement/statements using the codes given below

(a) only (i)　　　　(b) only (ii)

(c) only (iii)

(d) None of the (i), (ii) and (iii)

32. Which of the following correctly represents the technology of of AAD interceptor Missile test fired by India?

1. The missile is powered by solid propellant

2. The interceptor technology works on the basis of navigation system, mobile launcher etc.

3. It is capable of intercepting missiles up to an altitude of 50-80 km

Select the answer using the codes given below:

(a) 2 only　　　　(b) 3 only

(c) 1 and 2 only　　(d) 1, 2 and 3

33. Recently, BrahMos Cruise Missile was successfully launched. Consider the following statements with reference to it.

(i) It is the world's fastest supersonic cruise missile.

(ii) It was a joint venture of India's DRDO and Russia's NPO Mashinostroyeniya.

Which of the above statement/statements is/are correct?

(a) (i) only　　　　(b) (ii) only

(c) (i) and (ii) only　　(d) Neither (i) nor (ii)

34. With reference to Agni-IV Missile, which of the following statements is/are correct?　　**[IAS Prelim 2014]**

1. It is a surface-to-surface missile.

2. It is fuelled by liquid propellant only

3. It can deliver one-tonne nuclear warheads about 7500 km away

Select the correct answer using the code given below.

(a) 1 only　　　　(b) 2 and 3 only

(c) 1 and 3 only　　(d) 1, 2 and 3

35. The term 'IndARC', sometimes seen in the news, is the name of　　**[IAS Prelim 2015]**

(a) an indigenously developed radar system inducted into Indian Defence

(b) India's satellite to provide services to the countries of Indian Ocean Rim

(c) a scientific establishment set up by India in Antarctic region

(d) India's underwater observatory to scientifically study the Arctic region

36. What is "Terminal High Altitude Area Defense (THAAD)", sometimes seen in the news?　　**[IAS Prelim 2018]**

(a) An Israeli radar system

(b) India's indigenous anti-missile Programme

(c) An American anti missile system

(d) A defence collaboration between Japan and South Korea

ANSWER KEY															
1	(c)	2	(d)	3	(a)	4	(b)	5	(c)	6	(d)	7	(d)	8	(a)
9	(d)	10	(c)	11	(c)	12	(c)	13	(c)	14	(b)	15	(b)	16	(d)
17	(c)	18	(b)	19	(b)	20	(c)	21	(c)	22	(a)	23	(c)	24	(d)
25	(d)	26	(b)	27	(a)	28.	(d)	29.	(d)	30.	(b)	31	(a)	32	(c)
33	(c)	34	(a)	35	(d)	36	(c)								

Chapter 4

SPACE TECHNOLOGY & ADVANCEMENTS IN SCIENCE & TECHNOLOGY

It is the technology developed by the aerospace industry for implementation in spaceflight, satellites, space exploration, space stations and support infrastructure. plenty of daily services such as weather forecasting, remote sensing, GPS systems, satellite television, and long distance communications systems rely on space technology.

APPLICATION OF SPACE TECHNOLOGY

There are many applications of space technology such as:

Earth Observation

Satellite Communication

Disaster Management Support

Satellite Navigation

Climate and Environment

SPACE SHUTTLE

The primary vehicle for research and exploration is the space shuttle. The space shuttle takes off like a rocket, orbits the earth like a spacecraft and lands, like an aeroplane. It consists of an orbiter, an external tank and two solid rocket boosters.

ARTIFICIAL SATELLITES

An artificial satellite is a manufactured 'moon'. It circles the earth in space along a path called an orbit. An artificial satellite may be designed in almost any space. It does not have to be streamlined, because there is little or no air where it travels in space. Artificial satellite may be classified according to the jobs they do as : weather satellites, communications satellites, navigation satellites, scientific satellites and military satellites.

SPACE PROBES

Space Probes are the automated space craft which are operated and managed by robots so as to explore space after leaving Earth's orbit. They can reach the moon; enter into interplanetary space; act as fly by and last but not the least they can land on other planetary bodies.

ORBIT

An orbit can be a circular or eliptical path which is generally followed around an object in space. In object in an orbit is continuously moving unless and unfill some external force will be applied to it. More or less every celestial body in space has their own orbit.

A GEOSYNCHRONOUS ORBIT

A geosynchronous orbit (GEO) is an orbit about the Earth of a satellite with an orbital period that matches the rotation of the Earth on its axis (one sidereal day) of approximately 23 hours 56 minutes and 4 seconds, The synchronization of rotation and orbital period means that, for an observer on the surface of the Earth, an object in geosynchronous orbit returns to exactly the same position in the sky after a period of one sidereal day.

Geosynchronous Orbit (GEO) is the region in which satellites orbit at approximately 22,236 miles above the Earth's surface, in the plane of the equator, where near-geostationary orbits may be implemented. At this altitude, the orbital period is equal to the period of rotation of the Earth, so the satellite appears to move neither East nor west. When a geosynchronous orbital path remains above the Earth's equator (00 latitude) at all times, with a period and an orbital eccentricity of approximately zero.

JET ENGINE

A Jet engine is a machine that converts energy-rich, liquid fuel into a powerful pushing force called thrust. The thrust from one or more engines pushes a plane forward forcing air past its scientifically shaped wings to create an upword force called lift powers it into the sky its known as jet engine. It is also known as Reaction engine.

Reaction Engines idea was to design a device that could use the oxygen already present in the atmosphere through combustion like an ordinary jet engine. So jet engine uses the surrounding air for its oxygen supply and so is unsuitable for motion in space.

SPACECRAFT

A spacecraft is a vehicle, or machine designed to fly in outer space. Spacecraft are used for a variety of purposes, including communications, earth observation, meteorology, navigation, space colonization, planetary exploration, and transportation of humans and cargo. There are two types of spacecraft:

1. Manned spacecraft

As of 2018, only three nations have flown manned spacecraft: USSR/Russia, USA, and China. The first manned spacecraft was, Vostok which carried Soviet cosmonaut Yuri Gagarin into space in 1961, and completed a full Earth orbit. There were five other manned missions which used a Vostok spacecraft. The second manned spacecraft was named Freedom 7, and it performed a sub-orbital spaceflight in 1961 carrying American astronaut Alan

Shepard to an altitude of just over 187 kilometers (116 mi), other manned spacecraft include the Voskhod, Soyuz, Mir manned space stations.

2.   Unmanned spacecraft

Unmanned spacecraft are spacecraft without people ("man") on board, used for unmanned spaceflight.The unmanned spacecraft stations are Salyut 7 and cassini, and the ISS module Zarya were capable of unmanned remote guided station-keeping, and docking maneuvers with both resupply craft and new modules.

Cassini is an unmanned spacecraft sent to the planet Saturn. It is a Flagship-class NASA–ESA–ASI robotic spacecraft. Cassini is the fourth space probe to visit Saturn and the first to enter orbit, and its mission completed in 2017. It has studied the planet and its many natural satellites since arriving there in 2004.

NASA'S DEEP IMPACT SPACECRAFT

Deep impact is a NASA space probe, it was launched on a clear winter day in 12 January 2005 from Cape Canaveral air force station. NASA's Deep Impact spacecraft spanned 268 million miles (431 million kilometers) of deep space in 172 days, then reached out and touched comet Tempel 1.

NASA's Deep Impact space mission was employed to takes detailed pictures of Tempel-1 comet nucleus.

The collision between the coffee table-sized IMPACT and city-sized comet occurred on July 4, 2005.

SELENE-1

SELENE-1 is a lunar mission of JAXA (Japan Aerospace Exploration Agency). The mission objectives are the global survey of the moon, and to develop technologies for the lunar orbit insertion and spacecraft attitude and orbit control. The global survey of the moon is made for better understanding the origin and evolution of the moon, measuring the gravity field, elemental/chemical composition, etc. It also includes the measurement of the lunar and solar-terrestrial environment, and research on the possibility of future utilization of the moon. The nominal SELENE observation period is planned for one year.

BHUVAN

Bhuvan is a software application which allows users to explore a 2D/3D representation of the surface of the earth. ISRO launched the beta version of its web-based GIS tool, bhuvan, on august 12, 2009. Bhuvan offers detailed imagery of Indian locations compared to other virtual Globe software, with spatial resolutions ranging up to 1 meter.

Bhuvan, which uses high-resolution images, will comply with India's remote sensing data policy, which does not allow online mapping services to show sensitive locations such as military and nuclear installations. High-resolution images are those that show locations of 1 sq. m or less on earth.

THEMIS-MISSION

The time history of events and macro scale interactions during substorms (Themis) mission was originally a constellation of five NASA Satellites. These five NASA Satellites are Themis is A to Themis E.

The Name of the mission is acronym alluding to the titan, is known as themis.

The Themis mission, comprising five identical probes, aims to gain new insights into the colourful displays in high-latitude skies.

A US space agency (Nasa) mission to study auroras - the Northern Lights - has blasted off from Cape Canaveral in Florida, after it was delayed by wind.

GALILEO: EUROPE'S GLOBAL SATELLITE NAVIGATION SYSTEM

Galileo is Europe's Global Satellite Navigation System (GNSS), providing improved positioning and timing information with significant positive implications for many European services and users. For example:

- Galileo allows users to know their exact position with greater precision than what is offered by other available systems.
- The products that people use every day, from the navigation device in your car to a mobile phone, benefit from the increased accuracy that Galileo provides.
- Critical, emergency response-services benefit from Galileo.
- Galileo's services will make Europe's roads and railways safer and more efficient.
- It boosts European innovation, contributing to the creation of many new products and services, creating jobs and allowing Europe to own a greater share of the EUR 175 billion global GNSS market (Source: GSA Market Report Issue IV).

SPACE CENTRES AND UNITS

- Vikram Sarabhai Space Centre (VSSC) - Thumba (Thiruvananthapuram)
- ISRO Satellite Centre (ISAC) - Bengaluru
- SHAR Centre - Shriharikota (Andhra Pradesh)
- Liquid Propulsion Systems Centre (LPSC) - Bengaluru
- Space Application Centre - Ahemdabad
- Developmental and Educational Communication - Ahmedabad unit (DECU)
- ISRO Telemetry Tracking and Command Network (ISTRAC) - Bengaluru
- National Remote Sensing Agency (NRSA) - Hyderabad
- Master Control Facility (MCF) - Hassan (Karnataka)
- The Antrix Corporation Limited - Bengaluru
- North Eastern-Space Applications Centre (NE-SAC) - Shillong
- Physical Research Laboratory (PRL) - Ahmedabad
- Laboratory for Electro Optical System (LEOS)
- ISRO Internal System Unit (IISU)
- Indian Institute of Remote Sensing
- Regional Remote Sensing Service Centre (RRSC)
- Development and Eduction Communication (DECU)
- Space Application Centre (SAC)
- National Remote Sensing Centre (NRSC)

- ISRO Telemetry Racking and Command Network (ISTRAC)
- Indian Institue of Space Science and Technology (IIST)
- Antrix Corporation Limited.
- National Atmospheric Research Laboratory (NARL)
- Semi-Conductor Laboratory (SCL)

INDIAN SPACE PROGRAMME

Indian Space Programme have been initiated during 1960 when the space researches were generally carried out with the help of sounding rockets.

In 1969 Indian Space Research Organisation (ISRO) was formed which is known to be the pioneer institution for conducting space programmes in India. Later two other institution were added to the list named as Space Commission and Department of Space so as to gear up the space reseach activities. Today's India is facilitated with robust launch vehicle programmes for launching it indigenously.

In the initial stages of space programmes, satellite experiments such Aryabhatta, Bhaskar, Rohini and Apple were conducted. But with due course of time operational satellite programmes were also being executed. INSAT (Indian National Satellite System) and IRS (Indian Remote Servicing Satellite System) are the now among the major space programmes conducted by ISRO.

INSAT SYSTEM

The Indian National Satellite (INSAT) system is a multi-agency, multi-purpose and operational satellite system for domestic telecommunications, meteorological observations and data relay, nationwide direct satellite television broadcasting and nationwide radio and television distribution programme.

REMOTE SENSING

The term 'remote sensing' refers to the process of sensing, identifying and delineating various objects on ground from a distance without coming into direct physical contact with them. ISRO and the Indian Council of Agricultural Research conducted during 1974-75 a joint experiment called the Agricultural Resources Inventory and Survey Experiment (ARISE). Indian experimental satellites, Bhaskara I and II carried out remote sensing for land cover mapping, geology and vegetation cover of the country. Today, India has the largest group of remote sensing satellites providing services at both the national and global levels.

Indian Remote Sensing (IRS) Satellite System

The Indian Remote Sensing (IRS) satellite system is one of the largest constellations of remote sensing satellites in operation in the world today. The IRS programme commissioned with the launch of IRS-1A in 1988, presently includes thirteen satellites that in services continue to provide imageries in a variety of spatial resolutions ranging from better than one metre upto 506 kilometres.

CARTOSAT –2D	Launched on 15 Feb, 2017 by PSLV–C 36 (104 Satelities in on ago)
RESOURCESAT–2A	Lanched on on 7 Dec 2016 by PSLV–C36
SARAL	Launched on Feb 25, 2013 by PSLV-C20
RISAT-1	Launched on Apr 26, 2012 by PSLV-C19
Megha-Tropiques	Launched on Oct 12, 2011 by PSLV-C18
RESOURCESAT-2	Launched on Apr 20, 2011 by PSLV-C16
CARTOSAT-2B	Launched on July 12, 2010 by PSLV-C15
OCEANSAT-2	Launched on Sept 23, 2009 by PSLV-C14
RISAT-2	Launched on Apr 20, 2009 by PSLV-C12
CARTOSAT-2A	Launched on Apr 28, 2008 by PSLV-C9
CARTOSAT - 2	Launched on Jan 10, 2007 by PSLV-C7
CARTOSAT-1	Launched on May 05, 2005 by PSLV-C6
RESOURCESAT-1	Launched on Oct 17, 2003 by PSLV-C5

Oceansat-2 satellite

Indian Space Research Organization (ISRO) successfully launched the Oceansat-2 and six nano-satellites into a 720 km. intended Sun Synchronous Polar Orbit (SSPO) on September 23, 2009.

The main objectives of oceansat-2 are to study surface winds and ocean surface strata, observation of chlorophyll concentration, monitoring of phytoplankton blooms, study of atmospheric aerosol and suspended sediments. So we can say oceansat-2 satellite will help identify potential fishing zones, monitor the ocean, climate studies and provide inputs for weather forecasting. Example:

- Predicting the onset of monsoons
- Monitoring the pollution of coastal water
- Estimating the water vapour content in the Atmosphere.

Meteorological Satellite

INSAT-3D	Launched on Jul 26, 2013
INSAT-3A	Launched on Apr 10, 2003
KALPANA-1	Launched on Sep 12, 2002
GSAT-9	(South Asia Satellite) Launched on May 5,2017.

Launch Vehicle Technology

SLV: The indigenous capability for the development of satellite launch vehicle (SLV), was demonstrated through the first successful launch of SLV-3 in July 1980, carrying the 40-kilogram Rohini satellite.

ASLV: The Augumented Satellite Launch Vehicle (ASLV), basically derived from SLV-3, was originally meant for putting 150 Kilogram class technological/ scientific payloads into near-circular orbit.

PSLV: The PSLV, the country's first operational launch vehicle, is a four-stage rocket. The first stage is a solid propellant, the second stage is based on the liquid engine technology, the third stage is a solid propellant motor and the fourth, a liquid propellant stage.

GSLV: On March 28, 2001, the ISRO's efforts to launch the geosynchronous satellite launch vehicle ended in failure. On April 18, ISRO managed to prepare the GSLV again and launch it successfully from Sriharikota. The GSLV was commissioned after its successful second flight in 2003.

Export Promotion

Antrix Corporation Ltd. a wholly government-owned company, is the commercial arm of ISRO. It has been formed in Bengaluru to market technologies and services relating to assembly and sub-assemblies of satellite systems. Antrix has furthers expanded the international marketing of IRS data, with IRS coverage extending into the Latin American region and central Europe.

ISRO C25 CRYOGENIC UPPER STAGE OF GSLV MKIII TESTS

ISRO tested a Cryogenic Upper Stage for GSLV MkIII on January 25, 2017. The cryogenic stage designated as C25 was tested for a duration of 50 seconds at ISRO Propulsion Complex (IPRC) in Mahendragiri demonstrating all the stage operations. The performance of the Stage during the test was as predicted. This is the first test in a series of two tests. The next test is planned for flight duration of 640 seconds.

This 50 second test is a significant milestone in the development of indigenous cryogenic propulsion technology. The successful hot test of the stage in the first attempt itself demonstrates ISRO's ability to work in new areas like cryogenic technology.

The development of C25 cryogenic stage began with the approval of GSLV MKIII, the next generation launch vehicle of ISRO, capable of launching 4 ton class spacecraft in Geosynchronous Transfer Orbit (GTO). The vehicle consists of two solid strap-on motors (S200), one earth storable liquid core stage (L110) and the cryogenic stage upper stage (C25).

INDIAN SPACE MISSIONS

Space Missions (1975-2018)		
Satellite	**Launch Date**	**Launch Vehicle**
Aryabhata	19-Apr-75	u-11 Interkosmos
Bhaskara-I	7-Jun-79	C-1 Interkosmos
Rohini Technology Payload	10-Aug-79	SLV-3
Rohini RS-1	18-Jul-80	SLV-3
Rohini RS-D1	31-May-81	SLV-3
Ariane Passenger Payload Experiment	19-Jun-81	Ariane-1 (V-3)
Bhaskara -II	20-Nov-81	C-1 Intercosmos
INSAT-1A	10-Apr-82	Delta 3910 PAM-D
Rohini RS-D2	17-Apr-83	SLV-3
INSAT-1B	30-Aug-83	Shuttle [PAM-D]
Stretched Rohini Satellite Series (SROSS-1)	24-Mar-87	ASLV
IRS-1A	17-Mar-88	Vostok
Stretched Rohini Satellite Series (SROSS-2)	13-Jul-88	ASLV
INSAT-1C	21-Jul-88	Ariane-3
INSAT-1D	12-Jun-90	Delta 4925
IRS-1B	29-Aug-91	Vostok
INSAT-2DT	26-Feb-92	Ariane-44L H10
Stretched Rohini Satellite Series (SROSS-C)	20-May-92	ASLV
INSAT-2A	10-Jul-92	Ariane-44L H10
INSAT-2B	23-Jul-93	Ariane-44L H10+
IRS-1E	20-Sep-93	PSLV-D1
Stretched Rohini Satellite Series (SROSS-C2)	4-May-94	ASLV
IRS-P2	15-Oct-94	PSLV-D2
INSAT-2C	7-Dec-95	Ariane-44L H10-3
IRS-1C	29-Dec-95	Molniya
IRS-P3	21-Mar-96	PSLV-D3
INSAT-2D	4-Jun-97	Ariane-44L H10-3
IRS-1D	29-Sep-97	PSLV-C1
INSAT-2E	3-Apr-99	Ariane-42P H10-3
Oceansat-1 (IRS-P4)	26-May-99	PSLV-C2
INSAT-3B	22-Mar-00	Ariane-5G
GSAT-1	18-Apr-01	GSLV-D1
Technology Experiment Satellite (TES)	22-Oct-01	PSLV-C3
INSAT-3C	24-Jan-02	Ariane-42L H10-3
Kalpana-1 (METSAT)	12-Sep-02	PSLV-C4
INSAT-3A	10-Apr-03	Ariane-5G
GSAT-2	8-May-03	GSLV-D2
INSAT-3E	28-Sep-03	Ariane-5G
RESOURCESAT-1 (IRS-P6)	17-Oct-03	PSLV-C5
EDUSAT	20-Oct-04	GSLV-F01
HAMSAT	5-May-05	PSLV-C6
CARTOSAT-1	5-May-05	PSLV-C6
INSAT-4A	22-Dec-05	Ariane-5GS
INSAT-4C	10-Jul-06	GSLV-F02
CARTOSAT-2	10-Jan-07	PSLV-C7
Space Capsule Recovery Experiment (SRE-1)	10-Jan-07	PSLV-C7
INSAT-4B	12-Mar-07	Ariane-5ECA
INSAT-4CR	2-Sep-07	GSLV-F04
CARTOSAT-2A	28-Apr-08	PSLV-C9
IMS-1 (Third World Satellite – TWsat)	28-Apr-08	PSLV-C9
Chandrayaan-1	22-Oct-08	PSLV-C11
RISAT-2	20-Apr-09	PSLV-C12
ANUSAT	20-Apr-09	PSLV-C12
Oceansat-2 (IRS-P4)	23-Sep-09	PSLV-C14
GSAT-4	15-Apr-10	GSLV-D3
CARTOSAT-2B	12-Jul-10	PSLV-C15
StudSat	12-Jul-10	PSLV-C15
GSAT-5P / INSAT-4D	25-Dec-10	GSLV-F06
RESOURCESAT-2	20-Apr-11	PSLV-C16
Youthsat	20-Apr-11	PSLV-C16

GSAT-8 / INSAT-4G	21-May-11	Ariane-5 VA-202
GSAT-12	15-Jul-11	PSLV-C17
Megha-Tropiques	12-Oct-11	PSLV-C18
Jugnu	12-Oct-11	PSLV-C18
RISAT-1	26-Apr-12	PSLV-C19
SRMSAT	26-Apr-12	PSLV-C18
GSAT-10	29-Sep-12	Ariane-5 VA-209
SARAL	25-Feb-13	PSLV-C20
IRNSS-1A	1-Jul-13	PSLV-C22
INSAT-3D	26-Jul-13	Ariane-5
GSAT-7	30-Aug-13	Ariane-5
Mars Orbiter Mission (MOM)	5-Nov-13	PSLV-C25
GSAT-14	5-Jan-14	GSLV-D5
IRNSS-1B	4-Apr-14	PSLV-C24
IRNSS-1C	10-Nov-14	PSLV-C26
GSAT-16	7-Dec-14	Ariane-5
IRNSS-1D	28-Mar-15	PSLV-C27
GSAT-6	27-Aug-15	GSLV-D6
Astrosat	28-Sep-15	PSLV-C30
GSAT-15	11-Nov-15	Ariane 5 VA-227
IRNSS-1E	20-Jan-16	PSLV-C31
IRNSS-1F	10-Mar-16	PSLV-C32
IRNSS-1G	28-Apr-16	PSLV-C33
Corbo Set-2C	22-Jun-16	PSLV-C34
Insat 3DR	8-Sep-16	GSLV-F05
SCATSAT-1	26-Sep-16	PSLV-C35
GSAT-18	6-Oct-16	Ariane 5 ECA VA-231
RESOURCE SAT –2A	7–Dec–16	PSLV–36
CARTO SAT–2D	15–Feb -17	PSLV –C37
INS-1A (ISRO Nano-Satellite 1A)	15 Feb-17	PSLV-C 37
INS-1B (ISRO Nano-Satellite 1B)	15 Feb-17	PSLV-C 37
GSAT-9	5 May-17	GSLV-MK II
GSAT-19	5 June-17	GSLV-MK III
CartoSat-2E	23 June-17	PSLV-C 38
GSAT-17	29 June-17	Ariane-5 ECA
IRNSS-1H	2-Sept-17	PSLV-C 39
CartoSat-2E	10-Jan-18	PSLV-C40
MicroSat-TD	10-Jan-18	PSLV-C40
INS-1-C (ISRO Nano-Satellite 1C)	10-Jan-18	PSLV-C 40
GSAT-6A	29-March-18	GSLV-F08
IRNSS-1I	12 Apr-18	PSLV-C 41

IRNSS/NavIC

Indian Regional Navigation Satellite System (IRNSS) is a set of satellites independently being developed by India as a regional navigation satellite system which will provide India a regional positioning system similar to the GPS of USA, GLONASS of Russia, and GALILEO of European Union, BeiDU of China. It is renamed as "NavIC" (Navigation with Indian Constellation).

The system is designed to give position accuracy better than 20 m to users in its primary coverage area. It can also service regions extending up to 1500 km around India's boundary.

There are currently 6 IRNSS satellites (1A to 1I) in orbit. A, B, F, G are placed in a geosynchronous orbit, which means they seem to be at a fixed location above the Earth and they orbit along with the Earth. The remaining three, C, D, E, are located in geostationary orbit-they seem to be at a fixed location above the Earth along the equator and orbit along with the Earth. IRNSS-1H Satellite could not be placed into the orbit as mission was unsuccessful. The heat shield did not separate as a result of which satellite did not complete the fourth stage and mission deemed unsuccessful.

IRNSS-1A was the first of the seven satellites comprising the Navigation with Indian Constellation (NavIC) - (IRNSS-1G; IRNSS-1F; IRNSS-1E, IRNSS-1D, IRNSS-1C, IRNSS-1B; and IRNSS-1A). IRNSS-1A was replaced with IRNSS-1I after its three reubidium clocks turned dysfunctional.

These satellites help not just in land navigation but also in marine and aerial navigation. The data from these satellites can be used to give vehicle drivers visual and voice navigation assistance. They also help in disaster management and in proper time-keeping.

IRNSS will provide two types of services, namely, Standard Positioning Service (SPS) which is provided to all the users and Restricted Service (RS), which is an encrypted service provided only to the authorised users. The IRNSS System is expected to provide a position accuracy of better than 20 m in the primary service area.

ASTROSat

AstroSat is the Indian astronomy mission aimed at studying celestial sources in X-ray, optical and UV spectral bands simultaneously. The payloads cover the energy bands of Ultraviolet (both near and far range), limited optical and X-ray regime. Unique feature of AstroSat mission is that it enables the simultaneous multi-wavelength observations of various astronomical objects with a single satellite. Technically it is a mini version of NASA's famous Hubble Space Telescope.

AstroSat with a lift-off mass of 1515 kg was launched on September 28, 2015 into a 650 km orbit inclined at an angle of 6 deg to the equator by PSLV-C30 from Satish Dhawan Space Centre, Sriharikota. The minimum useful life of the AstroSat mission is expected to be 5 years.

The spacecraft control centre at Mission Operations Complex (MOX) of ISRO Telemetry, Tracking and Command Network

(ISTRAC), Bengaluru manages the satellite during its entire mission life. Scientific data gathered by five payloads of AstroSat are telemetered to the ground station at MOX. The data is then processed, archived and distributed by Indian Space Science Data Centre (ISSDC) located at Bylalu, near Bengaluru.

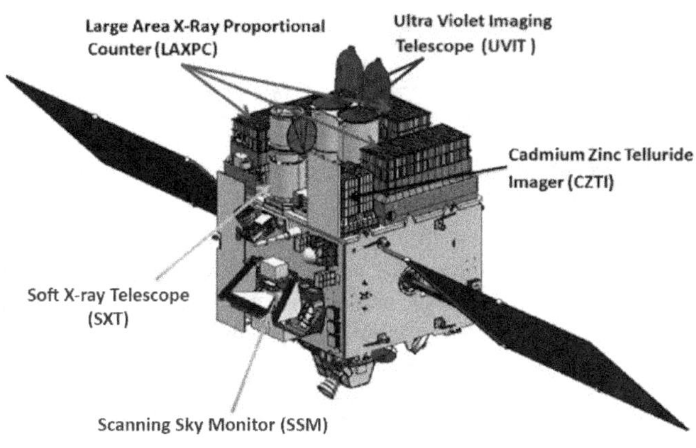

Fig. Astrosat

The scientific objectives of AstroSat mission include understanding of high energy processes in binary star systems containing neutron stars and black holes; estimation of magnetic fields of neutron stars; Study of star birth regions and high energy processes in star systems lying beyond our galaxy; detection of new briefly bright X-ray sources in the sky; perform a limited deep field survey of the Universe in the UV region.

RECENT SATELLITE LAUNCH BY SPACE AGENCIES

ISRO launches 31 satellites in one go

The first space mission of Indian Space Research Organisation (ISRO) in 2018 started on 11th January 2018 by beginning of 28-hour countdown to launch 31 satellites from Satish Dhawan Space Centre (SDSC), SHAR, Sriharikota (Andhra Pradesh).

The launch is unique as it is carrying 28 satellites from 6 foreign countries along with India's 3 satellites. India is launching its Cartosat-2 Series Satellite for earth observation along with one microsatellite and one Nanosatellite. Out of 28 foreign satellites 3 are Microsatellities while 25 are Nanosatellities from six countries Canada, Finland, France, Republic of Korea, United Kingdom and United States of America.

These satellites will be launched through the PSLV-C40 rocket. ISRO scientists are hopeful for a successful launch in the New Year aftermath of failed delivery of India's eighth navigation satellite in earth's lower orbit in August 2017.

The International customer satellites are being launched as part of the commercial arrangements between Antrix Corporation Limited (Antrix), a Government of India company under Department of Space (DOS), the commercial arm of ISRO and the International customer.

GSAT-6A Satellite

India's communications Satellite GSAT-6A was launched into its orbit. The launch took place from the Satish Dhawan Space Centre (SDSC) at SHAR, Sriharikota. GSAT-6A was lifted successfully into Geosynchronous Transfer Orbit (GTO) by Geosynchronous Satellite Launch Vehicle (GSLV-F08). With this launch the GSAT-6A joins a series of satellites for multi-media and mobile applications, hosting a payload comprising five C-by-S and five S-by-C-B and transponders optimized for Satellite Digital Multimedia Broadcasting. The satellite's capacity can also be used for strategic and social applications.

This also marked the fifth consecutive success achieved by GSLV carrying indigenously developed Cryogenic Upper Stage.

GSAT-6A is communications satellite which will be used for government and military purpose. The Satellite will be commissioned into service after the successful completion of orbit raising operations and its positioning in the designated slot in Geostationary Orbit following in-orbit testing of its payload.

IRNSS-1I

Indian Navigation Satellite IRNSS-1I was launched from ISRO's Polar Satellite Launch Vehicle from Satish Dhawan Space Centre, Sriharikota.

1,425 kg IRNSS-1I was successfully lifted off by using PSLV-C41. This was 43rd flight of PSLV and till this flight it has successfully launched 52 Indian satellites and 237 customer satellites abroad.

After separation from the launch vehicle the solar panels of IRNSS-1I were deployed automatically. ISRO's Master control Facility at Hassan in Karnataka then took over the control of the Indian navigation satellite.

NavIC or Indian Regional Navigation Satellite System is an independent regional navigation satellite system designed to provide position information in the Indian region and 1500 km around the Indian mainland.

ESA launches World's 1st satellite mission to survey Earth's winds

European Space Agency (ESA) launched Earth Explorer into Polar Orbit to measure winds around the globe. The Vega rocket carrying the Aeolus satellite lifted off from Europe's Spaceport in Kourou, French Guiana.

The novel mission is the fifth in the family of ESA's Earth Explorers, which address the most urgent Earth-science questions of present time. Aeolus carries the first instrument of its kind and uses a completely new approach to measuring the wind from space. Highlighted by the World Meteorological Organization, the lack of direct global wind measurements is one of the major deficits in the Global Observing System.

The launch of Aeolus will give scientists the information they need to understand how wind, pressure, temperature and humidity are interlinked. The mission will provide insight into how the wind influences the exchange of heat and moisture between Earth's surface and the atmosphere – important aspects for understanding climate change. Aeolus carries one of the most sophisticated instruments ever to be put into orbit. The first of its kind, the Aladin instrument includes revolutionary laser technology to generate pulses of ultraviolet light that are beamed down into the atmosphere to profile the world's winds – a completely new approach to measuring the wind from space.

Recent Updates in Space Technology
Multiple Burn Technology
It is the technology used for placing satellites in different orbits during a single launch. It employs switching off and switching on of a rcoket's engine in space. In December 2015 ISRO first time tested technology while flying its PSLV rocket. In June 2016,the technology was again demonstrated. ISRO launched 5 foreign and 3 domestic satellites in different orbits using the Multiple Burn Technology. The 320 ton PSLV rocket put its main cargo the 371 kg SCATSAT-1 for ocean and weather related studies-into a 730 km polar sun synchronous orbit, 17 minutes into the flight. The remaining 7 satellites placed in a 689 km polar orbit nearly 2 hours later.

Ice on Moon: Chandrayaan-1 data

The data from the India's first Chandrayaan confirmed the presence of ice deposits on lunar surface.

NASA Scientists have found frozen water deposits in the darkest and coldest parts of the Moon's Polar Regions using data from the India's Chandrayaan-1 spacecraft. The patchily distributed ice deposits could possibly be ancient.

With enough ice sitting at the surface within the top few mm -water would possibly be accessible as a resource for future expeditions to explore and even stay on the Moon, and potentially easier to access than the water detected beneath the Moon's surface.

At the southern pole, most of the ice is concentrated at lunar craters, while the northern pole's ice is more widely, but sparsely spread.

Scientists used data from NASA's Moon Mineralogy Mapper (M3) instrument to identify three specific signatures that definitively prove there is water ice at the surface of the Moon. M3, aboard the Chandrayaan-1 spacecraft, launched in 2008 by the Indian Space Research Organisation (ISRO), was uniquely equipped to confirm the presence of solid ice on the Moon.

Most of the new-found water ice lies in the shadows of craters near the poles, where the warmest temperatures never reach above minus 156 degrees Celsius. Due to the very small tilt of the Moon's rotation axis, sunlight never reaches these regions. Previous observations indirectly found possible signs of surface ice at the lunar South Pole, but these could have been explained by other phenomena, such as unusually reflective lunar soil.

RECENT ADVANCEMENTS IN SCIENCE & TECHNOLOGY

Large Hadron Collider (LHC)

European Organization for Nuclear Research, physicists and engineers (CERN) is largest physics laboratory in the world for probing the fundamental structure of the universe. It is one of Europe's first joint ventures and now the number of member states has reached up to 22. India is one among the associate Member States.

It is aimed to study the basic constituents of matter-the fundamental particles, using the world's largest and most complex scientific instruments. During the experimental conditions, the particles are made to collide together at close to the speed of light. The process gives the physicists clues about how the particles interact, and provides insights into the fundamental laws of nature.

The instruments used at CERN are purpose-built particle accelerators and detectors. Accelerators boost beams of particles to high energies before the beams are made to collide with each other or with stationary targets. Detectors observe and record the results of these collisions.

Seven experiments at the Large Hadron Collider (LHC) use detectors to analyse the myriad of particles produced by collisions in the accelerator. The biggest of these experiments, ATLAS and CMS, use general-purpose detectors to investigate the largest range of physics possible. COMPASS, NA61/SHINE, NA62, DIRAC, CLOUD are some of the non-LHC experiments.

Belle-II Experiment

The Belle-II experiment is one of the joint collaboration experimental projects of different nations aimed to study violations of the Standard Model of particle physics, specially the properties of B mesons. 700 scientists from 23 countries are part of this grand collaboration. Belle II is the successor to the Belle experiment, and is currently being commissioned at the SuperKEKB accelerator complex at The High Energy Accelerator Research Organisation (KEK) in Tsukuba, Ibaraki Prefecture, Japan. The Belle II detector was moved into the collision point of SuperKEKB) in April 2017 and it started taking data in early 2018. Over its running period, Belle II is expected to collect around 50 times more data than Belle, due mostly to a factor 40 increase in instantaneous luminosity provided by Super-KEKB over the original KEKB accelerator.

India and Belle Experiment

India is contributing significantly to the Belle-II experiment both on experimental and theoretical sides. The core of Belle-II is the highly sensitive particle detector has been built by Indian scientists from Mumbai's Tata Institute of Fundamental Research (TIFR).

Apart from TIFR, the Scientists from the Indian Institutes of Technology (Bhubaneswar, Chennai, Guwahati and Hyderabad); the Institute of Mathematical Sciences (Chennai) Panjab University(Chandigarh); Punjab Agricultural University

(Ludhiana); Malaviya National Institute of Technology (Jaipur); Indian Institute of Science Education and Research (Mohali) are participating in this multinational research

ITER

International Thermonuclear Experimental Reactor (ITER) is an international experimental fusion reactor at cadarache (France). The main aim of ITER is to demonstrate scientific and technological feasibility of fusion energy which have prominent role for production of electric energy in the future.

India and the ITER

India is one of the 7 partners. Other partners include USA, Japan, European Union, China, Republic of Korea and Russia. ITER-India is the Indian Domestic Agency formed with responsibility to provide ITER the Indian contribution.

India will be contributing like other partners about 9.1% of ITER construction cost (Host, European Union is providing 45%. Most of this will be in the form of components made by Indian industries and delivered to ITER for different experimental Purposes. Tokamak is an experimental machine for harnessing the fusion energy and ITER Tokamak will be the largest in them. As soon as access to the Tokamak building is completed, the scientists and engineers wil assemble, integrate and test the ITER fusion device. The successful integration and assembly of over 1 million components built in the ITER member's' factories around the world and delivered to the ITER site constitutes a tremendous logistics and engineering challenge. The ITER's first plasma is scheduled for 2025.

Gravitational Wave Research

The Laser Interferometer Gravitational-Wave Observatory (LIGO) is experimental facility for gravitational-wave research, providing opportunities for the broader scientific community to participate in detector development, observation, and data analysis. The capabilities of the LIGO detectors were greatly improved with the completion of the Advanced LIGO project in late 2014. The Advanced LIGO detectors will increase the sensitivity and observational range of LIGO by a factor of 10 over its predecessor, bringing 1000 times more galaxies into LIGO's observational range.

It is designed to open the field of gravitational-wave astrophysics through the direct detection of gravitational waves predicted by Einstein's General Theory of Relativity. LIGO's multi-kilometer-scale gravitational wave detectors use laser interferometry to measure the minute ripples in space-time caused by passing gravitational waves from cataclysmic cosmic sources such as the mergers of pairs of neutron stars or black holes, or by supernovae. LIGO consists of two widely separated interferometers within the United States—one in Hanford, Washington and the other in Livingston, Louisiana—operated in unison to detect gravitational waves.

On September 14, 2015, the National Science Foundation (NSF)-funded LIGO made the first-ever direct observation of gravitational waves—ripples in the fabric of space and time predicted by Albert Einstein 100 years earlier. This was a new era of scientific observation as cosmic event has been viewed in both gravitational waves and light. The scientists have directly detected gravitational waves—ripples in space-time—in addition to light from the spectacular collision of two neutron stars.

The discovery was made using the U.S.-based LIGO; the Europe-based Virgo detector; and some 70 ground and space-based observatories.

Key Scientists at LIGO, Rainer Weiss, Barry C. Barish and Kip S. Thorne awarded with Nobel Prize in Physics for contributions to the LIGO detector and the observation of gravitational waves.

The world's third advanced Laser Interferometer Gravitational wave Observatory (LIGO-India) will be set up in India in Maharashtra's Hingoli district. It is planned to be operational by the year 2025.

MULTIPLE CHOICE QUESTIONS

1. With reference to Indian satellites and their launchers, consider the following statements: **[IAS Prelim]**
   1. All the INSAT series of satellites were launched abroad
   2. PSLVs were used to launch IRS-series of satellites
   3. India used the indigenously built cryogenic engines for the first time for powering the third stage of GSLV
   4. GSAT, launched in the year 2001, has payloads to demonstrate digital broadcast and internet services
   Which of these statements are correct?
   (a) 1, 2, 3 and 4　　(b) 2, 3 and 4
   (c) 1, 2 and 4　　　(d) 1 and 3

2. **Assertion (A) :** Artificial satellites are always launched from the earth in the eastward direction.
   Reason (R) : The earth rotates from west to east and so the satellite attains the escape velocity. **[IAS Prelim]**
   (a) Both A and R are true and R is the correct explanation of A
   (b) Both A and R are true but R is not a correct explanation of A
   (c) A is true but R is false
   (d) A is false but R is true

3. Consider the following statements: **[IAS Prelim]**
   1. India launch its first full-fledged meteoro-logical satellite (METSAT) in September, 2002
   2. For the first time, the space vehicle PSLV C-4 carried a payload of more than 1000 kg into a geosynchronous orbit
   Which of these statement is/are correct?
   (a) Only 1　　　(b) Only 2
   (c) Both 1 and 2　　(d) Neither 1 nor 2

4. NASA's Deep Impact space mission was employed to take detailed pictures of which comet nucleus? **[IAS Prelim]**
   (a) Halley's Comet　　(b) Hale-Bopp
   (c) Hyakutake　　　(d) Tempel 1

5. Consider the following statements: **[IAS Prelim]**
   The satellite Oceansat-2 launched by India helps in
   1. estimating the water vapour content in the atmosphere.
   2. predicting the onset of monsoons.
   3. monitoring the pollution of coastal waters.
   Which of the statements given above is/are correct?
   (a) 1 and 2 only　　(b) 2 only
   (c) 1 and 3 only　　(d) 1, 2 and 3

6. Satellites used for telecommunication relay are kept in a geostationary orbit. A satellite is said to be in such as orbit when : **[IAS Prelim]**
   1. The orbit is geosynchronous.
   2. The orbit is circular.
   3. The orbit lies in the plane of the earth's equator.
   4. The orbit is at an altitude of 22,236.
   Select the correct answer using the codes given below :
   (a) 1, 2 and 3 only　　(b) 1, 3 and 4 only
   (c) 2 and 4 only　　　(d) 1, 2, 3 and 4

7. An artificial satellite orbiting around the Earth does not fall down. This is so because the attraction of Earth
   (a) does not exist at such distance **[IAS Prelim]**
   (b) is neutralized by the attraction of the moon
   (c) provides the necessary speed for its steady motion
   (d) provides the necessary acceleration for its motion

8. Which of the following pairs is/are correctly matched? **[IAS Prelim]**

	Spacecraft	Purpose
1.	Cassini-Huygens :	Orbiting the Venus and transmitting data to the Earth
2.	Messenger :	Mapping and investigating the Mercury
3.	Voyager 1 and 2 :	Exploring the outer solar system

   Select the correct answer using the code given below.
   (a) 1 only　　　(b) 2 and 3 only
   (c) 1 and 3 only　　(d) 1, 2 and 3

9. In the context of space technology, what is "Bhuvan", recently in the news? **[IAS Prelim]**
   (a) A mini satellite launched by ISRO for promoting the distance education in India
   (b) The name given to the next Moon Impact Probe, for Chandrayan-II
   (c) A geoportal of ISRO with 3 D imaging capabilities of India
   (d) A space telescope developed by India

10. Which among the following statements is/are correct regarding the failed launch of Geosynchronous Satellite Launch Vehicle (GSLV-F06)?
    1. This was the second consecutive failure of GSLV.
    2. The 2,300 kg satellite was to be used to boost television broadcast, telemedicine and tele-education.
    (a) 1 only　　　(b) 2 only
    (c) Both 1 and 2　　(d) Neither 1 nor 2

11. Satellites used for telecommunication relay are kept in a geostationary orbit. A satellite is said to be in such as orbit when :
    1. The orbit is geosynchronous.
    2. The orbit is circular.
    3. The orbit lies in the plane of the earth's equator.
    4. The orbit is at an altitude of 22,236.
    Select the correct answer using the codes given below:
    (a) 1, 2 and 3　　(b) 1, 3 and 4
    (c) 2 and 4　　　(d) 1, 2, 3 and 4

12. Consider the following statements:
    1. ISRO's Polar Satellite launch Vehicle (PSLV-C13) has successfully put five satellite in the orbit.
    2. This was the 16th Consecutive Successful fight of PSLV.
    Which of the above statement is/are correct?
    (a) 1 only　　　(b) 2 only
    (c) Both 1 and 2　　(d) Neither 1 nor 2

13. Consider the following statements regarding Indian polar research station:
    1. India established a research station named "Bharti" at Ny-Alesund in Svalbard region of Norway.
    2. India established a research station named "Himadri" in the Larsemann Hills region of East Antarctica.
    Which of the statements given above is/are correct?
    (a) 1 only　　　　　(b) 2 only
    (c) Both 1 and 2　　(d) Neither 1 nor 2

14. Which among the following statements is/are correct?
    1. The launch of GSAT-5P from Sriharikota was deferred after a minor leak in the Russian cryogenic engine on board the GSLV-F06 launch vehicle.
    2. ISRO has launched six GSLV rockets, of which statement have been unsuccessful.
    (a) 1 only　　　　　(b) 2 only
    (c) 1 and 2 both　　(d) None

15. In context of MEGHA-TROPIQUES what is correct?
    1. MEGHA-TROPIQUES is the new satellite that is a joint project between India and France.
    2. It will help study the life cycle of tropical convective systems over oceans and continents.
    3. It was launched in Oct 2011 using GSLV rockets over height of 800 km.
    (a) 1 and 2　　　　(b) 2 and 3
    (c) 1, 2 and 3　　　(d) 1 and 3

16. Russia has successfully launched a next-generation navigation satellite for its Glonass global communication system. Which among the following statements in this reference is/are correct?
    1. Glonass will not be integrated with the US Global Positioning System (GPS).
    2. Under an accord, Russia has agreed to share the Glonass Signal with India.
    (a) 1 only　　　　　(b) 2 only
    (c) 1 and 2 both　　(d) None

17. Consider the following statements:
    1. India's Second moon mission, Chandrayaan-II will carry Seven indigenous payloads.
    2. The '425 Crore mission was Scheduled to be launched in 2013.
    3. Chandrayaan-II, with a lift-off weight of 2,650 kg will be launched by GSLV from the Satish Dhawan Space Centre in Sriharikota
    4. ISRO's physical Research Laboratory is in Ahmedabad.
    Which of the above statement's are correct?
    (a) 1 and 4　　　　(b) 2 and 4
    (c) 1, 2 and 4　　　(d) 1, 2, 3 and 4

18. Consider the following statements with reference Aditya L1 Mission.
    1. Set to be launched by ISRO; it will be India's first solar mission.
    2. Aditya L1 satellite will be launched by using PSLV XL.

Select the correct statement/statements using the codes given below:
(a) 1 only　　　　　(b) 2 only
(c) Both 1 and 2　　(d) Neither 1 nor 2

19. Which of the following correctly explains the purpose of "EoTT equipment" proposed by Indian Railways?
    (a) Prevention of collision of train bogies
    (b) It is wireless communication between stations and train
    (c) Communication system driver and last wagon of train
    (d) Facility to run the train in low visibility conditions like fog

20. Holographic technology can be used in which of the following fields
    1. Engineering and Architecture
    2. Health and medicine
    3. Tradeshows
    Select the correct answer using the codes given below:
    (a) 1 and 2 only　　　(b) 2 and 3 only
    (c) 3 only　　　　　　(d) 1, 2 and 3

21. Consider the following statements:
    1. SARAS PT1N, has been developed by Hindustan Aeronautics Limited.
    2. It has been conceptualised to establish India's short-haul civil aviation market.
    Select the correct statement/statements using the codes given below:
    (a) 1 only　　　　　(b) 2 only
    (c) Both 1 and 2　　(d) Neither 1 nor 2

22. Read the following statements about Super Pressure Balloon Technology,
    1. Super Pressure Balloon Technology serves as low-cost, near-space access for scientific payloads
    2. The Super Pressure Balloon is made up of polyethylene film
    Select the correct statement/statements using the codes given below:
    (a) 1 only　　　　　(b) 2 only
    (c) Both 1 and 2　　(d) Neither 1 nor 2

23. Which of the following statements best describes the 'Synlight' which was recently in news?
    1. It is stated as world's largest Artificial sun
    2. The intensity of 'Synlight' is 10,000 times the intensity of Sunlight on Earth
    Select the correct answer using the codes given below:
    (a) 1 only　　　　　(b) 2 only
    (c) Both 1 and 2　　(d) Neither 1 nor 2

24. Select the most appropriate statements with reference to 'Multiple Burn Technology',
    1. It is related to usage of solid, liquid and cryogenic propellants in the same system.
    2. It is used during launching of satellites into multiple orbits using burning of different fuels.
    3. It refers to Switching 'off' and switching 'on' of engine to control height.

Select the correct answer using the codes given below:
(a) 1 only
(b) 2 only
(c) 3 only
(d) Both 2 and 3

25. Select the correct statements with reference to ISRO's GSLV MK III D1 rocket,
1. It can lift payloads of up to 4000 kg to Geosynchronous Transfer Orbit
2. It can lift payloads of up to 8000 kg into the Low Earth Orbit
3. Cryogenic upper stage engine is indigenously developed
4. Like GKLV MK II, it is based on solid, liquid and cryogenic propulsion system

Use the following codes to select your answer,
(a) 1, 2 and 3 only
(b) 2, 3 and 4 only
(c) 1, 3 and 4 only
(d) 1, 2, 3 and 4

26. Which of the following best describes the characteristics of gravitational waves?
(a) These are generated through one of the most energetic processes in core of the Earth
(b) The waves travel faster than the speed of light
(c) These waves are not dispersed during travel through space
(d) Gravitational waves display all the properties of light except speed

27. Which of the following best describes the purpose of NASA's SOFIA mission?
1. To study observations of celestial magnetic fields
2. To study Comet 46P/Writanen during its passage close to Earth
3. To study seasonal change on Mars with respect to change in methane levels

Select the correct answer using the codes given below:
(a) 1 and 2 only
(b) 2 and 3 only
(c) 1 and 3 only
(d) 1, 2 and 3

28. The Ministry of Environment and Forests has given environmental clearance to India-based Neutrino observatory project to be set up in
(a) Nilgiri hills
(b) Eastern Himalaya
(c) Bodi west hills
(d) Vindhyagiri hills

29. Select the correct answer from the following about 'AstroSat'?
(a) It is World's largest land observatory located in NASA premises
(b) It is World's Largest Astronomical Observatory
(c) It is India's first multi-wavelength Space Observatory
(d) It is resplacement of Hubble space Observatory

30. What is unique about "KalamSat"?
1. World's lightest satellite launched by NASA
2. World's first 3-D printed satellite launched by ISRO
3. It is developed to measure the radiation level in Space

Select the correct answer using the codes given below:
(a) 1 and 2 only
(b) 2 and 3 only
(c) 1 and 3 only
(d) 1, 2 and 3

31. Which of the following satellites has been dubbed as the 'South Asia' Satellite?
(a) GSAT-9
(b) GSAT-11
(c) GSAT-17
(d) GSAT-19

32. Select the main reason behind malfunctioning of IRNSS-1A,
(a) Failure of Heat shield to open
(b) Non-functioning of Rubidium clocks
(c) Dismantling of cesium atomic time-points
(d) Problem during multiple burn technology

33. What is the basis behind NASA's claim of presence of right chemicals to support life at Enceladus (Saturn's moon),
(a) Presence of thick ice-crust
(b) Hydrogen eruption from underground Ocean under the ice crust
(c) Presence of renants of ice crystals between core layers
(d) Presence of evaporated water crystals between crust and core

34. Which one of the following statements about a satellite orbiting around the Earth is correct?　　**[NDA - 2017-II]**
(a) Satellite is kept in orbit by remote control from ground station.
(b) Satellite is kept in orbit by retro-rocket and solar energy keeps it moving around the Earth.
(c) Satellite requires energy from solar panels and solid fuels for orbiting.
(d) Satellite does not require any enery for orbitin.

ANSWER KEY															
1	(a)	**2**	(c)	**3**	(c)	**4**	(d)	**5**	(d)	**6**	(a)	**7**	(d)	**8**	(b)
9	(c)	**10**	(c)	**11**	(a)	**12**	(b)	**13**	(d)	**14**	(a)	**15**	(a)	**16**	(b)
17	(d)	**18**	(c)	**19**	(c)	**20**	(d)	**21**	(b)	**22**	(d)	**23**	(c)	**24**	(c)
25	(c)	**26**	(c)	**27**	(d)	**28**	(c)	**29**	(c)	**30**	(c)	**31**	(a)	**32**	(b)
33	(b)	**34**	(d)												

Chapter 5

NUCLEAR SCIENCE TECHNOLOGY

Nuclear energy is the energy that comes from the core or the nucleus of an atom. The bonds which hold the atoms together contain a massive amount of energy. This energy must be released in order to make electricity. This energy can be freed in two ways: nuclear fission and nuclear fusion.

Uses of Nuclear energy

Today most people are aware of the important use of nuclear energy makes in cleanly providing a significant proportion of the world's electricity.

Applications of Nuclear Energy

Nuclear energy is the production of electric energy. Nuclear power plants are responsible for generating electricity. Nuclear fission reactions are generated in the nuclear reactors of the nuclear power plants. With these reactions thermal energy is obtained which will be transformed into mechanical energy and later into electrical energy.

There are many applications of nuclear energy where nuclear technology is used directly or indirectly. These are:

1. Military applications, nuclear weapons.
2. Nuclear medicine.
3. Gamma Sterilisation.
4. Smoke detectors
5. Radio therapy
6. Gamma radiography.
7. Industrial tracers.
8. Carbon Dating.

NUCLEAR REACTORS

A nuclear reactor, formerly known as an atomic pile, it is a device used to initiate and control a sustained nuclear chain reaction. Nuclear rectors are used at nuclear power plants for electricity generation and in propulsion of ships.

Nuclear reactors are divided into two categories:

- **Thermal Reactors:** Almost all of the current reactors which have been built use thermal neutrons to sustain the chain reaction. These reactors also contain neutron moderator that slows neutrons from fission
- **Fast Neutron Reactors:** Fast reactors contains no neutron moderator and use less-moderating primary coolants, because they use fast neutrons to cause fission in their fuel.

Types of Nuclear Reactors

Breeder Reactor

A breeder reactor is essentially a particular configura-tion of a fast reactor. The most common breeding reaction is an absorbtion reaction on uranium-238, where a plutonium-239 from non-fissionable uranium-238 is produced.

Pressurized Water Reactor – PWR

Pressurized water reactors use a reactor pressure vessel (RPV) to contain the nuclear fuel, moderator, control rods and coolant. They are cooled and moderated by high-pressure liquid water.

Boiling water reactor – BWR

A boiling water reactor is cooled and moderated by water like a PWR, but at a lower pressure (7MPa), which allows the water to boil inside the pressure vessel producing the steam that runs the turbines.

CANDU – Heavy Water Reactor

The CANDU reactor design (or PHWR – Pressurized Heavy Water Reactor) has been developed since the 1950s in Canada, and more recently also in India. These reactors are heavy water cooled and moderated pressurized water reactors. Instead of using a single large reactor vessel as in a PWR or BWR, the nuclear core is contained in hundreds of pressure tubes. PHWRs generally use natural uranium (0.7% U-235) oxide as fuel, hence needs a more efficient moderator, in this case heavy water (D_2O).

NUCLEAR POWER

Nuclear power for civil use is well established in India. Since building the two small boiling water reactors at Tarapur in the 1960s, its civil nuclear strategy has been directed towards complete independence in the nuclear fuel cycle, necessary because it is excluded from the 1970 Nuclear Non-Proliferation Treaty (NPT) due to it acquiring nuclear weapons capability after 1970.

ORGANISATION OF INDIA NUCLEAR ENERGY PROGRAM:

The Atomic Energy Commission was set up in August 1948 to look after atomic energy activities in the country. The functions of the Atomic Energy Commission are:

(i) To organize research in atomic science in the country;

(ii) To train, atomic scientists in the country;

(iii) To promote nuclear research in commissions own laboratories as well as in India;

(iv) To undertake prospecting of atomic minerals in India and to extract such minerals for use on industrial scale.

It has five research centres viz.

- Bhabha Atomic Research Centre (BARC), Mumbai
- Indira Gandhi Centre for Atomic Research (IGCAR), Kalpakkam (Tamil Nadu)
- Raja Ramanna Centre for Advanced Technology (RRCAT), Indore
- Variable Energy Cyclotron Centre (VECC), Kolkata
- Atomic Minerals Directorate for Exploration and Research (AMD), Hyderabad.

It also gives financial assistance to autonomous national institutes doing research in the field and has various other organizations under it.

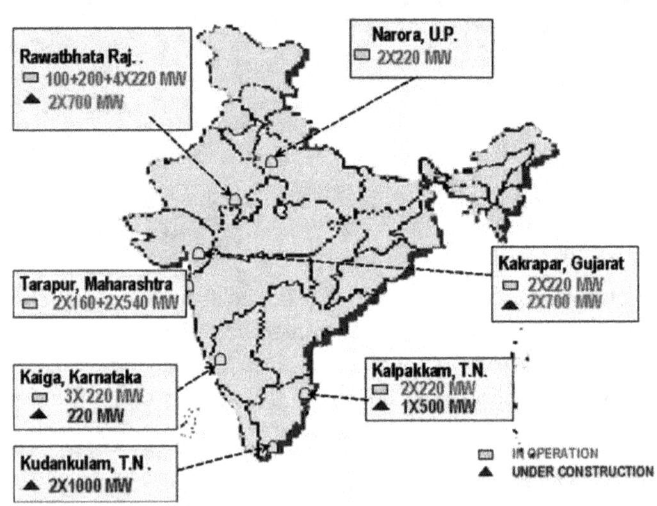

Fig. Location of Indian Nuclear power plants (operational & under construction)

NUCLEAR POWER PLANTS IN INDIA (OPERATIONAL)

S.N.	Unit	Type	Capacity (MWe)	Since
1.	TAPS-1 (Tarapur, Maharashtra)	BWR	160	28 October 1969
2.	TAPS-2 (Tarapur, Maharashtra)	BWR	160	28 October 1969
3.	TAPS-3 (Tarapur, Maharashtra)	PHWR	540	18 August 2006
4.	TAPS-4 (Tarapur, Maharashtra)	PHWR	540	12 September 2005
5.	RAPS-1 (Rawatbhata, Rajasthan)	PHWR	100	16 December 1973
6.	RAPS-2 (Rawatbhata, Rajasthan)	PHWR	200	1 April 1981
7.	RAPS-3 (Rawatbhata, Rajasthan)	PHWR	220	1 June 2000
8.	RAPS-4 (Rawatbhata, Rajasthan)	PHWR	220	23 December 2000
9.	RAPS-5 (Rawatbhata, Rajasthan)	PHWR	220	4 February 2010
10.	RAPS-6 (Rawatbhata, Rajasthan)	PHWR	220	31 March 2010
11.	MAPS-1 (Kalpakkam, Tamil Nadu)	PHWR	220	27 January 1984
12.	MAPS-2 (Kalpakkam, Tamil Nadu)	PHWR	220	21 March 1986
13.	NAPS-1 (Narora, Uttar Pradesh)	PHWR	220	1 January 1991
14.	NAPS-2 (Narora, Uttar Pradesh)	PHWR	220	1 July 1992
15.	KAPS-1 (Kakrapar, Gujarat)	PHWR	220	6 May 1993
16.	KAPS-2 (Kakrapar, Gujarat)	PHWR	220	1 September 1995
17.	KGS-1 (Kaiga, Karnataka)	PHWR	220	6 November 2000
18.	KGS-2 (Kaiga, Karnataka)	PHWR	220	6 May 2000
19.	KGS-3 (Kaiga, Karnataka)	PHWR	220	6 May 2007
20.	KGS-4 (Kaiga, Karnataka)	PHWR	220	20 January 2011
21.	KKNPP-1 (Kudankulam, Tamil Nadu)	VVER	1000	31 December 2014
22.	KKNPP-2 (Kudankulam, Tamil Nadu)	VVER	1000	31 March-2017
	Total Capacity		6780	

MULTIPLE CHOICE QUESTIONS

1. Consider the following organizations:

1. Atomic Minerals Directorate for Research & Exploration
2. Heavy Water Board
3. Indian Rare Earths Limited
4. Uranium Corporation of India

Which of these is/are under the Department of Atomic Energy?

(a) 1 only   (b) 1 and 4

(c) 2, 3 and 4   (d) 1, 2, 3 and 4

2. To meet its rapidly growing energy demand, some opine that India should pursue research and development on thorium as the future fuel of nuclear energy. In this context, what advantage does thorium hold over uranium?

1. Thorium is far more abundant in nature than uranium.
2. On the basis of per unit mass of mined mineral, thorium can generate more energy compared to natural uranium.
3. Thorium produces less harmful waste compared to uranium.

Which of the statements given above is/are correct?

(a) 1 only   (b) 2 and 3

(c) 1 and 3   (d) Neither 1 nor 2

3. Consider the following statements:

1. 10 Nuclear Power Plants of India comes under the AERB (Atomic energy regulatory Board).
2. Meckani committee recommended that the Nuclear Regulator be created as a statutory Body.
3. Kudankulam Nuclear Project will operate by AERB.

Which of the above statement are / is true?

(a) 1 and 2   (b) 1, 2 and 3

(c) 1 and 3   (d) 1 and 2

4. Consider the following statements : -

1. Cobalt - 60 was leaked when a worker cut open a piece of metal in a Delhi market this cobalt-60 is used for medical purposes, industrial radiography for nondestructive testing and in the food processing industry for irradiation process.
2. The Atomic Energy Regulatory Board (AERB) is meant to maintain a "Cradle to grave" System to keep track of such equipment, including through on-site inspection.

Which of the above statement is/are correct?

(a) 1 only

(b) 2 only

(c) Both 1 and 2

(d) None of the above.

5. Consider the following Statements :

1. The Fast Breeder test Reactor (FBTR) is at the heart of the Indira Gandhi Centre for Atomic Research (IGCAR) at kalpakkam, and it is a forerunner to the second stage of the country's nuclear power programme.
2. Fast Reactors use "Fast" (high energy) neutrons to sustain the fission process, in contrast to water cooled reactors that use thermal (low energy) neutrons. Fast reactors are commonly known as breeders because they breed more fuel than they consume.

Which of the above statements is /are correct ?

(a) 1 only   (b) 2 only

(c) Both 1 and 2   (d) Neither 1 nor 2

6. Consider the following statements

1. India has a published nuclear doctrine.
2. The doctrine advocates 'no-first-use' policy.
3. The authority to release nuclear weapons for use resides in the person of the President of India.

Which of the statements given above is/are correct?

(a) 1 only   (b) Both 1 and 2

(c) Both 2 and 3   (d) 1, 2 and 3

7. Consider the following statements:

1. India has 10 Pressurized Heavy Water Reactors (PHWRs)
2. The spent fuel from the PHWRs is reprocessed into plutonium.
3. All imported reactors are under the safeguards of the international Atomic Energy Agency (IAEA).

Which of the statements given above is/are correct?

(a) 1 only   (b) 2 only

(c) 2 and 3   (d) 1, 2 and 3

8. Consider the following statements:

1. CIRUS was the third Indian Research Reactor.
2. Fast Breeder Test Reactor is at Kalpakkam.

Correct statement/statements is/are

(a) 1 and 2   (b) 1 only

(c) 2 only   (d) None of them

9. Consider the following statements in relations to the nuclear reactors and choose the correct alternative:

1. The Pressurized Heavy Water Reactor (PHWR) uses natural Uranium as the Fuel.
2. The Fast Breader Reactor (FBR) uses liquid Sodium as the moderator.
3. The Advanced Heavy Water Reactor (AHWR) will be based on U233 as the Fuel.
4. The French Company Areva is building the European Pressurized Reactors (EPR) at Jaitapur in Maharashtra.

(a) 1, 3 and 4   (b) 2, 3 and 4

(c) 1, 2 and 4   (d) 1 and 4

10. The stages of India's Nuclear Power Programme differs with respect to:
1. Fuel used
2. Technology
3. Stage of development
(a) 1 and 2
(b) 2 and 3
(c) 1 and 2
(d) All

11. Identify the correct statement(s):
1. The Department of Atomic Energy is directly under the Prime Minister of India.
2. The Rajasthan Atomic Power Station (RAPS) is largest power producing nuclear site.
(a) 1 only
(b) 2 only
(c) Both 1 and 2
(d) None

12. The correct order of the countries from top to bottom in the Nuclear Safety Index is:
1. Belarus
2. France
3. Israel
4. U.K.
(a) 2, 4, 3 and 1
(b) 2, 3, 4 and 1
(c) 4, 1, 2 and 3
(d) 4, 3, 2 and 1

13. Consider the following statements:
1. The Nuclear Suppliers Group has 24 countries as its members.
2. India is a member of the Nuclear Suppliers Group.
Which of the statements given above is/are correct?
(a) 1 only
(b) 2 only
(c) 1 and 2 both
(d) None

14. Consider the following statements:
1. United States-India Peaceful Atomic Energy Cooperation Act, 2006 was named in honour of the Chairman of the House Committee on International Relations.
2. About 25% of world's total thorium reserves are in India.
Which of the statements given above is/are correct?
(a) 1 only
(b) 2 only
(c) 1 and 2 both
(d) None

15. Consider the following statements
1. India has 10 Pressurized Heavy Water Reactors (PHWRs).
2. The spent fuel from the PHWRs is reprocessed into plutonium.
3. All imported reactors are under the safeguards of the international Atomic Energy Agency (IAEA).
Which of the statements given above is/are correct?
(a) Only 1
(b) Only 2
(c) 2 and 3
(d) All of these

16. In the case of the nuclear disaster which of the following options for cooling the nuclear reactors may be adopted?
1. Pumping of water to the reactors.
2. Use of boric acid.
3. Taking out the fuel rods and keeping them in a cooling pond.
Select the correct answer using the codes given below
(a) Only 3
(b) 1 and 2
(c) 2 and 3
(d) All of these

17. Non-nuclear weapons of mass destruction
(a) are far less dangerous than nuclear weapons, so the international community is trying to eliminate nuclear weapons first.
(b) include chemical and biological weapons, which have been around for decades.
(c) are much easier to keep track of than nuclear weapons.
(d) are more difficult to build than nuclear weapons, so fewer states have them.

18. The Government of India is planning to establish a new independent nuclear safety regulatory authority. Who among the following will head this new authority?
(a) Prime Minister
(b) President
(c) Minister of Science & Technology
(d) A professional with extensive experience in atomic energy

19. Scientists at the Indira Gandhi centre for Atomic Research, Kalpakkam, have successfully extended the life of Fast Breeder Test Reactor (FBTR) by another 20 years. This centre is located in:
(a) Karnataka
(b) Gujarat
(c) Maharashtra
(d) Tamil Nadu

20. Heat is generated in a nuclear reactor (thermal) by
(a) Combustion of a nuclear fuel e.g. uranium.
(b) Fusion of atoms of uranium.
(c) Absorption of neutrons in uranium atoms.
(d) Fission of U-235 by neutrons.

21. Which one of the following metals is alloyed with sodium to transfer heat in a nuclear reactor? **[NDA (I) 2018]**
(a) Potassium
(b) Calcium
(c) Magnesium
(d) Strontium

ANSWER KEY															
1	(d)	**2**	(a)	**3**	(a)	**4**	(c)	**5**	(c)	**6**	(d)	**7**	(c)	**8**	(c)
9	(a)	**10**	(d)	**11**	(c)	**12**	(c)	**13**	(d)	**14**	(c)	**15**	(b)	**16**	(b)
17	(b)	**18**	(d)	**19**	(d)	**20**	(d)	**21**	(a)						

BIOTECHNOLOGY

Biotechnology is defined as any technological application that uses biological systems, living organisms, or derivatives thereof, to make or modify products or processes for specific use.

Principles of Biotechnology

Genetic engineering	Biochemical engineering
It is the manipulation of genes of an organism. Genetic engineering refers to artificial synthesis, isolation, modification, combination, addition and repair of the genetic material (DNA) to alter the phenotype of the host organism to suit human needs.	These are the processes that help the growth of desired microbe/eukaryotic cell in large quantities in a sterile medium (Tissue culture technique) for the manufacture and multiplication of biotechnological product (antibiotics, vaccines, enzymes, medicines, hormones, etc.)

RECOMBINANT DNA TECHNOLOGY

Recombinant DNA technology, popularly known as **'genetic engineering'** is a stream of biotechnology which deals with the manipulation of genetic material by man in vitro.

There are two distinct techniques for introducing foreign genetic material into plant cell genome — indirect and direct transfer.

The first is indirect transfer through a vector which requires –

- selection and isolation of the desirable fragment(s) of DNA which contains gene sequence(s) that needs to be cloned known as *insert;*
- Generation of *recombinant DNA* (r DNA) molecule by insertion of these inserts (DNA fragments) into a carrier DNA molecule, termed as *vector* (i.e., the bacterial *Agrobacterium tumefaciens*, a virus, a plasmid or any other vector) that can replicate within a host cell; Recombinant DNA (r DNA) = Vector + insert
- Introduction of the r DNA molecules into host cells.

The second, through direct introduction of DNA, involves –

- *Co-cultivation,* i.e., culturing the recipient protoplast with purified DNA
- *Electroporation,* i.e., application of electric impulses to change the porosity of protoplasts so that the directly imbibe the purified DNA.
- *Micro-injection,* i.e., direct injection of DNA fragments with the help of a micropipette. Other methods of gene transfer are – liposome mediated gene transfer, calcium phosphate precipitation method, transformation by ultrasonifation and transformation using pollen or pollen tube.

Thus, genetic engineering can be defined as the generation of new combination of heritable material by the insertion of desired genes or DNA of the cell, into any carrier system so as to allow their incorporation into a host organism in which they do not normally occur but in which they are able to perform normal behaviour and propagation.

Basic Tools of Recombinant DNA Technology

Enzymes

A number of specific kind of enzymes are employed in genetic engineering. These include lysing enzymes, cleaving enzymes, synthesizing enzyme and joining enzymes.

- *Lysing enzymes :* These are used to open up the cells to get DNA for genetic experiments. It is commonly used to dissolve the bacterial cell wall.
- *Cleaving enzyme :* These are used to break DNA molecule. They are further of 3 kinds—
  - **(i)** *Exonucleases* – which cut off nucleotides from 5' or 3' ends of DNA molecule;
  - **(ii)** *Restriction endonucleases* – which cleave DNA duplex at specific points called restriction sites in such a way that single-stranded free ends project from each fragment of DNA duplex. These single-stranded free ends are called **'sticky ends'** because they can join similar complementary ends of DNA fragment from some other source. Restriction endonuclease is called molecular scissors or a chemical scalpel.

3' - C T T A A G –5'   5' - G A A T T C - 3'

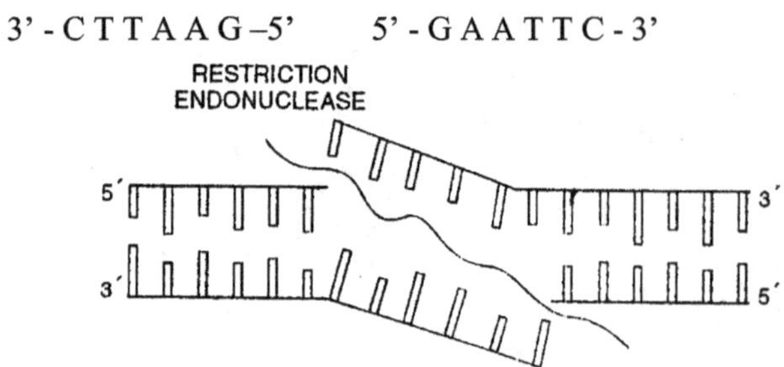

- *Joining enzyme:* These enzymes help in joining the DNA fragment. For example DNA ligase from *Escherichia coli* is used to join DNA fragments by forming a phosphodiester bond.

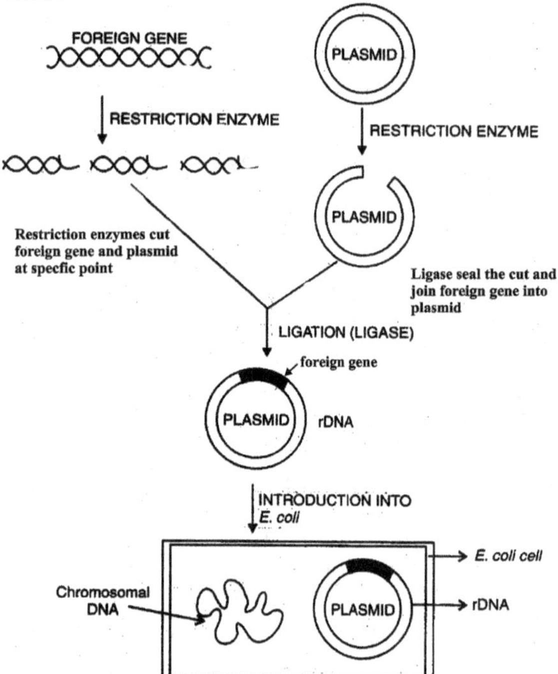

Vectors

- *Vectors* are cloning vehicles required to transfer DNA of interest from one organism to another.
- *Desirable properties of cloning vector* are -
  High copy number, Presence of origin of replication (Ori), Presence of selectable marker, Presence of unique recognition site or cloning site and Ability to sustain in bacterial cell
- *Ori* is sequence where replication starts and any piece of DNA linked here will be replicated. Ori also controls copy number of vector.
- *Selectable marker* allow to select those host cells that contain the vector amongst those which do not. Selectable markers helps in identifying eliminating nontransformants & selectively permitting the growth of transformants.
- *In cloning site,* vector should have single recognition site for restriction enzyme. Presence of more than one recognition site will cut the vector into many fragments.

- **Transformation efficiency** of vector is percentage of competent bacterial host cell receiving desired DNA at specific **recognition sequences** which are palindromic.

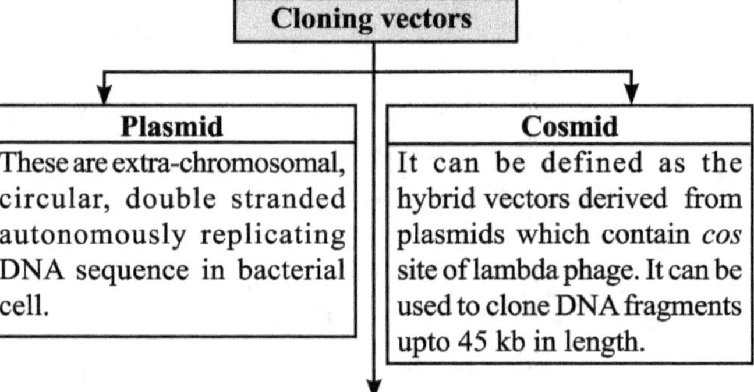

Plasmid	Cosmid
These are extra-chromosomal, circular, double stranded autonomously replicating DNA sequence in bacterial cell.	It can be defined as the hybrid vectors derived from plasmids which contain *cos* site of lambda phage. It can be used to clone DNA fragments upto 45 kb in length.

Bacteriophage
It is virus which infect bacteria. They have special sticky "cos" site to accept foreign DNA. As bacteriophage multiply faster, so transformation efficiency is higher in bacteriophage. Several bacteriophages are being used as cloning vectors but most commonly used are lambda (λ) phage and M 13 phage. These vectors can be used for large DNA fragments and can easily be detected at the time of cloning experiments.

Process of Recombinant Technology

Recombinant DNA (rDNA) is DNA created artificially by combining the DNA from two or more organisms into a single "recombinant" molecule. The term "recombinant DNA technology" also commonly known as 'DNA cloning,' 'molecular cloning' and 'gene cloning', refers to the transfer of a segment of DNA from one organism to another organism (the "host cell") where it reproduces.

Following are the steps in Recombinant DNA Technology

Step 1 : Isolation of genetic material
At first required DNA sequence from the donor cell is identified. Later the required DNA is cut by the help of restriction enzymes at specific site, which result is single stranded sequence with "stick ends".

Step 2: Cutting of DNA at specific locations
Second, cloning vectors from the host cell are identified and removed with the same restrictive enzyme applied to the donor DNA. Cloning vectors are DNA molecules in which another DNA fragment (i.e., foreign DNA) can be integrated and which are capable of independently replicating themselves and the foreign DNA once inserted into the host cell.

Step 3 : Amplification of Gene of interest using PCR
PCR stands for **Polymerase Chain Reaction**. It is the process of amplifying a desired gene of interest into a number of copies. In this reaction, multiple copies of the gene (or DNA) of interest is synthesised *in vitro* using two sets of primers (small chemically synthesised oligonucleotides that are complementary to the regions of DNA) and the enzyme DNA polymerase.

Step 4 : Insertion of Recombinant DNA into the Host Cell/Organism

There are several methods of introducing the ligated DNA into recipient cells. Recipient cells after making them 'competent' to receive, take up DNA present in its surrounding. So, if a recombinant DNA bearing gene for resistance to an antibiotic (e.g. ampicillin) is transferred into *E. coli* cells, the host cells become transformed into ampicillin-resistant cells.

Step 5 : Obtaining the Foreign Gene Product

After having cloned the gene of interest and having optimised the conditions to induce the expression of the target protein, one has to consider producing it on a large scale. If any protein encoding gene is expressed in a heterologous host, is called a **recombinant protein**.

APPLICATIONS OF BIOTECHNOLOGY

Bt COTTON

Bt means *Bacillus thuringiensis*. It is a gram positive dwelling bacterium. It produces crystal [Cry] protein. This Cry protein is toxic to larvae of certain insects. Each Cry protein is toxic to a different group of insects. The gene encoding cry protein is called **cry gene**. This Cry protein is isolated and transferred into several crops.

A crop expressing a **cry gene** is usually resistant to the group of insects for which the concerned Cry protein is toxic. There are a number of them, for example, the proteins encoded by the genes cryIAc and cryIAb control the cotton bollworms, that of cryIAb controls corn borer. Some strains of *Bacillus thuringiensis* produce proteins that kill certain insects such as lepidopterans (tobacco budworm, armyworm), coleopterans (beetles) and dipterans (flies, mosquitoes). *B. thuringiensis* forms protein crystals during a particular phase of their growth. These crystals contain a toxic insecticidal protein. The **Bt toxin** protein exist as inactive protoxins but once an insect ingest the inactive toxin, it is converted into an active form of toxin due to the alkaline pH of the gut which solubilise the crystals. The activated toxin binds to the surface of midgut epithelial cells and create pores that cause cell swelling and lysis and eventually cause death of the insect.

Problems related to GM foods

- The transgene product may cause toxicity and or produce allergies.

- The enzyme produced by the antibiotic resistance gene could cause allergies, since it is a foreign protein.

- The bacteria present in the alimentary canal of the humans could take up the antibiotic resistance gene that is present in the GM food.

Application of Biotechnology in Medicine

- The rDNA technology has been used in the production of safe and more effective therapeutic drugs.
- The recombinant therapeutics do not induce unwanted immunological responses, that are commonly observed with similar products isolated from non-human sources.

Genetically engineered insulin (humulin)

- Human insulin consists of two short polypeptide chains : chain A and chain B, linked by disulphide bridges.
- Insulin is secreted as prohormone which has to be processed before it becomes a mature and functional hormone.

DBT

The Department of Biotechnology or DBT was set up in 1986. It works under the Ministry of Science and Technology. It is responsible for administrating development and commercialization in the field of biotechnology and allied sectors of modern biology in India. The department has made significant achievements in the growth and application of biotechnology in the broad areas of agriculture, health care, animal sciences, environment, and industry.

DBT is responsible for Patenting of innovations, technology transfer to industries and close interaction with them have given a new direction to biotechnology research in India. It is also directly regulating R & D activities related with molecular biology of genetic disorders, brain research, plant genome research, development, validation and commercialisation of diagnostic kits and vaccines for communicable diseases, food biotechnology, biodiversity conservation and bio-prospecting, setting up of micro-propagation parks and biotechnology based initiatives.

Transgenic Animals

- Transgenic animals are those animals that have had their DNA manipulated to possess and express a foreign gene.
- Transgenic animals are used in the following ways :
  (i) Transgenic animals can be specifically designed to allow the study of how genes are regulated and how they affect the normal functions of the body and its development. e.g., Information is obtained about the biological role of insulin like growth factor.
  (ii) Transgenic animals are designed to increase our understanding of how genes contribute to the development of diseases; they are made to serve as models for human diseases.
  (iii) Transgenic mice are being developed for use in testing the safety of vaccines. (e.g. polio vaccine).
  (iv) Transgenic animals with more sensitivity to toxic substances are being developed to test the toxicity of drugs.

Transgenic Plants

Transgenic Plants (of some species) are easier to produce because plants have a lot of totipotent tissue (meristem) that can be grown in culture and then induced to develop into a whole plant. One of the most common methods utilizes a natural gene transfer system called the Ti-plasmid of *Agrobacterium tumefaciens* which transfers a piece of DNA called T-DNA into the genome of infected plants.

Table : Transgenic plants

Transgenic plants	Useful application
Bt Cotton	Pest resistance, herbicide tolerance and high yield. It is resistant to boll worm infestation.
Flavr Savr Tomato	Increased shelf-life (delayed ripening)
Golden rice	Vitamin A-rich
GM Potato	Higher protein content
GM Corn, GM Brinjal	Insect resistance
GM Soybean, GM Maize	Herbicide resistance
SmartStax GM Maize	Herbicide resistance and Pest resistance

SmartStax

SmartStax are genetically modified seeds which contain multiple transgene which protects the plant against various pests as well as provide resistance towards herbicides. It is produced with joint collaboration between two leading agrochemical/agrobiotech companies, Monsanto and Dow Agrosciences.

SmartStax includes eight transgenes. SmartStax-GM maize has 8 modified genes added to it, making it resistance to 2 types of herbicides and toxic to 6 different species of insects. It combines the *Bacillus thuringiensis* (Bt) traits found in VT Triple Pro and Herculex XTRA. VT Triple Pro contains Cry3Bb1 which targets corn rootworm species along with Cry1A.105 and Cry2Ab2 for control of Lepidoptera including European corn borer and corn earworm. Herculex XTRA contains Cry34/35Ab1 for control of corn rootworm and Cry1F for control of Lepidoptera including European corn borer and western bean cutworm. Additionally, SmartStax has tolerance of the herbicides glyphosate and glufosinate. Smartstax seeds also incorporated Monsanto's Acceleron Seed Treatment System and the seed coating contains the pyraclostrobin (fungicide) and Imidacloprid (neonicotinoid). Genuity (Monsanto) and Mycogen (Dow) are brand names under which SmartStax is sold.

GM crops and India

Bt cotton is the only GM crop permitted for cultivation in the country by the Central Government.

The safety aspects of genetically modified crops are assessed by the Institutional Biosafety Committees (IBSCs), Review Committee on Genetic Manipulation (RCGM) and Genetic Engineering Appraisal Committee (GEAC) constituted under Rules 1989 of Environment Protection Act (EPA) – 1986 based on Biosafety Guidelines and the Standard Operating Procedures.

GM crops are permitted for environmental release and cultivation only after undergoing elaborate food and environmental safety assessment following regulatory guidelines and standard operating procedures under Rules 1989 of EPA-1986 and no GM crop is allowed for cultivation, if it poses any risk to the environment including human and animal health. So far, only GM Mustard and Bt Brinjal have been recommended by GEAC to Ministry of Environment, Forests and Climate Change, Government of India for consideration for environmental release and cultivation.

GM Mustard- Dhara Mustard Hybrid-11

The Centre for Genetic Manipulation of Crop Plants (CGMCP), Delhi University South Campus, had submitted an application to the GEAC for the environmental release of GM mustard (*Brassica juncea*) hybrid DMH-11 and the use of parental events (varuna bn 3.6 and EH2 mod bs 2.99) for the development of a new generation of hybrids.

The variety –named as Dhara Mustard Hybrid-11 or DMH-11 which has been developed by a team of scientists from Delhi University led by former VC. It was developed by genetically modifying mustard variety "Varuna" and crossed it with an Eastern European line.

In GM mustard the genetic modification has been effected to simplify the breeding process. It uses a system of genes from soil bacterium that makes mustard –a self-pollinating plant, to better adapt it to hybridization than the current mustard crops in India.

GM cotton is the only genetically modified crop commercially allowed in India and if given go ahead, GM mustard would become India's first GM food crop.

No Commercial release of GM Mustard in India

A committee under Union Ministry of Environment and Forest has turned down commercial release of genetically modified mustard developed by Delhi University's Centre for Genetic Manipulation. After detailed discussion the application has been referred back to GEAC for re-examination, the committee has agreed that the applicant may be advised to undertake field demonstration in an area of 5 acres at 2-3 different location.

Ethical Issues

- Genetic modification of organisms can have unpredictable/undesirable effects when such organisms are introduced into the ecosystem.

- The modification and use of such organisms for public services has also resulted in problems with the granting of patents.

Biopiracy

- Basmati rice grown in India is distinct for its unique flavour and aroma, but an American company got patent rights on Basmati through the US patent and trademark office; the new variety of Basmati has been developed by this company by crossing an Indian variety with the semi-dwarf varieties.

- Now some nations are developing laws to prevent such unauthorised exploitation of their bioresources and traditional knowledge.

- Some such developed countries use the bioresources and traditional knowledge of the other countries without proper authorisation and/or compensation to the countries concerned (Biopiracy)

National Institutions related with field of Biotechnology

- Centre for DNA Fingerprinting and Diagnostics, Hyderabad
- National Institute of Animal Biotechnology, Hyderabad
- National Institute of Biomedical Genomics, Kalyani
- National Centre for Cell Science, Pune
- National Brain Research Centre, Manesar
- Rajiv Gandhi Centre for Biotechnology, Thiruvananthapuram
- National Institute of Immunology, Delhi
- National Institute of Plant Genome Research, New Delhi
- Translational Health Science and Technology Institute, Faridabad
- Institute of Life Sciences, Bhubaneswar
- Institute of Bio-resources and Sustainable Development, Imphal
- National Agri-Food Biotechnology Institute, Mohali
- Bharat Immunologicals and Biologicals Corporation Limited, Bulandshahar
- Indian Vaccine Corporation Limited, New Delhi
- Biotech Consortium India Limited, New Delhi

BIOINFORMATICS

Bioinformatics is the field of study that uses information technology to the study of living things, usually at the molecular level. It involves the use of computers to collect, organize and use biological informations. Besides collection, organization it also involves storage, retrieval, manipulation and modeling of data for analysis, prediction through the development of algorithms and software for biological informations.

Structural bioinformatics is the branch of bioinformatics and deals mainly with the analysis and prediction of 3-D structure of biological macromolecules (Deoxyribonucleic Acid, Ribonucleic acid, Proteins etc.). It deals with overviews about macromolecular 3-D structure such as comparisons of overall folds and local motifs, principles of molecular folding, evolution,

and binding interactions, and structure/function relationships, working both from experimentally solved structures and from computational models.

The greatest contribution of bioinformatics lies behind the successful completion of the Human Genome Project. Because of this the nature and priorities of bioinformatics research and applications have changed.

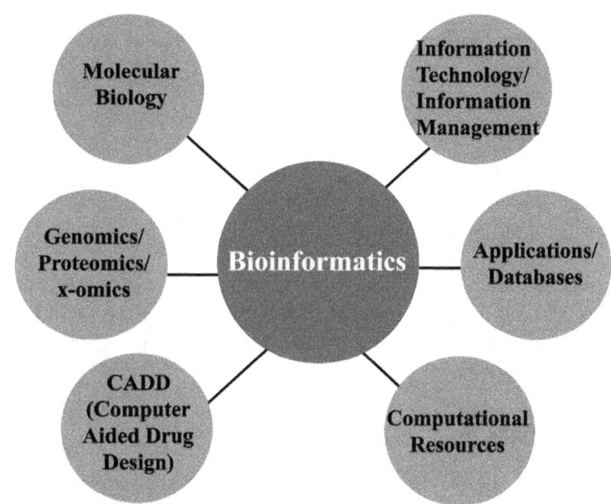

GENOMICS

Genomics is the study of the full genetic complement of an organism called the genome. It involves various methods including DNA sequencing methods, bioinformatics etc. to sequence, assemble, and analyse the structure and function of genomes.

TRANSCRIPTOMICS

Transcriptomics is the study of complete set of RNA transcripts known as transcriptome. Transcriptomes are studied using high-throughput methods, such as microarray analysis. Comparison of transcriptomes allows the identification of genes that are differentially expressed in distinct cell populations, or in response to different treatments.

PROTEOMICS

The term proteome describes the set of proteins encoded by the genome. The study of the proteome, called proteomics, now evokes not only all the proteins in any given cell, but also the set of all protein isoforms and modifications, the interactions between them, the structural description of proteins and their higher-order complexes. Proteomic experiments generally collect data on three properties of proteins in a sample: location, abundance/turnover and post-translational modifications. Depending on the experimental design, researchers may be directly interested in these data, or may use them to infer additional information.

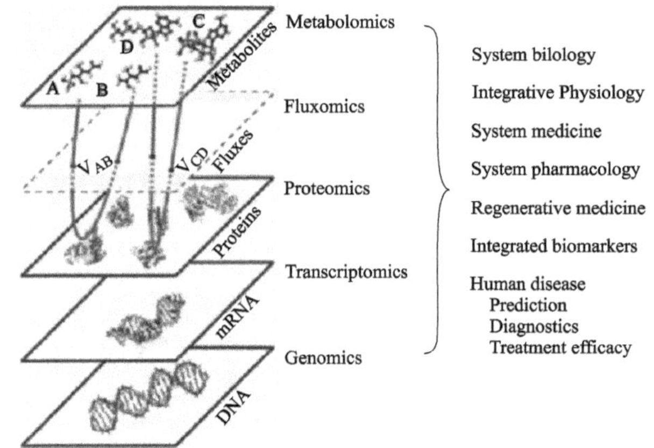

METABOLOMICS

Metabolomics describes the systematic identification and quantification of all the metabolites/metabolic products known as metabolome of a biological system like cell, tissue, organism etc.) at a specific point of time.

FLUXOMICS

Fluxomics determine the rates of metabolic reactions within the samples. Fluxomics provides a direct measure of the metabolic phenotype, namely the in vivo enzyme activity measured as the molar flux through each reaction in the network. It can be analysed using ^{13}C or ^{15}N labelled precursors introduced to the biological system.

DNA SEQUENCING

DNA sequencing refers to methods for determining the order of the nucleotides bases in chromosomal DNA. The first DNA sequence was obtained by using laboratories methods based on 2-D chromatography. With the development of dye based sequencing method with automated analysis, DNA sequencing has become easier and faster. The knowledge of DNA sequences of genes and other parts of the genome of organisms has become indispensable for basic research studying biological processes, as well as in applied fields such as diagnostic or forensic research.

Maxam-Gilbert sequencing Method

The method was developed by Allan Maxam and Walter Gilbert based on chemical modification of DNA and subsequent cleavage at specific bases. The method requires radioactive labelling at one end and purification of the DNA fragment to be sequenced. Chemical treatment generates breaks at a small proportions of one or two of the four nucleotide based in each of four reactions (G, A + G, C, C+T). Thus a series of labelled fragments is generated, from the radiolabelled end to the first 'cut' site in each molecule. The fragments in the four reactions are arranged side by side in gel DNA Representation 5 electrophoresis for size separation. To visualize the fragments, the gel is exposed to X-ray film for autoradiography, yielding a series of dark bands each corresponding to a radiolabelled DNA fragment, from which the sequence may be inferred.

Sanger's Chain-termination method

This method was developed by Frederick Sanger and coworkers and also known as Dideoxy method, since it uses dideoxynucleotide triphosphates (ddNTPs) as DNA chain terminators. The chain termination method requires a single-stranded DNA template, a DNA primer, a DNA polymerase, radioactively or fluorescently labelled nucleotides,and modified nucleotides that terminate DNA strand elongation. The DNA sample is divided into four separate sequencing reactions, containing all four of the standard deoxynucleotides (dATP, dGTP, dCTP, dTTP) and the DNA polymerase. To each reaction is added only one of the four dideoxynucleotide (ddATP, ddGTP, ddCTP, ddTTP) which are the chain terminating nucleotides, lacking a 3'-OH group required for the formation of a phosphodiester bond between two nucleotides, thus terminating DNA strand extension and resulting in DNA fragments of varying length.

NEXT-GENERATION SEQUENCING

Next-generation sequencing refers to high-throughput DNA sequencing technologies. Millions or billions of DNA strands can be sequenced in parallel, yielding substantially more throughput and minimizing the need for the fragment-cloning methods that are often used in Sanger sequencing of genomes. It involves sequencing techniques like, Illumina (Solexa) sequencing, Roche-454 sequencing etc. These technologies sequence nucleic acids at a rapid rate and are more economical than the previously used Sanger sequencing.

Illumina is based on dye terminators. In this, DNA molecule are first attached to primers on a slide and amplified, this is known as bridge amplification. The DNA can only be extended one nucleotide at a time. A camera takes images of the fluorescently labeled nucleotides, then the dye along with the terminal 3' blocker is chemically removed from the DNA, allowing the next cycle.

THE HUMAN GENOME PROJECT

The Human Genome Project was one of the landmark projects with the sole objective of determination of entire DNA sequence of human genome. This public funded project was initiated in 1990 and involved various laboratories. More than 18 different countries from across the globe had contributed to this massive project by the time of its completion.

The Human Genome Project was based on 2 key principles (International Human Genome Sequencing Consortium, 2001). First, it involved collaborators from various nations in an effort to move beyond borders, to establish an all-inclusive effort, and to benefit from diverse approaches. The group of publicly funded researchers that eventually assembled was known as International Human Genome Sequencing Consortium (IHGSC). Second, this project required that all human genome sequence information be freely and publicly available within 24 hours of its assembly. This founding principle ensured unrestricted access for scientists in academia and in industry, and it provided the means for rapid and novel discoveries by researchers of all types. During this project all 3.2 billion base pairs in the human genome were sequenced.

The Human Genome Project employed a two-phase approach to tackle the human genome sequence. In first phase or the shotgun phase human chromosomes were divided into DNA segments of an appropriate size, which were then further subdivided into smaller, overlapping DNA fragments that were sequenced. The Human Genome Project relied upon the physical map of the human genome established earlier, which served as a platform for generating and analyzing the massive amounts of DNA sequence data that emerged from the shotgun phase. Second phase involved filling in gaps and resolving DNA sequences in ambiguous areas not obtained during the shotgun phase.

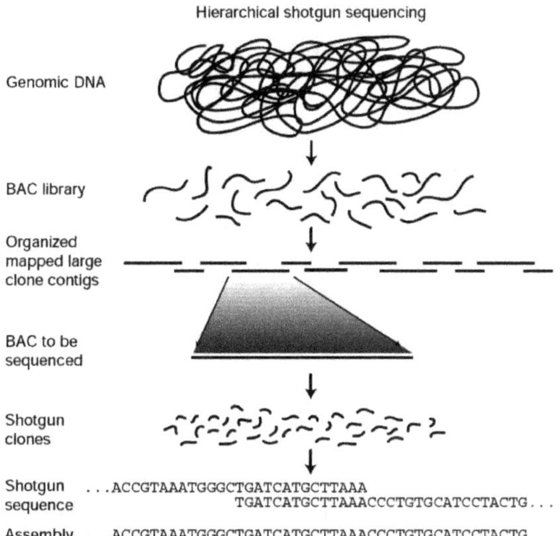

Fig. Shotgun sequencing method

Celera Genomics; a private biotechnology firm led by Dr. Craig Venter also entered the race for human genome sequencing. Although Celera used two independent data sets together with two distinct computational approaches to determine the sequence of the human genome. The first data set was generated by Celera derived from five different individuals. The second data set was obtained from the publicly funded Human Genome Project and was derived from the BAC contigs. The company used a whole-genome assembly method and a regional chromosome assembly method to sequence the human genome. The drafts of human genome sequence were published simultaneously by both groups in February 2001.

In second phase of the project the gaps filled and DNA sequences were resolved in ambiguous areas that were not solved during the earlier phase. It yielded 99% of the human genome in final form. The final form of the human genome contained 2.85 billion nucleotides, with a predicted error rate of 1 event per 100,000 bases sequenced. The final phase reduced the number of protein-encoding genes to around 25,000. Future challenges identified by the IHGSC during this phase included the identification of polymorphisms as a platform for understanding genetic links to human disease, the identification of functional elements within the genome (genes, proteins, elements involved in gene regulation, and structural elements), and the identification of gene and protein modules that act in concert with one another.

Genome Sequencing of Different Organisms

Organisms whose genome is sequenced			
Sr. No.	Organism	Genome size	Year of sequencing
1.	Bacteriophage φ × 174	5.38 kb	First genome sequenced (1977)
2.	Plasmid P^{BR} 322	4.3 kb	First plasmid sequenced (1979)
3.	Yeast chromosome III	315 kb	First chromosome sequenced (1992)
4.	*Haemophilus influenzae*	1.8 Mb	First genome of cellular organism to be sequenced (1995)
5.	*Sacharomyces cerevisiae* (Baker's Yeast)	12 MB	First eukaryotic organism to be sequenced (1996)
6.	*Arabidopsis thaliana* (Thale cress)	125 MB	First plant genome to be sequenced (2000)
7.	*Homo sapiens* (human)	3200 MB	First mammalian genome to be sequenced (2001)
8.	*Oryza sativa* (rice)	430 MB	First crop plant genome to be sequenced (2002)
9.	*Mus musculis* (mouse)	3300 MB	Animal model closest to human (2003)
10.	*P. falciparum*	22.9 MB	Malarial parasite (2002)
11.	*Azadirachta indica* (Neem)	364 MB	2011-12
12.	*Saccharum* spp.	800-900 MB (monoploid)	2018
13.	*Triticum aestivum* L. (Bread wheat var. chinese spring)	12-17 GB	2018

Microarray-based Comparative Genomic Hybridization (aCGH)

Many human genetic disorders result from unbalanced chromosomal abnormalities, in which there is net gain or loss of genetic material. In their attempts to identify such abnormalities, researchers are increasingly employing the technique known as array CGH (aCGH), which combines the principles of traditional comparative genomic hybridization with the use of microarrays. This technique facilitates simultaneous detection of multiple abnormalities and offers higher resolution than traditional cytogenetic methods, and it has allowed investigators to more closely focus on various types of rearrangements in particular regions of chromosomes.

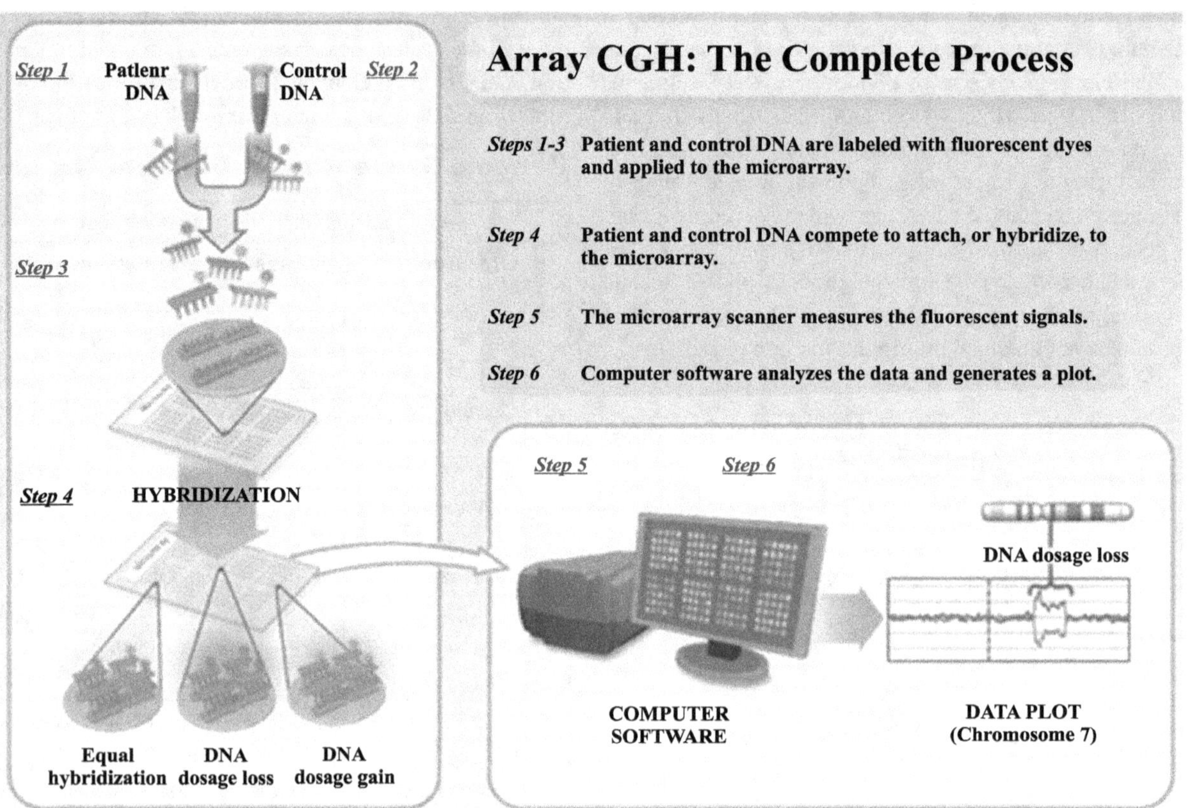

CRISPR-CAS 9 TECHNOLOGY

CRISPR-Cas9 technology is one of the recent technologies for editing genomes. It is useful for modify DNA sequences and edit genes. Its many potential applications include correcting genetic defects, treating and preventing the spread of diseases and improving crop yield and quality.

It stands for Clustered Regularly Interspaced Short Palindrome Repeats, and is the important part of a bacterial defense system and the basis for the CRISPR-Cas9 technology.

CRISPR-Cas9 technology involves the specialized DNA sequences or stretches known as CRISPRs, while Cas-9 component is an enzyme which acts like molecular scissors for Cutting specific DNA sequences.

The rapid progress and development related to CRISPR-Cas9 system for cell and molecular biology research has been remarkable and is due to the simplicity, high efficiency and versatility of this highly potential technology.

THREE PERSON BABY- MITOCHONDRIAL REPLACEMENT THERAPY

Mitochondrial replacement therapy (MRT) involves methodology to replace an oocyte with dysfunctional mitochondria with normal mitochondria. Mitochondrial replacement therapy gives an alternative opportunity to female carriers of mitochondrial disorders to have healthy children. The success of a promising experimental MRT involving a spindle transfer was first demonstrated in 2016 with the birth of a baby with the nuclear deoxyribonucleic acid (nDNA) of the mother and father and the mitochondria of a donor female egg.

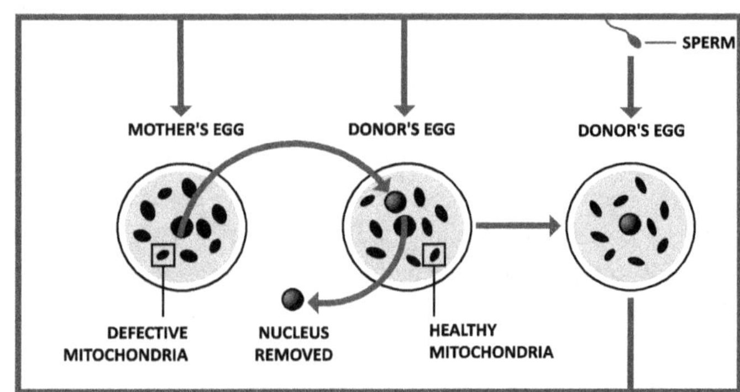

Fig. Concept behind three person babies

The Birth of such type of baby is popularly referred to as a three-person baby because the baby carries the genetic material of three different individuals (The father, the mother and the lady providing the healthy mitochondria).

RNA Interference (RNAi)

1. The central dogma

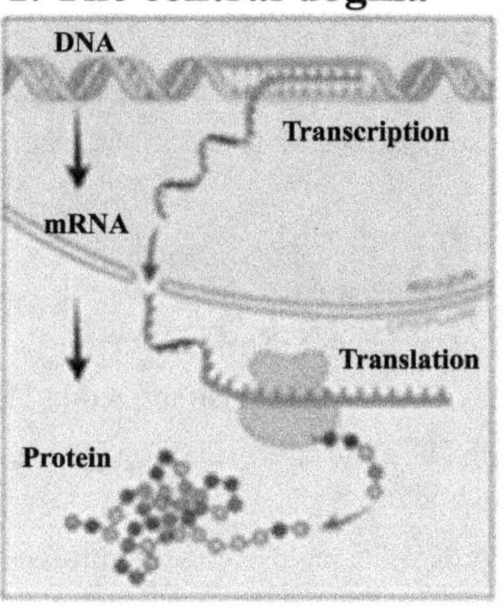

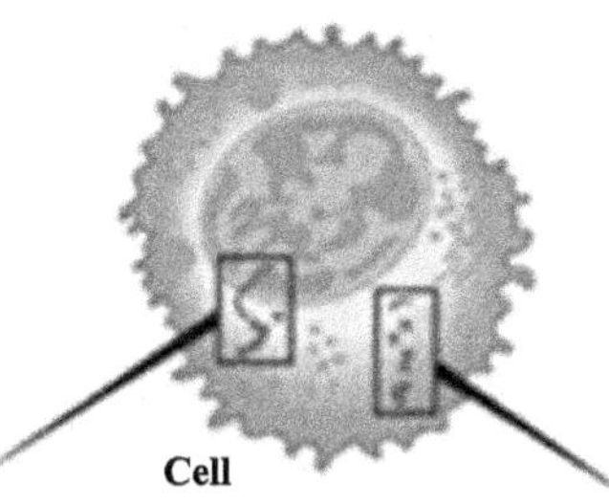

Our genome operation by sending information from double-stranded DNA in the nucleus, via single-stranded mRNA, to guide the synthesis of proteins in the cytoplasm

2. The experiment

RNA carrying the code for a muscle protein is injected into the worm *C. elegans*. Single-stranded RNA has no effect. But when double-stranded RNA is injected, the worm starts twitching in a similar way to worms carrying a defective gene for the muscle protein.

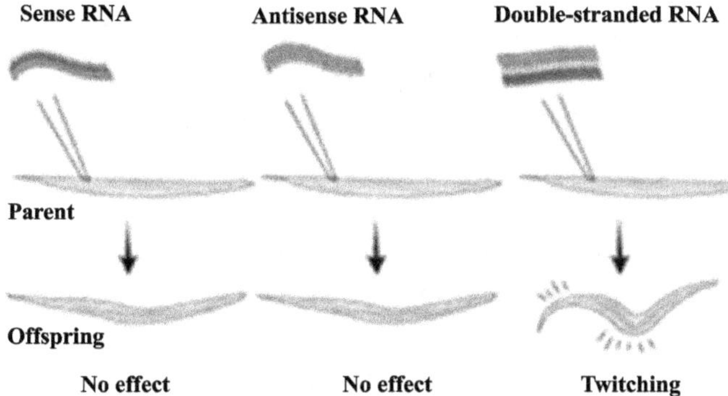

3. The RNAi mechanism

RNA interference (RNAi) is an important biological mechanism in the regulation of gene expression

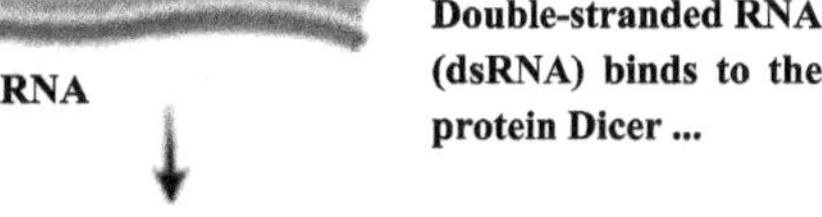

dsRNA

Double-stranded RNA (dsRNA) binds to the protein Dicer ...

... which cleaves dsRNA into smaller fragments.

One of the RNA strands is loaded into a RISC complex ...

...and links the complex to the mRNA strand by basepairing.

mRNA

mRNA is cleaved and destroyed. No protein can be synthesized.

4. Several processes in the cell use RNAi

A   When an RNA virus infects the cell, it injects its genome consisting of double-stranded RNA. RNA interference destroys the viral RNA, preventing the formation of new viruses.

B. Synthesis of many proteins is controlled by genes encoding micro RNA. After processing. microRNA, prevents the translation of mRNA to protein.

C. In the research laboratory. dsRNA molecules are tailor-made to activate the RISC complex to degrade mRNA for a specific gene.

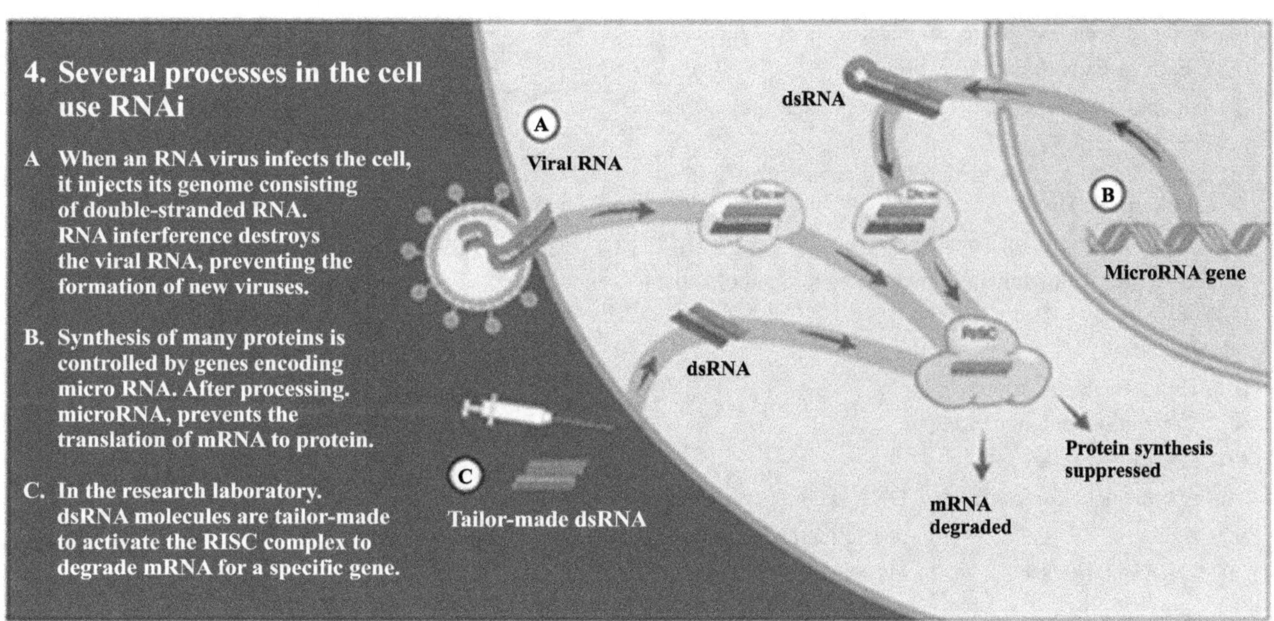

MULTIPLE CHOICE QUESTIONS

1. The bacteria generally used for genetic engineering is
   - (a) *Agrobacterium*
   - (b) *Bacillus*
   - (c) *Pseudomonas*
   - (d) *Clostridium*

2. *Bacillus thuringiensis* (Bt) strains have been used for designing novel –
   - (a) Bio-metallurgical techniques
   - (b) Bio-insecticidal plants
   - (c) Bio-mineralization processes
   - (d) Bio-fertilizers

3. Which of the following is false for Bt transgenic plant –
   - (a) Disease resistance
   - (b) Prepared by *Bacillus thuringiensis*
   - (c) It is recombinant type
   - (d) No such plant is known

4. First cloned animal is –
   - (a) Dog
   - (b) Molly
   - (c) Dolly sheep
   - (d) Polly sheep

5. Genetically engineered human insulin is prepared by using–
   - (a) E. coli
   - (b) Rhizopus
   - (b) Pseudomonas
   - (d) Yeast

6. Golden rice is a transgenic crop of the future with the following improved trait –
   - (a) High lysine (essential amino acid) content
   - (b) Insect resistance
   - (c) High protein content
   - (d) High vitamin-A content

7. Plasmid has been used as vector because
   - (a) both its ends show replication.
   - (b) it can move between prokaryotic and eukaryotic cells.
   - (c) it is circular DNA which have capacity to join to eukaryotic DNA.
   - (d) it has antibiotic resistance gene.

8. Which of the following is known as specific molecular scissors?
   - (a) Ligase
   - (b) Helicase
   - (c) Restriction endonuclease
   - (d) DNA polymerase

9. The enzyme used for joining two DNA fragments is called
   - (a) ligase
   - (b) restriction endonuclease
   - (c) DNA polymerase
   - (d) gyrase

10. Which of the following statement is incorrect regarding PCR?
    - (a) In PCR, two primers are used.
    - (b) *Taq* DNA polymerase is related for PCR.
    - (c) *Taq* DNA polymerase is not thermostable.
    - (d) Multiple copies of gene can be synthesized in PCR.

11. What is the aim of the DNA based technology (Use and Regulation) Bill, 2017?
    - (a) It aims to prevent misuse of DNA technology by regulating and standardizing DNA testing.
    - (b) It provides for collection of profiles and preservation of biological samples.
    - (c) It aims at setting up of new DNA testing authorized laboratories.
    - (d) None of the above.

12. RFLP and VNTR terms are associated with,
    1. DNA Damage
    2. DNA fingerprinting
    3. DNA profiling

    Select the correct answer using the codes given below:
    - (a) 1 only
    - (b) 2 only
    - (c) 2 and 3 only
    - (d) 1, 2 and 3

13. Read the following statements with reference to properties of Cryo-Electron Microscopy,
    1. It is method for imaging specimens at cryogenic temperature by Electron Microscopy.
    2. It is method for imaging frozen hydrated specimens at cryogenic temperature by Electron Microscopy using light source.

    Select the correct statement/statements using the codes given below:
    - (a) 1 only
    - (b) 2 only
    - (c) Both 1 and 2
    - (d) Neither 1 nor 2

14. Consider the following statements:
    1. Genetic Engineering Appraisal Committee (GEAC) is a statutory body under MOEFCC.
    2. India has so far permitted only GM cotton to be released into the environment.

    Select the correct statement/statements using the codes given below:
    - (a) 1 only
    - (b) 2 only
    - (c) Both 1 and 2
    - (d) Neither 1 nor 2

15. Which of the following professional(s) are more likely to run the risk of a permanent change in their cell's DNA?

1. Researchers using Carbon 14 isotope
2. X-ray technician
3. Coal miner
4. Dyer and painter

Select the correct answer by using the codes given below

Codes:

(a) 2 alone
(b) 1 , 2 and 3
(c) 1, 2 and 4
(d) 1, 3 and 4

16. Assertion (A) : Insect resistant transgenic cotton has been produced by inserting *Bt* gene.

Reason (R) : The *Bt* gene is derived from a bacterium.

(a) Both A and R are true and R is the correct explanation of A
(b) Both A and R are true but R is not a correct explanation of A
(c) A is true but R is false
(d) A is false but R is true

17. Assertion (A) : Dolly was the first cloned mammal.

Reason (R) : Dolly was produced by *in vitro* fertilization.

[IAS Prelim 1999]

(a) Both A and R are true and R is the correct explanation of A
(b) Both A and R are true but R is not a correct explanation of A
(c) A is true but R is false
(d) A is false but R is true

18. Insect-resistant cotton plants have been genetically engineered by inserting a gene from a/an

[IAS Prelim 2000]

(a) virus
(b) bacterium
(c) insect
(d) plant

19. Hybridoma technology is a new biotechnological approach for commercial production of **[IAS Prelim 2000]**

(a) monoclonal antibodies
(b) interferon
(c) antibiotics
(d) alcohol

20. The American multinational company, Monsanto, has produced an insect-resistant cotton variety that is undergoing field trials in India. A toxic gene from which one of the following bacteria has been transferred to this transgenic cotton? **[IAS Prelim 2001]**

(a) *Bacillus subtilis*
(b) *Bacillus thuringiensis*
(c) *Bacillus amyloliquefaciens*
(d) *Bacillus globii*

21. Genetically modified "golden rice" has been engineered to meet human nutritional requirements. Which one of the following statements best qualifies golden rice ?

[IAS Prelim 2010]

(a) The grains have been fortified with genes to provide three times higher grain yield per acre than other high yielding varieties
(b) Its grains contain pro-vitamin A which upon ingestion is converted to vitamin A in the human body
(c) Its modified genes cause the synthesis of all the nine essential amino acids
(d) Its modified genes cause the fortification of its grains with vitamin D.

22. Recently, "oil zapper" was in the news. What is it ?

[IAS Prelim 2011]

(a) It is an eco-friendly technology for the remediation of oily sludge and oil spills
(b) It is the latest technology developed for undersea oil exploration
(c) It is a genetically engineered high biofuel yielding maize variety
(d) It is the latest technology to control the accidentally caused flames from oil wells.

23. A genetically engineered form of brinjal, known as the Bt-brinjal, has been developed. The objective of this is

[IAS Prelim 2011]

(a) to make it pest-resistant.
(b) to improve its taste and nutritive qualities.
(c) to make it drought-resistant.
(d) to make its shelf-life longer.

24. With reference to 'stem cells', frequently in the news, which of the following statements is/are correct?

[IAS Prelim 2012]

1. Stem cells can be derived from mammals only.
2. Stem cells can be used for screening new drugs.
3. Stem cells can be used for medical therapies.

Select the correct answer using the codes given below :

(a) 1 and 2 only   (b) 2 and 3 only

(c) 3 only   (d) 1, 2 and 3

25. What are the reasons for the people's resistance to the introduction of Bt brinjal in India?   **[IAS Prelim 2012]**

1. Bt brinjal has been created by inserting a gene from a soil fungus into its genome.
2. The seeds of Bt brinjal are terminator seeds and therefore, the farmers have to buy the seeds before every season from the seed companies.
3. There is an apprehension that the consumption of Bt brinjal may have adverse impact on health.
4. There is some concern that the introduction of Bt brinjal may have adverse effect on the biodiversity.

Select the correct answer using the codes given below :

(a) 1, 2 and 3 only   (b) 2 and 3 only

(c) 3 and 4 only   (d) 1, 2, 3 and 4

26. Which one of the following statements about microbes is not correct ?   **[NDA - 2017-II]**

(a) They are used in sewage treatment plants.

(b) They are used in industrial fermenters for the production of beverages.

(c) No antibiotic has been obtained from any microbe.

(d) They are used to get many bioactive molecules for the treatment of diseases.

27. Golden rice is a genetically-modified crop plant where the incorporated gene is meant for biosynthesis of

    [NDA - 2017-II]

(a) Omega-3 fatty acids

(b) Vitamin A

(c) Vitamin B

(d) Vitamin C

ANSWER KEY															
1	(a)	**2**	(b)	**3**	(d)	**4**	(c)	**5**	(a)	**6**	(d)	**7**	(c)	**8**	(c)
9	(a)	**10**	(c)	**11**	(a)	**12**	(c)	**13**	(a)	**14**	(c)	**15**	(c)	**16**	(b)
17	(d)	**18**	(b)	**19**	(a)	**20**	(b)	**21**	(b)	**22**	(a)	**23**	(a)	**24**	(b)
25	(b)	**26**	(c)	**27**	(b)										